ENCYCLOPEDIA OF ELLIS ISLAND

ENCYCLOPEDIA OF ELLIS ISLAND

Barry Moreno

GREENWOOD PRESS
Westport, Connecticut · London

Library of Congress Cataloging-in-Publication Data

Moreno, Barry.
Encyclopedia of Ellis Island / Barry Moreno.
p. cm.
Includes bibliographical references (p.) and index.
ISBN 0–313–32682–7 (alk. paper)
1. Ellis Island Immigration Station (N.Y. and N.J.)—Encyclopedias.
2. United States—Emigration and immigration—History—Encyclopedias.
I. Title.
JV6484.M67 2004
304.8′73—dc22 2004054380

British Library Cataloguing in Publication Data is available.

Library of Congress Catalog Card Number: 2004054380

ISBN: 0–313–32682–7

First published in 2004

Greenwood Press, 88 Post Road West, Westport, CT 06881
An imprint of Greenwood Publishing Group, Inc.
www.greenwood.com

Printed in the United States of America

The paper used in this book complies with the Permanent Paper Standard issued by the National Information Standards Organization (Z39.48–1984).

10 9 8 7 6 5 4 3 2 1

To my young nephews,
Sergio and Victor Moreno

Contents

Acknowledgments	ix
Introduction	xi
Chronology	xxi
Alphabetical List of Entries	xxvii
List of Entries by Subject	xxxiii
List of Entries of Persons by Field of Endeavor or Background	xli
Encyclopedia	1
Appendix 1 Ellis Island: Its Organization and Some of Its Work	259
Appendix 2 Personnel Report of 1909	277
Appendix 3 Rules for the U.S. Immigrant Station at Ellis Island	283
Bibliography	305
Index	309

Acknowledgments

The first person to whom I must give thanks is Virginia Yans-McLaughlin, who when approached to write this book, declined and recommended me as the best person to undertake it. Since I had previously filled a notebook with plans for such a book, I was truly delighted when Wendi Schnaufer of Greenwood Press telephoned me on Professor Yans-McLaughlin's recommendation and asked if I would be interested in writing the book. Throughout my years at Ellis Island, I have had stimulating conversations and worked on numerous projects with many people, including a great variety of co-workers, authors, researchers, and specialists. I thank them all, especially museum staff members Diana R. Pardue, Jeffrey S. Dosik, Eric Byron, Janet Levine, Kevin Daley, George D. Tselos, Ken Glasgow, Sydney Onikul, Judith Giuriceo, Richard D. Holmes, Nora Mulrooney, Geraldine Santoro, Doug Tarr, Wiley Steve Thornton, Patricia Hom, Paul Roper, and Stephen Keene. Also former Ellis Island staff members Brian Feeney, Frank DePalo, Marcy Cohen Davidson, Paul Sigrist, Carl Rutberg, Robert Cecchi, Paul Kinney, Peter Stolz, George Hennessey, Steven Czarniecki, Felice Ciccione, and many others. Also helpful were Superintendent Cynthia Garrett, Deputy Superintendents Frank Mills and David Luchsinger, horticulturist Alfred Farrugio, concessions specialist Michael Conklin, and architect Don Fiorino, Deborah Falik, and our museum volunteers, including David H. Cassells, Charles B. Lemonick, North Peterson, Mary Fleming, John Kiyasu, Javier, Agramonte, and Joachim Baur.

The Statue of Liberty–Ellis Island Foundation has also been helpful, especially Peg Zitko, and Stephen A. Briganti and, at the American Family Immigration History Center, I must thank Catherine Daley and David Diakow, for their unfailing support.

Scholars, experts, and researchers have also been helpful indeed. These include historians Marian L. Smith, John Parascandola, Fitzhugh Mullan, Peter Mesenhoeller, Roger Daniels, and Robert Stein; archivists Brian G. Andersson, John Celardo, and the late Robert Morris; publisher and writer Loretto Dennis Szucs; Ellis Island immigrants Isabel Belarsky and Emmie Kremer; authors Tom Bernardin and Dennis Wepman; and documentary filmmaker Lorie Conway. I thank my wonderful editor, Wendi Schnaufer, at Greenwood Press, project editor, Judy Thurlow, at Capital City Press, and all those who have contributed to the development and production of this book.

Introduction

Ellis Island, located at the southern tip of Manhattan in New York Bay, is renowned as the major immigrant portal to the United States. Its historical importance cannot be overstated. Along with the Statue of Liberty, with which it now shares national monument status, Ellis Island is the most significant symbol of the opportunities that awaited immigrants arriving on U.S. shores. That Ellis Island has merited this encyclopedic treatment further demonstrates its enduring significance to U.S. history. Approximately 12 million immigrants, mostly Europeans, were processed on the island from 1892 through 1954. Their cultural contributions are celebrated as part of the American Dream. Their children and grandchildren became part of the American middle class. Today, perhaps 25 percent of Americans have an ancestor who was processed at Ellis Island. After extensive restoration, Ellis Island has a new purpose: it is the premier historical museum for immigration and genealogical research in this country and is a major tourist attraction and student group destination in New York.

Many reference books have been written about immigration in general, but this encyclopedia is the first reference book devoted to the subject of Ellis Island. General topics in this volume include children, languages and dialects, literature, wars, and women, along with specific laws, policies and procedures, notables and staff, organizations, buildings and rooms, and the various incarnations of its use until the founding of the current museum.

The need for this volume was dictated by the lack of well-organized and easily accessible publications that simplify the search for general knowledge of the island's history. The purpose of this encyclopedia is to remedy that situation.

Nonetheless, this volume is limited in its coverage simply because of the vastness of the story. The basic history is covered here with the emphasis on Ellis Island as an immigrant station from 1892 through 1954.

The criterion for entry selection was overall significance to the history of the island. Thus, for example, federal agencies, commissioners, various people, divisions, and diseases were all determined as vital to readers and researchers. Whenever possible, the entries have been named as they were known at Ellis Island. Hence, the entry on immigration inspectors is called "immigrant inspectors" because that was the term used on Ellis Island. The following brief, historical overview of the island will help put the contents of this encyclopedia in perspective.

THE EARLY HISTORY OF ELLIS ISLAND (1620–1890)

When the Dutch arrived, Ellis Island formed part of the domain of the Lenni Lenape Indians, who fished and gathered oysters from its shores. They called the sandbar *Kioshk*—Gull Island—for it was inhabited by many of these seafaring birds.

In the 1630s, Michael Paauw purchased the dreary isle from the tribe for "certain cargoes or parcels of goods." During these early years, the Dutch found the oyster beds rich and profitable, and the island came to be known as Little Oyster Island. The three-and-a-half-acre sandbar, however, attracted no settlers. In 1674, shortly after English colonial rule was made permanent by the Treaty of Westminster (ending the Third Anglo-Dutch War), the English governor, Sir Edmund Andros, granted Little Oyster Island to Captain William Dyre.

In 1686, Dyre and his wife Mary sold the island to Thomas and Patience Lloyd. After Lloyd's death about a decade later, the isle passed into other hands. A clue to one of the owners, perhaps, lies in the name the island bore around 1730—Bucking Island. In 1765, the execution of a pirate called Anderson gave the island two additional names—Anderson's Island and Gibbet Island.

It is believed that merchant and farmer Samuel Ellis acquired the island in 1774. One can safely assume that he was the proprietor by November 1778 when this notice was published:

Boat found adrift. The owner to apply to Garret Wouters at Mr. Ellis's Island.[1]

Ellis also attempted to sell the island around that time through an advertisement in *Loudon's New-York Packet*:

> *TO BE SOLD*
>
> By Samuel Ellis, no. 1, Greenwich Street, at the north river near the Bear Market, That pleasant situated Island called *Oyster Island*, lying in New York Bay, near Powle's Hook, together with all its improvements which are considerable; also, two lots of ground, one at the lower end of Queen street, joining Luke's wharf, the other in Greenwich street, between Petition and Dey streets, and a parcel of spars for masts, yards, brooms, bowsprits, & c. and a parcel of timber fit for pumps and buildings of docks; and a few barrels of excellent shad and herrings, and others of an inferior quality fit for shipping; and a few thousand of red herring of his own curing, that he will warrant to keep good in carrying to any part of the world, and a quantity of twine which he sell very low, which is the best sort of twine, for tyke nets. Also a large Pleasure Sleigh, almost new.[2]

After Ellis's death in 1794, the island was left to his heirs to fight over until an agreement to sell it to the state of New York for $10,000 was finally reached in 1808. The state, in turn, sold it to the federal government for the same sum. The Army Corps of Engineers erected a land battery on the island that was completed before the outbreak of the War of 1812.

The federal government had been interested in using Ellis Island for military purposes as early as 1794. By 1798, the military earthworks had been carried out on Ellis Island and it was used as a "rendezvous for the recruits of Artillerists & Engineers of the United States Army."[3]

After 1800, attention to military security in the harbor waned—this remained the case until 1807. Later that year, Colonel Jonathan Williams completed a survey of the harbor and reported the strategic value of Governor's Island, Ellis Island, and the tip of lower Manhattan. It was thanks to his report that the purchase of Ellis Island was effected in the next year.

During the War of 1812, Ellis Island and neighboring Bedloe's Island served as quarters for British soldiers captured as prisoners of war. In 1814, the fort on the island was named Fort Gibson in honor of Colonel James Gibson, who was killed by the British while fighting in Ohio.

In 1831, the abandoned island was the scene of the hanging of two pirates, George Gibbs and Thomas Wansley; the latter was an African American. Their bodies were sent to the College of Surgeons and Physicians for dissection. In 1839, another pirate, Cornelius Wilhelms of the ship *Braganza*, was hanged at Ellis Island.

Throughout the period the army and navy shared the island. In 1861, the army dismantled Fort Gibson, known as Battery Gibson. The navy continued using Ellis Island to store munitions.

In April 1890, complaints about the danger the naval magazines posed to the metropolitan area forced Congress to end Ellis Island's long association with the military. Congress now designated the island to be the site of the nation's first federal immigrant inspection station. A process of enlarging the island from its original three and a half acres through landfilling was carried out whenever new buildings were required.

The first immigrant station existed from 1892 through 1897; its wooden buildings were destroyed in a fire in the summer of 1897. Built primarily of steel, bricks, and limestone, the second immigrant station was fireproof. It opened in 1900 and remained in operation until the station was closed in 1954.

ELLIS ISLAND AS AN IMMIGRANT STATION (1892–1954)

When Ellis Island opened, it quickly became the center of mass migration to the New World from 1892 to 1924. At least 12 million foreigners were processed at the facility. The unpleasantness many persons encountered there was summed up in the immigrants' nickname for it: *isola della lacrime*, *Tränen Insel* (island of tears).

After passing New York quarantine inspection, the steamships from Europe and other parts of the world slowly entered New York harbor. Here they were met by a cutter from Ellis Island bearing officials from the Immigration Bureau's Boarding Division. These officials included one or two immigrant inspectors, assisted by clerks and interpreters; there was always a doctor or two, and sometimes a matron as well. When meeting a ship's officers, the inspectors ascertained all possible vital information about the passengers, including details about sick passengers and tips about suspicious ones. The boarding inspectors were given a handwritten copy of the ship's passenger list that had been prepared in advance by the steamship's purser and his assistants. Meanwhile, inspectors and clerks with the aid of the doctors checked first-class passengers with all decorum and courtesy; second-class passengers underwent the same processing with a little more suspicion and a little less decorum. Most of these travelers, especially those in first class, were businessmen, world travelers, distinguished persons, or entertainers. Only in second class were potential "immigrants" spotted. Immigration officials often encountered "suspicious persons" traveling in second class whom they detained and brought to Ellis Island for questioning and investigation. These often included women traveling alone or any person who was reported to them as behaving strangely or giving trouble during the voyage.

Steamships sailed slowly to their docks in Manhattan, Brooklyn, or Hoboken, where first- and second-class passengers who had passed immigration inspection aboard ship were now free to undergo customs and disembark. Third-class or steerage passengers, along with any first- or second-class detainees and possible stowaways, were prepared for transfer to Ellis Island for full inspection. Each received a large slip of paper—a tag—that was affixed to their coats or shirts and had to be worn in view at all times. The tag, often color-coded to indicate the steamship line, was inscribed with a manifest number of the passenger, the name of the steamship, and the immigrant's name. It was an easy, serviceable way of identifying and controlling a large crowd of people. When everything was ready, the large crowds of aliens, often exceeding 2,000 persons, were borne over to Ellis Island on small barges and ferries. The boarding division officials were able to achieve this with the aid of steamship employees.

Though many immigrants kept their personal belongings with them, others entrusted unwieldy trunks, cases, baskets, and boxes to the baggage master's men. In good weather, baggage workers could deposit large quantities of the immigrants' personal belongings near the entrance of the main building, and in bad weather they could be taken to the baggage master's office.

As the weary yet excited immigrants disembarked at Ellis Island, officials known as groupers shouted to them to form two lines, women and children in one and men in the other. This kind of discipline and order, often confusing or unnerving to immigrants, underscored the advanced crowd control technique that had been developed as a matter of necessity at the world's busiest immigration station. An Italian immigrant named Francesco Martoccia came to the United States in the early 1890s and in due time became a U.S. citizen. Around the year 1900, he began what was to be a lifelong career in the Immigration Bureau at Ellis Island, where he worked as an interpreter and then as an immigrant inspector. Many years later, he reminisced about the peak years of mass immigration at Ellis Island:

> *I can well remember, for at that time I was in the registry department, assigned to decide the eligibility of aliens to land. To make things run fairly smoothly in that mixed crowd of poor, bewildered immigrants. . . . Here in the main building, they were lined up: a motley crowd in colorful costumes, all ill at ease and wondering what was to happen to them.*[4]

Line Inspection

With the question of luggage at least temporarily settled, the doctors who worked for the U.S. Public Health Service could now begin the medical examination procedure famously known as line inspection. In good weather, some of the line inspection took place outside under the canopy. This procedure was an important step toward discovering an immigrant's state of health.

Posted near the entrance of the line, the first two doctors had a special technique to quickly identify signs of poor health. This was rather amusingly called the "six-second physical." Standing at a vantage point where the line of immigrants made a sharp turn, the doctor could observe an immigrant from three angles: front, profile, and rear. This gave the doctor the advantage of scrutinizing the immigrant's gait, posture, and mannerisms. In an instant, the doctor took in each immigrant's face, skin, hair, neck, hands, and fingers for any signs of disease or deformity. Blemishes, discoloration, and rashes of the skin, nervous twitches, an unusually pale or a flushed complexion, or sweating: any of these might give away the presence of disease or failing health. He watched for difficulty in breathing, coughing, or signs of feebleness. Next came an examination of the scalp and neck for signs of diseases such as favus or goiter or for common conditions such as hair lice. The doctor also tried to detect signs of mental instability, lunacy, or retardation. Sometimes a doctor would startle an immigrant by asking a few questions. The immigrant's reaction gave the doctor an inkling of the person's mental state.

The second set of doctors was posted halfway along the line. Known as an "eyeman," the physician's sole duty was to examine the immigrants' eyes carefully and watch for any visual impairment or sign of disease. Immigrants dreaded this man particularly because he always examined underneath the eyelid, a quick but slightly painful operation. This was done with the aid of a constantly cleaned and disinfected buttonhook. He looked under a person's eyelid for the telltale scabs of trachoma, a highly contagious disease that often leads to blindness. He also looked for signs of other eye diseases such as conjunctivitis or cataract.

Medical Detention and Hospitalization

Most people passed this medical scrutiny with no difficulty, for some, however, it was quite a different matter: their health seemed questionable. The doctors, using letters of the alphabet, created a code to indicate suspected health problems. Using a piece of chalk, a doctor wrote a letter or two on an alien's coat, shirt, or blouse. Some of the letters used, along with what they meant, included the following: *B* was for back, *Ct* for trachoma, *E* for eyes, *F* for face, *H* for heart, *K* for hernia, *L* for legs, *Pg* for pregnant, *S* for senile, *X* suspected mental problems or insanity. This also identified those who had to undergo full medical scrutiny in the examining rooms. At the completion of a full examination, a medical certificate was issued and co-signed by three doctors. Messengers and immigrants then took the certificates to the Registry Room (also known as the Great Hall) and handed them over to the responsible clerk on the floor. These documents were kept in readiness to help the inspector make a decision to admit or reject the alien when it was time for the interrogation. Immigrants found to be very sick or dangerously ill were hospitalized at once. Only after receiving medical care would they be sent on to undergo the immigration inspection in the Registry Room.

Primary Inspection

In spite of its importance, the medical examination was not the centerpiece of the Ellis Island experience; the doctors—known as medical officers and surgeons—merely supplied medical facts enabling the immigrant inspectors in the Registry Room to make informed decisions in landing, detaining, or excluding an alien with health problems. The inspectors were officers of the U.S. Bureau of Immigration, which supervised all affairs at Ellis Island. To undergo immigrant inspection, aliens were herded up the staircase to the Registry Room, grouped according to the ship they had sailed on and their manifest number. They were then directed to one of the inspection lines to slowly wait their turn at the front of the line.

Federal law required the immigrant inspector to exclude aliens suffering from any loathsome or dangerous contagious disease and all "morons, idiots, and lunatics." Others excluded were convicted criminals, dangerous radicals and anarchists, polygamists, prostitutes, and those guilty of moral turpitude. He used all the evidence available before making a decision: this might include the evidence of the freshly written medical certificate, a testimonial of good character, or a warning telegram from a foreign police force. There was also a restriction barring all persons "liable to become a public charge," a sweeping category that counted among its number vagabonds, professional beggars, unescorted women and girls, underage boys, and physically feeble persons, such as some elderly persons with no relatives or friends to take care of them. With these considerations in view, the inspector, sitting at a high desk at the front of the line, typically asked twenty-nine questions such as: What is your name? Age? Occupation or calling? Race? Country of origin? Do you understand English? Speak it? Read it? Write it? What is the name and address of your next of kin abroad? Ever been to the U.S. before? What is your destination? By whom was your fare paid? Are you a contract laborer? Polygamist? Anarchist? Convicted of any misdemeanor? Height? Color of skin? Eyes? Hair?

Eighty percent of the immigrants passed both the immigrant inspection and the medical examinations and were released to the ground floor to wait for a ferry to transport them to Manhattan or the Jersey City railway terminal. Of the 20 percent who were not immediately accepted, half went to the hospital for medical treatment and the other half were detained for legal reasons. Most detainees had no more than an overnight stay, while some had to wait for money to be cabled to them; for husbands, fathers, or guardians to pick them up; or for information such as the confirmation of an address before journeying to some far-off place in America. Immigrants who aroused suspicion, however, had to face more scrutiny, which could keep them at the island for weeks and lead to a long hearing before a board of special inquiry.

Detention and Exclusion

The immigrants detained on Ellis Island were typically fretful, unhappy, frustrated, or hostile. An incident at the station early on showed the disfavor directed at Italians. In the spring of 1896, inspectors freely detained and excluded large numbers of Italians, mostly penniless workingmen from the *mezzogiorno* (southern Italy), on the ground that they were paupers. This caused crowding in the detention quarters. To remedy this, officials had a temporary detention pen erected outside of the building. When 531 Italian aliens newly arrived on the steamers *Alesia* and *Bolivia* were ordered excluded and joined the throng in the pen, things began to turn nasty. Here is historian Thomas Pitkin's description of the incident:

> *One afternoon a crowd of them rushed the fence and began tearing off the pickets. The guards succeeded in beating them back with considerable difficulty. Senner [the commissioner], fearing more trouble, telegraphed Washington asking permission to employ armed constables on the island . . . the Washington office [then] appealed to the navy for protection at Ellis Island.*[5]

Commissioner Joseph Senner received a promise that marines at the Brooklyn navy yard would be available to assist him, however, things began to simmered down on the hot little island. A reporter from the *New York Tribune* came over to have a look at the Italians. Surveying them with a cold eye he declared them

> *A forlorn looking group, restless, depressed, degraded and penniless . . . it is pitiable indeed to watch their longing looks, hoping against hope as they do, for freedom. The most sympathetic, however, could but exclaim, as they look upon the groups, 'we don't want them; send them back!'*[6]

Detention and Immigrant Aid

Help came in many forms at Ellis Island. A kindly matron or a nurse or an interpreter or a messenger—anyone who looked like a fellow countryman (or even looked sympathetic)—might find himself buttonholed by a desperate immigrant anxious for someone to understand his problems and come to his aid or at least tell him what was going on. Detainees waited hours, days, and sometimes weeks before receiving a decision on whether they could stay in America. Men and women were assigned to separate quarters; the children remained with their mothers. These conditions made the work of missionaries, volunteers, and social workers especially welcome. Missionaries and port workers were permanently posted to Ellis Island, representing such groups as the YWCA, the Polish Society, the Methodist Church, the Hebrew Immigrant Aid Society, the National Council of Jewish Women, the Dutch Reformed Church, the Belgian Bureau, the German and Scandinavian Lutheran Churches, the Episcopal Church, and the Salvation Army. The island's most beloved Roman Catholic priests, Anthony Grogan (Irish) and Gaspare Moretti (Italian), were busy providing spiritual guidance every day—hearing confessions and singing mass. They also assisted immigrants in mundane affairs like getting sponsors or money and sometimes they wrote or read letters.

These and other missionaries and immigrant aid workers had their hands full with detainees and deportees who often did not understand U.S. regulations and were puzzled as to why they were detained. Others, especially the deportees, were usually better informed, since they had already lived in the United States for a while (from months to several years). They ended up at Ellis Island for deportation because they had violated the immigration laws of the country. Typical violations leading to arrest and deportation included illegal entry into the United States (usually by crossing the Canadian border without being inspected), committing a crime or moral offence, or becoming a public charge or vagrant.

Detainees Relax

Dull days in detention were made more bearable by special events such as concerts, religious services, and other activities. In 1909, the Austrian Society arranged a concert by soprano Madame Ernestine Schumann-Heink, and seven years later, the Italian Welfare Society sponsored a concert performed by famed opera star Enrico Caruso. Silent films were screened regularly; detainees could enjoy some of America's most popular screen stars: Douglas Fairbanks, Mary Pickford, Charlie Chaplin, Gloria Swanson, and William S. Hart. Immigrants also entertained themselves, the men played card games and soccer, while women sewed and kept an eye on their children. Christmas was a grand occasion at Ellis Island. Christian immigrants entering the Great Hall for the Christmas celebration saw an enormous Christmas tree with lovely ornaments, including a magnificent star on the topmost branch. They received presents such as apples, oranges, towels, and soap. In addition, men received shaving kits, ties, and tobacco, while the women received sewing materials and aprons. Boys received games and small toys, while girls were presented with dolls.

Jewish immigrants celebrated Passover, Yom Kippur, Sukkoth, and other holidays. Beginning in 1911, the Hebrew Immigrant Aid Society and the U.S. Bureau of Immigration maintained a kosher kitchen at Ellis Island that was supervised by a rabbi. These conditions made the dreary, uncertain days in detention somewhat less unpleasant. In the end, most detainees were approved to enter the country.

To the Immigrant Train

Most immigrants leaving Ellis Island were ferried to the railroad terminals in nearby Jersey City or Hoboken. There, steerage passengers were taken to the immigrant waiting room to wait for the special immigrant train that usually departed around 9:00 p.m. Their destinations might be as close as Trenton, Philadelphia, or Scranton, or as far away as the West Coast. Weary after a long sea voyage and their experience at Ellis Island, the sleepy immigrants found themselves spending the night in dirty, crowded coaches. The travelers were usually full of cheer and hope and, regardless of nationality, were willing to help each other. Mistakes in destination, in which the names of American states, towns, and streets were spelled using the phonetics of foreign languages, caused problems for train conductors. Thus the Wabash Railroad was sometimes written as "Vabassa," Jersey City as "Gersisi," and Brooklyn as "Bruccolino." This led to confusion, delays, and misdirection. Another problem arose when an immigrant gave the name of a relative or friend only to find, through the help of an immigrant aid society, that no such person existed; if the immigrant was lucky, he might learn that the relative or friend had changed his name.

The Chicago Railway Station

A major hub of railway transportation was Chicago, both as a destination and as a place to change trains. Immigrants found the depot of the Northwestern Railway Company remarkably well prepared to receive them. In 1912, the special immigrant waiting room was well ventilated and furnished with four large sofas, as well as numerous chairs and writing tables. The bathing and washing facilities for women and men were furnished with bathtubs and porcelain washing tubs. The nearby lunchroom provided hot tea and coffee with rolls for ten cents, while a complete meal could be had for thirty cents.

THE LATER YEARS AT ELLIS ISLAND

Southern and Eastern European immigration dropped sharply after the passage of the restrictive Immigration acts of 1921 and 1924 (laws that effectively halted the mass migration of these immigrants). The Kingdom of Italy, which had previously sent hundreds of thousands of immigrants each year, received a meager quota of 42,057 per annum under the 1921 law and, as if this were not enough of a blow, the regulation granted only 3,845 per year under the 1924 law. In addition, the Italian-speaking micronation of San Marino was given 100 per year. These immigrants, who were indistinguishable from Italians, followed the pattern of their resourceful cousins and settled in industrial cities like New York and Chicago. After this period, immigration through Ellis Island fell off drastically. Aside from the restrictive quotas, a new immigration policy provided for processing immigrants at American consulates in the country of origin, as well as permanently requiring the use of passports and visas, which had only been introduced on a selective basis at U.S. immigration stations after 1919. Over the next decades, Ellis Island was largely used for the detention and deportation of aliens. In the 1920s, the phenomenon of undocumented aliens began at Ellis Island, where thousands of such persons without passports were held and interrogated before their deportations. In the decades that followed, this policy hardened and became a common situation at Ellis Island. World War II brought a new crisis to Ellis Island: the arrival and interrogations of thousands of alien enemies arrested by the FBI. The alien enemies held at Ellis Island numbered in the low thousands and consisted of Germans, Italians, Japanese, as well as a few fascist Romanians and Hungarians. With the end of World War II, a rift between the Soviet Union and the United States and Western Europe brought about the Cold War. Thousands of aliens suspected of being communists were detained at Ellis Island. By the time Ellis Island was closed by the Immigration and Naturalization Service on November 12, 1954, its varied and sometimes controversial service to the nation was fully recognized.

The Ellis Island Restoration Project

After its closing, the station and its many buildings were left to decay. From 1956 to 1961, the General Services Administration made several unsuccessful attempts to sell the island to private investors. In 1965, responding to efforts by congressmen led by Senator Edmund S. Muskie, President Lyndon B. Johnson proclaimed Ellis Island a part of the Statue of Liberty National Monument and transferred it to the care of the National Park Service. But Congress provided no funds to care for the buildings, which were now in ruins. In addition, the National Park Service showed little interest in preserving the structures.

It was not until the 1970s that the importance of the historic buildings as a public monument became clearer. This was largely due to the efforts of Peter Sammartino, chairman of the Restore Ellis Island Committee. His cleanup campaign attracted public attention and the island was opened to visitors in 1976. From that year through 1984, 545,000 people visited Ellis Island and were moved by the power of the old ruin.

In the 1980s, a determined rehabilitation effort was at last launched. President Ronald Reagan was the force behind it and his plans to raise money though public donations were carried out with extraordinary success by Chrysler Chairman Lee A. Iacocca, who served as chairman of the Statue of Liberty–Ellis Island Foundation.

The success of the fund-raising campaign and the restoration of the main building led to its dedication as the Ellis Island Immigration Museum in 1990. Further steps to rehabilitate the remaining buildings on the island were begun in the 1990s and continue today.

HOW TO USE THE ENCYCLOPEDIA

The various lists of entry terms in the book's front matter will help readers identify the contents quickly. The index is key and should be used to locate the desired information. In addition, the A to Z enties have been cross-referenced through boldface type throughout the text. Convenient references have been included with many entries. There is also a separate selected bibliography. Three appendixes provide longer primary documents on the operation and rules of the immigration station as well as a personnel report.

NOTES

1. Sidney Berengarten, "Ellis Island" [ca. 1941], Manuscript collection, Statue of Liberty and Ellis Island Library, 9.
2. Berengarten, "Ellis Island," 7.
3. Berengarten, "Ellis Island," 13.
4. Edward Corsi, *In the Shadow of Liberty: The Chronicle of Ellis Island* (New York: Macmillan, 1935), 73.
5. Thomas M. Pitkin, *Keepers of the Gate: A History of Ellis Island* (New York: New York University Press, 1975), 25.
6. Pitkin, *Keepers of the Gate*, 25.

Chronology

1620 Up to this year, the island was used by the Lenni Lenape tribe of Native Americans. They named the island *Kioshk*, meaning Gull Island. The English called the Lenni Lenape Delaware Indians.

1620s The Dutch found the colony of New Netherland and the city of New Amsterdam.

1630 The Dutch West India Company, which owns the colony, buys the Oyster Islands from the Lenni Lenape. The first individual proprietor is Michael Paauw.

1664 England conquers New Netherland and renames it New York in honor of Prince James, the duke of York.

August 1673 The Dutch navy conquers New York and renames it New Orange in honor of the Dutch Royal Family.

February 1674 In the Treaty of Westminster, England regains New York and the Netherlands is given Surinam in South America.

1674–1679 Sir Edmund Andros, the English colonial governor of New York, grants Little Oyster Island to Captain William Dyre, the collector of customs. Dyre later served as mayor of New York from 1680 to 1682.

April 23, 1686 Captain Dyre sells the isle, now called Dyre's Island, to Thomas and Patience Lloyd.

October 1, 1691 The New York colonial legislature passes an act that includes a confirmation that the three oyster islands are within the boundaries of New York County.

1730 Governor John Montgomerie of New York grants a charter to New York City that includes Dyre's Island as a part of the city to be now officially known as Bucking Island.

1757 New York City officials consider Bucking Island for use as the site of a pest house (i.e., quarantine station).

1765 The notorious pirate Anderson is hanged on the island; other pirate hangings follow. This gives the isle new names, of which Anderson's Island and Gibbet Island are the most enduring.

November 18, 1774 Samuel Ellis, merchant, of 1 Greenwich Street, Manhattan, New York, buys the island.

January 20, 1785 Samuel Ellis offers the island for sale in *Loudon's New-York Packet*, a local newspaper printed by Samuel Loudon.

1794 Samuel Ellis dies. In his will he bequeaths the island to his daughter Catherine's unborn child with the proviso that the child must be a boy and must be named "Samuel Ellis." His daughter dutifully bears a son and names him after her father but the child dies in infancy.

Meanwhile, New York City grants the deed of Ellis Island to the State of New York for the purposes of constructing a fortification. Charles Vincent, a French engineer, builds the first military earthworks on the island.

1798 Ebenezer Stevens, working for the U.S. War Department, supervises further fortification work on "Ellis's Island." Observing that the island is still privately held by the Ellis family, he recommends that it be purchased by New York State and ceded to the U.S. government.

February 15, 1800 The State of New York passes an act ceding the jurisdiction of Governor's Island, Bedloe's Island, and Ellis Island to the U.S. government.

1806 One of Samuel Ellis's grandsons, Samuel Ellis Ryerson, deeds Ellis Island to John A. Berry in a questionable sale.

June 30, 1808 New York State gains control of Ellis Island through condemnation proceedings carried out by Governor Daniel D. Tompkins. The Ellis family is paid $10,000 for Ellis Island and the state immediately transfers the jurisdiction of the island to the U.S. government.

1811 Colonel Jonathan Williams, U.S. Corps of Army Engineers, finishes construction of the land battery at Ellis Island for defense of the harbor.

1812 A magazine and barracks are completed on Ellis Island and a small garrison of troops is stationed there. This work is done in time for the War of 1812.

1814 Governor Daniel D. Tompkins assumes command of the battery at Ellis Island and promptly names it Fort Gibson in honor of Colonel James Gibson, who was fatally wounded by the British in the Battle of Fort Erie.

1823 Fort Gibson is abandoned.

April 1831 Two pirates are executed on Ellis Island.

1833 The commissioners of New York and New Jersey meet in Manhattan and sign the Interstate Compact to resolve a boundary dispute over the Oyster Islands, New York harbor, and the Hudson River.

1834 The Interstate Compact is ratified by the two states' legislatures and approved by an act of Congress. Among its provisions is the agreement that Ellis and Bedloe's Islands remain a part of New York, but the submerged lands surrounding them belong to New Jersey.

1835 The U.S. Navy takes over the abandoned fortifications on Ellis Island and establishes a powder magazine.

June 22, 1839 Convicted pirate and murderer Cornelius Wilhelms is hanged on Ellis Island.

1841 The army regains jurisdiction of Ellis Island but the navy is permitted to continue operating its powder magazine.

1843 The army rearms Fort Gibson.

1847 The War Department rejects a request by the New York State emigration commissioners to use Ellis Island as the site of a convalescent home for immigrants.

1865–1866 The army dismantles Battery Gibson and withdraws from Ellis Island.

1868 The New York City publication *Harper's Weekly* warns that the navy's powder magazine at Ellis Island poses a danger to New York City.

1876 The New York *Sun* publishes an alarming exposé about the navy's explosives at Ellis Island.

1889 New stories about the Ellis Island explosives appear in the New York *World* and Jersey City newspapers.

1890 Congress passes a joint resolution ordering the removal of the navy's powder magazine from Ellis Island. An amendment is attached appropriating $75,000 to enable the secretary of the treasury to improve the island and construct a federal immigrant station there. President Harrison signed the resolution into law on April 11. By May 24, the powder and personnel have completed their move to Fort Wadsworth on Staten Island.

1891 Congress passes an immigration act creating the Office of the Superintendent of Immigration within the Department of the Treasury, taking effect on July 12. The Office of Immigration is authorized to control immigration at all ports at which foreigners entered the country. Colonel John B. Weber of Buffalo, New York, is appointed as commissioner of the Port of New York, with headquarters to be at Ellis Island. Meanwhile, the island has been slightly enlarged by landfill, and immigration buildings are being constructed there.

January 1, 1892 Colonel Weber opens Ellis Island and welcomes the first immigrant, Annie Moore of Ireland. By the end of the year, more than 400,000 immigrants have been processed at the station.

1893 Colonel Weber improves administrative procedures by requiring all steamship companies to add new questions to their manifests. President Grover Cleveland appoints Joseph Senner to succeed Weber as commissioner.

1895 The name Office of Immigration is changed to Bureau of Immigration.

1897 On the morning of June 15, the wooden buildings on Ellis Island are destroyed by fire. Immigrants and staff are evacuated and Senner transfers the processing of aliens to the aboard steamships and at piers. The Barge Office in Manhattan becomes the temporary headquarters for the Immigration Bureau and detained aliens.

President William McKinley appoints Thomas Fitchie to succeed Senner as commissioner.

1898 William Boring and Edward Tilton, New York City architects, win the contract to create the new fireproof immigrant station at the island.

December 17, 1900 Ellis Island reopens; 2,251 immigrants are examined.

1901 The powerhouse and the kitchen and laundry building are constructed on Island 1.

1901–1902 Scandals and corruption under Commissioner Fitchie forces President Theodore Roosevelt to launch an investigation on Ellis Island.

1902 President Roosevelt forces Fitchie to resign and appoints William Williams in his stead. Commissioner Williams institutes major reforms and improves the treatment of immigrants.

The hospital and laundry are built on Island 2.

September 16, 1903 President Roosevelt visits Ellis Island.

1904 The rear of the Main Building is extended by the addition of a railroad ticket office. Williams welcomes the new ferryboat *Ellis Island.*

1905 William Williams resigns in a dispute and President Roosevelt appoints Robert Watchorn as the new commissioner.

1907 More than 1 million aliens pass through Ellis Island, making it the peak immigration year at the station.

1909 President William Howard Taft reappoints William Williams as commissioner.

Contagious disease wards are completed on Island 3.

1910 President Taft visits Ellis Island.

1911 A dynamite blast in the harbor causes some minor damage at Ellis Island.

1913 President-elect Woodrow Wilson visits Ellis Island.

1914 President Wilson appoints Frederic Howe commissioner.

World War I begins in Europe, causing a sharp decline in immigration over the next four years.

1916 German saboteurs destroy a munitions depot at Black Tom Island, Jersey City, New Jersey. The tremendous explosion shatters the windows at Ellis Island. Island evacuated; no injuries.

1917 The United States declares war on Germany and its allies. Enemy aliens are interned at Ellis Island.

1918 The navy and the army use the majority of buildings at the station for their servicemen.

1919–1920 Red scare. Hundreds of anarchists and Bolsheviks are detained at Ellis Island prior to their deportations. Howe resigns in protest and President Wilson appoints Frederick A. Wallis as his successor. Mass immigration resumes.

1921 President Warren G. Harding appoints Robert E. Tod as the new commissioner. Immigrant quota system for foreign nations adopted.

1923 Tod resigns; President Harding appoints Henry H. Curran as commissioner.

1924 A new immigration act severely reduces the national quotas, ending mass immigration to the United States.

1926 President Calvin Coolidge appoints Benjamin M. Day commissioner of Ellis Island.

1929 Stock market crashes; Great Depression begins.

1930 The Hoover administration begins stricter enforcement of the immigration laws and increases detentions at Ellis Island.

1931 Benjamin Day resigns; President Hoover appoints Edward Corsi as commissioner.

1933: A special Ellis Island committee investigates conditions at the station. The Bureau of Immigration is amalgamated with the Bureau of Naturalization and renamed the Immigration and Naturalization Service.

1934 Edward Corsi resigns as commissioner; his successor was Rudolph Reimer. The Ellis Island Committee recommends the construction of better facilities at the station. Most of these recommendations are adopted and implemented.

The area of the island is increased to its present size of 27.5 acres.

1939 A Coast Guard training station opens on the island.

April 11, 1940 Commissioner Reimer presides over the fiftieth anniversary of Ellis Island's designation as an immigrant station. Reimer retires and the title of commissioner is no longer used. District Director Byron H. Uhl runs Ellis Island.

December 1941 With the entry of the United States into World War II, thousands of enemy aliens are interned at Ellis Island.

1942 Uhl retires and is succeeded by W. Frank Watkins as district director.

1943 Ellis Island ceases to be the headquarters of the Immigration and Naturalization Service for the New York area; the island remains only as a detention station.

1946 The Coast Guard withdraws from Ellis Island.

1947 The last wartime enemy aliens leave Ellis Island.

1949 Edward J. Shaughnessy becomes district director. Hearings for detained aliens are once again conducted at the island.

1950 The passage of the Internal Security Act over President Harry S. Truman's veto causes a flurry of detentions at Ellis Island.

1951 The Public Health Service closes the Immigrant Hospital complex at Ellis Island, maintaining medical care on a limited basis in the Main Building. The Coast Guard returns to Ellis Island.

November 12, 1954 Ellis Island is closed by the Immigration and Naturalization Service, as exceeding the needs of the service.

1955 On March 4, Ellis Island is determined to be surplus government property and on March 15 is transferred to the care of the General Services Administration.

1956–1959 The General Services Administration makes several unsuccessful attempts to sell Ellis Island.

May 11, 1965 President Lyndon B. Johnson declares Ellis Island a part of the Statue of Liberty National Monument under the jurisdiction of the National Park Service.

1966 Architect Philip Johnson recommends demolishing the majority of buildings at Ellis Island and the establishing a park and Wall of the 16 Million there.

1968 In June, the National Park Service issues a master plan for Ellis Island that recommends demolishing most of the historic buildings.

On August 11, due to lack of proper maintenance, the ferryboat *Ellis Island* sinks in its berth.

1973–1975 Public interest in the island instigated by Peter Sammartino leads to a cleanup campaign and repair on the island and some of its structures.

1982 President Ronald Reagan appoints Lee A. Iacocca chairman of the Statue of Liberty Centennial Commission, leading to the creation of the Statue of Liberty–Ellis Island Foundation.

May 1976–September 1984 Ellis Island is open to tourists.

1984 Restoration work begins on Island 1.

1987 President Reagan visits Ellis Island.

September 1990 The Ellis Island Immigration Museum is dedicated and opened to visitors.

1998 The U.S. Supreme Court splits the sovereignty of Ellis Island between New York and New Jersey. New Jersey receives the landfilled sections of the island, which compose a part of Island 1 and all of Island 2 and Island 3.

2001 Following the terrorist attacks on New York City that destroyed the World Trade Center, Ellis Island is closed from September 11 until December 18.

2004 Fort Wood and the pedestal of the Statue of Liberty reopen to the public on August 3 for the first time since September 11, 2001; the statue remains closed.

Alphabetical List of Entries

Abbreviations
Adamic, Louis
African Americans
American, Sadie
American Family Immigration History Center
American Museum of Immigration
American Red Cross
American Tract Society
Americanization Movement
Anarchists
Angel Island Immigrant Station
Animal House
Appeals
Army
Arrival
Assistant Commissioners
Austrian Society

Baer, Beulah
Baggage and Dormitory Building
Baggage Room
Baker, Percy A.
Bakery and Carpentry Shop
Barbusse, Henri
Barge Office
The Battery (Battery Park)
Belgian Bureau
Berkman, Alexander
Biddle, Francis
Births
Black Immigrants
Black Tom Explosion
Board of Review
Boarding Division
Boards of Special Inquiry
Bond Office
Bonds
Boody, Bertha M.
Boring, William A.
Boston Immigrant Station
Brandenburg, Broughton
Bremer, Edith Terry
Brownell, Herbert
Buck, Pearl S.
Buford
Buildings
Bureau of Immigration
Bureau of Immigration and Naturalization

Caminetti, Anthony
Canopy
Carol, Charles A.
Castle Clinton
Castle Garden
Castro, Cipriano
Celebrations
Certificates
Certificates of Registry
Chalk Mark Code
Chief Clerk
Children
Chinese Division
Chinese Exclusion Act
Christmas
Citizens
Clerks
Closing of Ellis Island
Coast Guard
Cold War
Commissioners
Commissioners-General
Concessions
Congressional Resolution of 1890

Contagious Disease Wards
Contagious Diseases
Contract Labor Laws
Corcoran, Emma
Corridors and Covered Passages
Corsi, Edward
Cortelyou, George
Cowen, Philip
Craigwell, Ernest
Crematory
Crime and Abuse
Criticism
Curran, Henry H.

Daughters of the American Revolution
Day, Benjamin M.
Deaths and Burials
Delaware Indians
Demolished Structures
Deportation
Deportation Cases
Deporting Division
Destinations
Detention Cases
Detention Conditions, 1930s
Detention Conditions, 1949
Detention Conditions, 1950s
Discharging Division
Diseases and Hospitalization
District Directors
Divisions
Doak, William N.
Docks
Dormitory
Duncan, Isadora

Elevators
Ellis, Samuel
Ellis Island
Ellis Island Chronicles
Ellis Island Committee
Ellis Island Immigration Museum
Employees' Quarters
Enemy Aliens
Escobar, José Dias d'
Evans-Gordon, Sir William
Exclusion
Executive Division
Eye Examinations

Famous Immigrants
Faris, James Edge
Feebleminded
Ferries and Boats
Ferro, Edward
Ferryboat *Ellis Island*
Ferry House
Ferry Service
Films and Documentaries
Fire of 1897
Firpo, Luis
First Immigrant Station
Food Service and Menus
Forman, Philip
Fort Gibson
Foxlee, Ludmila K.
Fry, Alfred Brooks

Gallico, Paul
Galvin, Thomas P.
Gatemen
Gateway
Geddes, Lord
General Hospital Building
General Services Administration
Gibran, Kahlil
Gibson, James
Gloucester City Immigrant Station
Goldman, Emma
Graffiti
Graham, Stephen
Grant, Madison
Great Hall
Greenstone, Cecilia
Grogan, Anthony J.
Groupers
Guards and Watchmen
Guastavino, Rafael (I)
Guastavino, Rafael (II)

Halifax Immigrant Station
Hall, Prescott

Harkavy, Alexander
Harrison, Benjamin
Head Tax
Hebrew Immigrant Aid Society
Heiser, Victor
Hendley, Charles M.
Hine, Lewis
Hope, Bob
Hospital Administration Building
Hospital Buildings
Hospital Extension
Hospital Outbuilding
Howe, Frederic C.
Hull, Harry
Husband, W. W.

Idiots
Imbeciles
Information Bureau
Immigrant Aid Societies
Immigrant Inspection Stations
Immigrant Inspectors
Immigration Act of 1882
Immigration Act of 1891
Immigration Act of 1893 (I)
Immigration Act of 1893 (II)
Immigration Act of 1895
Immigration Act of 1903
Immigration Act of 1907
Immigration Act of 1917
Immigration Act of 1918
Immigration Act of 1924
Immigration Act of 1965
Immigration Building
Immigration and Naturalization Service
Immigration Regulations
Immigration Restriction League
Immigration Restriction Movement
Immigration Statistics
Insane Persons
Inspection Division
Internal Security Act of 1950
Interpreters
Interview Corridor
Investigations
Island 1
Island 2
Island 3
Italian Welfare League

James, C. L. R.
James, Henry
Janitors' Division
Johnson, Albert
Johnson, Lyndon B.
Johnson, Philip
Junker, William E.
Jurisdiction

Keefe, Daniel J.
Khodja, Murad Mohammed
Kissing Post
Kitchen Building
Kitchen and Laundry Building
Knox, Howard A.
Krishnamurti, Jiddu

LaGuardia, Fiorello
Land, Paul H.
Landfill
Landing Agents
Landing Immigrants
Landis, Harry R.
Landscape and Vegetation
Languages and Dialects
Larned, Frank H.
Laundries
Laundry and Linen Exchange
Law Division
Lederhilger, John
Liable to Become a Public Charge
Libraries
Line Inspection
Linen Exchanges
Lipsitch, I. Irving
Literacy Tests
Literature and Reminiscences
Lloyd, Marie
Loathsome Contagious Diseases
Lodsin, Michael
Lugosi, Bela

MacCormack, Daniel W.
Main Building
Manifests
Marine Hospital Service
Marriages
Martoccia, Frank
Matthews, Alma
Matrons
Matrons' Division
McCarran, Patrick A.
McCarran-Walter Act
McDonald, Peter
McSweeney, Edward F.
Measles
Mechanical Division
Medical Certificates
Medical Division
Medical Officers
Mental Deficiency
Mental Room
Mental Testing
Messengers
MetaForm Incorporated
MetaForm Research Collection
Mezei, Ignac
Mikolainis, Peter
Miller, Watson B.
Minorities
Mission of Our Lady of the Rosary
Missionaries
Money Exchange
Moore, Annie
Moral Turpitude
Moretti, Gaspare
Mortuary and Autopsy Room
Mosher, Maud
Murray, Joseph E.
My Boy

Name Change Legend
Names
Narragansett
National Council of Jewish Women
National Monument
National Park Service
Navy
Nazis
NEGRO
Nevada
New Immigration Building
New York Chinese Office
New York City Mission Society
New York Detention Dormitory
New York District (INS)
New York Room
Nicknames
Night Division
North American Civic League for Immigrants
Novotny, Ann
Nurses

O'Beirne, James R.
Office Building and Laboratory
Office of Immigration
Oosterhoudt, Emma B.
Oral History Project
Owen, William Dale

Paauw, Michael
Palmer, Carleton H.
Passport Division
Passports
Peak Immigration Years
Peopling of America
Perkins, Frances
Peterssen, Arne
Pinza, Ezio
Pitkin, Thomas M.
Ports of Departure
Post, Louis F.
Postal Cards
Powderly, Terence V.
Power House
Pregnancies
Primary Inspection
Prisoners of War
Privilege Holders
Psychopathic Ward
Public Charge
Public Health and Marine Hospital Service
Public Health Service
Purcell, Anna

Quarantine
Quota Act of 1921
Quotas

Races and Peoples
Radicals
Railroad Ticket Office
Razofsky, Cecilia
Reagan, Ronald
Records
Recreation Hall
Recreation Shelter
Red Scare
Reed, David A.
Reentry Permits
Refugees
Registry Division
Registry Room
Registry Room Exhibit
Registry Room Views
Reimer, Rudolph
Renkiewicz, Frank
Restoration
Roosevelt, Eleanor
Roosevelt, Theodore

Safford, Victor
St. Joseph's Home for Polish Immigrants
St. Raphael Society for the Protection of German Immigrants
St. Raphael Society for the Protection of Italian Immigrants
Salmon, Thomas W.
Salvation Army
Sammartino, Peter
Sargent, Frank P.
Save Ellis Island!
Schooling
Second Immigrant Station
Semsey, Charles
Senner, Joseph H.
Sherman, Augustus F.
Silent Voices
Society for the Protection of Italian Immigrants
Sovereignty
Special Inquiry Division
Special Inspector
Sprague, E. K.
Squatters
Stabilization
Stairs of Separation
Statistical Division
Statue of Liberty
Statue of Liberty–Ellis Island Foundation
Steamship Companies
Steamship Emigration Agents
Steamships
Steerage
Steiner, Edward
Sterilization
Stowaways
Stump, Herman
Suicides
Superintendent of Immigration
Superintendent
Superintendents (NPS)
Surgeons
Surgeons' House
Swing, Joseph

Taft, William Howard
Tarsney Act of 1893
Tarsney, John C.
Taylor, James Knox
Theiss, Frederick A.
Through America's Gate
Tilson, Richard
Tilton, Edward L.
Tod, Robert E.
Trachoma
Tracy, Arthur
Treasurer's Office
Treasures from Home
Trenet, Charles
Tuberculosis

Uhl, Byron H.
Ullo, Lorenzo
Undocumented Alien
Uniforms
United Hebrew Charities
Unrau, Harlan D.

Vandalism

Waldo, Charles
Wallis, Frederick A.
Walter, Francis E.
Ward, Robert DeCourcy
Watchmen
Watchmen's and Gatemen's Division
Watchorn, Robert
Watkins, W. Frank
Weber, John B.
Wells, H. G.
White Slave Traffic Act
Williams, William
Within the Quota
Woman's Home Missionary Society
Women
Women's Christian Temperance Union
World Monuments Fund
World War I
World War II
Wright, Frank Lloyd

YMCA
YWCA

Zucker, Edward D.

List of Entries by Subject

Agencies
Army
Board of Review
Bureau of Immigration
Bureau of Immigration and Naturalization
Coast Guard
General Services Administration
Immigration and Naturalization Service
Marine Hospital Service
National Park Service
Navy
Office of Immigration
Public Health and Marine Hospital Service
Public Health Service

Buildings and Structures
Animal House
Baggage and Dormitory Building
Bakery and Carpentry Shop
Barge Office
Buildings
Canopy
Castle Clinton
Castle Garden
Contagious Disease Wards
Corridors and Covered Passages
Crematory
Demolished Structures
Docks
Ferry House
First Immigrant Station
Fort Gibson
General Hospital Building
Hospital Administration Building
Hospital Buildings
Hospital Extension
Hospital Outbuilding
Immigration Building
Kitchen Building
Kitchen and Laundry Building
Laundry and Linen Exchange
Main Building
Mortuary and Autopsy Room
Office Building and Laboratory
Power House
Psychopathic Ward
Railroad Ticket Office
Recreation Hall
Recreation Shelter
Second Immigrant Station
Statue of Liberty
Surgeons' House

Children
Births
Children
Christmas
Famous Immigrants
Kissing Post
Liable to Become a Public Charge
Measles
Oral History Project
Schooling
Stowaways

Crime
Black Tom Explosion
Crime and Abuse
Deportation
Investigations
Law Division
Moral Turpitude
Vandalism

Culture
Americanization Movement
Celebrations
Christmas
Ellis Island [film]
Films and Documentaries
Gateway [film]
Graffiti
Great Hall
Kissing Post
Languages and Dialects
Libraries
Literature and Reminiscences
Marriages
Minorities
Missionaries
My Boy [film]
Name Change Legend
Nicknames
Races and Peoples
Schooling
Within the Quota [musical]

Diseases and Health
Contagious Diseases
Diseases and Hospitalization
Eye Examinations
Feebleminded
Idiots
Imbeciles
Insane Persons
Line Inspection
Loathsome Contagious Diseases
Measles
Medical Certificates
Mental Deficiency
Pregnancies
Trachoma
Tuberculosis

Divisions
Boarding Division
Bond Office
Chinese Division
Deporting Division
Discharging Division
Divisions
Executive Division
Information Bureau
Inspection Division
Janitors' Division
Law Division
Matrons' Division
Mechanical Division
Medical Division
Night Division
Passport Division
Registry Division
Special Inquiry Division
Statistical Division
Treasurer's Office
Watchmen's and Gatemen's Division

Documents
Christmas
Crime and Abuse
Criticism
Deportation Cases
Detention Cases
Detention Conditions, 1930s
Detention Conditions, 1949
Detention Conditions, 1950s
Diseases and Hospitalization
Food Service and Menus
Foxlee, Ludmila K.
Immigration Regulations
Immigration Statistics

Interpreters
Mosher, Maud
Nazis
Records
Red Scare
Schooling
Trachoma

Ethnic and Racial Groups
African Americans
Black Immigrants
Chinese Division
Chinese Exclusion Act
Delaware Indians

Minorities
Races and Peoples

Ethnic Societies
Austrian Society
Belgian Bureau
Hebrew Immigrant Aid Society
Italian Welfare League
Mission of Our Lady of the Rosary (Irish)
National Council of Jewish Women
St. Joseph's Home for Polish Immigrants
St. Raphael Society for the Protection of German Immigrants
St. Raphael Society for the Protection of Italian Immigrants
Society for the Protection of Italian Immigrants
United Hebrew Charities

History
Americanization Movement
Army
Black Tom Explosion
Bureau of Immigration
Castle Clinton
Castle Garden
Closing of Ellis Island
Coast Guard
Cold War
Commissioners
Commissioners-General
Delaware Indians
Ellis, Samuel
Enemy Aliens
Famous Immigrants
Fire of 1897
First Immigrant Station
Fort Gibson
General Services Administration
Gibson, James
Immigration Restriction Movement
Literature and Reminiscences
Marine Hospital Service
Navy
Nazis
Office of Immigration
Oral History Project
Paauw, Michael
Public Health and Marine Hospital Service
Renkiewicz, Frank
Roosevelt, Theodore
Second Immigrant Station
Sherman, Augustus F.
Sovereignty
Superintendents of Immigration
World War I
World War II

Immigrant Aid Societies
American Red Cross
American Tract Society
Austrian Society
Belgian Bureau
Daughters of the American Revolution
Hebrew Immigrant Aid Society
Immigrant Aid Societies
Italian Welfare League
Mission of Our Lady of the Rosary
National Council of Jewish Women
New York City Mission Society
North American Civic League for Immigrants
St. Joseph's Home for Polish Immigrants
St. Raphael Society for the Protection of German Immigrants
St. Raphael Society for the Protection of Italian Immigrants
Salvation Army
Society for the Protection of Italian Immigrants
Woman's Home Missionary Society
Women's Christian Temperance Union
United Hebrew Charities

Immigrant Experience
Americanization Movement
Anarchists
Angel Island Immigrant Station
Appeals
Arrival
Births
Black Immigrants
Boards of Special Inquiry

Immigrant Experience *(continued)*
Bonds
Boston Immigrant Station
Castle Garden
Chalk Mark Code
Children
Contagious Diseases
Crime and Abuse
Criticism
Deaths and Burials
Deportation
Deportation Cases
Destinations
Detention Cases
Detention Conditions, 1930s
Detention Conditions, 1949
Detention Conditions, 1950s
Diseases and Hospitalization
Enemy Aliens
Exclusion
Eye Examinations
Famous Immigrants
Feebleminded
Ferries and Boats
Ferryboat *Ellis Island*
Films and Documentaries
Fire of 1897
Food Service and Menus
Gloucester City Immigrant Station
Graffiti
Great Hall
Halifax Immigrant Station
Head Tax
Immigrant Aid Societies
Interpreters
Interview Corridor
Investigations
Landing Agents
Landing Immigrants
Languages and Dialects
Liable to Become a Public Charge
Line Inspection
Literacy Tests
Literature and Reminiscences
Loathsome Contagious Diseases
Manifests
Marriages
Mental Room
Minorities
Missionaries
Money Exchange
Moral Turpitude
Name Change Legend
Nazis
Oral History Project
Passports
Postal Cards
Primary Inspection
Prisoners of War
Races and Peoples
Radicals
Railroad Ticket Office
Red Scare
Refugees
Registry Room
Schooling
Stairs of Separation
Steamship Emigration Agents
Steamship Companies
Steamships
Steerage
Stowaways
Suicides
Undocumented Alien
Women
World War I
World War II

Immigrant Inspection Stations
Angel Island Immigrant Station
Barge Office
Boston Immigrant Station
Castle Garden
Gloucester City Immigrant Station
Halifax Immigrant Station

Legislation
Chinese Exclusion Act
Congressional Resolution of 1890
Contract Labor Laws
Head Tax
Immigration Act of 1882

Immigration Act of 1891
Immigration Act of 1893 (I)
Immigration Act of 1893 (II)
Immigration Act of 1895
Immigration Act of 1903
Immigration Act of 1907
Immigration Act of 1917
Immigration Act of 1918
Immigration Act of 1924
Immigration Act of 1965
Internal Security Act of 1950
McCarran-Walter Act
National Monument
Quota Act of 1921
Tarsney Act of 1893
White Slave Traffic Act

Medical Service and Hygiene

American Red Cross
Animal House
Births
Boody, Bertha M.
Chalk Mark Code
Contagious Disease Wards
Contagious Diseases
Daughters of the American Revolution
Deaths and Burials
Deportation
Diseases and Hospitalization
Eye Examinations
Faris, James Edge
Feebleminded
General Hospital Building
Heiser, Victor
Hospital Administration Building
Hospital Buildings
Hospital Extension
Hospital Outbuilding
Idiots
Imbeciles
Immigration Regulations
Insane Persons
Interpreters
Island 2
Island 3
Laundry and Linen Exchange
Liable to Become a Public Charge
Line Inspection
Loathsome Contagious Diseases
Marine Hospital Service
Measles
Medical Certificates
Medical Division
Medical Officers
Mental Deficiency
Mental Room
Mental Testing
Mortuary and Autopsy Room
Navy
Nurses
Office Building and Laboratory
Pregnancies
Psychopathic Ward
Public Charge
Public Health Service
Public Health and Marine Hospital Service
Purcell, Anna
Quarantine
Recreation Hall
Recreation Shelter
Safford, Victor
Salmon, Thomas W.
Sprague, E. K.
Sterilization
Surgeons
Surgeons House
Theiss, Frederick A.
Trachoma
Tuberculosis
World War I

Military History

American Red Cross
Army
Coast Guard
Fort Gibson
Gibson, James
Navy
O'Beirne, James R.
Swing, Joseph

Military History *(continued)*
Weber, John B.
Williams, William
World War I
World War II
YMCA

Missionary Societies
American Tract Society
Austrian Society
Hebrew Immigrant Aid Society
Mission of Our Lady of the Rosary
National Council of Jewish Women
New York City Mission Society
St. Joseph's Home for Polish Immigrants
St. Raphael Society for the Protection of German Immigrants
St. Raphael Society for the Protection of Italian Immigrants
Salvation Army
United Hebrew Charities
Woman's Home Missionary Society
Women's Christian Temperance Union

Museums and Exhibitions
American Museum of Immigration
Baggage Room
Dormitory
Ellis Island Chronicles
Ellis Island Immigration Museum
Peak Immigration Years
Peopling of America
Registry Room Exhibit
Registry Room Views
Silent Voices
Through America's Gate
Treasures from Home

Occupations
Assistant Commissioners
Chief Clerks
Clerks
Commissioners
Commissioners-General
District Directors
Gatemen
Groupers
Guards
Immigrant Inspectors
Interpreters
Landing Agents
Matrons
Medical Officers
Messengers
Missionaries
Nurses
Privilege Holders
Special Inspectors
Superintendent of Immigration
Superintendents
Superintendents (NPS)
Surgeons
Watchmen

Ocean Crossing
Buford
Landing Agents
Nevada
Steamship Companies
Steamship Emigration Agents
Steamships
Steerage

Offices
Bond Office
New York Chinese Office
Railroad Ticket Office
Treasurer's Office

Places
Angel Island Immigrant Station [San Francisco]
Barge Office
The Battery (Battery Park)
Boston Immigrant Station
Castle Clinton
Castle Garden
Docks
Gloucester City Immigrant Station
Halifax Immigrant Station
Immigrant Inspection Stations
Island 1

Island 2
Island 3
Ports of Departure
Stairs of Separation
Statue of Liberty

Rehabilitation and Public Use
American Family Immigration History Center
Demolished Structures
Ellis Island Immigration Museum
General Services Administration
Graffiti
Johnson, Lyndon B.
Johnson, Philip
Jurisdiction
Landscape and Vegetation
MetaForm Incorporated
MetaForm Research Collection
Moore, Annie
National Monument
National Park Service
NEGRO
Oral History Project
Pitkin, Thomas M.
Reagan, Ronald
Restoration
Sammartino, Peter
Save Ellis Island!
Sherman, Augustus F.
Sovereignty
Statue of Liberty
Statue of Liberty–Ellis Island Foundation
Superintendents (NPS)
Unrau, Harlan D.
Vandalism
World Monuments Fund
Wright, Frank Lloyd

Rooms
Baggage Room
Great Hall
Interview Corridor
Laundries
Libraries
Linen Exchanges
Mental Room
Money Exchange
Mortuary and Autopsy Room
Railroad Ticket Office
Registry Room

Rules and Regulations
Abbreviations
Appeals
Arrival
Board of Review
Boards of Special Inquiry
Bonds
Certificates
Certificates of Registry
Chalk Mark Code
Children
Chinese Division
Citizens
Deaths and Burials
Deportation
Detention Cases
Diseases and Hospitalization
Divisions
Enemy Aliens
Exclusion
Eye Examinations
Head Tax
Immigrant Aid Societies
Immigration Regulations
Line Inspection
Literacy Tests
Manifests
Marriages
Mental Testing
Missionaries
Passports
Postal Cards
Primary Inspection
Prisoners of War
Privilege Holders
Quotas
Races and Peoples
Railroad Ticket Office
Refugees
Schooling
Stairs of Separation

Rules and Regulations (*continued*)
Steerage
Sterilization
Stowaways
Undocumented Alien
Uniforms
Women

Ships and Ferries
Buford
Docks
Ferries and Boats
Ferryboat *Ellis Island*
Ferry House
Ferry Service
Narragansett
Nevada
Steamships

Women
American, Sadie
Baer, Beulah
Births
Boody, Bertha M.
Bremer, Edith Terry
Buck, Pearl S.
Children
Christmas
Corcoran, Emma
Crime and Abuse
Daughters of the American Revolution
Deportation Cases
Detention Cases
Duncan, Isadora
Enemy Aliens
Food Service and Menus
Foxlee, Ludmila K.
Goldman, Emma
Greenstone, Cecilia
Immigrant Aid Societies
Kissing Post
Liable to Become a Public Charge
Lloyd, Marie
Marriages
Matthews, Alma
Matrons
Matrons' Division
Mission of Our Lady of the Rosary
Missionaries
Moore, Annie
Moral Turpitude
Mosher, Maud
National Council of Jewish Women
Novotny, Ann
Nurses
Oosterhoudt, Emma B.
Perkins, Frances
Pregnancies
Public Charge
Purcell, Anna
Razofsky, Cecilia
Roosevelt, Eleanor
Suicides
White Slave Traffic Act
Woman's Home Missionary Society
Women
Women's Christian Temperance Union
YWCA

List of Entries by Field of Endeavor or Background

Actors
Hope, Bob
Lugosi, Bela
Lloyd, Marie
Reagan, Ronald
Tracy, Arthur
Trenet, Charles

Anarchists
Berkman, Alexander
Goldman, Emma

Architects
Boring, William A.
Guastavino, Rafael (I)
Guastavino, Rafael (II)
Johnson, Philip
Taylor, James Knox
Tilton, Edward L.
Wright, Frank Lloyd

Assistant Commissioner-General
Larned, Frank H.

Assistant Commissioners
Landis, Harry R.
McSweeney, Edward F.
Murray, Joseph E.
O'Beirne, James R.
Uhl, Byron H.

Athletes
Firpo, Luis

Attorneys General
Biddle, Francis
Brownell, Herbert

Authors
Adamic, Louis
Baer, Beulah
Berkman, Alexander
Boody, Bertha M.
Brandenburg, Broughton
Buck, Pearl S.
Corsi, Edward
Cowen, Philip
Curran, Henry H.
Evans-Gordon, Sir William
Foxlee, Ludmila K.
Gallico, Paul
Gibran, Kahlil
Goldman, Emma
Graham, Stephen
Grant, Madison
Guastavino, Rafael (I)
Hall, Prescott
Harkavy, Alexander
Heiser, Victor
Hine, Lewis
Hope, Bob
Howe, Frederic C.
James, C. L. R.
James, Henry
Knox, Howard A.
Krishnamurti, Jiddu
LaGuardia, Fiorello
Mosher, Maud
Novotny, Ann
Palmer, Carleton H.
Pinza, Ezio
Pitkin, Thomas M.
Post, Louis F.
Powderly, Terence V.
Razofsky, Cecilia

Authors *(continued)*
Renkiewicz, Frank
Roosevelt, Theodore
Safford, Victor
Sammartino, Peter
Salmon, Thomas W.
Steiner, Edward
Tilton, Edward L.
Unrau, Harlan D.
Ward, Robert DeCourcy
Watchorn, Robert
Weber, John B.
Wells, H. G.

Chief Clerks
Sherman, Augustus F.
Uhl, Byron H.

Chief Inspectors
Cowen, Philip
Forman, Philip
Junker, William E.
Lederhilger, John
Zucker, Edward D.

Commissioners
Corsi, Edward
Curran, Henry H.
Day, Benjamin M.
Howe, Frederic C.
Reimer, Rudolph
Senner, Joseph H.
Tod, Robert E.
Uhl, Byron H.
Watchorn, Robert
Watkins, W. Frank
Wallis, Frederick A.
Weber, John B.
Williams, William

Commissioners-General
Caminetti, Anthony
Hull, Harry
Husband, W. W.
Keefe, Daniel J.
MacCormack, Daniel W.
Miller, Watson B.
Owen, William Dale
Powderly, Terence V.
Sargent, Frank P.
Stump, Herman
Swing, Joseph

Congressmen and Senators
Caminetti, Anthony
Harrison, Benjamin
Hull, Harry
Johnson, Albert
Johnson, Lyndon B.
LaGuardia, Fiorello
McCarran, Patrick A.
Reed, David A.
Tarsney, John C.
Stump, Herman
Walter, Francis E.
Weber, John B.

Critics
Brandenburg, Broughton
Corsi, Edward
Geddes, Lord
Goldman, Emma
Graham, Stephen
Grogan, Anthony J.
James, C. L. R.
James, Henry
LaGuardia, Fiorello
Wells, H.G.

Dancer
Duncan, Isadora

Deportees
Berkman, Alexander
Goldman, Emma
James, C. L. R.

Detainees
Adamic, Louis
Barbusse, Henri
Berkman, Alexander
Castro, Cipriano

Duncan, Isadora
Firpo, Luis
Goldman, Emma
James, C. L. R.
Krishnamurti, Jiddu
Lloyd, Marie
Mezei, Ignac
Pinza, Ezio
Trenet, Charles

Diplomats
Geddes, Lord

District Directors
Watkins, W. Frank
Uhl, Byron H.

Educator
Sammartino, Peter

Enemy Alien Suspect
Pinza, Ezio

Engineer
Fry, Alfred Brooks

Famous Immigrants
Adamic, Louis
Berkman, Alexander
Castro, Cipriano
Corsi, Edward
Gibran, Kahlil
Goldman, Emma
Hope, Bob
James, C. L. R.
Krishnamurti, Jiddu
Lugosi, Bela
Moore, Annie
Pinza, Ezio
Tracy, Arthur

First Lady
Roosevelt, Eleanor

Historians
Pitkin, Thomas M.
Unrau, Harlan D.

Immigrant Inspectors
Cowen, Philip
Ferro, Edward
Forman, Philip
Galvin, Thomas P.
Junker, William E.
Semsey, Charles
Uhl, Byron H.
Watchorn, Robert
Watkins, W. Frank
Waldo, Charles
Zucker, Edward D.

Immigrants/Aliens
Adamic, Louis
Barbusse, Henri
Berkman, Alexander
Carol, Charles A.
Castro, Cipriano
Corsi, Edward
Escobar, José Dias d'
Ferro, Edward
Firpo, Luis
Foxlee, Ludmila K.
Gibran, Kahlil
Goldman, Emma
Graham, Stephen
Greenstone, Cecilia
Grogan, Anthony J.
Guastavino, Rafael (I)
Guastavino, Rafael (II)
Harkavy, Alexander
Hope, Bob
James, C. L. R.
Khodja, Murad Mohammed
Krishnamurti, Jiddu
Land, Paul H.
Lederhilger, John
Lloyd, Marie
Lodsin, Michael
McSweeney, Edward F.
Martoccia, Frank
Mezei, Ignac
Mikolainis, Peter
Moore, Annie
Moretti, Gaspare

Immigrants/Aliens *(continued)*
O'Beirne, James R.
Peterssen, Arne
Pinza, Ezio
Semsey, Charles
Senner, Joseph H.
Steiner, Edward
Tracy, Arthur
Trenet, Charles
Ullo, Lorenzo
Waldo, Charles
Watchorn, Robert
Wells, H.G.

Interpreters
Ferro, Edward
LaGuardia, Fiorello
Martoccia, Frank
Mikolainis, Peter
Waldo, Charles

Marxists
Barbusse, Henri
James, C. L. R.

Matron
Mosher, Maud

Mayor
LaGuardia, Fiorello

Missionaries
American, Sadie
Bremer, Edith Terry
Carol, Charles A.
Foxlee, Ludmila K.
Grogan, Anthony J.
Greenstone, Cecilia
Harkavy, Alexander
Lipsitch, I. Irving
Lodsin, Michael
Matthews, Alma
Moretti, Gaspare
Razofsky, Cecilia

Novelists
Barbusse, Henri
Gallico, Paul
James, Henry
Wells, H.G.

Nurse
Purcell, Anna

Oral History Interviewees
Corcoran, Emma
Faris, James Edge
Ferro, Edward
Tracy, Arthur

Owners (Private)
Ellis, Samuel
Paauw, Michael

Physicians and Surgeons
Boody, Bertha M.
Faris, James Edge
Heiser, Victor
Safford, Victor
Salmon, Thomas W.
Sprague, E. K.

Political Detainees
Barbusse, Henri
Berkman, Alexander
Castro, Cipriano
Goldman, Emma
James, C. L. R.
Mezei, Ignac
Pinza, Ezio

Politicians
Caminetti, Anthony
Castro, Cipriano
Corsi, Edward
Curran, Henry H.
Evans-Gordon, Sir William
Geddes, Lord
Harrison, Benjamin
Hull, Harry
Johnson, Albert
Johnson, Lyndon B.
LaGuardia, Fiorello
McCarran, Patrick A.

Murray, Joseph E.
Reagan, Ronald
Reed, David A.
Roosevelt, Theodore
Stump, Herman
Taft, William Howard
Walter, Francis E.
Weber, John B.

Presidents
Harrison, Benjamin
Johnson, Lyndon B.
Reagan, Ronald
Roosevelt, Theodore
Taft, William Howard

Presidents (Foreign)
Castro, Cipriano

Priests
Grogan, Anthony J.
Moretti, Gaspare

Radicals
Barbusse, Henri
Berkman, Alexander
Goldman, Emma
James, C. L. R.

Restrictionists
Grant, Madison
Hall, Prescott
Johnson, Albert
Keefe, Daniel J.
McCarran, Patrick A.
Reed, David A.
Walter, Francis E.
Ward, Robert DeCourcy
Williams, William

Seamen
Lugosi, Bela
Peterssen, Arne

Secretaries
Baer, Beulah
Corcoran, Emma
Oosterhoudt, Emma B.

Secretary of Commerce and Labor
Cortelyou, George

Secretaries of Labor
Doak, William N.
Perkins, Frances

Singers
Lloyd, Marie
Pinza, Ezio
Tracy, Arthur
Trenet, Charles

Social Workers
American, Sadie
Bremer, Edith Terry
Foxlee, Ludmila K.
Greenstone, Cecilia
Harkavy, Alexander
Lipsitch, I. Irving
Matthews, Alma
Razofsky, Cecilia

Watchman
Tilson, Richard

Abbreviations. Along with the bureaucratic red tape for which Ellis Island is duly famous, a system of abbreviations was used there over the years. Here are a few examples associated with the **immigrant inspectors** and **clerks**: *A/R*, no passport; *CIV*, consular immigrant visa; *Crimson*, convicted before entry into U.S. of **moral turpitude**; *Do*, ditto; *EWI*, entered without visa; *IV*, immigrant visa; *LPC*, **liable to become a public charge**; *NoV*, no visa; *Rem Lon*, remained too long; *SI*, special inquiry; *Safekeeping*, detained for personal safety or to prevent from getting away; *Transit*, bound for another country and only passing through; *Vol. Dep.*, voluntary departure.

See also **Chalk Mark Code**

Adamic, Louis (b. Blato [Slovenia], Austria-Hungary, March 23, 1899; d. Milford, New Jersey, September 4, 1951). Louis Adamic arrived at Ellis Island on December 30, 1913, as a steerage passenger on the SS *Niagara*, a steamship of the French line. The following is a personal description of his experiences as a newly arrived immigrant at Ellis Island, which he wrote nineteen years later, in 1932.

Now and then I glanced at the noisy, picturesque, garlicky crowd on the steerage deck; people of perhaps a dozen nationalities milling around the capstans and steam-hissing winches, pushing toward the rails straining and stretching, catching a glimpse of the new country, of the city; lifting their children, even their infants, to give them a view of the Statue of Liberty; women weeping for joy, men falling on their knees in thanksgiving, and children screaming, wailing, dancing.

We docked somewhere in the East River, and I began to hear the distant rumble of the city's traffic.

Near by, too, I saw the great span of the Brooklyn Bridge. It looked huge and superb against the clear winter sky, with vessels passing under it. Steel! There was steel all about.

I had written Stefan ["Steve"] Radin, brother of my late friend Yanko, whose address in Brooklyn I happened to have, that I was due in New York on December 30, and would he meet me at Ellis Island, which Peter Molek had told me was the clearing-house for immigrants? In my letter I explained that I had witnessed the killing of his brother and had, as a result of my participation in the demonstration with Yanko, been imprisoned and expelled from school.

From the ship we were transferred on a lighter to Ellis Island, where I received a telegram from Steve that he was coming for me the next afternoon, when he had learned from the immigration authorities I was to be released, assuming I was found admissible. The day I spent on Ellis Island was an eternity. Rumors were current among immigrants of several nationalities that some of us would be refused admittance into the United States and sent back to Europe. For several hours I was in a cold seat on this account, although, so far as I knew, all my papers were in order and sewed away in the lining of my jacket were twenty-five dollars in American currency—the minimum amount required by law to be in the possession of every immigrant before entering the country. Then, having realized away some of these fears, I gradually worked up a panicky feeling that I might develop measles or smallpox, or some other such disease. I had heard that several hundred sick immigrants were quarantined on the island.

The first night in America I spent with hundreds of other recently arrived immigrants in an immense hall with tiers of narrow iron-and-canvas bunks, four deep. I was assigned to top bunk. Unlike most of the steerage immigrants I had no bedding with me and, the blanket which someone threw at me, was too thin to be effective against the blasts of cold air that rushed through the open windows; so that I shivered, sleepless all night, listening to snores and dream-monologues in perhaps a dozen different languages.

The bunk immediately beneath mine was occupied by a Turk who slept with his turban wound around his head. He was tall, thin, dark, bearded hollowed-faced and hook-nosed. At peace with Allah, he snored all night, producing a thin wheezing sound which, occasionally, for a moment or two, took on a deeper note.

I thought how curious it was that I should be spending a night in such proximity to a Turk, for Turks were traditional enemies of Balkan peoples, including my own nation. For centuries Turks had forayed into Slovenian territory, Now here I was trying to sleep directly above a Turk with only a sheet of canvas between us. (pp. 40–44)

REFERENCE: Adamic, Louis. 1932. *Laughing in the Jungle.* New York: Harper Brothers.

African Americans. Many African Americans were employed at Ellis Island. Solomon Johnson was an **immigrant inspector** from about 1908 until he retired in 1933; in 1926, Johnson earned the respectable salary of $2,300 per year. Another black official was Ernest Craigwell, a clerk in the **Statistical Division** from about 1903 through 1930. In 1909, he was listed as an underclerk at a salary of $900 per year. Over the years his income rose, though never as high as an immigrant inspector's. In 1906, he was photographed with Commissioner-General **Frank Sargent** and members of the Statistical Division staff.

But these men were exceptional, for most blacks occupied menial positions as common laborers and charwomen. They surprised Europeans that had never seen blacks.

American, Sadie (b. Chicago, 1862; d. New York, 1944). Social reformer. A founder of the **National Council of Jewish Women** (NCJW), Sadie American was originally from Chicago but moved to New York in 1900 to supervise efforts to aid Jewish girls and young women between the ages of fourteen and thirty-five. She assigned **Cecilia Greenstone**, **Cecilia Razofsky,** and other NCJW workers and volunteers to Ellis Island and the Lower East Side of Manhattan. She strove to protect these young women from crime and immorality. As a tribute to her success, she was appointed the U.S. delegate to the International White Slave Traffic Convention. In the NCJW, she served as corresponding secretary (1893–1905), executive secretary (1905–1914), and president of the New York section (from 1900 and many years thereafter).

American Family Immigration History Center (AFIHC). Opened in April 2001 by the **Statue of Liberty–Ellis Island Foundation**, this section of the **Ellis Island Immigration Museum** has a computer database with the records of twenty-two million passengers who entered the port of New York aboard ships from 1892 through 1924. Foreigners made up 17 million passengers, while the remainder were American citizens. The database provides researchers with such information as the passenger's complete name, his ethnicity, last residence, age at arrival, gender, marital status, the name of the vessel that brought him to America, and the port of departure. In addition, the database provides images of the original ship and manifest. The records of the computer database were copied from passenger lists held on microfilm in the U.S. National Archives by 12,000 volunteers from the Church of Jesus Christ of Latter-Day Saints (Mormon Church).

American Immigrant Wall of Honor. *See* **Statue of Liberty–Ellis Island Foundation**

American Museum of Immigration. The American Museum of Immigration was located on Liberty Island and was in operation from September 1972 until the National Park Service closed it in January 1991. The museum was founded by a group that included William H. Baldwin, Pierre S. duPont III, Alexander Hamilton, and General Ulysses S. Grant III. In 1955, the group began raising funds for museum construction with endorsements from prominent figures such as Vice President Richard M. Nixon, AFL-CIO union president George Meany, motion picture actor Edward G. Robinson, Twentieth Century-Fox Film Corporation chief executive Spyros P. Skouras, televi-

People can do genealogical research in the American Family Immigration History Center. Courtesy of the Ellis Island Immigration Museum.

sion host Ed Sullivan, and former immigration commissioner **Edward Corsi**. Although numerous ethnic societies, schools, and clubs contributed to the effort, the fund-raising was not successful. Eventually the federal government paid for the construction of the museum within the walls of Fort Wood at the base of the pedestal of the **Statue of Liberty**. Expensive construction work was carried out in the early 1960s that involved excavation within the walls of the fort and resulted in the destruction of valuable portions of its history that dated to the War of 1812.

The museum's advisory board of historians included Theodore Blegan, Allan Nevins, Carl Wittke, Oscar Handlin, John Higham, **Thomas M. Pitkin**, Rudolph Vecoli, John A. Krout, Horace M. Albright, and John Hope Franklin. They played an important role in planning the museum and its exhibits. Financial troubles and debates about the ethnic representations and the historic theme planned for the museum slowed its completion. It was opened by President Nixon during a formal ceremony on September 26, 1972.

The museum showed the demographic growth of the United States through immigration from the founding of the European colonies through the later years of **Castle Garden** and Ellis Island. Exhibits included photography, graphic designs, maps, engravings, and a wide variety of artifacts representing different periods of American history. Life-size mannequins represented colonists, pioneers who went west, ethnic fighting brigades from the Civil War, and so forth. There were also recordings of different immigrant types (as one approached mannequins they seemed to speak) and short historic films and different types of lighting in the various sections of the exhibit.

Thematically and chronologically, the American Museum of Immigration explored emigrants' reasons for leaving the Old World, such as advancing colonialism and land conquest, securing religious freedom, gaining wealth and prosperity, working as indentured servants, coming as criminals or slaves, or fleeing from poverty, famine, war, discrimination, and persecution.

The museum showcased the achievements of ethnic groups and their gifts to America. Thus the English, Scots, Welsh, Scotch-Irish, French, Dutch, Africans, Germans, Irish, Scandinavians, Chinese, Japanese, Eastern European Christians, Jews, Greeks, and Italians each received some measure of praise. In addition, the Indian wars, the African slave trade, slavery, the Revolutionary and Civil Wars, and other forms of military, social, political, and economic conflict were discussed and displayed.

Honored also were those who overcame hardship and struggle in the New World and created lasting settlements, developed agriculture, expanded trade and manufacturing, and waged war. Famous immigrants who were recognized include Baron Friedrich von Steuben, Tadeusz Kosciuszko, E. I. duPont, Alexander Graham Bell, Franz Siegel, Carl Schurz, Andrew Carnegie, Joseph Pulitzer, Nikola Tesla, Charles Proteus Steinmetz, Jacob Riis, Bert Williams, Al Jolson, Hideyo Noguchi, Wanda Landowska, and Rudolph Valentino.

The American Museum of Immigration, which did not enjoy continuous financial support from its founders, was closed shortly after the opening of the **Ellis Island Immigration Museum**.

REFERENCE: Blumberg, Barbara. 1985. *Celebrating the Immigrant: An Administrative History of the Statue of Liberty National Monument.* Boston: National Park Service.

American Red Cross. The Red Cross came to Ellis Island with the erection of the Red Cross house on Island 2 in 1915. It provided recreational and social services to U.S. servicemen and some immigrants from that year until 1924. These services included a library and reading room, performances, and lectures. The American Library Association donated books to the library. Religious services were offered including regular Roman Catholic masses given by Father **Anthony J. Grogan**. H. Edenborough was the director of the Red Cross activities at the island from 1919 until 1920. The Red Cross house was demolished in 1936 to make space for new constructions.

American Tract Society. This Protestant organization, founded in 1825, sent immigrant aid workers to Ellis Island for many years. Its representatives distributed foreign language tracts, books, and pamphlets to immigrants and aided newly arrived Christian immigrants. These publications were mainly gospel tracts.

Americanization Movement (c. 1917–1920s, 1930s–1950s). This nativist movement sought to compel foreigners living in the United States to learn English and American customs. At the height of its power, from 1917 through 1922, it was hostile toward Germany, Austria-Hungary, and German-speaking people throughout the United States. Following the end of **World War I**, it expanded into a vast patriotic movement that pressured immigrants of all nationalities to give up their foreign ways and traditions and become American. In the years 1918 through 1921, under its influence, twenty states passed laws creating Americanization programs.

At Ellis Island, the Americanization activities were conducted by such organizations as the **Daughters of the American Revolution** and the **YMCA**. It was actively supported by various Protestant missionaries, especially those from the Episcopal and Presbyterian Churches. Their goal was to teach newcomers American values through civics, history, and the English language. American law and heroes were extolled such as the Constitution, Bill of Rights, George Washington, Benjamin Franklin, and Abraham Lincoln. They also taught patriotic airs, including the National Anthem

CLEVELAND
MANY PEOPLES, ONE LANGUAGE
A
B
C
Come to the Public Schools
Learn the Language of America.
Prepare for American Citizenship.
Free Classes for both Men and Women.
Classes in the Evening and Afternoon.
Apply to nearest Public School or Library for further information.
Pridite v ljudske Šole!
Učite se ameriškega jezika!
Pripravljajte se za državljanstvo!
Razredi za moške in ženske!
Poduk zvečer in popoldne!
Vprašajte v bliznji publik šoli ali v čitalnici za nadeljna pójasnila.
Venite alle Scuole Pubbliche
Imparate la linqua di America. Preparate di diventare un cittadino Americano.
Ve ne sono classe per nomini e donne.
Le classe sono serali ed anche dopo mezzogiorno.
Andate alla scuola pubblica pui vicina o alla Biblioteca pubblica per altra informazione.
Zapisz się do Szkoły Publicznej
Ucz się języka angielskiego.
Przygotuj się do Obywatelstwa tego kraju.
Otwieramy klasy dla mężczyzn i kobiet wieczorami i po południu.
Zgłoś się do najblizszej Publicznej Szkoły lub Biblioteki po dalsze informacye.
Jöjjenek a Public Schoolokba
Tanulják meg Amerika nyelvét.
Készüljön amerikai polgárnak.
Osztályok ugy férfiak mint nök számára.
Elöadások délután es este.
Jelentkezzék a legközelebbi iskolában vagy könyvtárban bövebb felvilágositásert.
BOARD OF EDUCATION
EAST SIXTH AND ROCKWELL
IN CO-OPERATION WITH THE
CLEVELAND AMERICANIZATION COMMITTEE
(Mayor's Advisory War Committee)

The Cleveland Americanization Committee and the local board of education put out this poster encouraging the city's large immigrant population of Italians, Hungarians, Serbians, Croatians, and Jews to learn English. Courtesy of the Ellis Island Immigration Museum.

and "Hail Columbia," and well as the benefits and duties of citizenship. While the movement's popularity rose and fell at various times elsewhere in the nation, its influence on Ellis Island remained steady until the station closed in 1954.

REFERENCE: LeMay, Michael C. 1987. *From Open Door to Dutch Door: An Analysis of U.S. Immigration Policy since 1920*. New York: Praeger.

Anarchists. Those who advocated the violent overthrow of government by any means were greatly feared between 1870 and 1930. The assassinations of the Empress Elisabeth of Austria-Hungary (1897), and King Humbert I of Italy (1900) by avowed anarchists shocked Americans and people throughout the world. However, the real shock came when President William McKinley was killed in Buffalo in 1901 by Leon Czogolsz, a Slavic American who claimed to have become an anarchist after hearing the radical orator **Emma Goldman** give a speech. In the aftermath of the president's assassination, Congress included anarchists for exclusion in the **Immigration Act of 1903**. The first alien detained and excluded from entering the country because of his political opinions was the English anarchist and trade union organizer John Turner, who arrived in New York in October 1903 to begin a speaking tour of the country. A fortnight earlier the Secret Service had advised Commissioner-General **Frank P. Sargent** of his sailing and arrival date.

While in detention at Ellis Island, Turner was interviewed by a reporter from the New York *World*. The newspaperman found him to be a mild-mannered man. The exclusion of Turner sent out a warning to other well-known anarchists not to visit the United States. Previous to the Immigration Act of 1903, many prominent anarchists had visited the country on speaking engagements, the most famous of whom was Prince Peter Kropotkin, the Russian philosopher and author who had inspired no less an anarchist than Emma Goldman. In 1919, a group of 249 radicals and other undesirables—including Goldman and **Alexander Berkman**—were deported to Russia via Finland. The murder trial of the Italian immigrants Sacco and Vanzetti in the 1920s was the last great case involving anarchists. The powerful effects of the restrictive immigrant quota laws of 1920s and the Great Depression of the 1930s lessened the fear of foreign anarchists.

See also **Deportation Cases; Detention Cases; Red Scare**

REFERENCE: Preston, William, Jr. 1963. *Aliens and Dissenters: Federal Suppression of Radicals, 1903–1933*. Cambridge: Harvard University Press.

SUGGESTED READING: Conrad, Joseph. 1907. *The Secret Agent*. London: J.M. Dent; Conrad, Joseph. 1911. *Under Western Eyes*. London: J.M. Dent; Wallace, Edgar. 1905. *The Four Just Men*. London: The Tallis Press.

Angel Island Immigrant Station [San Francisco]. As the largest island in San Francisco Bay, Angel Island has been the headquarters of many federal government operations, from a **Public Health Service** quarantine hospital to an enemy alien prison camp during **World War II**. But its most famous role was that of San Francisco's best-known U.S. immigrant inspection station, a place comparable to Ellis Island. The station was opened when European immigration was at its height. With the upcoming inauguration of the Panama Canal, Europeans bound for California expected to be able to sail there via the canal instead of passing through New York's crowded Ellis Island Immigrant Station and traveling overland by train.

During its thirty years of operation (1910–1940), the portion of the island given over to the activities of the **Bureau of Immigration** saw some 175,000 Chinese detained there, the majority as "paper sons" and "paper daughters." Since it was illegal for Chinese people to immigrate to the United States under the **Chinese Exclusion Act**, most would-be immigrants had to take advantage of a loophole in the law that permitted the offspring of Chinese Americans to enter the country. The **boards of special inquiry** at the station responded to these claims by instituting long and arduous interrogations to ensure that the immigrant was not lying. Thus life at Angel Island for the majority of immigrants was marked by long periods of detention, feelings of frustration and hopelessness. Immigrants carved beautiful Chinese poems on the walls of detention areas at Angel Island to express their unhappiness and their plight.

In addition to the Chinese, about 25,000 Japanese as well as thousands of Indians, Koreans, Russians, Mexicans, Filipinos, Australians, New Zealanders, and others passed through Angel Island or were detained there.

Many of the **immigrant inspectors** and other employees of the Bureau of Immigration posted to Angel Island had transferred there from the Ellis Island station.

Angel Island was closed by the **Immigration and Naturalization Service** after a fire destroyed its administration building in 1940. In about 1970, Chinese graffiti was discovered on the walls of the barracks, prompting the California State Department of Parks and Recreation and the **National Park Service** (NPS) to preserve the site. In 1997, the NPS added Angel Island to the National Register of Historic Places.

See also **Chinese Division; New York Chinese Office**

References: Bamford, Mary. 1917. *Angel Island: The Ellis Island of the West.* Chicago: Women's American Baptist Home Mission Society; Lai, Him Mark, Genny Lim, and Judy Yung. 1980. *Island: Poetry and History of Chinese Immigrants on Angel Island, 1910–1940.* Repr., Seattle: University of Washington Press, 1997.

Animal House. The animal house was originally used as a mortuary (c. 1911–1930s). It was designed in the neo-Renaissance style by federal architect **James Knox Taylor** in 1908 and constructed in 1908–1909 but was not opened until 1911. It is a one-story building and is linked to the buildings of the **contagious disease wards** on **Island 3** by a central corridor.

As the center for certain types of bacteriological studies at Ellis Island, experiments on animals were conducted in this building. Guinea pigs and monkeys were inoculated with mumps and scarlet fever in order to study these diseases more carefully. In 1935, thirty-six male and twelve female guinea pigs were bought for experimentation there.

See also **Office Building and Laboratory**

Appeals. Appeals against excluding an alien could be made in writing by the dissenting member of the three-man board of special inquiry and sent to the **commissioner**. With certain exceptions, aliens themselves could file appeals against a board's decision to exclude the alien. According to **Bureau of Immigration** regulations:

Commissioner Robert Watchorn (seated left, holding document) presides over an appeal case, ca 1906. The man sitting across from him on the right is senior clerk Augustus Sherman. Courtesy of the Ellis Island Immigration Museum.

Appeals must be filed promptly. The immigration officer in charge may refuse to accept an appeal filed after the alien has been removed from an immigration station for deportation, provided the alien had a reasonable opportunity of appeal before such removal. Any appeal filed more than forty-eight hours after the time of an excluding decision may be rejected by the immigration officer in charge in his discretion.

See also **Exclusion**

REFERENCE: Herring, H.G., and D.H. Smith. 1924. *The Bureau of Immigration: Its History, Activities and Organization.* Baltimore: Johns Hopkins University Press.

Army. During **World War I**, the U.S. Army was assigned an extensive portion of Ellis Island, in effect twenty-one buildings. In a memorandum of understanding between the Departments of Labor, War, and Navy, dated February 17, 1918, the army received the general hospital buildings on Island 2, the **contagious disease wards** buildings on Island 3, and space in the **Main Building** and the **kitchen and laundry building** on Island 1. In the Main Building, the army occupied the **Registry Division** on the second floor and stairway two in the northeast tower leading to the third floor; all **Special Inquiry Division** board rooms and witness rooms on the north side, special inquiry detention rooms and the immigrants' dining room, kitchen and corridor, which formed a part of the kitchen and laundry building. On the third floor of the Main Building in the west wing, they received the upper special inquiry rooms, including the janitors' dormitory. On the same floor, in the east wing, was the Statistical Division's bookbindery room. The army assigned the station the name "United States Debarkation Hospital Number 1," for it was the nation's first and foremost hospital to serve wounded soldiers returning from the battlefields of France; Major Chester R. Haig was its commanding officer. It opened on March 8, 1918, and the medical detachment eventually exceeded 100 personnel. The army doctors and nurses also treated a large number of influenza cases. A total of 250 beds were assigned to the Debarkation Hospital. The detachment included surgeons and ward men and maintained separate surgical rooms. Surgical, ambulatory, and psychopathic cases were among the ailments treated. Many of the first patients to be shipped in from France that March were shell shock cases and those who had lost limbs or were otherwise maimed. An Ellis Island official later said that it "was horrible to hear them scream and moan" (Crookston et al. 1918). The women and men of the **American Red Cross** began operating at the hospital in May 1918 and distributed books, games, writing materials, sweets, tobacco, fruit, and occasionally tickets to vaudeville shows and theater plays in New York. The Red Cross also operated a boat plying the waters between Ellis Island and Manhattan. In addition, the Reverend Father **Anthony Grogan**, the priest in charge of the **Mission of Our Lady of the Rosary**, gave spiritual guidance to the military personnel of the Roman Catholic faith. He was a favorite with the detachment, just as he had long been with the immigrants. The **YMCA** set up a reading room furnished with a Victrola gramophone, billiard tables, a piano, a motion picture machine, and a stage that ensured many an amusing evening for the detachment and the patients. After Christmas 1918, the detachment began preparing for evacuation and bidding good-bye to Ellis Isle.

REFERENCES: Crookston, Harry N., Floyd P. Bixler, and Walter O. Given, eds. 1918. The pill box. Souvenir ed. Ellis Island, NY: USA Debarkation Hospital no. 1; Pitkin, Thomas. 1975. *Keepers of the Gate.* New York: New York University Press; Statue of Liberty and Ellis Island Library. Ellis Island during World War I. File Folder. Ellis Island, NY: Statue of Liberty and Ellis Island Library; Unrau, Harlan D. 1984. *The Historic Resource Study: Ellis Island/Statue of Liberty.* Vol. 3. Washington, DC: U.S. Dept. of Interior, National Park Service.

Arrival. Immigrants were transported to Ellis Island by barges and ferries from steamships docked at the piers of New York City and Hoboken, New Jersey. The **steamship companies** and the inspectors of the **Boarding Division** ensured that foreign passengers were safely brought to Ellis Island. In inclement weather, aliens stood under a majestic canopy at the southwest façade of the **Main Building**. It protected them from the elements as they

Large crowd of immigrants near the Main Building, ca 1904.
Courtesy of the Ellis Island Immigration Museum.

Immigrants carrying their suitcases, baskets, and bundles into the Main Building. Courtesy of the Ellis Island Immigration Museum.

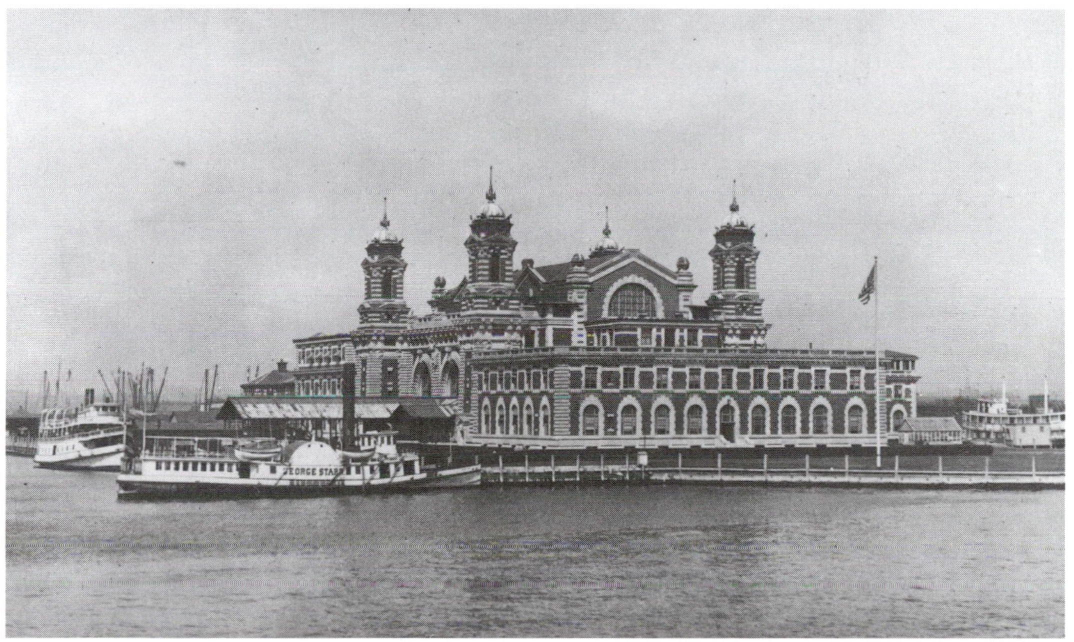

Transatlantic steamship companies were required to bring immigrants to Ellis Island. A couple of their barges are seen in this 1905 picture. Courtesy of the Ellis Island Immigration Museum.

proceeded from the ferry landing to the Main Building. Erected in 1903, its roof consisted of copper and glass skylights.

Assistant Commissioners. The assistant commissioner was the second highest-ranking official after the commissioner. His task was to keep an eye on events at Ellis Island for the commissioner and to correct and rectify all administrative errors brought to his attention or, to bring them to the attention of the commissioner. Further, he was required to be at all times prepared to serve as acting commissioner should the commissioner be absent. Over the years, the position was held by several men, including General **James R. O'Beirne** (1890–1893), **Edward F. McSweeney** (1893–1902), **Joseph E. Murray** (1902–1910), and **Byron H. Uhl** (1910–1940). From 1921 to 1925, **Harry L. Landis** served as a second assistant commissioner. He was succeeded, at least briefly, by **Percy A. Baker**.

See also **Executive Division**

Austrian Society. The Austrian Society was founded in 1898 by the Emperor Francis Joseph of Austria-Hungary to aid his Catholic subjects who had immigrated to the United States. The society was financed by donations and membership dues as well as by an annual subsidy of $5,000 from the Austro-Hungarian government. Not surprisingly, the organization was also known as the Austro-Hungarian Society.

The Austrian Society's membership included twenty-one priests and it employed three agents at Ellis Island; the agents chiefly aided Austro-Hungarian subjects held in detention or who were sick in the hospital. Although welcome as free boarders at the Austrian Society's immigrant home, those immigrants who were able to were asked to pay a nominal fee. Helping immigrants find jobs was an important activity. As a result of World War I, its services were suspended.

See also **Missionaries**

B

Baer, Beulah (b. 1889; d. 1985). Personnel officer from 1935 to 1945. Beulah Baer began working at the station as a time and pay clerk. By 1935, she had risen to the post of personnel officer. Many years later, she wrote her memoirs, *Facts, Scribbles, and Scraps* (1966), and reminisced about her job at Ellis Island, stating how much better it was to be a detained alien rather than an **Immigration and Naturalization Service** employee. She described favorite coworkers, including **Emma Oosterhoudt** (who was still alive in the 1960s) and supervisors Byron H. Uhl and Rudolph Reimer.

Baggage and Dormitory Building. Originally two stories in height, the baggage and dormitory building was planned in 1907 and constructed in 1908–1909. The third floor was added in 1913–1914, and an enclosed porch along the north side facing Manhattan was added in 1917. Federal architect **James Knox Taylor** designed the building in the beaux arts style, and the New York State Construction Company built it between March 1908 and February 1909.

The structure has a granite base and red Flemish bond brick walls trimmed in limestone. The roof is flat and covered with tar-coated roofing paper and trimmed with pressed copper cresting. The entire building measures 232.5 feet by 213.75. An iron-framed covered stairway from the second floor of the baggage and dormitory building runs across the courtyard to the first floor of the Main Building. Skylights from an open court above lighted the central area of the first floor.

From 1909 to 1954, this structure was the largest detention building for legal detainees.

The disposition of the baggage and dormitory building from 1909 to 1913 was as follows:

First floor: Public entrance lobby, baggage room, New York baggage room, customs house storage, scale room, fan room, three offices, six toilets, and a stair hall.

Second floor: Dormitory detention rooms and ten family detention rooms surround a central court. There was also a roof garden.

Third floor (1913–1914): Four detention wards (one for women) and three isolation wards.

The disposition of room space in 1926 was as follows:

First floor: Baggage room, baggage storage room, five offices, lunch packing room, railway baggage check office, Southern Pacific room, postal telegraph office, Western Union telegraph office, post office, steamship agents' room, railroad east ticket office, railroad west ticket office, money exchange, and the New York passage room.

Second floor: Vestibule, visitors' room (room 203), utensils room, three large dormitories (rooms 204, 206, 222), several small dormitories (rooms 209–218), one store room, the central light court, and the recreation porch.

Third floor: Four large dormitories (rooms A [305], B [303], C [332], D [330]), a matrons' room, and a nursery.

In 1932–1934, the baggage room on the first floor was replaced by a recreation room. On the second floor, dormitory room 222 was altered with the addition of six reading rooms, a laundry, and shower room. A sterilizer room was added to the third floor.

In 1951, there was a lunch counter, an express office, a detainees' dining room, a commissary storeroom, a dishwashing room, bakery shop, kosher kitchen, all located on the first floor.

Baggage Room (C102). This room located on the first floor of the **Main Building** in the **Ellis Island Immigration Museum** contains a large exhibit of immigrant luggage: suitcases, bags, baskets, valises, and cases. This exhibit includes large historical photographs of immigrants bearing luggage. There is a general information desk in the room as well as a station where recorded museum tour tape sets with headphones ("Acoustiguides") can be obtained, another desk providing information about programs offered by the **Statue of Liberty–Ellis Island Foundation**, such as the American Immigrant Wall of Honor, and the Ellis Island play. There is also a set of computer terminals in the baggage room that contains the database of the American Immigrant Wall of Honor.

During the height of immigration there was more than one baggage room and none occupied as large a space as the current baggage room does.

Baker, Percy A. (b. Brewster, New York, 1869; d. Brooklyn, New York, June 3, 1943). Superintendent of Ellis Island from 1919 to 1940; assistant commissioner from 1924 to 1926. Percy Baker began working at Ellis Island before the turn of the century and eventually became an **immigrant inspector** in the **Special Inquiry Division**; by 1908, he was the inspector in charge of that division. He was promoted to superintendent of Ellis Island in 1919. Later that year, Baker was instrumental in assisting in the expulsion of **Emma Goldman**, **Alexander Berkman,** and 247 other anarchists from the country. He also had several conversations with Goldman. In the 1930s, Commissioner **Edward Corsi** had many discussions with Superintendent Baker about the old days at Ellis Island. Baker told Corsi that

at times there have been twenty-five or thirty races in detention . . . the Italian cares nothing for the dried fish preferred by the Scandinavian and the Scandinavian has no use for spaghetti. The Greek wants his food sweetened and no one can make tea for an Englishman. The basis of all Asiatic and Malay food is rice, which they will mix with almost anything. The Chinese take to other foods but want rice in place of bread. The Mohammedan will eat no food across which the shadow of an infidel has fallen. And in big years it has been Superintendent Baker's problem to serve nine thousand meals per day, trying to please all.

Bread was bought at the rate of seven tons a day, both for these meals and for the box lunches formerly sold to immigrants departing for inland points. Those who did not buy box lunches usually found themselves at the mercy of grafters.

"What," I asked Superintendent Baker one day, "is the strangest case in your recollection?"

"There are so many," he replied, "that it is almost impossible to remember the names and dates. . . . Once I remember a young Italian girl arrived on a French ship. She announced she was on her way to her intended husband at Streator, Illinois. Of course we detained her. Washington was very strict in those days. We requested the man . . . to send affidavits as to his intentions and ability to provide for her. We permitted her to telegraph him under government supervision. A day or so after her detention a man appeared, saying he had come for her and that he was her brother. The case was cited for Special Inquiry in order that a record might be made. It was apparent to me that the man who alleged he was her brother was an imposter, so she was further detained pending receipt of the affidavits. The affidavits were received and at the hearing she again expressed her desire to join her intended husband at Streator. Everything being in order . . . we admitted her. Two weeks passed and nothing had been heard, when a communication was received from the man in Streator claiming his fiancée had not reached him.

Since a railroad ticket to Streator had been furnished her, it was easy for one of our officers to trace her journey. He reported a few days later that she had detrained at Buffalo. It was also discovered that her ticket had not been used beyond that point. The officer next set out to discover the alleged brother. The man was found in Brooklyn, but he had married the girl the day before. The man in Streator had paid the freight for the other fellow.

We finally learned that she had met the alleged brother at a steamship boarding house in Havre. He had taken a fast boat after they had fallen in love. . . . So far as I know the man in Streator is still waiting for a refund. (Corsi, 1935, pp. 121–122)

REFERENCES: Corsi, Edward. 1935. *In the Shadow of Liberty*. New York: Macmillan; *New York Times*. 1943. Percy Baker: Ellis Island official 36 years with Immigration Department. June 5.

Bakery and Carpentry Shop. In 1901, a temporary bakery and a carpentry shop made of wood were constructed on Island 1. In 1913, Congress appropriated $50,000 for construction of a new building to house both functions. Thus a new bakery and carpentry shop building was completed by June 1915, located in the same place as its old wooden predecessors. **Alfred Brooks Fry** designed it and its style is said to be utilitarian.

The building is two stories high and constructed of Flemish bond bricks over a steel framework; its foundation is constructed of granite and brick. On the first floor was a stoking pit, an oven room (with two peel ovens), one draw plate oven, a fuel room, an elevator machine room, a bakery, a lumber room, a general storage room, and an elevator. On the second floor were the paint shop, flour storage, sifters and blenders, a carpentry shop, three small rooms, and the elevator.

Barbusse, Henri (b. Asnières, France, May 17, 1873; d. Moscow, Russia, August 30, 1935). French novelist and journalist. The famous novelist Henri Barbusse was briefly detained at Ellis Island as a dangerous radical in September 1933; he was released quickly on the orders of Commissioner **Edward Corsi**. A prominent communist and pacifist, Barbusse had come to the United States to participate as a speaker at a major antiwar rally. Barbusse began his writing career as a journalist. He achieved fame for his realistic antiwar novel, *Under Fire* (1916), which won him the coveted Prix Goncourt, France's highest literary award. The book, which has been compared to Remarque's *All Quiet on the Western Front* (1929), was inspired by Barbusse's experiences as a soldier on the battlefields of World War I. His other novels, mostly of a political nature, include *Hell* (1908), *Le couteau entre les dents* (1921), *Chains* (1924), and *Le Judas de Jésus* (1927).

REFERENCE: Corsi, Edward. 1935. *In the Shadow of Liberty*. New York: Macmillan.

Barge Office. This Romanesque Revival building of granite was designed by James G. Hill and stood at the **Battery**, quite close to **Castle Garden**. The barge office was built in 1880–1882 and was opened on January 3, 1883, replacing an earlier federal building dating from 1860. It served as the Customs Service (Department of the Treasury) as a place where cabin passengers from steamships could comfortably have their luggage examined by federal customs inspectors. However, the building was hardly ever used, since most customs inspection was taken care of at the docks. In April 1890, the barge office became the nation's first federal immigrant inspection station, if only temporarily, when the Treasury Department began processing steerage class aliens there until Ellis Island opened in January 1892. After this, the barge office became a permanent part of the **Bureau of Immigration** and was supervised by the commissioner at Ellis Island. It served as the headquarters of the **Boarding Division** and the Manhattan dock for the **ferryboat *Ellis Island***. In 1911, under the supervision of chief engineer **A. B. Fry**, the building was knocked down and replaced by a new barge office designed by federal architect **James Knox Taylor**; this was completed in 1913.

The Battery [Battery Park]. The Battery, an area at the southernmost tip of Manhattan, was the landing place for millions of immigrants released from Ellis Island and **Castle Garden**. Its name comes from the days when it was the site of a land battery for harbor defense. Aside from Castle Garden, another important building at the Battery was the **barge office**, which served both as the docking place of the **ferryboat *Ellis Island*** and the office giving access to Ellis Island, from 1892 to 1954.

The Battery has served as a major hub of transportation not only for arriving immigrants but also for travelers going to and from Staten Island and Governor's Island, as well as soldiers who were stationed at Bedloe's Island (now Liberty Island). The Battery maintains a parklike atmosphere, and in recent decades various commemorative monuments and memorials have been put up there. In addition, millions of tourists go to the Battery every year to take the excursion boats to the **Statue of Liberty** and Ellis Island.

Belgian Bureau. The Belgian Bureau was established to provide help for Belgian immigrants arriving in the United States and was one of the immigrant aid societies associated with Ellis Island, from the first decade of the twentieth century. During World War I, financial support from the Belgian Relief Fund enabled the bureau to help Belgian refugees who were stranded in America or those fleeing Europe following the German invasion of Belgium in August 1914. The Belgian diplomat Louis de Sadeleer (1852–1924), who lived in the United States from 1914 until 1919, played an important role in this effort. The Belgian Bureau remained active at Ellis Island throughout the 1920s.

Berkman, Alexander (b. Vilnius, Lithuania [Russia], November 21, 1870; d. Nice, France, June 28, 1936). Anarchist. Alexander Berkman immigrated through **Castle Garden** in 1888 and settled in the Lower East Side of Manhattan. His attempt to assassinate industrialist Henry Clay Frick in 1892 landed him in prison for fourteen years. He believed in an ideal society based on voluntary anarchist collectivism. After his release in 1906, he became one of the nation's leading anarchists and became a close associate of **Emma Goldman**. With her and more than 200 radicals, he was arrested and detained incommunicado at Ellis Island in December 1919 and was then deported to Russia. During his exile, he continued to contribute articles to the Jewish Anarchist Federation of New York.

REFERENCE: Berkman, Alexander. 1912. *Prison Memoirs of an Anarchist*. New York: Mother Earth Publishing Association.

Biddle, Francis [Francis Beverely Biddle] (b. Paris, France, May 9, 1886; d. Hyannis, Massachusetts, October 4, 1968). U.S. attorney general from 1941 to 1945. As attorney general, Francis Biddle was responsible for and presided over the interrogations and interments of thousands of German, Italian, and Japanese **enemy aliens** at Ellis Island and other immigrant detention stations across the country. He also played a critical role in the internment of thousands of U.S. citizens of Japanese ancestry during the war. Prior to entering government service, he was a successful corporate lawyer. He also served as U.S. solicitor general from 1940 to 1941. Francis Biddle was the author of two memoirs, *A Casual Past* (1961) and *In Brief Authority* (1962).

Births. An estimated 500 immigrant infants were born at Ellis Island while their parents were in detention. In the majority of these cases, automatic U.S. citizenship for the infant was officially disallowed, and the child took the citizenship of his or her father. Birth records were always written up by the **Public Health Service** and sometimes by the city of New York.

Black Immigrants. An interesting feature of Ellis Island immigration history is the little known fact that thousands of Afro-Caribbean immigrants passed through the fabled station during the same years as the far greater waves of European immigration. Although most immigrants of color haled from the then European colonies Jamaica, Trinidad, and Guadeloupe, there were also numbers trickling in from other countries such as Venezuela, Ethiopia, and the Panama Canal Zone. An estimated 100,000 immigrants of black African heritage entered the United States through Ellis Island from 1892 through 1924. The

This African family passed through Ellis Island in 1909. Sherman Collection, courtesy of the Ellis Island Immigration Museum.

languages they spoke varied from English to French to Portuguese and Spanish, while many others spoke creolized dialects with grammatical systems originating in West Africa.

The heyday of this immigration coincided with the rising waves of immigrants arriving from southern and eastern Europe, and also from Lebanon and Armenia in Asia. African Caribbean people came to North America in search of the same things as most other immigrants. The primary goal for most was to improve their economic position. To this end, 85 percent of the newcomers flocked to New York, Massachusetts, and Florida, where they found jobs as laborers, servants and, in some cases, skilled artisans and clerical workers. English-speaking West Indians usually had a higher rate of literacy than other immigrants. In New York City, Harlem proved to be a Mecca for them, and they flourished in such fields as business, education, and the arts.

Because of cultural and linguistic differences, the black immigrants created their own communities quite apart from **African Americans**. In some cases, there was even some rivalry and hostility between the communities. Like their European counterparts, they found adjustment to the new country sometimes difficult. However, they were able to create and maintain a rich cultural and intellectual life in the United States. Powerful leaders emerged within their community such as Marcus Garvey, a Jamaican, who founded the Universal Negro Improvement Association, and the Trinidad-born poet Claude McKay, who was one of the central literary figures of the Harlem Renaissance in the 1920s. Both men entered this country through Ellis Island. On the other hand, one immigrant, a Trinidadian, was detained at the station for several months in 1952, for his leftist views. This was **C. L. R. James** (1901–1989), a noted historian. After some nine months at Ellis Island, during which time he wrote a book concerning his treatment, he was deported.

See also **Minorities**

References: Reid, Ira D. 1939. *The Negro Immigrant: His Background, Characteristics, and Social Adjustments, 1899–1937*. New York: Columbia University Press; Unrau, Harlan D. 1984. *The Historic Resource Study: Ellis Island/Statue of Liberty*. Vol. 1. Washington, DC: U.S. Department of the Interior, National Park Service; Watkins-Owens, Irma. 1996. *Blood Relations: Caribbean Immigrants and the Harlem Community, 1900–1930*. Bloomington: Indiana University Press.

Black Tom Explosion. Early on the morning of July 30, 1916, a series of explosions erupted at Black Tom Wharf, just behind Bedloe's Island and less than a mile from Ellis Island. They resulted in terrific fires that destroyed the wharf and fourteen barges at the piers of the National Storage Company. It was later proven that German saboteurs had set fire to the piles of munitions, TNT, and shells stored there for transfer to a Russian steamship bound for Europe. At Ellis Island the entrance doors to the **Main Building** were blown in, one of the dining rooms was wrecked, the windows of the **Executive Division** were all smashed, and there was a rain of shrapnel and burnt wood that fell everywhere. In addition, chief clerk **Augustus F. Sherman**'s cat was struck by glass.

In 1939, an international commission ordered Germany to pay an indemnity of $50 million to the United States.

See also **Fire of 1897**

Board of Review. This agency, which was in the Department of Labor (formerly the Department of Commerce and Labor), was located in the office of the secretary of labor in Washington; it reviewed all cases of aliens appealing the decisions to exclude them from the United States by the **boards of special inquiry** of the U.S. **Bureau of Immigration**. The board of review also reviewed the transcripts of hearings of aliens held under warrants of arrest. The board consisted of seven members, six of whom were appointed from the civil service by the Department of Labor and the Bureau of Immigration. The seventh member, who served as its chairman, was personally appointed by the secretary of labor.

Boarding Division. Inspectors, interpreters, doctors, and matrons of the Boarding Division went out to the newly arrived steamships to examine cabin passengers and to transport **steerage** and detained cabin-class passengers to Ellis Island. They reported to work each morning at the **barge office** and went out to each ship using the Immigration Bureau's cutter, *The Immigrant.* From 1929 until Ellis Island closed, the Boarding Division handled all **primary inspection** of newly arrived aliens who had not previously been inspected by American consular officials abroad. Essentially their task was to examine all arriving aliens on ships and, later, airplanes, and to discharge those found admissible. Those with questionable eligibility or requiring medical treatment were sent to Ellis Island. The division carried on this activity until the **closing of Ellis Island**.

Every morning and afternoon, *The Immigrant*, a government cutter, transported Boarding Division officers to meet newly arrived steamships. Courtesy of the Ellis Island Immigration Museum.

Boards of Special Inquiry. Boards of special inquiry were set up under the provisions of the **Immigration Act of 1893 (II)** and were composed of four inspectors. The centerpiece of the **Special Inquiry Division**, the four inspectors heard the cases of detained aliens and attempted to resolve them. Under a subsequent law, the **Immigration Act of 1903**, the number of board inspectors was reduced to three.

The cases that the boards dealt with mainly concerned immigrants who had failed to satisfy immigrant inspectors in the **registry room** as to whether they were "clearly and a beyond a doubt entitled to land" and previously landed aliens who were facing legal procedures such as deportation. The most common sort of cases handled by the boards included determining if an alien might become a **public charge** (e.g., women, children, stowaways, and the elderly), or if a physical defect might prevent an alien from earning a livelihood, or if he or she were guilty of **moral turpitude**, a criminal offence or harbored a radical political ideology (e.g., anarchism, bolshevism). In January 1912, the special inquiry inspectors were given written guidelines for conducting interrogations of detained aliens and witnesses. In February of the same year, forty-seven **Bureau of Immigration** employees at Ellis Island were officially authorized by the Department of Commerce and Labor in Washington to be appointed to the boards by the commissioner; the persons had all been selected in advance by Commissioner **William Williams**. Immigrants were often held three or four days or even longer in **detention** as they awaited their hearing. During the busiest years of immigration (1900–1924) there were between four and eight boards handling cases. Aside from the presiding immigrant inspectors, the chief of the **Registry Division** had to dispatch foreign language **interpreters** to translate for those aliens who understood no English, a state of affairs all too common at Ellis Island.

One session of a board of special inquiry. Sherman Collection, courtesy of the Ellis Island Immigration Museum.

Hostile critics of the boards publicly denounced them as "chambers of inquisition" and "star chambers," because the public was not permitted to attend any of their sessions. Commissioner Williams described the boards of special inquiry in his 1912 report, *Ellis Island: Its Organization and Some of Its Work.*

> Boards are appointed daily by the Commissioner in such numbers as the special inquiry work of the day may require. There may be from five to eight board in session. Each consists of three inspectors and has *authority to determine whether an alien who has been duly held shall be allowed to land or shall be deported* (section 25). The Chief of this division distributes the ones amongst the several boards and sees to it that the immigrants, their witnesses and all documentary evidence are produced as speedily as possible. Boards may dispose of cases upon the facts as they appear at the first hearing but often the interests of justice demand that a case shall be deferred for the production of further evidence. Even after exclusion has occurred a further hearing is granted whenever new and relevant evidence can be produced. Where a board feels itself bound to exclude through believing the case to have great merit, the chairman, in addition to notifying the immigrant of his right of appeal, may submit to the Commissioner a memorandum to this effect. Each board has at its disposal an interpreter, a messenger and a stenographer, and the daily board minutes vary, from 100 to 250 closely typewritten pages.

According to a statement made by Commissioner Williams in 1911, immigrants detained for special inquiry varied from 5 percent to 30 percent for each shipload. He added that out of a total of 5,000 immigrants arriving each day, 1,000 to 1,200 were held for special inquiry, and he noted how this added up day after day. Commissioner Williams reported that in 1910, there were 70,829 cases handled by the boards of special inquiry and observed that the great majority of immigrants were admitted but that the Ellis Island boards had excluded from admission to the country "a great deal of the riff-raff and scum which is constantly seeking to enter." Immigrants who were dissatisfied by the decision of a board of special inquiry were allowed to make an appeal to the **board of review** in Washington, DC.

REFERENCE: Williams, William. 1912. *Ellis Island: Its Organization and Some of Its Work*. N.p.

Bond Office. The bond office issued **bonds** for persons that were likely to become a public charge, some students, children under sixteen, and visitors whose cases seemed doubtful. The office was regularly in communication with surety firms, bondsmen, and schools. The usual amount of the bond was $500, although students were sometimes permitted to post a bond of $150. From the 1930s to the 1950s, the office was called the Bonding Division. In the 1930s and 1940s, Agatha LaBonde was chief of the bond office.

Bonding Division. *See* **Bond Office**

Bonds. Bonds were introduced at Ellis Island shortly after the turn of the century. The purpose of these bonds was to allow entry to an alien who, otherwise, was inadmissible due to lack of money or due to the fear that the immigrant might become a public charge. A bond might be required in the case of an alien who was simply passing through (in transit) the United States in order to reach another destination such as Newfoundland, Canada, Mexico, Cuba, or any other country of Latin America or the West Indies. A bond for insuring the alien's transit through and departure from the U.S. within 20 days was considered a wise precaution. The **Bureau of Immigration** regulations stipulated that

> Where the landing of an alien under bond is authorized, unless different instructions are given, the bond shall be in the sum of $500 and the alien shall not be released until it has been furnished and the immigration official in charge has satisfied himself of the responsibility of the sureties. If within a reasonable time after landing under bond a satisfactory bond is not furnished, instructions shall be requested of the bureau.
>
> . . . If the acceptance of a cash deposit is authorized, the deposit, unless different instructions are given, shall be in form of a postal money order and in the sum of $500. A receipt for the deposit shall be issued by the officer in charge, showing the object for which the money has been accepted and the disposition to be made thereof. The money order shall

then be transmitted to the department, by which it will be deposited in the postal savings bank in Washington, in such manner as to permit the interest accruing thereon to be semiannually and transmitted to the person making the cash deposit. (Smith and Herring, 1924)

Aliens who wished to appeal against a deportation order often had to obtain a bond in order to defray the government's cost of their continued maintenance at Ellis Island while their appeal was being considered. The regulations stipulated that

The amount of any bond under which an arrested alien may be released shall be $500, unless different instructions are provided by the department, which, prior to release, shall approve the bond, except that the approval of the local United States attorney or the Commissioner of Immigration or the inspector in charge of the district as to form and execution shall be sufficient to warrant the release of such alien pending approval of the bail bond by the Secretary of Labor. United States bonds may be accepted in lieu of sureties on bail bond, or sureties may deposit United States instead of justifying in real estate. Aliens who are unable to give bail shall be held in jail only in case no other secure place of detention can be found.

See also **Bond Office**

REFERENCE: Smith, Darrell, and Henry Herring. 1924. *The Bureau of Immigration.* Baltimore: Johns Hopkins University Press.

Boody, Bertha M. [Bertha May Boody] (b. 1877; d. 1943). Psychologist. Bertha M. Boody was the author of *A Psychological Study of Immigrant Children at Ellis Island* (1926). This work provides detailed information of immigrant nationalities in detention and offers interesting information on **schooling** at Ellis Island.

Boring, William A. [William Aciphron Boring] (b. Carlinville, Illinois, September 9, 1859; d. New York, May 5, 1937). Architect. **Edward L. Tilton** and William A. Boring were the designers of the main building at Ellis Island (1898–1900). Educated at several colleges, including Ecole des Beaux Arts in Paris and Columbia University, Boring began his career as an architect in Los Angeles in 1883. There he designed the Los Angeles Times Building, the University of Southern California, the Santa Monica Hotel, and the city's first firehouse in Olvera Street, now a museum. In 1890, he went to New York, where he became a member of the firm of McKim, Mead & White. He next went into partnership with Edward Tilton in 1891, under the name of Boring & Tilton. The two young architects had been students at the Ecole des Beaux Arts in Paris and had also worked at McKim, Mead & White. Though they achieved note as designers of residential buildings, they were also responsible for several prominent structures in Connecticut, including the First Church of Christ, Scientist, in Hartford, the Connecticut Institute for the Blind, and West Hartford's Institute for the Deaf. In 1898, the firm won the competition to build a fireproof immigrant station on Ellis Island. The firm won the Gold Medal of the Pan-American Exposition at Buffalo in 1901 for their design of the **Main Building**, the construction of which had been completed the year before. (They also won the Silver Medal of the Louisiana Purchase Exposition at Saint Louis in 1904.) The two men ended their partnership in 1903. As an independent architect, Boring designed houses and business and civic structures around the country. He joined Columbia University's School of Architecture as professor of design in 1916 and, three years later, was named the School's director. In his last years, he received many honors and closed his career with distinction in the position of dean of the School of Architecture in 1934.

See also **Tilton, Edward L.**

Boston Immigrant Station. The Boston Immigration Station was the headquarters of District 3 of the **Bureau of Immigration** and was opened in 1892. In 1924, the staff of sixty-four employees included the commissioner, the assistant commissioner, twenty-four inspectors, four interpreters, six clerks, an engineer, eight guards, five matrons, three charwomen, four laborers, and two telephone operators. One of the inspectors, Feri Felix Weiss, wrote a remarkably gossipy book about his experiences at the Boston station and his occasional postings to Ellis Island. It is colored by his dislike of various immigrant groups such as the Chinese and the Mormons.

REFERENCES: Smith, Darrell, and Henry Herring. 1924. *The Bureau of Immigration.* Baltimore: Johns Hopkins University Press; Weiss, F. F. 1921. *The Sieve or Revelations of the Man Mill, Being the Truth about American Immigration.* Boston: Page.

Brandenburg, Broughton [Earl Victor von Brandenburg] (b. 1876; d. ?). American author, journalist, and publicist. "Broughton Brandenburg" was a leading popular writer of the first decade of the twentieth century until he was arrested for larceny in 1908 for a letter he alleged to have been written by President Grover Cleveland (who had just died). At the time of his arrest, he dramatically told New York reporters that "it appeared that he was to be another Dreyfus." This was an attempt to make his plight appear as unjust as the famous treason case against Alfred Dreyfus, the French army captain. In the same year, Brandenburg's private life attracted further attention of the press: his scandalous public divorce, followed by his melodramatic kidnapping of his son from his ex-wife in St. Louis, for which he served a prison sentence. Crookedness led to another jail sentence in the 1920s, and in April 1933 the fifty-seven-year-old "ex-author" was convicted of theft and imprisoned in Sing Sing State Prison in New York. Despite these travails, Brandenburg was a pioneering writer on European emigrants and their treatment at Ellis Island. In 1903, he and his wife decided to study the Italians and so settled for a time in New York's Little Italy; then they went to Italy and lived among its people for a spell before embarking on their now famous journey with Italian emigrants at sea aboard a German steamer. What follows is an excerpt from Brandenburg's book, *Imported Americans*, detailing their arrival in the United States and their experience during immigrant inspection at Ellis Island.

Sunday fell on the 11th, and it was a pleasant day till afternoon, when it began to get rough. The ship's band was sent forward to play on the hurricane deck, in order to cheer up the emigrants, many of who were beginning to look very badly, and to endeavor to brace them up until port could be reached; for it is a great saving to the company to take as many passengers as possible to Ellis Island in a good state of health.

On this day occurred another medical inspection; and to make all of the health tickets appear to have been properly punched each passenger was inspected day by day, a steward whom I heard called Beppo went about and carefully punched any vacant spaces. Neither I nor my wife had gone by for the last three or four health inspections, having missed the call by being busy eating in the officer's cubby, Beppo punched out the full twelve days of the voyage at one punching. When those tickets were presented at Ellis Island there was nothing to show that their bearers had not been inspected each day. . . .

The night before, the joy among the emigrants that they were reaching the Promised Land was pitiful to see, mingled as it was with the terrible dread of being debarred.

There was little sleeping at night. About twelve at night, the women woke up the sleeping children, opened their packs, and took out finery on top of finery, and began to array the little ones to meet their fathers. My wife pleaded with Camela to stay in her bunk and wait for daylight at least, but Camela could not understand why she should wait and, at three o'clock, little Ina was brought on deck arrayed in her very best, and as clean as her mother could make her with a small bottle of water and a skirt combination of wash-rag and towel.

By six o'clock, all the baggage in the compartments had been hauled out and up on deck, and the hundreds of emigrants were gathered there, many trying to shave, others struggling for water in which to wash, and mothers who had been unable to dress their children to their satisfaction in the cramped quarters below were doing the job all over again, despite the chill air.

Happy, excited, enthusiastic as they were, there was still that dread among the people of the "Batteria," the name used to sum up all that pertained to Ellis Island. I saw more than one man with a little slip of notes in his hand carefully rehearsing his group in all that they were to say when the time came for examination, and by listening here and there I found that hundreds of useless lies were in preparation. Many, many persons, whose entry in the country would no way be hindered by even the strictest of enforcement of the letter of the emigration laws were trembling in their shoes and preparing to evade or defeat the purpose of questions which they had heard would be put to them. . . .

As we approached Sandy Hook, the alternate glee and depression of the groups were pathetic. . . .

The Steerage stewards and the interpreter under the direction of the junior officer appeared and ordered all the steerage passengers to pass up from the forward main deck to the hurricane deck and aft, leaving their baggage just where it was. Wild commotion broke forth, for this was preparatory action at last. Slowly, the chattering, excited hundreds were got aft and crowded into the space usually given to second-cabin passengers and, after a long wait there, while we approached quarantine, and the port doctor's boat came out, and the "Chamberlain" carrying the Ellis Island boarding-officers and a newspaperman or two, there were cries forward along the hurricane deck which indicated that the crowd was being passed back to steerage quarters.

I knew we were about to pass before the port doctor's deputy and the boarding-officers, and got our party together and into the line passing forward along the promenade deck. As we approached the forward end, we saw the dour German doctor standing with a grey-whiskered man in uniform, on whose cap front was the welcome golden-thread eagle design of the United States service. As we came nearly abreast of the them, I saw another official on the right-hand side, and turned my head slightly to see what was occurring on that side of the line. I caught a glimpse of steerage stewards beyond the officials, hurrying the emigrants down the companionway and, the next instant, received a heavy raking blow on the bridge of my nose and up my forehead. It partly stunned and dazed me, and I was merely conscious of stumbling on and having the spectacles which I wore for reading or distance-viewing hanging on the hook over one ear. Before I could even see, I was at the head of the companionway, and the stewards were hustling my wife down the steps. I gathered from what she was saying that the German doctor had struck me and, turning to look at him, saw he was looking after me with a sneer on his *face.* To go back would have been to spoil my investigations just at the last stage and, with a lamb-like meekness I went below, where my wife told how, having uncovered my head, as in the rule in passing the doctor, I had replaced my hat a second too soon as I turned to look to the right, and the German doctor had reached over her head and struck me with the back of his wrist, inflicting a heavy blow with the pretense of brushing my hat from my head.

When the inspection was finished, the great steamer got under way once more and, in the glorious sunlight of mid-forenoon, we steamed up between South Brooklyn and Staten Island, with the shipping, the houses, and the general contour of the harbor very plainly to be seen. On every hand were exclamation among the immigrants over the oddity wooden-built houses, over the beauty of the Staten Island shore places; and when the gigantic skyscrapers of lower Manhattan came into view, a strange serrated line against the sky, the people who had been to America before cried in joyful tones and pointed. . . .

Then there was the rush to port to see the Statue of Liberty and, when all had seen it, they stood with their eyes fixed for some minutes on the great beacon whose significance is so much to them, standing on the portals of the New World, and proclaiming the liberty, justice and equality they had never known, proclaiming a life in which they have an opportunity such as never could come to them elsewhere.

The majority of immigrants aboard who had been over before had landed previously at the Battery, and few knew Ellis Island to be the immigrant station, so that comparatively little attention was paid to it. Another odd thing was the effect the sight of the magnificence of New York had on the people who were destined for western and New England points. More than expressed an interest to remain in New York. . . .

In what seemed a very short space of time, we had steamed up the harbor, up North River, and were being warped into the North German Lloyd piers in Hoboken [New Jersey]. There were only a few people down to meet friends of the third-class, but the usual crowd awaited the first cabin passengers. Some of the Italians bore extra overcoats to give the shivering "greenhorns," as they called them—an American word that is current throughout the south of Italy and the Italian quarters of American cities.

We seemed to the eager immigrants an unreasonably long time of waiting passed while the customs officers were looking after the first class passengers and they were leaving the ship. When the way was clear, word was passed forward to get the immigrants ready to debark. First, however, Boarding Inspector Vance held a little tribunal at the rail forward on the hurricane deck, at which all persons had citizens' papers were to present them I watched him carefully as he proceeded with his task of picking out genuine citizens form the other sort and allowing them to leave the ship at the docks; and if all officials are as careful and thorough as he, then is the law enforced to its limit, and the many evasions of it which seem to exist are things no official or set of officials can prevent operating this side of the water. Here, again, I could not help seeing that deceit, evasion and trickery were possible, inasmuch as the inspector can only take the papers on the face of them, together with the immigrant's own statement; and if the gangs who smuggle aliens in on borrowed, transferred or forged citizens' papers have been careful enough in preparing and coaching their pupils, there is no way of apprehending the fraud at the port of arrival, nor would there be at the port of embarkation; but there would be no chance for any practices if the examinations were made in the community of the immigrant's residence.

Those whose citizenship was doubted by the inspector, and who had names familiar to him, were compelled to go to Ellis Island with them, or allow the families to go through the process alone.

At last we were summoned to pass aft and go ashore. One torrent of humanity poured up each companionway to the hurricane deck and aft, while a third stream went through the main dark alleyway, all lugging the preposterous bundles. The children, seeing sufficient excitement on foot to incite them to cry and, being by this time very hungry, began to yell with vigor. A frenzy seemed to possess some of the people as groups became separated. If a gangway had been set to a rail-port forward, there would have been little of the hullabaloo, but for a time it was frightful.

The steerage stewards kept up their brutality to the last. One woman was trying to get up the companionway with a child in one arm, her deck chair brought from home hung on the other, which also supported a large bundle. She blocked the passage for a moment. One of the stewards stained by it reached up, dragged her down, tore the chair off her arm, splitting her sleeve as he did so and scraping the skin off her wrist, and in his rage he broke the chair into a dozen pieces. The woman passed on sobbing, but cowed and without a threat.

As we passed down the gangway, an official stood there with a mechanical checker numbering the passengers, and uniformed watchmen directed the human flood pouring off the ship where to set down the baggage to await customs inspection.

The scene on the pier had something impressive in it, well worthy of a painter of great human scenes. The huge enclosed place, scantly lighted by a few apertures and massive with great beams and girders, was piled high in some places with freight, and all over the space from far up near the land end where a double rope was stretched to prevent immigrants from escaping without inspection, down to the pier head where the big door was open to allow the immigrants to pass out and aboard the barges waiting to convey them down the river again, to Ellis Island, was covered with immigrants customs inspectors, special Treasury detectives, Ellis Island officials, stevedores, ship's people, dock watchmen and vendors of apples, cakes, etc.

The dock employees were all German, some of them speaking very little English, and none that I saw using Italian. While their plan of keeping the immigrants in line in order to facilitate the inspection of baggage was all very good and quite the proper thing, the brutal method in which they enforced it was nothing short of reprehensible. The natural family and neighborhood groups were separated, and a part of the baggage was dumped in one place and apart in another. When the dock man had herded the off-coming immigrants in a mass along the south side of the pier with an overflow meeting forward of the gangway on the north, it was the natural thing for the parties to begin to hunt for each other and for leaders of groups to endeavor to assemble the baggage. . . .

In a few minutes we were having one more wrestling-match with the baggage. By this time the customs men had passed our heap and, when I did get an inspector and got it looked into, two trunks were held up for customs charges on account of all the provender packed in them, and the two musical instruments Antonio had bought in Naples were held. Unfortunately, the marks of the prices asked by the Neapolitan dealer was still on them and, though Antonio had got them just about one third, the customs appraiser later set a duty on them that totaled more than half the original cost. When we were through with the trunks, we found that the inspectors had passed over a part of the hand baggage. Two men standing by offered to mark it with chalk just as the inspectors mark it to show it has been inspected, and I was about to allow them to do it and then hand them over to my wife came up with the camera, and they turned and hurried away, going aboard the ship. I think they were either ship's people or part of the crew from some other boat of the North German Lloyd piers.

While we were waiting to get an inspector, we had time to buy something to eat from the fruit and cake vendors. . . . Few of the people aboard had eaten any breakfast because it was rumored among them they would land in time for breakfast and they had been looking forward to a good meal on shore.

One barge with power and another without, if I remember correctly, were lashed together; or there may have been a tug on the outer side of the second craft. Antonio and Camela, with the larger portion of the party, were hustled into the second barge, while my wife and squeezed into the second, little Ina with us. The great improvements in the way of heating, seating and hospital accommodation for the sick which Commissioner William Williams and his assistant Allen Robinson were then making were not yet in evidence in the barge on which we rode. We had to squat on the floor or sit on our baggage, smashed and crushed till the point of utter dissolution seemed not far away, so we stood up.

Slowly, we steamed down the river in mid-afternoon and, when we reached the slip at Ellis Island we merely tied up, for there were many barge-loads ahead of us, and we waited our turn to be unloaded and examined. . . .

Waiting, waiting, waiting, without food and without water; or, if there was water, we could not get to it on account of the crush of people. Children cried, mothers strove to hush them, the musically inclined sang or played, and then the sun went down while waited and still waited. My wife and one of the boys had walked into the space roped off around the plank which had been put aboard. Just then some of the youngsters who had tried to steal off the forward end of the barge, boylike, were chased back by the barge men, one of whom began rushing and pushing people in the open space back into the crowd—a very needless procedure, as there was no reason why that room there should not be utilized. . . .

Cooped up in the barge, we waited till the sun got down into the smoke of Bayonne and Elizabeth [New Jersey] and was a great red ball only, so dull that the eye could contemplate pleasantly. Then came the shadows of night and we began to dread that our turn to be disembarked would come so late that we should either be taken back to the steamer or be kept on the island until morning. Myriads of lights were shining in the great buildings. Each time the old ferry-boat floundered across from the battery it brought a crowd of friends of immigrants who had been summoned from New York and elsewhere to meet the newly arrived ones. All the races of Europe seemed to be represented in the crowds on the ferry-boat as it passed close to us when bound back to the Battery.

The babies had sobbed themselves to sleep, worn-out mothers sat with their heads dropped on the children they held to their breasts, and among the men mirth and song had died away, though now and then a voice would be inquiring if any one knew when or where we would get something to eat.

"All ready for the last Irenes," sang out a voice somewhere in the darkness up by the buildings, and there was a clatter of feet overhead on the wharf. The doors of the barge were opened. The barge hands dragged out the plank. The ropes restraining the crowd were dropped, and the weary hundreds, shouldering their bags yet once again, poured out of the barge onto the wharf. Knowing the way, I led those of our group who were with my wife and myself straight to the covered approach to the grand entrance to the building, and the strange assemblage of old world humanity streamed along behind us. . . .

Half-way up the stairs an interpreter stood telling the immigrants to get their health tickets ready, and so I knew that Ellis Island was having a "long day" and we were to be passed upon even if it took half the night. The majority of the people, having their hands full of bags, boxes, bundles, and children, carried their tickets in their teeth and, just at the head of the stairs stood a young doctor in the marine Hospital Service uniform, who took them, looked at them, and stamped them with the Ellis Island stamp. Considering the frauds in connection with these tickets at Naples and on board, the thoroughness used with them now was indeed futile.

Passing straight east from the head of the stairs, we turned into the south half of the great registry floor, which is divided, like the human body, into two great parts nearly alike, so that one ship's load can be handled one side and another ship's load on the other. In fact, as we came up, a quantity of people from the north of Europe were being examined in the north half.

Turning into a narrow railed-off lane, we encountered another doctor in uniform, who lifted hats or pushed back shawls to look for favus heads, keenly scrutinized the face and body for signs of disease or deformity, and passed us on. An old man, who limped in front of me, he marked with a bit of chalk on the coat lapel. At the end of the railed lane was a third uniformed doctor, a towel hanging beside him, a small instrument over which to turn up eyelids in his hand, and back of him basins of disinfectants. . . .

Concetta Formica was the only one of our party whom the doctors examined more than once. Her eyes were inflamed slightly, but she was passed. Just where we turned to the right, a stern looking woman inspector, with the badge, stood looking at the women who came up to select any whose moral character might be questioned, and one of her procedures was to ask each party as to the various relationships of the men and women in it. Her Italian was good.

Passing west, we came to the waiting-rooms, in which the groups which are entered on each sheet of the manifest are held until K sheet or L sheet, whatever their letter may be, is reached. Our party being so large, and some of the declarations which are used to fill out the items on the manifest having been made at Messina, some at Reggio di Calabria, and some at Naples, we were scattered through U, V and W groups.

We sank down on the wooden benches, thankful to get seats once more. Our eyes pained severely for some few minutes as a result of the turning up of the lids, but the pain passed.

Somewhere about nine o'clock an official came by and hurried out U group and passed it up into line along the railed way which led up to the Inspector who had U sheet, then came V group and then W. Knowing that the first into line would be the first passed, and having the task of gathering our people together out of the crowd as fast as they were passed, my wife and I hurried to the end of the lane and were among the first before the Inspector. Our papers were all straight, we were correctly entered on the manifest, and had abundant money, had been passed by the doctors, and were properly destined to New York, and so we passed in less than one minute. We were classed "New York Outsides" to distinguish us from the "New York Detained," who await the arrival of friends to receive them; "Railroads," who go to the stations for shipment; and "S.I.'s," by which is meant those unfortunates who are subjected to Special Inquiry in the semi-secret Special Inquiry Court, which is preliminary to being sent back, though, of course only a portion of "S.I.'s" are sent back.

By the kindness of the official at the head of the stairs by which we would have ordinarily have passed down and out to the ferry to take us to New York, we were allowed to drop our baggage behind a post and, standing out of the way of the crowd, pick out our people as they filtered through passed the inspectors. Salvatore Biajo came through marked "Railroad," and was passed along to get his railroad ticket order stamped, his money exchanged at the stand kept beside the stairs under contract by Post & Flagg, bankers, and, in a minute more, he had been moved on down the stairs to the railroad room, after I had had but the barest word with him. Antonio Genone, with a ticket for Philadelphia, came through without going over to the right to the railroad-ticket stamping official, and he was down the stairs and gone without even knowing that he was separated from us permanently.

We began to see why the three stairways were called "The Stairs of Separation." To their right is the money exchange, to the left are the Special Inquiry Room and the Telegraph offices. Here family parties with different destinations are separated without a minute's warning and often never see each other again. It seems heartless, but it is the only practical system for, if allowance was made for good-byes, the examination and distribution process would be blocked then and there by a dreadful crush. Special officers would be necessary to tear relatives forcibly from each other's arms. The stairs to the right lead to the railroad room, where tickets are arranged, baggage checked and cleared for customs, and the immigrants loaded on boats to be taken to the various railroad stations for shipment to different parts of the country. The central stair leads to the detention rooms, where immigrants are held pending the arrival of friends. The left descent is for those free to go to the ferry. . . .

Having passed the last barrier and got all the information I wanted on Ellis Island from the immigrant's point of view, it seemed time to declare myself and, so I informed the night chief inspector who I was and why I was there and requested that he discharge all our people to me so that I could take them over to New York, as I wanted to get the story of their first impressions of American soil by being with them when they landed in the greatest American city. The officials were highly amused and interested in the whole affair, showed me every courtesy, and in five minutes I was below at the gate of the detentions room with a written order for the entire party except the "Railroads," to be discharged to me; they were already gone. . . .

The more I saw of the inside of the great system on the Island the more I was struck with its thoroughness and the kindly, efficient manner in which the law was enforced. If undesirable immigrants are pouring into the United States through Ellis Island, it is not because the laws are not strict enough or the finest system that human ingenuity can devise for handling large masses is not brought into full play by honest and conscientious officials, to pick out the bad from the good. The whole trouble is that the undesirable immigrant comes up before the honest, intelligent official with a lie so carefully prepared that the official is helpless when he has nothing on which to rely but the testimony of the immigrant and his friends. Only in the home town can the truth be learned and the proper discrimination be made. Any other plan is fallacious. . . .

At last we were reassembled. The women had dried their tears. Under the inspiration of being at last within the barrier of being about to step on American soil and untrammeled, the party seemed to cast off its weariness and we passed out of the huge building, around to the ferry-boat and aboard. . . .

As we docked at the Barge Office, we had a slight wait until the returning officials, visitors and better class passengers on the deck overhead could be let off, and then we were released. We passed through the huge piles of immigrants' baggage, to which we must return on the morrow to get the heavy pieces of our own, and out to the street.

There was a stretch of Battery Park, the looming buildings about Bowling Green and on State Street, a real Broadway car and a fine L train roaring north on Sixth Avenue tracks, boys with ten-o'clock extras, and a thousand things that told us we were back home, once again in the best place of all. I was the head of the party leading the way to a Broadway car, for it was useless to try to go up on the L with all our encumbrances, and looked back at my wife. She was looking up at the trees and the buildings, and she said gently, 'Thank God! Thank God!'" (Brandenburg, 1904, pp. 198–200)

REFERENCE: Brandenburg, Broughton. 1904. *Imported Americans.* New York: Stokes.

Bremer, Edith Terry (b. September 10, 1885; d. 1964). Social reformer; founder and director of the **YWCA** Immigration Bureau and the National Institutes of Immigrant Welfare. Edith Terry Bremer supervised her organization's immigrant aid programs at Ellis Island (1911–1954). She concentrated her efforts to held unaided women and children, although her port workers, including **Ludmila K. Foxlee** and Johanna Cohrsen, aided women, men and, of course, children. Her organization also aided immigrants and refugees once they were released from Ellis Island, by offering English classes, housing, citizenship courses and recreational activities. She founded the National Institutes for Immigrant Welfare (NIIW) in 1911 and operated within the YWCA. However, desirous of being justified in aiding Catholics and Jews, she made the NIIW independent of the YWCA in 1933.

Brownell, Herbert (b. Peru, Nebraska, February 20, 1904; d. New York, May 1, 1996). U.S. attorney general (1953–1957). Attorney General Herbert Brownell authorized Gen. **Joseph Swing**, commissioner of the **Immigration and Naturalization Service**, to close Ellis Island and several other detention stations by November 1954. He also enforced the stringent immigration laws that brought so many aliens to Ellis Island in 1953 and 1954. Earlier in his career, Brownell served as New York state legislator (1933–1937), advisor to Governor Thomas E. Dewey, and was chairman of the Republican National Committee (1944–1946). His autobiography is entitled *Advising Ike: The Memoirs of Attorney General Herbert Brownell* (1993).

Buck, Pearl S. [Pearl Sydenstricker Buck] (b. Hillsboro, West Virginia, June 26, 1892; d. Vermont, March 6, 1973). Nobel Prize–winning novelist. In 1954, Miss Buck wrote a letter to the editor of the *New York Times* protesting the closing of Ellis Island:

> I have friends who have been held on Ellis Island pending the decisions as to their status in the United States. Their stay on Ellis Island was distressing enough, but now that Ellis Island has been closed for reasons of economy, we are told, their condition is most unfortunate. The men are sent to a house of detention in White Plains and the women to a prison, also in Westchester, N.Y. Here their plight is exactly the same as though they were common criminals. They are locked up with murderers, drug addicts and other degenerate types. Their food is inadequate, their bed mattresses dirty. They have little opportunity to get fresh air, and they must perform labor such as criminal prisoners perform. Attorney General Brownell has assured us that upon closing Ellis Island all persons would be treated with humaneness. This is not being done, although I understand that our federal government is paying New York State double the usual per diem allowance for food and acre, thus signifying that intentions are right. The sorry fact is, however, that intelligent and good persons are treated as though they had committed crimes. I am sure that the American people would not want this to happen. Moreover, it is inevitable that news of such treatment will go abroad and serve as bad propaganda for our country.

INS district director Edward J. Shaughnessy responded to these charges in a *New York Times* piece appearing on November 24, 1954:

> [A] careful study was made of the cases of all aliens detained at Ellis Island and the release of

all but forty-six was authorized, although normally we had been detaining between 200 to 300 daily. The cases cited by Miss Buck appeared to fall within the category requiring further detention. Of course, the cases of all detainees are constantly under study to determine the feasibility of continuing their detention or releasing them on bond or conditional parole or supervision with reasonable restrictions to ensure their availability when their presence is required by the Immigration and Naturalization Service. Miss Buck expresses concern about the conditions under which these undesirable detainees are housed in the Westchester County Jail at Eastview, N.Y. I may say that I personally inspected this facility before the transfer of our detainees was made. The detainees are housed in a modern structure immaculately maintained and classified by the Federal Bureau of Prisons as a Class A institution, so that its standards are high with respect to diet, cleanliness, security and treatment of its inmates.

REFERENCES: Buck, Pearl S. 1954. Letter to the editor. *New York Times*, November 16; Shaughnessy, Edward J. 1954. Letter to the editor. *New York Times*, November 24.

Buford. The United States Army Transport *Buford*, or "Soviet Ark," as the press called it, transported 249 radicals, including **Alexander Berkman** and **Emma Goldman**, as deportees to the Soviet Union late in December 1919. Since the vessel could not enter a Russian port, it only traveled as far as Finland.

The *Buford* had been constructed in Belfast, Ireland, in 1890 and originally christened as the SS *Mississippi.* In 1898, it was sold to the U.S. Army for use in the Spanish-American War and renamed the USAT *Buford.* It saw service in the newly acquired U.S. colonies as a result of the U.S. victory over Spain and was later sent to Mexico during the Pancho Villa crisis. During World War I, it was transferred temporarily to the navy and was used to bring home 4,700 U.S. soldiers from France. In September 1919, it was returned to the army. The vessel was painted white and had one funnel and two masts.

Aerial view of Ellis Island, 1920s. Courtesy of the Ellis Island Immigration Museum.

Aerial view of Ellis Island looking southeast, ca 1934. Courtesy of the Ellis Island Immigration Museum.

Buildings. As of 1980, the following forty-one buildings existed on Ellis Island. Those written in italics are no longer extant. On Island 1: **Main Building**, connecting wing, **baggage and dormitory building**, **kitchen and laundry building**, **power house**, *shed*, shelter (at fuel dock), *greenhouse*, *incinerator*, **bakery and carpentry shop**, *shed*, and passageway. At the head of the ferry basin between islands 1 and 2: passage, **ferry house**, and the new immigration building.

On Island 2: passageway, **laundry and linen exchange**, **psychopathic ward**, **general hospital building**, **hospital administration building**, and the **hospital extension** building.

Between islands 2 and 3: **recreation hall** and the **recreation shelter**.

Island 3: power house, **animal house**, **office building**, passageway, administration building, kitchen, eleven **contagious disease wards**, and staff house.

Bureau of Immigration. This federal agency administered immigration affairs from its headquarters in Washington, DC. Its field offices were called immigrant inspection stations and were located at the busiest U.S. seaports; the largest of these was on Ellis Island in New York harbor, the nation's busiest seaport.

The agency was first called the **Office of Immigration** and was officially established on July 12, 1891, under the authority of the **Immigration Act of 1891**, which had come into force in March of the same year. The key words giving birth to the agency appeared in section 7 of the act:

> The office of superintendent of immigration is hereby created and established, and the President, by and with the advice and consent of the Senate, is authorized and directed to appoint such officer,

whose salary shall be four thousand dollars per annum, payable monthly. The superintendent of immigration shall be an officer in the Treasury Department, under the control and supervision of the Secretary of the Treasury, to whom he shall make annual reports in writing, as the Secretary of the Treasury shall require. The Secretary shall provide the superintendent with a suitably furnished office in the city of Washington, and with such books of record and facilities for the discharging of the duties of his office as may be necessary. He shall have a chief clerk . . . and two first-class clerks.

In 1895, the Office of Immigration received a new name: the Bureau of Immigration. In 1903, the bureau was transferred from the Department of the Treasury to the newly created Department of Commerce and Labor and, in 1906, its name was changed to the **Bureau of Immigration and Naturalization**, expanding its activities. In 1913, the Departments of Commerce and Labor were established as separate entities; immigration went to the Department of Labor. In addition, the Bureau of Immigration and the Bureau of Naturalization split into two separate agencies within the Department of Labor. The Bureau of Immigration remained an independent agency until 1933, when it was once again united with naturalization under a new name: the **Immigration and Naturalization Service** (INS). In 1940, the INS was transferred from the Department of Labor to the Department of Justice. President Franklin D. Roosevelt intended this be but a temporary arrangement; after the end of World War II, he planned to transfer the agency to the Department of the Interior; his death in 1945, quickly brought an end to this plan. In 2003, the INS was split into four agencies divided between the Department of Justice and the newly created Department of Homeland Security.

See also **Commissioners; Commissioners-General**

REFERENCE: Immigration Act of 1891, *U.S. Statutes at Large* 26 (1891): 1084.

Bureau of Immigration and Naturalization. The Bureau of Immigration and Naturalization was the name of the united **Bureau of Immigration** and the newly created Bureau of Naturalization from 1906 through 1913; in the latter year, the two were separated and made independent agencies within the Department of Labor. But in 1933, they were once again united as the **Immigration and Naturalization Service**.

The Bureau of Immigration was responsible for the legal status of all aliens either entering or living in the United States, while the Bureau of Naturalization regulated applications for naturalization of foreigners seeking U.S. citizenship.

C

Caminetti, Anthony (b. Jackson, California, July 30, 1854; d. Jackson, California, November 17, 1923). Commissioner-General of immigration (1913–1921); lawyer and politician. Anthony Caminetti served as the commissioner-general of the Bureau of Immigration under President Woodrow Wilson, a period that included the anti-Bolshevik **red scare** years, during which so many radicals were expelled from the United States. Caminetti supported the aggressive deportation policy of his superiors in the Department of Labor, which exasperated and frustrated his commissioner at Ellis Island, **Frederic C. Howe**.

Caminetti, a prominent California Democrat, enjoyed a long career in public office, serving as the district attorney of Amador County (1878–1882); state assemblyman (1883–1885, 1896–1900); state senator (1885–1888, 1907–1913); and in the U.S. House of Representatives (1891–1995).

References: Biographical Directory of the United States Congress. Anthony Caminetti. Washington, DC: U.S. Government Printing Office; Giovinco, Joseph P. 1973. The California career of Anthony Caminetti, Italian-American politician. PhD diss., University of California.

Canopy. A large canopy was added at the entrance to the **Main Building** in June 1903. It sheltered arriving immigrants from inclement weather and benches were provided for them, and from 1911 until the 1920s, medical examinations took place there. The canopy was pulled down in 1932. A new canopy of steel and glass was erected at the entrance to the building in 1989.

Carol, Charles A. [Charles A. Karog] (b. Lithuania, 1889; d. New York, 1966). Missionary. Charles Carol emigrated from Lithuania in 1900 and was converted to the Protestant Episcopal religion. He was that church's missionary on Ellis Island from 1906 to 1954. In 1920s, he served on the Committee of Seven, the executive board for the twenty-nine **immigrant aid societies** then operating on Ellis Island. In the late 1940s and early 1950s, he served as an assistant librarian.

See also **Missionaries**

Castle Clinton National Monument (formerly **Castle Garden**). Long before it was opened to immigrants, Castle Garden was one of the best-known landmarks in New York. Located on the Manhattan waterfront at the **Battery**, it faces the entrance to New York known as the Narrows and blocked access to the entrance of the Hudson River. The circular, red sandstone building was designed by Colonel Jonathan Williams of the Army Corps of Engineers with the aid of eminent New York architect John McComb (1763–1853); the latter was responsible for the design of its entranceway and served as building contractor. The fortification was constructed between 1807 and 1811 as one of a chain of fortresses planned to protect New York from a naval attack. Surrounded by 35 feet (7.7 meters) of water, it stood 200 feet (61 meters) from the shore and was accessible to Manhattan via a wooden causeway and drawbridge. Its original name was South-West Battery, a name that attached itself to the land nearest the building; now its is known simply as the Battery or Battery Park. The South-West Battery was armed with twenty-eight cannons. Although armed and ready for hostilities during the War of 1812, the battery was never called on to fire a shot. In 1815, it was named in honor of Governor George Clinton of New York, who was a hero of the American Revolution and a close friend of President George Washington.

After briefly serving as the headquarters of the Third Military District of the United States (1815–1821), it was closed down and in 1823 was given to New York City. In 1824, it was renamed Castle Garden and opened as an attractive location for public festivities and performances. It later served under the same name as an immigrant station and finally as the city aquarium. The name Castle Clinton was restored to the edifice when President Truman declared it a national monument on August 12, 1946. After a proposal to installing an immigration history museum in it was rejected in the early 1950s, it remained closed until 1975. In that year it was reopened for small concerts and fairs and, soon afterwards, it became the location of the Circle Line ticket booth for those wishing to visit the Statue of Liberty and Ellis Island. A small **National Park Service** exhibit giving an overview of Castle Clinton's history was also installed in a room near the entrance gates of the castle.

Castle Garden. In 1824, **Castle Clinton** was renamed Castle Garden and was redesigned as a "place of resort" for New Yorkers; it opened on July 3 of that year. A newspaper described its interior as having the appearance of a "fanciful garden, tastefully ornamented with shrubs and flowers." This aspect was enhanced with the installation of a fountain. A series of illustrious performers appeared at the Castle, including Jenny Lind, the Swedish singer celebrated as the Swedish Nightingale; and Maria Montez, the Irish-born dancer who was formerly mistress to King Ludwig of Bavaria.

This was America's first immigrant receiving station and was operated not by the federal government but by the state of New York. Its historic importance is underlined by the 8 million immigrants who were processed there, which makes it the second busiest immigration depot in the history of the United States. Castle Garden was originally built as a fort in the early nineteenth century and was first named South-West Battery and then **Castle Clinton**. Known by Germans, Jews, and central and eastern Europeans as *kessel garden* and Greeks as *kasi gardi.* After Castle Garden was closed, the name lived on in emigrants' minds, for it was long thought that Ellis Island

Castle Garden and Battery Park, ca 1880s. Courtesy of the Ellis Island Immigration Museum.

was merely a new "Castle Garden." To many, the term *castle garden* signified a crowded place where a confusion of voices disturbed the silence.

Employees from Castle Garden who went on to work at the barge office and Ellis Island included Samuel C. Tompkins (clerk, Executive Bureau), John J. Simpson (superintendent, Landing Bureau), **Charles Semsey** (clerk, Landing Bureau), Sven A. Smith (clerk, Landing Bureau), Anna Prokupek (clerk, Information Bureau; at Ellis Island she was in the Information and Discharging divisions, through 1920), Mrs. Sloper (head matron), Mrs. Regina Stucklen (matron; later head matron), Charles Eichler (boarding officer), and Phillip Herrlich (boarding officer). The titles refer to the position they held at Castle Garden in 1890. **Peter McDonald**, an employee of the Castle Garden baggage concession, also went on to work at the barge office and Ellis Island.

References: Moreno, Barry. 2003. Castle Garden: The forgotten gateway. *Ancestry*. March–April; Svejda, George J. 1968. *Castle Garden as an Immigrant Depot, 1855–1890*. Washington, DC: National Park Service.

Castro, Cipriano [Cipriano Castro Ruiz] (b. Capacho, Táchira, Venezuela, October 12, 1858; d. Santurce, Puerto Rico, December 4, 1924). President of Venezuela (1899–1908); military officer. The detention of Cipriano Castro was one of the famous cases in the history of Ellis Island. General Castro was overthrown from the presidency of his country during a medical trip to Berlin, Germany, in 1908. His policies while in office had alienated the western creditor nations, including the United States. President Theodore Roosevelt had a particularly poor relationship with the general.

On December 31, 1912, the stateless political exile arrived in New York on board the *Touraine*, sailing from Le Havre, France. Exactly one week earlier, Ellis Island officials received a telegram on former President Castro from the **Bureau of Immigration** instructing them to "detain and examine carefully, not releasing in any event until Bureau has been communicated with." The chief of the **Boarding Division** was immediately sent a "lookout order," together with the advisory that Castro was traveling as "Luis Ruiz." On December 28, Ellis Island's commissioner received the further orders from the Washington Bureau he had been awaiting. Instructions included the following: "whether or not any specific reason is ascertained for his exclusion under the immigration law, Castro should be detained until the case can be referred to the Department for decision." Inspectors Moore and Samuel Eppler of the **Special Inquiry Division** questioned him about his rule or misrule in Venezuela; the general denied the most extreme accusations and refused to answer questions that did not concern the United States. In later January, a board of special inquiry chaired by Eppler ordered General Castro excluded. A few days later, Charles Nagel, the secretary of Commerce and Labor, upheld this decision.

However, Castro's lawyers immediately appealed to the federal district court, which, on February 15, 1913, ordered the Bureau of Immigration to release Castro at once. Secretary Nagel decided not to appeal against the decision and ordered Castro released two days later. He remained in New York and completed his business, departing on March 15. He settled in Puerto Rico in 1916.

Reference: Corsi, Edward. 1935. *In the Shadow of Liberty*. New York: Macmillan.

Celebrations. National and religious celebrations were observed at Ellis Island, especially for the detained aliens. Independence Day and New Year's Day were especially popular. There were also ethnic events such as a Ukrainian festival that was held in the **Great Hall** in 1916. Religious observances were also observed at the station, especially **Christmas**, for which much documentation exists. For Jewish detainees, Passover, Yom Kippur, Sukkoth, and other holy days were observed. The kosher kitchen staff, under the supervision of a rabbi, prepared food that was appropriate for these occasions.

Certificates. A document certifying the state of an immigrant's health, namely a **medical certificate** or a document certifying an immigrant's right to reside in the United States, known as a **certificate of registry**. At Ellis Island, the **Medical Division** issued medical certificates and certificates of registry were issued by the **Registry Division**. Medical certificates were issued to immigrants who were detained during **line inspection** and escorted to examination rooms for a more detailed medical inspection; certificates were also issued to immigrants who were hospitalized. After being co-signed by three surgeons of the **Medical Division**, the certificate were then sent to the chief inspectors of either the **Registry Division** or **Special Inquiry Division** for further action.

Certificates of Registry. A certificate of registry was a document that certified an immigrant's right to live in the United States, and thus was desirable for any illegal alien or any immigrant whose presence in the country might be interpreted as doubtful. Introduced under the Immigration Act of 1929, it authorized the voluntary registry of aliens for whom there was no record of admission in the United States. This especially applied to persons who had entered the United States by crossing a point at the Canadian or Mexican borders, and had evaded immigrant inspection and paying the **head tax**. It also was for those immigrants for whom no immigration record could be found and illegal aliens of good moral character, who were not subject to deportation, and able to meet other legal requirements. The law stipulated that an immigrant had to meet four requirements in order to be eligible for a certificate of registry:

1. He must show that he entered the United States prior to June 3, 1921.
2. He must show that he has resided in the United States since such entry.
3. He must show that he is a person of good character.
4. He must show that he is not subject to deportation. (p. 91)

At Ellis Island, inspectors of the **Registry Division** carried out the administration of this program. However, Ellis Island officials imposed extra obligations on applicants for the certificates of registry such as requiring them to submit excessive documentary proofs, including landing cards, tax records and receipts, school papers, marriage and birth certificates, bank books, and other personal and financial records. All of these were designed to prove continuous residence in the country. By 1933, some of the more exacting practices were dispensed with and individual inspectors relied on their discretion in issuing certificates. Fees for certificates of registry ran as high as $20.00.

REFERENCE: Palmer, Carleton. *Report of the Ellis Island Committee.* March 1934.

Chalk Mark Code. The Ellis Island surgeons developed a simple alphabetical code for marking aliens suspected of illnesses during **line inspection**. Using a piece of chalk, the doctor would make a mark or write a word on the alien's clothing. The alien was then removed from the line by a medical attendant to undergo a thorough examination for a suspected illness or condition. The following is an excerpt from E. H. Mullan's description of the system.

> Many inattentive and stupid-looking aliens are questioned by the medical officer in the various languages as to their age, destination and nationality. Often simple questions in addition and multiplication are propounded. Should the immigrant appear stupid and inattentive to such an extent that mental defect is suspected, an X is made on his coat at the anterior aspect of his right shoulder. Should definite signs of mental disease be observed, a circle X would be used instead of the plain X. In like manner, a chalk mark is placed on the anterior aspect of the right shoulder in all cases where physical deformity or disease is suspected.
>
> In this connection, B would indicate back; C, conjunctivitis; CT, trachoma; E, eyes; F, face; Ft, feet; G, goiter; H, heart; K, hernia; L, lameness; N, neck; P, physical and lungs; Pg, pregnancy; Sc, scalp; S, senility. The words hands, measles, nails, skin, temperature, vision, voice, which are often used, are written out in full.

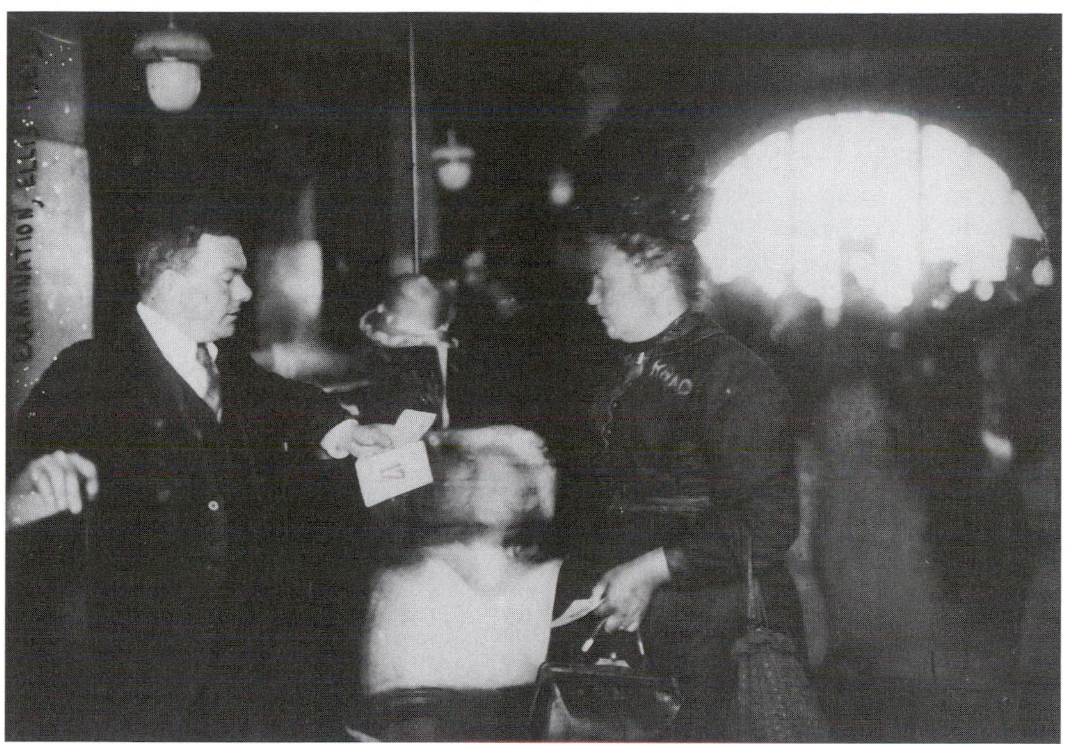

Chalk markings on this woman's clothing show that she was detained for an extensive medical examination before she appeared before the inspector in the Registry Room here.
Courtesy of the Ellis Island Immigration Museum.

. . . Corneal opacities, nysstagmus, squint, bulging eyes, the wearing of eye glasses, clumsiness, and other signs on the part of the alien, will be sufficient cause for him to be chalked marked with "Vision." He will then be taken out of the line by an attendant and his vision will be carefully examined. If the alien passes through this line without receiving a chalk mark, he has successfully passed the medical inspection and off he goes to the upper hall.

See also **Abbreviations; Line Inspection**

REFERENCE: Mullan, E. H. 1917. Mental examination of immigrants. Administration and line inspection at Ellis Island. Washington: Public Health Service.

Chief Clerk. The chief clerk's office was near the commissioner's office and as such was a part of the **Executive Division**. The holder of this post had supervision over all of the clerks and the **Special Inquiry Division** stenographers at Ellis Island, controlled the station's correspondence, prepared appeal cases for the commissioner's review, and issued instructions to the **Deporting Division** pursuant to the commissioner's decision. Although the chief clerk was officially only equivalent to a chief of division, he was in fact the third most powerful official at Ellis Island. Only the commissioner and the assistant commissioner were superior to him. This was evident from the 1890s through about 1921. The incumbent of the position had much to do with its influence. Prominent chief clerks included Clarence W. Cady (1890s), **Byron H. Uhl** (1909), and **Augustus F. Sherman** (1909–1921), Samuel J. Eppler (1921–1925).The position was abolished around 1925.

Children. Hundreds of thousands of immigrant children passed through Ellis Island in the company of their parents, guardians, and siblings. Some children entered as stowaways. Others were orphans and had to have sponsors to enter the country, and when released, they were put aboard immigrant trains to go to their new homes in the United States. Many children were detained at Ellis Island when they were sick and had to be hospitalized. Common illnesses for which they were detained included **measles**, scarlet fever, chickenpox, mumps, diphtheria, and **trachoma**. However, it was just as likely that another family member might be the cause of the delay at the station, such as a parent or another child in the family. In this case, it was common to detain the whole family temporarily during the period of hospitalization. If a child under the age of twelve was excluded or deported, an adult had to accompany him; older children—especially boys—were thought able to return to Europe or elsewhere alone.

The **Bureau of Immigration** was forced to call on the missionaries and immigrant aid workers to make the life of detainees at least slightly bearable. Immigrant schoolrooms and kindergartens operated at various times through the years; the Congregational Church operated one schoolroom in the 1920s. The Bureau of Immigration set up a roof garden on the **Main Building** for adults and children just after the turn of the twentieth century. Although this roof garden was closed in 1911, another one was eventually set up in the **baggage and dormitory building**. There was also a playground set up outdoors, behind the Main Building. It included a sandbox, two slides (one for big children and one for small children), and swings. In addition, boys often played football, both European (soccer) and American, and both boys and girls played other games and sports, usually in separate groups. Neither nationality, ethnicity nor race seemed to be a barrier among children, and a great mixture could be found playing all sorts of games. Photographic collections of immigrant children at Ellis Island are held by several institutions including the **Ellis Island Immigration Museum**, the Library of Congress, the National Archives, the State Historical Society of Wisconsin, and Louisiana State University.

See also **Schooling**

Chinese Division. The work of the Chinese Division at Ellis Island was to prevent the illegal entry of Chinese immigrants into New

Chinese immigrants with an Ellis Island nurse, 1920s. Courtesy of the Ellis Island Immigration Museum.

York harbor and the greater metropolitan area. Its immigrant inspectors were called Chinese inspectors.

Because New York City had a large population of Chinese immigrants, the inspectors of the Chinese Division were always busy. Chinese affairs at Ellis Island, including enforcement of the **Chinese Exclusion Act**, were originally handled by the **Special Inquiry Division**, as far back as the 1890s. For many years Chinese were brought to Ellis Island as illegal aliens, stowaways, and deportees. In the 1920s and 1930s, the Immigration officers conducted raids in Chinatown based on tips and other information they received. In 1941 list of some 900 aliens being deported from Ellis Island, well over 100 were Chinese. Many were undocumented aliens being deported to Canada, others were simply alien seamen who had overstayed their shore leave.

The **Bureau of Immigration** also operated a **New York Chinese Office** in Manhattan. The Chinese Division at Ellis Island was established in about 1920 or earlier and continued in operation until 1951. Chiefs of the Chinese Division included **Edward D. Zucker** and Eugene W. Willard.

REFERENCE: Corsi, Edward. 1935. *In the Shadow of Liberty*. New York: Macmillan.

Chinese Exclusion Act (May 6, 1882; 22 Statute 58). The Chinese Exclusion Act suspended the immigration of Chinese laborers for ten years. The law required laborers who had resided here but then returned to China to show a certificate of eligibility on reentering the country. This law also prohibited the Chinese from becoming U.S. citizens. Congress continued renewing the Chinese Exclusion laws until those laws still on the books were at last repealed on December 17, 1943 (57 Statute 600).

The **Special Inquiry Division** and the **Chinese Division** long enforced these laws at Ellis Island. The same policies were also enforced at all other stations of the **Bureau of Immigration**, especially **Angel Island Immigrant Station** (San Francisco), Seattle, Honolulu, Los Angeles (Terminal Island), Portland (Oregon), Montreal, New Orleans, and the **Boston Immigrant Station**.

Christmas. Christmas was observed each year at Ellis Island through religious services, festivities, and gift giving. Celebrations for the holiday were organized chiefly for detainees and deportees. The Roman Catholic Church and the various Eastern Orthodox and Protestant churches and denominations offered separate religious services in accordance with their respective traditions. There offerings were commonly presided over by foreign-born clergymen who could speak fluently in such foreign languages as Italian, Polish, German, French, Greek, Danish, Norwegian, Swedish, Dutch, Spanish, and Portuguese; naturally, many services were also offered in English for British and Irish detainees. Notable priests presiding at Christmas over the years including the Reverend Fathers S. Cynalewski, **Anthony Grogan**, and **Gaspare Moretti**; among Protestant ministers and evangelists were the Reverend Georg Doering of the German Lutheran Church, the Reverend W. A. Dalton, and Brigadier Thomas Johnson of the **Salvation Army**. In addition, New York Bible Society missionary **Charles A. Carol** helped organize services on behalf of the Protestant Episcopal Church and, for many years, handed out Christian tracts in a variety of languages to immigrants at the station. In the 1940s and 1950s, Carol helped run the Ellis Island library. Because Christmas festivities were directed at detained aliens who were often at the point of being excluded or deported, Christmas messages were often somber. This was especially the case during the two administrations of Commissioner **William Williams**, who was an unyielding enforcer of immigration restriction policies. Speaking to Italian detainees on Christmas 1910, Father Moretti said:

> I have spoken at Ellis Island before, but never was there at a time when I felt so bad as now. There are so many detained here. You have crossed the

ocean, endured hardships and dangers to come to the country discovered by your fellow countryman. You have found the door closed. You have had your hope in the land of liberty shattered. To those who will finally get in, I would say, you must live to be a credit to your country and the land of your adoption. (Moreno 2003, p. 68)

Years later, **Ludmila K. Foxlee**, a **YWCA** port worker, provided the following description of the aid given to detainees at Ellis Island during Christmases in the 1920s and 1930s. Although Foxlee specifically deals with holiday conditions in the post–World War I years, her description is nearly similar to Christmases dating back to the turn of the century.

Christmas was regularly observed on the island. Missionary societies sent toys and fruit for the children. The General Committee of Immigrant Aid decided to buy small, useful articles for the adults, so that everyone could have a Christmas gift. An appeal was made for bags about eighteen by eighteen inches with a draw string at the top, made of bright cotton prints. Girls bags contained a doll, towel, washcloth and soap, a game, a set of toy dishes, three handkerchiefs, a writing tablet, a pencil box, and a pair of stockings. Women received a sewing bag, needles and thread, pins and safety pins, scissors and buttons, a bead necklace, an apron, a bath towel and washcloth, tooth brush and tooth paste, soap, a writing tablet and a pencil, stockings and three handkerchiefs.

For men the bags contained a comfort bag (with needles, thread, some buttons, et cetera), a safety razor, tooth brush, tooth paste, pins, safety pins, washcloth and soap, a towel, a game, a writing tablet and pencil, a pair of socks, and three handkerchiefs. For boys the bags were similar to those for the girls, with a game substituted for the doll. A Christmas tree with lights and a silver star brightened the hall. Benches in long rows with an aisle in the middle accommodated the detained. Chairs stood at the side of the hall for the General Committee of Immigrant Aid and their friends. A musical program occupied the major part of the afternoon, and the talent was donated. For two successive Christmases, a group of Social Service workers appeared in national costumes and sang English, Italian, German, Polish, Spanish and Czechoslovak carols. However, the Commissioner decided later that professional talent must be provided. He persuaded a broadcasting company to present a musical program, and that was heard coast to coast. The radio company provided a full orchestra and a Metropolitan Opera soprano to a sing a Puccini aria. The grandeur had no visible affect on the audience. After the program, the immigrants were given their bags and an orange. (1968, pp. 7–8)

In December 1927, the *New York Times* reported that at the Christmas festivity, Santa Claus entertained 300 aliens and 100 guests in the main detention room. At the Christmas festival of 1930, accordionist Charles Albera performed "Happy Days," "Sweet Jenny Lee," "Woman in the Shoe," "Betty Co-Ed," "The Stein Song," and "My Treasure Waltz."

REFERENCES: Foxlee, Ludmila K. 1968. How they came: The drama of Ellis Island, 1920–1935. Manuscript Collection, Ellis Island Library, Statue of Liberty N.M.; Moreno, Barry. 1992. Ellis Island Christmases. Manuscript Collection, Ellis Island Library, Statue of Liberty N.M.; Moreno, Barry. 2003. *Italian Americans.* Hauppage, New York: Barron's; *New York Times.* 1927. Christmas at hand: Ellis Island has party. December 24.

Citizens. Steamship passengers claiming to be "U.S. citizens" on the ground that they had been born in the United States were required to "state with accuracy their place of birth" at the time that they embarked at a foreign port. Likewise those claiming to be U.S. citizens through naturalization were expected "to furnish the date of their naturalization papers and the name of the court which issued them" before embarking for the United States. If the steamship agent were satisfied that the passenger was a citizen, he was then permitted to write the person's name on the special manifest sheets reserved for U.S. citizens. But if the agent was suspicious of the claim, he was instructed to write the name of the person on the manifest for alien passengers, and, if desired, add the words "Claims U.S. citizenship."

Clerks. Clerks worked in a variety of divisions and offices at Ellis Island, including those that were assigned to assist during **primary inspection**. Other important clerical posts were in the **Special Inquiry Division**, where clerks worked as stenographers and typists (called typewriters prior to World War I). In his 1909 report (see appendix), **Special Inspector** Roger O'Donnell described the work of the fifteen male stenographers as "arduous, exacting and expert, the work being in the order of court reporting, demanding the acquirement of high speed in stenography and rapid typewritten transcriptions." That year, the **Executive Division**, the division to which all clerks actually belonged, included a staff of five senior clerks, seven clerks, nine junior clerks, and eight under clerks. A large complement of Executive Division clerks was assigned to the **Statistical Division** (thirty-seven), and eighteen others were in the **Special Inquiry Division**, five in the Information and Discharging Division, three in the **Deporting Division**, one in the Sanitary Division, one in the **Night Division**, two in the **Mechanical Division**, and one in the Chief Executive's Office (chief clerk). Clerks were assigned to the **Registry Division** as needed. The clerks were all under the supervision of the **chief clerk**, who exercised considerable authority. Notable chief clerks included **Byron H. Uhl** and **Augustus F. Sherman**.

Closing of Ellis Island. The first serious discussions for closing Ellis Island began as early as 1937–1939; however, world crises and U.S. domestic security concerns forestalled it. Plans for closing the station once again became serious in May 1954. At that time, an **Immigration and Naturalization Service** (INS) study showed that the island open was no longer economically advantageous to the government since only a few hundred aliens were kept there. It was also observed that closing the station would save the Justice Department the expense of maintaining the many buildings, the power plant, and the Ellis Island ferry, as well as end plans to buy second ferry and install modern conveniences in the buildings such as modern air conditioning, which were being planned. Following this, **Joseph Swing**, the commissioner of Immigration and Naturalization, wrote Attorney General **Herbert Brownell** on July 28, 1954, recommending that Ellis Island be closed and all INS operations be transferred to the INS district headquarters office building at 70 Columbus Avenue in Manhattan.

In September and October, laborers cleaned up the island and INS staff began moving government items. In late October and November, seven officers and thirty inmates from the Bureau of Prisons removed heavy equipment, such as furniture, kitchen equipment, refrigerators, laundry equipment, plumbing, carpentry, water coolers, lockers, glass, paint, iron, steel, janitorial supplies, fittings, wire cables, linoleum, food, cutlery, crockery, clothing, bedding, and athletic equipment.

On October 15, 1954, the INS officially filed its final major report: *Report of Excess Real Property.* It declared that Ellis Island had thirty-five buildings with a floor area of 513,013 square feet; 6,435 lineal feet of masonry sea walls; its water system consisted of two miles of main and two 250,000 gallon outdoor water tanks; 640 lineal feet of sewage lines; three incinerators; two fuel oil storage tanks, the larger of which held 130,000 gallons and the smaller 75,000 gallons; 6,000 lineal feet of electric main feeders; 88,000 square feet of paved walkways; and 7,000 lineal feet of chained fencing measuring 10 feet in height. The estimated value of the island's 27.5 acres was put at $260,000, the structures at $5,877,000, and the old **ferryboat *Ellis Island*** at $103,000. Thus the Immigration and Naturalization Service calculated the whole property at $6,137,000.

On November 11, 1954, Attorney General Brownell announced new administrative procedures to cut detentions to a minimum by releasing most suspicious aliens on conditional parole or bond instead of ordering their immediate detention. Meanwhile aliens were being removed from Ellis Island, some were released under the new policy and others detained elsewhere, including jails. By November 12, the last aliens were taken away from Ellis Island. The very last person was **Arne Peterssen**, a

Norwegian seaman who had overstayed his shore leave. Articles appeared in many publications, including assessing the importance of Ellis Island as its service to the nation so abruptly ended. Some of the best-known articles appeared in the *American Mercury* (December 1954), the *Boston Globe* (November 15, 1954), and the *New York Times* (several articles, November 13–16, 1954). Novelist **Pearl S. Buck** criticized the closing of Ellis Island because a number of detainees were sent to jails as a result of it.

The **ferryboat *Ellis Island*** made its final boat run from the Battery to its slip at Ellis Island on November 29, 1954. The pilot was Captain Raymond P. Ives. INS guards were posted to the island, traveling there daily by courtesy of the Coast Guard. In March 1955, the INS officially turned over jurisdiction of Ellis Island to the **General Services Administration**, ending its historic sixty-two-year association with Ellis Island.

REFERENCE: Unrau, Harlan D. 1984. *The Historic Resource Study: Ellis Island/Statue of Liberty.* Vol. 3. Washington, DC: U.S. Department of the Interior, National Park Service.

Coast Guard. In September 1939, following the outbreak of war in Europe, the Coast Guard was ordered to begin patrolling the East Coast. Needing a suitable place to train and provide residential quarters for its men, the force requested the use of a portion of Ellis Island for the purpose. Secretary of Labor **Frances Perkins** granted them the use of the **baggage and dormitory building** and outside recreation areas. In April 1942, they were permitted to move into the **barge office** and by December of that year, they had been granted the use of other buildings, including one wing of the **ferry house** (where they had training classes). Approximately 3,000 officers and 60,000 men were trained at Ellis Island during **World War II**; they withdrew from the

Coastguardsmen at Ellis Island in 1952. Second from the left is Ralph Hornberger. Hornberger Collection. Courtesy of the Ellis Island Immigration Museum.

station on August 15, 1946, and moved all remaining functions to St. George, Staten Island. The Coast Guard had five commanders at Ellis Island: Arthur W. Davis (1939–1940); Randolf Ridgley III (1940–1942); Richard M. Hoyle (1942–1944); Herbert F. Walsh (1944–1945); and Joseph Mazzotta (1945–1946).

The Coast Guard returned to Ellis Island in 1951–1954. During this period the hospital buildings on **Island 2**, which had just been abandoned by the **Public Health Service**, were in use.

REFERENCES: Cassells, David H. The Coast Guard on Ellis Island. Manuscript Collection, Ellis Island Library, Statue of Liberty N.M.; U.S. Coast Guard. 1946. The Coast Guard at Ellis Island. Manuscript Collection, Ellis Island Library, Statue of Liberty N.M.; Unrau, Harlan D. 1984. *The Historic Resource Study: Ellis Island/Statue of Liberty.* Vol. 3. Washington, DC: U.S. Department of the Interior, National Park Service.

Cold War. The early years of the Cold War (1946–1955) had an important impact on Ellis Island's last years as an immigration station. The period was dominated by the fear of communism (the **red scare**) and a fierce hostility toward the Soviet Union, which was the most powerful communist nation. Because of this, immigrants with any ties to leftist or "un-American" organizations were regularly suspected of being communist spies or saboteurs, and found themselves under Federal Bureau of Investigation (FBI) surveillance. Many of the more serious cases underwent long FBI and **Immigration and Naturalization Service** (INS) interrogations, and found themselves facing deportation at Ellis Island. However, the heightened security also affected incoming tourists and others entering the country for only short visits. Well-known aliens held at Ellis Island as result of Cold War tensions included **Ignac Mezei**, Ellen Knauff, and **C. L. R. James**, while British novelist Graham Greene, who had been detained by INS agents in Puerto Rico, came near to being detained on the island.

REFERENCE: Stein, Robert. 1997. Rethinking an American symbol: Ellis Island when it stopped welcoming immigrants. Master's thesis, Hunter College. Manuscript Collection, Ellis Island Library, Statue of Liberty N.M.

Commissioners. The commissioner was the highest ranking **Bureau of Immigration** official at Ellis Island. The incumbent of this post was in charge of all that went on at the station. Although he managed the operation as a whole through the **Executive Division**, he also supervised all other **divisions** at the station, including the **Public Health Service** staff, which was known as the **Medical Division**. The commissioner appointed all division chiefs and certain other officials. He conducted all external affairs of the station, including all relations with his superiors in Washington, DC. He also heard appeals against decisions of the **Special Inquiry Division** handled delicate cases often involving international political figures, criminals, or celebrities. The position was originally created in 1890 as the "superintendent of immigration." It was changed to commissioner in 1891 when Congress assigned the title "superintendent' to the head of the Bureau of Immigration in Washington, DC. The rank was also conferred on the heads of all of the busiest immigrant inspection stations, including those at Boston and Philadelphia. The following excerpt of the Immigration Act of 1894 (28 Statute L., 372, 390) describes the post of commissioner.

> The commissioners of immigration at the several ports shall be appointed by the President, by and with the advice and consent of the Senate, to hold their office for the term of four years, unless sooner removed, and until their successors are appointed; and nominations shall be made to the Senate by the President as soon as practicable after the passage of this act.

In 1940, commissioners were no longer appointed for Ellis Island and the district director effectively became the island's chief. The commissioners of immigration at Ellis Island were **John B. Weber** (1890–1893), **Joseph H. Senner** (1893–1897), Thomas Fitchie (1897–1902), **William Williams** (1902–1905), **Robert Watchorn** (1905–1909), **William Wil-**

liams (1909–1913), **Frederic C. Howe** (1914–1919), **Frederick A. Wallis** (1920–1921), **Robert E. Tod** (1921–1923), **Henry H. Curran** (1923–1926), **Benjamin M. Day** (1926–1931), **Edward Corsi** (1931–1934), **Rudolph Reimer** (1934–1940). The district directors were **Byron H. Uhl** (1933–1942), **W. Frank Watkins** (1942–1949), and Edward J. Shaughnessy (1949–1954).

REFERENCE: Immigration Act of 1894, *U.S. Statutes at Large* 28 (1894): 372, 390.

Commissioners-General. The commissioner-general of immigration was the highest-ranking officer of the **Bureau of Immigration**. The officer was created under the provisions of the **Immigration Act of 1891** and was originally styled "superintendent of immigration." This was changed to commissioner-general under the **Immigration Act of 1895**. The commissioner-general supervised all of the port commissioners of immigrations, including the commissioner of immigration at Ellis Island.

In 1895, the title of superintendent was dropped in favor of commissioner-general, which remained in use until it was changed to "commissioner" in about 1940; at that time, also, the port commissioners title was changed to district director. Prominent commissioners-general over the years included **Herman Stump**, **Terence V. Powderley**, **Frank P. Sargent**, **Daniel J. Keefe**, **Anthony Caminetti**, and **W. W. Husband**.

Concessions. Concessions for trade and other necessities have been granted under contract to many firms at Ellis Island as far back as 1891–1992. The concessionaires throughout the immigration years were called **privilege holders** and offered vital services to immigrants that the **Bureau of Immigration** either was unable or did not chose to provide. These included providing or selling meals and refreshments, railway and steamboat tickets, changing foreign money into American dollars, and sending telegrams. The operations were lucrative and extensive but they ended with the **closing of Ellis Island** in 1954.

Since the opening of the **Ellis Island Immigration Museum** in 1990, the **National Park Service** has granted concessions to several firms, including Circle Line to provide ferry service from Manhattan and Jersey City, and the Aramark Corporation to operate a food and gift concession. Other private firms have provided various maintenance services at the museum.

Congressional Resolution of 1890 (26 Statute 670). On April 11, 1890, President Benjamin Harrison approved the Joint Resolution of Congress designating Ellis Island as the site of the first federal immigrant inspection station.

The resolution authorized the U.S. Navy to remove its powder magazine from Ellis Island and install it elsewhere (e.g., Fort Wadsworth, Staten Island), for which it appropriated $75,000. Another $75,000 was appropriated for the secretary of the treasury to improve Ellis Island for immigration purposes. When the funds for Ellis Island ran out, Congress appropriated more money for it in the Sundry Civil Appropriation Act of 1890 and the Deficiency Act of 1890. The navy completed its removal of the equipment and explosives transferred the island to the Department of the Treasury on May 24, 1890.

REFERENCE: Pike, Henry. 1963. *Ellis Island: Its Legal Status.* Washington, DC: Office of the General Counsel, General Services Administration.

Contagious Disease Wards. The contagious disease hospital and wards are located on **Island 3**. The complex comprises eleven separate buildings, containing twenty-two medical wards. The wards were numbered 11 through 28; wards 1 through 10 were in the general **hospital buildings** on **Island 2**.

The isolation wards were as follows:

Ward 11: Pneumonia, whooping cough, and measles cases (29 beds)
Ward 12: Measles cases (30 beds)
Ward 13: Scarlet fever, diphtheria, mumps, and chicken pox cases (20 beds)

Contagious disease wards on Island 3, circa 1912. Courtesy of the Ellis Island Immigration Museum.

Ward 14: Closed (24 beds)
Ward 15: Tuberculosis and Public Health Service beneficiary cases (15 beds)
Ward 16: Tuberculosis overflow cases (20 beds)
Ward 17: Male trachoma cases (24 beds)
Ward 18: Female trachoma cases (24 beds)
Wards 19 and 20: Closed
Wards 21 and 22: Closed/storage
Ward 23: Sick aliens held under warrant (close detention) (stowaways) (20 beds)
Ward 24: Sick aliens held under warrant (close detention) (stowaways) (20 beds)
Ward 25: Male trachoma cases (22 beds)
Ward 26: Favus, nail, and scalp disease cases (22 beds)
Wards 27 and 28: Venereal disease cases

In 1907, Commissioner **Robert Watchorn** and Chief Surgeon George W. Stoner reported to the **Bureau of Immigration** that the medical buildings were inadequate. The commissioner-general promptly requested funds to enlarge the medical complex. The new facilities were designed in the neo-Renaissance style by federal architect James Knox Taylor and built from June 1908 through May 1909; they were not put to use until June 1911. Each hospital building is two stories high and stands on a granite base and is constructed of red brick with stucco coating. The inside of the buildings has linoleum over wooden floors, metal doors and frames, plaster walls, and tile ceilings.

The hospital complex includes an **office building and laboratory** (1909), mortuary/animal house (1908), power house/laundry (1907), measles wards A–H (renamed wards 11–26, in 1919), isolation wards J–L (wards 27–32), administration building (1907), **kitchen building** (1907), and a staff house (1908). A corridor running the length of Island 3 connects these buildings. Conditions treated were measles, pneumonia, whooping cough, scarlet fever, diphtheria, mumps, chicken pox, trachoma; tuberculosis; favus, nail, and scalp diseases; and venereal diseases.

The staff house (72 ft. by 47 ft.) is two and a half stories high and made of stuccoed brick walls over a steel frame. The house was used by surgeons.

See also **Contagious Diseases; Diseases and Hospitalization; Hospital Buildings; Loathsome Contagious Diseases; Trachoma; Tuberculosis**

Contagious Diseases. The Public Health Service issued classification lists of immigrant-related diseases sometimes referred to as the immigrant nomenclature. The list was broken down into three categories: the most dangerous, causing mandatory exclusion, were assigned to Class A; diseases affecting one's ability to earn a living (exclusion at immigrant inspectors' discretion), Class B; and diseases that did not result in exclusion, Class C.

In 1903, Class A dangerous contagious diseases were trachoma and pulmonary tuberculosis. In 1910, the list included trachoma, filariasis, hookworm, and amœba coli infection. Tuberculosis was broken down into those occurring in three parts of the body: the respiratory tract, the intestinal tract, and the genito-urinary tract. The 1917 list had trachoma, filariasis, amœbiasis, leishmaniasis, and four diseases newly added in that year: schistosomiasis, sleeping sickness, paragonomiasis, and clonorchiasis. The 1930 list of Class A diseases was virtually unchanged from its predecessor. The Class B and C lists did not include dangerous contagious diseases.

See also **Contagious Disease Wards; Diseases and Hospitalization; Line Inspection; Loathsome Contagious Diseases; Trachoma; Tuberculosis**

Contract Labor Laws. The Contract Labor Act of 1885 (23 Statute L, 332; enacted on February 26, 1885) prohibited contracted laborers from entering the United States; its purpose was to protect American workers from having to compete with foreigners for jobs. The Contract Labor Act of 1885 provided

> That from and after passage of this act it shall be unlawful for any person, company, partnership or corporation in any manner whatsoever to prepay the transportation or in any way assist or encourage the importation or migration of any alien or aliens, any foreigner or foreigners, into the United States, its Territories or the District of Columbia, under contract or agreement, parole or special, express or implied, made previous to the importation or migration of such alien or aliens, foreigner or foreigners, to perform labor or service of any kind in the United States, its Territories or the District of Columbia.

Only actors, artists, lecturers, skilled workmen for industries not yet established in the United States, private secretaries, and domestic or personal servants were exempted. The law allowed relatives or friends to help aliens come to the United States.

The Contract Labor Act of 1887 (24 Statute 414) assigned the enforcement of the law to the Treasury Department, which stationed contract labor inspectors at **Castle Garden**, Boston, and in certain other states. The Contract Labor Act of 1888 provided that foreign contract laborers be deported within a year of their arrival in the United States and rewarded informers with money. The **Immigration Act of 1895** empowered the **Bureau of Immigration** to enforce the contract labor law.

Contract labor inspectors at Ellis Island were given separate office and detention space. In 1914, there were two contract labor inspectors at the island and in the early 1920s, only one was assigned there. For many years, Augustus P. Schell was the special inspector of Contract Labor Cases (1905–1920s). Other contract labor inspectors included Joseph F. Frayne and Nicholas D. Collins, who served in the 1920s and 1930s.

In Washington, the bureau maintained the Contract Labor Division, which examined the evidence submitted and supervised all investigations. From 1892 through 1954, 41,937 contract laborers were barred from the entering the United States. Between 1892 and 1900, 5,792 were excluded; in 1901–1910, 12,991 were excluded; 1911–1920, 15,417 were excluded; 1921–1930, 6,274 were excluded; 1931–1940, 1,235 were excluded; and in 1941–1954, 117 were excluded.

REFERENCE: Contract Labor Act of 1885, *U.S. Statutes at Large* 23 (1885): 332.

Corcoran, Emma (b. 1885; d. 1980). Clerk, Statistical Division; secretary, Executive Division (1904–1916). Emma Corcoran was interviewed in the 1970s for the Ellis Island Oral

History Project and, among other matters, reminisced about one of her supervisors, Chief Clerk Augustus Sherman.

Corridors and Covered Passages. Nearly every building at Ellis Island is connected to others by a series of corridors and enclosed passages. On **Island 1**, Corridor 1, designed by Boring and Tilton in 1901, joins the **Main Building**, the **kitchen and laundry building**, and the **ferry house**. It is made of red bricks laid in Flemish bond.

Corridor 2 leads from the kitchen and laundry to the **baggage and dormitory building**. Built in 1909, it has a steel frame and red bricks laid in Flemish bond. The passage has arched windows on the ground level and flat-headed windows on the second floor; a third floor passage was added in 1914.

The enclosed stairway linking the first floor of the **Main Building** to the second floor of the **baggage and dormitory building** was constructed in 1924. Aliens, their friends and relations, and immigration officials used this stairway.

One corridor as it looks today. Photo by M. Johnson, National Park Service, Statue of Liberty National Monument. Courtesy of the Ellis Island Immigration Museum.

Two connecting outside covered passages lead from the baggage and dormitory building to the power and ferry houses; the latter was designed by Boring & Tilton in 1901.

Covered Passage 6, dating from 1909, joins the Main Building and the baggage and dormitory building.

Covered Passages 7A and 7B were built in 1934–1936 and connect the ferry house and the **immigration building**.

Covered Passage 8A, constructed in 1901, connects the **general hospital building** to the **hospital outbuilding**; the **psychopathic ward** was connected to it at the time it was added.

Covered Passages 8B and 8C, constructed in 1934, lead from **Island 2** to **Island 3**.

The last corridor, built in 1909, links the structures of the contagious disease hospital complex on **Island 3**: the power house and laundry, **office building and laboratory**, animal house/mortuary, administration building, kitchen building, measles wards, isolation wards, and the staff house.

Corsi, Edward [Edoardo Corsi] (b. Capestrano, Abruzzi, Italy, December 29, 1896; d. Phoenicia, New York, December 13, 1965). Commissioner of immigration, Ellis Island (1931–1934). The son of Filippo Corsi, an Italian politician who died in 1903, Corsi came to the United States with his mother, stepfather, and siblings as steerage passengers on board the SS *Florida* in 1907. His stepfather worked as a manual laborer. Corsi was educated at Fordham University Law School and worked for a time as a foreign correspondent in Mexico for *Outlook* magazine (1923–1924). He worked as correspondent in Italy for the *New World* in 1928. In 1930, he entered federal government service as the supervisor of the New York

Commissioner Edward Corsi in the early 1930s. Author's Collection.

census. His success at the job led to his appointment by President Herbert Hoover as the commissioner of immigration at the port of New York in 1931. After leaving the Immigration and Naturalization Service in 1934, he wrote his memoirs, *In the Shadow of Liberty: The Chronicle of Ellis Island*, which was published in the next year. The following is an excerpt from this extraordinary book.

My first impression of the new world will always remain etched in my memory, particularly that hazy October morning when I first saw Ellis Island. The steamer *Florida*, fourteen days out of Naples, filled to capacity with sixteen hundred natives of Italy, had weathered one of the worst storms in our captain's memory; and glad we were, both children and grown-ups, to leave the open sea and come at last through the Narrows into the Bay. . . . Passengers all about us were crowded against the rail. Jabbered conversation, sharp cries, laughs and cheers—a steadily rising din filled the air. Mothers and fathers lifted up the babies so that they too could see, off to the left, the Statue of Liberty . . . I felt resentment toward this Ellis Island ahead of us, where we could already see many people crowded into a small enclosure. It could not be a good place. It would have better if we had stayed in our comfortable home in the Abruzzi, back in Italy. To come made mother cry. I looked around the deck and saw that many women were crying. Our little vessel coasted into the slip at Ellis Island. The passengers began to move. We moved with them and as we stepped from the gangplank to the land, all silent and subdued, I knew that my parents were thinking what as I was, 'What is next?'

. . . Ellis Island in 1907 represented a cross-section of all the races of the world. Five thousand persons disembarked on that October day when my mother, my stepfather, and we four children landed there from the *General Putnam*.

We took our places in the long line and went submissively through the routine of answering interpreters' questions and receiving medical examinations. We were in line early and told that our case would be considered in a few hours, so we avoided the necessity of staying overnight, an ordeal which my mother had long been dreading. Soon we were permitted to pass. . . .

My stepfather's brother was waiting for us. It was from him that the alluring accounts of opportunities in the United States had come to our family in Italy. And we looked to him for guidance.

Crossing the harbor on the ferry, I was first struck by the fact that American men did not wear beards. In contrast with my own fellow-countrymen I thought they looked almost like women. I felt that we were superior to them. Also on this boat I saw my first negro. But these wonders melted into insignificance when we arrived at the Battery and our first elevated trains appeared on the scene. There could be nothing in America superior to these! (Corsi, 1935, p. 22)

New York's mayor, **Fiorello LaGuardia**, appointed Corsi director of emergency relief in 1934 and in 1935 named him deputy welfare director for the city. In 1938, Corsi entered politics when he vied unsuccessfully for the U.S. Senate. In 1943, Governor Thomas Dewey appointed him as the state of New York's commissioner of industrial affairs. In 1952, Corsi made one last fling in politics by trying to unseat New York City's new mayor, Vincent R. Impellitteri. In 1954, President Dwight D. Eisenhower brought Corsi back into the federal government when he appointed him special assistant for refugee and immigration problems, under Secretary of State John Foster Dulles; however, Corsi clashed with Dulles and was forced to resign in 1955. After this fiasco, he accepted appointment as executive vice president of the executive of the American Museum of Immigration, an unpaid position to support fund-raising for the **American Museum of Immigration** to be built on Liberty Island. In 1958, he was appointed a member of the New York State unemployment appeals board by Governor W. Averill Harriman and in 1964 cut a dashing figure as director of the New York World's Fair; he also enthusiastically endorsed a proposal to make Ellis Island a national monument within the **National Park Service**. The following year, Corsi was tragically killed in an automobile crash in Phoenicia, New York (*New York Times* 1965).

See also **Commissioners**

References: Corsi, Edward. 1935. *In the Shadow of Liberty.* New York: Macmillan; *New York Times.* 1965. Edward Corsi, 68, dies in crash; held city, state and U.S. posts. December 14.

Cortelyou, George [George Bruce Cortelyou] (b. New York, New York, July 26, 1862; d. Huntington, New York, October 23, 1940). Secretary of commerce and labor (1903–1904). Secretary Cortelyou oversaw the transfer of the **Bureau of Immigration** from the Treasury Department to the newly created Commerce and Labor Department in 1903. Although only briefly in charge of the department, Cortelyou still left an imprint on it. Cortelyou also served as stenographer to President Grover Cleveland (1895–1897); aide and secretary to President William McKinley (1897–1901); secretary to President **Theodore Roosevelt** (1901–1903); postmaster general (1905–1907); secretary of the treasury (1907–1909).

Cowen, Philip (b. July 26, 1853, New York; d. April 20, 1943, New Rochelle, New York). Journalist, editor, immigrant inspector (1905–1927). Cowen was the editor of the *American Hebrew* (1879–1906). During this time he published the works of Emma Lazarus (*Songs of a Semite*), Alexander Kohut, Oscar S. Strauss, as well as his own. Needing an effective advocate for Jewish immigrants at Ellis Island, **Frank Sargent** and **Robert Watchorn** offered a position of immigrant inspector to Cowen; he was posted to the **Special Inquiry Division**. In 1906, he was dispatched to Russia to investigate the conditions causing the mass exodus of Jews, which was causing somewhat of a crisis at Ellis Island. On his return, he reported that the Russian government was responsible for the massacres (pogroms) that were causing the emigration. Inspector Cowen later worked in the Information Division, which, among other services, provided employment advice to immigrants seeking jobs. In 1932, he published his autobiography, *Memories of an American Jew.* In it he recalled his days at Ellis Island.

> Twenty-five years ago Ellis Island was worth visiting, not "to see the animals," as some people went, but to note the kindly care with which the immigrant was treated, and to observed at close range the future builders of America. To each one who came to the Island out of genuine interest in the newcomer, all the several commissioners under whom I served were please to give the fullest opportunity for observation. This was particularly true of Commissioner Robert Watchorn, who presided during the high-tide of immigration. . . .
>
> I was assigned to special details from time to time, some of which were very important. . . . Another important detail was to investigate the treatment of the immigrants by railroad on their way from Ellis Island to their destination. A slight reduction was made to the immigrant in his railroad fare when he went to a group by barge from Ellis Island to the railroad stations on the North River. The accommodation was very inferior, however, and the immigrant was exploited.
>
> Commissioner Watchorn believed, considering the large number of passengers that were sent daily from Ellis Island, that steamship companies could well afford to give either lower rates or better accommodations. He filed a complaint with the Interstate Commerce Commission and a hearing was granted. I was the only witness to be heard. I told of my posing as an immigrant who arrived one morning at the Island at ten o'clock, went down to the railroad room and bought my ticket to Philadelphia for $2.50.
>
> There, I waited with the other passengers, eating with them till 4.40 o'clock, when we went on a barge to the Pennsylvania Station. . . . I had to wait at the

Penn Station—till a late hour, buying my food and drink at prices higher than at Ellis Island. The water was not fit to drink; I could not send a telegraph home; the cars were filthy and not properly supervised; there was no chance to get a bed, and a lot of et ceteras. We arrived at Philadelphia Station at 1.10 in the morning, having been on the way from Ellis Island since ten in the morning of the day previous. I reentered the station at Philadelphia, bought a ticket to New York for the same price, $2.50, got a Pullman sleeper, telegraphed home, got plenty of fresh water and could buy food, reaching home in two hours. This was, of course, and aggravated or exaggerated case. The railroad company could not help the delay till five o'clock on the Island; but once in their hands it should not have taken till 1.15 to reach Philadelphia, at the same price as the regular fare. . . .

It often happened that immigrants were admitted under a bond, and the immigration authorities would occasionally look them up to see if they were becoming public charges. If so, a warrant was issued that resulted in deportation. Otherwise, the bond might be canceled and their admission be made permanent.

The Board of Special Inquiry is only a quasi-legal tribunal. It is not governed by the ordinary rules of legal procedure. The alien is kept from contact with friends until there has been a preliminary hearing, where he may have friends or counsel to intervene. As a general thing, the immigrant tells the truth. Not so the witnesses that appear on his behalf. They want to make an impression of importance before the board and to overstate their earnings and savings. In the earlier days of my service, it was a common thing for them to show false bank books on the many immigrant banks then existing or money that they had borrowed for the occasion—there were many persons who made a lucrative business of loaning money for this purpose, and we found them standing at the Battery waiting for the friend to return from testifying before the board—usually with his greenhorn—in order to get back the money. . . .

The immigration authorities have always given particular attention to the discharge of girls, and the welfare societies of various groups at Ellis Island have been encouraged to look after those in which they were interested, to see that they reached their destination and that those of proper age went to school. The social workers mingled with the girls after discharge by the inspectors, saw that they had good addresses to go to or, if they were not clear, verified them; saw to that they purchased food for the journey and telegraphed to their relatives. The finest work of this kind was performed by the National Council of Jewish Women for the single girls and the Hebrew Immigrant Aid Society for the married women and children with them. At the time of which I speak this work was done mainly at Ellis Island, as the great part of immigration entered through that station . . . Commissioner Watchorn, while there, gave permission to the national bodies interested in girls to list their arrivals. To Sadie American, for many years the national secretary of the Council of Jewish Women, is due this fine, humanitarian piece of work. This was continued later, under the direction of Miss Florina Lasker, by her able assistant, Miss Cecilia Razofsky. . . .

During the height of immigration, Ellis Island was provided with a corps of interpreters who covered pretty well every civilized tongue yet, from time to time, there came along a people that taxed the ability of our staff. . . .

In complicated cases it was possible to get a satisfactory record only if there was an interpreter who fully understood the immigrant and could make himself fully understood by him. . . .

In 1907, when the immigration was at its height, we handled at Ellis Island 5,000 as a steady number in a day. I have seen it run to 5,800, but that was the limit. The largest number of inspectors that could be out to work was twenty-one, and that averaged 250 immigrants an inspector; when the ships crowded in on us, arriving immigrants were compelled to remain on board ship for two or three days. During the twenty-four hours of March 27, 1907, there arrived 16,050 passengers. . . . On May 2, 1907, as we went to the island in the morning, we found eleven ships on the list, with 16,209 passengers, while during the day four more arrived making the total number of passengers 21,755.

The Philip Cowen papers are in the American Jewish Historical Society at the Center for Jewish History in New York City.

REFERENCE: Cowen, Philip. 1932. *Memories of an American Jew.* New York: International.

Craigwell, Ernest (b. Washington, DC, 1870; d. ?). Clerk, Statistical Division (1903–1930s). Although Ernest Craigwell was one of the many African Americans employed at Ellis Island, he was one of the few in a white-collar position. His colleague, Solomon Johnson, was an immigrant inspector for many years and retired in 1933; there were also a number of black hospital attendants. Almost all other blacks at the station were laborers or charwomen.

Crematory. The crematory was the incinerator on Island 1 where all garbage and refuse was burned in the furnace. Items contaminated by patients of the contagious disease wards were always destroyed in the incinerator. The crematory was built in 1901 and the dilapidated remains of it were demolished in 1985.

Crime and Abuse. Corruption was rampant at Ellis Island and the **barge office** during the administration of Commissioner Thomas Fitchie (1832–1905) and his unscrupulous deputy, Edward F. McSweeney. Lesser members of the staff took advantage of the flagrant disregard of decency.

One mysterious case was the murder of Isadore Termini, an elderly Italian immigrant, who disappeared from detention at the barge office in May 1900. Some weeks later, his body was found floating in the harbor by the Jersey Central railroad terminal, across from Ellis Island.

In a January 1902 investigative report some of the many offences were described.

> The following robberies of immigrants have recently taken place at Ellis Island and, although it is possible that some of them have been committed by other detained persons, it would seem that some system should have been in operation to prevent robbery of the immigrants who are temporarily wards of the Government.
>
> 1. Josef Gojes, arr. per s/s Cassel, Dec. 14, 1901, robbed of $20 in the dormitory on the night of Dec. 15th or Dec. 16th.
>
> 2. Constancia Zielinska, arr. per s/s Amsterdam, Nov. 12, 1901, robbed of shawl, 20 pr. Scapulars, 8 religious medals, 2 pictures, 1 pillow case and one quilt; stolen from basket trunk in the baggage room at Ellis Island.
>
> 3. Gustav Lichtenberger, arr. s/s LaGascogne, May 20, 1900, $5 taken from him by an employee at Ellis Island.
>
> 4. Julius F. von Vesteneck, an Interpreter, recently relieved an immigrant woman of $1, but was permitted to resign instead of being dismissed under charges."
>
> Among the numerous outrages visited on Ellis Island's immigrants was the insult of Joseph el Koussa. El Koussa was a passenger on board the steamship Patricia that docked in the port of New York on 13 July 1901. The investigations of 1902 showed that when his son, Khalil el-Koussa, came to fetch his father he was threatened and driven out of the main building by a gateman named Thomas Wall. (Ellis Island Investigations)

The most dramatic investigation led to the downfall of the Fitchie-McSweeney regime at the station. The numerous complaints and accusations of corruption at Ellis Island finally came to a head when President Theodore Roosevelt ordered the **Bureau of Immigration** to remove the bad apples from Ellis Island. Chinese Inspector Roger O'Donnell headed the investigative team from Washington.

The cases mentioned came out in the investigations along with graver testimonies against Assistant Commissioner **Edward F. McSweeney**, chiefs **John Lederhilger**, Herrlich, Richard Horan, Philip S. Biglin, Inspectors Frank B. Macatee, Creuzet Vance, Albert Wank, Matron Helen A. Taylor, and several others. McSweeney was recognized as the dominant corrupting force at the station, Lederhilger as his chief crony, the other chiefs as passive figures who accepted the dictates of dishonesty without a murmur. Wank was proved to be the chief bribe taker (he discharged aliens as U.S. citizens at the piers if they paid him a few dollars); Taylor was called on the carpet for her abusive temper.

McSweeney, Lederhilger, and Wank were forced to resign; the others took heed and presumably mended their ways.

In July 1902, Vaclav Vacek, an immigrant who had gone on to Omaha, Nebraska, complained that he had been deliberately shortchanged by a telegraph clerk at Ellis Island. He claimed that when he gave the clerk his $20 gold piece, he only received two gold coins worth $15 as change. Commissioner **William Williams** sent for John Kuklis Jr., who confessed his guilt. He was remanded to Ludlow Street jail, where he awaited trial. The commissioner then posted this notice for all employees to see:

Swindling immigrants is contemptible business and whoever does this, under whatever form, should be despised. It is the duty of all Government officials to go out of their way to protect immigrants against every kind of imposition. Let everyone at Ellis Island clearly understand that all impositions, whenever detected, will be punished as severely as the law permits. (Pitkin, p. 66)

In October 1921, Commissioner **Frederick A. Wallis** punished several employees for "irregularities" Here is an excerpt from his report on their conduct.

1. Dennis P. Sheehan, Watchman: Accepted money from persons calling on behalf of detained aliens.
2. Frank Behnkin, Watchman: Accepted money from persons calling on behalf of detained aliens.
3. Nicholas Grazimono, Watchman: Accepted $20 from immigrant woman; jumped bail of $500; warrant issued; referred to U.S. District Attorney.
4. Herman Pincus, Watchman: Admitted acceptance of cash bribe to release immigrant.
5. Leonardo Lombardo, Laborer: Robbed baggage.
6. Edward V. Hanlon, Watchman: Short changed immigrants in sending telegrams.
7. Daniel Radice, Watchman: Asleep on post. Accepted gratuities.
8. Arthur R. Hogan, Watchman: accepted money from persons calling in behalf of detained aliens.
9. Louis Burkhardt, Inspector: Admitted as citizens at $25 per head; held under $5,000 bail; in hands of U.S. District Attorney. This will doubtless lead to other convictions.
10. Augustus P. Schell, Inspector: Guilty of many irregularities proven by affidavits.
11. Some time ago $495 disappeared from the Treasurer's Office. The amount has not been recovered nor has the thief been apprehended. The matter is now in the hands of detectives. Mr. Budde, formerly in charge of the Treasurer's Office, is unable to give any clue whatever. A few weeks later several other amounts disappeared. Three envelopes containing $25 each and one containing $50 were missing, it is supposed, on the same day. When asked for a balance and a checking up of all the case in the Treasurer's Office, Mr. Budde informed that a striking of a balance and checking up of the money had not been done for probably fifteen years.
12. The larger part of the exploitation of immigrants is carried on by persons having no official connection whatever with the Station. Not long ago a certain Mr. Rose represented himself as "Inspector Green." He later pleaded guilty in the U.S. Court to such misrepresentation and given sixty days.

Social Service workers have also been apprehended for misconduct. An Italian Social Worker was removed last fall for accepting money from immigrants. A social worker in the employ of the Hebrew Immigrant Aid Society was discharged for accepting fees in connection with the making of appeals.

A person was apprehended and imprisoned for selling passes to Ellis Island to people desiring to come to the station to meet arriving immigrants. (Ellis Island Investigations)

In another case, Assistant Commissioner **Byron Uhl** was compelled to discharge Inspector Jeremiah B. Fitzgerald from the bureau in November 1921. Aside from **Hebrew Immigrant Aid Society**, several members of other immigrant aid and missionary societies were occasionally accused of irregular or activities or unacceptable conduct. These included the **Austrian Society**'s Home, the Swedish Immigrant Home, **St. Joseph's Home for Polish Immigrants**, the German Lutheran Home, and the Irish Immigrant Society. Most of them were accused of making financial gains on immigrants by making them pay excessive fees and running a labor exchange out of the so-called homes. Especially criticized for this was the Reverend H. Berkemeir of the German Lutheran Home and the Reverend Joseph L'Etauche of the Polish Home.

Many other scandals and investigations occurred over the years. A familiar one that appeared many times from the 1890s through the 1930s was the selling of false citizenship papers, fake passports, and other forgeries. It was not until the 1940s that the level of abuse began to wane.

See also **Criticism; Ullo, Lorenzo; Watkins, W. Frank**

REFERENCES: Corsi, Edward. 1935. *In the Shadow of Liberty.* New York, Macmillan; Pitkin, Thomas. 1975. *Keepers of the Gate.* New York: New York University Press; Statue of Liberty N.M. Library. "Ellis Island Investigations," file 109; Shapiro, Mary J. 1986. *Gateway to Liberty.* New York: Random House; Unrau, Harlan D. 1978. *The Historic Resource Study: Ellis Island/Statue of Liberty.*

Washington, DC: U.S. Department of the Interior, National Park Service.

Criticism. In 1910, a journalist wrote an article that was saved by Commissioner **William Williams**. It described conditions at Ellis Island under that commissioner's management in the following unflattering terms.

"Devil's Isle"—The American Immigrants' Inquisition Scandal

Map-Makers write it down Ellis Island but immigrants to New York call it "Devil's Isle"—appropriately, as I can testify, writes an *Answers* reader. For, having to visit the State at a time when practically every berth in every transatlantic liner was taken, I was forced to travel as an immigrant.

I trust that I shall never again have to submit to such indignities as I was subjected to on my arrival across the "Pond."

Before being officially received on American soil, immigrants to New York are taken over on steam-packet to Ellis Island. When this vessel arrives alongside the liner, loud orders are given to the immigrants: *All form in line for the shore! Close up! Step this way with your green health-cards handy! Bring all your hand baggage with you!*

Each immigrant has been given a green health-card by the ship's doctor after examination. These cards are now to pinned on a conspicuous part of the person.

Once disembarked on Ellis Island, we move along in single file till we pass through the portals of an immense hall, divided by stout wire netting into alleyways and pens like cattleyard. This intricate mass we traverse several times, getting shuffled up with the passengers of French and German boats.

Suddenly, there is a cry of *Halt!* And then a specialist examines us for trachoma, folding back each eyelid in a very rough manner. Next, proceeding in single file, we are individually chalked. My brand is a capital *S*, which, I suppose, stands for *senile. P* means *pulmonary*; *Ex* means *excema.* A man chalked *Face* had a large wart thereon. *Gait* is lame; *Vision* wears an eyeglass.

The rams are now separated from the ewes, the men filing to the right, the women to the left. What happens to the ladies, I do not know; but it is not pleasant, to judge by the squealing, crying, and protesting we can hear.

I find myself one of fifty white, black, red, and yellow immigrants. *Strip!* comes the order. *Take everything off and line up as you were born!* I protest. I am a Britisher. *No matter!* comes the answer. *Line up naked like the rest!* We strip and, one by one, pass up for inspection. I am tested and told to *Cough! Cough again!* And then, as something is written on my paper, to *Pass along and dress! Take this report with you!*

The ladies join us and we kick our heels for a space. Then our papers are taken from us and copies in a letter-press, the originals being filed for further inspection. Next, a strip of paper, with the word *Certificate* is pinned on our shoulders. Some have already passed along; but just as my turn arrives the officials tell us that they are going to knock off for one hour for lunch, and walk through the folding glass doors marked *No Admittance* puffing their cigarettes.

I begin to light up. *No smoking allowed!*, snaps an attendant. I ask for a drink. *First to the right, first to the left!* I follow these directions and find an iron pipe without a nozzle. There is no glass. The water flows, and you just put your mouth to the pipe.

When the hour has expired the officiating medico resumes his chair. I am asked, *Are you married? Where is your wife? What have you come to America for? What do you intend to do now you're here?*, etc. Then the certificate is torn from my shoulder and I march along to the last pen, cheerfully marked *Hospital Cases.* Here I remain for another hour and a half.

Altogether I spend four and a half hours at Ellis Island. Once outside the *Hall of Tears*, I inquired for my cabin trunk. I was told to go to the nether regions; so, mentally consigning the said trunk to that warm place, I went across myself to South Ferry, New York. (*Answers*, n.d.)

See also **Buck, Pearl S.; Crime and Abuse; Deportation Cases; Detention Cases; Goldman, Emma; Immigration Restriction League; James, C. L. R.; Nazis; Women's Christian Temperance Union**

Curran, Henry H. [Henry Hastings Curran] (b. New York, November 8, 1877; d. New York, April 8, 1966). Commissioner of immigration, Ellis Island (1923–1926); lawyer, politician, judge. President Warren G. Harding appointed Curran to the post of commissioner on the recommendation of Senator James Wadsworth. Curran realized that the new job "would be walking into a furnace." His fears quickly bore fruit, for directly after assuming office, Sir Auckland Geddes, the British ambassador, issued a highly unflattering report on conditions at Ellis Island. A kindly administrator, Commissioner Curran initiated many improvements at the station and established a more positive relationship with the immigrant aid society workers than had been the case with his immediate predecessor, **Robert E. Tod**. However, he had difficulties with his superior, Commissioner-General **W. W. Husband**, in Washington, whom he accused of delaying his reforms and allowing detention cases to languish at Ellis Island unnecessarily long. For example, in a letter to Husband he cited the case of two detainees, Mr. and Mrs. Einsiedler, who had been on Ellis Island for five months. Curran wrote that they had "become so indigenous to the soil of Ellis Island that Mr. Einsiedler has mastered the American game of basket ball and is now the leader in alien outdoor sports here. Mrs. Einsiedler has been occupied having a baby at Ellis Island. I do not know what will happen next. But I do know that this case could have been decided before this time."

During a long career in the public service, Curran became a city alderman in 1911, borough president of Manhattan in 1919; in 1921 he was the Republican candidate for mayor of the city of New York, but was defeated by John F. Hylan by a plurality of 400,000 votes. In the 1930s, he served as deputy mayor of New York under **Fiorello LaGuardia** and then as chief magistrate (1939–1945) and judge of the Court of Special Sessions (1945–1947).

REFERENCE: Curran, Henry H. 1941. *Pillar to Post.* New York: Charles Scribner's Sons.

D

Daughters of the American Revolution (National Society of the Daughters of the American Revolution—DAR). Patriotic genealogical organization in which participants gain the right of membership exclusively through ancestors who served the country during the American War of Independence. The DAR operated important occupational therapy units at Ellis Island for nearly thirty years. The operation began with the founding of occupational therapy for detained immigrants in 1923. During the Great Depression, the DAR opened another unit in the hospital at the request of the **Public Health Service**. The occupational unit for immigrants was discontinued with the decline of immigration in 1941. In 1943, when Ellis Island's tubercular patients were transferred to the Public Health Service hospital on Staten Island, the DAR extended services there. The DAR services were eventually moved to Long Island. At Ellis Island, the DAR organized activities to make the life of detainees less tedious. To this end, they set up sewing circles and offered lessons in American civics and the English language. Elizabeth Estes and Lucille Boss taught sewing classes in the 1930s and 1940s.When the DAR extended its occupational therapy activities to the Ellis Island hospital in 1934, it offered care to patients suffering from arthritis, cardiac and genitourinary diseases, skin, blood, and respiratory conditions, tuberculosis, and neuro-psychiatric illnesses. On the average, the DAR staff consisted of three trained therapists, a secretary, and many volunteers and, in the 1940s, several New York University students who had come to the island to receive their clinical training. In that decade, Mrs. H. Stebbins Smith directed the DAR activities on Ellis Island.

See also **Immigrant Aid Societies**

Day, Benjamin M. [Benjamin Mulford Day] (b. North Plainfield, New Jersey, January 24, 1886; d. New York, February 1, 1976). Commissioner, Ellis Island (April 1926–September 1931). During Day's period in office, the immigration quota system, visa regulations, and immigration inspections at American consulates abroad became standardized. The operation at Ellis Island slowly altered from being America's once bustling "golden door" to a place of detention and deportation for undesirable aliens. Day resigned in 1931, not long after **William Doak** became secretary of labor and introduced an aggressive anti-immigrant policy at Ellis Island. A lawyer by profession, Day also served as chief deputy collector of the Internal Revenue Service in New York City (1921–1925) and later held the presidency of the New York Society for the Prevention of Crime (1940–1943).

Deaths and Burials. A total of 3,500 immigrants died at Ellis Island, 1,400 of them children. The deaths were attributed to numerous causes, including scarlet fever, tuberculosis, and heart disease. When an immigrant died in the Ellis Island hospital, the chief nurse summoned the medical officer. The patient's medical record was then filled in with the appropriate information, the deceased was covered with a shroud, and an identity tag was tied to the wrist. The corpse was then transported to the morgue. Should the patient have died of a contagious disease, his body was tied up in a sheet that had been soaked in a disinfectant solution and wrung out; an identity tag was then tied to sheet, prior to removal from the ward. Upon arrival, the undertaker drew up a receipt for the body, which he gave to the hospital registrar; the latter personage was responsible for the proper carrying out of all authorized procedures. If relatives wished, a religious service could be performed.

Over the years, several local undertakers had contracts to remove bodies of deceased immigrants from Ellis Island; one of these was J. C. van Mater, who was contracted in 1930 to bury the dead in Mount Hope Cemetery, Westchester, New York.

The following is a sample of the contract between the **Public Health Service** and Thomas M. Quinn, a New York City undertaker for immigrants who had died at the Ellis Island hospital, which was known officially as U.S. Marine Hospital 43. This contract covered the burial of all immigrants who died at the hospital during fiscal year 1924. It dates from 1923.

To the Surgeon General, Public Health Service
LOCAL BURIAL

Sir:

I hereby agree to provide a respectable burial in St. Michael's, St. John's, St. Mary's or Mt. Olivet Cemetery, in a part thereof not used for the burial of paupers, for a patients of the Public Health Service dying at U.S. Marine Hospital #43, during the fiscal year ending June 30, 1924, at a rate of $94.00 for each burial.

The burial specified includes the following:

1. *Shaving, washing and dressing the body (clothing not to be furnished by the undertaker).*
2. *Coffin or casket, net and plain, properly lined, with six handles, and finished in mahogany or other approved color or cloth covered, same to be of approved quality, and manufactured by a reputable manufacturer of coffins and caskets # 5 N.Y. & Brooklyn Casket Co.*
   (State here make and type or casket bid upon)
   (a) outside box for above coffin or casket.
3. *A separate grave for each body.*
4. *Headboard or metal marker properly set up which shall bear the number of the grave, name of deceased, age and the letters U.S.P.H.S.*

The following additional charges will be made when the service specified is ordered and furnished: Thoroughlyembalmingthebody(arteriallyandits cavities) with a good disinfectant standard embalming fluid, $2.00; Furnishing Shroud, $2.00

PREPARATION OF DECEASED BODY FOR SHIPMENT

(When necessary for deceased claimants of the Bureau of War Risk Insurance)

I hereby agree to prepare for shipment, in a proper and respectable manner, the body of any deceased patient of the Bureau of War Risk Insurance dying in U.S. marine Hospital #43 or Sanitarium at New York City, at the rate of $69.00 for each body prepared for shipment.

The preparation specifies the following:

1. *Procuring the necessary permits.*
2. *Transportation of the body necessary for its delivery to the express company or other designated common carrier and its shipment as directed by the proper officer of the Public Health Service, no charge to be paid for shipment to be made Government bill lading.*
3. *Embalming as specified above, shaving, washing, dressing.*
4. *Coffin or casket as specified in paragraph 2 for local burial.*
5. *Strong wood shipping box provided with three pairs of strong handles.*

The following additional charges will be made when the service specified is ordered and furnished:

Shroud . . . $5.00

Hermetically sealing the coffin or casket provided above . . . $25.00

(sgd) Thomas M. Quinn (Unrau 1984, pp. 649, 731–732)

See also **Suicides**

REFERENCE: Unrau, Harlan D. 1984. *The Historic Resource Study: Ellis Island/Statue of Liberty.* Vol. 2. Washington, DC: U.S. Department of the Interior, National Park Service.

Delaware Indians. The Delaware Indians (more correctly, the Lenni Lenape) were among the native inhabitants of New Jersey when the Dutch and Swedes came to the area early in the seventeenth century. Gull Island or *Kioshk* (Ellis Island) and Minnesais (Liberty Island) were part of their land. There they gathered the sea creatures of the Hudson River estuary that surrounded Ellis Island: oysters, clams, blue mussels, striped bass, sturgeon, flounder, and bluefish.

In 1630, the Dutch West India Company

bought the island for "certain cargoes or parcels of goods" from the Delaware. It was then transferred to **Michael Paauw**, an official of the company who lived in Holland. Paauw eventually sold his possessions to the company. In these far-off days of the Dutch colony of Nieuw Nederland (1620s–1664), the abundance of oysters round the surrounding tidal flats gave Ellis Islands and the other nearby isles and shoals an interesting name: the "oyster islands." Ellis Island, then three and a half acres in size, was called Little Oyster Island, while its larger neighbor of ten acres, Liberty Island, was called Great Oyster Island.

Years passed and, in 1985 and 1986, **National Park Service** officials found human remains on Ellis Island. Anthropologists from the Museum of Natural History in New York and New York University concluded that the remains were of prehistoric Americans, most likely Delaware Indians.

National Park Service archaeologist Dick Hsu and anthropologist Muriel Crespi notified the National Council of American Indians of the discovery. In June 1987, Delaware Indians (now living in Oklahoma and Ontario, Canada) came and sanctified the remains on Ellis Island. In 2003, the Delaware Indians returned and buried the remains in a ceremony on Ellis Island.

Demolished Structures. The following buildings are regarded as the most important ones to have been demolished: the **surgeons' house** (extant 1901–1936), Red Cross house (1915–1936), **Island 1** greenhouses (1910–1935; and 1935–1985), **Island 1** crematories/incinerators (1901–1911; and 1911–1985), and two Island 1 water tanks (1929–1985).

Deportation. Procedure of expelling an alien from a country. Although the United States had empowered the president to deport undesirable aliens in the early years of the republic, it was not until 1893 that detailed regulations for the procedure were set in place. The Immigration Service handled deportation all such cases. Only a person who had previously entered the country was subject to deportation. The deportation of aliens by the **Bureau of Immigration** was authorized under the **Immigration Act of 1891**. From the 1910s through the 1950s, deportees often traveled in "deportation parties" that were brought to New York on trains from cities and town throughout the nation or on Southern Pacific steamboats coming up from New Orleans. On reaching the docks of New York, the deportees were tagged. They then walked carrying their baggage to a government tugboat or a barge taking them to Ellis Island. At the island, they were escorted into a room where immigration officers made identifications. Immigrants who were being deported for insanity were sent to the hospital. The rest of the deportees were divided into groups, the criminals detained in separate quarters. Men were also held in special quarters while women were sent to wait with other detained females. When possible, prostitutes were held in a room reserved for them alone. Money was taken from all deportees and held for safekeeping.

On October 8, 1933, the *New York Times* reported on the rise of deportation work at Ellis Island and three types of aliens commonly deported from there:

> First are the voluntary deportees, aliens arrived since 1930 who can prove that they are destitute. In 1932, 1,000 were sent out. Second are the criminal aliens, aliens here less than five years who have been sentenced to one year's imprisonment, or aliens, regardless of when they arrived, who have had two such sentences. They automatically face deportation at the expiration of their sentence. The third group deported are those aliens who have been found here illegally.
>
> It is the Island's deportation work which brings charges of delays and stories of four or six months' detention of individuals. A foreign nation is not eager to receive one of its citizens who is perhaps an ex-criminal and insists on the most accurate and complete proof of his citizenship. Months sometimes elapse before all the papers are in order.
>
> In 1932, 511 criminals were deported, most of them from New York state.

It is the deportation business also, new on the Island since the World War, which has given some of the corridors in one large building there the appearance of a jail. Some of the guards are armed, doors are locked and windows barred. An attempt is made to keep any of the jail atmosphere from reaching those immigrants, mostly women and children, who are awaiting permission to enter the country or who are going back at their own request. They are kept entirely separate, in waiting hall, mess hall and dormitories, from the deportees. They have different playgrounds, complete freedom to telephone, to move about, and to see friends and relatives at any hour of the day; the privileges are new, introduced within the past two years. . . .

The government provides quarters and food, bedding and medical attention. But one of the severest criticisms is directed at the fact that the government does nothing to help the alien keep busy and contented during his stay. Social service groups and religious organizations step in, in cooperation with the commissioner, and provide materials for sewing, games, Sunday concerts, reading, they also provide clothing.

See also **Boards of Special Inquiry; Deporting Division; Exclusion; Special Inquiry Division; Tilson, Richard**

REFERENCE: *New York Times*. 1933. October 8.

Reverend Father Joseph Vasilion, an Eastern Orthodox priest, was deported in January 1908. Sherman Collection, courtesy of the Ellis Island Immigration Museum.

Deportation Cases. The following are a few actual descriptions of deportation cases. Since deportation was attended with a feeling of frustration and rejection, it often gave rise to bitterness, which is more than evident in the case of Mark Glanvill.

The Glanvills, a South African family and thus British subjects, emigrated from Cape Town via Southampton, England, and were detained at Ellis Island from July 23 to July 26, 1921. Mark Glanvill (b. 1889), a secretary on his way to study at the YMCA college, and a native of England, arrived with his wife Evelyn and their infant son, Mark. They were excluded because of their baby, who was ill. On their return to South Africa, Glanvill wrote a scathing letter to the U.S. Bureau of Immigration denouncing the treatment he alleged that he and his family received at their hands. What follows is a portion of Glanvill's letter.

We arrived in New York Harbour per the *R.M.S.P. Orduna* on July 22nd, second cabin. As is customary, the passengers lined up to pass the Immigration Officers. Where our turn came, the official, without question, curtly told us that we were "over the quota" and would have to await word from Washington—particulars having been telegraphed there. We did not anticipate any difficulty and were quite content to wait on board for the expected word. We were not of course permitted to land. The next afternoon we were called before a different official on the boat who told us that it would necessary for us to go to Ellis Island. He stated we certainly would be released the next morning, that it would be very comfortable there for us. We were concerned about our baby boy and questioned the official regarding conditions on the Island. He assured us that it was an excellent place at which we would be well treated and be able to get all things necessary.

We went to the Island willingly believing it would be only a matter of a few hours before being released. We were taken by a representative of the Royal Mail Steam Packet Company to the Island. Our reception there was almost insolent. We were made to stand about for an hour and given no assistance with baggage extremely heavy and cumbersome. A woman (so called matron) conducted us through long passages and corridors. She was sharp and totally unsympathetic to Mrs. Glanvill and baby; we began to grow suspicious. The aspect of the building so far as we had seen it was prison-like, but as we marched along it grew more and more so. Presently, we reached a wide passage completely blocked by a seething mass of humanity, filthy in the extreme—Europe's worst, negroes, Asiatics—dregs of humanity; the were pushing and yelling and cursing, men and women alike. Women with tiny babies in their arms were jammed in the mass. They were responding to the supper bell. Little we knew it even then, these were to be our companions. We were shown into a cell almost the size of a large double room with window barred with a strong steel mesh. We realized then we were virtually prisoners.

The cell just mentioned was for day use.

Day Cell. Our particular cell contained about twenty-seven persons, men and women, with seating accommodation for about fifteen. As stated, the window was fenced in. Our cell was one of some eight in that particular corridor and had access to the other cells in it, but the cells were all crowded and the corridor was the general standing place for the overflow. Each cell had a lavatory—naturally in a vile condition—*common to both sexes and with butaswingdoorwithoutfastenings.* Menandwomen used it frequently, apparently unconcerned. The floors of the cell were paved and an attempt was made to keep them clean, but the occupants were too many and indifferent and muck soon accumulated. The smell in the cell was abominable.

Night Cell. Cells a little larger than the day ones. Thirty-seven slept together and I believe in some cases more. I was confined with steerage people—mostly Greeks; the stench was terrible. The bunks were of iron, one above the other, three high with little space between, covered with dirty canvas. No mattresses or pillows were provided. Blankets were not given, but filthy ones were to be found lying on the bunks. The blankets were ridden with lice and were gritty. Mice ran over the floor at night; little sleep was to be had. The din of the hundreds sleeping in close proximity (the night cells surrounded a big hall and had open tops in most cases) was terrific and continued until a later hour. We were all marched to bed at 6.30 and locked in; the cell doors were usually opened about 6 a.m. Mrs. Glanvill and baby experienced similar treatment as described, but in her case she was turned out at 5.15 a.m.

One evening the British people were put together in night cells, but only after much protest, and it worked only once. It was quite impossible to get a bath. I could get neither towel nor soap.

Meals. After being turned out of the night cells, we were made to stand around in corridors for an hour and a half. We could never understand the reason. The bell then went for breakfast and of course there was the usual rush and push. It must be here stated the food on the Island was not bad. It was extremely coarse and unpalatable. We were fortunate in being put in the care of an attendant, who did his best. We were allowed to purchase milk, others were not so fortunate. We all ate together, many hundreds yelling, screaming and grabbing—general pandemonium.

The Porch. Part mornings and part evenings we were all allowed out on a large porch overlooking the Harbour. The statue of Liberty could plainly be seen if one cared to look at it. The porch was caged in with the same steel mesh. It was used by hundreds at a time and was always crowded and in a filthy condition. Once on the porch we were not allowed in to conveniences. It is not possible to imagine the condition of the floor with many children cooped up without access to lavatories.

Officials. We found the officials invariably insolent and cruel. Guards treated women without regard to their sex—yelled and pushed them to and fro. The women attendants were callous and different. The cleaners were mostly coloured men who were insulting in their treatment.

Board of Enquiry. We arrived on the Island on the Saturday and, on the Monday, we were taken before a Board. Before our turn came, we sat on benches and noted the treatment of other classes by the Board. The members of the board were curt and the chairman sarcastic and vulgar. When our turn came we were treated with respect, but hurriedly. We were told that we could not be released because of baby. Evidently at this point they were prepared to release my wife and self. We were then told we were 'excluded.' An outside official told us this meant our doom. Later on in the day, I was told I might appeal, but that likely it would take nine days—and then perhaps be unsuccessful.

By this time, the health of my wife, a delicate and refined woman, was giving way. Baby was getting ill. Instant action to obtain release was necessary. I was desperate when fortunately I learnt that there was a Canadian representative on the Island. Having serving with the Canadians during the war, I thought he might be able to arrange our release to proceed to Canada. This, however, he could not do, but he suggested and advised that we appealed to the Commissioner of the Island to be deported. I did this through him stating I would pay my own fare back to England. The Canadian arranged everything and on the Tuesday, we were taken under guard to the *Aquitania*, where we remained in his custody until the boat sailed.

Before closing, let me state that we were allowed access to neither telephone nor telegraph. I fought hard to interview the Y.M.C.A. man on the Island and it took two days to get a message to him. It was with great difficulty I got a message to the Canadian representative. Guards are everywhere. Prison conditions existed throughout. The whole experience was cruel, revolting and humiliating. For one night, Mrs. Glanvill went to hospital, baby not being well. She and baby were treated in a shameful way. The nurses shook their fists in her face when she appealed for food for baby. She returned on the point of collapse. . . .

The object of my visit to the United States was to complete a course at the Y.M.C.A. College, Springfield, Mass. I had been studying at this college over two years prior to the war. I left there to enlist in Canada in 1914. I had my credentials but was not given an opportunity to exhibit them. I had £100 in English notes on the Island and $150.00 awaiting me at the 23rd Street Y.M.C.A., New York. (Unrau 1984, pp. 1117–1120)

To make matters worse, Evelyn Glanvill, the thirty-one-year-old wife of Mark Glanvill, filed her own complaint against the **Bureau of Immigration** through her own government of South Africa, which accordingly took diplomatic action against the United States. What follows is an excerpt of her scathing attack against America's immigration procedures.

Thank God, we are now free again and away from the horrors of Ellis Island. Every night I awake in terror, dreaming that we are back again in prison.

The details of our life there were so horrible I feel too stunned still to describe them. It was such a shock that it will leave a mark on one for life.

Our poor innocent baby suffered. There were no baths, no fresh air, nor a sleeping place for it except in my arms. It was terrifically hot and the stench abominable. I felt my strength ebbing fast, and the life would have killed us had we remained a day or two longer. I really felt like committing suicide to get away from the horrors of cruelty and disease and the terrible filth. We were herded with thousands of foreigners.

We were yelled at, pushed and cursed from morning to night, and driven from one cell to another for unknown reasons.

I could not believe that such a hell existed on earth, or that free British subjects could be treated so.

Our only means of escape was begging to be deported to England, on which plea we succeeded after four days of these horrors. (Unrau 1984, pp. 1117–1120)

See also **Anarchists; Goldman, Emma; James, C. L. R.**

REFERENCES: *Statement of Treatment Meted Out to Mark Glanvill, English Born . . . 1921.* Immigration and Naturalization Service, National Archives, General Immigration Files, Record Group 85; Unrau, Harlan D. 1984. *The Historic Resource Study: Ellis Island/Statue of Liberty.* Vol. 3. Washington, DC: U.S. Department of the Interior, National Park Service.

Deporting Division. Also called the Deportation Division, its task was to guard all immigrants in its charge and, when the time came, conduct such aliens safely to their ships for **deportation**, either aboard a small boat, taking them from Ellis Island directly to the ship, or by a horse-drawn wagon, automobile, or other vehicle driving from the barge office to the appropriate pier. The division was generally divided into three departments, the day watch, the night watch, and the deporting squad. In 1903, this division of twenty-five men was presided over by a chief inspector, assisted by two inspectors. The remaining employees were clerks, watchmen, gatemen, and messengers. The division dealt with excluded and deferred aliens. Deferred aliens (i.e., detained) were those whom the **Special Inquiry Division** was still awaiting further evidence on before making a final decision to exclude or admit. Deferred and excluded men were kept in separate rooms, while the women shared a room. When an alien was excluded, his detention card was delivered to the clerk of the Deporting Division who then copied the information in the record book of deferred and excluded aliens. Then taking out a blue deportation card (form 1509), he would copy the same information on it. He then wrote down the action of the **board of special inquiry** on the special inquiry sheets, and in the books of the Information Bureau. Both cards were then placed in the excluded card case, which contained separate compartments for each steamship line. The detention cards of deferred were handled likewise, except that no deportation card was prepared, and the detention card was placed in the deferred card case instead. The deporting watch or squad consisted of five men at all times (early watch, 6 a.m.– noon; late watch, noon–7 p.m.; night watch, 7 p.m.–6 a.m). The aliens were counted at each change of the watch. In addition, every Monday and Thursday, the early watch performed a complete roll call. In 1909, the division's structure looked like this: three inspectors, twenty-one watchmen, and three clerks. In 1924, there was a staff of thirty-six in this division, an inspector in charge (i.e., chief inspector), twenty-nine inspectors, two interpreters, three guards, and one clerk. The day after a ship's sailing, a representative from the division went to the steamship offices and pier to make certain that the excluded aliens had sailed with the ship and not escaped. Each week the division sent a weekly report of its deportation cases to the **Statistical Division**.

See also **Deportation; Ellis Island; Tilson, Richard**

Destinations. The leading destinations named by immigrants bound for the United States in the 1899 through 1910 period by state were New York (2,994,358; 31.4 percent), Pennsylvania (1,737,059; 18.2 percent), Illinois (722,059; 7.6 percent), Massachusetts (719,887; 7.5 percent), New Jersey (489,533; 5.1 percent), Ohio (407,285; 4.3 percent), Connecticut (245,636; 2.6 percent), California (237,795; 2.5 percent), Michigan (233,824; 2.4 percent), Minnesota (182,558; 1.9 percent), Wisconsin (150,162; 1.6 percent), Missouri (123,045; 1.3 percent), Washington (111,814; 1.2 percent), Rhode Island (98,635; 1 percent), Texas (75,807), Maryland (71,265), Florida (66,612), Arizona (13,414).

The states cited, especially those in the Northeast, were sometimes only temporary destinations, before immigrants moved on to other places, which even included one of the Canadian provinces.

Certain nationalities favored particular regions and states in which to settle. For instance, Germans preferred the northeastern, West Coast, and midwestern states, such as Pennsylvania, Ohio, Indiana, Michigan, Illinois, and Wisconsin; large numbers also settled in Missouri, Kansas, Iowa, and California. The Irish concentrated in the northeastern and midwestern states, especially New York, Massachusetts, and Illinois. The Italians preferred the northeastern states, especially New York, New Jersey, Pennsylvania, and Delaware. Polish Catholics and Russian Jews both favored the northeastern states, especially New York, New Jersey, and Pennsylvania. Canadian immigrants preferred New England, followed by the Northeast, Midwest, and Pacific Coast. Scandinavian immigrants settled heavily in the Midwest, especially Minnesota, Illinois, Wisconsin, Iowa, Nebraska, Montana, and the Dakotas.

REFERENCE: Dillingham, William, et al. 1911. *Reports of the Immigration Commission.* Washington: Government Printing Office.

Detention Cases. The following selected detention cases reveal the very different reactions of foreigners to the conditions at Ellis Island over the years. The first case is that of Sydney H. Bass (1911), a Methodist minister from England; others were the Russian émigré Constantin Oberoutcheff (1923) and a French lady, F. M. Lalande (1923).

The following is an excerpt of the testimony Sydney Bass gave before the House Committee on Rules on May 29, 1911. In it, the thirty-year-old minister of the Methodist Episcopal Church complained of the treatment he received at Ellis Island when he arrived in the United States on January 12, 1911. His purpose for coming was to serve as the pastor for four Methodist churches in Harrison Valley, Pennsylvania.

> I arrived at Ellis Island about 8.30 on the following morning, when I went in line, single file, with

Detention pen on roof of Main Building, where detained immigrants could go in nice weather. STLI Collection, National Park Service, Statue of Liberty National Monument. Courtesy of the Ellis Island Immigration Museum.

the other immigrants. I make no complaint about these things. I do not complain about the immigration law and I always endeavor to carry out all the requirements of the law.

On arriving at Ellis Island the first thing that occurred that gave us an indication of what I might expect was the porter putting us in line and calling out: *Get on upstairs, you cattle. You will soon have a nice little pen.*

Then I went to the first inspector, and he said: *Are you an American citizen?* I said: *No, sir; British.* He said: *What is your occupation?* I said: *My profession is that of a minister of the Gospel.* He said: *Right. Go in there*, and he put me in the first pen.

The whole of the building, as I saw it at first, struck me very favorably as a magnificent public building, and I was highly impressed as I went through the preliminary part with the efficiency of the staff. In the first instance I thought the thing was carried out in a wonderfully methodical manner, and I was quite pleased.

Then, of course, I had my medical examination, and I took my certificate, which showed that I had had infantile paralysis of the right leg. I explained to the doctor, facetiously, that I did not preach with my feet, and he said: *All right. You can straighten them out with the immigration authorities.*

I may say that I had securities worth some hundreds of dollars in my pocket and $60 in cash. . . .

After going through the various pens, I arrived at 9.30 in the common room and that is the basis of the bulk of my complaint. . . . There is awful congestion there, and it is the height of cruelty to heard people together in such crowded, congested quarters, under such unsanitary conditions, where there is not sufficient air space. . . . I objected to being placed there in such close proximity with the filthiest people of all nations, covered with dirt and vermin there, I can not guarantee that I did not take a considerable amount away with me from Ellis Island.

On arriving at the final door before I went into the common room I was permitted to send a telegram. They wrote it for me, and charged me 35 cents. I did not get it free. I did not require it free; and I did not see anything of the official post cards, although I do not say that there were not any.

I found the hours to be as follows: 4 a.m., breakfast—I got into the common room about 4.15 or 4.20—1 p.m. dinner, and 5 p.m., supper; and 7.30 p.m., we went to bed. Please notice, nine hours in the morning breathing that foul atmosphere on an empty stomach.

The official to whom I was speaking, just outside of the common room, struck me as being one of those petty officials. . . . I saw some of the results of giving men of that sort a little power. When I had been in the common room for one hour I saw the door open for a moment, and I slipped out and asked him for permission to wire to the British consul, and for permission to wire to Messrs. Eaton and Mains, of the Methodist Episcopal Book Room, prominent officials in my church. I was peremptorily ordered back into the common room. There were 600 people in that little room, crowded together. It seemed to me the most like the black hole of Calcutta of anything that I have seen since reading about that historical occurrence in the Indian mutiny. . . .

The worst feature of all was the common room. I was there on the first day from 9.30 in the morning until 7.30 at night, standing all the time, except occasionally when I sat on the ground. I said to the inspector, *It seems an anomaly to hold me up for a bad leg and then make me stand on it all those hours.*

On the second day I was there from 4.20 a.m. till 10.30 a.m. When my name was called, I had difficulty in getting out of the crowded room. Then I went to stay in board of special inquiry room No. 2. My case did not come on until after dinner. We had dinner at 12 o'clock (from the common room it is 1 o'clock). At 10.30 I found that cases were going on, and after dinner the cases began again at 12.30 o'clock.

I had been detained for 28 hours before my case was called at all, after I had specifically stated to the first inspector I met that I was minister of the gospel and I had my certificate of successes in examinations and my conference credentials in my possession as well as my property.

I then went before the board of special inquiry, and they seemed to give me apparently a very fair hearing. I spoke as I am speaking to you now, without interruption; but the refused to look at my conference credentials during the hearing, and at the conclusion of it I was unanimously ordered to be deported as an alien without visible means of support and as liable to become a public charge. Of course my means of support are invisible.

That was shortly after 1 o'clock. They then gave me better quarters. I complained bitterly before the board about the dastardly treatment in putting 4 English ladies and 16 English gentlemen in that common room while I was there, and about putting them in such crowded quarters with so many other people.

Yours was an excellent suggestion, if you will permit me to say it, about looking into things a little bit on the other side. I went before the American consul and a medical man there. The American consul thoroughly protects your interests at Southampton and is a very courteous gentleman. . . .

I was put in better quarters after that complaint. Commissioner Sherman [*sic*] told me, when I said it was very disgraceful to put English ladies in that filthy place, *All right; we are going to alter it right now.* I said, *High time that you did; I did not know that you were chairman of the board.*

When I was in the common room, for three hours I was standing hemmed in on all four sides by Italian immigrants very much taller than I, I being short. They were eating garlic and you can imagine how offensive it was. It was very unpleasant. It made it difficult for me to breathe. The smell was worse than I ever smelled before, and I have worked at my profession in slums of our large towns in England. You could almost taste and feel it, as well as smell it.

I asked permission to wire, as I have said, and they refused me. During all the time I was there not a single visitor came in the room, but an Irishman was in charge who, in keeping order, knocked the immigrants on the head with a brush. A great deal goes on there that Commissioner Williams does not hear of and probably does not know about. . . .

On one occasion an inspector who came in ordered all of the men out of that part of the room in which the urinals were situated. Previous to that several of the Englishmen (including myself) had retired there continuously in order to get a little fresh air. The atmosphere in the urinals was better than in any other part of the common room.

At night, just before going to bed, I objected as any self-respecting Englishman or Americans or those self-respecting Germans we heard of yesterday would do under similar circumstances. I objected very much to going down into the sort of quarters that I could see, by prophetic vision, they were taking me to. I stayed there by the place that is like a little ticket office and told the official in charge that I objected very much to going down there and protested against English people being herded together in such close quarters with so many others. I am glad to say that they thought the request was a reasonable one, and I succeeded in getting the 16 Englishmen put in tolerably decent room up over the balcony.

. . . . I did not get a mattress but a mat, impregnated with salt and disinfectant—which was probably necessary.

We were not compelled to 'sleep' on them. I did not sleep a wink all night; but we were compelled to lie upon them. There were distant screams all night from women. It was the most terrible night I have ever experienced in whole life. I had altogether about 40 hours of this thing and it seems to me even now like half of my life.

I did not have any access at all from that common room to a restaurant. I did not see a restaurant while I was there. There may be one, but if so I could not get to it to buy anything. No one went out of the common room at all until their case was called.

My great objection is to be the people being herded there and kept there in such congested quarters. Some of those people had been kept there six days from the steamship *Batavia*, they told me, being daily (4 a.m. to 7.30 p.m.) in this common room.

When I went to the better quarters to which they assigned me after my complaint, I found two girls, each about 19 years old. One of them was a Primitive Methodist and the other was Roman Catholic. They never had any religious instruction or help. They had been there over a month. . . .

The temperature appeared to be about 100 in the common room when it was nearly zero outside. There were just a few benches that were occupied at the first possible moment in the morning, and the rest of the people stood up all day. Probably not 40 out of the 600 could sit down. The air was fresh in the morning after about 10 minutes after we arrived. I believe that the officials do all in their power to disinfect and clean during the night, but, as you can understand, within a few minutes after you arrive in the morning the air is bad again.

I am complaining about the things that any self-respecting Englishman or any citizen of any other nation would complain about. There were 4 English ladies and 16 English gentlemen there. Some of the fellows took turns at breathing through the floor. The air that came through the holes in the floor was better. I spent about a quarter of an hour lying full length on the floor breathing through a sort of little ventilator or air shaft in the middle of the side of the room, near the door. . . .

I may say, with reference to that, that I was insured just before leaving England in one of the leading English companies whose medical man gave me a first-class health certificate. I am very sure that, from going through Ellis Island, I will not be able to get such again for some time, anyway. (Unrau 1984, pp. 1117–1120)

Another detention case was that of a fifty-eight-year-old Russian, Constantin M. Oberoutcheff, the former military commander of Kiev under during the premiership of Alexandr Kerensky. Oberoutcheff arrived in February 1923 with his wife, Olga, as passengers on board the SS *Orbita*, sailing from Cherbourg, France. His story was published in the August 4, 1923, issue of *Literary Digest*.

Considering the fact that multitudes of immigrants are handled on Ellis Island daily, conditions there, except for the prison atmosphere, are quite tolerable. The rooms are spacious and well-ventilated, altho frequently overcrowded. They can not boast of a high degree of cleanliness, but the circumstances under which they operate are quite exhausting. . . .

The passengers of the first and second cabins were landed first and taken to a large prison-like building. We were led to a large room and handed over to the authorities. The roll was called and the official left us.

In the large reception-room we sat on benches apart from the mass of third-class passengers. At the doors were officials at their desks questioning the immigrants in their turn. We were not kept waiting long; an official called the roll of the second-class arrivals and handed each of us a pass for second-class accommodations. To be candid, it was only when we were in the dining-room that I noticed the distinction that was made between immigrants of the different cabins. First and second-class passengers were seated on chairs; the less fortunate third-class on benches. A similar distinction was made in the rations.

Our case came up when the clock began to strike twelve, and was consequently put off until after lunch. We were removed to another room, where a crowd of people stood in expectation. The doors of the room were locked. In the center of the room, a pedlar was selling writing-paper, postage stamps, and apples. I was about to make my first American purchase of some apples when we were called for dinner. Several corridors led to our spacious dining-room. The dinner was tasty and plentiful. It consisted of soup, roast, vegetables, bread and butter, and coffee. The third-class immigrants were seated apart and I noticed that their menu was not as well chosen as ours of the first and second class, nor was it as generous. (Unrau 1984, pp. 1117–1120)

The following is Oberoutcheff's description of the detention quarters at Ellis Island.

Our doors were not locked, but they were guarded and the watchman allowed us to leave only for an airing in our corridor. In the rooms for third-class passengers, the men and women were kept apart. These rooms are often overcrowded to the point of suffocation . . .

All this contributed to the constant noise in the corridor and rooms, so that it was absolutely impossible to concentrate upon any thought or even to read intelligently. The suspense and forced idleness are the greatest ordeals of all those sentenced to wait on Ellis Island.

It was on a Wednesday, the day set for entertainment. At 7 o'clock in the evening, we were ordered to attend a motion-picture show. The cabin-passengers were seated on the balcony and those of the third-class in the orchestra. This compulsory attendance of a picture show amazed me. After the picture show, we were taken to our sleeping-quarters, which were on the same floor. The beds in the sleeping-quarters were of the triple-deck kind. We were given four blankets each, but no pillows or sheets which indispensable comfort would require.

My lot was cast in a room of Italians; a jolly company, to be sure. No provision was made there to accommodate people with families, and men and women are kept separately. I asked the attendant to put me in the non-smoking bedroom, but my request did not avail me.

The immigrants are treated in a cold and formal way but with without insult. If the unnecessary shouting by attendants upon transferring immigrants from one room to another would subside a bit, the impression upon the troubled minds of the newcomers would not be so intimidating. When I asked a negro worker to wipe the water which his pail left on a bench, he answered me harshly that there were other benches to sit on. (Unrau 1984, pp. 1117–1120)

Yet another detainee was Madame F. M. Lalande, also held at Ellis Island in 1923. Described as a Frenchwoman of "education and refinement," her story was told in the March 8, 1924, edition of the *Literary Digest.*

> After a life of travels and study, knowing five languages, it might have been supposed that I had seen everything worthy of interest, yet I had lately an excellent opportunity to study an institution unique in the world and extremely interesting. I mean Ellis Island.
>
> The construction is vast and imposing tho often crowded by the immense quantity of emigrants, whose absolute ignorance prevents many to appreciate that the short the short detention is not only imposed for the security of the United States but for their own welfare.
>
> The ladies and gentlemen in charge of the immigrants have inexhaustible patience and kindness. The large admission hall is (in the evening) used as a concert (once a week) and cinema . . . also Sundays a Catholic, a Protestant and Jewish service are held, so any creed can be followed. All this free. Above, all around the hall, is a balcony. This have white tiles walls and floors, porcelain lavabos and baths. There are two hospital, a kindergarden, medical attendance all free as well as board logging, entertainment, etc., etc. Interrogation rooms, dining rooms, kitchen, trunk rooms, etc., are on the ground floor. Besides breakfast (coffee, eggs, bread, butter, jam) (lunch—meat, vegetables, cheese, tea), dinner (soup, meat, etc.) there are (morning, afternoon, evening) free distributions of the best sweet fresh milk and crackers. Many days, thirty of those enormous cans are needed (they contain fifty gallons each, I was told). Six hundred and fifty employees are daily in attendance. Eighteen languages are interpreted. From morning till night, colored men and women clean incessantly. Towels are changed daily. Sheets three times a week.
>
> I leave to a competent man the estimate of the daily expense of such an establishment, and I should thank heartily an expert to compare Ellis Island to anything of the same sort, any other nation in the wide world has to offer. (Unrau 1984, pp. 1117–1120)

Other well-known detainees included former Venezuelan president **Cipriano Castro** (1912–1913); English suffragette Emmeline Pankhurst (1913); **Louis Adamic** (1913); anarchists **Alexander Berkman** and **Emma Goldman** (1919); the Baroness Mara de Lilier-Steinheil, an outraged Russian noblewoman who was held for three days in August 1923 and compared Ellis Island to her earlier imprisonment in Bolshevik jails; champion Argentine boxer **Luis Firpo** (1924); Lithuanian politician Constantine Norkus (1925); former Yugoslav banker and politician August Kosutic (1930); Spanish wrestler Primo Carnera (1930); Yiddish singer Sidor Belarsky (1930); the Austrian Trapp Family Singers (1938); the royal imposter Harry Gerguson, who posed successfully for years as "Prince Michael Romanoff" (1932), Soviet communist Irene Raissa Browder (1940); Italian-born gangster Charles "Lucky" Luciano (1946); French scientist and leftist Irene Joliot-Curie (1948); French singer **Charles Trenet** (1948); Italian conductor Victor de Sabata (1950); opera singers Fedora Barbieri, Boris Christoff, and Zinka Milanov; Czech actor George Voskovec (1951), and Trinidadian Marxist **C. L. R. James** (1952).

See also **Deportation Cases**

REFERENCE: Unrau, Harlan D. 1984. *The Historic Resource Study: Ellis Island/Statue of Liberty.* Vol. 3 Washington, DC: U.S. Department of Interior, National Park Service.

Detention Conditions, 1930s. According to the *Report of the Ellis Island Committee* (1934), the following conditions existed in detention. On arriving at Ellis Island, immigrants were examined by doctors in the **Main Building** and then either hospitalized across the slip or sent to detention in the **registry room**.

Large trunks and baggage were stored in the railroad room and receipts for them were issued by an agent at the exchange desk. Large amounts of money could be deposited in the Treasury Division. Detainees could receive callers daily at 10:00 a.m. and 2:00 p.m. An alien who urgently needed to go into New York City to fetch valuables or belongings would be accompanied by a guard or a matron.

Sleeping quarters were on the balcony level (third floor) and the second floor. Husbands and wives slept in separate quarters. Immigrants retired at 8:00 p.m. and lights were put out at 9:00 or 9:30 p.m. They rose at 6:00 a.m.

and breakfasted at 7:30 a.m. Dinner (lunch) was served at noon and supper at 5:30 p.m. Bathtubs and showers and toilets were available for use. Aliens had access to the lavatories and the government laundry to wash their clothes. For breakfast hot cereal, milk, fruit, bread and butter, were served; for luncheon there was soup, meat, potatoes, a pudding, cake for dessert, and ice cream twice a week. For supper, a typical meal might be meat, macaroni and cheese, bread, and butter, and coffee. Special kosher meals were served to Jews and halal meals to Muslims.

REFERENCE: Palmer, Carleton H., ed. 1934. *Report of the Ellis Island Committee.* Repr., New York: Ozer, 1971.

Detention Conditions, 1949. Frances W. Kerr, a writer in the Special Articles Section at the Department of State, wrote the following description of conditions for detained aliens at Ellis Island.

The average detention period for all types of cases at Ellis Island is 8½ to 10 days. . . . Of the detainees, about one-third are applicants for admission to the United States as visitors or under immigration quotas. They may be permitted to enter the country after meeting certain immigration requirements. Are [And] two-thirds are the unqualifiedly inadmissible who are detained for deportation. Some of the latter cannot be immediately deported because their own countries refuse to receive them. Detainees at Ellis Island get free food and shelter, and medical care day and night. The hospital on the island cost U.S. taxpayers $9.75 a patient a day.

Detainees may have visitors every day. They have only to request passes that admit their relatives and friends. . . . There is not forced activity at the detention center. Alien residents do not even have to make their own beds unless they wish to. Those who want to work receive ten cents an hour . . . but are not allowed to work more than eight hours a day.

There were 330 persons living on the island March 15, 1949. Maximum capacity is 1,500. Every person occupies a single bed. No double- or triple-tiered bunks are used. Single men sleep in large, well-lighted, well-ventilated dormitories. Single women are housed—two to six persons to the room—in large rooms with wash bowls and connecting private toilets. Bathrooms have private showers and bathtubs. Families occupy spacious rooms with single beds, baby beds, bureaus, tables and rocking chairs. The rooms are kept scrupulously clean. Floors are of tile or linoleum. Each person receives two clean blankets on arrival. Bed linen is changed every week.

Certain undesirable aliens, including some with criminal records, are restricted to special quarters that include dormitories and a day room with connecting sun porch.

In winter the rooms and dormitories are kept at a comfortable temperature by central heating. . . . In summer the buildings are cool because of high ceilings, many windows and breezes from the harbor.

The central recreation hall **[registry room]**, where aliens spend much of the time, is a two storied room, 125 feet by 175 feet, with a balcony . . . the recreation hall contains a piano, tables and chairs; facilities for reading, writing and playing games, and a blackboard for English classes. During daylight, detainees go outdoors whenever they wish for exercise.

Laundry facilities, including washtubs, clotheslines and electric irons are provided. A sewing room is available. So is a kitchen for heating milk for babies or making tea, day or night. The food at Ellis Island is prepared in modern kitchens equipped with electric stoves, refrigerators, meat lockers, electric dishwashers, and bakery equipment. The food is of first quality and is purchased through the sources used by the United States Army and Navy. Servings are ample, providing 4,100 calories a day. This compares with an average of 3,300 calories for United States civilians. Meals are served in cafeteria style on trays. Each person carries his tray of food to the table and returns the empty tray to the pantry. High chairs are provided for babies. Children receive milk with their meals, and milk and crackers at 11 a.m., 4 p.m. and bedtime.

The diet at Ellis Island caters to national and religious preferences. Rice and potatoes are often served at the same meal, since certain nationalities do not like potatoes. Kosher food is provided for persons of the Jewish faith. Kosher cooks, using a special kitchen and special utensils, prepare the food. A rabbi comes to Ellis Island for the Jewish holidays.

Ellis Island has its own post office, telegraph office and railroad-ticket office.

Religious services are held in the chapel, which is equipped with an electric organ, a piano, and a special altar and confessional for Roman Catholics. Services are held on Sundays as follows: Catholic, 9 to 10 a.m.; Protestant, 11 a.m. to 12 noon; Christian Science, 1 to 2 p.m.; Lutheran, 2 to 3 p.m. Services also are held for those of the Jewish faith.

Motion pictures are shown twice a week. The **Salvation Army** maintains a 20,000 volume library and reading room at the center.

Supplementing the services of the United States Government at the island is the Social Service Group, composed of representatives of the Protestant Episcopal Church, the Lutheran Church and Catholic and Jewish welfare organizations. These welfare workers maintain a school and kindergarten and provide a teacher. The schoolroom is equipped with desks, piano and blackboard.

Since detainees are not allowed to leave the island unaccompanied, the social service workers do personal shopping and errands for them. They also distribute newspapers and magazines, clothing and toys; inform relatives of needs of detained immigrants; obtain from relatives affidavits and money on behalf of detainees; provide Christmas gifts and celebrations; visit hospital patients and advise relatives of the parents' progress; provide free notary service.

The welfare workers are permitted to appear before the Board of Special Inquiry in behalf of the detainees; they draw up necessary documents. Their files are full of letters of appreciation for their services.

The social workers see that no person leaves Ellis Island without clothing suitable for the locality to which he is going. They purchase railroad tickets, locate baggage, arrange temporary shelter, and make contacts with their own organizations in other communities so that the Americanization services may be carried on when detainees who are permitted to remain in the United States leave the island.

See also **Enemy Aliens**

REFERENCE: Kerr, Frances W. 1949. Ellis Island. *Immigration and Naturalization Service Monthly Review*, May.

Detention Conditions, 1950s. In a December 1952 Immigration and Naturalization Service report, Ellis Island was described as a "self-contained city." It boasted a 200-seat chapel for religious observances. About one-third of the detainees were applying for admission to the United States as visitors or quota immigrants. The remaining two-thirds were excluded or awaiting deportation. A few were temporarily in limbo because no country would take them. The former **registry room** was now called the passengers' hall. Measuring 175 feet in length and 125 feet in width, it provided spacious accommodations as a day room, where aliens relaxed, read, and played. The room was equipped with a piano, a television set, ping pong and billiard tables, as well as chairs and tables. In the three-acre outdoor playing field, men played soccer and women and children played volleyball. Sleeping accommodations were described as "excellent." Single men slept in large, well-lighted, well-ventilated dormitories, and single women were assigned two to six to a room, each of which was equipped with wash bowels and connecting private toilets. Bathrooms had private showers and bathtubs. Families were assigned spacious rooms with single beds, baby beds, bureaus, tables, and rocking chairs.

Despite these conditions, some aliens still plotted to escape. On April 3, 1953, the *New York Times* reported the escape of three young men—a Dutchman, a Belgian, and a Spaniard—who managed to get away only to be captured by the Hoboken police (New Jersey). The police officials described the escape:

> The escape plan hinged on a plastic shower curtain taken from a dormitory bathroom. The men wrapped dry clothing in the curtain Wednesday night and put the bundle on a ledge outside their third-floor window.
>
> About midnight, they tied the sheets and blankets together and slid to the ground. They dodged patrolling guards and dived into the bay.
>
> The swim took four hours. At the pier, the three men dressed in dry clothing from the waterproof bundle. The Spaniard went his separate way. (*New York Times* 1953)

From December 24, 1952, to July 31, 1953, 1,012 aliens facing exclusion were held on the island, of which 237 were special inquiry cases, 8 were stowaways, 730 were temporary detainees, and 37 aliens were being held for safekeeping.

The Salvation Army's Ellis Island library (founded in 1916) held 23,000 volumes, of which 6,850 were works of fiction, 308 on historical topics, 740 general works, 2,010 works of natural science, 500 on religious topics, 125 philosophical works, 250 philological texts, 480 biographies; 3,675 were foreign language publications.

REFERENCE: *New York Times*. 1953. April 3.

Discharging Division. The Discharging Division, also known as the Information and Discharging Division, was responsible for releasing temporarily detained immigrants from Ellis Island. The division was headed by an inspector and had clerks and matrons on its staff. Files were kept of all aliens being held for release. In 1901, waiting rooms or sheds for immigrants going to New York and for immigrants' friends were constructed near the **Main** and **kitchen and laundry buildings**.

Diseases and Hospitalization. The medical examination of immigrants at Ellis Island consisted of **line inspection** and thorough physical and mental examinations, often called "second inspection." This second examination was reserved for immigrants who failed to satisfy the **surgeons** as to their good health. The following are excerpts from the *Book of Instructions for the Medical Inspection of Immigrants*, which was issued in 1903 by direction of the surgeon general. Its general rules and descriptions applied to all immigrant inspection stations where the **Public Health Service** had a presence, including Boston, New York, Philadelphia, Detroit, Montreal, Miami, New Orleans, Galveston, San Francisco, Los Angeles, Seattle, and Honolulu.

> For the purpose of carrying out the provisions of the immigration law, diseased, abnormal, crippled, and deformed aliens may be regarded as divisible in two classes.
>
> *Class A—Those who are excluded from admission into the country by reason . . . of a disease or abnormal condition . . . expressly declared by the law . . . to constitute a ground for such exclusion.*
>
> *Class B—Those who present some disease or defect, physical or mental, which may be regarded as conclusive or contributory evidence to justify the exclusion, by the proper immigration authorities, of the person in question as an alien "likely to become a public charge."*
>
> *In accordance with the present law, aliens of Class A must fall within one of the four subdivisions of that class, viz.:*
>
> *(1) Persons suffering from dangerous contagious diseases.*
> *(2) Persons suffering from loathsome diseases.*
> *(3) Insane persons.*
> *(4) Idiots.*
>
> Care should be taken to see that the form of the medical certificate in every case is such as to enable the immigration officers to see clearly in which class the alien in question belongs, and caution should exercised especially in placing an alien in any of the

Patients and nurses. Courtesy of the Ellis Island Immigration Museum.

subdivisions of Class A, because boards of Special Inquiry have no alternative but to exclude in such cases.

The medical examination should be made by daylight and never, except in an emergency, attempted in poorly lighted rooms or by artificial light. The preliminary line inspection should be conducted on an even, level surface, so that the passengers may not be tempted to look where they are stepping. A basin containing disinfecting solution should be placed near the examiner, so that he may disinfect his hands after handling cases of trachoma, favus, etc. care should taken to prevent crowding, to maintain a single file evenly spaced, with the individuals well separated.

Whenever it can be possibly avoided, immigrants should not be permitted to take the their baggage with them while undergoing inspection, because it interferes with the view of the examiner. There should be abundant lighting coming from behind the examiner. Direct sunshine or its reflection from the water directly in the faces of the approaching passengers must be avoided, as it causes them to squint or look down. Care should be taken to obviate the necessity of the passenger passing from a shadow into a light or vice versa. The file should make a right angle turn immediately in front of the examiner's position. This enables the examiner to observe both sides and the back of the passenger in the shortest possible time, besides bringing out lameness, defective eyesight (through passenger's efforts to adjust his vision to a new course), artificial eyes, corneal opacities or roughened cornea (through light striking the eye at changing angles of incidence as the passenger turns). A clear view of the eyes may be secured by holding up a finger or some small object in front of the passenger just before he reaches the examiner. The examiner should not permit a passenger to approach nearer than 12 to 15 feet before beginning the scrutiny. In making this preliminary scrutiny, it is well to follow a systematic plan. It is usually well to commence at the feet and proceed upward, reserving the matter of the eyes as the last feature to be inspected.

Cases turned aside for special examination, as well as any others to whom the attention of the examiner has been brought, should be subjected to a sufficiently thorough physical examination to determine whether there are other defects besides those which primarily attracted attention. The examiner should detain any alien or aliens as long as may be necessary to insure a correct diagnosis.

The following mental or physical conditions should be placed in the class indicated by the outline given below.

CLASS A

Subdivision I—"Dangerous Contagious Diseases"

1. Trachoma—*For the purposes of this circular, the term "trachoma" is used to designate a diseased condition of the conjunctiva, characterized by a muco-purulent discharge, firm persistent hyperplastic granulations, and exhibiting a tendency to be associated with atrophy of the conjunctiva with scar formation, roughened corneæ, adhesive bands of cicatricial tissue, entropion, pannus or even marked evidence of inflammatory processes, not due to external traumatism. Examiners are therefore instructed to regard as trachoma any case wherein the conjunctiva presents firm, well-marked granulations which do not have a tendency to disappear when the case is placed in hygienic surroundings a few days, or does not yield rapidly to ordinary treatment, even though there be no evidence of active inflammation at the time of the examination, nor appreciable discharge, nor yet signs of degenerative or destructive processes. Examiners are also instructed to regard as a possible case of trachoma any person who presents an active inflammatory condition of the conjunctiva accompanied by a discharge or a thickened infiltrated condition of the lids, and to hold such case until by treatment or otherwise the examination may be satisfactorily concluded. Cases of acute inflammation of the conjunctiva presenting a granular appearance of the lids should be regarded as suspicious and final judgement be withheld until the case has been under observation for a period of at least two weeks.*

In view of the present state of medical science as to the etiology of trachoma, an immigrant should not be regarded as suffering with that disease whose conjunctiva presents only a granular appearance and a discharge both of which rapidly and entirely disappear.

Suggestions—*The eyelids should be everted in all cases which show any of the following conditions: roughened cornea, corneal opacities, corneal ulcers, cloudiness of the media, lids which seem thickened at the location of the tarsal cartilage, entropion, lids which have a tendency to droop or do not raise simultaneously with the eyeball as the person looks up, pannus, and any eye which shows signs of acute conjunctival congestion. It should also be remembered that large numbers of cases of trachoma are found among Syrians, Greeks, Armenians, Russians, and Finns, and that, especially among the lattermentionedrace,manycasesoftrachomaarefound which give no outward evidence of the disease.*

The cul-de-sac should be brought into view, because it frequently happens that an eye which is otherwise normal will have the cul-de-sac filled with granulations. Marginal blepharitis rarely accompanies trachoma. If both are present, the granulations of trachoma will be found farther back on the lid in the cul-de-sac.

Prognosis—*The following class of cases may be regarded as practically incurable. Any case showing extensive areas of granulation, associated with any one or all of the following conditions: infiltration, well-marked evidence of degenerative changes, pannus, roughened cornea, entropion, and cases which present numerous so-called "sago-like" bodies. Cases which do not show marked improvement after several weeks' treatment, cases which show a strumous diathesis, cases which present a grayish semitransparent or so-called ground-glass appearance. This is especially true of trachoma found in the Finnish race.*

Caution should also be exercised in making definite prognosis even in the most favorable cases, because treatment is generally very disappointing.

2. Pulmonary Tuberculosis—*In view of the large amount of literature on the subject of tuberculosis, it is not deemed necessary to formulate special suggestions for its detection. No case of pulmonary tuberculosis should be certified as "dangerous contagious" unless the clinical symptoms are well marked and the tubercle bacillus has been found in the sputum. For the disposition of aliens suspected of having pulmonary tuberculosis but in which the bacillus can not be found, see list of diseases under Class B, "Aliens excluded as likely to become public charges."*

In every case of pulmonary tuberculosis certified as "dangerous contagious disease," a slide showing tubercle bacilli in the sputum should be prepared, properly labeled, and preserved.

Subdivision II—"Loathsome Diseases"

1. Favus—*Cases of favus should not be certified unless they present clinical as well as microscopical evidence of the disease. A slide of a culture tube, properly labeled should be preserved in every case certified. . . . In most instances, material for microscopical examination is best obtained by carefully lifting the cup and selecting the soft material immediately beneath it. As it is possible during the time occupied by the ocean voyage to remove temporarily by skillful manipulation all positive clinical evidence of this disease and to make the microscopical diagnosis extremely difficult, care should be taken not to permit these specially prepared cases in which the disease is still active to pass the examination. All scalps showing signs of recent treatment and presenting areas of loss of hair, slight incrustations about the openings of the hair follicles, the hairs often being loose, and the remaining presumably healthy hairs imparting to the hand as sensation as though fine wire was being touched, should be regarded as suspicious and held under examination for a period of one to three weeks without washing or treatment, providing attempts at diagnosis give negative results in the meantime. In all cases suspected of being favus, the fingernails should be carefully examined. If likewise diseased, they will also probably furnish material for confirming the diagnosis.*

Cases of recovered favus seen among immigrants seldom have much hair left. The scalp will be pale, withoutreddenedareas.Thecuticlewillhaveaglazed appearance, the underlying tissue being atrophied. The remaining hairs will be firmly fixed and coarse.

Caution should be exercised in expressing an opinion as to the length of time necessary to effect a cure.

After the head has been shaved, the disease will usually be found to involve a greater area than was previously apparent. For a child or even a person under 20 years of age with a thick growth of hair, a year's treatment with daily attention in hospital under most approved methods will often prove fruitless. In an older person with little remaining hair, the prognosis may be made with more safety. No person having been under treatment for favus should be discharged as recovered until treatment has been suspended at least four weeks and at the end of which period there has been no return of the disease.

2. Syphilis—*Cases of active syphilis in which there can be no question as to the diagnosis should be certified immediately.*

3. Gonorrhea—*Cases of this disease are ordinarily held for hospital treatment until they have recovered. In the event of there being obstacles in the way of hospital treatment, the case should be certified.*

4. Leprosy—*Generally held at quarantine: if not, certify.*

Subdivision III—"Insane Persons"

The following definition of insanity may be accepted for guidance: Insanity is a deranged and abnormal condition of the mental faculties, accompanied by delusions or hallucinations or illusions, or manifesting in homicidal or suicidal tendencies or persistent mental depression, or inability to distinguish between right and wrong.

In the case of immigrants, particularly the ignorant representatives of emotional races, due allowance should be made for temporary demonstrations ofexcitement,fearorgrief,andreliancechieflyplaced upon absolute assurance of the existence of delusions or persistent refusal to talk or continued abstinence from eating.

Persons suffering from acute attacks of delirium tremens should be certified as insane. Those presenting less active evidence of alcoholism should be regarded as coming under the heading of likely to become public charges, as should also cases of simple epilepsy or hysteria.

At least two officers should concur in a certificate of insanity, and when this is impractical the medical officer should recommend the employment of a local physician in good standing, and they shall jointly sign the certificate.

The evidence on which a certificate of insanity is based should be made a matter of permanent record. It should always include, among other things, the physical appearance, character of hallucinations, delusions or illusions, and a brief history of the peculiarities noted while the case was under observation.

Subdivision IV—"Idiots"

The following definition of an idiot may be accepted for guidance:

An idiot is a person exhibiting such a degree of mental defect, either inherited or developed during the early period of life, as incapacitates the individual for self-maintenance or ability to properly care for himself or his interests. (Richardson)

Idiocy is a defect of mind which is either congenital or during to causes operating during the first few years of life, before there has been the development of the mental faculties, and may exist in different degrees. ("Standard Dictionary" by Maudsley, 'Responsibility in Mental Diseases,' chapter 3, p. 66)

In case of persons of impaired mentality to whom the term "idiot" or "insane," as above defined, is inapplicable, certificates should be made in such terms as may be deemed best calculated to convey an idea of the degree of disability in each particular case.

CLASS B

"Aliens Excluded as Likely to Become a Public Charge"

Under this head should be included all diseases and deformities which are likely to render a person unable to earn a living. The certificate in each case should be sufficiently explicit to enable the inspector whose duty it is to pass final judgement on these cases to form an opinion as to what degree the disease or deformity will affect the immigrant's ability to earn a living.

The need for clearness in all certificates rendered under Class B will be better understood when it is remembered that the Board of Special Inquiry must base its opinion on the certificate rendered, which will in a great measure determine whether the immigrant certified should be excluded, released in bond or released unconditionally.

It is to be observed that a medical certificate frequently constitutes the sole testimony on which the Board of Special Inquiry, composed of non-medical men, will decide whether the alien concerned does or does not belong to one of the excluded classes; that such certificate, once issued, becomes a part of the permanent records of the Treasury Department: that it is made the subject of legal comment and in official scrutiny is every case of appeal, and is always likely to be placed in evidence in habeas corpus proceedings, actions in tort, or other suits at law, both civil or criminal.

Therefore, in the class of cases excluded as likely to become public charges the greatest care should be taken.–

First—To give technical diagnosis, following the official nomenclature of diseases, whenever practicable.

Second—To make, in addition to this statement, such explanation or comment, in plain language, as may be deemed necessary to enable the Board of Special Inquiry or the appellate authority to form an intelligent opinion as to the extent of the alien's disability.

Whenever it may appear advisable for the medical officer to supplement his certificate by further explanatory statements, written or verbal, he will that every such supplementary statement is correctly incorporated in the permanent records of the case.

From the very nature of the subject, it be apparent that it is impossible to name all the diseases or deformities which may be classed under this heading. A few of the most common causes are given below.

1. Hernia—*In writing certificates for hernia, the following points should be borne in mind: (a) Occupation and the extent to which the hernia is likely to affect the immigrant's to earn a living must be considered. (b) Probability of an early operation; in the latter case, application for treatment would probably be made at a charity hospital, in which event the alien would become a public charge for at least several months.*

2. Valvular Heart Disease—*Well marked cases of heart disease may usually detected at the preliminary inspection by the incurved nails, thickened condition about the lobes of the ears and the alæ nasi, associated with indistinctness of these parts, dyspnœa, and a peculiar pallor. In cases of persons whose face, neck or extremities suggest an appearance of faulty nutrition, the heart should always be examined. As a matter of routine, it is best to examine the heart in all persons held for the second inspection. In writing certificates for heart cases, it should always be remembered that such cases are*

extremely likely to become worse, and in that event they may become inmates of charity hospitals or institutions, where they will probably be public charges for a great length of time.

3. Pregnancy—*Every pregnant woman should be turned aside for the second inspection, a record stating the probable number of months that she is pregnant should be made, and the same be reported to the examining immigrant inspector, whose duty it is to ascertain whether she is legitimately pregnant. In the event of her being illegitimately pregnant, a certificate stating her physical condition should be made. Pregnant women who are so far advanced that further travel would be attended with serious risk, should be detained and the immigration officials notified as to the examiner's opinion in the matter.*

4. Poor Physique—*Under this head should be placed cases in which it is evident from their physical condition that they will be unable to earn a living at manual labor. Cases of so-called "chicken breast," especially those having the physical signs of pulmonary tuberculosis, but in which the tubercle bacillus can not be found in the sputum, should be certified under this head.*

5. Chronic Rheumatism—*The large number of persons suffering from this disease, found in hospitals, homes for incurables, etc., should lead the examiner to be very careful in making the certificates in these cases.*

6. Nervous Affections—*The large number of persons suffering from locomotor ataxia, spastic paraplegia, and other incurable nervous diseases, who are the recipients of public charity, should lead the examiner to be very careful to watch for these cases. At the preliminary inspection, the examiner should make it a rule to have all children who are being carried placed on their feet in order to see whether they are able to walk. Many cases of infantile paralysis have been detected in this way.*

7. Malignant Diseases—*Cases of carcinoma, sarcoma, etc., which can not be placed under the head of 'Loathsome' should be placed under this head, and the extreme probability of their being incurable can not be too strongly emphasized in the certificate.*

8. Deformities—*All cases in which there are deformities which are liable to interfere with the afflicted one earning a living should be certified, the degree of disability being stated in each case. The deformities usually found are kyphosis, lordosis, scoliosis, mutilation of the extremities, etc.*

9. Senility and Debility—*Senile persons who are unlikely to be able to provide and cared for themselves should be certified. Cases of extreme debility which will evidently not be cured by treatment in hospital should be certified, the prognosis being stated in each case.*

10. Varicose Veins—*Whenever an immigrant with well-marked varicose veins, especially when affecting the lower extremities, he should be certified. The tendency to ulcer formation should be pointed out, and special stress should be laid upon the fact that these cases often require many months of hospital treatment.*

11. Eyesight—*Serious defects of vision, including refractive errors of high degree, optic atrophy, choroiditis, retinitis pigmentosa, etc., should be certified. Whenever the inability to see clearly appears to be independent of distance, the eyes should be examined with the opthalmoscope.*

12. General Considerations—*Any disease of deformity which can not be placed in any of the above classes, but which will interfere with an immigrant's ability to earn a living, should be certified. Terminal conditions resulting from previous inflammatory diseases of the eye, and which can not be placed in the 'Dangerous Contagious' class, should be included under this head. For example, scar formation of the conjunctiva, entropion, infiltration of the cornea, etc. Whenever the examiner has any doubt as to the likelihood of a person being a public charge through a disease or deformity, he should write a certificate in that case, because the Board of Special Inquiry is charged with assuming the responsibility of disposing of the cases.*

Hospital Cases

All cases should be recommended for treatment in hospital when in the opinion of the examiner –

First—*A more extended examiner than is possible at the place of inspection is necessary to order to complete a diagnosis.*

Second—*The immigrant, owing to his mental or physical state is not in condition to travel.*

It is also suggested that the examiner recommend to the Commissioner for detention in hospital any immigrant who is afflicted with a disease on account of which he is likely to seek charity treatment.

In dealing with communicable diseases, he should endeavor in every possible way to secure conformity to the United States quarantine laws and the sanitary laws and ordinances in which he may be stationed. (Unrau, pp. 652–660)

Ellis Island physician Alfred C. Reed wrote an article called "The Medical Side of Immigration," which appeared in the April 1912 issue of *Popular Science Monthly.* In it he mentioned diseases encountered at Ellis Island.

First among these might be placed trachoma, a disease of the eyelids characterized by extreme resistance to treatment, very chronic course and most serious results. Most of the immigrant cases occur in Russians, Austrians and Italians, although it is of common occurrence in oriental and Mediterranean countries. It causes a large percentage of the blindness in Syria and Egypt. Its contagious nature, together with the resulting scarring of the lids and blindness, make its recognition imperative. The hookworm (*Uncinaria*) has received much attention lately so it has been found so widely distributed through the mountains of the south, the mines of California, the middle west, etc. It is a minute parasitic intestinal worm about three fifths of an inch long and, under the microscope, shows relatively enormous and powerful chitinous jaws by means of which it attaches itself to the intestinal walls. The saliva of the hookworm has the curious property of preventing coagulation of blood like leech extract, and when its is remembered that the worms may vary in number from several hundred to a thousand or more, and that each worm moves frequently from place to place on the intestinal wall, it is apparent how excessive and continuous is the drain on the blood and lymph juices. The result is an extreme anemia which brings in its wake a varied multitude of bodily ills, and may eventuate fatally, meanwhile having incapacitated the victim for mental or physical work.

Infection can spread rapidly from a single case. Not many hookworm carriers have been discovered among immigrants, probably because the facilities for their detection is so meager. But the heavy immigration from countries where uncinaria is abundant, as well as the recent suggestive work of Dr. H.M. Manning at the Ellis Island Immigrant Hospital, indicate that there is a constant stream of fresh infection pouring in. Indisputably routine examination for hookworms should be instituted. The same can be said of other intestinal parasites as tapeworms, pin worms, whip worms, eel worms and others. One of the tapeworms, the so-called fish worm (*dibothriocephalus latus*) leads to an anemia fully as severe as that for the hookworm.

. . . Most cases of trachoma and mental or organic nervous disease are sent to the hospital and are kept under care and observation to facilitate an accurate diagnosis. Seldom indeed does the alien suffer from too harsh a medical judgement. He is given the benefit of the doubt always. For example, if a case of defective vision is found to be 3/20 normal, it would be certified as perhaps 5/20 normal. . . .

The exclusion of Class A aliens is mandatory because of a definite specified defect or disease. Class B (aliens) . . . possess some defect or disease . . . likely to interfere with the ability to earn a living. Class C aliens . . . present a defect or disease of still lesser seriousness, nor affecting ability to earn a living but which nonetheless, must be certified for the information of the immigration inspectors.

The following were the orders given to the **Public Health and Marine Hospital Service** in assisting the **Bureau of Immigration** in the inspection of immigrants. President Theodore Roosevelt and the secretary of the treasury approved this document on November 21, 1902.

IMMIGRATION

804. When requested by the Bureau of Immigration, the Surgeon-General will detail a regular officer of the Public Health and Marine-Hospital Service for the medical examination of immigrants. The examination will be conducted in conjunction with the inspection instituted by the Commissioner of Immigration.

805. Officers detailed for the purpose of inspecting immigrants shall be governed by the general regulations of the Public Health and Marine-Hospital Service as far as applicable. The specific duties of officers engaged in this work shall be according to the requirements embodied in the Official Book of Instructions for the Medical Inspection of Immigrants. . . .

806. Medical officers examining immigrants shall have charge of the medical inspection and shall be responsible for its efficiency. They will recommend for detention in hospital or otherwise all cases in which observation is necessary. Immigrants detained shall be visited by the medical examiner as often as he may deem necessary in order that the inspection may be completed as speedily as possible.

807. The medical officer in charge will certify to the Commissioner of Immigration all insane persons, idiots, persons suffering from a loathsome or dangerous contagious disease, and all persons whose mental or physical condition will affect their ability to earn a living.

808. The medical officer shall furnish the Commissioner of Immigration such information as he may require concerning the physical condition of any immigrant, and he shall conduct the medical inspection in such manner as to expedite, as far as practicable, the work of landing immigrants. When requested, he shall give advice on sanitary matters relating to immigrants.

809. The Commissioner of Immigration will furnish adequate facilities for conducting the medical inspection, including when necessary, a proper office and equipment therefor[e].

810. Should an appeal be taken from the diagnosis in a case of idiocy or a case classified as 'loathsome' or as 'dangerous contagious' and an additional opinion is desired by the Bureau of Immigration, the immigrant shall be brought before the board provided for in paragraph 813, and its decision shall be final.

811. Should an appeal be taken from the diagnosis in a medical case classified as 'Likely to become a public charge,' the officer in charge of the medical inspection will again examine the case and transmit his opinion in writing to the Commissioner of Immigration.

REFERENCES: *Book of Instructions for the Medical Inspection of Immigrants.* 1903. Washington, DC: Marine Hospital Service; Immigrant inspection document. 1902. November 21; Reed, Alfred C. 1912. The medical side of immigration. *Popular Science Monthly.* April; Unrau, Harlan D. 1984. *The Historic Resource Study: Ellis Island/Statue of Liberty.* Vol. 3 Washington, DC: U.S. Department of Interior, National Park Service

District Commissioners. *See* **Commissioners**

District Directors. From 1933 to 1940, the district director was the second in command to the commissioner. However, after Rudolph Reimer retired in 1940, the district director assumed full authority at the station and was the chief executive officer of the Southern District of New York. The chiefs of Ellis Island who held the title of district director include **Byron H. Uhl** and Edward Shaughnessy.

Divisions. The workforce was assigned to various divisions in the bureaucracy in order to ensure control and efficiency. The following seventeen divisions existed at the station in 1903 and comprised 350 employees: **Executive**, **Boarding**, **Medical**, **Registry**, **Special Inquiry**, **Information**, **Discharging**, **Deportation**, **Statistical**, **Treasurer's**, **Watchmen's and Gatesmen's**, **Matrons'**, Engineers', Laborers', **Night**, Marine, and Miscellaneous. In 1912, there were eleven divisions: Executive, Medical, Boarding, Registry, Information, Special Inquiry, Deporting, Statistical, Mechanical, **Janitors'** (laborers and charwomen), Night. In 1924, 493 employees worked at Ellis Island; the divisions were these: Boarding, Deporting, Executive, Treasurer's, Information, Janitors', **Law**, Matrons', Night, Power Plant (same as Engineers'), Record (formerly Statistical), Registry, Special Inquiry, Superintendents. The Marine Division seems to have been put in the Superintendent's Division after 1922. The chief of Special Inquiry supervised the **Chinese Division**.

Doak, William N. [William Nuckles Doak] (b. Wythe County, Virginia, December 12, 1882; d. McLean, Virginia, October 23, 1933). U.S. secretary of labor (1930–1933). Serving President Herbert Hoover, Doak was a strong enforcer of immigration restriction laws and kept a firm hand on their enforcement at Ellis Island. Although his policies aroused opposition from many quarters, he prevailed in increasing the number of immigrants deported and excluded. Before holding this post, he had served as vice president of the Brotherhood of Railroad Trainmen.

Docks. The docks were located on **Island 1** and the sliver of land where the **ferry house** stands. By 1907, there was the ferry slip dock, barge docks along the boardwalk in front of the **Main Building**, and at the entrance to the slip. The fog bell also stood at the entrance.

The railroad dock taking immigrants to the Central Jersey railroad terminal in Jersey City was located behind the Main Building. The Central Jersey railroad terminal was built in 1889 and served passengers until 1962. It is now a museum.

See also **Arrival; Ferries and Boats**

Dormitory (C307). The dormitory room is a permanent exhibit of the **Ellis Island Immigration Museum** and is located on the third floor overlooking the balcony. The exhibit is located in one of the former dormitories. It features bedding and other items of the kind used at Ellis Island.

Typical scene of immigrants embarking at one of the Ellis Island docks.
Courtesy of the Ellis Island Immigration Museum.

Duncan, Isadora (b. San Francisco, Calif., May 27, 1878; d. Nice, France, September 14, 1927). American dancer and choreographer. Early in October 1922, the world famous star was detained at Ellis Island with her Soviet husband, Sergei Esenin. The Immigration Bureau detained her under the Cable Act of 1916, which ruled that an American woman who married a foreigner took the citizenship of her husband. As well as arriving during the height of the **red scare** with a Soviet communist husband, she also lived with him before they married. The Esenins were released after a two-hour interrogation. Duncan's producer, Sol Hurok, fetched them off the island. A combination of anti-Bolshevism and the moral code of the day played a part in the affair.

E

Elevators. The Otis Elevator Company installed a freight elevator in the stairwell of the northeast tower in April 1901. It held a maximum load of 2,500 pounds. It appears to have been powered by a worm-geared electric traction machine. When the third floor was added and the **Special Inquiry Division** moved part of its operation there, a passenger elevator was installed. This one was located in the stairwell of the southwest tower. Commissioner **William Williams** reported: "Witnesses, applicants for interviews, visitors and employees are constantly passing up and down. When the board rooms are established on the third floor, it will involve a climb of eight flights of steps, much confusion and considerable hardship." This elevator had a twenty horsepower motor and was completed in December 1910; it received a new motor in 1934.

Another elevator was operating in the Main Building by the 1920s and 1930s. It was a self-service passenger car and located in the east end of the building.

Ellis, Samuel (b. Wales, 1712 ?; d. New York, 1794). Merchant and farmer; proprietor of Ellis Island, for whom it was named. Samuel Ellis, a Tory colonist, owned Ellis Island from about 1774 until his death. His address was 1 Greenwich Street, Manhattan. On January 20, 1785, he published an advertising notice in *Loudon's New-York Packet*, offering to sell the island. "To be Sold By Samuel Ellis, no. 1, Greenwich street, at the north river near the Bear Market. That pleasant situated Island, Oyster Island, lying in New York Bay, near Powle's Hook, together with all its improvements, which are considerable." However, it was still among his possessions at the time of his death in 1794; in his will and last testament, he bequeathed it to the child of one of his daughters, Catherine Westervelt, with the proviso that the child would have to be a boy to receive the property and that the boy must be named "Samuel Ellis." Mrs. Westervelt duly gave birth to a son and named him "Samuel Ellis Westervelt"; however, the child died in infancy and the claims to the island became a struggle between Mrs. Westervelt, her sisters, and their respective families.

Ellis Island (1936 motion picture; 67 minutes). This B movie, a comic thriller, features two inspectors of the Ellis Island deporting squad who get entangled in a web of gangsters, deportees, and a missing $1 million in stolen money. The film opens with the robbery of the Metropolitan Federal Bank in 1926, shortly followed by the capture and imprisonment of the criminals. Only the whereabouts of the money remains a mystery. The next scene opens ten years later, when the criminals are being taken to Ellis Island for deportation. The remainder is filled with excitement and intrigue and ends with a chase scene in the country.

Produced by the Invincible Pictures Corporation, it stars Donald Cook, Johnny Arthur, Joyce Compton, Peggy Shannon, Jack LaRue, Bradley Page, George Rosener, Maurice Black, and Monte Vandergrift. Arthur T. Horman wrote the original story. The producer of *Ellis Island* was Maury M. Cohen and the director was Phil Rosen. The picture includes rather good re-creations of Ellis Island and includes footage of the ferryboat and the canopy from about 1930.

Ellis Island Chronicles (Rooms E305–309). Located in the east wing of the main building, *Ellis Island Chronicles* is a permanent exhibition of the **Ellis Island Immigration Museum**. It chronicles the geological origins, pre-Columbian use of Ellis Island and colonial proprietors, especially **Samuel Ellis**. Three large models showing how Ellis Island was enlarged over the years (1890s–1950s) form a major part of the exhibition. In addition, the original pilot's wheel and another artifact from the old **ferryboat *Ellis Island*** are also on display. The remainder of the exhibits consists of photographs and graphics chronicling the history of immigration and Ellis Island, including information on landfill operations, architecture and construction, laws, the commissioners, detainees, wartime, enemy aliens, the Edward Laning mural, and the **closing of Ellis Island.**

Ellis Island Committee. The Ellis Island Committee was set up by Secretary of Labor **Frances Perkins** in 1933 to investigate Ellis Island and find ways of improving conditions there. Many of its suggestions were adopted, including demolishing the Red Cross house and the old ferry house, constructing a new **ferry house** and the new immigration building, carrying out landfill operations, landscaping the grounds, and doing extensive maintenance and repair work.

The committee worked closely with Commissioner **Edward Corsi** and found his administration efficient. Among the fifty-two committee members were **Carleton H. Palmer** (chairman), Joseph P. Chamberlain (vice chairman), Mrs. Daniel O'Day (vice chairman), Chester H. Aldrich, Mrs. Vincent Astor, Dr. S. Josephine Baker, Frederic R. Coudert, Mrs. E. Marshall Field, Mrs. Charles Dana Gibson, Israel Goldstein, Nathan Hirsch, Foster Kennedy, Franklin B. Kirkbride, Arnold Knapp, Mrs. Alexander Kohut, Mrs. Henry Goddard Leach, Read Lewis, Francis J. McConnell, Mrs. Maurice T. Moore, Mrs. Carleton H. Palmer, Angelo Patri, George A. Soper, S. D. Wallach, and Helen Arthur, secretary.

REFERENCE: *Report of the Ellis Island Committee*, March 1934. Repr. Jerome S. Ozer, 1971.

Ellis Island Immigration Museum. The Ellis Island Immigration Museum was dedicated on September 10, 1990. The museum is divided into permanent exhibits on each of the three floors of the **Main Building**. The museum was planned by the **National Park Service** and researched and designed by **MetaForm Incorporated**. A national fund-raising campaign to pay for the museum was carried out by the **Statue of Liberty–Ellis Island Foundation** throughout the 1980s.

The museum's permanent exhibits are designed to tell the story of Ellis Island and immigration to the United States between 1892 and 1954.

At the entrance to the Main Building is a new canopy that gives an idea of what the historic **canopy** that once surmounted the entrance to the building was like.

In the central area of the first floor are the **Baggage Room** and **Peopling of America/ Railroad Ticket Office** exhibit. The space also includes an information desk and a service desk for the Statue of Liberty–Ellis Island Foundation. Computer terminals connect to a database of the 600,000 names inscribed on the American Immigrant Wall of Honor located on the outside of building. In addition, a cinema (Theater 1), a cafeteria, and a souvenir gift shop are located in the east wing of the building. The west wing is the headquarters of the **American Family Immigration History Center** (AFIHC), which has a database of 22 million immigrants and American travelers who entered the port of New York between 1892 and 1924.

The second floor of the museum contains the most extensive exhibitions. In the central section is the **Registry Room**, containing ap-

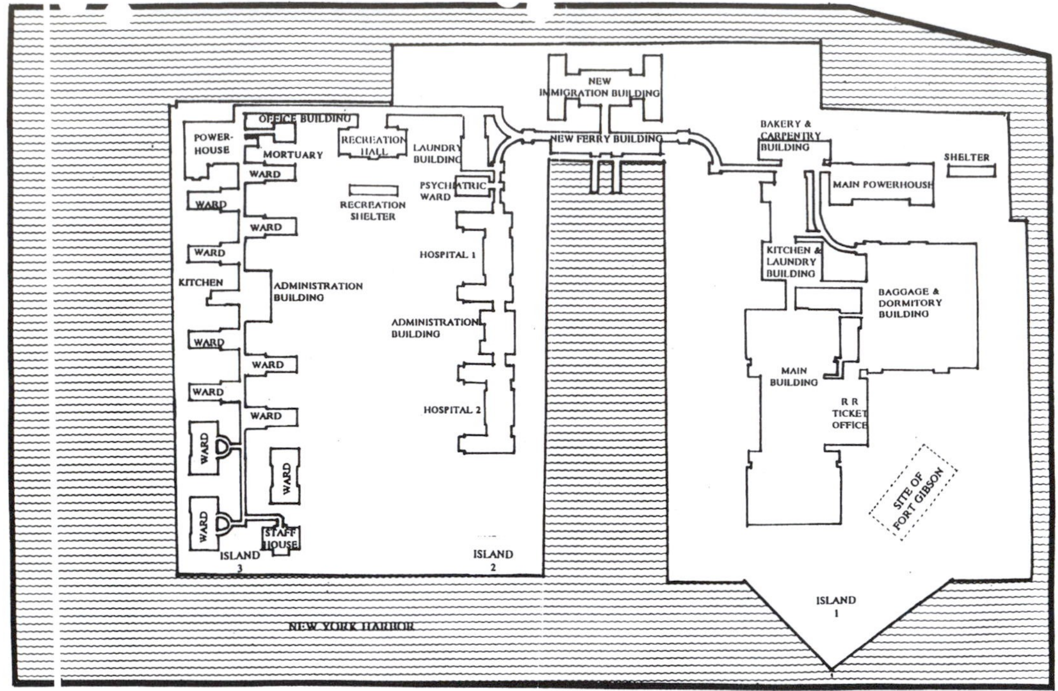

Ellis Island Historic District plan. Courtesy of the Ellis Island Immigration Museum.

proximately twenty original benches, the original three chandeliers, and reproductions of the inspectors' desks.

In the east wing is the **Peak Immigration Years** exhibit and in the west wing, **Through America's Gate**. In addition, there is a second cinema (Theater 2) in the east wing.

The third floor balcony level has **Registry Room Views** photographic exhibit, the **Dormitory** exhibit, and the temporary exhibit galleries. In the east wing are three exhibits: **Ellis Island Chronicles**, **Treasures from Home**, and **Silent Voices**.

The west wing of the third floor houses the Graffiti Columns exhibit (inscriptions and drawings left by detainees); the Oral History Listening Room and the studio of the Ellis Island Oral History Project; and the reference library, reading room, and museum curatorial offices of the chief of museum services, exhibits curator, oral historian, and archivist.

The area once occupied by the Sherman Gallery (1990–2000), which was named in honor of **Augustus F. Sherman**, is now the location of the American Immigration Family History Center.

The National Park Service and the Statue of Liberty–Ellis Island Foundation are currently expanding the museum into the **kitchen and laundry building**.

Ellis Island Oral History Project. *See* **Oral History Project**

Ellis Island Resolution of 1890. *See* **Congressional Resolution of 1890**

Employees' Quarters. Residential quarters were provided to certain employees of the **Public Health Service** on Island 2 and Island 3 throughout the years. For instance, in January 1924, the following quarters on **Island 2** were in use: the third floor of the **hospital administration building**, which housed nurses and maids, and the **surgeons' house**, where male attendants lived. On **Island 3**, the second floor of the staff house was used by married commissioned medical officers (surgeons), acting assistant surgeons, unmarried interns, and dietitians, and the third floor of the contagious disease **hospital administration building** housed all female nurses (including head nurses). Male nurses lived on the first floor of the laboratory building, and maids and male attendants lived on the second floor of the **laundry** building. Male attendants also had quarters in **contagious disease wards** 22, 28, 30, and 32.

With the exception of select medical personnel during the early years of the station, who were originally allotted the staff house and other quarters on Island 3, **Bureau of Immigration** employees were not usually allotted quarters because after-hours service was maintained by members of the **Night Division**, who came on duty late in the afternoon and continued working until relieved by the day staff the next morning.

Enemy Aliens (World War I). *See* **World War I**

Enemy Aliens (World War II). Immediately before and during World War II, more sophisticated procedures were set up to address the perceived threat of potential spies and saboteurs. The Justice Department had charge of the search and discovery of such persons. Its agencies—the Federal Bureau of Investigation (FBI), the U.S. Office of the Attorney General, and the **Immigration and Naturalization Service** (INS)—played a crucial role to ensure success.

On the outbreak of war between Germany and Poland in September 1939, President Franklin D. Roosevelt authorized FBI director J. Edgar Hoover to compile a list of alien enemies to be apprehended in the event of war. In addition, the government took two other significant steps to ensure national security, both of which were carried out in June 1940. On June 14, Congress approved President Roosevelt's Reorganization Plan No. V (54 Statute 230), transferring the INS to the Justice Department. On June 28, Congress passed the Alien Registration Act (Smith Act). Swiftly approved by the president, this law required all resident aliens and aliens applying for a visa to be registered and fingerprinted. Early in 1941, FBI agents were dispatched to Ellis Island to open a permanent office.

Shortly after the attack on Pearl Harbor, President Roosevelt signed proclamations identifying all citizens of Japan, Germany, and Italy residing in the United States as "alien enemies." This affected nearly a million aliens, who had already been registered and fingerprinted under the Alien Registration Act, which was itself a precautionary measure that had been implemented in the previous year. Overnight, 600,000 Italians, 300,000 Germans, and 90,000 Japanese—none of whom had become U.S. citizens—were transformed into alien enemies. Attorney General **Francis Biddle** authorized the FBI to increase surveillance of people of these nationalities and to apprehend those suspected to be potentially dangerous; custody was assigned to the INS and the army.

Ellis Island was a major detention facility for civilian enemy aliens; they were held in accordance with the regulations set up under the Geneva Convention of 1929. Within a few weeks of the Pearl Harbor bombing, 279 Japanese, 248 German, and 81 Italian enemy aliens were detained at Ellis Island.

Some months later, Hungarians, Romanians, and Bulgarians, whose home countries had been forced to join alliances with Nazi Germany, were likewise proclaimed enemy aliens. In February 1942, a further step was taken: all enemy aliens were required to register as such with the INS and were given alien enemy certificates. The Justice Department then set up alien enemy hearing boards in federal districts nationwide. One of the boards was set up at Ellis Island. Presided over by U.S. attorneys, the boards examined evidence collected by the FBI and heard the testimony of accused aliens and other persons. The Alien Enemy

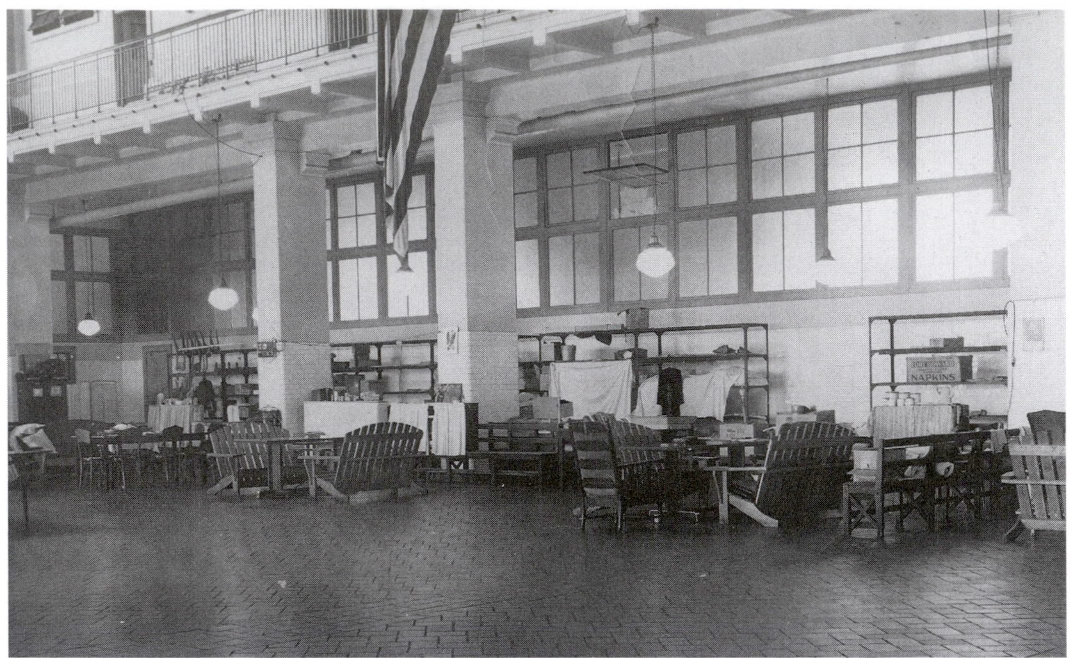

During World War II, German enemy aliens used the Registry Room as their daytime parlor. Courtesy of the INS and the Ellis Island Immigration Museum.

Control Unit in Washington, DC, then reviewed each case for a final decision. Many aliens were either released unconditionally or paroled; 50 percent were interned. Women and children internees were put in the permanent custody of the INS at immigration stations, including those located in Boston, Gloucester City (New Jersey), Detroit, Seattle, San Francisco, Los Angeles (San Pedro), Crystal City (Texas), and Fort Lincoln (North Dakota). Those interned in New York City were held at Ellis Island.

Interned men—considered potentially more dangerous—were placed in custody of the Department of War and sent to army-run internment camps in the interior of the United States. However, beginning in June 1943, the government was forced to send the male internees back to INS stations in order to make room for the thousands of enemy soldiers who had been captured by the British and American armed forces. Although not ideal for prolonged internment, Ellis Island did qualify under the provisions of the Geneva Convention. As many as 6,000 enemy aliens spent time at the station; in some cases, detainees preferred to remain on Ellis Island to be near their families and friends living in New York.

As it became clear that the great number of detainees would become a part of daily life, attention was drawn to the lack of space and amenities. As a corrective, the grand registry room was commandeered for use of German families and the balcony dormitory rooms were occupied by Japanese and Europeans. From time to time, other rooms in the Main Building were transformed into temporary habitations of the accused. Further, the addition of more playing fields and the introduction of a greater variety of games enhanced the recreation space. Another complaint that arose was that of food quality, detainees having expressed dissatisfaction with the food supplied by contractors. The government's solution was to set up a cafeteria and allow enemy aliens to work there for nominal pay. From then on, the typical offerings included German, Italian, central European, or Japanese dishes. Under the Geneva Convention, war prisoners, such as the internees at Ellis Island, were permitted to choose a spokesman from their own ranks. The spokesmen who emerged, often highly adept in upholding the rights of prisoners of war, sometimes gained significant concessions at Ellis Island. The **Nazis**, for example, were allowed to celebrate Adolf Hitler's birthday each year, and they were even permitted to receive expense money from the German government through the Swiss embassy.

Additionally, the federal government persuaded several Latin American republics to turn over thousands of Germans, Italians, and Japanese residing in their countries to U.S. custody. These persons were shipped to the United States and many were held at Ellis Island. In December 1945, for instance, more than 400 Germans from Latin America were being held at Ellis Island. While in the United States, many detainees lost their personal property and citizenship in such countries as Peru and Brazil. After the war, many were forbidden to return to Latin America and chose to be repatriated to Europe or Japan.

Noted enemy aliens detained at Ellis Island during World War II included Fritz Kuhn of the German-American Bund, refugee writer Jan Valtin (author of *Out of the Night*), and Italian opera singer **Ezio Pinza**. The latter two were later proved innocent. In November 1945, President Harry Truman signed a proclamation ordering the return of alien enemies to their home countries, The Alien Enemy Program at Ellis Island came to an end in 1947.

REFERENCES: *Annual Reports of the Immigration and Naturalization Service: 1943–1947*. Washington, DC: U.S. Department of Justice; Friedman, Max Paul. 2003. *Nazis and Good Neighbors: The United States Campaign against the Germans of Latin America in World War II*. Cambridge: Cambridge University Press; Moreno, Barry. 1997. *Ellis Island during the Second World War.* Ellis Island, NY: National Park Service, Statue of Liberty N.M.; Smith, Arthur Lee. 1965. *The Deutschtum of Nazi Germany and the United States*. The Hague: M. Nijhoff; Stephan, Alexander. 1995. *Im Visier des FBI: Deutsche Exilschriftsteller in den Akten amerikanischer Geheimdienste*. Stuttgart: Metzler.

Escobar, José Dias d' (b. Horta, Fayal, Azores Islands, Portugal, March 1878; d. 1950?). Interpreter (Portuguese and Spanish) (1918–1940). While employed as an interpreter at Ellis Island, José d'Escobar wrote many poems that he recited at the retirement parties for his fellow **Bureau of Immigration** officials. For this, he was called the poet of Ellis Island.

D'Escobar, one of the best known Portuguese journalists in the United States, served as editor of *America*, a Portuguese language journal that promoted U.S. goods for export to merchants in Portugal, the Brazil, and the Portuguese colonies, such as Mozambique and Angola. It was one of the many foreign language publications of the National Association of Manufacturers. With offices at the Portuguese News Service on Park Row, Escobar also translated documents into Spanish, French, and Italian, as well as Portuguese and English. Escobar held a law degree in Portugal.

Evans-Gordon, Sir William [Major Sir William Eden Evans-Gordon] (b. Great Britain, 1857; d. London, England, October 13, 1913). British politician and soldier. After serving as an army officer, Sir William Evans-Gordon entered public life through his interest in the rise of Jewish immigration into England between 1890 and 1914. Because a large percentage of the Jews were refugees and settled in the East End of London, Evans-Gordon organized public meetings in London; this led to the formation of the British Brothers League, a nativist group opposed to foreign immigration. On the strength of these activities, Evans-Gordon won election to Parliament as the Member for Stepny, London, in 1900. As an MP, he served as one of the five members of the Royal Commission on Alien Immigration. As a royal commissioner, he investigated emigration conditions in Russia by visiting many Jewish and peasant communities there, including Grodno. He also investigated the transportation of emigrants across Poland and Austria to the German ports and Jewish immigration to the United

States, especially New York City, the headquarters of the American apparel industry (which attracted many Jews). He examined the U.S. **Immigration Act of 1891** and the alien inspection at Ellis Island, and he corresponded with the **Immigration Restriction League**. Armed with the results of this study, he published his book, *The Alien Immigrant* (1903), and introduced Great Britain's first important immigration restriction bill to Parliament, which was adopted as the Aliens Act of 1905. He was also instrumental in the adoption of the more restrictive Aliens Act of 1914. In addition, Evans-Gordon favored the founding of a Jewish homeland in either Palestine or Uganda.

REFERENCE: Evans-Gordon, Major W. 1903. *The Alien Immigrant.* London: William Heinemann.

Exclusion. Exclusion was the result of an unfavorable assessment during **primary inspection** based on a variety of evidence, possibly medical, legal, or both. In effect it barred an immigrant from entering the country. Exclusion was sometimes called deportation, because aliens were sent away from the port of entry. However, this should not be confused with the legal process of **deportation**. The decision to exclude an alien was made only by the **boards of special inquiry**, the commissioners of immigration, the **Bureau of Immigration**, the **board of review**, and/or the cabinet secretary responsible to the president for immigration such as the secretaries of the treasury (1890–1903), of commerce and labor (1903–1913), of labor (1913–1940), and the attorney general (1940–1954). Immigrants and a dissenting member of a board of special inquiry were both permitted to lodge an appeal to the commissioner against exclusion order of a board. The regulations governing exclusion included the following:

> Whenever, either before or after receipt of a decision from the bureau or the department affirming an excluding decision, the local immigration officials learn of new evidence of such relevancy and materiality as in their opinion to require that, in justice to the alien or the United States, it be considered by the board, they may stay deportation and request the bureau's permission to reopen the case, at the same time briefly stating the general nature of the new evidence.

From 1892 through 1954, the number of immigrants excluded and the reasons for exclusion were the following.

1892–1900: 22,515 aliens were excluded, including 15,070 considered likely to become a public charge (LPC); 5,792 contract laborers; 1,309 mental or physical defectives; 89 for moral turpitude; and 65 criminals.

1901–1910: 108,211 aliens were excluded, including 63,311 LPC; 24,425 mental or physical defectives; 12,991 contract laborers; 1,681 criminals; 1,277 for moral turpitude; and 10 subversives or anarchists.

1911–1920: 178,109 were excluded, including 90,045 LPC; 42,129 mental or physical defectives; 15,417 contract laborers; 5,083 for illiteracy; 4,824 for moral turpitude; 4,353 criminals; 1,904 stowaways; and 27 subversives or anarchists.

1921–1930: 189,307 aliens were excluded, including 94,084 for illegal entry or as an undocumented aliens; 37,175 LPC; 11,044 mental or physical defectives; 8,447 stowaways; 8,202 for illiteracy; 6,274 contract laborers; 2,082 criminals; 1,281 for moral turpitude; and 9 subversives or anarchists.

1931–1940: 68,217 aliens were excluded, including 47,858 for illegal entry or as undocumented aliens; 12,519 LPC; 2,126 stowaways; 1,530 mental or physical defectives; 1,261 criminals; 1,235 contract laborers; 258 for illiteracy; 253 for moral turpitude; and 5 subversives or anarchists.

1941–1950: 30,263 aliens were excluded, including 22,441 for illegal entry or as undocumented aliens; 3,182 stowaways; 1,134 criminals; 1,072 LPC; 1,021 mental or physical defectives; 219 contract laborers; 108 for illiteracy; 80 for moral turpitude; and 60 subversives.

1951–1954: 13,678 aliens were excluded, including 10,530 for illegal entry or as undocumented aliens; 1,184 criminals; 661 mental or physical defectives; 244 stowaways; 197 subversives; 120 LPC; 117 for moral turpitude; 9 contract laborers; and 9 for illiteracy.

See also **Appeals**

REFERENCE: Bennett, Marion T. 1963. *American Immigration Policies*. Washington, DC: Public Affairs Press.

Executive Division. The Executive Division comprised employees assigned to the commissioner's personal office and was directly presided over by that high official himself. In 1912, a fairly typical year, the staff consisted of the following: commissioner, assistant commissioner, **superintendent**, chief clerk, attorney, law clerk, treasurer, civil engineer, storekeeper, **clerks**, stenographers, **matrons**, **messengers**, the time clerk, telegram clerks, and the telephone operator. In addition, any employee not specifically assigned to another division was automatically part of the Executive Division. In 1912, this included plumbers, carpenters, painters, tile setters, elevator operators, gardeners, and pilots. In other years, such personnel were assigned to other divisions. The Executive Division had varying numbers of employees in different years. In 1914 there were fifty-one employees, in 1921, seventy-eight employees, and in 1922, sixty. The superintendent had charge of daily operations over the divisional chiefs and all other employees, and he carried out all bureaucratic regulations and instructions of the commissioner to ensure as smooth an operation as possible. The Executive Division carried on the work of the commissioner and the executives under him. Thus, the Executive Division handled the station's correspondence, budget and accounts, personnel, maintenance and repairs, purchasing of supplies, appeal cases of detainees, applications to admit aliens under a bond, most legal and quasi-legal matters (except actual litigation, which was handled by U.S. attorneys), warrants to arrest illegal aliens, and public relations, including the press and, beginning in the 1920s, radio.

See also **Commissioners; Appendix 1: Ellis Island: Its Organization and Some of Its Work**

Eye Examinations. All aliens underwent a quick examination of the eyes during **line inspection**. A medical officer of the **Public Health Service**, known as the "eye man" everted immigrants' eyelids and carefully examined the eye for any sign of defective vision or of the presence of any disease. Doctors were especially looking for signs of **trachoma** and conjunctivitis, two highly contagious diseases. Three means of lifting up the eyelids were used at Ellis Island. One was simply to use the forefinger and thumb, another was to use a buttonhook, and a third alternative was to use a special kind of forceps. Doctors cleaned their hands and medical instruments in a disinfectant solution.

See also **Chalk Mark Code; Diseases and Hospitalization; Line Inspection**

Immigrants' eyes were scrutinized for any sign of trachoma, cataracts, or conjunctivitis. Courtesy of the Ellis Island Immigration Museum.

F

Famous Immigrants. Although she did nothing exceptional in her life, Ireland's **Annie Moore** (1892) became a legendary figure simply for having been the first immigrant to be inspected and passed through Ellis Island. Other well-known Irish immigrants to follow in her footsteps were actor Brian Donlevy (Waldo Bruce Donlevy, 1900); the two priests Edward Flanagan (1904) of Boys Town fame and Timothy Manning, cardinal archbishop of Los Angeles; New York City mayor William O'Dwyer (1910); dancer, singer, and movie actress Ruby Keeler (Canada); and motion picture actor George Brent (1922).

Hungary's **Bela Lugosi** entered the country as an illegal alien while serving on the crew of the SS *Graf Tisza Istvan.* He jumped ship at New Orleans in October 1920 and finally submitted to immigrant inspection at Ellis Island in March 1921.

Other famous Ellis Island immigrants include actor Alan Mowbray (who, though he was a second-class passenger, was temporarily taken to Ellis Island for questioning by a board of special inquiry); actor Donald Crisp (Scotland, 1906), union leaders Philip Murray (Scotland, 1911), James Reston (Scotland, 1922), and Douglas Fraser (1922), actors James Finlayson (Scotland, 1916) and Andy Clyde (Scotland, 1923), and singer Annie Ross (Scotland); actor E. E. Clive (Wales, 1912), football coach Knute Rockne (Knut Rokne; Norway, 1893), novelist Ole Rölvaag (Norway, 1896), actors Warner Oland (Werner Ohlund; Sweden, 1894) and Karl Dane (Rasmus Karl Gottlieb; Denmark, ca. 1916), pianist Victor Borge (Denmark, 1940). Bishop Francis Hodur (Poland, 1893), composer Irving Berlin (Israel Beilin; Russia, 1893), writer Mary Antin (Russia, 1894), Supreme Court associate justice Felix Frankfurter (Austria, 1894), singer and vaudeville star Al Jolson (Asa Yoelson; Lithuania, 1894), poet Kahlil Gibran (Syria, 1895), union activist Pauline Newman (Poland, 1901), New York City mayor Vincent R. Impellitteri (Italy, 1901), novelist Anzia Yezierska (Poland, 1901), gangster Frank Costello (Italy, 1902), actor Antonio Moreno (Spain, 1902), bodybuilder Charles Atlas (Angelo Siciliano; Italy, 1903), film director Frank Capra (Italy, 1903), actor Edward G. Robinson (Emmanuel Goldenberg; Romania, 1903), Father Edward J. Flanagan (Ireland, 1904), cosmetologist Max Factor (Russia, 1904), Admiral Hyman G. Rickover (Poland, 1904), New York City mayor Abraham Beame (England, 1906), impresario Sol Hurok (Russia, 1906), gangsters Charles "Lucky" Luciano (Salvatore Lucania; Italy, 1906) and Meyer Lansky (Russia, 1906), actress Claudette Colbert (Lily Chauchoin; France, 1906), novelist Henry Roth (Ukraine, 1906), singer **Arthur Tracy** (Russia, 1906), historian Samuel Noah Kramer (Russia, 1906), comedian **Bob Hope** (England, 1908), San Francisco mayor George Christopher (George Christopheles; Greece, 1910), union leader David Dubinsky (Poland, 1911), painter Alfred Levitt (Ukraine, 1911), writer **Louis Adamic** (Slovenia, 1913), composer/bandleader Xavier Cugat (Cuba, 1915), wrestler Mike Mazurki (Ukraine, 1915), Ettore Boiardi ("Chef Boyardee"; Italy 1915), writer/illustrator Ludwig Bemelmans (Austria, 1916), exiled politician **Cipriano Castro** (Venezuela, 1912), engineer/inventor Igor Sikorsky (Russia, 1919), actor Ricardo Cortez (Jacob Kranz; Austria, 1920), abstract painter Arshile Gorky (Vosdanig Adoian; Armenia, 1920; briefly detained for suspected mental defect and tuberculosis), spiritual writer Neville Goddard (Barbados, 1921), poet Claude McKay (Jamaica, 1921), industrialist John Kluge (Germany, 1922), science fiction novelist Isaac Asimov (Russia, 1923), writer George Papashvily (Georgia, 1923), religious philospher **Jiddu Krishnamurti** (India, 1926), novelist Ayn Rand (Russia 1926), singer Sidor Belarsky (Russia 1930), fashion designer Pauline Trigère (France, 1937), the Trapp Family Singers (Austria, 1938), painter Mark Rothko (Russia, 1913), and actor George Voskovec (Czechoslovakia, 1953).

REFERENCE: Moreno, Barry. 2003. *Ellis Island.* Charleston, SC: Arcadia.

Faris, James Edge (b. Charlottesburg, Virginia, 1889; d. Fort Manse, Virginia, January 20, 1952). Surgeon, U.S. **Public Health Service**. James Faris was working at Ellis Island during the **Black Tom** Wharf explosions of July 1916. His son, James Faris Jr., was born at Ellis Island on July 26, 1922. Faris was serving as the director of the quarantine hospital at Fort Manse, Virginia, at the time of his death.

Feebleminded. Category of mental deficiency certified as such by doctors of the **Public Health Service**. The term was adopted officially in 1907. Eugene H. Mullan, an Ellis Island physician, wrote that feebleminded immigrants were persons whose "common knowledge, retentiveness of memory, reasoning power, learning capacity and general reactions are severely or distinctly below normal. The feebleminded alien learns with difficulty, his attention may be at fault, he may exhibit peculiar and subnormal mental traits, all of which point to an awkward mentality, which is beyond hope of much improvement. His appearance, stigmata, and physical signs may confirm such diagnosis. It is further believed by the certifying officer that his mental condition will decidedly handicap him among his fellows in the struggle for existence."

See also **Mental Testing**

REFERENCE: Mullen, E. H. 1917. *Mental Examination of Immigrants.* Washington, DC: U.S. Public Health Service.

Ferries and Boats. Several ferries and boats were used at Ellis Island through the years. The ***Narragansett*** was used after the fire of 1897, while the *Samoset* was used for general purposes. The major vessels included the steamer *John G. Carlisle* in the 1890s through the early years of the twentieth century and the *Ellis Island,* which operated from 1904 through 1954. When the *Ellis Island* was being repaired or overhauled, it was replaced by an old steamboat called the *Minnehanock.* The *John G. Carlisle* was named in honor of the Kentucky-born secretary of the treasury (1893–1897) and was the primary staff boat until the **ferryboat *Ellis Island*** was added to the marine force.

For many years, the **Boarding Division** used a cutter called the *Immigrant*, which took inspectors and other officials out to ocean liners in the harbor.

Ferro, Edward (b. Sicily, Italy, 1894; d. 1968). Immigrant inspector and interpreter (1920–1957). Edward Ferro emigrated from Sicily and arrived at Ellis Island in 1906. He attended Columbia University and became a pharmacist. He served in the army during World War I and, following his return to New York, was hired by the Bureau of Immigration as an interpreter of Sicilian and Italian at Ellis Island. During the 1920s, he worked in the **Registry Division**. By 1926, he was an immigrant inspector.

Ferryboat *Ellis Island*. The ferryboat *Ellis Island* was used to transport employees of Ellis Island, immigrants released from Ellis Island, and supplies. The boat's Manhattan dock was at the **Barge Office**.

In the 1890s, and just after the turn of the century, the **Bureau of Immigration** used boats such as the *John G. Carlisle* and the *Samoset* to

Two barges docked at Ellis Island directly across from the general Hospital buildings.
The nurses' cottage is the small building on the left.
Courtesy of the Ellis Island Immigration Museum.

Ferryboat *Ellis Island*. Courtesy of the Ellis Island Immigration Museum.

transport staff to Ellis Island. However, Congress appropriated $110,000 for a government ferryboat and the contract for building its was awarded to Harland & Hollingsworth, a firm in Wilmington, Delaware. Specifications called for a structural steel framework and hull and a wooden superstructure. Ellis Island's supervising engineer, William M. Foist, ensured that these specifications were met during the phases of construction, from August 1903 through March 1904. When construction was completed and the boat found to be satisfactory, a ceremony was arranged for its christening. Mabel Sargent, daughter of Commissioner-General **Frank Sargent**, did the honors with a bottle of champagne in Wilmington, Delaware, on March 19, 1904, in the presence of Commissioner-General Sargent, Secretary of Commerce and Labor **George Cortelyou**, and Commissioner **William Williams**, U.S. senators, and other dignitaries. The ship arrived in New York harbor on May 8 and was put into service in June.

The vessel was 160 feet in length. It had two decks and two pilot houses at each end of the upper deck; there were rubber tile floors and the deck rails were made of white oak. The lower deck had accommodations for about 1,000 passengers and baggage. In addition, there was a special room for insane persons. The boat was reputedly the first to be built without accommodations for horses. The seats in the main cabin and upper cabins were made of slotted oak. The commissioner's cabin was similar but it also had an upholstered locker seat and swinging oak tables and chairs. The engines and quarters for the crew were down in the hull. The ship's exterior was painted black.

The ferry operated eighteen hours a day and made the trip from Ellis Island to the Battery in twenty minutes.

A tragic accident occurred on the ferry in September 1913, when Inspector **Charles Waldo** and another employee fell overboard and drowned.

Around 1928, the *Ellis Island* began to bring immigrants to Ellis Island for inspection and continued to do so until the station closed. Previously, barges and other small boats had transported them to the island, but with the severe drop in immigration after the adoption of the Immigration Act of 1924, the *Ellis Island* assumed the task.

In 1946, Herbert L. Booth of the Maintenance Section at Ellis Island wrote, "Statistics show that all employees who miss the boat in the morning and work at Ellis Island do so by a margin of 30 seconds. . . . If the schedule were changed by one minute apparently nobody would ever be late. There is no record of any employee missing the boat from Ellis Island going home."

By November 29, 1954, the last run of the Ellis Island, the boat had logged nearly one million miles after fifty years of service.

The *Ellis Island*, left in its berth at the island, was deteriorating by 1956 and her condition worsened in the 1960s. Considerable amounts of water accumulated in her bilges, and half-hearted attempts to pump it out by the General Services Administration and the National Park Service were ineffectual. The ferry sank during a storm on August 10–11, 1968. Attempts by the U.S. Navy to raise her in the late 1980s were unsuccessful and the boat's hull remains in its watery grave at Ellis Island.

The many captains of the ferryboat included John J. Halpin (ca. 1904–1917), Frank M. Dienst (1917–1938), Alfred Jacobson (1917–1942), Menzo J. Kellenbach (1938–1952), Herbert J. Nichols (1938–1950), James F. Ryan (1940s), Nils J. Anderson (1930s–1954), Raymond P. Ives (1942–1955), Arthur O'Toole (1943–1954), William J. McKinney (1951–1955), and Ronald Whelan (b. 1920; served as a deck hand, 1941–1943 and 1945–1953; captain, 1953–1954). Immigrant **Murad Khodja** was among the many deckhands who worked aboard the *Ellis Island*.

Ferry House (ferry building). All three ferry houses have occupied the same space. The original ferry house was part of the first immigrant station and was destroyed in the fire of

The old Ferry House, 1908. National Archives.

1897. The second ferry house was constructed in 1901 and stood during the heyday of immigration through Ellis Island. In 1933, it was somewhat dilapidated, and was damaged in a severe windstorm that year. It was pulled down in 1935 and replaced by a new structure that was

Ferry House and ferry dock, 1942. In the background, from left to right, are the insane asylum and the Hospital Outbuilding. Courtesy of the INS and the Ellis Island Immigration Museum.

designed in the Works Progress Administration modern style by architects Louis A. Simon and Chester Aldrich. Construction was completed in 1936. The center section of the building contained a waiting room for passengers that included high-backed wooden benches at each corner; officials of the U.S. Customs Service occupied the left wing. The right wing contained a lunchroom, kitchen, and lavatories. A lead-sheathed cupola or tower of two tiers surmounts the building. The sheathing has a geometrical design at the first tier, which is surmounted by eagles cast in lead, one at each of its four corners. Throughout the years, these ferry houses mainly served the riders of the **ferryboat *Ellis Island*.** The Boarding Division handled all primary inspections for cabin-class passengers aboard steamships. At each corner of the waiting room are high-backed oak benches.

The building was restored between 2003 and 2004 and opened to the public in 2005.

Ferry Service. Tourists were transported to Ellis Island aboard the ferryboats of the Circle Line Company from 1976 to 1984 and since September 1990, when the Ellis Island Immigration Museum opened to the general public. The company has likewise served visitors to the Statue of Liberty since 1953. The ferryboats include *Miss Ellis Island*, *Miss Liberty*, and *Miss Circle Line*. The founders of the company were Irish immigrants.

See also **Ferries and Boats**

Films and Documentaries. Notable dramatic films featuring Ellis Island include ***My Boy*** (1921), ***Ellis Island*** (1936), and ***Gateway*** (1938). The immigrant station played a small role in *Anything Can Happen* (1952), which starred José Ferrer. It was mentioned in a humorous vein in *With a Song in My Heart* (1952), the classic biography of singing legend Jane Froman.

Film shorts and documentaries include *Emigrants Landing at Ellis Island* (1903; 2 min.) and *Arrival of Emigrants at Ellis Island* (1906; 3 min.), both by Thomas Edison; *An Island Called Ellis* (1967), narrated by José Ferrer; *Ellis Island* (1979), narrated by Georges Perec (with Tom Bernardin); *Island of Hope, Island of Tears* (1990), narrated by Gene Hackman; *Ellis Island: Every Man's Monument* (1991), narrated by Telly Savalas; and *Ellis Island* (1998), produced by the History Channel.

Fire of 1897. The great fire of 1897 destroyed nearly all the buildings at Ellis Island and closed down the island for immigrant inspection for three and a half years. The fire was discovered in the Main Building of the **first immigrant station** at 12:38 a.m. on June 15 by a watchman. The fire was believed to have broken out in the furnace. There were 191 immigrants on the island—136 in detention dormitories and 55 in hospital, including several Hindus and a number of European Mormons. The Night Division consisted of a superintendent, six guards, two engineers, four firemen, a matron, an apothecary, a cook, three nurses, three railway watchmen caring for the baggage, and three restaurant workers.

The flames ate their way through the pine wood structure. Several other structures, including the cook house and hospitals, were also destroyed in the conflagration. All detained immigrants were evacuated safely and no lives were lost.

As the flames and smoke subsided, Colonel **Herman Stump**, the commissioner-general, came by train from Washington to inspect the damage. He expressed his support for Commissioner Joseph Senner, who showed him around. Immigrants arriving directly after the fire were diverted to the **Barge Office** for inspection.

Firpo, Luis [Luis Angel Firpo] (b. Jujuy, Argentina, 1894; d. Buenos Aires, Argentina, 1960). Boxer. The world famous prizefighter arrived in New York in July 1924 as a passenger aboard the SS *American Legion*, out of Buenos Aires; he was briefly detained at Ellis Island for passport irregularities. His secretary, Eduardo Carbone,

Remains of the Ellis Island immigrant station after the fire of June 1897. Courtesy of the Ellis Island Immigration Museum.

and trainer, Julio J. Bacquerisa, were also detained. Carbone and Bacquerisa were held overnight for an appearance before a board of special inquiry. Firpo, hailed as the "savage bull of the Pampas," was the undisputed father of Argentine boxing and fought against American champions Jack Dempsey and Jess Willard.

First Immigrant Station (January 1, 1892–June 15, 1897). Following its selection by Congress as the site of the first federally operated immigration station in April 1890, along with a $75,000 appropriation, plans were made to enlarge the island through landfill and to construct all necessary buildings, docks, and landing stages. Five of the old arsenal buildings on the island were retained for use in the new immigration station: (1) the powder magazine (shell house number 1), which was a brick building dating from 1854 through1868; (2) the keeper's cottage (pre-1886); (3) the barracks or shell house number 2 (1812); the naval magazine or shell house number 5 (ca. 1844); and a second naval magazine (1854–1886). The old gunners quarters was used as a temporary construction office. In late 1890, the powder magazine was slightly enlarged and became the insane hospital; the keeper's cottage became the surgeon's quarters; early in 1891, the barracks, which was newly sheathed with metal and slate, became the detention building; the naval magazine was converted to service as the restaurant building; and the second magazine, with thick stone and mortar walls, became the storage vault for immigration records. In 1891, two new buildings were constructed on the island, the **Main Building** and the boiler house. Designed by J. Bachmeyer, assistant to the superintendent of repairs for federal buildings in New York City, the Main Building was the primary structure at the first immigration station, and would later serve as a model for the Main Building of the **second immigrant station**. The firm of Sheridan and Byrne constructed the Main Building in 1891; the primary material for its framework and exterior was North Carolina pinewood, while the interior was composed of resinous pine and spruce. Plans also required that the wooden building's exterior be sheathed in galvanized iron, but it is unclear whether this was completely done. The building was

Federal architect J. Bachmeyer designed the original immigrant inspection building at Ellis Island. Courtesy of the Ellis Island Immigration Museum.

distinguished by high, slate-covered roofs and four decorative towers at each of the four corners. Also built in 1891 by Sheridan and Byrne, the boiler house was a single-story wooden building surmounted by a four-sided smokestack. The building, also made of North Carolina pine, was sheathed in galvanized iron. Its purpose at the station was to provide steam heating and electricity for lighting and to store water. The Main Building and the boiler house were basically completed by November 1891. The floor plan of the vast central area on the first floor of the Main Building was known as the baggage room, the primary purpose for which it was used. This level was also the entrance for the lines of arriving immigrants, who climbed stairs to the registry department above. The east end contained the customs inspectors' office, the customs baggage room, and a vault, while the west end contained a large room used by immigrants to exit the building and a smaller room and a private office. Upstairs on the second floor, the central area had four large waiting spaces for immigrants, the Registry Department, three detention rooms, the office of the superintendent of landing, the telegraph office, the money exchange, a lobby, and toilets. The east end of the second floor was given over to a physicians room, the treasurer's room, the commissioner's private office, the secretary's room, the stationery room, a vault, a conference room or general office, the contract labor department, the assistant commissioner's office, and three other offices for clerks and other staff. The third floor had only a gallery walkway for looking down at the central area of immigrants and registry staff below. The west end of the second floor contained the New York room, the local ticket office, the Information Bureau, the capacious western ticket office, and toilets. Other buildings for the station were built in 1892 and 1893. These were the tank and coal house, built of bricks, concrete, wood, and corrugated galvanized iron, and the hospital, which was primarily constructed of wood. The hospital quadrangle (completed in 1893) consisted of the kitchen and insane hospital; Hospital D (medical office); Hospital C (included a maternity ward, patients dining room, doctors and nurses rooms, and an accouchement, or delivery room); Hospital B (for surgeries, disinfecting, post mortems, bathhouse, laundry, and storage); and Building E (refectory). By 1897, the island had been enlarged by two and three-quarters acres to a total of fourteen acres; it also had two new constructions, an outdoor detention pen and a new pier. In addition, telegraph and telephone cables had been laid to Manhattan via Governor's Island. The station was completely destroyed in a fire just after midnight on June 15, 1897.

See also **Fire of 1897**

REFERENCE: Ehrenkrantz Group. 1978. *Historic Structures Report: Ellis Island.* New York: Ehrenkrantz Group.

Food Service and Menus. Food on Ellis Island was provided by concessionaires under government contract. Meals were provided to detainees free of cost, the bills being settled by the government. In a 1908 food concession contract, the following specifications for meals were described. All menus for breakfasts, lunches, and suppers were served in rotation on successive days.

Breakfasts: (*a*) Boiled rice, oatmeal, farina, cracked wheat, or cornmeal mush served with milk and sugar or syrup; (*b*) meat hash or baked beans and pork or fried fish; (*c*) fresh bread and butter; (*d*) a bowl of tea or coffee, with milk or sugar, as desired.

Dinners (i.e. lunches): (*a*) Vegetable, pea, bean, lentil, tomato, ox tail, or macaroni soup; (*b*) fresh bread and butter; (*c*) roast or fried beef, pork or mutton or corned beef, served with mashed potatoes or peeled boiled potatoes, and one other vegetable: lima beans, mashed turnips, carrots, peas, corn or succotash. Kosher meat or fish with potatoes, and one other vegetable, was also available. Fresh fish, baked or boiled, was served on days officially specified. (*d*) A bowl of tea and coffee, with milk and sugar, as desired.

Suppers: (*a*) Beef stew, mutton stew, baked pork and beans, or meat hash. (*b*) Stewed prunes, apple sauce, pie, bread pudding with raisins, rice pudding, or tapioca pudding; (*c*) fresh bread, spread with wholesome butter. (*d*) A bowl of tea or coffee, with milk and sugar, if desired. Salt, pepper and properly prepared mustard was on every table.

Children under the age of two were supplied, free of charge, "such milk and crackers as they may need." Foods for special diets were prepared separately in the kitchens of the general hospital and contagious disease wards.

See also **Privilege Holders**

REFERENCE: *Exclusive Privileges of Furnishing Food to Aliens and Maintaining a Restaurant at Ellis Island, New York Harbor. (Terms, Conditions, Limitations, and Specifications).* 1908. Washington, DC: Government Printing Office.

Forman, Philip (b. 1895; d. 1978). Chief of detention and deportation (1935–1950s). Philip Forman had worked as a inspector in the

Women and children eat in the detainees' dining room.
Courtesy of the Ellis Island Immigration Museum.

Deporting Division for some time when temporarily suspended from duty following the widely publicized escape from Ellis Island of the imposter Prince Michael Romanoff in 1932. But he was quickly forgiven and was eventually appointed chief of his division. From World War II until Ellis Island closed, his title was chief of detention, deportation, and parole. He ended his career as a federal judge. Forman's father, Emil Forman, also had a long career at the station. He was an interpreter of Croatian, Bohemian (Czech), Slovenian, German, and Hungarian. Emil Forman was assigned to the **Registry Division** for some thirty years (1904–1934).

Fort Gibson. Fortress at Ellis Island. The fortification took the shape of a horseshoe and was capable of holding fourteen heavy guns and a bomb battery of four guns. In 1808, construction was begun under the supervision of Colonel Jonathan Williams and was completed by March 1812, just in time for America's second war with Great Britain. The new fort also had a gunpowder magazine and was manned by a garrison of 182 artillerymen who lived in the barracks; officers lived in adjoining but separate quarters. Although well set up, the only enemy the fort encountered were captured British soldiers who were occasionally brought there for temporary confinement. In the fall of 1814, the battery was named Fort Gibson to honor the memory of Colonel James Gibson, who had just been killed in Canada by British troops during the Battle of Fort Erie. After the war, its most notable service was for use as an army recruiting depot. From 1835 through 1841, the navy took over the island, largely using it as a supply depot for gunpowder for American warships. In 1841, the army regained jurisdiction of the island, but permitted the navy to control the magazine to store its munitions. But the fort had already been demoted to battery status, following the naming of an army post in Oklahoma Territory as Fort Gibson in 1832. In 1842, the army repaired the battery and also constructed a hotshot furnace; within a year, Battery Gibson was once again "armed and equipped" for military duty. Over the years, both army and navy continued to share the island. During the Civil War, the navy built more gunpowder magazines on the island and the army installed ten heavy new guns and two howitzers to help guard the approaches to New York. In 1867 or 1868, the army, uneasy with the large number of naval munitions, withdrew its small garrison from the island, leaving it completely to the navy, which then increased its stock of munitions held there. In 1868, a reporter from the New York *Sun*, warning of the danger to New York City and the surrounding area, visited the facility and stated that there were 3,000 barrels of black powder and gun shells. There was also a magazine in Battery Gibson and six other large magazine buildings. In 1876, Augustus Hardenburgh, a congressman from New Jersey, introduced a bill that compelled the navy to remove all munitions from Ellis Island, expressing a concern for the safety of Jersey City, Hoboken, and other populated areas. This failed. It was not until the Johnstown flood disaster in 1889 that New Jersey officials began to look seriously at the naval magazine as a potential threat to their communities. This resulted in the introduction of a joint resolution of congress promoted by Senator John McPherson of New Jersey calling for the removal of the navy's munitions arsenal from Ellis Island. Coincidentally, the legislators and high officials in the Harrison administration were in search of a site for the nation's first federally operated immigration station to replace New York's Castle Garden. Consensus held that Ellis Island would be the best choice, so the joint resolution was amended with an appropriation of $75,000 to enable the secretary of the treasury to make the island suitable for immigration purposes. This was approved by both houses of Congress and signed into law by President Benjamin Harrison on April 11, 1890. Within a few weeks the navy evacuated the site and removed all munitions to Fort Wadsworth on Staten Island; the

Treasury Department formally assumed control of the island on May 24 but did not dismantle the battery. This was proven in 1992 when archaeologists discovered a section of its remains under the soil. Located in the northeast part of Ellis Island near the Main Building, it is now preserved as part of America's military history.

See also **Gibson, James**

Foxlee, Ludmila K. [Ludmila Kucharova Foxlee] (b. August 13, 1885, Bohemia, Austria-Hungary; d. 1971, New Jersey). Social worker at Ellis Island who served the Young Women's Christian Association (YWCA) (October 1920–1933) and then the National Institute of Immigrant Welfare (December 1933–1937). Foxlee made her mark at Ellis Island by assisting thousands of Central European men and women of various Christian faiths—Roman Catholic, Eastern Orthodox, and Protestant. From 1920 to 1937, she kept meticulous records and handled an extraordinary number of cases. In the 1920s, Foxlee attracted the attention of the press by posing with newly arrived immigrants in colorful peasant clothes and then immediately afterward in stylish American dress—all to underline the popular desire among immigrant women and children to transform themselves as quickly as possible from "greenhorn" to American. In 1926, Foxlee's efforts were rewarded when the government of Czechoslovakia conferred on her the Order of the White Lion. She spoke Czech, Russian, Polish, Serbian, Croatian, and German.

Foxlee was herself an Ellis Island immigrant, having passed through the station with her family in 1894. Her father was a Czech and her mother an Austrian. In 1907, she married English immigrant John Foxlee who was a designer and, in 1918, a farmer in New Jersey. In 1934, Foxlee opened a sideline antiques business in Madison, New Jersey. This eventually took up more of her time and lead to her resignation from welfare work in 1937. In 1936, she wrote a twelve-page article called "A Social Worker's Ellis Island," in which she disclosed her personal experiences with immigrants who had got themselves into difficulties and were doomed to deportation. In 1968, she completed her memoir, *How They Came: The Drama of Ellis Island.* The following is an excerpt from her memoir:

YWCA social worker Ludmila Foxlee poses in peasant garb with three children in the 1920s. Courtesy of the Ellis Island Immigration Museum.

> An intelligent Slovak woman related to us her experience while traveling third-class from Prague, Czechoslovakia, to Rotterdam, The Netherlands, in 1920. She said:
>
> Three days and three nights were spent riding in local trains from Prague to Rotterdam. At Oldenzaal, four stations distant from Rotterdam, all our baggage was taken from without an explanation why this was done. We were marched to the barracks near the railway station and there were sent into compartments with walls of canvas and told to undress. Our dresses were put on hangars and sent to the disinfection plant. We walked to another room wrapped in blankets. These were taken from us, so that we all stood there naked. A woman with a bucket and a large brush such as is used in whitewashing, brushed our bodies from neck to feet with a strong carbolic disinfectant. There

were about forty of us. It occurred to no one to ask how we felt about having to expose our bodies to the eyes of thirty-nine women and girls of all ages.

After this, we were sent under a hot shower bath and given soap and a towel to wash our bodies. Then a woman with a bucket of crude oil came to apply the oil to our heads. We were then, at eleven p.m., sent to bed and told that we could wash our heads in the morning. We found the barracks to be a kind of shed with beds along one side of it and tables along the other. Each woman was assigned a bed with a number. The rough mattress and the two dirty blankets on the bed were infested with vermin that promptly found its way to our heads. The baggage was returned to us broken, with handles torn off, with broken locks, and our clothes creased in the steaming, to which they were subjected.

We lived in these barracks three days. As long as there were any vermin on our heads, we could not depart. Breakfast consisted of a small quantity of black coffee and a piece of bread; the midday meal was a stew with white bread. The stew appeared inedible to me. In the evening, we were given salt herrings, marmalade, bread and tea. After three days, we were transported to a hotel in Rotterdam, where they served stew all the time, but at least the tables were covered with cloths and the service was decent. Here, we waited four days during which doctors examined our eyes and scalps. A charge of one dollar was made for the cleaning of the scalp, and those who paid and submitted to the cleaning were passed as ready to embark; their card was stamped "Head Cleaned." Those who could not pass the physical test or had wrong papers were led away. No attention was paid to their lamentations.

We embarked at seven p.m., after our baggage was disinfected again. In the steerage of the steamship, I found myself in a large cabin that had two rows of bunks on each side, one above the other. About five persons could sleep on each tier, but there no division between the beds, and one went in head first. We had to stow our baggage under the bunks, and when the sea was rough our baggage and shoes flew back and forth across the floor. There was a rough mattress, and the two blankets were infected with vermin; there were no pillows. Some of the women in our cabin possessed no understanding of cleanliness; they made a privy of the cabin.

We ate at tables that stood under a ceiling that was the floor of the deck above us. That floor was made of boards that did not fit together tightly and permitted dirt to fall through the crevices onto our tables. Those who ate on the deck below us had the same difficulty and dirt carried on shoes fell into their food. Any complaint made was answered by the seamen who served us, who said that we should have sailed in the second class if we wanted better treatment, that human being did not travel in the steerage; only animals did.

There were only four washstands in the whole steerage and these were accessible only in the forenoon. The doctors avoided the steerage and only when a woman became seriously ill was she carried to the second class to be examined by the doctor.

Breakfast consisted of coffee, bread, cheese, marmalade, butter, but if one did not hasten to take his share of the food on the table, aggressive individuals snatched up everything and nothing left for backward ones. Stew was served daily for luncheon, also an evil smelling fish aspic and peas that were not edible; and coffee. For supper, there were beans, fish conserve and hash. Dessert was not served. On Sundays, the only addition to the menu was four hard-tack biscuits that were thrown on each bed.

See also **Immigrant Aid Societies; Missionaries; YWCA**

REFERENCE: Foxlee, Ludmila K. 1968. *How They Came: The Drama of Ellis Island*. Ellis Island, NY: Statue of Liberty and Ellis Island Library.

Fry, Alfred Brooks (b. New York, May 3, 1860; d. Coronado, California, 1933). Marine engineer and naval officer; superintendent of federal buildings, New York City; and consulting engineer, Ellis Island (1895–1915). After a seven-year apprenticeship in drafting and engineering jobs at sea, Alfred Fry entered federal service as an assistant engineer in the Department of the Treasury in 1886, and rose to the highest levels throughout his long career, ending with his retirement. From 1900 through 1917, he served as superintendent of federal buildings in New York and was also an expert on canal and sewage engineering. During the Spanish American War, he served as an acting chief engineer with the navy and attained the rank of lieutenant commander; he served as a marine engineer with the navy during World War I; he retired with the rank of rear admiral. In the early 1920s, he was a consulting engineer in the Canal Zone, Panama. His wife, the former Emma Sheridan, was a well-known actress of the American stage during the late Victorian period.

See also **Barge Office**

G

Gallico, Paul (b. New York, July 26, 1897; d. Monaco, July 15, 1976). Novelist. In an amusing passage in his novel *Mrs. 'Arris Goes to New York* (1960), Paul Gallico has his fictional characters discuss Ellis Island.

> Mr. Bayswater, who is a chauffeur and an old friend of Mrs. Harris, put down a copy of the Rolls-Royce monthly bulletin . . . and snorted,
>
> ". . . Wait until you come up against the United States Immigration Inspectors—they'll put you through it. I'll never forget the first time I came over. It was after the war. They had me sweating. You never head of Ellis Island? It's a kind of gaol where they can pop you if they don't like the look of your face. Wait till you sit down with those lads. If there's so much of a bit of a blur on you passport or a comma misplaced, you're for it."
>
> [Mrs. Harris] said to Mrs. Tidder, "Garn, I don't believe it. It's just people talking. It's a free country, ain't it?"
>
> "Not when you're trying to get into it," Mr. Bayswater observed. "Proper Spanish Inquisition, that's what it is. How much have you got? Who are you with? Where are you going? For how long? Have you ever committed a crime? Are you a Communist? If not, then what are you? Why? Haven't you got a home in England—what are coming over here for? Then they start in over your papers. Heaven 'elp if there's anything wrong with them. You can cool your heels behind bars on their ruddy island until someone comes and fetches you out." (Gallico, pp. 141–142)

Gallico's other novels include *Mrs. 'Arris Goes to Paris* (1958), *Mrs. 'Arris Goes to Parliament* (1965), *The Snow Goose* (1941), and *The Poseidon Adventure* (1969).

See also **Literature and Reminiscences**

REFERENCES: Gallico, Paul. 1960. *Mrs. 'Arris Goes to New York.* New York: Doubleday; Wepman, Dennis. 2002. *Immigration: From the Founding of Virginia to the Closing of Ellis Island.* New York: Facts on File.

Galvin, Thomas P. (b. 1895; d. January 29, 1978). Immigrant inspector (1932–1948); Law Division (1932–1934); Special Inquiry Division (1934–1948). Thomas P. Galvin joined the **Bureau of Immigration** as an immigrant inspector in Detroit, where he served on the Ambassador Bridge between the United States and Canada. At his own request, he was transferred to Ellis Island, New York, where he was assigned to the **Law Division**. There he investigated immigrants' status and conducted hearings for aliens under warrant of arrest, occasionally resulting in actual deportations. After two years in the Law Division, he was transferred to the **Special Inquiry Division**. There he served on various boards of special inquiry, and often as chairman. At Ellis Island, he met Alice Mahedy, a stenographer and secretary to Edward Barnes, chief of the Law Division. She and Galvin were married in 1936. In 1948, the Galvins moved to Tampa, Florida, where Galvin became chief inspector of arrivals and departures. He retired from this position in 1960. His widow had fond memories of Ellis Island and said, "The happiest days of my life were spent on Ellis Island. They had radio shows and Christmas parties that were wonderful." (Bolino, pp. 100–101)

REFERENCE: Bolino, August C. 1990. *The Ellis Island Source Book.* 2d ed. Washington, DC: Kensington Historical Press.

Gatemen. The gatemen maintained order among the thousands of immigrants arriving each day. They worked at the **Barge Office**, controlling access through the gate to the **ferryboat *Ellis Island***; at the Ellis Island dock, where barges arrived with thousands of immigrants; at the ferry house, where immigrants were discharged and visitors received; and they also kept order inside the overcrowded **Main Building**. They were called groupers because they were responsible for keeping groups of immigrant passengers from steamships from mixing with passengers from another ship. They worked in the **Watchmen's and Gatemen's Division** but could be assigned to other divisions as needed.

Gateway (Twentieth Century Fox, 1938). Released in time to amuse summer audiences in August 1938, this unusual feature film starred Don Ameche in the role of a war correspondent returning home aboard a transatlantic steamship. Although quite unconvincing, the story line was amusing and gave viewers a sense of the goings on at Ellis Island. When the drama starts, the ship is nearing the end of its voyage. At this point, Ameche encounters an enchanting Irish immigrant girl from third class, and starts what seems a harmless shipboard flirtation. The dashing American reporter then invites the immigrants to join him at a party in the first-class section—and now the trouble begins, for when this is found out it results in a shipboard row. At dockside, this ridiculous problem continues to escalate, and finally veteran actor Harry Carey, portraying the commissioner of immigration, orders the straying Irish lass, and even the whole group of eccentric, mostly wealthy foreign tourists to be sent to Ellis Island for investigation. The romantically smitten Ameche gallantly throws away his U.S. passport and joins the detainees, who are portrayed

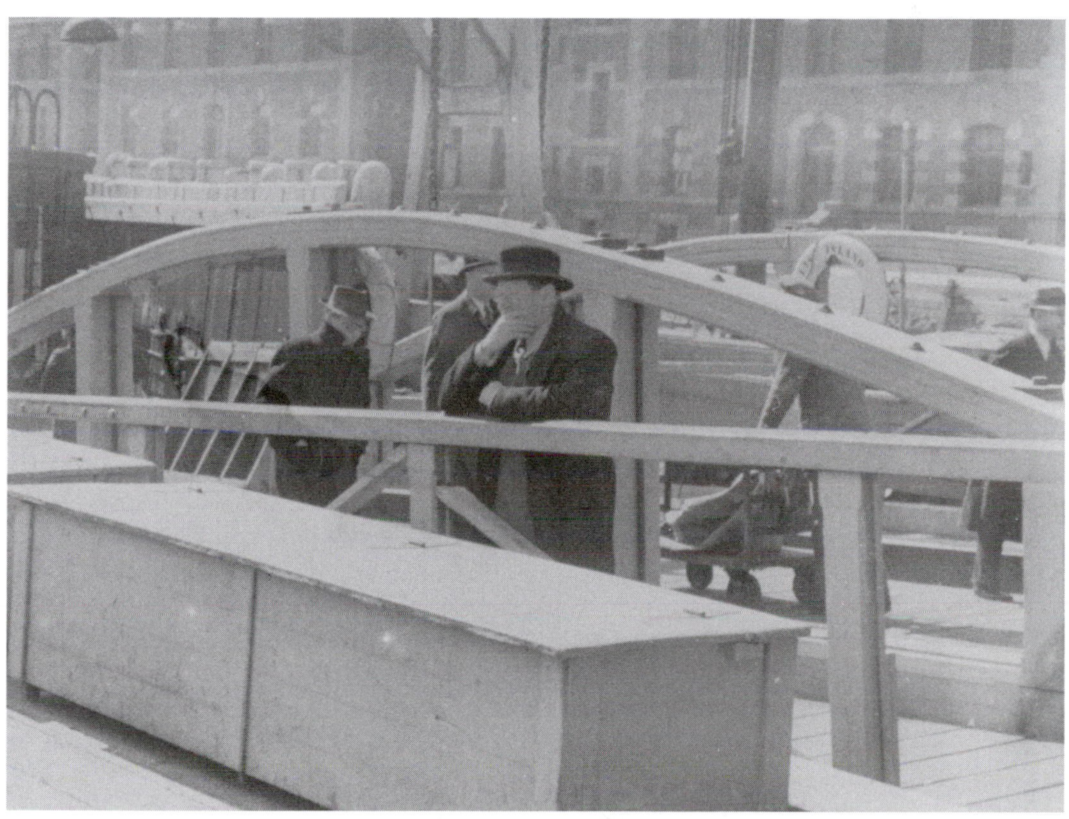

Film actor Gregory Ratoff directed the scenes of the motion picture *Gateway* that were shot at Ellis Island, 1938. In the film, Ratoff played the role of Prince Michael Boris Alexis, a Russian imposter. Courtesy of the Ellis Island Immigration Museum.

by some of Hollywood's best character actors, including Binnie Barnes (as a worldly upper-class English divorcee), Gregory Ratoff (as a phony and comic Russian prince, based on famous imposter "Prince" Michael Romanoff), John Carradine (as a ranting revolutionary), E. E. Clive, and even the famous ventriloquist's dummy, Charlie McCarthy (without Edgar Bergen). Actress Arleen Whelan, a relative newcomer to Hollywood, portrays the Irish girl. There are good day and night distance shots of the Main Building on Ellis Island; some filming was also done on the island itself. The immigration building's interior rooms, including the Registry Room, were re-created in a Hollywood set. The climax of the film featured a dramatic escape at nightfall orchestrated by the fanatical leader of the refugees, played melodramatically by John Carradine. There is also a terrible fire in Battery Park that lights up the dark sky unforgettably. Lamar Trotti wrote the final screenplay based on an original story ("Ellis Island") that had been submitted to Twentieth Century Fox executives by immigrant writer Walter Reisch. The film's producer was Darryl F. Zanuck. Gregory Ratoff directed the scenes filmed on Ellis Island. Although it was more expensive to make than its 1936 predecessor, ***Ellis Island***, its story line is far less realistic.

See also **Films and Documentaries**

Geddes, Lord [Rt. Hon. Sir Auckland Campbell Geddes, First Baron Geddes] (b. Scotland, June 27, 1879, Great Britain; d. 1954). British ambassador to the United States (1920–1924); cabinet minister, surgeon, soldier, and industrialist. Sir Auckland Geddes was the British ambassador to the United States whose personal tour of inspection at Ellis Island in 1922 resulted in a controversial report that he composed for the foreign secretary, Lord Curzon, which contributed to a strain in relations between Great Britain and the United States. Geddes's report, *Despatch from His Majesty's Ambassador at Washington Reporting on Conditions at Ellis Island Immigration Station*, which was later issued as a parliamentary paper (August 1923), dealt with the manner in which the U.S. government handled immigrants at its chief station; quite naturally, the author was especially interested in the treatment there of His Majesty's subjects. Geddes came to Ellis Island early in December 1922 at the invitation of the secretary of labor, James J. Davis, who personally conducted him through the facility. Commissioner **Robert Tod** welcomed both gentlemen and was also present during the tour. Although Geddes warmly praised Commissioner Tod in his report, he roundly criticized the station for its low standard of cleanliness and the "diabolic" and time-consuming method of appeal in cases of exclusion. He also noted the locked doors, the "wire cages," the dirt in the corners, unsavory smells, and the "make-shift facilities for medical examination." The visit satisfied him that immigrants could not be separated by nationality with any degree of efficiency.

Lord Geddes, a Scotsman, began his career as a professor of anatomy and taught at Edinburgh University, the Royal College of Surgeons (Dublin), and McGill University (Canada). He served as a Unionist Member of Parliament from 1917 until 1920. His abilities were quickly recognized and he was brought into the government as minister of reconstruction in 1919 and president of the board of trade from 1919 until 1920. From 1920 through 1924, he was the British ambassador to the United States. Geddes was knighted by King George V in 1917 and was created knight grand commander of the Order of St. Michael and St. George for his diplomatic services to the Crown in 1922. In 1942, King George VI raised him to the peerage as Baron Geddes.

REFERENCE: Geddes, Sir A. 1923. *Despatch from His Majesty's Ambassador at Washington Reporting on Conditions at Ellis Island Immigration Station*. London: Parliamentary Paper (Foreign Office).

General Hospital Building. Also known as Hospital 1 and the main hospital building, this

General Hospital complex. Courtesy of the Ellis Island Immigration Museum.

structure was designed in the beaux arts style by the architects **William A. Boring** and **Edward L. Tilton** in 1897 and 1899. It was erected at a cost of $150,000 by contractor David A. Garber of New York City. It was completed in April 1901, although repairs delayed its opening. The building is composed of a three-and-a-half-story central pavilion and two and a half wings. The entire structure is made of masonry on a frame of steel. The foundation is of rusticated granite and the upper levels are of red brick laid in Flemish bond. The dormer windows have brick and limestone walls and are trimmed in copper. Chimneys and copper-trimmed skylights punctuate the roof. Two-story iron and steel porches are attached to the southern ends of the wings. The building had two wards with enclosed porches for men, a dining room, a surgeons' dining room, a kitchen, dispensary, study, and living quarters.

General Services Administration. The General Services Administration (GSA), founded in 1949, is the federal agency whose primary responsibility is to care for unused government property, especially real estate. When Ellis Island was officially abandoned "as excess to the needs of the Immigration and Naturalization Service" on March 15, 1955, the GSA assumed control of the station after having ascertained that no other branch of the federal government wished to make use of it. Over the next eighteen months the agency made it available to a state or local governmental agency or to a nonprofit organization for public use. Receiving no satisfactory replies, the GSA announced that Ellis Island was for sale to the general public. This was in September 1956. When the offer elicited denunciations for attempting to sell a national landmark, the GSA quickly retreated. After failing to attract nonprofit or governmental interest in the island, the agency again tried to sell it (1958–1959). After the three bids were rejected, the agency turned to the U.S. Department of Health, Education, and Welfare for help in attracting potential nonprofit proprietors. Offers came from Ellis Island for Higher Education to set up a coeducational liberal arts college for 1,000 resident students; the Training School at Vineland, New Jersey, to established a medical center for diagnosis of mentally retarded children and for training medical professionals; the

International University Foundation, which proposed to create a American Immigration Library and Museum, spanning the years from 1890 through 1950; and Theodore Granik, who wanted to use Ellis Island for the Golden Age Center, providing housing, health, and education for the elderly. After a careful study of these proposals, HEW rejected them.

Commercial offers came. For instance, the Damon, Doudt Corporation offered to buy Ellis Island for $2.1 million in cash in order to begin construction of a city of the future designed by **Frank Lloyd Wright**; the Sol G. Atlas Realty Investment Company offered over $1 million to build a resort hotel, a marina and boathouse, a middle-income housing project, cultural facilities, a museum of immigration, and recreational facilities. Both British and Greek investors expressed interest in residential and commercial development of the island.

Other groups and individuals made a variety of suggestions. These included converting the island into a marine center and nautical high school, establishing a veterans convalescent home and rest camp, opening a treatment center for narcotics addicts, setting up a Bible center, creating a Boys Island, and establishing an International Cathedral for Peace Prayers.

Soon Senator Edward S. Muskie led the way for Ellis Island to be declared a national monument in the **National Park Service** (NPS). After investigating Ellis Island with other legislators, hosting public meetings, and arranging for the NPS to study the possibilities of adding the landmark to the Park Service, Muskie persuaded President Lyndon Johnson to declare it a national monument on May 11, 1965.

Gibran, Kahlil (b. Bishara, Lebanon, January 6, 1883; d. New York, April 10, 1931). Poet and painter. Kahlil Gibran received primary inspection at Ellis Island on June 25, 1895, with his mother, Kamila Gibran, and siblings. They were detained overnight before proceeding to Boston. Gibran became famous as a Christian mystic poet and writer. His most celebrated work is *The Prophet*, which has sold 10 million copies since its publication in 1923. He died at St. Vincent's Hospital in Manhattan.

Gibson, James (b. 1781, Delaware; d. 1814, Canada). Soldier. Governor Daniel D. Tompkins of New York named the battery on Ellis Island "Fort Gibson" in honor of this soldier late in 1814, just after James Gibson was killed in one of the final battles fought in the War of 1812. Gibson was graduated from West Point in 1808 and was posted as a lieutenant with the U.S. Light Artillery, an elite regiment. When the War of 1812 broke out, he was a captain. His first important combat experience was in the Battle of Queenstown Heights, in which he and other American soldiers were captured by the British. His release came as part of an agreement in which the two sides exchanged prisoners. Gibson's bravery and competence were swiftly recognized by his superiors, and, in July 1813, he was appointed inspector general of the army; in the following year, he was promoted to the rank of colonel and put in command of the 4th Rifle Regiment. In August, the regiment was assigned to the U.S. Army Left Division, which was under the command of General Porter, who was positioning his forces for an invasion and conquest of Canada. Although Colonel Gibson successfully stormed the first of the British batteries in a surprise assault, the enemy rallied in time to put a gallant defense of the second battery—an engagement that cost Gibson his life. In his report on Colonel Gibson's death, General Porter eulogized the hero in these words: "Colonel Gibson fully sustained the high military reputation which he had before so justly acquired." In 1829, a portrait of the Gibson painted by Jacob Eicholtz (after a miniature in the possession of his widow) was unveiled in the Delaware Legislative Hall, where it remains to this day.

See also **Fort Gibson**

Gloucester City Immigrant Station (New Jersey). Located just south of Ellis Island, this immigrant inspection station of the U.S. **Bureau of Immigration** was the headquarters of District 6 of the Bureau, and was responsible for southern New Jersey and eastern Pennsylvania, including the city of Philadelphia. In 1924, there were twenty-six employees, headed by a commissioner. Other employees were an assistant commissioner, seven immigrant inspectors, two clerks, an interpreter, an engineer, a stationary fireman, five guards, three laborers, a matron, and a charwoman. During World War II, Gloucester City was a leading enemy alien internment camp of the **Immigration and Naturalization Service**.

Goldman, Emma (b. Kaunas, Lithuania [Russia], June 27, 1869; d. Toronto, Canada, May 14, 1940). Anarchist. A prominent anarchist and feminist, Emma Goldman came to the United States as a girl of sixteen in 1885, passing through **Castle Garden**. She settled in Rochester, New York. During the **red scare**, she and over 200 other suspected radicals, including **Alexander Berkman**, were arrested and brought to Ellis Island and then summarily deported to Russia aboard the SS *Buford*, which only took them as far as Finland. She described her experiences of being held incommunicado at Ellis Island in a chapter of her autobiography, *Living My Life*. In February 1934, the veteran anarchist returned to the United States to give a series of lectures around the country. During her visit to New York she recalled her treatment at Ellis Island.

"I enjoyed writing pamphlets in those days but I was afraid my writings would be taken from me that I waited until everyone had gone to bed at Ellis Island, and when they were sleeping, I got up, turned on the light and wrote. On the night we were taken away I was writing a pamphlet on deportation at 2.00 a.m. I did not dream that we should be going for several days. In fact, I had spoken with Superintendent Baker and others, telling them we should like to know a day or two before our deportations in order that we might send for our clothes and personal belongings. You see—many of us had been jerked up wherever we were found, and not permitted to communicate in any manner with our relatives until after we reached the Island. . . . As I said, I was writing the pamphlet when a rap sounded on my door. It was once of the coldest nights of the year. I hurriedly hid the manuscript I was working upon and went to the door. An official said: "Get your things together—you're being taken to the deportation boat!"

Those who were sleeping were pulled from their beds. We were marched between two long lines of soldiers with loaded guns to the cutter. We had to stand in the freezing cold. When two hours had elapsed we reached the "Buford." Two hours later we were heading out to sea, and none of us knew where we were being taken."(Corsi, pp. 198–199)

REFERENCE: Corsi, Edward. 1935. *In the Shadow of Liberty*. New York: Macmillan.

Graffiti. Over the years, various messages were scribbled on walls, columns, partitions, and doors by detained aliens. Only some of these have been preserved. Many of the specimens were discovered when the buildings at Ellis Island were studied for variations in architectural design in the late 1970s and 1980s. The graffiti were inscribed between 1901 and 1954. The older graffiti are located on the second and third floors in the west wing of the **Main Building**; later graffiti, primarily from the period 1950 through 1954, appear on the first, second, and third floors of the **Baggage and Dormitory building**. In addition to the various inscriptions, there are many cartoon-like drawings; images appearing in these drawings include an immigration official, faces and bodies, a flower, a swastika, a Cuban flag, and a steamship. The graffiti are quite diverse and appear in several languages, including Italian, French, Finnish, Greek, Chinese, Korean, Spanish, German, Serbo-Croatian, and English. The following foreign countries (presumably the native lands of the writers) are also written out: Italy, Mexico, Peru, Cuba, Holland, Israel, and Finland. Cities listed included Havana and Lima. There are also numerous personal names, including G. Scuka, Salvatore Giglio, Osvaldo Barrios (Cuban), Oscar Villar (Cuban), Pauli Jauhiainen (Finnish), Kauko Kinnunen (Finnish), "Juan de L . . . " "George . . . ," "Daniel." Messages inscribed include "What a Life," "Viva Mussolini," "Adolf Hitler," "Jesus Seminario Lima Peru," "Pinta Sis Haifa, Israel," "La Libertad no . . . ," "Viva Cuba," and "Un jour il n'existera plus ce Forcat? Il y aura un changement! Qui ne tardera pas." The graffiti discovered in the Main Building was preserved in the mid-1980s by National Park Service conservator Christy Cunningham.

REFERENCE: Beyer, Blinder, Belle/Anderson, Notter, Finegold. 1988. *Historic Structure Report: The Main Building.* Vol. 1. Washington, DC: U.S. Government Printing Office.

Graham, Stephen (b. Edinburgh, Scotland, March 16, 1884; d. London, England, March 15, 1975). Scottish travel writer. In 1913, Stephen Graham got a taste of an emigrant's life by traveling in the steerage of a White Star Line vessel from Liverpool to New York and enduring immigrant inspection at Ellis Island. These experiences are described in his book, *With Poor Immigrants to America* (1914). The following is an excerpt:

"The day of the emigrant's arrival in New York was the nearest earthly likeness to the final Day of Judgement, when we have to prove our fitness to enter Heaven. . . . It was the hardest day since leaving Europe and home. From 5 a.m., when we had breakfast, to three in the afternoon, when we landed at the Battery, we were driven in herds from one place to another, ranged into single files, passed in review before doctors, pocked in the eyes by the eye-inspectors, cross-questioned by the pocket-inspectors, vice detectives, and blue-book compilers.

Nobody had slept the night before. Those who appreciated America for the first time stood on the open deck and stared at the lights of Long Island. Others packed their trunks. Lovers took long adieus and promised to write one another letters. There was a hum of talking in the cabins, a continual pattering of feet in the gangways, a splashing of water in the lavatories where cleanly emigrants were trying to wash their whole bodies at hand basins. At last the bell rang for breakfast; we made that meal before dawn. When it was finished we all went up on the forward deck to see what America looked like by morning light. A little after six, we were all chased to the after-deck and made to file past two detectives and an officer. The detectives eyed us; the officer counted to see that no one was hiding.

At seven o'clock, our boat lifted anchor and we glided up the still waters of the harbour. The whole prow was a black mass of passengers staring at the ferry-boats, the distant factories and sky-scrapers. Every point of vantage was seized, and some scores of emigrants were clinging to the rigging. At length, we came into sight of the green-grey statue of Liberty, far away and diminutive at first but, later on, a celestial figure in a blaze of sunlight. An American waved a starry flag in greeting, and some emigrants were disposed to cheer while some shed silent tears. Many, however, did not know what the statue was. I heard one Russian telling another that it was the tombstone of [Christopher] Columbus.

We carried out at eight, and in a pushing crowd prepared to disembark. At 8.30, we were quick-marched out of the ship to the Customs Wharf and there ranged in six or seven long lines. All the officials were running and hustling, shouting out, 'Come on!' 'Hurry!' 'Move along!' and clapping their hands. Our trunks were examined and chalked marked on the run—no delving for diamonds—and then we were quick marched further to a waiting ferry-boat. Here, for the time being, hustle ended. We waited three-quarters of an hour in the seatless ferry, and everyone was anxiously speculating on the coming ordeal of medical and pocket examination. At a quarter to ten we steamed for Ellis Island. We were then marched to another ferry-boat, and expected to be transported somewhere else, but this second vessel was simply a floating waiting-room. We were crushed and almost suffocated upon it. A hot sun beat upon its wooden roof; the windows in the sides were fixed; we could not move an inch from the places where we were awkwardly standing, for the boxes and baskets were so thick about our feet; babies kept crying sadly, at irritated emigrants swore at the sound of them. All were thinking—'Shall I get through?' 'Have I enough money?' 'Shall I pass the doctor?' and for a whole hour, in the heat and noise of discomfort, we were kept thinking thus. At a quarter past eleven we were released in detachments. Every twenty minutes each and every passenger picked up his luggage and tried to stampede through the party, a lucky few would bolt past the officer in charge, and the rest would flood back heart-broken desperate looks on their faces. Every time they failed to get included in the outgoing party, the emigrants seemed to feel that they had lost their chance of a job or that America was a failure or their coming there was a great mistake. At last, at a quarter-past eleven, it was my turn to rush out and find what Fate and America had in store for me.

Once more, it was 'Quick march!' and hurrying about with bags and baskets on our hands, we were put into to lines. Then we slowly filed up to a doctor who turned our eyelids inside out with a metal instrument. Another doctor scanned faces and hands for skin diseases, and then we carried our ship-inspection cards to an official who stamped them. We passed into the vast hall of judgement, and were classified and put into lines again, this time according to our nationality. It was interesting to observe at the very threshold of the United States the mechanical obsession of the American people. This ranging and guiding and hurrying and sifting was like nothing so much as the screening of coal in a great breaker tower.

It is not good to be like a hurrying, bumping, wandering piece of coal being mechanically guided to the sacks of its type and size, but such is the lot of the immigrant at Ellis Island.

But we had now reached a point in the examination when we could rest. In our new lines we were marched into stalls and were allowed to sit and look about us and, in comparative ease, await the pleasure of officials. The hall of judgement was crowned by two immense American flags. The centre, and indeed the great body of the hall, was filled with immigrants in their stalls, a long series of classified third-class men and women. The walls of the hall were booking-offices, bank counters, inspectors' tables, stools of statisticians. Up above was a visitors' gallery where journalists and the curious might promenade and talk about the melting-pot and America, 'the refuge of the oppressed.' Down below, among the clerks offices, were exits; one gate led to Freedom and New York, another to quarantine (sic) a third to the railway ferry, a fourth to the hospital and dining-room, to the place where unsuitable emigrants were imprisoned until there is a ship to take them back to their native land.

Somewhere also there was a place where marriages were solemnised. Engaged couples were there made man and wife before landing in New York. I was helping a girl who struggled with a huge basket and a detective asked me if she were my sweetheart. If I could have said, 'Yes,' as like as not we'd have been married off before we land. America is extremely solicitous about the welfare of women, especially of poor unmarried women who come to her shores. So many women fall into the clutches of evil directly they land in the New World. The authorities generally refuse to admit a poor, friendless girl, though there is a great demand for female labour all over the United States, and it is easy to get a place and earn an honest living. . . . At three in afternoon I stood in another ferry-boat, and with a crowd of approved immigrants passed (to) the City of New York. Success had melted most of us and, though we were terribly hungry, we had words and confidences for one another on the ferry-boat. We were ready to help one another to any extent in our power. That is what it feels like to have passed the Last Day and still believe in Heaven, to pass Ellis Island and still believe in America."

This versatile author wrote many other books including *Vagabond in the Caucasus* (1911), *A Tramp's Scetches* (1912), *London Nights* (1926), *Quo Vadis, Europa?* (1927), *Peter the Great* (1929), *Stalin* (1931), *Ivan the Terrible* (1932), *Thinking of Living* (1949), *Summing up on Russia* (1951), *Pay As You Run* (1955), and his autobiography, *Part of the Wonderful Scene* (1964).

REFERENCE: Graham, Stephen. 1914. *With Poor Immigrants to America.* New York: Macmillan.

Grant, Madison (b. New York, November 19, 1865; d. New York, May 30, 1937). Lawyer and author. Madison Grant was one of the nation's most influential anti-immigrant nativists and a powerful advocate that the "white race" was divided into superior and inferior levels. He strongly opposed accepting large numbers of southern and eastern European immigrants, whom he considered inferior to northern and western Europeans. He was particularly critical of Jews. In 1909, he wrote a letter to Commissioner **William Williams** congratulating him for his "effort to secure proper enforcement of the laws and regulations of immigration." Grant was the author of *The Passing of the Great Race* (1916), a highly influential book and a best-seller in its day (it sold nearly 16,000 copies by the mid-1920s), and served as the vice chairman of the **Immigration Restriction League** (1922–1937). As a prominent league member, he successfully lobbied for the passage of the **Immigration Act of 1924**, which completely ended mass immigration to the United States.

See also **Immigration Restriction**

REFERENCES: Friedman, Walter. 1995. Madison Grant. In *Encyclopedia of New York City*, ed. Kenneth T. Jackson. New Haven: Yale University Press; Le May, Michael. 1987. *From Dutch Door to Open Door: An Analysis of U.S. Immigration Policy since 1820.* New York: Praeger; Pitkin, Thomas M. 1975. *Keepers of the Gate: A History of Ellis Island.* New York: New York University Press.

Great Hall. This popular term is sometimes applied to the **Registry Room**, where the primary inspection of immigrants took place. The room was also popularly known as the examination hall. Occasionally the **Main Building** itself was referred to as the Great Hall.

Greenstone, Cecilia [Cecilia Greenstone Arnow] (b. Bialystock, [Russian] Poland, November 18, 1887; d. New York, 1971). Immigrant aid worker (1907–1919) employed by the **National Council of Jewish Women** (NCJW). Greenstone spent much of her time seeking ways to help the large numbers of young Jewish women and girls arriving at the station. She was conversant in five languages, including her native Yiddish. As a young immigrant, Greenstone attracted the attention of **Sadie American**, who founded NCJW's immigrant aid work, and was hired and posted to Ellis Island. At the station, Greenstone won the trust and confidence of not only immigrant girls but also of officials of the **Hebrew Immigrant Aid Society**. In 1914, at the eve of World War I, Greenstone was dispatched to Russia to accompany an immigrant home. But the sudden outbreak of war in Europe halted her mission and she found herself stranded in Liverpool, England. Return to New York was the only solution. Greenstone retired from Ellis Island to get married. Years later, admirers of her work dubbed her the "angel of Ellis Island."

Cecilia Greenstone and the National Council of Jewish Women and the Hebrew Immigrant Aid Society provided much assistance to their co-religionists at Ellis Island. Courtesy of the Ellis Island Immigration Museum.

REFERENCES: Peterson, Jesse. 1997. Cecilia Greenstone: Ellis Island Agent. Manuscript Collection, Ellis Island Library, Statue of Liberty N.M.; Berman, John. 2003. *Ellis Island.* New York: Barnes & Noble Books; Moreno, Barry. 2003. *Ellis Island.* Charleston, SC: Arcadia.

Grogan, Anthony J. (b. June 1873, County Cork, Ireland; d. August 25, 1930, Dublin, Ireland). Roman Catholic priest. Father Grogan was the chaplain of Irish immigrants at Ellis Island from 1900 until his death in 1930. Grogan immigrated to the United States in the early 1890s and, after his ordination to the priesthood, was assigned as an assistant priest to the Mission of Our Lady of the Rosary directly across the road from the Battery and Barge Office. This was in 1898. After serving with the mission's pastor, Father Henry and agent Patrick McCool, Grogan was eventually elevated to pastor; the post also included the directorship of the Home for Irish Immigrant Girls (later known also as the Catholic Refuge for Irish Immigrants) and the chaplain's role to the Irish at Ellis Island. His daily presence in a span of thirty years won him the confidence and affection of both the Immigration Service and the immigrants. Grogan was so much a part of Ellis Island that the *New York Times* (1930), quoting an old Ellis Island joke, wrote that "he was the first thing an immigrant looks for after the Statue of Liberty." During World War I, Grogan served as the chaplain of the U.S. military forces on Ellis Island and in 1918 officiated at a mass held in Battery Park for American soldiers killed during the war. In the 1920s, Grogan became a steadfast defender of Ellis Island before the press and the public. His consistent praise of the commissioners, inspectors, and other workers at the station was widely publicized at a time when most press reports emphasized complaints, abuse, and scandal. In 1930, Grogan sailed to Ireland to finalize plans for American participation in the Eucharistic Congress of 1932. He spent a week with his brother Jeremiah Grogan in Screggan, Tullamore, then went on to Dublin, where he suddenly became ill and died. His popularity in New York was so great that the requiem mass for him was held in St. Patrick's Cathedral, where he received honors from the Knights of Columbus and the Friendly Sons of Saint Patrick.

See also **Immigrant Aid Societies; Missionaries**

REFERENCE: *The New York Times*. 1930. Rev. Anthony Grogan dies. August 29.

Groupers. Although "grouper" was not an official job title, it was used at Ellis Island for many years. Officially groupers were designated as **messengers**, **watchmen,** or **gatemen**; generally speaking, they carried out whatever was needed in respect to the crowds of aliens arriving, being examined on the registry floor or held in detention. Their task was to keep aliens from different steamships in their respective groups and to prevent them from mixing with passengers from other ships. Every day groupers directed traffic at Ellis Island and kept good order as far as was possible. They were assigned to the **Watchmen's and Gatemen's Division**.

Guards and Watchmen. Guards and watchmen cared for people detained pending deportation. They were commonly assigned to the **Watchmen's and Gatemen's Division**, **Deporting Division,** and **Night Division**. Fisticuffs occasionally were required in this job. Thomas Wall was a watchman (1890s–1921), and superintendents of the watch included Charles E. Murphy (1890s–1900) and Richard Tilson (1900–1917).

Guastavino, Rafael (I) (Rafael Guastavino y Moreno) (b. Valencia, Spain, March 1, 1842; d. Asheville, North Carolina, February 2, 1908). Architect and designer. Rafael Guastavino y Moreno's pioneering work and designs are the basis of the magnificent vaulted ceiling in the **Registry Room** that was installed by the Guastavino Company, then headed by his son, **Rafael Guastavino (II)**. Rafael Guastavino y Moreno brought the technique of Catalan vaulting to the United States and introduced modifications to it that gained him recognition as an innovator. Guastavino's special approach to the technology included his use of Portland cement instead of gypsum in its construction. Guastavino, the son of a carpenter, was educated at the School of Builders in Barcelona and then trained as an apprentice at engineering and architectural firms. After being qualified, he set up offices as an architect and a builder in the 1860s and designed many textile factories and elegant houses. He was a pioneer in the construction of fireproof buildings and argued that use of cohesive masonry in tile was the most effective way of protecting buildings from potential fire damage. His views met with praise and he presented his theory in the form of a lecture ("Improving the Healthfulness of Industrial Towns") at the U.S. Centennial Exhibition at Philadelphia in 1876; the judges were impressed and conferred on him the Medal of Merit. The Great Chicago Fire of 1871 had made fireproofing a major issue for American architects and engineers. Continuing American interest in his ideas prompted Guastavino to immigrate to the United States with his family in 1881. Settling in New York, he soon went into business as an architect and, after a series of successful commissions, he incorporated the Guastavino Fireproof Construction Company in 1889. Guastavino's many projects include the Batllo Factory (Barcelona, 1869), Progress Club (New York, 1883), Boston

Public Library arcade ceiling and dome (1889), St. Joseph's Seminary (Yonkers, NY, 1892), U.S. Army War College (Washington, DC, 1905), U.S. House of Representatives Office Building rotunda dome (1905), Gorham Building (New York, 1905–1906), Pennsylvania Railroad Station (New York, 1905–1909), U.S. Customs House elliptical dome (New York, 1906), Cathedral of St. John the Divine (New York, 1907–1910). Guastavino built an estate for himself and his family in Asheville, North Carolina, where he died in 1908.

REFERENCES: Guastavino, Rafael. 1892. *Essay on the Theory and History of Cohesive Construction, Applied Especially to the Timbrel Vault.* Boston: Ticknor; Anonymous. 1893. The cohesive construction: Its past, its present, its future? *American Architect and Building News* (August 26): 125–129; Collins, George R. 1968. The transfer of thin masonry vaulting from Spain to America. *Journal of the Society of Architectural Historians* (October): 176–201; Parks, Janet, and Alan G. Neumann. 1996. *The Old World Builds the New: The Guastavino Company and the Technology of the Catalan Vault, 1885–1962.* New York: Avery Architectural and Fine Arts Library/ Wallach Art Gallery, Columbia University; Serra, Montserrat. 1996. Un Innovador in Nova York. *El Temps* (May 20): 68–75.

Guastavino, Rafael (II) (Rafael Guastavino y Esposito) (b. Barcelona, Spain, May 12, 1872; d. Bay Shore, Long Island, New York, October 20, 1950). Architect; son of **Rafael Guastavino**. The younger Guastavino was trained by his architect father and inherited the Guastavino Company after his father's death in 1908. He applied his father's innovative tile vaulting techniques in constructing the vaulted ceiling in the **Registry Room** at Ellis Island in 1918, as well as in his other projects. He was contracted for this job by the **Bureau of Immigration** based on the agency's 1917 specifications. Aside from his work at Ellis Island, the younger Guastavino's projects included the Vanderbilt Hotel (New York, 1912), Grand Central Terminal restaurant and foyer (New York, 1913), Federal Reserve Bank (New York, 1924), National Shrine of the Immaculate Conception (Washington, DC, 1920s, 1956–1962), Nebraska State Capitol, House of Representatives wall panels and barrel vaults (Lincoln, 1929), Western Union Building (New York, 1929), and the Cloisters Museum (New York, 1934–1938). After his death the Guastavino Company continued to operate until 1962. When the family closed the business, it donated the company archives to Columbia University.

See also **Guastavino, Rafael (I)**

REFERENCE: Parks, Janet, and Alan G. Neumann. 1996. *The Old World Builds the New: The Guastavino Company and the Technology of the Catalan Vault, 1885–1962.* New York: Avery Architectural and Fine Arts Library/Wallach Art Gallery, Columbia University.

H

Halifax Immigrant Station (Nova Scotia, Canada). This immigrant inspection station of the U.S. **Bureau of Immigration** was a part of the Canadian Border District, withheadquarters at Montreal. This station was often the first stop for European steamships on their way to New York. In 1924, a chief inspector, an inspector, a clerk, and a charwoman were employed there.

Hall, Prescott [Prescott Farnsworth Hall] (b. Boston, Massachusetts, September 27, 1868; d. Brookline, Massachusetts, May 28, 1921). Lawyer, author. A leading nativist, Prescott Hall was a one of the founders of the **Immigration Restriction League** and served as its secretary (1896–1921). Objecting to the southern and eastern European immigrants as inferior to northern and western Europeans, he and his fellow members used their considerable social and intellectual influence to bring about the enactment of laws to end mass immigration to the United States. Hall and his colleagues were particularly interested in the nation's biggest immigration station, Ellis Island, and watched events there closely. They enjoyed good relations with Commissioner **Joseph Senner**. Hall was delighted with the strong enforcement of the immigration laws carried out by Commissioner **William Williams** in his second administration. On July 14, 1909, Hall wrote Williams: "I can't help writing you at this time to express my admiration of the way things are going at Ellis Island. Nothing has made me so happy for a long time as feeling that you are there and seeing, as far as I do from the papers, how you are cleaning things up (Pitkin, p. 62)." Prescott Hall wrote several books, including *Immigration and Its Effects on the United States* (1906). He was also chairman of the immigration committee of the American Genetic Association (1911–1921).

References: LeMay, Michael C. 1987. *From Open Door to Dutch Door: An Analysis of U.S. Immigration Policy since 1820*. New York: Praeger; Pitkin, Thomas M. 1975. *Keepers of the Gate: A History of Ellis Island*. New York: New York University Press.

Harkavy, Alexander (b. Novogrudek, Belarus [Russia], 1863; d. 1939). Representative, **Hebrew Immigrant Aid Society** (1904–1909); lexicographer, scholar, writer, lecturer. Alexander Harkavy improved the level of aid accorded to the growing number of Jewish immigrants and refugees who were arriving at Ellis Island during the period of the pogroms and other persecutions to which Jews were subjected in the Russian Empire and eastern Europe. Harkavy's attentions to the people set the standard for his successors in the many years that followed. Additionally, his Ellis Island work was made even more successful thanks to the esteem Commissioner **William Williams** held him in. Harkavy had an international reputation as an expert in the Yiddish language and produced many works, including the famous *Yiddish-English-Hebrew Dictionary* (1925). He came to the United States following the pogroms of 1881. In Russia, he had learned Hebrew, Russian, Syriac, and German, as well as his native Yiddish.

Harrison, Benjamin (b. Ohio, 1831; d. Indianapolis, Indiana, 1901). President of the United States (1889–1893). President Benjamin Harrison was deeply involved in the debate over the possibility of the federal government taking control of immigration from the states. He signed the **Congressional Resolution of 1890** and the **Immigration Act of 1891** into law. Further, he appointed Colonel **John B. Weber** as the first federal superintendent/commissioner of immigration of the port of New York.

Head Tax. The head tax was a poll tax imposed on each immigrant entering the United States. The **Immigration Act of 1882** imposed the first federal head tax of fifty cents.

The money was used to pay for examining immigrants, and, in the 1880s through 1891, to pay for the relief of those in distress. The U.S. Treasury received the money from collectors of customs posted at U.S. seaports and distributed the funds to state immigration officials, the largest state recipient being New York. After the creation of the federal **Bureau of Immigration** in 1891, the money was disbursed to that agency exclusively; as before, the money increased or decreased based how many aliens inspectors and doctors examined each year. The **Immigration Act of 1907** increased the head tax to $4.00. The Immigration Act of 1909 abolished the use of the head tax as an "immigrant fund" for the Immigration Bureau. Henceforth, the money went directly into the federal treasury, and Congress appropriated money in the federal budget for immigration affairs. Under the **Immigration Act of 1917**, the head tax was increased to $8.00. To encourage the immigration of agricultural laborers to the United States during World War I and World War II, the head taxes for 1918, 1943, and 1944 were waived. The head tax continued to be periodically increased and was still being collected when Ellis Island closed in 1954.

A NICE RECEPTION FOR LIBERTY.

In this cartoon, Liberty is asked to pay the head tax before she will permitted to mount her pedestal. This was attack on the government's policy of extending this tax to almost all foreigners entering the country. Courtesy of the Ellis Island Immigration Museum.

REFERENCES: Pitkin, Thomas M. 1975. *Keepers of the Gate: A History of Ellis Island.* New York: New York University Press; Unrau, Harlan D. 1984. *The Historic Resource Study: Ellis Island/Statue of Liberty.* Vol. 1. Washington, DC: U.S. Department of Interior, National Park Service.

Hebrew Immigrant Aid Society (HIAS). One of the leading societies to offer aid to immigrants at Ellis Island. In the 1890s and in the first years after the turn of the century, HIAS representatives were not always available. But starting in 1904, the HIAS presence improved and this paved the way for the coming of **Alexander Harkavy**, the distinguished writer and lexicographer of the Yiddish language. Harkavy's dedicated work as executive director at the station increased the prestige of HIAS in the Jewish Lower East Side and enabled large numbers of detained Jews to avoid exclusion and deportation. Throughout the years other prominent HIAS officials assigned to their Ellis Island Bureau included general manager **Irving Lipsitch** (1914–1920s), general manager, Helen Barth (1914–1918), Isaac Asofsky (1920s–1954), Samuel Littman (1910s), Samuel Frommer (1910s), S. Paley (kosher cook, 1911–1920s), Sadie Schwartz (kosher cook, 1920s–1930s), and William Neubau (October 1920–December 1954). In 1916, Ellis Island Bureau's telephone number on the island was 6306 Broad. The foremost task of HIAS was to assist and comfort Jewish immigrants, particularly those who were detained. HIAS helped Jewish aliens file appeals against exclusion and deportation. In the 1930s and 1940s, they also helped Jewish refugees change their status from nonimmigrant visitors to permanent residents. For example, the agency's Ellis Island Bureau aided 848 Jews involved in 441 appeal cases between January and June 1941; however, the problems were many, including no immigrant visa (186 cases), likely to become a public charge (88), physically defective (81), holds an expired passport (20), contract laborer (5), stowaway (3) and venereal disease (2). Of these 441 appeal cases, 221 were admitted as "visitors under bond," 40 were admitted as immigrants, 22 were paroled (conditionally admitted), and most of the 90 remaining cases left the United States. HIAS also sponsored Jewish religious observances such as Passover, Yom Kippur, Rosh Hashanah, Sukkoth, and Chanukah. In addition, in 1911, it founded the Ellis Island kosher kitchen, which served breakfast, dinner (lunch), and supper every day of the week. HIAS paid the wages of the cook and the rabbi who was the kitchen's kashruth supervisor, while the supplies, food, and other four kitchen workers were paid for by the government. In 1940, the kitchen served 85,794 meals. The kosher kitchen remained in service until Ellis Island closed in November 1954. *See also* **Harkavy, Alexander; Immigrant Aid Societies; Missionaries; National Council of Jewish Women**

REFERENCE: Krantz, Suzanne, comp. 1983. *HIAS Ellis Island Bureau Documents.* New York: YIVO Archives.

Heiser, Victor [Victor George Heiser] (b. Johnstown, Pennsylvania, February 5, 1873; d. February 27, 1972). Physician, surgeon, author. After completing his medical studies, Victor Heiser joined the Marine Hospital Service and began a long career working in the field of immigration. His assignments included the Boston Immigrant Station, Ellis Island, the Canadian Border, Naples, Italy, and the Far East. Realizing the vital importance of good health in the workforce, Heiser wrote in his best-selling autobiography, "I believed that health should be regarded from economic as well as from the humanitarian viewpoint. To be without it was to be without earning power."

His published works include *Leprosy: Its Treatment in the Philippines* (1914), *An American Doctor's Odyssey* (1936), *You're the Doctor* (1939), and *Toughen Up, America!* (1941).

REFERENCE: Heiser, Victor. 1936. *An American Doctor's Odyssey: Adventures in Forty-five Countries.* New York: W.W. Norton.

Hendley, Charles M. (b. Cincinnati, Ohio, February 13, 1852; d. ?). Civil servant; private secretary to William Windom, secretary of the treasury. Charles M. Hendley represented Secretary Windom at the opening of Ellis Island as an immigrant inspection station on January 1, 1892. Hendley inspected the first immigrant to pass through Ellis Island, **Annie Moore**. Hendley enjoyed a long career as an executive clerk and secretary at the White House, beginning in 1877, during which time he served several presidents, including Rutherford B. Hayes, Chester Alan Arthur, and Grover Cleveland. He went to the Treasury Department during the administration of **Benjamin Harrison**. Hendley was the author of *Trifles of Travel* (1924).

Hine, Lewis [Lewis Wickes Hine] (b. Oshkosh, Wisconsin, September 26, 1874; d. Dobbs Ferry, New York, November 4, 1940). Photographer. Lewis Hine used his photography to promote social reform. He took pictures of immigrants at Ellis Island in 1905 and 1926, and possibly on other occasions. The most complete collection of his work is at the International Museum of Photography, George Eastman House, in Rochester, New York. The National Archives and the New York Public Library also hold selections of his photography.

Hope, Bob [Leslie Townes Hope] (b. Eltham, England, May 29, 1903; d. Hollywood, California, 2003). Comedian; star of vaudeville, Broadway, radio, and motion pictures. Leslie (later Bob) Hope sailed to America with his mother and brothers in March 1908. Their ship was delayed in the outer waters of New York harbor because of thick fog, but when they finally disembarked at Ellis Island, the immigrant inspector landed them without ceremony and they were transferred to an immigrant train bound for Cleveland.

On the steamship, the Hopes occupied a steerage compartment directly above the main drive shaft. It was hot and noisy and hard to sleep. When time came for the customary vaccination of the immigrants on board, Avis Hope lined her sons up, but Leslie bolted. The four-year-old was cornered and returned to the line up where, amid his howling, the needle pricked.

Hospital Administration Building. The three-and-a-half-story hospital administration building was designed by federal architect **James Knox Taylor** in 1905–1906 and was built in 1906–1907. The base is composed of rusticated granite and the walls are Flemish bond bricks and limestone. Two chimneys rise from the ridge of the roof. The building was initially used as a regular hospital, but after the construction of the new hospital extension in 1909, it was turned over to medical administration.

The first floor included the vestibule, three wards (medical reception rooms), a nurses' room, a dining room, an attendants' dining room, a corridor, a staircase hall, an elevator, and two toilets and two bathrooms.

The second floor was divided into three wards, one nurses' room, an attendants' room, a dining room, an interns' room, a linen room, a corridor, a staircase hall, an elevator, two toilets and bathrooms each. Quarters for nurses and interns were on this floor.

The third floor was arranged as follows: three dormitories (thirteen bedrooms), the hall, one nurses' room, one attendants' dining room, one dining room, one maternity ward, one ward, the linen room, a corridor, a staircase hall, an elevator, and two toilets and bathrooms each.

Hospital Buildings. Designated officially by the **Public Health Service** as U.S. Marine Hospital 43, the Ellis Island Immigrant Hospital consisted of more than thirty buildings and structures on Islands 2 and 3. The general medical complex was located on **Island 2** and consisted of the **laundry and linen exchange** also called the **hospital outbuilding** (1907), the **psychopathic ward** (1907), the **general hospital building** (1901), the **hospital administration building** (1908), and the **hospital extension** building (1909). The **contagious disease wards** were on Island 3.

The entire hospital consisted of 28 wards and 650 beds, and it had an emergency bed capacity of 100. The space area per bed averaged 59 square feet. In January 1924, the ward use and capacity of the hospitals on Island 2 were as follows:

Ward 1: Female pediatric and medical cases (37 beds)
Ward 2: Obstetrical and female medical cases (30 beds)
Ward 3: Admissions for women and children (23 beds)
Ward 4: Male and female mental cases (31 beds)
Ward 5: Male medical cases (34 beds)
Ward 6: Medical cases (less serious) (36 beds)
Ward 7: Public Health Service beneficiary cases (19 beds)
Ward 8: Closed
Ward 9: Female psychopathic cases (16 beds)
War 10: Male psychopathic cases (16 beds)

Hospital Extension. Also known as Hospital 2, the hospital extension has a granite facing at the basement level; the upper structure is built of red bricks laid in a Flemish bond and trimmed in limestone. The building is composed of a central pavilion three and a half stories high and wings two and a half stories high. The hospital extension was designed in the beaux arts style by federal architect **James Knox Taylor** in 1907 and 1908 and was erected during 1908 and 1909; it measures 142 feet by 83 feet.

The hospital extension contained medical wards with dressing rooms, bathrooms, toilets,

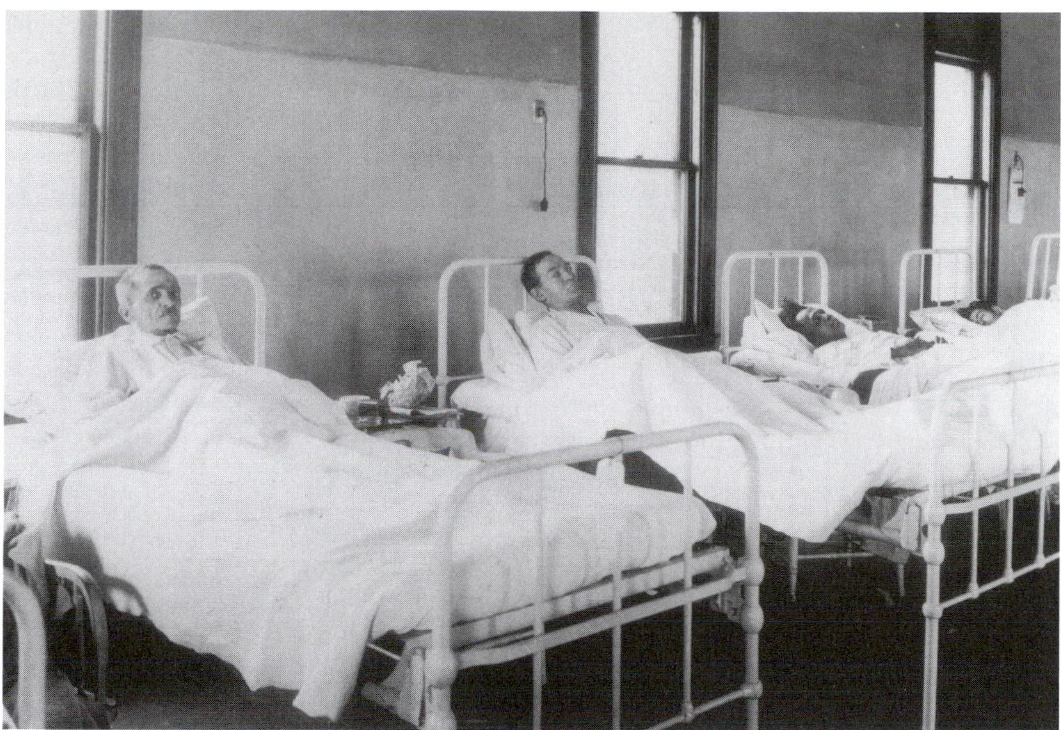

Men's ward of the Ellis Island hospital. Courtesy of the Ellis Island Immigration Museum.

and enclosed porches, in addition to offices and sitting rooms. A pergola led from this building to the **surgeons' house**.

Hospital Outbuilding. Designed in the beaux arts style by architect **James Knox Taylor** in 1898 and constructed by the firm of Attilio Pasquini of New York City in November 1901. It is rectangular with a brick-bearing wall structure and an upper frame of steel. The exterior is clad in red brisk laid in Flemish bond and trimmed with brick quoins and limestone. It is a part of the general hospital complex on **Island 2**. The building included a laundry, linen exchange, boiler room, mortuary, and autopsy room. It was also known as the **laundry and linen exchange**.

Hospitalization. *See* **Diseases and Hospitalization**

Howe, Frederic C. [Frederic Clemson Howe] (b. Meadville, Pennsylvania, 1868; d. Martha's Vineyard, Massachusetts, August 3, 1940). Commissioner of immigration, Ellis Island (1914–1919); lawyer, author, critic, reformer. Frederic C. Howe was a major liberal reform commissioner who attempted to put right things he regarded as wrongs. Consequently he became a controversial figure at Ellis Island, especially during the **red scare** following the Bolshevik Revolution in Russia. The aggressively anti-Bolshevik policy adopted by the Wilson administration brought about the summary arrest and expulsion via Ellis Island of hundreds of foreign-born radicals.

An example of Howe's reforms occurred in his first year in office. Among these were games and sporting activities organized for men, women, and children; Sunday and holiday concerts performed by well-known singing societies and famed artists such as Enrico Caruso. Other events included weekly silent films in the **Registry Room** supplied by the Home Missions Council; classes in knitting and other handicrafts; "to which the women eagerly applied themselves"; and kindergarten classes for detained children. Detained men were organized in groups of fifteen to make doormats from "waste material from the cables" (Unrau, p. 756). Howe also brought in the **YMCA** to offer calisthenics classes and New York City schoolteachers to give courses in elementary topics such as English, hygiene, and motherhood. In addition, during the winter of 1914 and 1915, Howe dispatched members of his staff over to the Battery to round up 750 vagabonds and immigrants found along the waterfront and bring them to Ellis Island. They were given beds and sold breakfasts of "coffee and bread at a cost of five cents." The **ferryboat *Ellis Island*** provided a 7:30 p.m. run for vagabonds who wanted a bed on Ellis Island. This service continued throughout the winter.

In his obituary in the *New York Times*, the news writer mentioned Howe's work at Ellis Island: "As United States commissioner of immigration, port of New York, in 1914–19, Howe conceived the idea of a federal employment service and, in 1916, organized the first bureau in New York which was administered by employees of the immigration service. The project was later taken over as an activity of the immigration service of the Department of Labor in various parts of the country."

Howe was a prolific author of sociological and political studies, including *The City: Hope and Democracy*, *Privilege and Democracy in America*, *Revolution and Democracy*, and his autobiography, *Confessions of a Reformer*.

REFERENCES: *New York Times*. 1940. Dr. F. C. Howe dead; noted liberal, 72—leader in civic reforms. August 3; Howe, Frederic C. 1925. *Confessions of a Reformer.* New York: Charles Scribner's Sons; Unrau, Harlan D. 1984. *The Historic Resource Study: Ellis Island/Statue of Liberty.* Washington, DC: U.S. Department of Interior, National Park Service.

Hull, Harry [Harry Edward Hull] (b. Belvidere, New York, March 12, 1864; d. Washington, DC, January 16, 1938). Commissioner-general of immigration (1925–1933). Harry Hull was commissioner-general under President Calvin Coolidge. During his term of office, immigration fell to its lowest levels in a century, as a result of the restrictive **Immigration Act of 1924**. He continued in office during the presidency of Herbert Hoover. By the end of his term of office, Ellis Island had become primarily a deportation and detention station.

Hull come to politics after having been a successful businessman in Iowa. He entered politics there, serving as a Republican congressman from 1915 to 1925.

Husband, W. W. [William Walter Husband] (b. East Highgate, Vermont, September 28, 1871; d. St. Johnsbury, Vermont, July 31, 1942). Commissioner-general of immigration (1921–1925). W. W. Husband gained national recognition as an expert on immigration questions through his many years as a journalist, editor, and critic. He was appointed clerk of the Senate Immigration Committee by Senator William P. Dillingham (1903) and served as executive secretary of the U.S. Immigration Commission (1907–1911). In 1912, he became chief of the Contract Labor Division in the Department of Commerce and Labor, and he investigated emigration conditions in Europe for the department. During World War I, he worked with the **American Red Cross** as the associate director of relief to prisoners of war abroad. He then served on the committee in Berlin that repatriated sick and wounded prisoners of war. In addition, he edited his own publication, *Immigration Journal.* As commissioner-general of immigration, he sought to improve conditions at Ellis Island. He also served as second assistant secretary of labor under President Warren G. Harding.

REFERENCE: *New York Times.* 1942. Walter Husband, served in capital: Immigration ex-commissioner and former aide to secretary of labor dies at 70. August 1.

I

Idiots. A class of aliens barred from entering the United States on grounds of mental deficiency. From 1892 through 1907, 211 persons were excluded for this reason; 38 cases occurred in 1905, 92 in 1906, and 29 in 1907. These were the busiest years for such cases. From 1908 through 1931, a total of 184 more were excluded, the busiest year of which was 1908, when 20 were turned away. Thus from 1892 through 1931 a grand total of 395 persons were certified as "idiots" and excluded from the United States.

Imbeciles. This category of mentally deficient immigrants was added to statistical summaries in 1908, when 45 were excluded. Other busy years for excluding this type of alien were 1909 (42), 1910 (40), 1911 (26), 1912 (44), 1913 (54), 1914 (68), 1915 (27), 1921 (31), and 1922 (35). From 1908 through 1931, a total of 542 persons were certified as "imbeciles" and thereby excluded from entering the country.

Immigrant Aid Societies. Throughout the years numerous organizations offered aid to immigrants at Ellis Island. Some maintained agents on the island and at the piers, while others sent occasional representatives; all sent assistance to immigrants, including money, clothing, books, periodicals, food, religious items, and other presents. A number of these societies were carryovers from **Castle Garden** days and included most of the **missionaries**.

In 1915, Commissioner **Frederic Howe** made the following report concerning immigrant aid.

> There are forty missionary and immigrant-aid societies having representatives at Ellis Island. Of the immigrant-aid societies, fifteen maintain immigrant homes in New York City, where arriving and departing aliens may secure board and lodging. During the past year there have been discharged to these homes and societies 1,290 aliens—267 males and 1,023 females. Periodical inspections of these homes by this office has tended to raise the standard of service and help extended to the immigrants. Some of the homes, however, act as ticket agents of the steamship companies. This practice is incompatible with the purposes for which they are granted the privilege of representation at Ellis Island and should be discontinued. (Unrau, pp. 758–759)

During **World War I**, the societies and missionaries united into different groups in order to provide better service. Starting in about 1916, a general committee on immigrant aid operated whose members were the representatives of the leading societies and missions on the island. In April 1920, its seven members represented twenty-nine organizations. The seven were Alma Matthews, Father Anthony Grogan, Charles Carol, Michael Kley (HIAS), Mr. Ricciardi (Italian Society), Mr. Cestari (Albanians and others), and Elsa Alsburg (NCJW). The last four members appealed against exclusion and deportation orders.

In 1934, the committee was expanded to fourteen members: Cecilia Razofsky Davidson, Isaac L. Asofsky, Edith Terry Bremer, Florence G. Cassidy, Jane Perry Clark, Raymond E. Cole, Ruth Larned, Thomas F. Mulholland, Carlotta N. V. Schiapelli, Marian Schibsby, David W. Wainhouse, George L. Warren, Aghavnie Y. Yeghenian, and Katherine E. Young.

Immigrant aid organizations at Ellis Island included American Red Cross, Belgian Bureau, Bulgarian Society, Clara de Hirsch Home for Immigrant Girls, **Daughters of the American Revolution** (DAR), German Society, Greek

Society, Hungarian Home, Hungarian Relief Society, **Italian Welfare League**, National Institutes of Immigrant Welfare, Polish National Alliance, Slavonic Immigrant Society, **Society for the Protection of Italian Immigrants**, and the Travelers' Aid Society (Port Department).

Prominent immigrant aid officials included Virginia M. Murray (1900–1910) of the Travelers Aid Society; Elizabeth G. Gardiner (1919–1924) and Ruby Brown Douglas (1930s) of the American Red Cross; for the DAR there was Lucille Boss, whose assistants included Elizabeth Estes and Isabel Rittenhouse. Mrs. H. Stebbins Smith, national chairman of the DAR in the 1940s, personally inspected her organization's activities weekly. The National Institute for Immigrant Welfare was represented by several workers, including port director **Edith Terry Bremer** (1911–1954) and her able deputies, **Ludmila K. Foxlee** (1933–1937), who mainly aided eastern Europeans, Johanna Cohrsen, who ran the German Bureau for decades, and Elizabeth G. Niewiadomsky, head of the Russian Bureau.

In spite of the valuable services and the many sterling characters who dedicated themselves to aiding the newcomers, some representatives of immigrant aid societies and missionaries were involved in improprieties, mostly exploiting them for financial gain. Reports of such cases were common from the time Ellis Island opened until the beginning of World War I, when immigration waned. After the war, more cases arose, but by the 1930s, with fewer immigrants, reports of abuses became rare. Commissioners Thomas Fitchie (1901) and **William Williams** (1910) both investigated the immigrant aid societies. The following is an excerpt from Commissioner Williams's investigative report.

> I found that the trustees of some (not all) of these societies had confided the management to incompetent or corrupt underlings with the usual results in such cases and the additional disgraceful result that a government station was being used as a base for carrying on various practices of the meanest kind. I use advisedly the word "meanest," because they were perpetrated against helpless, ignorant immigrants. Some of these practices included housing them in quarters of extreme filth at a charge of about $1 a day; exposing girls to coarse, vulgar treatment, turning them over to improper persons, and reporting fictitious addresses as to where they were sent; treating immigrants in an unfriendly, even brutal manner; taking their money on deposit and refusing to surrender it on request, and (in one instance) advising an immigrant to loan his to a missionary's bankrupt friend. It is difficult to find words adequately to express the contempt one must have for persons who would knowingly do such things or allow them to be done. All such as were found guilty were duly punished and their misdeeds exposed to the press. An immigrant society which is not conducted on a high plane of efficiency and decency by managers whose own sense of duty will make them unwilling to see it conducted in any other way is obviously not fit to be represented at a government station, and it ought not to be necessary (as it has been) to tell persons supposedly engaged in philanthropic business such elementary truths. I may add that there are at Ellis Island several societies which are conducted in a model way and also missionaries whose work is disinterested and excellent. These could add still further to their usefulness if they would band together for the purpose of assisting the Government in detecting black sheep and the missionary for revenue, whose presence should be as unpleasant to them as it is to the commissioner.

Violations caused some immigrant societies to be barred at least temporarily from Ellis Island. These included the Austro-Hungarian Society Home (1904), the Swedish Immigrant Home (1909), and St. Joseph's Home for Polish Immigrants (1909).

REFERENCES: Willliams, William. 1910. Annual report of the commissioner-general of immigration. *Reports of the Department of Commerce and Labor.* Washington, DC; Unrau, Harlan D. 1984. *The Historic Resource Study: Ellis Island/Statue of Liberty.* Washington, DC: U.S. Department of Interior, National Park Service.

Immigrant Inspection. *See* **Line Inspection; Primary Inspection**

Immigrant Inspection Stations. Soon after the Bureau of Immigration was created under the Immigration Act of 1891, twenty-four immigrant inspection stations were established at U.S. ports and the Mexican (1894) and

Canadian (1895) borders. The station at Ellis Island, New York, was the largest station in the service throughout its entire history (January 1, 1892–November 12, 1954). Other stations that opened in the 1890s were in Boston, Philadelphia, Baltimore, and Montreal. Medical inspections by Marine Hospital Service physicians were begun simultaneously at these stations. The national headquarters of the Bureau of Immigration was in Washington, DC, and from there it administered all of the inspection stations as field offices. By 1924, the following immigrant inspection stations existed (the location of the main office and number of personnel at headquarters appear in parentheses). District 1—Canadian border: 52 stations, including Halifax, Nova Scotia, and Quebec City (Montreal immigrant station, staff of 40); District 2—Portland, Maine: one station (Portland immigrant station, staff of 4); District 3—Boston, Massachusetts: four stations (Boston immigrant station, staff of 64); District 4—Ellis Island, New York: one station (Ellis Island immigrant station, staff of 552); District 5—Buffalo, New York: eight stations (Buffalo immigrant station, staff of 26); District 6—Gloucester City, New Jersey: one station (Gloucester City immigrant station, staff of 26); District 7—Pittsburgh, Pennsylvania: one station (Pittsburgh immigrant station, staff of five); District 8—Baltimore, Maryland: one station (Baltimore immigrant station, staff of 16); District 9—Norfolk, Virginia, plus two substations (Norfolk immigrant station, staff of seven); District 10—Jacksonville, Florida, plus thirteen substations, including Key West, Miami, Tampa, Savannah, Georgia, Charleston, South Carolina (Jacksonville immigrant station, staff of five); District 11—Detroit, Michigan, plus seven substations, including Toledo, Ohio (Detroit immigrant station, staff of 32); District 12—Cincinnati, Ohio: one station (Cincinnati immigrant station, staff of three); District 13—Atlanta, Georgia: one station (Atlanta immigrant station: staff of three); District 14—Chicago, Illinois: one station (Chicago immigrant station: staff of 16); District 15—St. Louis, Missouri: one station (St. Louis immigrant station: staff of three); District 16—Memphis, Tennessee: one station (Memphis immigrant station: staff of two); District 17—New Orleans, Louisiana, plus four substations, including Mobile, Alabama, and Pensacola, Florida (New Orleans immigrant station: staff of 25); District 18—Winnipeg, Minnesota, plus twenty-two substations throughout North Dakota and Minnesota (Winnipeg immigrant station: staff of 13); District 19—Minneapolis, Minnesota (Minneapolis immigrant station, staff of six); District 20—Omaha, Nebraska (Omaha immigrant station, staff of two); District 21—Kansas City, Missouri (Kansas City immigrant station: staff of three); District 22—San Antonio, Texas, plus thirteen substations, including Brownsville, Del Rio, Eagle Pass, Fort Worth, and Laredo (San Antonio immigrant station, staff of 14); District 23—Helena, Montana (Helena immigrant station, staff of two); District 24—Denver, Colorado (Denver immigrant station, staff of three); District 25—El Paso, Texas, plus seventeen substations, including Albuquerque, New Mexico, Douglas, Nogales, Phoenix, Tucson, Arizona (El Paso immigrant station, staff of 53); District 26—Spokane, Washington, plus ten substations (Spokane immigrant station, staff of five); District 27—Salt Lake City, Utah (Salt Lake City immigrant station, staff of one); District 28—Seattle, Washington, plus thirteen substations, including Tacoma and Vancouver, British Columbia (Seattle immigrant station, staff of 50); District 29—Portland, Oregon, plus two substations (Portland immigrant station, staff of 8); District 30—San Francisco, California, plus substations at Sacramento, Eureka, and Fresno (San Francisco immigrant station and Angel Island, staff of 132); District 31—Los Angeles, California, plus fourteen substations, including Calexico, San Diego, San Pedro (Terminal Island), Santa Barbara and Yuma, Arizona (Los Angeles immigrant station, staff of 15); District 32—Ketchikan, Alaska, plus seven substations, including

Juneau (Ketchikan immigrant station, staff of four); District 33—San Juan, Puerto Rico, plus nine substations, including Ponce (San Juan immigrant station, staff of nine); District 34—Honolulu, Hawaii, plus two substations (Honolulu immigrant station, staff of 28); District 35—Galveston, Texas, plus three substations, including Port Arthur (Galveston immigrant station, staff of eight). In addition, there was a Chinese office in Manhattan, New York, which worked closely with Ellis Island officials in dealing with the large number of Chinese in the city and to enforce the Chinese Exclusion Act of 1882 (New York Chinese Office, staff of 16). In 1933, President Franklin D. Roosevelt unified the Bureau of Immigration and the Naturalization to form a single Immigration and Naturalization Service. A consequence of this administrative change was the replacement of the thirty-five immigrant inspection stations by twenty-two stations; as a part of this change, Ellis Island, New York, became District 3.

REFERENCE: Smith, Darrell, and Henry Herring. 1924. *The Bureau of Immigration*. Baltimore, MD: Johns Hopkins University Press.

Immigrant Inspectors. The work of immigrant inspectors was manifold and conducted in several departments, including the **Registry Division**, the **Boarding Division**, and the **Special Inquiry Division**. The registry inspectors performed the best-known function: they interrogated the steerage passengers that composed the vast majority of immigrants passing through Ellis Island. They determined whether they were "beyond a doubt qualified to land." This task was called **primary inspection** and took place in the **Registry Room** of the **Main Building.** The Boarding Division performed the same task with first- and second-class passengers aboard the steamships. They then transported all steerage passengers and first- and second-class detainees to Ellis Island. Inspectors of the Registry and Boarding Divisions detained for special inquiry any alien they thought might not be qualified to land. The special inquiry inspectors formed boards and investigated and decided whether to admit or exclude problem cases.

What follows is a partial list of men who actually worked as immigrant inspectors at Ellis Island; their approximate years of service, previous jobs, and place of birth are included, where known. Eugene P. Abbott (watchman, 1903; inspector, Special Inquiry Division, 1908, and Boarding Division, 1920s–1930s); Wells F. Andrews (1920s); Najeeb Arbeely (1890–1920s); Jacob Auerbach (b. Poland; inspector, 1930–1942); **Percy A. Baker**; Edward J. Barnes (chief, Law Division, 1930s); Karl Bawor (1900–1914); Charles L. Behlert (1920s–1933); Habib A. Bishara (b. 1879; Registry Division, 1917–1940s); William Bock (1892–1920s); August Bostroem (1892–1910; b. Russia); John Breffit (1900–1905; b. England); Michael F. Brophy (1905–1933); William W. Brown (1890s–1929; chief, Law Division), Charles W. Bryant (watchman, 1901; inspector, Special Inquiry Division, 1915–1930s); Richard M. Burke (1900–1930s; Special Inquiry Division); Louis Burkhardt (1910–dismissed 1922); Grover D. Bushman (1920s–1933); Richard W. Conradson (1890–1920); Thomas J. Conry (1920s); **Philip Cowen**; Robert S. Crater (1890s–1915); Lucien Daileader (1920s); Chauncey M. DePuy (chief of Appeals, Hearing and Files Division, 1920s); Daniel Downing (1910–1930s); Joseph DiMiceli (1906–1933); Roman Dobler (b. Germany, 1848; inspector, 1890s–1905; superintendent, 1905–1912; chief, Boarding Division, 1914–1918; senior inspector, 1918–1920s), Charles G. Eichler (1890; chief, Statistics and Record Division, 1899–1903); Charles F. English (1910–1933); Samuel Eppler (1890s–1920s); William Feder (Boarding Division, 1920s–1930s); Max Felstyner (1920–1950s); **Edward Ferro**; Isador Fisch (1920s–1930s); Jeremiah B. Fitzgerald (1903–dismissed, 1921); Edward L. Flannery (1890s–1920s); **Philip Forman**; **Thomas P. Galvin** (1932–1948); Frank Hayes (clerk typist, warrant cases, 1906; chief, Special Inquiry Division, 1920s); Samuel Hays (senior inspector, 1892–1897); David Healy (b.

Canada; inspector, 1906–died 1916;); Oscar W. Henn (1920s); Phillip E. Herrlich (Boarding Division, 1890; chief, 1890s–1906); Arthur S. Hibler (1920s), Howard M. Jackson (1920s); Vincent F. Jankovski (asst. insp., 1900–1902; inspector, 1902–1933; chief, Registry Division, 1914), Alexander Jeannison (1920s); Solomon Johnson (1905–1933); Charles I. Jones (1900–1930); William E. Junker; John Kaba (Boarding Division,1910–1930s); William M. Kanzer (1920s–1930s); Patrick King (1908–1940s; Boarding Division); Max Klein (1920s); Monroe Klein (chief, Passport Division, late 1930s–1940s); Peter Laird (1890s); Edward J. LaPointe (1920s); William Leonard (1903–dismissed 1922); Henry M. Luick (1920s–1930s); Patrick Lynch (1920s); Frank B. Macatee (1892–1920s; Registry Division, 1890s–1906, Special Inquiry Division, 1906–1920s); Vivian G. MacIntosh, (1912–1930s); John J. McKee (1890s–1933; chief, Boarding Division, 1930–1933); Hyman A. Mintzer (Chinese Division, 1920s); John R. Montgomery (Boarding Division, 1920s; chief 1930s–1940s); John J. O'Connor (1890s–1930); Roger O'Donnell (Chinese Division, 1900–1908; special immigrant inspector, 1908–1910); Joseph M.W. Olding (Boarding Division, 1920s); Charles P. Parbury (inspector, 1900–1940; b. Belgium); Vincent Piaggio (Registry Division, 1903–1930s); William C. Pearsall (inspector, 1890s–1920s; chief of Registry Division, 1926); John Raczkiewicz (1892–resigned 1916); John A. W. Richardson (Registry Division, 1915–1930s); Olaf L. Root (1920s); Homer W. Rotz (1900–1915; also served in Seattle, 1915–1930s); Joseph Scarinzi (1910–1930s); William Scarlett (1904–1920s); Charles Semsey (1890–1907), Louis Sillen (Boarding Division, 1941–1954; senior detention officer); John J. Simpson (1890s); Sven A. Smith (b. Sweden; inspector, 1890–1930); Harvey E. Snider (gatekeeper, 1900; clerk, 1903; inspector, 1907–1920s), Luther C. Steward (1900–transferred to Kansas City, July 1916); Andrew Tedesco (b. Hungary; laborer, 1900; Boarding Division inspector, 1905; chief inspector, White Slave investigations, 1910); Clarence A. Thompson (1890–1920); Samuel C. Tompkins (1890–1910); Gideon B. Travis (1920s), Giuseppe Tufarolo (1920s); William Tuller (Record Division: clerk, 1902; chief clerk; chief of the division, 1920s–1933); Frederick A. Tuttle (gatekeeper, 1900; clerk, 1902; inspector, 1906; chief, Primary Inspection, 1918–1920; chief, Boarding Division, 1920; chief, Information Division, 1920s; chief, Consolidated Division (Registry, Information, Discharge and Special Inquiry, 1926; retired 1933); D. T. Van Duzer (1890s); Edward Van Ingen (1890s–1908; also attorney, he handled bids for contracting in the Law Division) Albert Wank (Boarding and Special Inquiry divisions, 1894–1901; b. Austria; formerly held the rank of captain in the Austrian Imperial Army); William S. Watson (Registry Division, 1905–1930s; Arabic interpreter, 1890s–1905); John R. Watts (Boarding Division, 1920s), Eugene W. Willard (1920s–1933); Frank Zahajsky (Boarding Division, 1920s–1930s); **Edward D. Zucker**; and William J. Zucker (Boarding Division, 1920s–1950s).

Immigration Act of 1882 (August 3, 1882; 22 Statute 214). The Immigration Act of 1882 was the first general U.S. immigration restriction law covering several classes of immigrants deemed inadmissible for entry into the United States. The law also imposed a **head tax** of fifty cents for all immigrants planning to settle in the United States. Those excluded under this law were "any convict, lunatic, idiot, or any person unable to take care of himself or herself without becoming a public charge." All such types were to be returned to their countries at the expense of the shipping companies that brought them to the shores of the United States. Immigrants who had been convicted of a political offense were exempt for exclusion under this law's provisions.

Immigration Act of 1891 (March 3, 1891; 26 Statute 1084). This law was the most comprehensive immigration legislation of the nineteenth century and is historically significant because it put the control of immigration squarely in the hands of the federal government control over immigration, thus ending the control that individual states had previously exercised. The law also provided for immigrant inspection, the exclusion and deportation of immigrants, the establishment of immigration regulations and boards of special inquiry. It also created the **Bureau of Immigration** as an agency within the Department of the Treasury. The law also excluded the following types of immigrants from exclusion from the United States:

> "[A]ll idiots, insane persons, paupers or persons likely to become a public charge, persons suffering from a loathsome or a dangerous contagious disease, persons who have been convicted of a felony or other infamous crime or misdemeanor involving moral turpitude, polygamists, and also any person whose ticket or passage is paid by others to come, unless it is affirmatively and satisfactorily shown on special inquiry that such person does not belong to one of the foregoing excluded classes, or to the class of contract laborers excluded by the act of February twenty-sixth eighteen hundred and eighty-five, but this section shall not be held to exclude persons living in the United States from sending for a relative or friend who is not of the excluded classes under such regulations as the Secretary of the Treasury may prescribe: Provided, that nothing in this act shall be construed to apply to or exclude persons convicted of a political offence."

Immigration Act of 1893 (I) (February 15, 1893; 27 Statute 449, 452). This law authorized the president to prohibit the entry into the United States all persons and property from foreign countries where cholera and or other infectious or contagious diseases were known to exist.

Immigration Act of 1893 (II) (March 3, 1893; 27 Statute 569). Under this law all commanding ship officers bringing immigrants to the United States were required to deliver to immigration officers manifests of lists of alien passengers with detailed information on each person. It empowered the immigrant inspectors to detain and bring any doubtful immigrant before a board of special inquiry composed of four inspectors. A vote of at least three members was required to accept or reject the alien. A dissenting inspector either for or against the majority could appeal to the commissioner. The law also required that the American consul at the port of embarkation verify the manifest of alien passengers, to ensure that the immigrants had received physical examinations before boarding the vessel and were not ineligible to emigrate to the United States.

Immigration Act of 1895 (28 Statue L, 764, 780). This law changed the name of the **Office of Immigration** to the **Bureau of Immigration** and likewise altered the titles of the agency's top officials. The highest official, the superintendent of immigration was restyled commissioner-general of immigration. In addition, he was given responsibility of enforcing the **contract labor laws**.

Immigration Act of 1903 (32 Statute 1213). This statue of March 3, 1903, was enacted to codify all previous federal immigration laws and include a new restriction on immigration. Containing thirty-nine sections, it strengthened bureaucratic procedures such as immigrant inspection, **detention**, and **deportation**. It also excluded persons who held certain political views regarded as radical; this was primarily aimed at **anarchists**, but was also used against Bolsheviks and communists. This was a significant departure from previous U.S. policy, which had previously welcomed any immigrant regardless of his or her politics. In sum, the following were excluded. On medical grounds: "Idiots, insane persons, epileptics, and persons who have been insane within five years previous; person who have had one or two attacks of insanity at any time previously . . . persons afflicted with a loathsome or a dangerous contagious disease." On economic grounds: "paupers, persons likely to become a public charge, and professional beggars; contracted foreign laborers, including those whose ticket or passage had been paid by some another persons."

On criminal or moral grounds: "persons . . . convicted of a felony or other crime or misdemeanor involving moral turpitude, polygamists, prostitutes, and persons who procure or attempt to bring in prostitutes or women for the purposes of prostitution." On racist grounds, it upheld the "the laws relating to exclusion of persons of Chinese descent." On political grounds it excluded "anarchists, or persons who believe in or advocate the overthrow of the United States or of all government or of all forms of law, or the assassination of public officials." Immigrants exempt from exclusion were those whose fare was paid for by a relative, any person whose employment was of such as a type as could not be found the United States, and all "actors, artists, lecturers, singers, ministers of any religious denomination, professors for colleges or seminaries, persons belonging to any recognized learned profession, or persons employed strictly as personal or domestic servants." The Immigration Act of 1903 also reduced the size of the boards of special inquiry from four to three members. The vote of two members could decide a case, while the dissenter could appeal to the commissioner, if he wished. The law also authorized the **Bureau of Immigration** to impose a $100 fine on steamship and other transportation companies that brought to America an alien afflicted with a loathsome or contagious disease, the illness of which could easily have been detected by a doctor overseas. Most of the details of this codified statue were included on the advice of Commissioner **William Williams**.

Immigration Act of 1907 (February 20, 1907; 34 Statute 898). The Immigration Act of 1907 raised the head tax for immigrants to $4.00 and expanded the classes of immigrants to be excluded from entering the United States. The new groups barred were imbeciles, "feeble-minded" persons, persons with physical or mental defects that might make it difficult for them to earn a livelihood, persons with tuberculosis, children unaccompanied by a parent, anyone who admitting that he had committed a crime prior to entering the United States, persons whose tickets had been paid for by a foreign government or any private organization, and all children under the age of sixteen unless accompanied by or going to one or both parents. This law also required the government to maintain emigration statistics of departing aliens, took away the right of physically or mental disabled immigrants from appealing against a decision of the boards of special inquiry. It also required steamship lines to improve sanitary conditions aboard ships and established a Joint Immigration Commission of Congress. Additionally, it excused professional actors, artists, lecturers, singers, clergy, professors, and domestic servants from exclusion under the contract labor laws.

See also **Statistical Division**

Reference: Unrau, Harlan D. 1984. *The Historic Resource Study: Ellis Island/Statue of Liberty*. Vol. 1. Washington, DC: U.S. Department of Interior, National Park Service.

Immigration Act of 1917 (February 5, 1917; 39 Statute 874). Influenced by the findings of the Dillingham Commission, this statute was enacted over the veto of President Woodrow Wilson. It repealed the immigration acts of 1903 and 1907 and all other laws inconsistent with its provisions. Further, it introduced a literacy test for immigrants in English or another language and barred Asian immigration. It excluded from entering the United States all immigrants found to be idiots; imbeciles; feeble-minded; anyone who had one or more attacks of insanity; persons of constitutional psychopathic inferiority; chronic alcoholics; paupers; professional beggars; vagrants; the tubercular; persons with a loathsome or contagious disease; anyone with a physical or mental defect that may affect his ability to earn a living; those who have committed a crime involving moral turpitude; polygamists; anarchists; those who believe in or advocate the overthrow of the government; those who believe in the assassination of public officials; those who advocate the destruction of property; those affiliated with any organization teaching the foregoing views; prostitutes; procurers and pimps; contracted laborers, skilled or unskilled (but exempted were professional actors, artists, lecturers, singers, nurses, ministers, professors, members of the learned professions and domestic servants); laborers who come in response to advertisements for laborers published abroad; persons likely to become a public charge; persons who had previously been deported (unless approved by the attorney general); persons whose ticket or passage was paid by another unless it is known that they do not belong to an excluded class; persons whose passage is paid by any corporation, association, society, municipality, foreign government, except aliens in transit; stowaways; children under sixteen years of age unaccompanied by a parent or parents, or not coming to a parent; Asiatic immigrants not already barred under the Chinese exclusion laws and the gentlemen's agreement with Japan (exceptions to this law: government officials, ministers, missionaries, lawyers, physicians, students, authors, artists, merchants, travelers for curiosity or pleasure, and their legal wives and children under sixteen years of age, so long as they maintain their status or occupation at entry, in which event they shall be deported; persons over sixteen years who cannot read some language (excepted were alien's relatives over the age of 55; also exempted were political or religious refugees and those previously admitted or were in transit).

Immigration Act of 1918 (40 Statute 1012). This law was leveled against **anarchists** and persons advocating the overthrow of government by force or violence. It also excluded persons who advocated assaulting or assassinating government officials "because of their official character;" those advocating the unlawful damage, injury, or destruction of property; or those advocating acts of sabotage. It granted the federal government more power to deport aliens who had already settled in the United States. The provisions now made deportable aliens associated with the proscribed doctrines based on belief, membership in subversive organizations, or writing or publishing proscribed literature. Aliens deported for these reasons were forbidden ever to return to the United States, and those who did so were automatically guilty of a felony.

Immigration Act of 1924 (May 26, 1924; 43 Statute 1530). This was the most important immigration restriction law in U.S. history. Its provisions required that no more than 2 percent of the proportion of a nationality living in the United States in the year 1890 could enter the country annually. This law thus ended mass migration to the United States and drastically changed conditions at Ellis Island. **Line inspection** was no longer necessary, scores of employees were discharged, and certain previous laws no longer needed to be upheld with such rigor. Further, Ellis Island was soon transformed into the federal government's chief deporting station for undesirable aliens.

This law reduced the annual quota set forth in the 1921 measure from 357,803 to only 164,677. Hence western and northern Europe received 85.6 percent of the slots for quotas, while southern and eastern Europe received 12.4 percent.

Only the independent nations of the Western Hemisphere were exempt from the quota regulations; thus immigrants from those countries entered the United States as nonquota immigrants. All quota and nonquota immigrants had to obtain an immigrant visa to enter the country. American consuls stationed abroad issued immigrant visas. The Immigration Act of 1924 remained in force until the passage of the **Immigration Act of 1965**, which did away with preferential quotas.

Immigration Act of 1965. This law repealed the preferential quotas favoring western and northern European immigrants over eastern and southern Europeans, a policy that was adopted under the **Immigration Act of 1924**.

It was approved by President **Lyndon B. Johnson**.

Immigration Building. This building stands behind the **ferry house** and was erected on new **landfill** and was planned during 1934 and 1935 by Treasury Department supervisory architect Louis A. Simon and consulting architect Chester Aldrich. Designed in the WPA modern style, it was constructed during 1935 and 1936. It is linked to the ferry house by a passageway. It was intended for the use of aliens detained for minor problems and voluntary repatriates. It was a way of segregating them from deportees and criminals. However, after completion, the building was not put in use. The Coast Guard used the building from 1939 through 1946.

Rooms in the building included a large sitting room and barber shop; upstairs there were ten dormitories and two sun porches with skylights.

Immigration and Naturalization Service. When the **Bureau of Immigration** was reunited with the Bureau of Naturalization in 1933, the combination was named the Immigration and Naturalization Service (INS). As the INS, the agency had greater reach and responsibilities, as naturalizations and the detention and recording of aliens had expanded since the two bureaus had last been united from 1906 through 1913 as the **Bureau of Immigration and Naturalization**.

The Immigration and Naturalization Service was transferred from the Department of Labor to the Department of Justice in 1940 and was abolished in 2003. Its successors are the Bureau of Immigration and Customs Enforcement, which is responsible for illegal aliens, detention and deportation; the Bureau of Citizenship and Immigration Services, which is responsible for naturalizations, asylum, and refugee affairs; the Bureau of Customs and Border Protection, which is responsible for the Border Patrol and immigrant inspections on the Canadian and Mexican borders; and the Office of Immigration Statistics. These agencies are in the U.S. Department of Homeland Security.

See also **New York District (INS)**

Immigration Regulations. On April 25, 1893, the secretary of the treasury issued the following regulations to the **Bureau of Immigration**. These regulations, despite the passage of years and occasional modifications, remained the standard for the inspection of aliens until of the adoption of the **Immigration Act of 1924**.

Article 1 authorized the collectors of customs to continue collecting the **head tax** duty of fifty cents for each and every foreign passenger coming to the United States by steam or sail vessel from a foreign port, except for vessels employed exclusively between the ports of the United States, Canada, and Mexico, which had been exempt from the head tax as of 1884. *Article 2* dealt with depositing the head tax money and keeping accounts. *Article 3* empowered the collectors of customs to enforce federal immigration laws at any place along the Canadian frontier in the absence of officers of the Bureau of Immigration.

Article 4 authorized immigration officials to remove temporarily from vessels all foreigners and take them to a place of immigrant inspection. It further stated that immigrants so taken should not be regarded as having landed in the United States pending their questioning by the authorities. *Article 5* ordered the commissioner of immigration to record the name of immigrants prohibited from entering the country. Both the reason for the exclusion and an order in the form of a written notice requiring the vessel to return the prohibited immigrants "to the port whence they came." *Article 6* authorized the Bureau of Immigration to exclude the public from all board of special inquiry hearings. However, if an immigrant were excluded by a decision of a board of special inquiry or if he should file for an appeal against a decision, he was given the right of conferring with friends of counsel "in such as manner as the commissioner may deem proper."

Article 7 allowed any immigrant claiming to be "aggrieved by the decision of the inspection officers" to file an appeal, which effectively stayed the immigration deportation. The appeal had to be submitted in writing to the commissioner, specifying the grounds on which the appeal was made. The commissioner was then instructed to forward the appeal the Department of the Treasury in Washington, DC, "with all the evidence in the case and his views thereon." Further, this article authorized "any examining inspector dissenting from a decision to admit an immigrant" to file a written appeal against it, which was to be submitted to the commissioner, who was required to forward it "to the Department in like manner as in cases of appeal by an immigrant." *Article 8* declared that once the department in Washington, DC, had rendered a judgment on an appeal, the immigrant was to be "at once landed or deported" in accordance with the decision made. In the case of those ordered deported, officials of the steamship line were to be informed and the alien was to placed aboard one of its vessels "to be returned as aforesaid." *Article 9* assigned the expenses for the keep and maintenance of immigrants ordered deported to the steamship line responsible for having brought such immigrants to this country.

Article 10 instructed the responsible officials of vessels to notify the commissioner twenty-four hours before sailing of their proposed hour sailing, so that the commissioner could place on board "all immigrants to be returned by such vessel aforesaid." Any official of the steamship line refusing in any way to cooperate with this arrangement were to be declared guilty of a misdemeanor and "fined not less than $300 for each and every offence and . . . shall not have clearance from any port of the United States while any such fine is unpaid." *Article 11* barred immigrants from entering the United States on a ship coming from a port contaminated with an infectious disease without having first been separately quarantined and under medical observation at the port of embarkation for at least five days, and their clothing, baggage, and personal effects disinfected before being stowed aboard ship. *Article 12* decreed that the master or commanding officer of the vessel should make a manifest or list of immigrant passenger with nineteen questions to be answered of each passenger at the port of embarkation. On arrival at an American port, this manifest or list should be delivered to the commissioner of immigration. The following are the nineteen questions:

1. Full name
2. Age
3. Sex
4. Whether married or single
5. Calling or occupation
6. Whether able to read or write
7. Nationality
8. Last residence
9. Seaport for landing in the United States
10. Final destination in the United States
11. Whether having a ticket through to such final destination
12. Whether the immigrant has paid his own passage or whether it has been paid by other persons or by any corporation, society, municipality, or government
13. Whether in possession of money; and, if so, whether upward of $30, and how much, if $30 or less
14. Whether going to join a relative; and, if so, what relative, and his name and address
15. Whether ever before in the United States; and, if so, when and where
16. Whether ever in prison, or almshouse, or supported by charity
17. Whether a polygamist
18. Whether under contract, express or implied, to perform labor in the United States
19. The immigrant's condition of health, mentally and physically, and whether deformed or crippled; and, if so, from what cause

Article 13 ordered that immigrants would be listed in convenient groups and no one list or manifest was to have more than thirty names per page; and that each immigrant be given a ticket identification for the use of immigration officials on arrival at U.S. ports. The ticket was required to have written on it the name of the passenger, a number or letter designating the list and the passenger's name on that list, "for convenience of identification on arrival." Further, each list or manifest was required to be declared true on the oath or affirmation of the master of the vessel or the first or second officer, and of the ship's surgeon or medical officer. Each of these affidavits was to be attached to each list or manifest.

Article 14 imposed a fine on any steamship line failing to submit lists or manifests of immigrant passengers; the fine was $100 for each immigrant qualified to enter the United States, "or said immigrant shall not be so permitted to enter the United States, but shall be returned like other excluded persons." *Article 15* stipulated that the filing date of the certificate required by section 8 be filed with the secretary of the treasury on the first days of January and July of each year. *Article 16* ruled on the effective dates of these rules; the majority were to take effect immediately; sections 7 and 11 were to take effect on May 3, 1893.

The above regulations were then supplemented by Bureau of Immigration rules issued on November 29, 1893, by Superintendent (later Commissioner-General) Herman Stump. They were included in Departmental Circular 177.

1. All alien immigrants before they are landed shall be inspected and examined, as by law provided, on shipboard or at a suitable place provided for the convenience of the owners of vessels transporting them and the comfort of the immigrant, where they may be temporarily placed while undergoing such examination. During such time and until finally discharged and landed, said immigrants shall be deemed and be treated, as on shipboard, and the owners, consignee, or master of the vessel transporting shall be liable for all expenses incurred in lodging, feeding and caring for them, or said immigrants may be remanded onboard ship or taken onboard ship by the master thereof, who shall be responsible for their safe-keeping.

2. Upon arrival, all alien immigrants shall be inspected and examined without unnecessary delay. Those qualified to land shall be promptly discharged. Those detailed for special inquiry shall have a speedy hearing and be either discharged or ordered deported. If an appeal is prayed, the record of proceedings shall at once be transmitted to the Superintendent of Immigration in Washington. All expenses incurred in lodging, feeding, and maintaining alien immigrants during the period covered by these proceedings shall be borne by the steamship company, owners, or master of the vessels transporting them. No appeal shall be received or transmitted which is applied to after the immigrant has been transferred from the immigrant station to be deported.

3. Upon arrival of an alien immigrant, helpless from sickness, physical debility or infancy, who is detained for further inquiry, one person only—if necessary—shall be detained to look after and care for such helpless immigrant, the natural guardian or relative to be selected; the transportation company to the responsible for their maintenance whilst so detained. The remainder of the family—if any—shall proceed on their journey or defray their own expenses.

4. In case of an immigrant not qualified to land, but who would be entitled upon proof of certain facts, such as the case of a woman who claims to have a husband, father or brother, residents of this country, able and willing to support her, she may be detained a reasonable time until such husband, father or brother can be communicated with; the transportation company to be responsible for her maintenance in such and like cases until a final decision is reached.

5. Immigrants qualified to land shall be promptly discharged and landed and, if they desire to wait for friends or remittances, they may be permitted to do so upon payment of all costs and expenses, which should not be charged to the transportation company. In cases where an immigrant qualified to land is unable, from accident or unavoidable circumstances to immediately continue his journey, and is without sufficient means to defray the expenses of the enforced delay, the Commissioner of Immigration may, in his discretion, pay said expense, reporting said case to the Bureau of Immigration with reasons for his action, and ask that such expense be paid out of the "immigrant fund."

6. That in case of the arrival of sick and disabled immigrants unable to travel, said immigrants shall be removed to hospitals provide for their case, and shall be maintained at the expense of the owner or master of the vessel transporting them until suffi-

ciently recovered either to be landed or deported and, whilst detained in hospital shall not be considered as landed until examined and discharged, or said immigrants shall remain on shipboard until able and ready to be landed or deported.

Immigration Restriction League. The Immigration Restriction League (IRL) was founded in Boston in 1894 by three Harvard graduates, **Prescott Hall** (secretary, 1894–1921), **Robert De Courcy Ward** (secretary), and Charles Warren. They were soon joined by John Fiske, Nathaniel Shaler, and Henry Cabot Lodge. The league was created to oppose what its founders believed to be an invasion of the United States by "undesirable immigrants" who threatened the American way of life, which at the time was primarily dominated by Protestant citizens of Anglo-Saxon ancestry. Often called the "new immigrants," the newcomers for whom the IRL expressed such horror and distaste were peoples primarily from eastern and southern Europe, such as Slavs, Jews, Hungarians, Romanians, Italians, Greeks, Albanians, Spaniards, Portuguese, and Gypsies (Roma). Also "undesirable" were peoples coming from the Near and Far East, such as Arabs, Turks, Egyptians, Armenians, Persians, Indians, and Japanese. The league also opposed the immigration of Spanish Americans, Brazilians, Africans, and West Indian blacks. For the next thirty-five years, the IRL was the nation's most powerful lobby against this type of immigration, whom they labeled as unfit for assimilation into American society because of racial inferiority, cultural and ethnic backwardness, and a tendency towards moral degeneracy. Many leading anthropologists, sociologists, biologists, organized labor, patriotic societies, law enforcement officials, and charities generally endorsed their views, which gave the league considerable influence in Congress. Thus the eventual passage of immigration restriction legislation such as the **Immigration Act of 1917,** the **Quota Act of 1921**, and the landmark **Immigration Act of 1924** came as no surprise. Throughout the years, the league argued strongly in favor of the adoption of a literacy requirement for immigrants, since it was known that most of the new immigrants were illiterate in the native languages and dialects. The league supported a succession of literacy bills (1896, 1898, 1902, 1906, and 1909) in Congress that failed to be enacted. Finally, the league tasted victory with the passage and approval of the Immigration Act of 1917. This law made minimal literacy in any language a requirement for an immigrant to enter the United States. In addition to the members mentioned above, others within the league's inner circle included **Madison Grant**, Owen Wister, Henry Holt, Robert Treat Paine, and John Farwell Moors; the latter served as its president. At Ellis Island, they received support from Commissioner **Joseph Senner** in the 1890s. For many years the IRL was opposed by the relatively ineffectual National Liberal Immigration League, which was founded in 1906.

See also **Evans-Gordon, Sir William; Immigration Restriction Movement**

REFERENCES: Coakley, J. F., et al. 2002. Immigration Restriction League Records Guide. Collection of Houghton Library, Harvard University; LeMay, Michael C. 1987. *From Open Door to Dutch Door: An Analysis of U.S. Immigration Policy since 1820.* New York: Praeger; Ward, Robert DeCourcy. 1904. The restriction of immigration. *North American Revue*, 226–237.

Immigration Restriction Movement. The movement to restrict immigration began with opposition to Chinese immigration to California and resulted in the adoption of the Chinese Exclusion Act of 1882. Subsequently, opposition to rising numbers of southern and eastern European immigrants became a primary factor in the strength of the movement. Racism and Anglo-Saxon chauvinism were powerful elements in the movement. In addition, there was a fear that immigrants from such regions were bringing "foreign" diseases (typhus, cholera, trachoma, varieties of tuberculosis, etc.) and dangerous political beliefs such as anarchism, syndicalism, socialism, and bolshevism). In addition, many feared growing populations of Cath-

Harold Cargill drew this anti-immigration cartoon showing the Mother Countries taking advantage of Uncle Sam's "open arms" policy on immigration, ca 1920. Courtesy of the Ellis Island Immigration Museum.

Many American workers feared immigrants as competitors for jobs in industry and manufacturing. This cartoon underlines the fact that most immigrants were not interested in agricultural work. Courtesy of the Ellis Island Immigration Museum.

olics and Jews in Protestant America. In 1894, Senator Henry Cabot Lodge (R-MA) joined other nativists to found the **Immigration Restriction League** in Boston and in 1896 he successfully pushed through Congress an immigration restriction literacy bill, which was vetoed by President Grover Cleveland. Further attempts to cut immigration by imposing a literacy requirement failed to pass in 1898, 1902, 1906, and 1909. On the West Coast, the Japanese Exclusion League, supported by Senator Hiram Johnson (R-CA), added to the anti-immigrant fever. In 1903, two immigration acts became law. One act (32 Statute 1213), added epileptics, prostitutes, and professional beggars to the list of aliens to be excluded from the country. The second law (32 Statute 828) transferred the **Bureau of Immigration** from the Department of the Treasury to the newly formed Department of Commerce and Labor. In 1917, opposition to a literacy requirement for immigrants was finally overcome when the provision was included in the **Immigration Act of 1917**. This law required immigrants to be able read and effectively barred Asians from immigrating into the United States.

The forces opposing immigration united after the war and had a temporary measure, the **Quota Act of 1921**, enacted into law. But the greatest achievement of the restrictionist movement came in the passage of the powerful **Immigration Act of 1924**, which barred mass migration into the United States for decades. Subsequently, a variety of supportive restrictions laws were enacted including the National Origins Act of 1929, the Philippine Independence Act of 1934 (48 Statute 456), **Internal Security Act of 1950**, and the Immigration and Naturalization Act of 1952, which did away with the racist provision barring Asians from becoming U.S. citizens.

See also **Evans-Gordon, Sir William; Grant, Madison; Johnson, Albert; McCarran, Patrick A. ; Quota Act of 1921; Reed, David A.; Walter, Francis E.; Ward, Robert DeCourcy**

Immigration Statistics. The following are the immigration statistics for the port of New York, the vast majority of which passed through Ellis Island. The totals for the entire country appear in brackets.

1892—445,987 [579,663]
1893—343,422 [439,730]
1894—219,046 [285,631]
1895—190,928 [258,536]
1896—263,709 [343,267]
1897—180,556 [230,832]
1898—178,748 [229,299]
1899—242,573 [311,715]
1900—341,712 [448,572]
1901—388,931 [487,918]
1902—493,262 [648,743]
1903—631,835 [857,046]
1904—606,019 [812,870]
1905—788,219 [1,026,499]
1906—880,036 [1,100,735]
1907—1,004,756 [1,285,349]
1908—585,970 [782,870]
1909—580,617 [751,786]
1910—786,094 [1,041,570]
1911—637,003 [878,587]
1912—605,151 [838,172]
1913—892,653 [1,197,892]
1914—878,052 [1,218,480]
1915—178,416 [326,700]
1916—141,390 [298,826]
1917—129,446 [295,403]
1918—28,867 [110,618]
1919—26,731 [141,132]
1920—225,206 [430,001]
1921—560,971 [805,228]
1922—209,778 [309,556]
1923—295,473 [522,919]
1924—315,587 [706,896]

Total immigration for the United States between 1892 and 1924 was 20,003,041, of which 14,277,144 (71.4 percent of total) arrived at New York harbor and passed through Ellis Island.

1925—137,492 [294,314]
1926—149,289 [304,488]
1927—165,510 [335,175]
1928—157,887 [307,255]
1929—158,238 [279,678]
1930—147,982 [241,700]
1931—63,392 [97,139]
1932—21,500 [35,576]
1933—12,944 [23,068]
1934—17,574 [29,470]
1935—23,173 [34,956]
1936—23,434 [36,329]
1937—31,644 [50,244]
1938—44,846 [67,395]
1939—62,035 [82,998]
1940—48,408 [70,756]
1941—23,622 [51,776]
1942—10,173 [28,781]
1943—1,089 [23,725]
1944—1,075 [28,551]
1945—2,636 [38,119]
1946—52,050 [108,721]
1947—83,884 [147,292]
1948—104,665 [170,570]
1949—113,050 [188,317]
1950—166,849 [249,187]
1951—142,903 [205,717]
1952—183,222 [265,520]
1953—87,483 [170,434]
1954—98,813 [208,177]

See also **Destinations; Races and Peoples**

REFERENCE: Unrau, Harlan D. 1984. *The Historic Resource Study: Ellis Island/Statue of Liberty*. Vol. 1. Washington, DC: U.S. Department of Interior, National Park Service.

Information Bureau. Also known as the Information Division, the Information Bureau kept indexes of all active cases of aliens held or discharged from Ellis Island. The chief inspector, several clerks, and other assistants answered inquiries from immigrants' friends and relatives who called at Ellis Island in person, sent a letter or telegram or telephoned. On ascertaining an alien's status, it referred callers to the appropriate department or office, such as the hospital, an immigrant society, the **Deporting Division**, **Discharging Division**, or

Executive Division. Its clerks also issued passes to visited detainees in the many departments or offices at the station. A long-serving clerk there was Anna Prokupek (1892–1920s). The bureau was located on the first floor in the west wing of the **Main Building**. For many years, refreshments could be purchased in a small cafeteria adjacent to the bureau. The division dated from 1892 and continued operating until the station closed in 1954. By the latter year, it had been renamed the Information Unit and was absorbed by the Mails, Files, and Information Section.

See also **Discharging Division**

Insane Persons. Immigrants certified as insane comprised a large number of foreigners who were excluded from the United States. The largest number of such exclusions occurred in the following years: 189 (1907), 175 (1913), 172 (1914), 169 (1910), 159 (1908), 141 (1909), 139 (1906), 123 (1916), 112 (1917), and 111 (1911). In all other years less than 100 persons were excluded for this reason. The total number of such exclusions for 1892 through 1931 was 2,012. Aliens were excluded under this provision during the whole period in which Ellis Island was opened.

See also **Mental Testing; Psychopathic Ward**

Inspection. *See* **Line Inspection; Primary Inspection**

Inspection Division. The **Registry Division** was renamed the Inspection Division in about 1929. The **immigrant inspectors** of this division made the primary examinations of aliens entering the United States whose papers were not in order or had not been inspected at American consulates abroad. The former **Special Inquiry Division** was also amalgamated within this division. The Inspection Division remained active until the **closing of Ellis Island**.

Inspectors. *See* **Immigrant Inspectors**

Internal Security Act of 1950. Passed by Congress on September 22, 1950, this law required all communist front organizations to register with the U.S. Department of Justice. It had a strong impact on immigration since it barred all members of totalitarian organizations from immigrating to the United States or gaining U.S. citizenship. Thus all communists and fascists (including Nazis and Falangists) were barred from entering the country as immigrants, resulting in Ellis Island's return to the limelight. During the latter part of 1950 and the spring of 1951, hundreds of immigrants, refugees, and foreign visitors were summarily taken from steamships and airplanes, directly on arrival in New York, and detained at Ellis Island. Often, admission to membership in such organizations as the Hitler Youth or the Chinese Communist Party did not reflect personal political views but rather the social pressures forced upon residents of a totalitarian state. All such detainees had to satisfactorily explain their wartime activities and their political affiliations to immigration inspectors or face exclusion. The overcrowding at Ellis Island and the treatment of foreigners under the new law aroused a good deal of criticism and public debate. Under this pressure, Congress partly backed down by passing an amendment to the Internal Security Act on March 28, 1951. This amendment exempted all persons from the Internal Security Act if certain conditions existed at the time of their affiliation with a fascist or communist organization. Thus anyone who had been a member under the age of sixteen, had been forced into membership through a national law, had joined in order to obtain food, work, or a livelihood, and former members who had actively opposed totalitarianism for the past five years. Aside from its effect on immigration, the Internal Security also prohibited communists from working in defense industries and granted the president the power to intern them in the event of a national emergency. The author of this law was Senator Patrick A. McCarran (D-NV), one of the nation's leading hawks. He was responsible for another stringently anticommunist law, the Immigration and Naturalization Act of 1952. Commonly known as the McCarran-Walter Act, it placed further constraints on immigrants or naturalized citizens identified by the government as subversive.

REFERENCES: Bennett, Marion T. 1963. *American Immigration Policies: A History*. Washington, DC: Public Affairs; Caute, David. 1978. *The Great Fear: The Anti-Communist Purge under Truman and Eisenhower.* New York: Simon & Schuster.

Internment. *See* **Enemy Aliens; Nazis; World War I; World War II**

Interpreters. Interpreters translated and interpreted for immigrants who could not communicate in English. Both the **Bureau of Immigration** and the **Public Health Service** employed interpreters. On the bureau staff, they were usually assigned to the **Registry Division** and aided the immigrant inspectors in interrogated non–English speaking immigrants. Many were themselves immigrants and some had entered the United States through **Castle Garden** or Ellis Island. The U.S. Civil Service Commission's examination for interpreters in 1914 was divided into six subjects: linguistic ability (50 percent), spelling ability (10 percent), knowledge of arithmetic (10 percent), letter writing (10 percent), penmanship (10 percent), and copying from texts (10 percent). They were required to be U.S. citizens of at least eighteen years of age and had to submit a recent photograph of themselves to the government.

The following list drawn up by Commissioner **William Williams** shows the number of languages known by interpreters as of January 1911. Arabic (Syrian)—2; Albanian—2; Armenian—2; Bohemian Czech—4; Bosnian—1; Bulgarian—5; Croatian—7; Dalmatian—2; Danish—2; Dutch—1; Finnish—1; Flemish 1; French—14; German—14; Greek—8; Herzegovinian—1; Italian—11; Lithuanian—2; Macedonian—1; Magyar (Hungarian)—4; Montenegrin—4; Moravian Czech—1; Norwegian—2; Persian (Farsi)—1; Polish—6; Portuguese—1; Roumanian—4; Russian—6; Ruthenian—4; Servian (Serbian)—6; Slovak—7; Slovenian—2; Spanish—2; Swedish—3; Turkish—6; Yiddish—9.

On January 3, 1911, Commissioner William Williams made the following remarks about the interpreters in correspondence with the commissioner-general:

> Thirty-six interpreters are given credit in the above table for languages with which they are but slightly acquainted. For instance, they may be able to speak them but cannot read or write them. Again, some may be able to read them but cannot speak them.
>
> Thirty-six interpreters are in one sense a large number, but in another is not. There are twenty inspection lines, all of them full during numerous successive days in the year, and there are always four (special inquiry) boards, usually six and sometimes eight. Then there is the Boarding Division with the poor quality of people arriving in the second cabin (placed there often on advice that they could not enter through the steerage). And there are also the appeals before the Commissioner, requiring the presence of one or more interpreters between 11 a.m. and 1 or 2.30 p.m. every day. I should add that there are a number of investigations in New York City which it falls to the lot of the interpreters to make. You will perhaps have to take my word for it that we are very short of interpreters, but in giving it I assure you it is based on full knowledge of the situation. The Chief of the Registry Division is constantly having to surrender men to the boards and vice versa, at a time when both of them need the men. With the 20 lines filled, one-third of them we will say with immigrants knowing only Slavic languages, it is obviously impossible for our interpreters who know Slavic languages to be on all those lines, let alone to be doing board work or the other kind of work which it may be imperative for them to do at that particular time. What happens is this: Our inspectors cope with the situation as best they can, and that means in some instances that they cannot cope with it. Many who can ask the ordinary questions are all at sea when it comes to inquiring of the immigrants as to the condition of health of the members of the family remaining abroad, etc. Nor can they ask whether any accompanying members of the family came second cabin, as so often they do when they are sick and ineligible.

Thus it comes as no surprise that immigrant inspectors were encouraged to learn one or more foreign languages on their own time.

Prominent among the Ellis Island interpreters were Domenico J. Andreaccio (Italian; 1890s–1930s; b. Italy), August J. Arachtingi (Turkish; 1900–1920; b. Turkey), Marie N. Arbeely (Arabic and French; 1908–1921), Peter Bacigalupo (Italian, 1890–1905), Samuel D. Barbari (Arabic, French), Habib A. Bishara (Arabic, French, Turkish; 1905–1917; immigrant inspector, 1917–1940s), John Thomas Braun (German and six other languages; 1900–1908), John J. Camara (1905–1917), Emile Carpentier (French and German; 1912–1917) Cesare Casarico (Italian, French, and Spanish; 1910–1917), Demetrios Christopher (Greek, Turkish, French; 1903–1920s; b. Turkey), Vincent Daukszys (Russian, Polish, and Lithuanian), Father De Javannes (French, Italian, and Spanish; read and translated Latin), F. C. DiGiovanni (Italian; 1903–1915), Joseph Di Miceli (Italian interpreter, 1890s–1903; immigrant inspector, 1903–1930s; b. Italy), N. Driller (Hebrew, Yiddish, German, and Polish; 1920s), A. Dwozecki (Lithuanian, Polish and Russian, 1920s), **José Dias d'Escobar** (Portuguese and Spanish, 1918–1930s), John A. Fenger (1915–1917), José Ferreira do Valle (Portuguese, 1900–1905; native of Brazil), **Edward Ferro** (Italian, 1919–early 1920s), Emil Forman (Croatian, Czech, Slovenian, and German), Carl Freund (German; 1890–1899), Abraham M. Friptu (Yiddish, Romanian and French; 1920s–1930s), Anthony Galletta (1942–1954), Nahum Greenberg (1916), George Grunik (Hungarian; 1900–1914; b. Hungary), Joseph Gyory (Hungarian, German; 1900–1930), Charles J. Hedberg (1892–1999), C. S. Ingalls (Armenian, Turkish, and Persian; 1920s), Vincent F. Jankovski (Estonian and Russian, etc., 1903–1933), Louis Jenik (Czech and German; 1890s–1905), Louis Kaye (clerk, Verifications, 1929; inspector, 1930–1940), Joseph Kratky (German; 1892–1900; b. Austria), **Fiorello H. LaGuardia** (Italian, French, Yiddish, and Serbo-Croatian), J. Lassoe (Danish, Norwegian, and Swedish), Elias Lazaretti (Italian; 1914–1917), Solomon Lubliner (1890s–1905; b. Russian Poland); **Frank Martoccia** (Italian, 1899–1938; b. Italy), Domianus Maskeviczious (Russian; 1900–1905; b. Russia), B. Matusek (Slovak and Czech), **Peter Mikolainis** (Lithuanian, Russian, German, etc.), Kosta D. Momiroff (Russian), F. Mordt (Norwegian, Danish and Swedish; 1920s), B. K. Moscopoulos (Greek; 1890s; b. Greece), Julius Nazar (Turkish; 1903; b. Turkey), Desiderius Nemeth (Hungarian, 1903), Edward L. Newman (1917), Einar Nordenstreng (Scandinavian languages and French; 1912–1923, fired), Andrea Palmieri (1890–1999), Vincent Piaggio (Italian, 1903), John Peeters (Flemish and Dutch; 1900–1910; b. Belgium); Nicola Prisco (Italian, 1903; b. Italy), Sigmund Radwaner (Romanian, Yiddish, Greek, Italian, and German, 1920s), Selim S. Sadah (Turkish; 1900–1905; b. Turkey), George E. Schubert (German; 1890s–1903; inspector, 1903; b. Austria), Daniel Schwartz (German; messenger, 1900–1903; interpreter, 1903–1906; b. Austria), Alicibiades A. Seraphic (Greek, 1900–1905; b. Turkey), Cyprian Shanowsky (Russian, 1920s–1930s; b. Russia), Ichiro Shirato (Japanese, 1935–1945), Julius Stierheim (German and Hungarian; 1900–1914; b. Hungary), Ernest Stoltenberger (German, 1913), Is. Van Lier (Dutch, Spanish, German and French), Frank Varallo (Italian, 1890s), Angelo P. G. Viglezzi (Italian; 1911–d. May 11, 1916) J. Vogels (Flemish, Dutch, and French), Ruben Volovick (Russian, Yiddish and Ruthenian, etc.; 1905–1935), Hendric M. F. von Stamp (Danish; 1895–1905; b. Denmark), Julius F. von Vesterneck (German; 1890s–1901; b. Germany), G. P. Voskanyan (Armenian and Turkish, 1920s–1930s), **Charles Waldo** (Finnish; 1890s–1905; inspector, 1905–1913), William S. Watson (Arabic; 1890s–1905), Adam Wetzler (1890–1899), Mrs. Eleonora Yovtcheff (Bulgarian, Italian, Greek, and Turkish).

The following is a selection of employees working in other positions at Ellis Island who were also fluent in foreign languages. Inspector Najeeb Arbeely (Arabic and French; 1890–1920s), Inspector Richard W. Conradson (Swedish, 1892–1920s), Sven A. Smith (Swedish, Norwegian, and Danish; 1892–1930; b. Sweden); **Joseph H. Senner** (German; 1893–1997); John Lederhilger (German, 1890s–1902; b. Germany); **Lorenzo Ullo** (Maltese; 1890s–1902); Inspector Albert Wank (German; 1893–1901; b. Austria), Inspector Isador Fisch (Polish, Yiddish, and German, 1920s); Inspector Vincent Piaggio (Italian); Inspector Giuseppe C. Tufarolo (Italian; 1920s); Inspector William S. Watson (Arabic; interpreter, 1890s–1906; inspector, 1906–1920s); Matron Mary Angone (Italian; 1914–1922); Inspector Jacob Auerbach (Yiddish, German, and Polish; 1930–1942), **Edward Corsi** (Italian; 1931–1934).

The interpreters of the Chinese Division were consultants from Chinatown and were Chinese.

The Public Health Service rated certain languages as the most important to aid in the medical examination of aliens in the **Main Building**. In a letter to the surgeon general, dated November 4, 1914, Dr. L. L. Williams, chief medical officer of Ellis Island, wrote of requirements of new interpreters to be appointed:

> The languages with which they should be familiar are named below in the order of their importance, viz.: Italian, Polish, Yiddish and German, Greek, Russian, Croatian and Slovenian, Lithuanian, Ruthenian and Hungarian. Each of the five interpreters should be able to speak at least two of the languages named and it is very desirable that all of those named should be spoken by the five interpreters collectively, if practicable.
>
> In addition to these languages, a knowledge of Portuguese, Spanish, French, Turkish and Syrian, and Scandinavian languages, would increase the usefulness of any of the candidates. (Ellis Island employees file)

REFERENCES: Ellis Island employees file. Ellis Island, NY: Statue of Liberty and Ellis Island Library; *William Williams to the Commissioner General of Immigration, January 3, 1911.* National Archives. General Immigration Files, Record Group 85.

Interview Corridor. A corridor in the west wing of the **Main Building** where detained immigrants met and conversed with visiting relatives and friends. Such detainees were in the custody of the **Deporting Division**.

Investigations. Ellis Island officials investigated such matters as fraud, corruption, theft, immorality, and illegal entry. Investigations of suspicious aliens included anyone suspected of **moral turpitude**, criminal background or activity, of being a pauper or misrepresenting the money one possessed, violating the contract labor laws, lying to immigration officers, escaping from Ellis Island, holding forged passports or visas, having radical political beliefs, being a polygamist or bigamist, being involved in espionage, and so forth.

Among the most important special investigations conducted by the Ellis Island **commissioners**, special inspectors, and high officials from the Washington office of the **Bureau of Immigration** were those of Colonel **John B. Weber**, who traveled to Europe to study the causes of the rising Jewish emigration from eastern Europe; of **Joseph H. Senner**, who studied and wrote on the causes of the increasing levels of Italian emigration; of **Terence V. Powderly**, who investigated working conditions in Europe and the many ways in which immigrants evaded the contract labor laws; of Thomas Fitchie, who examined corruption in the **immigrant aid societies**; of **special inspector** Roger O'Donnell, who investigated many crimes and Chinese cases, as well as the corruption ad illegalities under the regime of Commissioner Thomas Fitchie; **William Williams**, who studied in immense detail corruption at Ellis Island itself; of **Philip Cowen**, who investigated conditions in tsarist Russia and Austro-Hungarian Galicia, where he interviewed witnesses to the 1905 pogroms and looked into the daily life of the Jews; and of **Robert Watchorn**, who traveled with John Trenor to Europe, where, in 1907 and 1908, they investigated the origins and causes of the Italian criminal league known as the Black Hand (*la mano nera*). In addition, in 1922, the

Immigration Bureau sent Lillian Russell, the beloved stage actress known as America's Beauty, to study emigration conditions in Europe.

In later years, officials sent directly from Washington, DC, conducted most major investigations of crime at Ellis Island. For example, in the 1930s, the INS investigated naturalization frauds that had been taking place on a major scale for several years.

See also **Crime and Abuse; Ullo, Lorenzo**

Island 1. Island 1 is the original 3.3-acre Ellis Island plus enlargement through **landfill**. From 1890 to 1892, the island was enlarged to 11.07 acres. The **Main Building**, the **baggage and dormitory building**, the **kitchen and laundry building**, the **power house**, the **bakery and carpentry shop** are on this part of Ellis Island.

Structures demolished include the coal hoist and coal bins behind the **ferry house** (1901), a pump house (1901), the incinerator (1902–1985), a wood frame dormitory barracks (1901–1909), a shed for immigrants' friends, immigrants waiting room shed, outside privies, an oil tank, two water tanks, the life boat dock, three guard houses, and the original bakery and carpentry shop.

Island 2. Island 2 was added in 1898 and measures 3.31 acres, increasing Ellis Island to 15.52 acres. The breakwater was added in 1890 and a new seawall was built in 1916–1917. Contractor Warren Rosevelt carried out all crib work, dredging, and landfill operations from January through December 1898. The fill consisted of earth, stone, rubble from the **first immigrant station**, which had been destroyed in the previous year.

Structures erected on there were several **hospital buildings**, the **surgeons' house**, and later the Red Cross house (1915).

Island 3. This island was created by landfilling in 1905–1906 and consists of 4.75 acres. Buildings include the contagious diseases and isolation wards, consisting of eleven hospital buildings housing twenty-two wards, the staff house (1908), **mortuary and autopsy room**, the **animal house** (1908), **kitchen** (1907), **office building and laboratory** (1909), and corridors from the power house to measles wards.

Italian Welfare League. Beginning in the early 1920s, the Italian Welfare League provided aid to Italian immigrants at Ellis Island. The organization continued this work over the years; the **World War II** years were particularly harrowing as all Italian immigrants were labeled **enemy aliens** and several hundred were arrested and brought to Ellis Island, including the renowned opera singer Ezio Pinza in 1942.

In addition, the league provided help for many Italian communities across the nation (some were called Little Italies). This assistance included translating English, finding employment, making arrangements for schooling, helping with naturalization, and teaching the newcomers about American customs and social practices. Angela Carlozzi Rossi served as the league's secretary and treasurer at Ellis Island (1930–1949).

See also **Immigrant Aid Societies; St. Raphael Society for the Protection of Italian Immigrants**

J

James, C. L. R. (Cyril Lionel Robert James) (b. Trinidad, [British West Indies], 1901; d. England, 1989). West Indian Marxist writer and critic C. L. R. James was arrested by the FBI and held at Ellis Island as a dangerous subversive from June 10 through October 7, 1952. During his stay he wrote a remarkable book called *Mariners, Renegades, and Castaways* in which he used the voyage of the *Pequod* in Herman Melville's novel *Moby Dick* as a symbol of modern civilization seeking its destiny. In chapter seven "A Natural but Necessary Conclusion," he discussed at length his plight as a detained alien at Ellis Island and his relations with fellow detainees, immigration officers, and the general atmosphere at the station. He had lived in the United States since 1938. James was famous for his opposition to colonialism and the oppression of peoples of sub-Saharan Africa and the African diaspora. His most famous book is *Black Jacobins* (1938).

REFERENCE: James, C. L. R. 1985. *Mariners, Renegades, and Castaways: The Story of Herman Melville and the World We Live In*. London: Allison & Busby.

James, Henry (b. 1843, New York; d. 1916, England). British American novelist. After an absence of twenty-one years, this expatriate writer returned for a visit to his native United States from 1904 through 1905. The literary result of this visit is the admirable book, *The American Scene* (1907), in which James tries to discover a forgotten country in scenes of a new life made different by many forces, not the least of which was immigration. This perhaps aroused in him the curiosity that prompted his visit to the immigration station in the bay. He was received by Commissioner **William Williams** and was astonished at the scene on the island, leaving behind a vivid and thoughtful remembrance of the place.

> The terrible little Ellis Island, the first harbour of refuge and stage of patience for the million or so of immigrants annually knocking at our official door. Before this door, which opens to them there only with a hundred forms and ceremonies, grindings, and grumblings of the key, they stand appealing and waiting, marshalled, herded, divided, subdivided, sorted, sifted, searched, fumigated, for longer or shorter periods—the effect of all which prodigious process, an intendedly "scientific" feeding of the mill, is again to give the earnest observer a thousand more things to think of than he can pretend to retail. The impression of Ellis Island, in fine, would be—as I find throughout that so many of my impressions would be—a chapter by itself; and with a particular page for recognition of the degree in which the liberal hospitality of the eminent Commissioner of this wonderful service, to whom I had been introduced, helped to make the interest of the whole watched drama poignant and unforgettable. It is a drama that goes on, without pause, day by day, and year by year, this visible act of ingurgitation on the part of our body politic and social, and constituting really an appeal to amazement beyond that of any sword-swallowing or fire-swallowing of the circus. The wonder that one couldn't keep down was the thought that these two or three hours of one's own chance vision of the business were but a tick of two of the mighty clock, the clock that never, never stops—least of all when it strikes, for a sign of so much winding-up, some louder hour of our national fate than usual. I think indeed that the simplest account of the action of Ellis Island on the spirit of any sensitive citizen who may have happened to "look in" is that he comes back from his visit not at all the same person that he went. He has eaten of the tree knowledge, and the taste will be for ever in his mouth. He had thought he knew before, thought he had the sense of the degree in which it is his

American fate to share the sanctity of his American consciousness, the intimacy of his American patriotism, with the inconceivable alien; but the truth had never come home to him with any such force. In the lurid light projected upon it by those courts of dismay it shakes him—or I like at least to imagine it shakes him—to the depths of his being; I like to think of him, I positively have to think of him, as going about ever afterwards with a new look, for those who can see it, in his face, the outward sign of the new chill in his heart. So is stamped, for detection, the questionably privileged person who has had an apparition, seen a ghost in his supposedly safe old house. Let not the unwary, therefore, visit Ellis Island.

Following his departure from the island and his wanderings about New York City, James was troubled by the changes he saw nearly everywhere and haunted by a feeling of both "possession and dispossession" in his own country. Before his death, James himself assumed the cloak of the permanent immigrant when he was naturalized as a British subject shortly before his death. James's most famous novels include *Washington Square*, *The Europeans*, *The Ambassadors*, *The Wings of the Dove*, and *The Golden Bowl.*

See also **Literature and Reminiscences; Wells, H. G.**

REFERENCE: James, Henry. 1907. *The American Scene.* London: Harper and Brothers; New York: Penguin Books, 1994.

Janitors' Division (Laborers' Division). This division was headed by an official called the janitor, who supervised a staff consisting of laborers and charwomen. In 1903, there were forty-five male laborers and nine charwomen, with ten laborers and five charwomen assigned to night duty. A head charwoman supervised the female workers.

The first duty of this force was to keep the buildings and outside grounds of the island clean by day and by night. The day force left the **Barge Office** for work on the 6:20 a.m. boat and departed for home on the 5:30 p.m. boat run. The laborers brushed up beds, changed blankets, swept dormitory floors, scrubbed and washed floors and toilets with Carbolene disinfectant; they mopped floors, then brushed the beds with a solution of equal parts of turpentine and kerosene oil (at least every other day). Likewise, they toiled in the men's deferred room, the women's excluded room, the New York detained room, the discharging bureau, the callers' waiting room, the missionaries' room, all toilets (where they also replaced the cloth towels), all rooms, all corridors, and the sidewalks outside of the buildings. A pair of laborers made the rounds of emptying every can of rubbish, from room to room. The mounting waste and rubbish was then burned in the furnace. Teams of laborers also washed windows every ten days and every morning and filled the ice coolers that stood in every office.

The janitor reported to the chief of the **Deporting Division** in the early years but after 1910 he reported directly to the **superintendent**. Charwomen were responsible for emptying wastebaskets in the women's toilets, dusting, sweeping, and cleaning railings in the gallery and the staircases.

Night jobs were divided into three squads and included sweeping, flushing, and mopping all day rooms in the building, including the board rooms, Special Inquiry rooms, toilets, Deportation Bureau, registry floor, Medical Division, corridors, and passageways. Carbolene disinfectant was used as necessary.

The workforce tended to increase as immigration rose. In 1914, there were fifty-nine laborers and eighteen charwomen at Ellis Island. In 1921, there were a hundred laborers and sixteen charwomen; and in 1922, after the passage of the **Quota Act**, there were sixty-seven laborers and fifteen charwomen. In 1924, there were forty-four laborers, twelve charwomen (plus the head charwoman), and a gardener to supervisor the care of the lawn and other vegetation. As for the ethnic composition of these workers, records indicate that many of the laborers were white and black and the majority of the charwomen were Irish.

Men holding the position of janitor before World War I included Peter D. Herrick and James Beggs, who was born in Ireland.

See also **New York District (INS)**

Johnson, Albert (b. Springfield, Illinois, March 5, 1869; d. American Lake, Washington, January 17, 1957). Journalist; U.S. Representative (1913–1933). As chairman of the House Committee on Immigration and Naturalization, Congressman Johnson cosponsored the **Immigration Act of 1924** (Johnson-Reed Act), which effectively ended mass immigration into the United States for more than forty years. Johnson began his career as a newspaper reporter in St. Louis and later became a prominent news editor for several papers, including the *New Haven Register*, the *Washington Post*, and the *Tacoma News*.

See also **Immigration Act of 1924; Immigration Restriction; Reed, David A.**

REFERENCE: Biographical Directory of the United States Congress. 1989. Washington, DC: U.S. Government Printing Office.

Johnson, Lyndon B. [Lyndon Baines Johnson] (b. Texas, August 27, 1908; d. Texas, January 22, 1973). President of the United States (1963–1969). President Johnson took the first step in preserving Ellis Island when he issued presidential proclamation 3656 on May 11, 1965, which officially added Ellis Island to the Statue of Liberty National Monument.

Johnson, Philip [Philip Cortelyou Johnson] (b. Cleveland, Ohio, July 8, 1906). Architect. In 1965, Secretary of the Interior Stewart Udall asked Philip Johnson to redesign Ellis Island so that it could more easily fit into the national park system. Johnson's plan, announced at Federal Hall National Memorial on Wall Street, Manhattan, in February 1966, called for the island to be turned into a place of romantic ruins. The more important of the buildings decaying on the island would be partially stabilized in order to make them nostalgically attractive for future visitors; all the other structures and buildings would be consigned to oblivion. In addition, a 130-foot-high circular Wall of the 16 Million was to be constructed on the south side of the island, bearing the names of all immigrants who had been inspected at Ellis Island. Visitors would walk up spiral ramps to find the inscribed names of immigrants. Johnson also planned for the construction of gardens, a reflecting pool, a viewing platform facing the skyline of Manhattan, and a restaurant. Ethnic dancers and picnickers would also be accommodated. Although the scheme, which would destroy the island's unique character, was praised as "triumphant" by Secretary Udall, Congress never appropriated funds for it. Thus the island remained neglected until the 1980s.

See also **Restoration**

REFERENCES: Novotny, Ann. 1971. *Strangers at the Door.* Riverside, CT: Chatham; Pitkin, Tho-

Architect Philip Johnson's 1966 proposal for Ellis Island called for the demolishing of many historic structures, including the contagious disease wards, the morgue and the baggage and dormitory building. Courtesy of the Ellis Island Immigration Museum.

mas M. 1975. *Keepers of the Gate.* New York: New York University Press.

Junker, William E. (b. 1865; d. 1922). Chief inspector, Statistical Division (1906—1922). William E. Junker had a checkered career at Ellis Island in which he demonstrated on the one hand quite exceptional abilities as an administrator, while on the other, he suffered from occasional dishonesty. Hired as an assistant inspector in 1894, he was discovered to have been accepting bribes from the French Line in 1901 during a bureau investigation of corruption at Ellis Island. A scandal in 1922 resulted in his demotion from chief of the **Statistical Division** to mere inspector.

Jurisdiction. Ellis Island has been under the jurisdiction of the U.S. government immediately after its purchase from the heirs of **Samuel Ellis** for $10,000 in June 1808. Since that time it has been cared for by several federal agencies. These have been the Department of War (1808–1868); the Department of the Navy (1868–1890); the Department of the Treasury (1890–1903), through its **Office of Immigration** (1891–1895) and **Bureau of Immigration** (1895–1903); the Department of Commerce and Labor (1903–1913), through the Bureau of Immigration (1903–1906), and then Bureau of Immigration and Naturalization (1906–1913); the Department of Labor (1913–1940), through the Bureau of Immigration (1913–1933), and Immigration and Naturalization Service (1933–1940); the Department of Justice (1940–1955), through the Immigration and Naturalization Service; the **General Services Administration** (1955–1965); and, since May 11, 1965, the Department of the Interior, through its **National Park Service**.

In addition, Ellis Island was located entirely in the State of New York, from the War of Independence through 1998. Since the latter date, a part of Island 1 is in the State of New York and all the land-filled areas, including a portion of Island 1 and all of Island 2 and Island 3, are in New Jersey.

See also **National Monument; National Park Service; Sovereignty**

K

Keefe, Daniel J. [Daniel Joseph Keefe] (b. Willow Springs, Illinois, September 27, 1852; d. Elmhurst, Illinois, January 2, 1929). Commissioner-general of immigration (1908–1913). Daniel J. Keefe was commissioner-general at a time when the immigrant rush to America was still in full force, although numbers had dropped after 1907: that incomparable year in which 1 million immigrants passed through Ellis Island. Keefe's background as a trade union leader caused him to favor a strict interpretation of the immigration laws to protect American workers. However, he was disappointed in this when President William H. Taft vetoed the literacy bill in 1909. Near the end of Keefe's tenure, hundreds of immigrants were killed when the *Titanic* sank.

Keefe worked his way up from his beginnings as a longshoreman. His work as a union activist led to his election as president of the Lumber Unloaders' Association when he was thirty years old. He rose even higher in union leadership as president of the National Longshoremen's Association (1893–1908) and as a member of the executive council of the American Federation of Labor (1903–1908). After serving as commissioner-general, Keefe was a conciliation commissioner at the Department of Labor and worked on labor dispute cases for the U.S. Shipping Board Merchant Fleet Corporation (1921–1925).

Khodja, Murad Mohammed [Murad Mohammed Kadri Khodja] (b. Algiers, Algeria, May 1, 1885; d. France, 1970). Deckhand, **ferryboat *Ellis Island*.** Khodja, a fireman aboard merchant ships, arrived in New York as a French subject in May 1919, where he presented his seaman's identification card to the officers of the **Bureau of Immigration**. He resumed his seaman's duties aboard such vessels as *Harkness* and the *Eastern Admiral.* He established New York as his place of residence and applied for U.S. citizenship by June 1927. He received citizenship by about 1929 and was hired as an Immigration Service deckhand at Ellis Island. He remained there through the 1930s and was a member of the U.S. Immigration Service Beneficial Association. He eventually returned to France.

Kissing Post. The kissing post (or kissing gate) is located on the first floor in the west wing of the **Main Building**. Immigrants met their relatives and friends there. In an interview in the early 1930s with Commissioner **Edward Corsi**, Italian interpreter **Frank Martoccia**, who had worked at the station for some thirty years, described it this way:

> Incidentally, as you may have heard, there is a post at Ellis Island that through long usage has come to earn the name of "The Kissing Post." It is probably the spot of greatest interest on the Island, and if the immigrants recall it afterwards it is always, I am sure, with fondness. For myself, I found it a real joy to watch some of the tender scenes that took place there.
>
> There was a line of desks where the inspectors stood with their back towards the windows and facing the wall. Further back, behind a partition, one waited outside for detained aliens. As the aliens were brought out, the witnesses were brought in to be examined as to their rights of claim. If the inspector found no hitch, they were allowed to join each other. This, because of the arrangement of the partitions, usually took place at "The Kissing Post," where friends, sweethearts, husbands and wives, parents

and children would embrace and kiss and shed tears for pure joy. (Corsi 1935, p. 87)

Calling it the kissing gate, old-time matron **Maud Mosher** wrote about it in 1910.

> There are many joyful meetings at this place that the officers call it the Kissing Gate. The manner in which the people of different nationalities greet each other after a separation of years is one of the interesting studies at the island. The Italian kisses his children but scarcely speaks to his wife, never embraces or kisses her in public. The Hungarian and Slavish people put their arms around one another and weep. The Jew of all countries kisses his wife and children as though he owned all the kisses in the world and intended to use them all up quick.

Currently, the kissing post is a favorite visitor area at the **Ellis Island Immigration Museum**.

REFERENCES: Corsi, Edward. 1935. *In the Shadow of Liberty*. New York: Macmillan; Mosher, Maud. 1910. Ellis Island as the matron sees it. Manuscript Collection, Ellis Island Library, Statue of Liberty N.M.

Kitchen Building. The Public Health Service maintained one kitchen on Island 2 and one kitchen on Island 3. Workers consisted of a chief cook, assistant cooks and kitchenmen, a clerk, and a storekeeper. Several waitresses were assigned to the personnel dining room. Food was partly obtained under a contract (e.g., milk and bread), and partly through direct purchase on the open market (e.g., vegetables, eggs, fish, and meat). Storage facilities for food, such as pantries, were insufficient, while the refrigeration units were neither large enough nor cold enough to keep foods for very long. Dishes, pots, cutlery, and kitchen utensils were washed by hand until Autosan machines were installed in 1923. Utensils and dishes in the kitchen of the **contagious disease ward** on **Island 3** were put through a "utensil sterilizer" and were never taken off the island.

Depending on their state of health, patients received one of four diets: regular, light, liquid, or special. Nurses and ward maids brought the food to serving rooms on covered trolleys and portable thermos boxes that kept food hot (or at least warm). From the serving rooms, the food was conveyed on trays into the hospital wards.

See also **Food Service and Menus; Privilege Holders**

Kitchen and Laundry Building. Formerly known as the kitchen, laundry, and bathhouse building, this steel-framed structure was made of red bricks with limestone and bluestone trims. It measures 104.5 feet by 30 feet to its west end and 68.5 feet by 109 feet to its northeast end; it also has a northern addition that is 22.5 feet by 92 feet. Designed by architects **William A. Boring** and **Edward L. Tilton** in the beaux arts style, the two-and-one-half-story building primarily served as a kitchen, restaurant, bathhouse, and laundry. It was designed in 1898 and 1900 and constructed in 1900 and 1901.

The laundry, kitchen employees' dining room, storekeeper's office, commissioner's dining room, and pantry were on the first floor while a kitchen and immigrants' dining room, along with a chapel, library, and schoolroom, could be found on the second. A larger dining room seating 1,000 immigrants was added to the upper floor in 1908. The structure is connected to the **Main Building** by means of a two-story passageway.

In later years, the commissioner's dining room and a barber shop were located on the ground floor. The old laundry machines and other equipment remained on the ground floor until it was rehabilitated in 1994. The building now contains the offices of the superintendent, the U.S. Park Police, the interpretive rangers, and the administrative and maintenance divisions. The upper level provides storage space for museum objects. There are plans to install a demographic exhibit on the second floor of the building.

Knox, Howard A. [Howard Andrew Knox] (b. Romeo, Michigan, March 7, 1885; d. Jersey City, New Jersey, July 27, 1949). Physician. Knox served as a Public Health Service assistant sur-

Howard A. Knox administers one of his psychological tests to an immigrant. Courtesy of the Ellis Island Immigration Museum.

geon at Ellis Island (1912–1916). Knox, who was under the direct influence of Henry Herbert Goddard, created a variety of mental tests designed to measure the intelligence of races, all of which were based on the intelligence quotient (IQ) tests created by Alfred Binet in France. Goddard introduced the tests to the United States and selected immigrants of Ellis Island as objects for experimentation. Knox's task was to develop IQ tests for foreigners of a variety of ethnic and cultural backgrounds, which, to him, demonstrated varying levels of intelligence among the peoples of eastern and southern Europe, whom he regarded as different in race, a common view of the age. In a real sense, Knox's test of immigrants was the trial ground for a procedure destined to be a common one in the United States. During his four years at Ellis Island, he wrote twenty-seven papers and articles about mental testing.

After receiving his medical degree in 1908, Knox became an army surgeon in Texas. He resigned his military commission in 1910 and returned to the East, ostensibly to care for his mother. After four years with the Public Health Service, he resigned after not being promoted past assistant surgeon. In 1916, he settled in New Jersey and became a general practitioner in Bayonne. After marrying his fourth and last wife, he set up a practice in southern New Jersey.

References: Knox, Howard A. 1913. The moron and the study of alien defectives. *Journal of the American Medical Association*, 60 (January 11): 105–106; Knox, Howard A. 1914. A scale based on the work at Ellis Island for estimating mental defect. *JAMA*, 62 (March 7): 741–747; Knox, Howard A. 1914. A comparative study of the imaginative power in the mental defective. *Medical Record* 85 (April

25): 748–751; Richardson, John. 2002. *The life and work of Howard Andrew Knox, the neglected pioneer of performance tests.* Ellis Island, NY: Statue of Liberty and Ellis Island Library.

Krishnamurti, Jiddu (b. Madras, India, 1895; d. Ojai, California, 1986). Spiritual leader and philosopher. When Krishnamurti, the famed messianic world teacher of the Theosophical Society, arrived in New York aboard the RMS *Majestic* with Annie Besant in August 1926, he found himself detained for questioning at Ellis Island. Immigration officials had received anonymous charges of moral turpitude against the distinguished visitor. However, interrogations with both Krishnamurti and Besant satisfied Commissioner Benjamin M. Day that none of the charges involved him personally and he was quickly released.

L

Laboratory. *See* **Office Building and Laboratory**

LaGuardia, Fiorello [Fiorello Raffaele Enrico LaGuardia] (b. New York, December 11, 1882; d. New York, September 20, 1947). Interpreter, **Registry Division**; mayor of New York City (1934–1945). Before he achieved political fame, Fiorello LaGuardia began his career as a federal employee, first for the State Department's Consular Service and then for the **Bureau of Immigration**. His first official contact with emigrants was at Fiume, Austria-Hungary, where he worked as the American consul from 1903 to 1906. There he caused an uproar with Cunard Line officials when he demanded that emigrant passengers undergo medical inspections before boarding ships. In 1907, the Bureau of Immigration hired him as an interpreter at Ellis Island. He was qualified to interpret Italian, Serbo-Croatian, German, and Yiddish; he was also spoke some French. Like the other employees, he rushed to work aboard the 8:40 a.m. run of the **ferryboat *Ellis Island*** and once on the island went to his locker to change into his interpreter's uniform. The six-day-a-week job was absorbing and exciting and LaGuardia was in his element. The bureaucracy and the rules that so easily barred immigrants on technicalities often exasperated him. His supervisors disapproved of his feisty manner yet were impressed by his work. In 1909, he was one of thirteen interpreters who earned $1,200 a year. In a February 1910 report to the **commissioner general** in Washington, DC, Commissioner **William Williams** expressed his approval of LaGuardia in these words:

> Mr. LaGuardia is energetic, intelligent and familiar with a number of foreign languages. Against him there may be said that he is inclined to be peppery; that with some of the Board Members, he is inclined to be argumentative, but he has been spoken to about this and it is not a defect of the first order. For some months past he has been assigned to the duty at the Night Court, where his knowledge of languages and typewriting have been made especially valuable. Inspector Tedesco is receiving $200 additional per annum to cover costs of meals, etc., while assigned to this special duty and Inspector Schlamm received a like allowance while he was on duty at the Night Court. Aside from fact that Mr. LaGuardia should receive like consideration in this respect, I think that his abilities place him in the higher grade of interpreters, which under the existing scheme is $1400 per annum. I, therefore, suggest his regular promotion to the $1380 grade.

The result of this favorable recommendation was that LaGuardia's salary was raised to $1,260, far below what was requested. Not surprisingly, LaGuardia left the Bureau of Immigration to become a full-time interpreter at night court and began practicing law. Over the years, he remained a friend to several of his Ellis Island coworkers, including **Byron Uhl** and **Frank Martoccia** and visited Ellis Island several times while he was mayor of New York City (1934–1945).

REFERENCE: Ellis Island employees file. Ellis Island, NY: Statue of Liberty and Ellis Island Library.

Land, Paul H. (b. Germany, 1871; d. New York, New York, 1952). Harbor missionary, German Lutheran Church. Reverend Paul H. Land began his missionary work among German Protestants at Ellis Island in 1906 and continued after World War II ended. He delivered the German Address at the **Christmas** festival of 1910.

Landfill. Until 1890, Ellis Island was 3.3 acres in size. In that year, its size was enlarged through landfill operations that eventually brought it to its present 27.5 acres. The first stage of land-filling took place between 1890 and 1892, and enlarged the island to 11.07 acres, by using a mixture of mud, clayey sand, and gravel. During the second stage (1894–1996), it was expanded to 14.2 acres. The material used was clayey sand, loam, and cinders from the power house. A third stage of land-filling took place from 1897 to December 1898, bringing the size to 15.52 acres with dirt and stone. These last two phases created **Island 2**, directly across the slip. **Island 3** was created by the fourth phase of landfill operations, taking place from 1905 to 1906; its 4.75 acres increased Ellis Island to 20.27 acres. The material used was cellar dirt, stones, clay, old masonry, along with 70,000 cubic yards of earth and sand, built behind 1.2 cubic feet of cribwork and stones. Islands 2 and 3 were connected by a narrow wooden gangway that measured fifty feet in length.

Between 1923 and 1924 the watery "lagoon" between Islands 2 and 3 was filled in, measuring 4.10 acres. The operation employed cinders and hot ash from the powerhouse and was not completed until about 1932. Counting additional landfill operations on the north side and behind the **ferry house** (1934–1936), the island achieved its full 27.5 acres. The last work was done by laborers employed by the Works Progress Administration.

REFERENCES: National Park Service. 2000. *Cultural Landscapes Inventory: Ellis Island.* Olmsted Center for Landscape Preservation; National Park Service. 2002. *Cultural Landscape Report for Ellis Island.* Olmsted Center for Landscape Preservation.

Aerial view shows the effects of landfilling at Ellis Island, ca 1915.
Courtesy of the Ellis Island Immigration Museum.

Landing Agents. Landing agents were employees of the steamship companies and were allotted office space on the first floor of the **Main Building**. The agents kept an eye out for each crowd of immigrants who had been passengers aboard their company's steamships and watched to see that they satisfied the immigrant inspectors. They also accepted bills for the detention of aliens submitted by the **Statistical Division** and answered questions and criticism concerning passengers and the responsibility of the steamship line. In addition, landing agents accepted and ensured the execution of orders for railway and steamboat tickets held by immigrant passengers. They often worked closely with missionaries and immigrant aid workers as well as with inspectors, interpreters, and other **Bureau of Immigration** officials.

See also **Landing Immigrants**

Landing Immigrants (to land; landing; landed). The term "to land" was simply a declaration that an immigrant was admitted to the United States. This term refers to the disembarkation of ship passengers onto terra firma; for immigration purposes the term came to have a highly significant meaning, for its governmental use was restricted to judging the qualifications of a ship's foreign passengers for admission into the country. Since the 1870s, the federal government had barred criminals, prostitutes, insane persons, and others as undesirable immigrants. The federal government reserved the right to refuse "to land" such persons and compelled them to remain aboard ship and depart from the port and from the country. During the nineteenth century, the State of New York immigration commissioners used the term officially and named one of its bureaucratic departments at **Castle Garden** the Landing Bureau; this term was used at Ellis Island in its first few years of operation. In the early 1890s, John J. Simpson was called the superintendent of landing.

Through the years, Ellis Island was often called "immigrant landing station" (1892–1954). Federal immigration laws and regulations ordered inspectors and senior officials of the **Bureau of Immigration** to exclude all aliens who were not "clearly and beyond a doubt entitled to *land.*"

The shipping companies, which transported foreign passengers to the United States aboard their ships, maintained **landing agents** at Castle Garden, Ellis Island, and other immigrant inspection stations. The agents tried to ensure that their passengers landed with as little trouble as possible and helped them with such problems as lost baggage and disputed railroad ticket orders.

Landis, Harry R. [Harry Raymond Landis] (b. Rock Creek, Ohio, 1881; d. Norwalk, Connecticut, April 30, 1950). Assistant commissioner (1921–1924). Harry R. Landis joined **Byron H. Uhl** at Ellis Island, and both men held the rank of assistant commissioner. Landis joined the **Bureau of Immigration** in 1907. After leaving Ellis Island, he received the highest post at the Chicago immigrant station—inspector-in-charge. He retired in 1945 as district director for the Immigration and Naturalization Service on the eastern Canadian border.

Landscape and Vegetation. Ellis Island originally consisted of 3.3 acres and was enlarged by a series of landfill operations enlarging **Island 1** and creating **Island 2** and **Island 3**. Today the island measures 27.5 acres.

The original vegetation was salt marsh cordgrass, salt grass, and salt meadow hay. The character changed drastically after 1890 with the enlargement of the space, the construction of buildings, and paving and heavy human occupation. The most carefully planted and manicured vegetation was cultivated around the **Main Building**, where a lawn, hedgerows, and flowers were maintained after 1900. During the late 1930s, the Works Progress Administration provided funding for landscape work on the island. The implementation of the master plan of the 1930s introduced scores of London plane trees that geometrically lined the walkways and open spaces.

After the **Immigration and Naturalization Service** abandoned Ellis Island, vegetation ran riot and the island and buildings were soon overgrown with vines such as English ivy, euonymus, and Virginia creeper; shrubs such as forsythia, lilac, privet, and yews; trees such as London plane, birch, elm, and oak; and woody plants such as cherries. Beargrass was also present as well as invasive weeds like sumac and poison ivy.

In 1990s, the National Park Service reestablished a manicured landscape around the Main Building, with London plane trees and ornamental plantings that included tulips and violets. Islands 2 and 3 were also brought under control.

Reference: National Park Service. 2000. *Cultural Landscape Inventory: Ellis Island.* Olmsted Center for Landscape Preservation.

Languages and Dialects. Out of necessity and the demands of the work, a wide variety of foreign languages and dialects were interpreted and translated at Ellis Island. The work was carried out by specially qualified officials of the **Bureau of Immigration** and the **Public Health Service** called **interpreters**. In addition, many other federal employees at the station—immigrant inspectors, clerks, matrons, watchmen, gatekeepers, groupers, messengers, doctors, nurses, charwomen, and so on—were fluent or familiar with one or more foreign languages. Immigrant aid workers, missionaries, and steamship agents augmented the linguistic pool, although they were seldom allowed to act as official interpreters at registry floor examinations, special inquiry hearings, appeals, or investigations. The languages interpreted at Ellis Island included Italian, Polish, Yiddish, German, French, Russian, Slovak, Hungarian, Greek, Ukrainian, Croatian, Lithuanian, Serbian, Slovenian, Finnish, Latvian (Lettish), Swedish, Romanian, Czech, Bulgarian, Norwegian, Danish, Portuguese, Armenian, Turkish, Spanish, Arabic, Dutch, Flemish, Estonian, Hebrew, Chinese, and Persian (Farsi).

Other languages encountered at Ellis Island were Albanian, Amharic, Basque, Burmese, Catalan, Chinese, Estonian, Frisian, Gaelic, Icelandic, Japanese, Korean, Ladino, Malay, Maltese, Pashto, Romany (Gypsy), Sardinian, and Welsh.

Various dialects were widely spoken among the immigrants, since the majority did not speak the standard languages of their own countries. These dialects included many variations of Italian (Sicilian was especially distinct), the Slavonic languages, German, Yiddish, Hungarian, Russian, French, Dutch, Romanian, Portuguese, Spanish (especially Galician), Greek, Turkish, Arabic, and Persian.

Larned, Frank H. (b. 1861; d. Baltimore, Maryland, June 21, 1937). Assistant commissioner-general of immigration (1902–1914). Larned began his public service career as an assistant clerk in the newly created **Bureau of Immigration** in 1891. As assistant commissioner-general in Washington, he exerted an important influence at Ellis Island, especially during the long illness and the death of Commissioner-General **Frank P. Sargent** in 1908. His previous training in Europe aided his early career. In 1922, he moved into the State Department's Consular Service and served as vice consul in London from 1922 to 1929 and consul in Toronto from 1929 until his retirement in 1932.

Reference: *New York Times.* 1937. Frank H. Larned, 76, retired U.S. consul (dies). June 23.

Laundries. Three laundries were in operation at the station. One was located in the **kitchen and laundry building** on **Island 1**. The remaining two were in the medical complex: one in the **hospital outbuilding** (also known as the **laundry and linen exchange**) on **Island 2**; and one in the **contagious disease ward** on **Island 3**. The Island 3 laundry was closed in 1922. Laundry equipment included washing machines, mangles, and dryers.

Laundry and Linen Exchange/Hospital Outbuilding interior today. Courtesy of the Ellis Island Immigration Museum.

Laundry and Linen Exchange. Measuring 60.5 feet by 48 feet, the laundry and linen exchange building was constructed in 1901; it was designed by the supervising architect of the Treasury Department and was constructed by the Attilio Pasquini Company. Its foundation is of bluestone and its walls are red brick Flemish. It was also known as the **hospital outbuilding** and contained a laundry, linen exchange, and autopsy room. A fire destroyed the laundry in May 1921 and in the next year a new laundry plant was installed. The new laundry machinery consisted of two washers, two extractors, two washtubs, one collar shaper, one collar droner, one starch cooker, one flat-iron worker, one dryer, five electric irons and boards, and two double body pressers. With a workforce of fourteen, the new laundry could process from 2,000 to 3,000 pieces of laundry each day.

At the linen exchange, soiled linen was exchanged for clean and sent to the laundry for washing. Damaged linen was mended or disposed. The staff consisted of two women, a supervisor and a seamstress. Two electric sewing machines were used for repairing linen. There was also a boiler room in the building.

See also **Linen Exchanges**

Law Division. The Law Division was originally known as the Law Office and as such was a part of the **Executive Division** (1892–1920s). During these years it was headed by a law clerk, who was frequently answerable to the **chief clerk**. The work of the division involved preparing immigration cases for the U.S. Attorney's office, preparing warrants of deportation, and drawing up concession contracts.

In about 1925, the Law Office was made a full division under a chief inspector. During these years, its work mostly involved the investigation of deportation cases, arranging bail bonds in warrant cases, investigating fraudulent **reentry permits**, and drawing up concession contracts.

Lederhilger, John (b. Germany). Chief of the **Registry Division** (1895–1902). Lederhilger was hired by Commissioner **Joseph Senner**. A former detective with the New York Police Department, Lederhilger used the powerful position of chief clerk to carry out a variety of illicit activities, both at Ellis Island and the **Barge Office**. In this regard, he was in collusion with Assistant Commissioner **Edward F. McSweeny**. As chief of the registry division, Lederhilger enjoyed investigating suspicious aliens, sometimes going out to the steamships with the boarding inspectors and sometimes going into seedy streets in Manhattan to investigate or sniff out criminals and other suspicious aliens.

Liable to Become a Public Charge (LPC). A category of immigrant deemed inadmissible for entry into the United States under the **Immigration Act of 1891** and subsequent legislation. It was the task of **Registry Division** inspectors to determine whether an alien might become a public charge at American institutions such as almshouses—due to poor health, disease, mental defect, or lack of funds—or a recipient of any other public charity due to the inability to survive financially or take care of his family through his own efforts. Immigrants certified by doctors of the **Public Health Service** as having certain diseases or physical conditions could also be excluded by officials of the **Bureau of Immigration** as "liable to become public charge" (LPC). LPC categorization prevented the immigration not only of paupers and sick persons but also large numbers of "unescorted" women and girls, underage boys and, sometimes, the elderly. The leading groups excluded as LPC on grounds of health (certified as Class B and C) between 1908 and 1930 were the following: Greeks; Romanians; Turks; Bulgarians, Serbs, and Montenegrins; Dalmatians, Bosnians, and Herzegovinians; Croats and Slovenians; Ruthenians; Bohemians and Moravians; and Welsh.

Libraries. Although several libraries existed at Ellis Island over the years, the one established in 1916 under Commissioner **Frederic Howe** was the most enduring, lasting until the station was closed in November 1954. Missionaries, immigrant aid societies, social welfare organizations, the New York Public Library, and private individuals donated the books and periodicals, which were in several languages. Immigrants often were allowed to keep them on leaving Ellis Island (they often wanted something to read on long journeys by train, boat, or steamship).

In 1942, there were 10,222 books and 2,968 periodicals as well as large numbers of religious tracts, pamphlets, and manuals. That year 3,882 books circulated and 620 persons visited the facility. The **American Tract Society**, the **YWCA**, the **Daughters of the American Revolution**, and the Protestant Episcopal Church were among many organizations that sponsored the library.

Over the years, the library's quarters changed on more than one occasion, when it also discarded worn-out and soiled books. In addition, beginning in 1917, there was a hospital library at the extreme end of Island 3. The American Library Association (ALA), as part of its library war service, supplied books. The **American Red Cross** set up a library in the Red Cross house during **World War I**; the ALA donated 500 novels to this collection. The ALA sent

The Red Cross Library primarily served convalescing soldiers at the end of World War I. Courtesy of the Ellis Island Immigration Museum.

Welfare library decorated with plants, a globe, paintings, and a display of periodicals. Courtesy of the Ellis Island Immigration Museum.

3,000 volumes to Ellis Island, 800 in 22 foreign languages.

The current reference library dates from the 1970s and was originally on Liberty Island. Later, librarian Harvey Dixon moved it to the **kitchen and laundry building**. When his successor, Won Kim, left the National Park Service in September 1987, he closed it and stored the books and files in the **immigration building**. In April 1988, a library technician was hired and reopened it on the first floor of the **hospital administration building**. In 1992, he moved the collection to a specially designed space on the third floor of the **Main Building**. The collection consists of 4,000 books, many thousands of photographs and slides, technical reports, unpublished manuscripts, periodicals, films, video and audio recordings, the Gino Speranza Collection, and extensive research files on the history, immigration, and ethnic groups of Ellis Island, as well as the history of the Statue of Liberty.

Line Inspection. Line inspection was a brief medical inspection of immigrants unique to Ellis Island. It was devised in response to the thousands of aliens who arrived daily at the port of New York and had to be examined for the presence of illnesses or physical conditions that barred admission to the United States. Surgeons of the **Marine Hospital Service** (later renamed the **Public Health Service**) conducted all medical inspections. Other immigration stations—such as those at Boston, Baltimore, Philadelphia, New Orleans, Galveston, San Francisco, or Seattle—did not require line inspection because they did not handle the volume that Ellis Island did.

The following is a description of the line inspection in 1912 from one of the physicians, Alfred C. Reed:

> Incoming immigrants pass in single file down two lines. Each of these lines makes a right-angled turn midway in its course. At this turn stands a medical officer. He sees each person directly from the front as he approaches, and his glance travels rapidly from feet to hand. In this rapid glance, he notes the gait, attitude, (the) presence of flat feet, lameness, stiffness at ankle, knee, or hip, malformations of the body; observes the neck for goiter, muscular development, scars, enlarged glands, texture of skin and, finally, as the immigrant comes up face to face, the examiner notes the abnormalities of the features, eruptions, scars, paralysis, expressions, etc. As the

immigrant turns, in following the line, the examiner has a side view, noting the ears, scalp, side of neck, examining the hands for deformity and paralysis, and if anything about the individual seems suspicious, he is asked several questions. It is surprising often a mental aberration will show itself in the reaction of the person to an unexpected question. As the immigrant passes on, the examiner has a rear view which may reveal spinal deformity or lameness. In case any positive or suspicious evidence of defect is observed, the immigrant receives a chalk mark indicating the nature of the suspicious circumstance.

At the end of each line stands a second medical officer who does nothing but inspect eyes. He everts the eyelids of every person passing the line, looking for signs of trachoma, and also notes the presence of cataract, blindness, defective vision, and acute conditions requiring hospital care and any other abnormalities. All cases which have been marked on the line are separated from the others and sent to the medical examining rooms for careful examination and diagnosis. When it is remembered that often 5,000 immigrants pass in a day, it is clear that the medical officers not only are kept busy but that see an unusually wide variety of cases.

After careful examination, the nature of the defect or disease found, is put in the form of a medical certificate which must be signed by at least three physicians on duty. It is not within the province of the medical officer to pass judgement on the eligibility of the immigrant for admission. The medical certificate merely states the diagnosis, leaving to the immigration inspector in the registry division the duty of deciding the question of admission. In the inspector's consideration are not alone the medical report, but all other data concerning the applicant, such as age, money in his possession, previous record, liability to become a public charge, and his sponsors.

In 1917, another Ellis Island surgeon, Eugene H. Mullan, offered a detailed description of line inspection.

Administration and Line Inspection at Ellis Island

Immigrants not traveling in the cabin . . . are first brought to Ellis Island in order to undergo an examination to determine their fitness for admission. The average immigrant remains at Ellis Island two to three hours, during which time he undergoes an examination by the Public Health Service in order to determine his mental and physical condition, and by the Immigration Service in order to find if he is otherwise admissible.

Immigrants are brought to Ellis Island by means of barges. As soon as they land at Ellis Island, they undergo the medical inspection and examination which are conducted by the officers of the Public Health Service.

Line Inspection

Upon entering . . . immigrants are guided by an attendant into the different inspection lines. These lines, separated by iron railings, are four in number at their proximal end and two in number at their distal end. Each pair of lines, after extending a distance of fifteen feet, terminates in a single line which is perpendicular to them. The two single or distal lines are approximately fifteen feet in length.

Four medical officers, who carry on the general inspection, are stationed each in one of the four proximal lines, and two medical officers stand at the extreme ends of the two distal lines or just where these lines merge into two common exits.

At this merging point stands an attendant whose duty it is to separate the chalk-marked aliens from those who are not chalk-marked. Accordingly, immigrants who have passed the medical inspection are guided into the exit which leads to the upper hall of the Immigration Service, while the chalked-marked ones pass through the exit which leads to the examination department of the Public Health Service. . . . Every immigrant in undergoing the medical inspection passed two medical officers. As above stated, the officer who occupies the proximal position carries on the general inspection.

It is the function of this officer to look for all defects, both mental and physical, in the passing immigrant. As the immigrant approaches, the officer gives him a quick glance. Experience enables him in that one glance to take in six details, namely, the scalp, face, neck, hands, gait and general condition, both mental and physical. Should any of these details not come into view, the alien is halted and the officer satisfies himself that no suspicious sign or symptom exists regarding that particular detail. For instance, if the immigrant is wearing a high collar, the officer opens the collar or unbuttons the upper shirt button and sees whether a goiter, tumor or other abnormality exists. A face showing harelip, partial or complete is always stopped in order to see if a cleft palate, a certifiable condition, is present.

It often happens that an alien's hand can not be distinctly seen: it may be covered by his hat, it may be hidden beneath his coat, or it may be deeply embedded in blankets, shawls or other luggage. In all the physical details in the medical inspection of immigrants, it is perhaps the most important to watch the hands. In many cases, where the hands can not be plainly seen at a glance further searching has revealed a deformed forearm, mutilated or paralyzed hand, loss of fingers, or favus nails.

Likewise, if the alien approaches the officer with hat on he must be halted, hat removed, and scalp observed in order to exclude the presence of favus, ringworm, or other skin diseases of this region of the body. Pompadours are always a suspicious sign. Beneath such long growths of hair are frequently seen areas of favus. The slightest bit of lameness shows itself in an unevenness of gait or a bobbing up-and-down motion. After constantly observing the passing of thousands of immigrants the experienced eye of an examiner will quickly detect the irregularity in gait. Where the alien carries luggage on his shoulder and back, it may be necessary to make him drop his parcels and to walk 5 or 10 feet in order to exclude suspicious gait or spinal curvature. Immigrants at times carry large parcels in both arms and over their shoulders in order that the gait resulting from a shortened extremity or ankylosed joint may escape notice. In like manner they maneuver in attempting to conceal the gaits of Little's disease, spastic paralysis and other nervous disorders. All children over 2 years of age are taken from their mother's arms and are made to walk. As a matter of routine, hats and caps of all children are removed, their scalps are inspected and, in many cases, are palpated. If care is not exercised in this detail, ringworm and other scalp conditions are apt to escape the attention of the *examiner.*

Immigrants that are thin and of uncertain physical make-up are stopped while the officer comes to a conclusion as to the advisability of detaining them for further examination. A correct judgement is often arrived at in these cases by the officer placing his hands against the back and chest of the alien, so as to obtain an idea of the thoracic thickness and also by feeling the alien's arm. Very often a thin and haggard face will show on palpation a thick thorax and a large, muscular arm.

Many inattentive and stupid-looking aliens are questioned by the medical officer in the various languages as to their age, destination and nationality. Often simple questions in addition and multiplication are propounded. Should the immigrant appear stupid and inattentive to such an extent that mental defect is suspected, an X is made on his coat at the anterior aspect of his right shoulder. Should definite signs of mental disease be observed, a circle X would be used instead of the plain X. In like manner, a chalk mark is place on the anterior aspect of the right shoulder in all cases where physical deformity or disease is suspected.

In this connection, B would indicate back; C, conjunctivitis; CT, trachoma; E, eyes; F, face; Ft, feet; G, goiter; H, heart; K, hernia; L, lameness; N, neck; P, physical and lungs; Pg, pregnancy; Sc, scalp; S, senility. The words hands, measles, nails, skin, temperature, vision, voice, which are often used, are written out in full.

The alien after passing the scrutiny of the first medical officer passes on to the end of the line, where he is quickly inspected again by the second examiner. This examiner is known in service parlance as "the eye man." He stands at the end of the line with his back to the window and faces the approaching alien. This position affords good light, which is so essential for eye examinations. The approaching alien is scrutinized by the eye man immediately in front of whom the alien comes to a standstill. The officer will frequently ask a question or two so as to ascertain the condition of the immigrant's mentality. He may pick up a symptom, mental or physical, that has been overlooked by the first examiner.

He looks carefully at the eyeball in order to detect signs of defect or disease of that organ and then quickly everts the upper lids in search of conjunctivitis and trachoma. Corneal opacities, nysstagmus, squint, bulging eyes, the wearing of eye glasses, clumsiness, and other signs on the part of the alien, will be sufficient cause for him to be chalked marked with "Vision." He will then be taken out of the line by an attendant and his vision will be carefully examined. If the alien passes through this line without receiving a chalk mark, he has successfully passed the medical inspection and off he goes to the upper hall, there to undergo another examination by officers of the Immigration Service, who take every means to see that he is not an anarchist, bigamist, pauper, criminal, or otherwise unfit.

Roughly speaking, from 15 to 20 per cent of the immigrants are chalk-marked by the medical officers, and it is these chalk-marked individuals who must undergo a second and more thorough examination in the examination rooms of the Public Health Service. The aliens marked X and circle X are place in the mental room. The other marked aliens are placed in the two physical rooms, one for the men and the other for the women. . . . At the line inspection, about 9 out of 100 immigrants are set aside as mental suspects in order to undergo the secondary or "weeding-out process." At the termination of the line inspection, the line officers go to the different examination rooms. 2 or three of them usually proceeds to the mental room and there conduct the secondary mental inspection or, as it is sometimes styled, "the weeding-out" process." (pp. 773–746)

See also **Diseases and Hospitalization; Mental Testing**

References: Mullan, E. H. 1917. Mental examination of immigrants: Administration and line inspection at Ellis Island. *Public Health Reports* (May 18); Reed, Alfred C. 1912. The medical side of immigration. *Popular Science Monthly* (April).

Linen Exchanges. Each of the **laundries** at Ellis Island had a linen exchange. Two women operated each exchange, one was the supervisor and the other a seamstress. Soiled linen was brought and exchanged for clean. All linen from the contagious disease hospital was put through a steam pressure sterilizer before being sent into the laundry.

Lipsitch, I. Irving. Representative of the Hebrew Immigrant Aid Society (HIAS, 1909–1914). Irving Lipsitch was responsible for persuading President William H. Taft to authorize a kosher kitchen at Ellis Island in 1911. He also set up an effective follow-up system to keep track of every Jewish immigrant who landed at the Port of New York. All aliens were classified and registered by HIAS and their names were forwarded in advance to their destinations to help find lodgings, employment, schooling in English, and other social services. Lipsitch was also an attorney.

Literacy Tests. Following the passage of the **Immigration Act of 1917**, immigrants were required to be able to read at least forty words in a language. The reading tests were printed on index cards in the various languages of the immigrants and administered by inspectors and interpreters of the **Registry Division**.

The following are a few of the languages included and the texts selected for the reading tests. For Arabic, Job 1: 18–19; for Croatian, Job 1: 13–14; for Dutch, Proverbs 12: 17–18; for Finnish (Gothic script), 1 Kings 11: 1; for Italian, Psalm 8: 2; for Polish, Hebrews 13: 1; for Russian, Psalm 17: 8–10; for Syriac, Psalm 119: 15–19; and for Yiddish, Joshua 9: 12. Literacy tests were given in many other languages, including Armenian, Bulgarian, Chinese, Czech, Danish, English, Estonian, Flemish, French, German, Greek, Lettish, Lithuanian, Norwegian, Portuguese, Romanian, Serbian, Slovak, Spanish, Swedish, Turkish, Ukrainian, and Welsh.

Political and religious refugees escaping persecution were exempt from this law.

See also **Languages and Dialects**

Literature and Reminiscences. A number of immigrants have written about their experiences. Some are in the form of autobiographies, memoirs, newspaper interviews, **Oral History Project**, and radio and filmed broadcasts. Others are recounted not by the immigrants themselves but rather by those to whom they have told their stories such as journalists, authors, social workers, and government officials. The stories usually cover emigration conditions in the old country, reasons for leaving home, means of transportation, including train journeys, traveling across the sea in steamships, usually in **steerage**, the arrival at the Port of New York, immigrant inspection at Ellis Island, and settling in the United States. Notable published reminiscences include *The Story of an Emigrant* (1892) by Hans Mattson, *The Making of an American* (1901) by Jacob Riis, *From Plotzk to Boston* (1899) by Mary Antin, *The Soul of an Immigrant* (1928) by Constantine Panuzio, *Son of Italy* (1924) by Pascal d'Angelo, *A Long Way from Home* (1937) by Claude McKay, *Laughing in the Jungle* (1932) by Louis Adamic, *Red Ribbon on a White Horse* (1950) by Anzia Yezierska, *The Log Book of a Young Immigrant* (1939) by Laurence M. Larson, *The Sound of Music* by Maria von Trapp, *Chinatown Family* by Lin Yutang, *Mariners, Renegades and Castaways* by **C. L. R. James**, *Lost Paradise* by Samuel Chotzinoff, *Moorings Old and New* by Paul Knaplund, and an unpublished manuscript, "Autobiography of the Street Singer" by **Arthur Tracy**. Other important memoirs were penned by Edward Steiner, Marcus E. Ravage, George Santayana, Edward Bok, Konrad Bercovici, William O'Dwyer, Luigi Barzini, and George Mardikian. Some immigrants wrote bits and pieces of their memoirs in the guise of fiction. These include Ole Rolvaag, Abraham Cahan, Isaac B. Singer, Anzia Yezierska, George Papashvily, and Jacob Auerbach. Other important writers were Broughton Brandenburg (*Imported Americans*), and Stephan Graham (*With Poor Immigrants to America*). Prominent among biographies of immigrants written by their children is Virginia Haroutunian's *Orphan in the Sand*, which tells the story of her mother, Victoria Haroutunian. Immigration officials also penned books revealing books on the subject; authors of these books include Ellis Island officials **Victor Safford**, **John B. Weber**, **Frederic C. Howe**, Feri Felix Weiss, **Edward Corsi**, **Victor Heiser**, **Terence V. Powderly**, **Henry H. Curran**, **Fiorello LaGuardia**, and **Robert Watchorn**. In addition, government historian **Thomas M. Pitkin** produced an important academic work on the station, which included firsthand accounts. Later oral history compilations were published in book form by editors David Brownstone and colleagues (*Island of Hope, Island of Tears*), Joan Morrison and Charlotte Zabusky (*American Mosaic*), Peter Morton Coan (*Ellis Island Interviews*), and Bruce Stave and John F. Sutherland with Aldo Salerno (*From the Old Country*).

Lloyd, Marie (b. London, England, February 12, 1870; d. October 7, 1922). Music hall and vaudeville comedienne. In December 1913, Marie Lloyd came for a six-month vaudeville tour of the United States, accompanied by her lover, Bernard Dillon; they were traveling as "Mr. and Mrs. Dillon." When questioned by boarding inspectors whether she and young Dillon were married, she confessed that they were not. They were immediately taken to Ellis Island. The next morning her case came before a board of special inquiry that promptly excluded her on grounds of moral turpitude. She was to remain detained at Ellis Island until the next Saturday, when her ship, the RMS *Olympic*, would sail for England. This created a sensation. Negotiations with her solicitors and the Immigration Bureau continued until, at the last moment, a compromise was reached. The bureau offered her permission to enter the country and complete her theatrical engagements, provided they paid an enormous bail of £300 each. Furthermore, the couple would have to reside in separate residences during their American stay. Lloyd promptly consented. When two months later she received word that her legal husband had died in England, she and Dillon were married at the British consulate in Portland, Oregon, in February 1914.

Loathsome Contagious Diseases. Loathsome contagious diseases, the very appearance of which "excited abhorrence in others," were labeled Class A diseases. Immigrants certified with any one of them were forbidden admittance into the country. The category of loathsome contagious diseases included the following chronic illnesses: favus (scalp and nail fungus), ringworm, parasitic fungal diseases, Madura foot, leprosy, and venereal diseases.

See also **Diseases and Hospitalization; Line Inspection; Public Health Service**

Lodsin, Michael [Michael Ivan Lodsin] (b. Courland, Latvia, 1862; d. New York, 1918). Missionary, New York Bible Society (Baptist, 1890s–1918). Michael Lodsin was known to his fellow Protestants as the "evangelist to the Russians." He was famous (or notorious, since Jewish groups and others complained) for handing out tracts and Bibles to immigrants in their native languages. He had himself immigrated through Ellis Island from Russia in 1893 and became a U.S. citizen in 1912. Lodsin was fluent in twelve languages, including Lettish, Russian, German, and Yiddish. In December 1905, the short, mustachioed Lodsin, Commissioner **Robert Watchorn**, and a crowd of detainees were photographed grouped around the Christmas tree in the **Registry Room**.

LPC. *See* **Liable to Become a Public Charge**

Lugosi, Bela [Bela Ferenc Deszö Blasco] (b. Lugos, Austria-Hungary, October 20, 1882; d. Hollywood, California, August 16, 1956). Actor. Bela Lugosi is one of the few **famous immigrants** to enter the United States illegally. Lugosi was a seaman aboard the SS *Graf Tisza Istvan*, which he had boarded at the port of Triest. When members of the ship's crew were given shore leave at the port of New Orleans, Lugosi was the only seaman not to return to the vessel. His action was immediately reported to the **Bureau of Immigration**. Lugosi made his way to New York City, where he joined the Hungarian community on the Upper East Side. He turned himself in to the immigration authorities in March 1921 and was interrogated at Ellis Island by Inspector John A.W. Richardson. In order to avoid arousing the suspicions of the inspector, Lugosi claimed to be a Romanian rather than a Hungarian. Being in excellent health and paying his **head tax**, he was admitted without any serious difficulties.

REFERENCE: Famous Immigrants File. *Immigration Manifest of Bela Lugosi.* Statue of Liberty and Ellis Island Library.

M

MacCormack, Daniel W. (b. Wick, Scotland, 1880; d. Washington, DC, January 1, 1937). Commissioner-general of immigration. During his tenure, Daniel MacCormack oversaw the unification of the bureaus of immigration and naturalization as the Immigration and Naturalization Service (INS) and major improvements on Ellis Island as a result of recommendations presented by the **Ellis Island Committee**. At his death, Secretary of Labor **Frances Perkins** paid tribute to him for reorganizing and humanizing the immigration and naturalization agencies.

MacCormack immigrated to the United States with his family when he was nine. He served in the U.S. Army and attained the rank of colonel. He also achieved success as an engineer, financier (he founded the Fiduciary Trust Company), and diplomat.

REFERENCE: *New York Times.* 1937. Daniel M'Cormack dead in capital: Head of immigration and naturalization service since March of 1933. . . . His death "desperate loss," says Miss Perkins. January 1.

Main Building. The Main Building was the first structure to replace the **first immigrant station** that had been destroyed in a great fire of 1897. Funds were authorized for its construction in 1897 and it was built from 1898 through 1900; it was opened on December 17, 1900. The Main Building was designed in the grand beaux arts classical style by architects **William A. Boring** and **Edward L. Tilton**. In 1905–1906, a railroad ticket office was added to its rear. In 1911, a third story was added to the west wing and, in 1913–1914, a third story was added to the east wing. The building was primarily used for the examination, processing, and registration of immigrants. It currently houses the **Ellis Island Immigration Museum**.

Like European railway stations, the Main Building was capable of accommodating crowds flowing through its passageways, staircases, and **Registry Room**. Its arched windows were a hallmark of the great French railway stations of the nineteenth century. The central section of the Main Building is buttressed at each corner by four magnificent towers and is believed to have been suggested by the Electricity Building, which was one of the glories of the World's Columbian Exhibition of 1893. The east and west wings of the building served as annexes to the central section's main function of checking baggage and directing crowds up to the Registry Room for primary inspection. There were various special inquiry and medical examination rooms, as well as detention rooms, dormitories, offices, and waiting rooms. The three-story building is a construction of Flemish bond red brick walls over a steel frame trimmed in limestone and granite. It measures 390 feet by 172.5 feet. The building's most powerful sculptural ornamentation is seen in the eagles mounted atop the piers between the central arches; directly beneath the eagles are escutcheons. There are also a series of masks on the arched keystones, as well as distinctive moldings and lintels at the entrance doors to the towers, and on the belfries. The magnificent **canopy** at the entrance to the building was added by June 1903; it was pulled down in 1932.

The following describes conditions exactly as they were in 1907, its busiest year ever. Access to all upper floors was reached by means of the

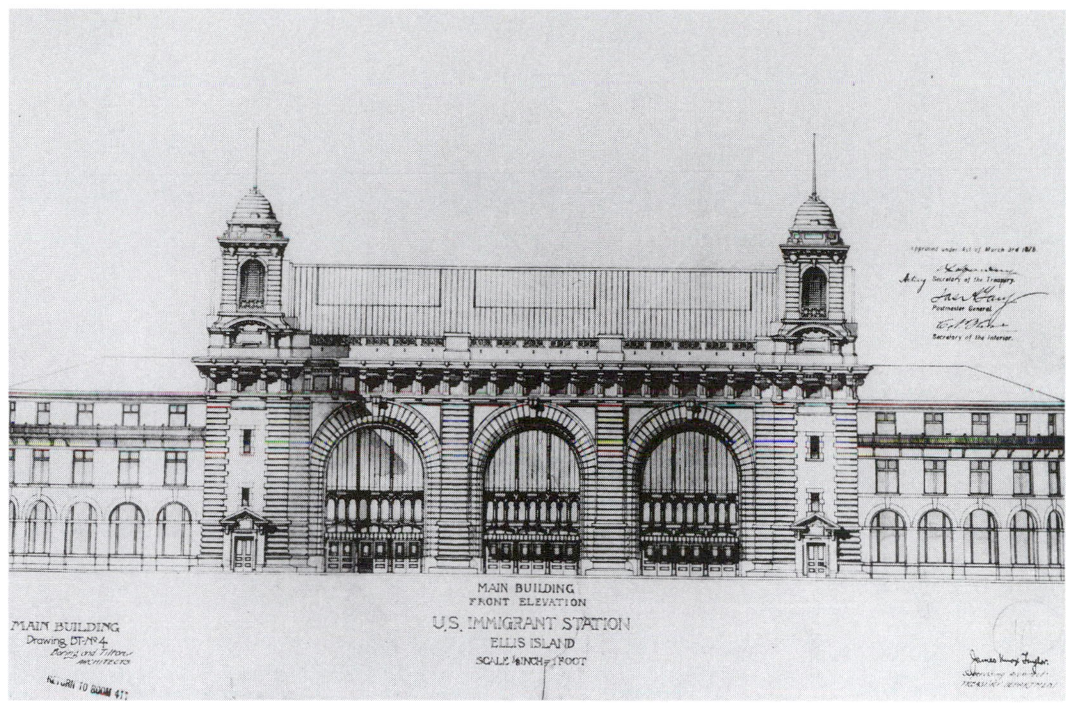

Part of Boring and Tilton's 1897 design for the Main Building (left, west wing; right, east wing). Courtesy of the Ellis Island Immigration Museum.

staircases in the four towers. In addition, an elevator in the southwest tower of the building carried inspectors, interpreters, witnesses, aliens, visitors, and others to the second floor.

First Floor. The east wing was occupied by the medical examination rooms, a medical office, the chief surgeon's office, the medical sitting room, the certificates office, the medical examiners' sitting room and adjoining locker room, the hospital cases detention room, the statistical office vault (files), a staff room, and three special medical examination rooms.

In the center or middle section of the building was found the vestibule at the canopied entrance, the immigrant examination walkways, the staircases leading to the second floor Registry Room, the U.S. Customs inspectors' office, the immigrants' waiting room; the immigrants' hand baggage room; the storeroom for clothes; a waiting room adjoining three offices (the missionaries quarters, the **Immigrant Aid Societies room**, and the landing agents' room), the railroad east waiting room, the railroad east ticket office, a railroad general office, and a small baggage office. These railroad rooms were for northeastern travelers.

Behind the central area of the first floor was a long passage way and behind this, the large railroad room (railroad ticket office), where national railroad lines sold tickets.

The west wing of the first floor consisted of the Information Bureau, a waiting room for friends and relatives calling for immigrants, the Discharging Division, a small room for the **National Council of Jewish Women**; and crossing a wide corridor led to the huge New York temporarily detained room. There was a also a railroad ticket office in this area.

Second Floor. This floor was the most important place on Ellis Island, for it was here where **primary inspection** took place. The middle space, officially called the **Registry Room** (unofficially, the Great Hall) was composed of pens that formed alleyways for immigrants to

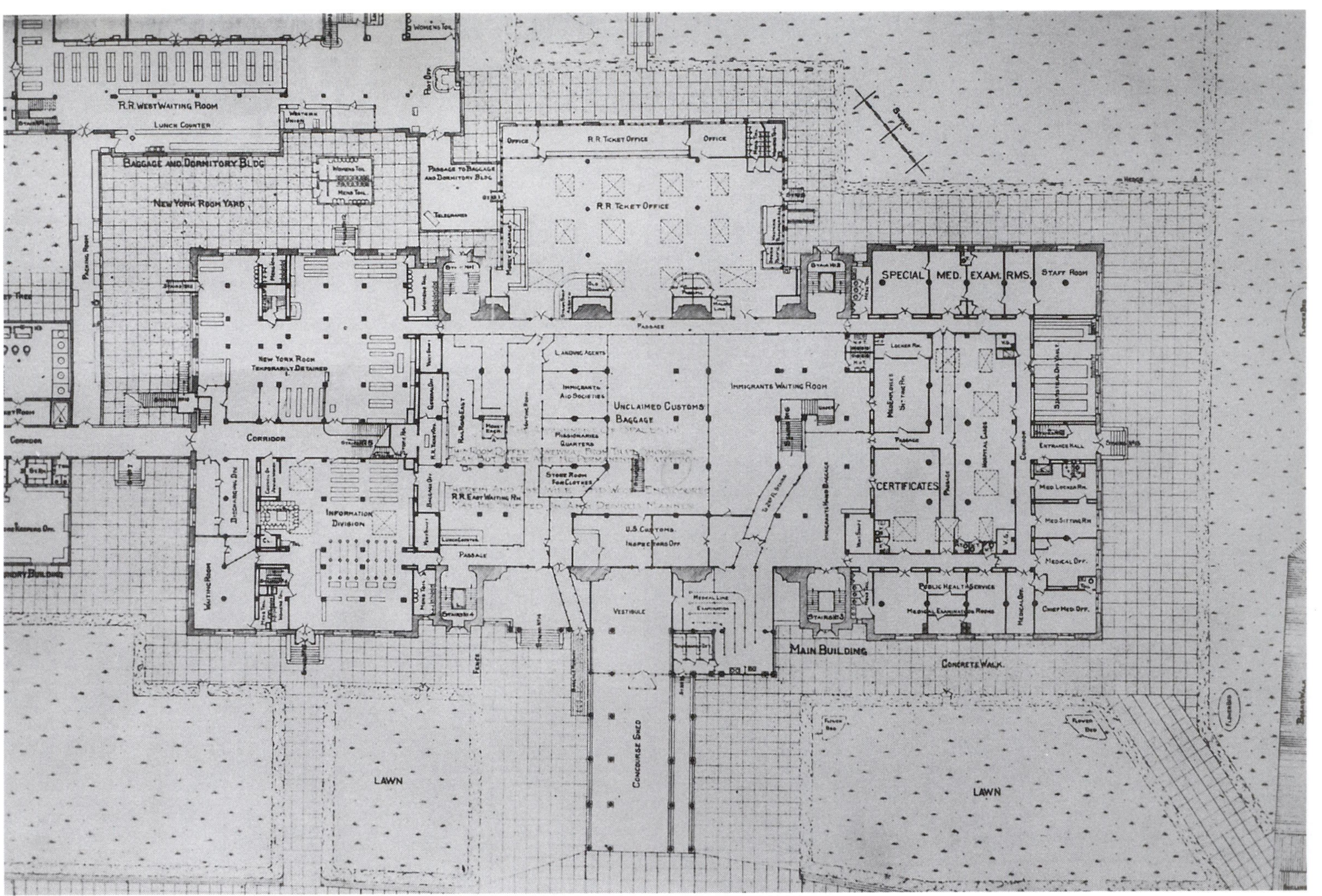

First-floor plan of the Main Building. Courtesy of the Ellis Island Immigration Museum.

form queues in. These pens kept the crowd under control and prevented wandering and confusion which otherwise would have been the case. Even though the immigrants crowded in the room at any one time may have come from the same vessel, they may have spoken different languages and, therefore, would scarcely have been able offer assistance to one another. The entrance staircase to this room was located in the central portion. There was also an elevator in the northeast tower; however, this was seldom if ever used by arriving aliens. The east end of the Registry Room was occupied by a cagelike matron's pen in which to detain women and children aliens for medical examinations or questioning, and a cagelike doctor's pen in which males with suspected conditions were detained. The east wing of this floor contained important medical and immigration offices. An open door near the doctor's pen led straight to medical examination rooms, the laboratory, and a general office. There were also toilets near the two Registry Room pens. The southeast end contained the offices of immigration officials. The first office just off of the Registry Room was a toilet, then came a large clerk's office. Next was the assistant commissioner's office, the main office, then the commissioner's secretary's office, which led into the commissioner's private office, which had an entrance vestibule and a private lavatory. The next offices down the hall were those of the treasurer, the chief engineer, and the restaurant keeper (located behind a stairwell). The next room was a large lounge, followed by rooms in the northeast end. These were the offices of the statistician, the chief inspectors, and a large office given over to the Contract Labor Bureau. Here, only the northeast tower had an elevator; however, all four towers had staircases. The west end of the Registry Room was the location of fourteen inspectors desks, where immigrants were interrogated. Behind these desks were two telegraph rooms, a post office, the money exchange, a clerk's office, and the steamship companies' emigrants' space. In the middle of this area were the **stairs of separation** leading down to the first floor. The west wing was occupied by the Special Inquiry Division offices and detention rooms that were intimately connected with the work done by the immigrant inspectors in the Registry Room. In the west wing were the following rooms: Special Inquiry Division secretaries' office, two examination rooms for boards of special inquiry, one witness room, three special inquiry detention rooms, one large dining room for detained immigrants, one hearing room for contract labor suspects, the excluded women's detention room, and the New York detention dormitory. There were also two lavatories and a linen room for bedding supplies.

Third Floor. Here the central area was empty space rising above to the vaulted ceiling. The floor area was the balcony where people could look down on the second floor Registry Room. The rooms on the balcony level were all dormitories for detained aliens. The south side balcony dormitories were for women and those on the north side were for men. The visitors' gallery was at the west end of the balcony. Behind this were a few offices and a door which led outside onto the west wing promenade roof. The east end of the balcony led to another dormitory and a few supply rooms. A door led to the east wing's outside promenade roof.

Years later, the arrangements in the building underwent various changes. The **Black Tom** Wharf Explosion (1916), World War I, and passage of the restrictive immigration law of 1924 brought about modifications in the appearance and use of space in certain rooms of the building. The following is a description of the Main Building, as it was appeared in 1924.

First Floor. The entrance to the Main Building led to a staircase connecting to the Registry Room on the second floor. On either side of the inside entrance were vestibules. Both of these gave access to the various offices and rooms that occupied the central area of the first floor. This central space was occupied by the unclaimed

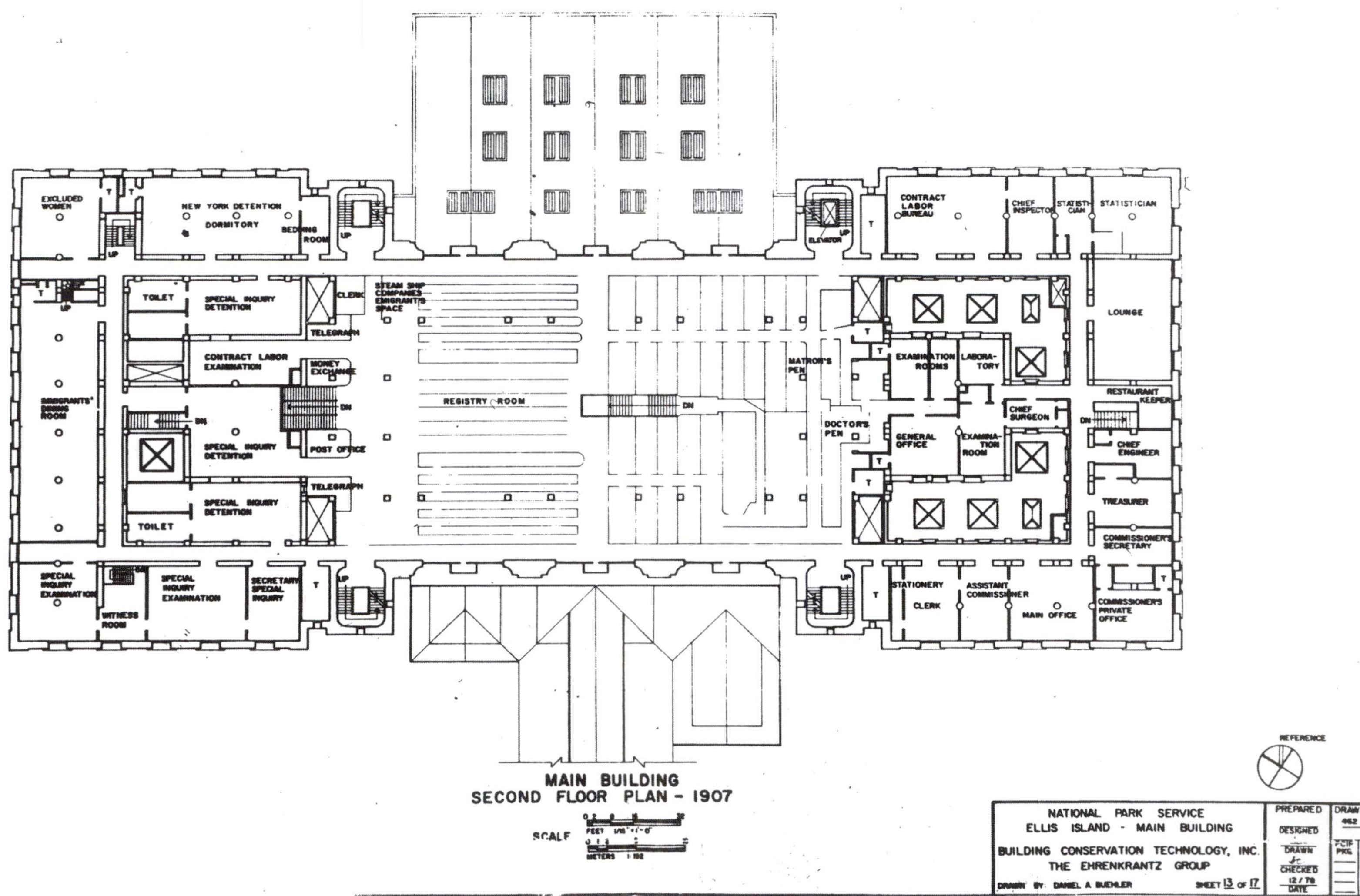

Second-floor plan of the Main Building. Courtesy of the Ellis Island Immigration Museum.

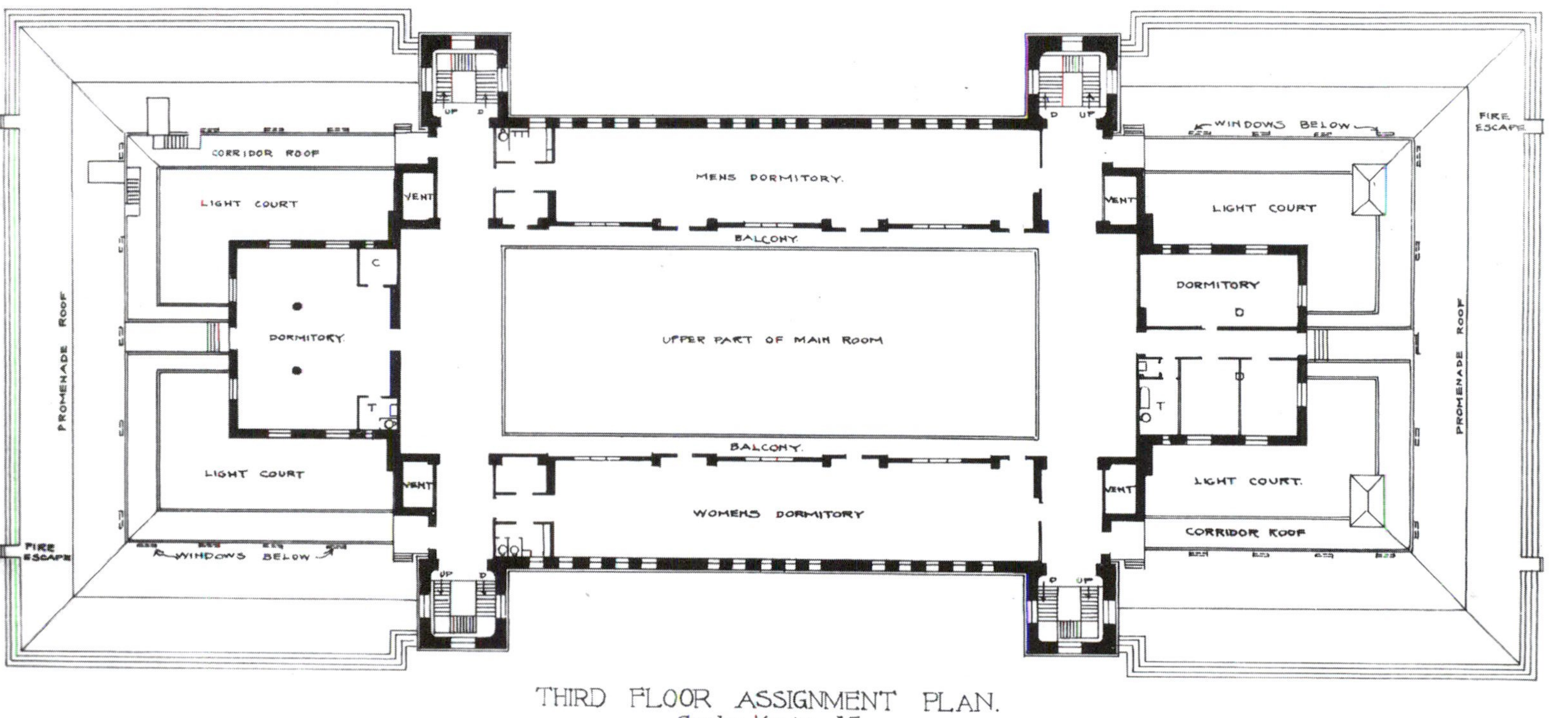

Third-floor plan of the Main Building. Courtesy of the Ellis Island Immigration Museum.

baggage room, landing agent's office, Immigrant Aid Societies office, missionaries' quarters, the clothes room, railroad east waiting room, the immigrants' hand baggage area, and an immigrant's waiting room. Behind the baggage room was the large railroad room, which was also known as the **railroad ticket office**. The east wing of this floor was divided into a variety of offices, mostly occupied by the **Public Health Service**. The separate offices in this wing were three medical examination rooms, two medical offices, the chief surgeon's office, medical sitting room, entrance office, the statistical division's vault, a staff room, three special medical examination rooms, the mental room, medical staff sitting room, and the medical certificates office.

In the west wing of the first floor were the following rooms/spaces: lobby, eastern passengers' bureau, Italian bureau, bureau of information, a cafeteria, waiting room for callers (friends and relatives of immigrants), Discharging Division, telegraph office, National Council of Jewish Women, New York detention room, and ticket office.

Second Floor. The east wing was divided into the following rooms: re-hearings room, superintendent's office, chief clerk's office, commissioner's private office (including a vault and toilet), assistant commissioner's office (**Byron H. Uhl**), the second assistant commissioner's office (**Harry R. Landis**), correspondence clerks room, records office, a main office, appeals room, treasurer's room, time clerk's office, Canadian office, contract labor office, ladies' retiring room, matrons' room, charwomen's room, a storeroom, and separate toilets for immigrants and staff members.

The Registry Room was divided into a temporary detention room on the south side and a special inquiry room on the north.

The west wing consisted of seven board of special inquiry hearing rooms, one witness room, a Special Inquiry Division office, a Deporting Division office and a Deporting Division room, two waiting rooms, one male employees' locker room, one female employees' locker room, toilets, and two other locker rooms.

Third Floor. The east wing consisted of the offices of the Statistical Division, the Chinese Division, four detention dormitories, and three toilets.

The balcony section was divided into the men's dormitories on the south side and the Women's on the north side. There was also a visitors' gallery overlooking the Registry Room.

The west wing was divided into a large inspectors' room (north side), a drafting room, the upper special inquiry room, dormitories, and toilets.

From 1939 to 1942, the basement of the Main Building consisted of the plumbers' shop, laborers' quarters and supply room, gardeners' quarters, tile shop, records storage room, and pipe storage room.

The *first floor* of the Main Building consisted of the following rooms: the information office, the welfare agencies office, the post office, the Works Progress Administration clerical project office, the laborers' dressing room, the Record Division, Medical Division, Parole Division, washrooms, toilets, and utility closets. On the *second floor* the old Registry Room was soon renamed passenger hall. From December 1941 and throughout the remainder of World War II, it used as a day detention room for alien enemy families. The office space in the two wings consisted of the offices of the **district director** (i.e., **commissioner**), the assistant district director, and an administrative assistant. There was also the correspondence office, the files room, the treasurer's office, extension of stay office, bond office, detention and special inquiry offices and rooms. There were also dressing rooms for matrons and guards.

The *third floor* consisted of dormitories for immigrant passengers; but during the war they were used exclusively for alien enemies.

Manifests. First required under federal law by the Passenger Act of 1819, a manifest was prepared by the shipping clerks and bore the names of every passenger aboard every vessel and was then submitted to the federal collector of customs at American seaports. Under the Immigration Act of 1893 (II), the masters or commanding officers of all vessels arriving at U.S. ports were required to deliver to federal immigration officers lists or manifests of all alien passengers made at the time and place of embarkation. The information to be filled in at foreign ports included the following: full name; age; sex; marital status; calling or occupation; whether able to read or write; nationality; last residence; name of seaport for landing in the United States; final destination; whether has a ticket to final destination; whether the immigrant paid his own passage or not; amount of money in hand and how much (more or less than $30); name of relative or friend immigrant is going to (if applicable); whether immigrant has ever before been in the United States; whether immigrant has ever been in prison, an almshouse or supported by charity; whether a polygamist; whether under contract as a laborer; condition of health, mental and physical, and whether crippled or deformed and, if so, from what cause. The manifests were arranged into first class, second class, and steerage (sometimes called third class); there were also pages with the names of the ship's crew (alien seamen), and passengers who were U.S. citizens. Each page of the manifest contained information on thirty passengers. On embarkation or during the voyage at sea, the steamship officers were required to give each passenger a ticket bearing the passenger's name, coded with a letter or number designating the passenger list and his number on the list. The manifest or list was then verified by the signature and oath or affirmation of the master of the vessel or the first or second officer under his command; the ship's surgeon or other medical officer was required to do likewise. These affidavits were then attached to the manifest. Failure to carry out these regulations before arrival at a U.S. port resulted in the imposition of a fine of $100 for each immigrant destined for the United States. If the fine was not paid, the passengers were to be automatically excluded.

In 1943 and 1944, the National Archives helped the Record Division copy disintegrating records, including 14,000 volumes of ship manifests and other documents, for the years 1897 to 1942. The documents were all microfilmed.

Marine Hospital Service. This agency of the federal government, founded in 1798, was originally responsible for the care of sailors, naval officers, and marines. The Marine Hospital Service was the original name of the **Public Health Service** when it was assigned to provide medical care to aliens immigrants in 1891. The service hospital at Ellis Island was officially known as Marine Hospital Number 43. After being called the **Public Health and Marine Hospital Service** for a number of years, the agency was renamed the Public Health Service in 1912. The service began caring for sick aliens at Ellis Island from the first day that the station opened in 1892 until it was closed in 1954. After the **Fire of 1897** destroyed the original wooden hospital, the first fireproof hospital building was opened in 1902, and more buildings were added until 1915. The staff included **surgeons** (doctors), **nurses**, orderlies, attendants, physical therapists, ward maids, cooks, social workers, and others.

Marriages. An interesting phenomenon at Ellis Island was the large influx of young women joining their intended husbands and the subsequent marriages that were orchestrated and arranged by the **Bureau of Immigration**. Because the immigration laws did not allow immigrant inspectors to admit these unescorted females without benefit of marriage, large numbers found themselves detained at Ellis Island if their fiancés were late in coming to call for them. Once the men arrived and were brought into the Information Division, a meeting would quickly be arranged and the two were expected to recognize each other and agree to an immediate wedding. If both consented, the immigration officials, sometimes with the aid of missionaries, made arrangements for the ceremony to be carried out at once. The couple was then escorted by an inspector, interpreter, or other officials to New York's city hall on Park Row, Manhattan, and then often to a religious institution such as the Leo House on 23rd Street, also in Manhattan. With the cooperation and aid of the various missionaries and city officials, thousands of young women were wed before immigration officials relinquished custody of them. The Roman Catholic Church, the Protestant dominations, the Eastern Orthodox churches, and Jewish organizations played an important role in assisting such marriages. The city of New York also played a key role, as is evident in this reminiscence of former interpreter **Fiorello LaGuardia**: "I was assigned to only a few of these. . . . I would escort the bridegroom and his bride to the City Hall to see that they were properly married and then give the bride clearance for admission to the country. In a few instances the aldermen were drunk. Some of the aldermen would insert into their reading of the marriage ceremony remarks they considered funny and sometimes used lewd language, much to the amusement of the red-faced, cheap 'tinhorn' politicians who hung around them to watch the so called fun."

REFERENCE: LaGuardia, Fiorello. 1948. *The Making of an Insurgent: An Autobiography, 1882–1919.* Philadelphia: J.B. Lippincott.

Martoccia, Frank [Francesco Martoccia] (b. Italy, 1867; d. New York, 1954). Interpreter, **Registry Division** (1903–1936). Frank Martoccia began as an **interpreter** at Ellis Island in the 1890s. He was a fluent in Italian, and also could effectively communicate in Spanish, French, German, and Polish. He trained **Fiorello LaGuardia** as an interpreter when the future New York City mayor was hired by the Immigration Bureau in 1907. In 1909, Martoccia was one of thirty-one interpreters at the station and earned $1,400 per year. His reminiscences were published in the form of an interview with Commissioner **Edward Corsi** in *In the Shadow of Liberty*, authored by Corsi (1935, pp. 71–92). Before emigrating to the United States in the 1890s, Martoccia had been a barber in Italy.

REFERENCE: Corsi, Edward. 1935. *In the Shadow of Liberty.* New York: Macmillan.

Matthews, Alma (b. 1868?). Missionary, Methodist Church. Alma Matthews was a missionary at Ellis Island for many years. In the 1920s, she was a leading member of the **Women's Home Missionary Society** and at the station she served on the Ellis Island Committee on Immigrant Aid. Matthews was remembered for many things, including distributing clothes to aliens and providing them with fruit and sweets. Most of the help she provided was for women and children.

Matrons. The matrons helped immigrant women and girls while at Ellis Island, both those passing through in a few hours and those who were held in detention. The matrons also watched for suspicious women who might be involved in some intrigue, suspicious activity or moral turpitude, or crime—anything and everything that smacked of impropriety. They offered sympathy to detained women and children and listened to the individual cases of troubles, misery, and frustration. Perhaps the first matron at Ellis Island was Mrs. Sloper, who had worked earlier at **Castle Garden**. Other well-known matrons from the 1890s through 1914 were Regina Stucklen, **Maud Mosher,** and Helen A. Taylor, who according to an investigation in 1901 was "notorious for her ungovernable temper," which included slapping people in the face.

REFERENCE: Ellis Island investigations file. Ellis Island, NY: Statue of Liberty and Ellis Island Library.

Matrons' Division. In 1903, the Matrons' Division consisted of one head matron and nine **matrons**, five of whom were assigned to the **Boarding Division** to help women cabin passengers meet their friends on the dock, directing them to appropriate lodgings, railway terminals, and so forth. Part of this duty was to watch for indications of immoral relations between women passengers and men.

The other matrons were posted to Ellis Island where they helped female and children immigrants held for special medical examination or in detention. Thus they worked with the **Medical Division** during **line inspection**, the Temporary Detention Division, and the **Discharging Division**. They also investigated women suspected of immoral character while posted to Ellis Island.

In 1914, there were twenty matrons on staff; in 1921, twenty-five matrons; in 1922, twenty-one matrons; and in 1924, fifteen matrons and the chief matron, who was now the special woman inspector in charge.

McCarran, Patrick A. (Patrick Anthony McCarran) (b. near Reno, Nevada, 1876; d. Hawthorne, Nevada, September 1954). Politician, lawyer, sheep rancher. This powerful senator sponsored the **Internal Security Act of 1950** and the Immigration and Naturalization Act of 1952. The latter was popularly known as the **McCarran-Walter Act**. McCarran was the son of Irish Catholic immigrants who settled in Nevada as sheep ranchers. A prominent Democrat, McCarran was held back by political rivals until his election to the U.S. Senate in Franklin D. Roosevelt's landslide victory of 1932. Prior to that he was in and out of state elective offices. He served as state legislator (1902–1904), district attorney in Tonopah, a justice of the Nevada Supreme Court (elected 1912), and chief justice (1917–1919). His twenty-one years in the Senate (1933–1954) established his power base in Nevada and his reputation as a leading conservative Democrat. He was an early critic of President Roosevelt's New Deal legislation and a pioneer in civil aviation legislation. He sponsored the Civil Aeronautics Act of 1938, the Federal Airport Act, and the National Aircraft Theft Act. After World War II, he emerged as a leading anticommunist. In the Senate, he served as chairman of the powerful Judiciary committee.

See also **Walter, Francis E.**

REFERENCES: Hopkins, A. D. 1999. Pat McCarran: Perennial politician. In The first 100 persons who shaped southern Nevada. *Las Vegas Review-Journal.* http://www.1st100.com/part2/mccarran.html; Wepman, Dennis. 2002. *Immigration: From the Founding of Virginia to the Closing of Ellis Island.* New York: Facts on File.

McCarran-Walter Act (Immigration and Naturalization Act of 1952). This law replaced the severely restrictive **Immigration Act of 1924**, and was sponsored by Senator **Patrick McCarran** and Congressman **Francis Walter**. Although more liberal than the previous law, the McCarran-Walter Act perpetuated quotas favoring northwestern European immigrants over other immigrants entering under quotas. The law repealed the long-standing ban on Asians becoming U.S. citizens; however, the new law adversely affected black immigration from the European colonies in the West Indies by limiting immigrants from each colony to a quota of 100 persons each year. At the time, Great Britain, France, and the Netherlands had colonial possessions in the Caribbean region. No quotas were imposed on immigrants from the independent nations of the Western Hemisphere. The McCarran-Walter Act barred the admission of thirty-one classes of aliens: (1) feebleminded aliens; (2) insane persons; (3) aliens who had any attacks of insanity; (4) aliens afflicted with a psychopathic personality, epilepsy, or a mental defect; (5) narcotic drug addicts or chronic alcoholics; (6) aliens afflicted with tuberculosis in any form or with leprosy or any dangerous contagious disease; (7) aliens with disease or defect that may prevent them from earning a livelihood; (8) paupers, professional beggars, or vagrants; (9) aliens convicted of or admitting to a crime of moral turpitude (other than purely political), unless the crime was committed five years or more before applying for an American visa and the applicant was eighteen or under when the crime was committed; (10) aliens convicted of two or more nonpolitical offenses imposing imprisonment of five years or more; (11) polygamists; (12) prostitutes, procurers, and pimps; (13) aliens coming to the United States to engage in any immoral sexual act; (14) aliens seeking to enter the country to engage in kinds of skilled or unskilled labor that the secretary of Labor has certified as already sufficiently filled or that the entry of new immigrant workers might adversely affect wages and working conditions; (15) aliens likely to become a public charge; (16) previously excluded or deported aliens, unless their new application for entry has been approved by the attorney general; (17) aliens who have previously been excluded or deported, including those who have been "removed" (i.e., deported) for having fallen into distress or as enemy aliens; (18) stowaways; (19) aliens who have sought visas by fraud or willful misrepresentation of a material fact; (20) aliens who at the time of application for admission have no valid entry document, such as a current visa, reentry permit, or border crossing identification card; (21) aliens who have come from countries under the quota, yet have no valid quota visa; (22) aliens ineligible for citizenship and those who have left the United States to avoid military service (this provision does not apply to nonimmigrant aliens); (23) aliens convicted of possession of or traffic in illicit narcotic drugs; (24) aliens who have not resided for at least two years in the country from where they seek to migrate; (25) aliens who cannot read or understand some language or dialect, with the exception of permanent U.S. residents returning from a temporary visit abroad, or those under sixteen years of age or unable to read, or close relatives of U.S. citizens, or resident aliens or refugees; (26) nonimmigrant aliens with passports that expire within six months; (27) aliens identified by the consular officer or the attorney general as seeking to enter to engage in activities prejudicial to the public interest; (28) anarchists, aliens who advocate or teach opposition to organized government, members or affiliates of the Communist Party or another totalitarian party, and advocates of the principles of communism or totalitarianism; and aliens required to register under the Subversive Activities Control Act, subject to the previously noted exceptions; (29) aliens for whom there is a reasonable ground to believe that they would engage in subversive activities; (30) any alien accompanying another alien that has been excluded or deported and certified as helpless, and thus in need of guardianship and protection; (31) any alien who shall have knowingly and for gain encouraged or assisted any other alien to enter the United States in violation of law.

REFERENCES: LeMay, Michael C. 1987. *From Open Door to Dutch Door: An Analysis of U.S. Immigration Policy since 1820*. New York: Praeger; Unrau, Harlan D. 1984. *The Historic Resource Study: Ellis Island/Statue of Liberty*. Vol. 1. Washington, DC: U.S. Department of Interior, National Park Service.

McDonald, Peter (b. 1849; d. New York, 1918). Baggage master (1892–1918). Beginning his work as a helper in the baggage office for the Old Dominion Line at **Castle Garden** in the early 1870s, Peter McDonald became baggage master there in 1877 and continued in the same occupation at the **Barge Office** and Ellis Island. At Ellis Island, he had charge of the hand baggage room on the ground floor of the Main Building and the various railroad and steamship lines (especially the Old Dominion Line) paid his wages. Known as "Peter Mac," he, accompanied by his helpers, handled the immigrants' personal belongings. Over the years he gained some fluency in half a dozen foreign languages. In a newspaper interview he said,

> It's I that doesn't have to ask a man what his nationality is. I take one look at the baggage and can tell by the way the knots are tied around the bundles whether the owner's a Swede, a Swiss, an Italian or an Irishman. Take for instance the Danes, Swedes and Norwegians. They always bring more with them than anyone else. . . . Mattresses, feather beds, bedsteads, bureaus, chests of drawers, and . . . kitchen chairs . . . are included in their belongings and no matter how much we tell them about what it will cost to carry the stuff out West, where they are going, they hang on to it for dear life.
>
> The baggage of the English, Irish and the French

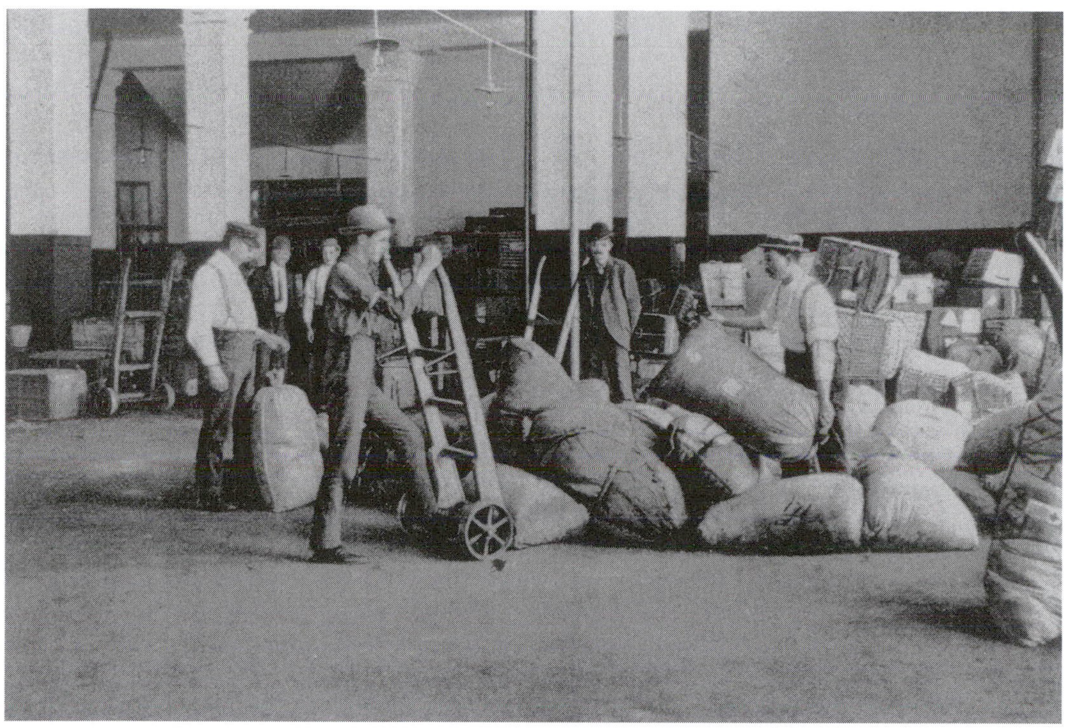

Ellis Island's long-serving baggage master, Peter McDonald (far left), is seen with some of his assistants in the early twentieth century. Courtesy of the Ellis Island Immigration Museum.

come here in better shape than from any other country and is the most modern kind of stuff.

A Greek or Arab thinks the best way to bring baggage here is to get it in the biggest bundle he can. They put five or six hundred pounds of their stuff together and then, after lacing it all up, wrap the whole thing in rugs and shawls. It's a load for six men sometimes.

For years, the immigrants from Spain and Portugal, who have been coming here to settle in the far West and South, brought their entire kitchens, seeds, and plants from their homes. They come here to be farmers and have the idea that seeds are unknown here.

The Polish immigrants carry the least baggage.... They never have their things checked through the baggage room or at least not very often.

There are a lot of funny things happen here on the island. The other day I was fixing labels on the baggage of an Italian bound for Oakland, California, when suddenly I taken off my feet by another Italian throwing his arms around the fellow I was attending. After they finished weeping and kissing each other they told me their story. They came here twenty years ago as boys and went to work as laborers building the railroads. They were friends for years but got separated on the Coast.... Both prospered, bought farms but never returned to Italy until this year.... It took me a half hour to separate them and get their baggage together.

REFERENCE: *New York Evening Telegram*. 1912. Baggage in fifty languages fails to rattle "Peter Mac." December 29.

McSweeney, Edward F. (b. Marlboro, Massachusetts, 1865; d. Framingham, Massachusetts, November 18, 1928). Assistant commissioner (1893–1902). Edward F. McSweeney was the dominant force at Ellis Island during the administration of Commissioner Thomas Fitchie (1897–1902). During these years, Ellis Island and the Barge Office gained the reputation for corruption, dishonesty, and abuse. McSweeney was regarded as largely responsible for this. One of his closest henchmen was **John Lederhilger**, chief of the **Registry Division**. President **Theodore Roosevelt** and Commissioner **William Williams** forced McSweeney to resign. His successor was Roosevelt's political crony, **Joseph E. Murray**. McSweeney entered federal service as an inspector at Ellis Island in 1892 and was selected as assistant commissioner under **Joseph H. Senner**.

Measles. A highly contagious disease that primarily affects children. The mortality rate from this disease at Ellis Island was 30 percent, according to **Victor Safford** in his book, *Immigration Problems*. Safford noted that previous to the opening of measles wards at Ellis Island, immigrants had had to be transported to city hospitals, which took excessive time and contributed to the failure of recovery. But with the establishment of the eleven measles wards as a part of the **contagious disease wards**, the possibility of saving more infected persons improved.

REFERENCE: Safford, Victor. 1925. Immigration Problems: Personal Experiences of an Official. New York: Dodd, Mead.

Mechanical Division. The Mechanical Division operated the **power house** and all other mechanical plants on Ellis Island. From the 1890s through about 1911, it was called the Engineer's Division, and after that it was renamed the Mechanical Division. In 1903, the division consisted of an engineer in chief, assistant engineers, firemen, wiremen, dynamo tenders, a plumber, coal passers (laborers), and a machinist who was in charge of the refrigerating plant. According to Commissioner **William Williams**, in a report he issued in 1912, the Mechanical Division cared for the elaborate light, heat, and power planet, the refrigerating plant, all electric wires, bells and batteries, and all fire lines and apparatus, as well as the heating and lighting of all buildings at Ellis Island. Further, he stated that 15,000 tons of coal were consumed each year. The staff of fifty employees under the supervision of a chief engineer was "composed of engineers, firemen, wiremen, dynamo tenders, machinists and laborers." In the 1890s until 1903, the employees worked a sixteen-hour shift and then were off duty for twenty-four hours before reporting back to work. In 1903, Commissioner Williams changed this arrangement by adding a midnight boat run from the **Barge Office** to Ellis Island. With this reform, the employees were divided into three watches, each of which was on duty for eight hours. Before changing a shift the employees were required to "examine the water in the boilers, the feed pumps, engines, dynamos, and all other machinery . . . in winter the heating apparatus" and so forth.

REFERENCE: Williams, William. 1912. *Ellis Island: Its Organization and Some of Its Work*. Ellis Island, NY: Statue of Liberty and Ellis Island Library.

Medical Certificates. These documents certified the medical state of an alien at Ellis Island. They were written up for aliens who had been singled out during **line inspection** and taken to the physical or mental examination rooms for more thorough examinations, and then found to be suffering from a disease or condition; immigrants detained in the hospitals across the ferry slip from the **Main Building** were also certified. To certify an alien for a Class A condition—"insane," or an "idiot" or as suffering from a "dangerous contagious" or "loathsome" disease—meant that the doctors could not or would not undertake a cure for it and that the **immigrant inspector** would have to exclude or deport the alien. In the case of those certified for Class B conditions, exclusion was not conclusive.

A signed copy of the medical certificate was then given to the immigrant for presentation to an immigrant inspector or sent by a messenger to the **Registry Division**, usually to the registration floor or the **Great Hall**, an immigrant inspector would take into consideration the findings of the document along with other facts pertaining to the case. As already noted, immigrants certified as suffering from a dangerous, contagious, or loathsome disease could never be landed. However, for immigrants certified as suffering from less dangerous conditions, the immigrant inspector had the prerogative to accept or reject an alien and could practically ignore medical certificates that suggested exclusion.

See also **Diseases and Hospitalization; Line Inspection**

Medical Division. The Public Health Service staff, designated by the **Bureau of Immigra-**

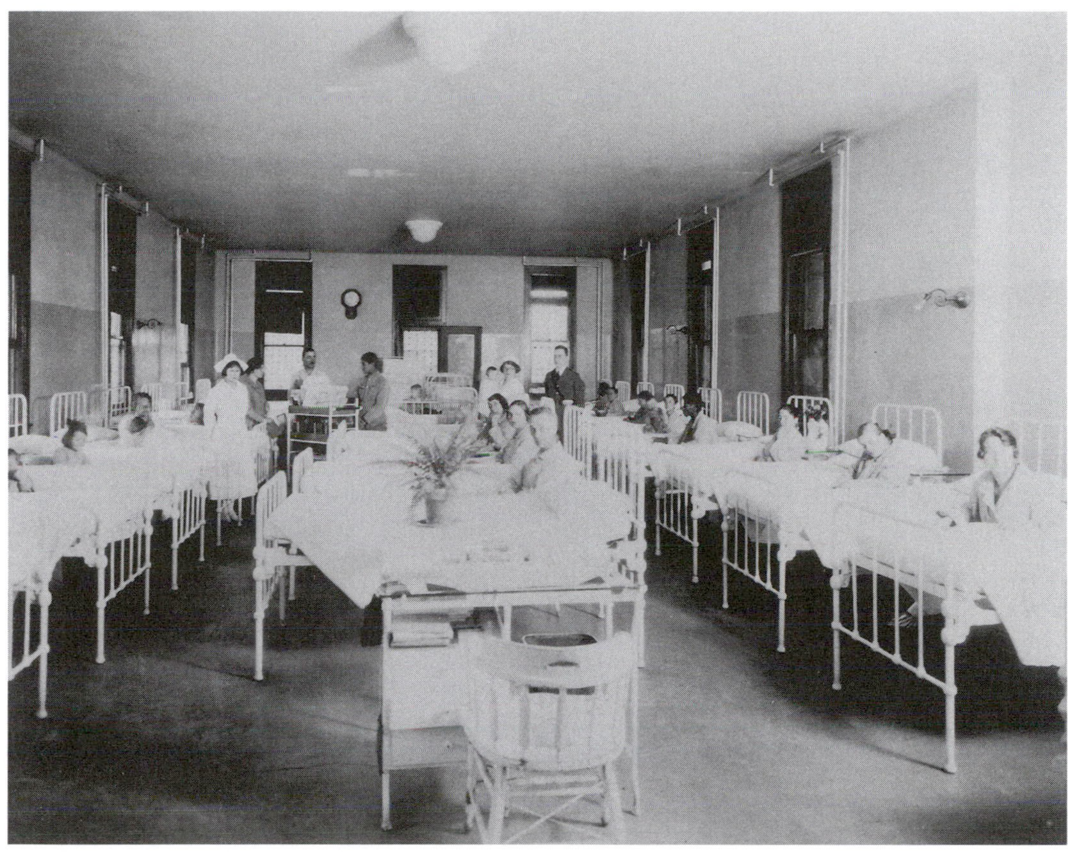

Patients in one of the women's wards. Courtesy of the Ellis Island Immigration Museum.

tion as the Medical Division, was divided into three distinct operations at the Ellis Island station: surgeons and attendants posted to the **Main Building** and a more varied medical team assigned to the hospitals on Islands 2 and 3. The third group consisted of a small detachment assigned to the Boarding Division; they kept private rooms and an infirmary at the **Barge Office**.

The medical force in the Main Building handled the routine line inspection of all newly arrived immigrants and operated the physical examination rooms and the mental room, where immigrants suspected of poor health or disease received more thorough examinations.

The hospital force was divided between those who were assigned to the general immigrant hospital on Island 2 and those assigned to the contagious disease hospital on Island 3. In 1951, the **Public Health Service** closed these hospital buildings and moved the entire medical operation into the east wing of the Main Building.

The head of the **Medical Division** was called the chief medical officer, although he also known as the chief surgeon. The other physicians were also surgeons.

In 1910, the following Public Health Service surgeons were assigned to Ellis Island:

George W. Stoner was the chief medical officer for the entire station. The following surgeons were assigned to assist the **Boarding Division** in cabin inspections aboard arriving steamships: D. E. Robinson, Emil Krulish, A. J. Nute, J. G. Wilson, H. M. Friedman, and J. M Delgado. The following surgeons were assigned to duty in the general immigrant hospital on Island 2: John McMullen, M. C. Guthrie, R. A. Herring, and J. P. Leake. Assigned to line inspection were the following surgeons: M. H. Foster, L. P. H. Bahrenburg, Herbert M. Manning, R. D. Spratt, E. H. Mullan, F. A. Ashford, Carlisle P. Knight, and W. O. Wetmore. In addition to the surgeons, the hospitals on Islands 2 and 3 had a pharmacist, T.V. O'Gorman, and forty-seven medical attendants, of which eighteen were women; in the Main Building, there was one pharmacist, W. F. Macdowell, and twenty medical attendants, including one woman.

In March 1923, there were two surgeons; three past assistant surgeons; five assistant surgeons; five medical interns; two administrative assistants (personnel officer and materiel officer; several attending specialists (ear, nose, and throat; dermatology; oral surgery; ophthalmology; neurology; general surgery; orthopedic surgery); nine clerical workers and property workers, one druggist; two chief nurses (M. V. Daly and E. G. Cartledge); fourteen head nurses; thirty nurses; one chief dietician (H. L. Gillum); three dieticians; two laboratory assistants; two chief cooks; six cooks; 208 attendants, including laundresses, laundrymen, janitors, orderlies, ward maids, kitchenmen, waitresses, clinical workers, a messenger, linen warden and assistant, and one chief librarian (C. B. Tompkins). The total personnel numbered 311.

The following breakdown of the medical operation at Ellis Island in 1913 accounts for all employees except the surgeons and the medical attendants.

The following employees were assigned to the Main Building:

1. Medical office: one assistant pharmacist, two clerks, and two stenographers
2. Certificate room: one chief attendant and six assistants
3. Male examination room: one attendant
4. Female examination room: one matron
5. Line inspection: one stamper and four distributors (attendants)
6. Baggage: two baggage handlers
7. Alley man: one alleyman
8. Barge office: one attendant
9. Interpreters: five interpreters

The following employees were required in the general immigrant hospital on Island 2. In the hospital administrative building offices there was one office attendant/clerk, one matron nurse, one assistant matron, one night matron, one dispensary attendant, and one stenographer. In the laundry, there was one laundryman, one assistant laundryman, and four laundry helpers. In the kitchen, there was the chief cook, two assistant cooks, two kitchenmen, and two pantrymen. In the hospital wards, there were twenty-four male and female ward nurses, twelve orderlies, thirteen ward maids, and two waitresses. The other employees on duty were two switchboard operators (one each for day and night duty), one night watchman, one janitor, one messenger, one ambulance orderly, four porters for general work, two hallmen, one linen woman, and six maids for general work.

The types of employees required in the **contagious disease ward** on Island 3 were the following. In the office building, there was one office attendant/clerk, one dispensary attendant, one day orderly, one night orderly, two night watchmen, and one matron nurse. In the laundry, there was one laundryman and two laundry assistants. In the kitchen, there was a chief cook, one assistant cook, and one kitchenman. In the dining rooms, there were two waitresses. In the hospital wards, there were five female head nurses, eleven female nurses, and thirteen ward maids. In addition, the facility had a janitor, five porters, five hallmen, and one seamstress.

Reference: Unrau, Harlan D. 1984. *The Historic Resource Study: Ellis Island/Statue of Liberty.* Washington, DC: U.S. Department of Interior, National Park Service.

Medical Inspection. *See* **Diseases and Hospitalization; Line Inspection**

Medical Officers. "Medical officer" is another term for the **surgeons** of the **Public Health Service** who had charge of the medical affairs at Ellis Island and all other federal immigrant inspection stations. By custom, tradition, and regulation they held commissions equivalent to those of the U.S. Navy. This was further shown in the military **uniforms** they were required to wear.

Mental Deficiency. Immigrants certified for feeblemindedness, idiocy, or insanity were labeled mentally defective. Such persons were inadmissible to the country and had to be excluded under the immigration laws. The leading nationalities excluded or deported as mentally defective between 1899 and 1930 were the following: Irish; Russians; Spaniards; English; French; Armenians, Cubans; black Africans; Dutch and Flemish; Scots; Dalmatians, Bosnians and Herzegovinians; and Czechs.

See also **Diseases and Hospitalization; Line Inspection; Mental Testing**

Mental Room. In 1912, the mental room consisted of two examining desks and eighteen benches for suspected mental defectives to sit on. The benches were arranged in rows and directly faced the examining desks. Although the room could comfortably accommodate 108 aliens, space often had to be found for twice as many. At one point, it was located on the second floor of the **Main Building**.

Mental Testing. The detection of **mental deficiency** was a part of the test for fitness that doctors of the **Marine Hospital Service** and **Public Health Service** applied to incoming aliens at Ellis Island. Doctors stopped and questioned inattentive and "stupid-looking" aliens in their own languages, asking their age, destination, and nationality. Simple mathematical questions were also asked, such as, How many are 15 and 15? To children under twelve, the question might be asked to add 4 and 4; very small children were often asked their names or how old they were. These brief exchanges gave medical officers an impression of the individual's attentiveness, alertness, reasoning ability, and emotional reactions. Those appearing feebleminded were marked with the letter X on the upper right hand side of their coat. Doctors were also looking for signs of maniacal psychosis, which were usually suggested by striking eccentricity in dress and mannerism, constant talkativeness and joking, facetiousness, keenness, excitement, impatience, impudence, unruliness, flightiness, nervousness, restlessness, egotism, excessive signs of mirth, smiling and laughter, vulgarity, screaming and shouting, and annoying other immigrants. Signs of depressive psychosis were commonly suggested by slow speech, low voice, trembling articulation, a look of sadness on the face, crying or weeping, perplexity, difficulty in thinking, and slow movements. Signs of alcoholism, drug abuse (opium, cocaine, etc.), paresis, and organic dementia were shown by surliness, apprehensiveness, untidiness, intoxication or suggestions of it, confusion, aimlessness, dullness, stupidity, an expressionless face, ataxia, stuttering and tremulous speech, extraordinary calmness, joviality, lying, grandiosity, sullenness, fussiness, and physical symptoms such as can be observed in the eyes. Various kinds of dementia, mental deficiency, and epilepsy were suggested by facial scars, curious rashes, stupidity, confusion, talking to oneself, incoherence, objecting to having the eyelids turned up for examination, silly laughter, nail biting, hallucinating, and other peculiarities. If a greater certainty of mental disease was suspected, the letter X was circled. Stereotyped assumptions about the behavior of peoples of certain racial types also guided physicians in making judgments. Dr. E. H. Mullan wrote, "Those who have inspected immigrants know that almost every race has its own type of reaction during the line inspection . . . If an Englishman reacts to a questions in the manner of an Irishman, his lack of mental balance would be suspected. . . . If the Italian responded . . . as the Finn responds, (he) would in all probability be suffering with a depressive psychosis." When talking with suspected persons, the doctors were always watching the person's facial expressions. Those marked with an X or a circle X were immediately removed from the line inspection by attendants and taken to the **mental room**.

According to Berth M. Booby, about 500 examinations were conducted each month, some immigrants being examined twice or even three times. As indicated, many questions were asked. Here are few more examples: Is it morning or afternoon? How many legs has a dog? How many legs has a horse? Which would you throw overboard and why—food or gold? Tests conducted with detained immigrant children at the Ellis Island school included the following.

1. Card sorting, in which playing cards are used. The cards were dealt and the immigrant sorted them into piles first by colors and then by the suits, diamonds, hearts, clubs, and spades. Errors and timing were rated.
2. Drawing circles, crosses, and stars.
3. Tying a bowknot.

PHS physicians associated with mental testing at Ellis Island included **Howard A. Knox**, Eugene H. Mullan, Alfred C. Reed, **Thomas W. Salmon**, **Bertha M. Boody**, and Robert Leslie (1912–1914).

REFERENCE: Boody, Bertha M. 1926. *A Psychological Study of Immigrant Children at Ellis Island.* Baltimore: Williams & Walker.

Messengers. Messengers were assigned to several divisions, including the **Executive Division**, the **Special Inquiry Division**, the **Registry Division,** and the **Watchmen's and Gatemen's Division**. Messengers delivered messages, escorted witnesses to the elevator, and up the staircases to the boards of Special Inquiry hearing rooms on the second floor and called them in when they were required to testify or state their case. Messengers also assisted the **watchmen**, **gatemen,** and **groupers** in keeping order and helping immigrants with their baggage.

MetaForm Incorporated. This exhibition designing firm was hired by the **National Park Service** as a part of the Liberty/Ellis Island Collaborative to conceptualize, research, curate, and design the exhibits of the **Ellis Island Immigration Museum** in the 1980s. The museum was completed and opened to the public in September 1990. The firm also designed the Statue of Liberty exhibit (with exhibit text by Marvin Trachtenberg). Located on Liberty Island, this exhibit opened in July 1986 as part of the Statue of Liberty restoration.

The MetaForm research staff for Ellis Island consisted of Phyllis Montgomery (director of research and chief curator), Mary Angela E. Hardwick (senior researcher and curator), Fred Wasserman (senior researcher and curator), Elizabeth G. Wilmerding (registrar), Suzanne Considine (assistant researcher), Silvia Koner (assistant researcher), and Mary J. Shapiro (exhibit text writer). From 1985 to 1990, this team researched and gathered a vast array of material for the new museum. On completing the project, they turned over all materials gathered to the Museum Services Division at Ellis Island, including information that did not find its way into the final exhibits. With exhibit designer Ivan Chermayeff, the research team composed a museum book and a souvenir booklet for the Ellis Island Immigration Museum.

See also **MetaForm Research Collection**

REFERENCE: Chermayeff, Ivan, Fred Wasserman, and Mary J. Shapiro. 1991. *Ellis Island: An Illustrated History of the Immigrant Experience.* New York: Macmillan.

MetaForm Research Collection. The MetaForm Research Collection contains materials that were researched or acquired by **MetaForm Incorporated**, the firm that was engaged by the **National Park Service** to create exhibits for the **Ellis Island Immigration Museum**. The research collection is now National Park Service property and located at Ellis Island, where it is in the care of the Museum Services Division. The collection consists of forty-six boxes, including the Exhibit Text and Final Technical Design Package volumes that contain the text exactly as it appears in the permanent exhibits of the museum. The Final Technical Design Package also contains lists of illustrations and artifacts on display. However, later changes to the exhibits are not reflected in these documents. The collection includes the prints of photographs used for the displays as well as a large number of historic photographs that were not selected.

Reference Materials. Box 1 contains reference materials, including lists of donors and lenders, oral history audiotapes created by the Murray Street Enterprise, domestic and foreign photo houses, copies of historic Ellis Island articles, the **Immigration and Naturalization Service** Index to the Subject Correspondence Files, 1906–1932 (National Archives, Record Group 85), and the two museum exhibit volumes mentioned above.

Photographs. Box 2 contains the photographs that were selected for inclusion in the **Peak Immigration Years** exhibit (1880–1924), and Box 3 contains photographs that were not selected for that exhibit. Box 4 contains the photographs selected for the **Through America's Gate** exhibit, and Box 5 has the nonselected photos for that exhibit. Box 6 comprises both selected and nonselected photographs of several exhibits: **Baggage Room**, **Peopling of America**, the third floor photo murals in the east wing of the museum, **Dormitory** exhibit, **Registry Room Views**, **Ellis Island Chronicles**, **Silent Voices**, Restoration and miscellaneous pictures. Box 7 contains the selected and nonselected photographs of the **Treasures from Home** exhibit and the Family Album Walls. Box 8 holds the negatives and color transparencies of the selected and nonselected artifacts of the Peak Immigration Years: 1880–1924 exhibit, as well as potential Silent Voices artifacts and miscellaneous MetaForm items. Box 9 contains negatives and transparencies of selected and nonselected items used in the Baggage Room, Peopling of America, Ellis Island Chronicles, Restoration, Treasures from Home, and Family Album Walls, and the Through America's Gate exhibits, including the **Robert Watchorn** portraits obtained from his hometown of Alfreton in Derbyshire, England.

Donor and Lenders Lists. Box 10 contains the A–F lists of the museum donors and lenders of items on exhibit, including the addresses of the family groups displayed in the Treasures from Home gallery; Box 11 contains the G–M donor/lender lists; Box 12, the N–S lists; and Box 13, the T–Z lists.

Artifacts. Boxes 14 and 15 contain the files of the artifacts that were selected and nonselected for the Peak Immigration Years exhibit, including passports, vintage charts, maps, and timetables. Box 16 contains the artifact files of those items not selected for display, including **Castle Garden** papers, naturalization documents, and sheet music. Boxes 17 and 18 hold the Through America's Gate files both of artifacts selected for display and those not selected; Box 18 also holds nonselected artifact files for selected items of the Baggage Room, and Registry Room exhibits, and the selected and nonselected items of the Ellis Island Chronicles exhibit. Boxes 19 through 21 hold binders with photographs of the selected artifacts of the Treasures from Home exhibit, while Box 22 contains binders of photographs of artifacts and photos that were not selected for the Treasures from Home, Silent Voices, and Through America's Gate exhibits.

Research Files. Box 23 holds the research files of the Peak Immigration Years exhibit including Leaving the Homeland and Passage to America (includes steamship steerage and manifests) galleries. Box 24 holds research files for the following Peak Immigration Year galleries: Ports of Entry, Across the Land, and The Closing Door. Box 25, contains the research files for the Peak Immigration Years gallery called At Work in America, while Box 26 hold the files of the Between 2 Worlds gallery and Box 27 the files of The Go-Beweens, New Americans, and the oral history excerpts for the entire Peak Immigration Years exhibit. Box 28 contains photocopies of each picture and many of the artifacts displayed in the Peak Immigration Years galleries, including passports, steamship tickets and postal cards, and naturalization papers. Box 29 holds the research files for the Baggage Room;

Registry Room; and Through America's Gate exhibits, including the Arrival, Medical Inspection, Legal Inspection, and **Boards of Special Inquiry** galleries. Box 30 holds the files of the following galleries of the Through America's Gate exhibit: Free to Land, **Money Exchange**, Box Lunch, **Mental Testing**, Medical Care, and **Immigrant Aid Societies**. Box 31 contains more research files for the Immigrant Aid Societies gallery. Box 32 holds the files of more Through America's Gate galleries: Detention & Rejection, Food, Sanitation, **Graffiti**; this box also contains the oral history excerpts for the Baggage Room, Registry Room Views, and Through America's Gate exhibits.

Box 33 has the research files for the Dormitory and Ellis Island Chronicles exhibits, including the latter's galleries: Early Years (1600–1890), **Castle Garden**, Early Years–America's New Gateway, Brick and Stone and Years of Turmoil galleries; and Box 34 holds the files of the End of an Era (1925–1954), Ellis Island Ferry galleries, as well as the files for the six models of Ellis Island's growth in display cases, including a list of the construction drawings for them from the Denver Service Center of the National Park Service. This box also contains some research files for the Silent Voices and Restoration exhibits. Boxes 35 and 36 contain research files for the Peopling of America exhibit.

Box 37 contains general research files, such as the Ellis Island paintings of Martha Walter and Ellis Island articles from the press. Box 38 holds variety of immigration subjects, including information on black people, Chinese, Filipinos, Japanese, folk art, genealogy, contemporary immigration, and the Lower East Side Tenement Museum.

Box 39 also contains general research information on immigration; its subjects are pre–Ellis Island immigration, Puerto Ricans, return migration, first-person accounts from oral history interviews, and quotations culled from letters.

Box 40 holds the workbooks of the Freedom's Doors exhibit from the Balch Institute for Ethnic Studies and has information on the historic immigrant inspection stations at Boston, New York, Philadelphia, Baltimore, Miami, New Orleans, San Francisco, and Los Angeles. Box 41 hold the negatives, prints, and transparencies from the Albert Carcieri Collection, articles on immigration conferences held in 1986, photocopies of political cartoons on immigration themes from John Barbieri, and two binders of photocopies of still pictures research conducted by Guggenheim Productions for the museum's film, *Island of Hope, Island of Tears*. Box 42 contains information on Commissioner **William Williams**'s papers, calendar of photographs, and scrapbooks in the New York Public Library. Box 43 holds a portion of the **Harlan Unrau** Papers. Box 44 contains original newspaper stories about Ellis Island. Box 45 holds prints made by Alexander Alland of images from his collection, the rights of which may now be held by Culver Pictures. Box 46 has stray information of searching for Ellis Island artifacts, as well as oversize prints of images, some of which were selected for display.

REFERENCE: Wasserman, Fred. June 1992. Meta-Form Research Collection: Guide to the collection. Museum Services Division, Ellis Island Immigration Museum, Statue of Liberty N.M.

Mezei, Ignac (b. Hungary, May 2, 1897; d. Budapest, Hungary, October 1976). Cabinetmaker. Ignac Mezei, the "man without a country," was detained at Ellis Island for two lengthy stays that drew wide public attention and gave rise to considerable legal debate. He was detained there from February 9, 1950, until May 10, 1952, and from April 22, 1953, through August 11, 1954. The Immigration and Naturalization Service (INS) endeavored to deport him at least seventeen times, alleging that he endangered the internal security of the United States. Although they refused to clarify their position, it was clear that he was suspected of being a communist spy. In a statement, the agency described him as "an alien of uncertain antecedents whose parents were Hungarian or Rumanian but who claims to have been born in Gibraltar." Although Mezei had lived in the United States since the 1920s, he did not speak English well. Mezei immigrated to the United States in 1923, settled in Buffalo, New York, and eventually married a naturalized U.S. citizen—Julia Mezei (1901–1996). During this period, he became an active member of a Hungarian benevolent society, which eventually amalgamated with a leftist group known as the International Workers Order. Mezei served as president of this organization's Buffalo branch (1939–1945). In 1948, he returned to Europe to visit his dying mother, who, he said, lived in Romania. However, he only got as far as Hungary, where he stayed for more than a year and a half, claiming that Communist authorities detained him. He was eventually released and went to France, where he applied for an American visa. After some difficulty, he managed to get one and sailed back to the United States aboard the *Isle de France.* When he arrived in New York harbor on February 9, 1950, he was immediately taken to Ellis Island. Although Mezei was later described by Ellis Island guards as a "nice man," he himself remarked, "You don't do nothing on Ellis Island, you go crazy!" He was finally released from INS custody in 1954 and eventually returned to Hungary.

See also **Radicals**

Mikolainis, Peter [Petras Mikolainis] (b. Ciziskés, Vilkaviskis, Lithuania, May 26, 1868; d. Brooklyn, New York, January 7, 1934). Interpreter (1903–1913). Fluent in Lithuanian, German, Polish, and Russian, Peter Mikolainis immigrated to the United States in 1896, attained citizenship by 1901, and was hired as an **interpreter** at Ellis Island by Commissioner **William Williams** on October 2, 1903; his salary was $1,000 per year. Like most interpreters, he was attached to the **Registry Division** and his chief work was to assist inspectors to interrogate non–English speaking immigrants; in his case, Lithuanians and others with whom he could converse in their native language or dialect. In April 1913, Mikolainis resigned from the **Bureau of Immigration** to embark on a new career; his last day of work at Ellis Island was May 8. His salary by then was $1,300 per year.

Mikolainis's work at Ellis Island was insignificant in comparison to his ceaseless labors for the Lithuanian nation before and after he immigrated. A dedicated nationalist, he used every means at his disposal to fight the imperial Russian decree that outlawed Lithuanian-language publications from appearing in Lithuania and other parts of the Russian empire. This policy of Russification (1864–1904) caused a sense of outrage among a large section of the population, but many were afraid of the tsarist police spies and other imperial authorities that might punish them for disobedience. Mikolainis joined the fight against Russia when he moved to East Prussia, where he became a bookseller and adopted the alias Matthias Noveski, a supposed U.S. citizen from Wanamie, Pennsylvania. Under this guise, he operated bookshops, first briefly in Ragnit and then for a longer time in Tilsit, which proved to be a better location. From this German base, he organized an extensive underground network of smugglers; in the province of Sulwalki, seventeen collaborators smuggled Lithuanian-language books and newspapers across the frontier into Lithuania. The operation remained remarkably successful most of the time, and it was not until German border surveillance cracked down on the operation in 1896 that the police compelled him to close his bookshop. His solution was to flee to the United States. He settled in Pennsylvania, and he married Eva in 1898 and became a U.S. citizen in 1901. From 1897 to 1900 and 1902 to 1903, he was the editor of the ethnic newspaper *Vienybe Lietuninky* (Lithuanian Unity). He also served as the secretary of the Lithuanian Patriots Association (1896–1900), which enabled him to publish and send books to Lithuania; one of the smuggling routes he orchestrated was from New York to Finland or Sweden to St. Petersburg and thence to Lithuania. He was also an active force in the Lithuanian Alliance of America. In 1901, he decided that it was time to return to Europe and promptly went back into the book smuggling business in Tilsit. However, he quickly found himself at odds with local German publishers who were making a profit in the lucrative Lithuanian book smuggling trade. In 1902, his rivals banded together and prompted German authorities to force Mikolainis to return to the United States. Mikolainis and his family moved to Brooklyn, New York, and he was hired as an interpreter for the U.S. Bureau of Immigration at Ellis Island. After resigning from that position, he went into business as a notary public; he also handled general business matters, such as immigration questions and real estate. Mikolainis remained active in Lithuanian affairs until his death. On May 23, 1933, only months before his death, he was decorated by the government of Lithuania as a knight of the Order of the Grand Duke Gedimas in recognition of his meritorious service to Lithuania.

REFERENCE: *Encyclopedia Lituanica.* 1973. Mikolainis, Peter. New York: Juozas Kapocius.

Miller, Watson B. (b. Renssalaer, New York, 1878; d. Washington, DC, February 11, 1961). Commissioner of Immigration and Naturalization (1947–1950). Watson B. Miller was President Harry S. Truman's commissioner, and during his term the Cold War and the **red scare** colored the activities of the Immigration and Naturalization Service. In addition, the service was looking for a means of closing Ellis Island completely.

Miller was active in service positions for many years, first as an army captain during World War I and later as the director of the American Legion Rehabilitation Commission (1923–1941). He entered government service during World War II and held the posts of assistant administrator of the Federal Security Administration (1941–1945) and administrator (1945–1947).

Sikhs from India were among the many non-Europeans to pass through Ellis Island. Others included Africans, Arabs, Armenians, Chinese, Japanese, Koreans, Persians, and Turks. Sherman Collection. Courtesy of the Ellis Island Immigration Museum.

Minorities. Historically, the term "minority" is problematic because many European immigrants formed an ethnic minority once they settled in this country. The southern Italians, Slavs, Jews, Greeks, and Hungarians were regarded as minorities in the early years of their immigration. Their languages, customs, and religions set them apart from the Anglo-Saxon majority. They experienced discrimination, suspicion, segregation, and dislike, as well as fascination and curiosity.

In addition to these large groups of immigrants, there were also significant numbers of peoples who fit today's understanding of minority groups. Thousands of these people—Africans, Asians, and Latin Americans—passed through Ellis Island at the same time as the great waves of Europeans were entering.

In 1893 "oriental" passengers from the steamship *Guildhall*, sailing from Alexandria, Egypt, were brought to Ellis Island for inspection. The group was made up of performers from Cairo, led by the famed soothsayer Mohamet Nur, and were on their way to represent a Cairo street scene at the World's Columbian Exposition in Chicago. Aside from Nur, who was a Sudanese, the group included Egyptians and Nubians.

The steady flow of unusual immigrants continued for decades. They included Armenians, Turks, Georgians, Persians, Hindus, Sikhs, Zoroastrians (Parsees), and Gypsies (Roma); Syrians, Lebanese, Iraqis, Egyptians, Algerians, and Moroccans; Ethiopians, Somalis, and Afro-Caribbeans (West Indian blacks); mulattos or mixed-races persons of various nationalities; Chinese, Japanese, Koreans, Burmese; Cubans, Puerto Ricans, Mexicans, Dominicans, Argentines, and other Latin Americans.

See also **Black Immigrants; Chinese Division**

Mission of Our Lady of the Rosary (Mission of the Immaculate Virgin for the Safekeeping of Irish Girls). Located at 7 State Street in lower Manhattan, directly across from Battery Park, the Mission of Our Lady of the Rosary was founded in 1881. It was dedicated to helping immigrant Irish girls and women. The mission sent representatives to **Castle Garden** from 1881 to 1890 and to Ellis Island from 1892 through the 1930s. The first chaplain was Father John J. Riordan. In the 1890s, his successor, Father M. J. Henry, went to the island regularly. Missionary agent Patrick McCool assisted him at the island. Father Henry was soon joined by young Father **Anthony J. Grogan**, who eventually succeeded him as pastor and chaplain at the mission. By 1908, 100,000 Irish girls had received welcome aid from the mission, all free of charge.

For his part, Grogan was one of the most popular **missionaries** at Ellis Island and remained there until his death in 1932.

Missionaries. At Ellis Island missionaries helped aliens in need at a vulnerable point in their lives. They provided temporary shelter for discharged aliens at their immigrant "homes" and directed them to various jobs. They also helped immigrants by writing letters and sending telegrams for them. Each religious group was usually restricted to assisting their coreligionists and was asked not to proselytize to immigrants of other faiths or beliefs. The presence of missionaries at Ellis Island was inherited from the **Castle Garden** immigrant depot, where they had worked for many years. The following organizations permanently stationed or sent missionaries to Ellis Island nearly every day.

Since the majority of Ellis Island immigrants were Catholics, the Roman Catholic Church had a strong presence on the island. Missionaries came from the Irish **Mission of Our Lady of the Rosary**, the **St. Joseph's Home for Polish Immigrants**, the **St. Raphael Society for the Protection of Italian Immigrants**, the **St. Raphael Society for the Protection of German Immigrants**, St. Raphael Society for the Protection of Ruthenian Immigrants, the **Austrian Society**, and the National Catholic Welfare Conference, among others.

After the Catholics, the second largest religious group was the Jews. They had help from the **Hebrew Immigrant Aid Society** and the **National Council of Jewish Women**.

Missionaries from the Eastern Orthodox churches were represented by agents from organizations such as the Greek Society.

Protestant missionary societies included the Baptist Home Missionary Society, **American Tract Society**, Domestic Missions of the Reformed Church, Congregational Home Missionary Society, Danish Evangelical Lutheran Church, Holland Immigration Bureau of the Dutch Reformed Church, Evangelical Home Mission Council, Danish Mission Home, Deutsche Lutheranische Emigrantes Haus (German Lutheran Emigrant Home), Lutheran Pilger House, **Woman's Home Missionary Society** of the Methodist Episcopal Church (with the Immigrant Girl's Home at 9 State Street), **Salvation Army**, **YMCA**, **YWCA**, **Women's Christian Temperance Union**, **New York**

Missionaries played an active role in aiding foreigners at Ellis Island. In this May 1908 picture Protestant clergymen, the Reverend Father Anthony Grogan of the Catholic Church, and Hebrew Immigrant Aid Society officials, are shown. Sherman Collection, courtesy of the Ellis Island Immigration Museum.

City Mission Society of the Protestant Episcopal Church, Presbyterian Board of Home Missions, the New York Bible Society, Svenska Lutheran Immigrant Hemmet, Swedish Baptist Home Missions, and Swedish Missionaries.

Over the years well-known missionaries working at Ellis Island included Father Giacamo Gambera, Father **Anthony Grogan**, Father **Gaspare Moretti**, Father S. Cynalewski, and Father Leo Kwasniewski, and Irish missionary agent Patrick McCool; Reverend W. A. Dalton; Reverend H. J. Berkemeier, and Reverend George Doering for the German Lutheran Church (1892–1914); Bruce M. Mohler and Thomas F. Mulholland (director, 1920–1940s), for the National Catholic Welfare Conference; Angela Carlozzi Rossi (secretary and treasurer, 1930s–1940s) of the Italian Welfare League; Baptist Reverend Ernest Jackson (1892–1921) and evangelist **Michael Lodsin** (1890s–1918) for the New York Bible Society; Colonel Helen R. Bastedo, Captain Fritz Nelson, Amalia Fuhr, and Brigadier General Thomas Johnson for the Salvation Army; Harry Force (who played the piano on Sundays, 1903–1906) and **Charles A. Carol** served the Episcopal Church; **Alexander Harkavy**, **Irving Lipsitch**, Michael Kley, Samuel Frommer, and William M. Neubau for HIAS; **Sadie American** (director), **Cecilia Razofsky** (1905–1910), Florina Lasker (1905–1910), **Cecilia Greenstone** (1907–1919), and Anna M. Kaufman (1926–1954), for the NCJW; **Ludmila K. Foxlee**, and Mrs. Athena Marmaroff (1913–1940s; she was fluent in seven languages and under stood twelve) of the **Women's Christian Temperance Union**, **Alma Matthews** (she was said to be stone deaf and had charge of the old clothes, sweets, and fruit), and Reverend John Kveetin (1930s–1940s) of the American Tract Society. Another long-serving immigrant aid worker was Jenny F. Pratt, who represented the Congregational and Christian Churches (1930s–1954). Rev. John Evans was the chaplain for the Protestant Episcopal Church, Seaman's Institute, at Ellis Island from 1946 to 1953. His sermons emphasized Americanization.

See also **Immigrant Aid Societies**

Money Exchange. The foreign money exchange was operated by a single privilege holder in a contract with the federal government (**Bureau of Immigration**).

The rates of exchange were based on "the prevailing rates recognized by the most reputable money exchange houses of New York City." Foreign coins of gold and silver, as well as paper money, were exchanged for U.S. currency. The concessionaire received a small fee of 1 percent or less of the value of the currency exchanged. The foreign currency most commonly exchanged were British pounds and guineas, German Reich marks, French francs and napoleons, Dutch guilders, Belgian francs, Swiss francs, Italian lire, Russian rubles, Greek drachmas, Danish , Norwegian , and Swedish kronor, Finnish marks, Polish zlotys, Czechoslovak kronen, Austrian schillings, Turkish pounds, Spanish pesetas, and Portuguese escudos.

Checks and bank drafts could be cashed, including the paychecks of the federal employees at the station.

Interpreters were always available to assist immigrants at the Money Exchange. Courtesy of the Ellis Island Immigration Museum.

Companies holding the concession were Francis J. Scully in the 1890s, Post & Flagg (1902–1905; George B. Post Jr., partner), and American Express (1905–1954).

See also **Privilege Holders**

Moore, Annie [Mrs. Patrick O'Connell] (b. Cork, Ireland, January 1, 1877; d. Texas, 1923). Annie Moore, the first immigrant to be inspected at Ellis Island, arrived in New York as a steerage passenger aboard the SS *Nevada*, with her two young brothers, eleven-year-old Anthony and seven-year-old Philip. **Charles M. Hendley**, an important official of the Treasury Department in Washington, conducted the primary inspection by which she and her brothers were admitted to the country. Superintendent **John B. Weber** presented her with a ten-dollar gold piece after delivering a warm speech of welcome to the United States. Annie and her brothers were released to their parents, Mr. and Mrs. Matthew Moore, who had come to Ellis Island to fetch them. An older son, Thomas Moore, had come to the United States earlier with their parents. The Moores resided at 32 Monroe Street in Manhattan. They eventually moved to Indiana and then westward to Texas and New Mexico. Annie Moore married Patrick O'Connell in Waco, Texas; the couple had eight children, three of whom died at birth. Patrick O'Connell died of influenza in 1919. Annie Moore O'Connell was accidentally killed by a train while visiting her sick bother.

Statue of Annie Moore from Ireland, the first immigrant to pass through Ellis Island, at the Ellis Island Immigration Museum. Courtesy of the Ellis Island Immigration Museum.

In 1993, a bronze statue of Annie Moore was unveiled at the **Ellis Island Immigration Museum** by President Mary Robinson of Ireland. The sculptor was Jeanne Rhynhart, who also sculpted a companion piece that stands in Cobh, Cork, Ireland, and represents Annie and her two brothers departing their homeland for America. President Robinson unveiled it on February 8, 1993, in the presence of M. Ann Belkov, superintendent of the Statue of Liberty National Monument and Ellis Island. The Irish American Cultural Institute and the Cobh Heritage Trust commissioned the sculptures.

Annie Moore's story has inspired fiction writers Eithne Lochry of Ireland and Eve Bunting of the United States to produce juvenile novels about her. In addition, there is now an "Annie Moore's Pub and Restaurant" near Grand Central Station in Manhattan as well as other places named in honor of the Irish immigrant.

REFERENCE: *New York Tribune.* 1892. Annie's golden greeting: The first immigrant to land on Ellis Island got $10—she was a little Irish girl come to join her parents. January 2.

Moral Turpitude. Moral turpitude first appeared in the **Immigration Act of 1891**. The bureau asserted that all of the following embraced moral turpitude: adultery, lewd and lascivious cohabitation, sodomy, rape, prostitution, bigamy, fraud, larceny, embezzlement, burglary, receiving stolen property, obtaining money under false pretences, conspiring to defraud, and perjury. There were cases at Ellis Island involving immigrants that were deported or excluded for all of these offences.

Noted cases involving moral turpitude were

the detentions of **Marie Lloyd** and the Countess of Cathcart for traveling aboard their steamships with their male companions and of **Charles Trenet** for homosexuality. Indian spiritual leader **Jiddu Krishnamurti** was briefly detained to answer charges of moral turpitude, which, in his case, were quickly found to be false.

REFERENCE: Clark, Jane Perry. 1931. *Deportations of Aliens from the United States to Europe.* New York: Columbia University Press.

Moretti, Gaspare (b. Italy, 1880; d. 1924). Missionary. Father Gaspare Moretti, one of the most beloved priests at Ellis Island, was a talented photographer and produced a large number of pictures of Italian immigrants and life in Little Italy. Father Moretti was the director of **St. Raphael Society for the Protection of Italian Immigrants** and their chaplain at Ellis Island (1905–1921). In 1910, during the second administration of Commissioner **William Williams**, Father Moretti delivered the Italian Address at the Christmas Festival at Ellis Island. The following is an excerpt from his remarks:

> I have spoken on Ellis Island before, but never was there a time when I felt so bad a now. There are so many detained here. You have crossed the ocean, endured hardships and danger to come to the country discovered by your countryman. You have found the door closed. You have had your hope in the land of liberty shattered. To those who will finally get in, I would say, you must live to be a credit to your country and to the land of your adoption.

The Italians received his address with cheers and great displays of enthusiasm.

REFERENCES: Aleandri, Emelise. 2002. *Little Italy.* Charleston, SC: Arcadia; *New York Times.* 1910. Ellis Island Christmas Festival. December 24.

Mortuaries. *See* **Animal House; Hospital Outbuilding; Mortuary and Autopsy Room**

Mortuary and Autopsy Room. In 1936, the engine room on the first floor of the power house on **Island 3** was converted into a mortuary and autopsy room. The autopsy room contained a table on which to perform autopsies that was surrounded on one side by an observation platform. Eight cadavers each could be stored in eight refrigerated body storage units set in the wall like cupboards. There was also an autopsy room and mortuary in the **hospital outbuilding** on **Island 2**. It opened in 1901.

See also **Deaths and Burials**

Mosher, Maud (b. Streator, Illinois, 1871; d. ?). Matron (October 15, 1903–June 15, 1907). Maud Mosher was a matron assigned to the **Boarding Division** to protect foreign girls and young women from the white slave traffic. Her second assignment was in the Temporary Detention Division on Ellis Island. Her career apparently began in Wichita, Kansas, where she worked as a schoolmistress in 1892. She next worked as an assistant clerk in the Indian Service at Wichita from April 26, 1893, until July 15, 1900. She then worked variously as a commercial teacher, a principal, and a traveling saleswoman. She briefly returned to the Indian Service in the capacity of matron, June 1902 through October 1903, whereupon she entered the **Bureau of Immigration** and was posted at Ellis Island. Mosher kept an extensive diary of her experiences at Ellis Island. In 1910, she wrote several amusing articles about her experiences as a matron at Ellis Island in the *Coming Nation*, a well-known periodical of the time. She wrote about diverse immigrants, including italians, irish, hungarians, french, english, and west indians. at the time she penned her articles, she was living in chicago, illinois.

Here is an excerpt from her first article in which she tells of unexpectedly receiving a letter from the Bureau of Immigration offering her a job at Ellis Island; at the time she was a matron in the Indian Service:

> It was as surprising as a thunderbolt out of a clear sky. Had it been a position on the moon it could not have seemed more improbable—would I accept a position as matron at Ellis Island, qualified for Boarding Duty, answer immediately, etc.
>
> I knew nothing about the Immigration service. To be sure, I had heard that Ellis Island was the place where the immigrants were examined the same

as old Castle Garden—but Boarding Duty, what could it mean?

After some further correspondence with the Commissioner at Ellis Island the spirit of adventure prompted me to accept the position.

About her arrival in New York she wrote,

The conductor on the train told me that the terminal of the railroad was in Jersey City and that I would have to take a ferry boat to New York, "just follow the crowd" from the depot. I did so and went into what seemed to be a fairly pleasant waiting room. The crowd sat down, so did I. They waited, so did I. By and bye, they all rose and went toward a door and I supposed the ferry boat had arrived, so I went to the door also when someone near me said, "Well we are in New York at last," and so we were, instead of it being a waiting room, as I thought it was, it was the ferry and we had been crossing the North River while I thought we were waiting for the boat.

. . . It was after midnight when we reached a hotel. In the morning I asked the maid in the hall how to get to the Barge Office where I had been directed by the Commissioner in order to get to the boat to the Island.

"Ye do go down Broadway, ye'll know ut when ye see ut because the buildin's are so high. Ye go over straight east until ye git there, thin ye go down Broadway until ye come to the Battery, thin ye are at the Barge Office. Ye'll know ut on account of the immigrants comin' out and waitin' on the strate. Ony policemin will tell ye if ye are afraid."

For a wonder I arrived at the Barge Office without losing my way, went onboard the Ellis Island boat, passed ever so many watchmen who asked me ever so many questions and finally found my way to the Commissioner's office. . . .

Next the Matron in Charge took me round the Island explaining things. . . . She said that they were not very busy that day as there were only about three thousand immigrants to be examined. To me it looked as though all the poor people of Europe had come in on that day.

Out in Kansas no one was so very wealthy but no one was so very poor. . . . In all my life I had never seen people so desperately poor except some of the reservation Indians and we always thought they were so poor because they were an uncivilized people—but these were people from the civilized countries of Europe, so of course, they must be civilized. That is what Americans think . . . yet many of these immigrants . . . are no more civilized than our North American Indians, the reservation Indians, I mean, the real "old timers," as we used to call them in the Indian Service.

As I stood and watched the immigrants coming in, it look as though they would never cease, every minute was an hour, and the line, two by two, kept moving on. The Doctors were examining their eyes and scalps at one place . . . on the line. 2 Matrons, very grave and dignified, stood there looking and occasionally taking some woman or woman and man out of the ranks. Officers stood at different places giving strange commands in foreign tongues. Little children were crying, tugging at the mother's skirts, the tears making streaks down their tired dirty faces, some of the many babies were screaming. Men and women and children were also bending under burdens which seemed almost beyond their strength to carry—bags, bundles, great packs, valises without handles tied together with rope, little tin trunks, great baskets, cooking utensils. . . .

So many look weak and starved, so many were filthy and dirty . . . so low and degraded looking, and so poor, so dreadfully poor! And I—I had to stay, I had to stay. . . .

[Next day]

When I reported for duty, the Matron in Charge introduced me to a Matron and told her, Show her the ropes. . . . As I soon learned that the way of doing anything seemed to be of much more importance than . . . doing the duty itself.

Every day the terrible feeling of being in a place from which there was no escape grew upon me. The noise and confusion, the curt commands of the officers, the Sundays the same as other days—for the Sabbath is not observed at Ellis Island—the thousands of poor people arriving every day, the misery of the deported.

The tears were always so near my eyes that I just had to keep on smiling to keep them from flowing.

The text that follows is an excerpt from Mosher's diary. In it, she refers to several coworkers of the Boarding Division. A few are identifiable from personnel lists. They are Chief Inspector William W. Brown, Matron Sarah E. Waters, Inspector John J. O'Connor, Inspector Philip S. Biglin, Inspector William C. Pearsall, and Inspector Frank B. Macatee.

Dec. 21, 1904

My long day but as I was sick all day went home at 1.45 by permission of Mr. Brown. The "Kroonland" came up Mrs. Waters went to pier for it. Mrs. Mooney traded her next late day with me.

Went on cutter as usual in morning but was ordered off by Mr. O'Connor. I was at the table in the dining cabin when Mr. O'C. came in and said in his usual harsh, brutal manner when delivering an order to the matrons. "Miss Mosher the Capt. will not permit you to board the ships in this weather and he wishes you to go ashore." I got up without a word and went. I don't know when I ever felt so humiliated—Messrs. Biglin, Pearsall, McAtee and Tappin were present.

Dec. 22, 1904

Asked Mr. O'Connor if I would be allowed to go on cutter today & he said I would have to ask Capt. Newcome—Capt. N. came in and said: There is nothing down there for you and I don't want you on the cutter when there is no ship for you.

I said to Mr. O'C. "I do not wish to be ordered away from the table again, that is a humiliation I will not stand for." Of course, he flew into his usual rage.

REFERENCE: Mosher, Maud. *Maud Mosher Papers.* Ellis Island, NY: Statue of Liberty and Ellis Island Library.

Murray, Joseph E. (b. Ireland, 1839). Assistant commissioner (1902–1909); politician. Joseph E. Murray, a close political associate of President **Theodore Roosevelt**, was appointed assistant commissioner over the objections of Commissioner **William Williams**, who eventually resigned in protest. Murray continued in the position through the administration of **Robert Watchorn** but promptly submitted his resignation in person to William Williams, on the latter's return to office in 1909.

Joseph Murray was responsible for Theodore Roosevelt's entry into the realm of politics, having serving as his first campaign manager (1881).

My Boy. Featuring child star Jackie Coogan (1914–1984), this 1921 melodramatic film dealt with the chaos in postwar Europe and the subsequent flow of refugees to the United States. In the picture, Coogan portrays the immigrant orphan boy Jackie, whose father died sometime during the war and whose mother died during the voyage to America. On arrival in New York, Jackie is promptly detained at Ellis Island. The Ellis Island sequences appear to have been actually filmed at the station. Jackie somehow escapes from the immigration authorities and attaches himself to Captain Bill (Claude Gillingwater), a rundown old ne'er-do-well who suffers from rheumatism. The old captain has little to offer the boy, as he is broke and behind on his room rent. This wretched state of poverty deepens until the lad is saved at the last hour. The film ends on a happy note when it is discovered that Jackie is the long-lost grandson of Mrs. J. Montague Blair, a lady of great wealth. *My Boy,* produced by Sol Lesser and directed by Victor Heerman and Albert Austin, was not nearly as successful or popular as Coogan's first feature film, *The Kid* (1921), in which he starred opposite Charlie Chaplin.

See also **Films and Documentaries**

N

Name Change Legend. Passenger names were recorded on manifests prepared by the officials of the steamship companies that brought foreigners to the United States. These officials, mostly ticket agents and pursers, required no special identification from passengers and simply accepted the names the immigrants gave them.

Immigrant inspectors accepted these names as recorded in the ship's manifests and never altered them unless persuaded that a mistake had been made in spelling or rendering the name. Nonetheless, the original mistake was never entirely scratched out and remained legible. These manifests can be examined at the National Archives and Records Administration and at the **American Family Immigration History Center** at Ellis Island.

Immigrants, however, changed their own names at a fairly high rate. The changes came in the form of spelling modifications, such as shortening Schimmelpfennig to Shimmel, Vigliosi to Vigo, Lewandowski to Levand, Martoccia to Martocci, Eichenlaub to Aiken, and Birnbaum to Burns. They also anglicized their names, thus a Christopheles became Christopher, Blanco became White, Piccolo became Little, and Weisskopf became Whitehead.

Names were also changed completely because some immigrants thought that in America it was convenient to have an "American name." However, they resumed their original name when traveling abroad and visiting their native land. Because there were so few identification documents used in those days, one could go by any name one chose.

REFERENCES: LaSorte, Michael. 1985. *Images of the Italian Greenhorn Experience.* Philadelphia: Temple University Press; Smith, Marian L. 2002. American names: Declaring independence. http://www.ins.usdoj.gov/ (5/12/04)

Names. Ellis Island has been known by many names throughout history. The earliest name attributed to it is *Kioshk*, a word from the Delaware Indians meaning Gull Island. After the founding of the Dutch colony of New Netherland in the 1620s, the island was known as one of the oyster islands or Little Oyster Island. This was a used as a convenient descriptive term for the island the next two centuries, since its official name changed so often. The first official name in colonial days seems to have been Paauw Island (1630), in honor of its first European proprietor, Michael Paauw, one of the directors of the Dutch West India Company. After the Netherlands lost the colony to the Duke of York in 1664, the island's name, which had drifted back to Oyster Island, was renamed Dyre's Island when William Dyre, a prominent colonial official, obtained title to it in the 1670s. But by 1691, it was once again referred to as one of the three oyster islands. In a colonial document drawn in 1730, the island was described as Bucking Island, a name apparently given it by English colonial officials. In 1765, the island was given the name Gibbet Island and, for a while, Anderson's Island, when a notorious pirate called Anderson was tried, condemned, and hanged there. The name Gibbet Island was used for as long as pirates were executed there. Meanwhile, New York City merchant **Samuel Ellis** acquired the island in 1774 and his name was eventually added to this list of names; by the time of the War of 1812, it was the preferred name for the island.

See also **Nicknames**

Narragansett. This steamboat was the property of the Providence and Stonington Line. In January 1898, several months after the disastrous **Fire of 1897** completely destroyed the immigration station at Ellis Island, this steamboat was quickly brought into commission and was moored to the wharf at Ellis Island to provide detention quarters for immigrants. Its interior was refurbished to accommodate 800 detained aliens and doctors, nurses, and attendants of the **Marine Hospital Service**. It remained in use until the reopening of Ellis Island in 1900.

National Council of Jewish Women. The National Council of Jewish Women (NCJW) began aiding Jewish girls at Ellis Island in 1904. **Sadie American**, one of the organization's leaders, arranged for this to happen. The National Council was given a private room in the west wing on the first floor of the **Main Building**, so that women could be attended to with some degree of privacy. The NCJW prepared them to take train journeys and meet relations and friends, and helped with detention or deportation problems. Over the years, the National Council's many representatives maintained close contact with their counterparts in the **Hebrew Immigrant Aid Society**, other societies and the immigration authorities. Prominent NCJW representatives at the station included **Cecilia Greenstone**, **Cecilia Razofsky** (1891–1968), Elsa Alsburg, and Anna M. Kaufman (service: 1926–1954). The organization remained at the station until about 1950.

National Monument. On May 11, 1965, President **Lyndon B. Johnson** issued proclamation 3656 decreeing that Ellis Island was "added to and made part of the Statue of Liberty National Monument." Effective as of that date, Ellis Island was placed under the jurisdiction of the **National Park Service** (NPS), U.S. Department of the Interior. This proclamation was officially published in the Federal Register on May 13, 1965.

In 1976, Ellis Island was added to the National Register for Historic Places by the NPS and, in 1993, the New York City Landmarks Preservation Commission designated it as the Ellis Island Historic District.

National Park Service (NPS). This federal agency of the U.S. Department of the Interior has been responsible for the care and administration of Ellis Island since May 11, 1965, when President **Lyndon B. Johnson** proclaimed Ellis Island a national monument under the provisions of the Antiquities Act of 1906. The agency, which was created in 1916, administers national parks, battlefields, historic sites, memorials, monuments, parkways, recreation areas, and other areas. Because of its complicated history and extensive decaying buildings, Ellis Island became a challenge to the Park Service, which had primarily focused on the areas of military history and domestic affairs. Ellis Island, on the other hand, told the story of mass migration from a variety of European nations, most of which had little direct connection to major U.S. history sites. Nonetheless, the service persevered, and NPS historian **Thomas M. Pitkin**, who had previously been involved in the creation of the **American Museum of Immigration**, issued a major historical study of Ellis Island in 1966; a master plan for Ellis Island prepared by other officials soon followed (1968). With the prodding of Dr. **Peter Sammartino**, the Park Service launched a cleanup campaign of the island and opened it to limited visitation (1976–1984).

In the 1980s, with the support and guidance of President **Ronald Reagan**, **restoration** work was begun at Ellis Island. In 1982, the president appointed Lee A. Iacocca, the chairman of Chrysler Motors, to raise the funds necessary to restore the Statue of Liberty and the four buildings on Ellis Island. This resulted in

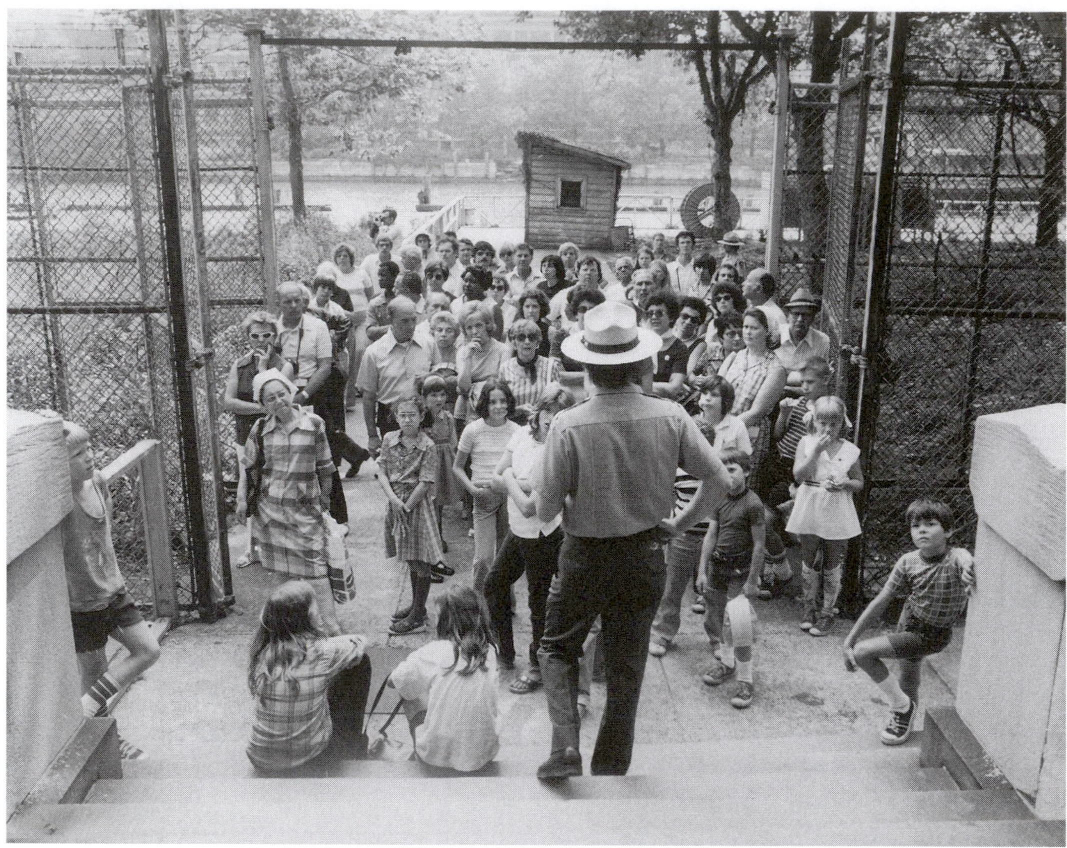

Park technician Gerald Price addressing visitors at Ellis Island, June 1976. Photo by Richard Patterson. Courtesy of the National Park Service, Ellis Island Immigration Museum.

the creation of the **Statue of Liberty–Ellis Island Foundation**, which eventually raised more than $500 million for Ellis Island and the Statue of Liberty. Restoration work at the former immigrant station including drying out the dampness in the **Main Building**, repairing the damaged structure, and installing the museum exhibits designed by **MetaForm Incorporated**.

President Reagan visited Ellis Island in April 1987. The **Ellis Island Immigration Museum** was at last completed and dedicated on September 10, 1990, by Vice President Dan Quayle (standing in for President George H. W. Bush). Iacocca and other officials also played a prominent role in the event.

But the National Park Service has remained committed to restoration of the many other buildings at Ellis Island that have not received restoration support. Beginning in 1999, with the aid of the state of New Jersey, the abandoned buildings on Islands 2 and 3 began to be stabilized. In 2001, the NPS entered into an agreement with **Save Ellis Island!** to begin fund-raising for the complete restoration of these buildings.

Navy. During **World War I**, the Bureau of Navigation of the U.S. Navy was in urgent need of sanitary and ample accommodations for sailors to be received in New York and shipped overseas to the war in Europe. Using the facilities at Ellis Island was vital in fighting the war because the Port of New York was the country's central shipping base for the **navy** and merchant marine, the headquarters of all the big troop transports and escorting cruisers. In addition, 75 percent of the merchant ships requiring armed guards were fitted out, sailed from, and returned to New York. According to a naval memorandum of December 26, 1917, addressed to Secretary of the Navy Josephus Daniels, "Ellis Island is peculiarly, favorably situated in the lower harbor and the facilities of the buildings are peculiarly well adapted for the handling and isolation of such cases of sickness as may appear among so many men, has excellent boating and landing facilities for the transportation of handling large drafts, and all the buildings, heating arrangements, et cetera, are now ready." In January 1918, Secretary of Labor William B. Wilson granted the navy permission to use a limited portion of the island since the situation was urgent. Retired naval Captain A. C. Hodgson was appointed to investigate Ellis Island to see whether it was suitable for naval use. With two other officers to assist him, he went to Ellis Island on January 17, 1918. Deeply impressed by the extent of the station, its buildings and grounds, he strongly recommended that the navy make every effort to secure the whole island. In the end, the secretary of Labor decided to give certain portions of the island to the **army** and navy. In a memorandum of understanding, dated February 17, 1918, between the departments of Labor, Navy, and War, the navy took over the entire **baggage and dormitory building**, the **railroad ticket office** complete, and, on the first floor of the **Main Building**, medical examination rooms 43, 44, and 45.

Nazis. A good number, but by no means all, of the Germans detained as "enemy aliens" at Ellis Island during World War II were sympathetic to the Third Reich, while others strongly supported it. The following is a magazine piece that was published about the pro-Nazi presence at Ellis Island:

> Last July, an officer of the British Merchant Marine was taken ill when his ship arrived in New York and was sent to the Marine Hospital on Ellis Island. By the time he was well again his ship had left, so he was removed to the Immigration and Detention Station on the island and put in the Passenger Room to await its return. There . . . (he) found himself in the midst of a large group of men and women, all of whom spoke German and frequently gave the Nazi salute. He was dumbfounded. In vain he tried to find an official who would move him away from these people who were loyal to the enemy he had been fighting. At dinnertime, he was expected to sit at a long table with all the Nazis. He flatly refused—which the Nazis thought highly amusing. Later he found out that since Pearl Harbor, the Passenger Room had been used mainly for married enemy aliens detained on the island.
>
> The same thing has happened often to torpedoed seamen of Allied nations who lose their papers and are brought to Ellis Island to be cleared. Frequently, they have to wait for weeks in the midst of Nazis who are either offensive or who try to indoctrinate them with the Nazi philosophy.
>
> I heard this from a man who has had ample opportunity to learn what is going on in the detention station, as well as in several internment camps for enemy aliens. An anti-Nazi of long standing, he was arrested by mistake. The Nazis interned in this country knew of his opposition to their doctrine and, before he was freed, he had been thoroughly beaten up. He showed me documentary proof of the puzzling conditions in American internment camps—affidavits of witnesses and countless reports and letters that he had been forwarding to our authorities.
>
> Who are these men and women who have been put in American internment camps? Attorney General Francis Biddle says that the average German citizen living in this country has not been touched and that only dangerous or potentially dangerous enemy aliens have been interned. . . .
>
> These people were interned after Pearl Harbor. Then Hearing Boards formed in all districts of the United States and evidence collected by the FBI was presented against those arrested. Their cases were finally reviewed by the Enemy Alien Control Unit, after which many of them were either released unconditionally or paroled. Only fifty percent of those originally taken to the immigration stations were finally sent to camps and, of these, some have since been released. . . .
>
> At first, these prisoners were under the supervision of the Army. By June of 1943, however, all the Army prison camps were need for captured Axis soldiers and the civil internees, about five thousand

in all, were put under the supervision of the Immigration and Naturalization Service. . . . In many cases, Germans with American wives and children were allowed to bring their families to live with them.

A number of Nazi American big shots are in these internment camps today. For one, there is Fritz Kuhn, who has finished his jail sentence. With him is his whole family. There is Kurt Ludecke, author of *I Knew Hitler*, the first official representative of the Nazi Party in this country. Fittingly enough, he has become a camp librarian. Doctor Hesselbein, author of, *Hitler Was Right*, is now probably pondering whether he wrote the right book. The once famous Princess Stephanie von Hohenlohe does knitting in camp and will finish quite a few sweaters and shawls, for she is certainly in for the duration. Other prominent Nazis are Doctor Degener of the German–American Board of Trade and Doctor Wuensche, a top of the Hamburg–American Line, have already been sent back to Germany, in exchange for American citizens. All . . . are inconspicuous in their present circumstances. They behave quietly, blending into the background and it seems that someone higher up has ordered them to do so.

The Geneva Prisoner of War Convention of July 27, 1929, did not deal with civil internees. After Pearl Harbor, however, the United States and Germany arranged to extend the provisions of the Geneva Convention to civil internees. . . .

One of the most important rules is contained in Article 43: *In every place where there are prisoners of war, they shall be allowed to appoint agents entrusted with representing them with military authorities and protecting Powers. This appointment shall be subject to the approval of the military authority.* It is this so-called . . . spokesman who becomes the Führer of the camp. By obtaining the post of spokesman, the key men of the party (who are never the publicized big shots) can make sure there is no dissension among the rank and file.

American officials have been able to do very little about the authority of the spokesman. Indeed, they appear to have wanted to do very little.

Up to the beginning of 1944, the most prominent among the German spokesmen was Herr Ernst Kerkhof, who carried the unofficial title of *Gauleiter of Ellis Island.* Most of those interned there felt that he was more powerful than some American officials. He ran the lives of all the Nazis on Ellis Island and saw to it that Hitler's birthday was celebrated with all the trimmings. When it became known that the saboteurs who had come here in a U-boat were to be executed, Kerkhof ordered twenty-hours of general mourning.

Among the accomplishments of Kerkhof was a Nazi Christmas party in 1943, to which the German government contributed $600 expense money. Kerkhof had made the demand for this contribution via the Swiss Legation, which has taken over German interests in this country (as the Swiss Legation in Berlin has taken over American interests). Some of the money was to be used for the celebration; the rest was to be given to Nazis. Later, Kerkhof had everyone sign a receipt or an acknowledgment. Thus he obtained a proof that all these internees indirectly received money from the German government—a document that may come in handy someday to keep unreliable Nazis in line. When the Department of Justice asked for a copy of these "receipts," Kerkhof refused.

. . . There is nothing in the Geneva Convention that says anti-Nazis must be forced to attend entertainments that ridicule democratic ideals. Yet this happened in at least one case, when an anti-Nazi German was conducted to such an entertainment by a dozen Nazis who then arrayed themselves behind him so he could not leave. . . .

They have their own code, these Nazi internees. They still believe themselves the Master Race, and even object to being served by American Negroes. At the detention station on Ellis Island, the Swiss Legation was compelled to recommend to American authorities the removal of colored men. It was done.

. . . The FBI has done a magnificent job of trapping and arresting dangerous enemy aliens all over the United States, but nothing has been done to disturb their activities once they were in camp. . . . Paradoxical as it may seem, a great deal of espionage is conducted by these people in internment camps; they find out a lot about what is going on outside.

As already mentioned, Allied sailors occasionally must spend considerable time on Ellis Island. It is easy enough for Nazis who peak perfect English to approach them and get them to talk. . . . Nazi agents from different parts of the country have met and pooled information. . . . There are numerous ways of smuggling intelligence out of camps. The least dramatic is to wait till an inmate is released—which happens constantly.

. . . Quite a few guards have been discovered to be Nazi sympathizers. . . . There are conferences with "friendly lawyers" and visits of relatives. On Ellis Island these visits take place in a very large room where it is impossible for the guards to overhear what is being said. Even if they could hear, they wouldn't understand, because the guards do not speak German."

See also **Enemy Aliens**

REFERENCE: Riess, Curt. 1944. *The Nazis Carry On—Behind Barbed Wire* (exclusive inside story). Original publication information unknown. Ellis Island detention file. Ellis Island, NY: Statue of Liberty and Ellis Island Library.

NEGRO (National Economic Growth and Reconstruction Organization). This African American self-help organization was headquartered on Ellis Island from 1970 to 1971 and had bold goals for Ellis Island that were never achieved due to the lack of funds. Early in 1970, Thomas William Matthew, the founder and president of NEGRO, applied to the **National Park Service** for permission to clean up Ellis Island and establish business operations there. When summer came, Matthew grew impatient, as no word had yet been received. Matthew then quietly landed on the island with a large group of squatters of men, women, and children. During their twelve-day stay at the island, the sixty-three squatters set up a packaging business that grossed $1,500 from activities. Following their departure, they secured a five-year permit from the National Park Service and returned to Ellis Island in September 1970. The permit gave them the use of the south side of the island. NEGRO made the following statement about its goals for Ellis Island:

> Restore and maintain the Main Building as the Ellis Island Immigration Museum. It is through this building that the parents and grandparents of millions of Americans entered this country. It is the symbol of the melting pot concept of Americans. We would:
>
> (a) In cooperation with currently existing historical societies and museums create exhibitions enabling Americans to retrace their ancestors' steps providing a permanent record of the immigration experience.
>
> (b) In cooperation with ethnic groups and societies, provide facilities for suitable ethnic celebrations and programs throughout the year.
>
> (c) Develop suitable eating, lounge and comfort facilities for tourists.
>
> (d) Landscape the area around the Main Building so as to meet tourist, ethnic groups' and aesthetic needs.
>
> (e) Provide transportation for tourists and ethnic groups no only to and from Manhattan but also to and from adjacent New Jersey.
>
> We propose to organize tourists and ethnic activities so that the Ellis Island Immigration Museum may be self-supporting. Any initial deficit would be met through subsidy by the productive industries on the island insuring no financial dependence on any major community off the island. (Unrau, pp. 1185–1186)

Matthew also wanted to set up a work and rehabilitation center for as many as 7,000 former drug addicts, ex-convicts, and welfare recipients. His idea was to convert several of the abandoned buildings for use as factories where these people could assemble electronic equipment, package chemical products and be employed at other light industry jobs. However, NEGRO vacated Ellis Island in September 1971. Their permit was terminated April 1973, after federal officials found major health and safety violations in the areas of the island where NEGRO had been operating.

Matthew, who founded NEGRO in 1964, described the organization as a national self-help program that would use black power constructively, "to build a people in pride, dignity and self-respect through economic independence." Between 1964 and 1970, he set up a chain of twenty-seven labor-intensive industries that grossed $4 million each year and provided work to nearly 3,000 workers. Matthew, a prominent black activist, was also involved in many other projects, including the founding of an African American bus line and the Interfaith Hospital, which was located in Queens. He had previously occupied a public school in Manhattan and was pardoned by President Richard M. Nixon after he was convicted of not paying income tax. In later years, he devoted his attention to his medical practice as a neurosurgeon and general practitioner in Brooklyn.

REFERENCES: *New York Times*. 1970. Negro's tactician. August 20; Novotny, Ann. 1971. *Strangers at the Door.* Riverside, CT: Chatham; Unrau, Harlan D. 1984. *The Historic Resource Study: Ellis Island/Statue of Liberty*. Vol. 3. Washington, DC: U.S. Department of Interior, National Park Service.

Nevada. The *Nevada*, a steamship of the Guion Line, was the vessel that brought **Annie Moore**, the first immigrant to be inspected at Ellis Island, to the United States. Moore was one of 148 passengers who made the passage. She and her brothers Anthony and Philip boarded the *Nevada* at Deepwater Quay, Queenstown (now Cobh), Ireland, on December 20, 1891. The vessel arrived at the Port of New York on the evening of December 31, and the passengers were brought to Ellis Island for inspection on January 1, 1892.

New Immigration Building. *See* **Immigration Building**

New York Chinese Office. This field office or branch of the **Bureau of Immigration** was operated and organized in much the same manner as the bureau's thirty-five major immigrant inspection stations. Located in Manhattan, the staff of the Chinese office included a chief inspector, Chinese inspectors, clerks, interpreters, and guards.

See also **Chinese Division; Chinese Exclusion Act; Immigrant Inspection Stations**

New York City Mission Society. The New York City Mission Society provided aid to immigrants at Ellis Island for many years and with other groups shared space in the missionary room on the first floor of the **Main Building**. The organization was sponsored by the Protestant Episcopal Church.

SUGGESTED READING: Romita, Paul, et al. 2003. *New York City Mission Society.* Charleston, SC: Arcadia.

New York Detention Dormitory. This dormitory was located on the second floor, on the north side of the west wing. It existed from 1900 through the early 1920s, when it was replaced by boardrooms of the **Special Inquiry Division**. The dormitory was used by temporarily detained immigrants; their day room was the **New York room** on the first floor.

New York District (INS). In 1943, the New York District headquarters of the Immigration and Naturalization Service, which had previously been on Ellis Island, was transferred to 70 Columbus Avenue, Manhattan. From that time until 1954, the Immigration and Naturalization Service offices were in Brooklyn, and the **Barge Office** in Manhattan. Suboffices were at Idlewild and LaGuardia airports, Albany, New York, and Newark, New Jersey. Ellis Island was both a suboffice and the district detention station.

The head of the New York District was the **district director**. The district's operations were administered by him through the Investigations Division (nationality, citizenship, seamen, and smuggling), Adjudications Division (control and entry of aliens into the country; expulsion of illegal aliens; immigrant status and naturalizations), and the Detention, Deportation, and Parole Division. In addition, the administrative services office at headquarters was responsible for the fiscal section; mail, files, records and information section; services and supply section; and the maintenance section. the many departments at Ellis Island included the warrant processing unit and the subversive unit, as well as detention, deportation and parole, and maintenance.

In the 1940s, the maintenance section of the Administrative Services Division handled what had once been the work of the Janitors' and Laborers' Division. The section was assigned to the power plant, the ferryboat, automobile repairs, the laundry, the maintenance office, and buildings and grounds.

The buildings and grounds unit had alterations, repairs, upkeep, and maintenance of the buildings and grounds and marine shore structures at the island. A superintendent directed a force of seventy that included laborers, charwomen, carpenters, electricians, painters, mechanics, gardeners and masons. Herbert L. Booth was chief of the maintenance section in the 1940s. His office force consisted of Henry Friedland and Annette Gold. In his 1945–1946 report, he stated that Ellis Island was an "isolated community of about 3,000."

New York Room. The New York room for the temporarily detained was located on the first floor of the **Main Building**. It occupied the greater area of the west wing's northern section from 1900 to 1924. A smaller space in the same area was utilized after the enactment of the **Immigration Act of 1924**. It served as a general dayroom for aliens awaiting the arrival of relatives or friends. The **Discharging Division** and the **Information Bureau** were responsible for immigrants held in this room. Women, the elderly, and children were commonly held temporarily. Clerks in the Information Bureau sent telegrams or letters to relatives or friends in greater New York or other parts of the country to come for them. Persons calling for immigrants brought the letter or telegram to the **Barge Office** and, on the strength of it, were allowed to come to the station aboard the **ferryboat *Ellis Island***. At the island, they were directed to the Information Division, where a clerk checked a file and directed the visitor to the adjacent visitors waiting room. Not long after, the immigrant was brought from the New York room to the Discharging Division to identify the visitor and, if all went well, the immigrant left with his or her relative or friend at once.

Nicknames. Ellis Island has had several nicknames including the following: **Castle Garden**, Kasa Garda (Slavic), Kasa Gardi (Greek), Kessel Garten (German and Yiddish), Island of Hope, Island of Tears, isola della lacrime (Italian), Tränsel Insel and Insel der Tränen (German), *la batteria* (the battery), Doorway to America, Eastern Gate, Gateway to America, and the Golden Door.

See also **Names**

Night Division. The Night Division was charged with caring for Ellis Island after business hours. The staff consisted of an immigrant inspector, two or three matrons, twenty guards, and a crew of laborers and charwomen from the **Janitors' Division**. In 1942, the Night Division was consolidated with the **Deporting Division** and part of the Inspection Division to form the Detention Division.

See also **Appendix 1: Ellis Island: Its Organization and Some of Its Work**

North American Civic League for Immigrants. This organization originated in Boston but established a branch in New York City to help aliens who had been released from Ellis Island. By 1911, they had set up an "excellent guide and transfer system at Ellis Island," which safely escorted immigrants from the Ellis Island ferryboat through the **Barge Office**, past Battery Park and to various destinations in New York. Their work was praised by Commissioner **William Williams**. The League also published a booklet entitled *Messages for New Comers to the United States*, which, among other things advised the immigrant to "keep everything clean and sweet about your person, your home and your street. This is your best protection against disease . . . in America, as in other countries, nothing is more necessary to the ambitious as good health."

See also **Appendix 1: Ellis Island: Its Organization and Some of Its Work**

REFERENCES: Fairchild, Amy L. 2003. *Science at the Borders*. Baltimore: Johns Hopkins University Press; North American Civic League for Immigrants. 1913. *Messages for New Comers to the United States*. Teacher's edition. Boston; Pitkin, Thomas, M. 1975. *Keepers of the Gate*. New York: New York University Press.

Novotny, Ann (b. 1936; d. December 1982). Writer. Ann Novotny was the author of one of the first popular histories of Ellis Island to be published. Her *Strangers at the Door: Ellis Island, Castle Garden and the Great Migration to America* appeared in 1971. It was published by Chatham Press. She was directly influenced by the work of National Park Service historians **Thomas Pitkin** and George Svejda and personally interviewed well-known Ellis Island immigrants Spyros Skouras and David Dubinsky, as well as the widows of Marcus Garvey and Ben Shahn. Her book was for many years used as a way of introducing newly hired Statue of Liberty interpretive rangers to the station's history. Ann Novotny's other books include *White House Weddings* (1966) and *Alice's World* (1975).

Nurses. The nurses at Ellis Island were employed by the **Public Health Service** (PHS); a few worked with the **American Red Cross**. Hierarchically, one chief nurse was assigned to the General Hospital and one chief nurse was assigned to the contagious disease hospital. Next, there were several head nurses to supervisor the thirty or so ordinary nurses. Nurses lived in various quarters at Ellis Island and according to PHS regulations they were required to return to the hospital from New York City or New Jersey on or before the last Ellis Island ferry run (12:30 a.m.). All-night passes could be issued only by the Chief Nurse, but were seldom requested.

The following is the list of instructions given to chief nurses at Ellis Island for the years 1922–1924. (1) Make routine duty assignments to nurses, maids, and orderlies. (2) Grant leaves of absence for periods not to exceed one day at a time with the approval of the Chief Medical Officer. (3) Arrange annual leaves for staff members and report all cases of illness. (4) Maintain discipline, good morale, and proper sanitary standards of all female employees, including their individual quarters. (5) Maintain economic use of linens and supplies. (6) Inspect all wards and operating rooms, and ensure the cleanliness and physical comfort of patients. (7) Submit efficiency reports each month as required by the bureau. (8) Cooperate with dieticians to ensure efficient service of foods to patients. (9) Supervise disinfecting and preparation of hospital rooms, bedding, linen, and clothing to guard against infection.

Male and female nurses of Ellis Island, ca 1920. Courtesy of the Ellis Island Immigration Museum.

According to a staff report for the **contagious disease wards** issued on October 14, 1913, by Dr. L. L. Williams, there were five chief nurses, ten other nurses, and twelve ward maids employed. The chief nurses were paid $50 per month, the nurses $40 monthly, and the ward maids from between $25 and $35 monthly.

A numerous contingent of women and men were employed as PHS nurses at Ellis Island. The women were spinsters. In the 1920s chief nurses included Ellen C. Cartledge (contagious disease hospital, 1920s) and Margaret V. Daly (chief nurse, General Hospital, 1920s). Listed as head nurses in the same decade were Ida Bonitz (b. 1889), Olive Bott (b. 1895), William A. Boyer (b. 1884), R. B. Chase (female), Mabel B. Haworth, Michael G. Gaffey, A. Eileen O'Brien, Katharine E. O'Connell (b. 1890), Edward Powers, **Anna Purcell**, and Laura Lomas Wurm. Among the numerous nurses of the 1920s were Beatrice C. Bona, Ina Delaney, Julia A. Dunne (b. 1892; promoted to a head nurse position in 1924) Antonio DiStefano (b. 1890), Gaynelle Finks, Mary Fitzpatrick, Marie Flanagan, Arthur Foulds (b. 1885), Ruth Franzen (b. 1889), Edmund W. Harrington, Ida Holbrook, Joseph Klein (b. 1896), Ossia Knapp (b. 1896), Frances R. Mather (b. 1896), and Joseph Woolley.

The hospital nutritionist at the period was Dr. Louise Gilum (1892–1982), who later taught at the University of California at Berkeley. Another employee working in the field of nutrition was Eleanor Irwin (b. 1910), who worked at Ellis Island from 1939 until 1952; she made a return visit to the station in 1988. The head of the hospital's clinical service in the early to middle 1920s was Bertha Josephine Fulton (b. 1899), who also was employed by the Red Cross and spoke French and German. Her assistant was Adela Girdner. A psychiatric worker was Edith van Doorn (b. 1882); she also worked with the Red Cross and was fluent in Dutch, German, French, and Russian.

See also **Medical Division**

O'Beirne, James R. [James Rowan O'Beirne] (b. Ballagh, Roscommon, Ireland, 1844; d. February 18, 1917). Assistant commissioner, Ellis Island (1890–1893). As the chief assistant to Commissioner **John B. Weber**, General James O'Beirne was posted to Ellis Island in its first days as an immigrant depot. O'Beirne's reputation at the island, however, was diminished by his tendency to bluster. For example, the *New York Times* and other newspapers, in March 1892, had a field day when O'Beirne had a brief moment of power when Colonel Weber went away to Washington on government business. According to the *Times*, O'Beirne ordered the registry clerks to exclude any alien with less than $10.00 for "railroad fare." This promptly resulted in some 300 aliens being excluded from entering the country and caused disorder, anger, confusion, and overcrowding at the station. On his return, declaring that O'Beirne had no authority to alter immigration inspection policy, Weber reversed the ruling and released all aliens detained for exclusion under O'Beirne's orders. O'Beirne had a distinguished career as an army officer during the Civil War, having fought valiantly at Fair Oaks, Virginia (1862), and other engagements. He served as a private in the 7th New York Militia, a lieutenant in the Irish Rifles (37th New York Volunteer Infantry). While in the 22nd U.S. Veteran Reserve Corps he was brevetted quickly through the ranks to brigadier general of volunteers by September 1865. He was also the last provost marshal of the District of Columbia and played a role in the pursuit and capture of President Abraham Lincoln's assassin, John Wilkes Booth.

REFERENCES: Prime, John Andrew. James Rowan O'Beirne. http://www.shreve.net/-japrime/37thnyvi/jrobeirne.htm (5/9/04); *New York Times*. 1892. General O'Beirne. March 28.

Office Building and Laboratory. Located on **Island 3**, the office building and laboratory was designed in the neo-Renaissance style by architect **James Knox Taylor** in 1908. It was constructed in 1909 and opened in 1911. The laboratory and offices were on the second floor. The building is made of a steel frame steel and red bricks with a stucco coating and limestone trim, and measures 45 feet by 45 feet. The laboratory, one flight up, has cupboard shelves and benches made of varnished oak and the floor has white and black tiles laid in the pattern of a diamond. The routine examinations of specimens and bacteriological research were carried out there. Experiments on animals were done only in the **animal house**. In addition, the building contained a dispensary and pharmacist's quarters on the ground floor. In later years, these quarters were assigned to male nurses. The office building and laboratory was stabilized in 1999.

See **Diseases and Hospitalization; Stabilization**

Office of Immigration. The Office of Immigration was the original name of the **Bureau of Immigration**. The office was established within the Department of the Treasury under the provisions of the **Immigration Act of 1891**. Based in Washington, the head of the agency was called the superintendent of immigration and, for this reason, the agency was also sometimes called the Office of the Superintendent of Immigration. The superintendent had charge of twenty-four immigrant inspection stations; the largest of these was at Ellis Island in New York harbor. The administrators of the individual stations were called commissioners or inspectors in charge. Dissatisfaction with the agency's rather weak identity led Congress to introduce new provisions regarding names and titles. Under the **Immigration Act of 1895**, the Office of Immigration was renamed the Bureau of Immigration and the superintendent of immigration was restyled commissioner-general of immigration. He was also given the power to enforce the contract labor laws.

REFERENCE: Smith, Darrell, and Henry Herring. 1924. *The Bureau of Immigration*. Baltimore: Johns Hopkins University Press.

Oosterhoudt, Emma B. Typist, clerk, then secretary, **Executive Division** (1903–1942). Emma Oosterhoudt had a long career at Ellis Island, serving as the secretary to Assistant Commissioner **Byron H. Uhl** (1911–1930). She then served as secretary to Commissioners **Benjamin M. Day** (1930–1931), **Edward Corsi** (1931–1934), Rudolph Reimer (1934–1940), and Byron H. Uhl (1940–1942). In an April 1910 personnel report, Commissioner **William Williams** described her thus:

> Miss Oosterhoudt has been at Ellis Island since February 1903. She prepares records on appeals and arranges the details of transmitting same to the Bureau. Her work is heavy and of a responsible character; and she does it with great accuracy. Like may others, she frequently arrives by the 8.20 a.m. boat. Last July, these appeals ran up to over 50 a day. Today, there were 25. She is very competent.

REFERENCE: William, Williams. 1910. *Personnel Report*. Ellis Island, NY: Statue of Liberty and Ellis Island Library.

Oral History Project. The Ellis Island Oral History Project interviews are available to researchers and the general public at the Oral History Listening Room located in the Reference Library on the third floor, west wing of the **Ellis Island Immigration Museum**. People wishing to use the interviews, both as recordings or on-screen transcripts, may do so at the specially designed computer stations in this room. Simple instructions on the computer screens help users to find interviews and pertinent information. The Oral History Project contains interviews with about 2,000 immigrants, former Ellis Island employees, and **World War II** coastguardsmen. It is an ongoing project and was launched in 1973.

Many immigrants have been interviewed, including Isabel Belarky (Russia), Maljan Chavoor (Turkey), Millvina Dean (England), Artemio Hernández (Cuba), Emmie Kremer (Germany), Dr. Muriel Petioni (West Indies), Manny Steen (Ireland), **Arthur Tracy** (Russia), Elda del Bino Willetts (Italy), and George Zemanovic (Czechoslovakia). Various persons who once worked at Ellis Island have been interviewed, including former immigrant inspector Jacob Auerbach, former clerk **Emma Corcoran**, former nurse Ina Delaney, surgeons T. Bruce Anderson, Grover Kempf, Robert Leslie, John Thill, Salvation Army Brigadier General Thomas Johnson, former social worker and Japanese interpreter Ichiro Shirato, and the island's former Episcopal chaplain, Reverend John Evans. Coastguardsmen interviewed include David H. Cassells (World War II), and Ralph Hornberger (Korean War), while Charles DeLeo, Brian Feeney, Paul Sigrist, and Paul Weinbaum number among Park Service employees who have been interviewed

Owen, William Dale (b. 1846; d. 1906). Superintendent of Immigration (1891–1893). William Dale Owen was the first head of the **Office of Immigration**, which later became the **Bureau of Immigration** and the **Immigration and Naturalization Service**. A Republican, he was appointed by President **Benjamin Harrison**. During his tenure the office was set up in Washington and the first federal immigrant station was established at Ellis Island, New York. Superintendent Owens's deputy there was Colonel **John B. Weber**. Owen also supervised the opening of immigrant stations at Boston, Philadelphia, and Baltimore.

P

Paauw, Michael. Dutch colonial shipper, "patroon," and official of the Dutch West India Company; proprietor of Ellis Island. In 1629, Michael Paauw was given a large grant of land in New Netherland by the Dutch West India Company, which included the Oyster Islands. The larger two of these islands later became known as Bedloe's Island and Ellis Island. Paauw's estate was known as Pavonia, a Latinized version of his name. Paauw never visited his possessions in the New World.

Palmer, Carleton H. (b. March 21, 1891, Brooklyn, New York; d. May 1971). Chairman of the Ellis Island Committee. One of the nation's leading drug manufacturers, Carleton Palmer was appointed to chair the **Ellis Island Committee** created by Secretary of Labor **Frances Perkins** in June 1933. Its task was to investigate the conditions at Ellis Island and the welfare of immigrants and then submit recommendations for the guidance of the Department of Labor. The result was the 149-page *Report of the Ellis Island Committee* printed in March 1934. It had an important impact on the station's future. Palmer became the president of E. R. Squibb & Sons in 1915 and served as its chairman of the board of directors from 1941 until his death.

Passport Division. The Passport Division opened at Ellis Island in about 1926. Its task was to obtain passports from the embassies and consulates of deportees, as these documents were required before sending an unwanted alien back to his homeland. Foreign consular officials were sometimes quite reluctant to issue a passport to a deportee with a bad record. Some detainees spent months at Ellis Island as the Passport Division clerks pressed reluctant foreign consulates for passports for deportees who claimed citizenship from their countries. When a consulate refused to issue one, the Immigration Bureau usually had no alternative but to release the alien from Ellis Island.

Passports. This documentary requirement was originally applied only to Chinese and Japanese laborers who desired to enter and work temporarily in American possessions such as the Panama Canal Zone and Hawaii. For reasons of national security, foreign passports were temporarily required of all aliens entering the country in 1917 and 1918. The rule was revived in 1921 on a permanent basis. The quota law of that year also required visas to be issued by American consuls to qualified aliens.

Interestingly, Italy required it citizens to apply for a passport (*il passaporto rosso*) to leave Italy as early as 1888; Greece and Romania also adopted this practice. None of these documents were required to enter the United States until 1921.

Peak Immigration Years (Rooms E202, E209–218). One of the permanent exhibitions of the **Ellis Island Immigration Museum**. It is located on the second floor in the east wing of the **Main Building**, an area that once housed the offices of the **commissioner** of immigration, the **Executive Division**, the **Statistics Division**, and rooms used by chief inspectors and their staffs. The exhibit tells the story of international migration into the United States from 1880 through 1924, the heyday of migration via steamship. Although the story is primarily a European one, the exhibit includes graphics and other information on journeys from the Asia, the Middle East, the Americas, and sub-Saharan Africa. Peak Immigration Years comprises twelve exhibit galleries (rooms) containing extensive photography, graphics, maps, posters, and various artifacts. In the adjoining space that forms a large outer corridor or atrium (E202) is displayed a selection of photomurals of immigrant portraits originally taken by **Augustus Sherman** and Lewis Hine. Each gallery of the Peak Immigration Years exhibit covers one or more of the primary themes of immigration history, each of which is individually titled. The following is a brief description of each gallery in this exhibit.

Leaving the Homeland (E209–210) covers emigration from the old country. On display in this gallery are images of maps; charts; countries of origin in Europe (especially from southern and eastern Europe, and Russia); scenes of poverty, and old world violence and hatreds against religious minorities, specifically Jews and Armenians; journeys by carts, wagons, and trains from emigrants' homes to seaports; letters about America; a poster warning German women and girls to beware of being dishonored and sexually exploited in America; and quotes from emigrants' reminiscences, including Golda Meir's (Israeli prime minister). There is also a large graphic display on one of the walls of the names for America in a variety of languages, including Italian, German, Greek, Russian, Yiddish, and French. The Passage to America gallery (E211) focuses on railroads and steamship lines and includes scenes of European, Asian, and Caribbean ports; steerage and cabin-class accommodations; the arrival of steamers in New York harbor; original British manifests; a variety of foreign passports from European nations as well as from the Ottoman Empire and other parts of the world; postal cards of famous steamships; and posters, leaflets, and papers from a variety of sources, in several languages including Italian, Romanian, and German. Ports of Entry deals with **Castle Garden** and federal immigrant inspection stations. Across the Land tells the story of immigrant settlements in the United States. The Closing Door explores story of **immigration restriction movement**s and laws and includes historic anti-immigrant political cartoons as well as photographs. At Work in America highlights labor conditions for immigrants in the United States and the common types of work that different nationalities took up. Between 2 Worlds concentrates both on assimilation and retention of foreign traditions in America, and includes "ethnic" music and examples of the immigrant press of olden days. The Go-Betweens gallery examines immigrant amusements, schools, and street life. The last gallery of the exhibit, New Americans, shows the process of assimilation through learning English, serving in the military, supporting the nation's political goals, and acquiring citizenship.

Peopling of America (Room C103). Located in the former **railroad ticket office** on the first floor of the **Ellis Island Immigration Museum**, the Peopling of America exhibit describes the demographic changes caused by colonization and immigration to the United States. It features a map showing the original homelands of the many Native American tribes and nations whose land comprised North America (The First Americans: Indian Tribal Groups), a map showing the slave trade from Africa (Forced Migration: The Atlantic Slave Trade), and a globe of the world migration (Millions on the Move: Worldwide Migration). Other exhibits show the statistics of immigration to the United States by decade (The Growth of Nation), the geographic sources of immigrants, statistics on the gender of immigrants, European colonization, migration to the West, an ethnic origins database of the U.S. population from the Bureau of the Census, an American flag of faces, and a word tree, showing the non–Anglo Saxon origins of selected English words.

Plans are afoot to move part of this exhibit to

the second floor of the **kitchen and laundry building**.

Perkins, Frances (b. Boston, Massachusetts, April 10, 1882; d. New York, May 14, 1965). Secretary of Labor (1933–1945). In 1933, Secretary Frances Perkins authorized the investigation of the station of the **Ellis Island Committee** and improved conditions at the station during her administration of the **Immigration and Naturalization Service** (INS). In 1940, she supported the transfer of the INS from her care to that of the Department of Justice.

Peterssen, Arne. Arne Peterssen, a Norwegian seaman, was the last alien to be held at Ellis Island. His release on November 12, 1954, effectively ended Ellis Island's service as a U.S. immigration station. Peterssen had overstayed his shore leave from the ship aboard which he served as a crewmember. He was ordered to return to Norway no later than December 10, 1954.

REFERENCE: *New York Times.* 1954. Last alien leaves Ellis Island. November 13.

Physicians. *See* **Medical Officers; Surgeons**

Pinza, Ezio [Fortunato Pinza] (b. Rome, Italy, May 18, 1892; d. Stamford, Connecticut, May 7, 1957). Opera singer. On March 12, 1942, the famed baritone Ezio Pinza was arrested by FBI agents as an Italian enemy alien and taken directly to the federal courthouse at lower Manhattan's Foley Square, where he was searched, photographed, fingerprinted, and interrogated. Then the same to FBI agents took him down to the **ferryboat *Ellis Island*** at the **Barge Office** dock and handed him over to the custody of uniformed guards. The opera singer described his experience on Ellis Island:

> There were one hundred and twenty-six of us, Italians, Germans, Japanese, milling around in the enormous barrack-like room on Ellis Island. Most of us were bewildered and frightened, desperate for solace and despairing at our helplessness. Our misery was still further intensified by the untidiness to which were reduced: all suspenders, belts, shoelaces and other objects that might help a would-be suicide had been taken away from us.
>
> Many of the internees recognized me and wondered why I had been brought in, for I had never taken part in political activity. Whatever the degree of their own guilt, they were all touchingly solicitous of me, especially the Italians. They introduced me to card game called *scopa* and welcomed me as a partner whenever I wished to play.
>
> The men I was with came from different walks of life: workingmen, professional soldiers, and intellectuals. 1 man was a member of a noble German family who, far from resenting the incarceration . . . justified it . . . as a necessity dictated by centuries of experience with enemy espionage . . . he discussed our plight with the detachment of a scientist peaking of insects. . . . Every newspaper in New York carried the story of my arrest under sensational headlines. . . . Even *The New York Times* frontpaged it as a "hot" story with my photo thrown in: *Ezio Pinza Seized as Enemy Alien; FBI Takes Singer to Ellis Island.* (Pinza, pp. 208–210)

The FBI accused the singer of being a fascist enemy agent based on at least five points.

1. He owned a ring with a Nazi Swastika on it.
2. He had a boat equipped with a radio that received and sent out secret messages.
3. He was a personal friend of Benito Mussolini, the Italian Prime Minister.
4. He sent coded messages while singing at the Metropolitan Opera House in a radio broadcast each Saturday afternoon. The code was allegedly based upon the changing tempo of his voice while singing.
5. In 1935 he organized a collection of gold and silver for the benefit of the Italian government.

More careful investigations by the FBI disproved the allegations and indicated that Pinza's accuser at the Metropolitan Opera House was motivated more by jealousy than patriotism. The government was soon convinced of his innocence and Pinza was released from custody on June 4, 1942.

See also **Enemy Aliens**

REFERENCE: Pinza, Ezio. 1958. *An Autobiography.* With Robert Magidoff. New York: Rinehart.

Pitkin, Thomas M. [Thomas Monroe Pitkin] (b. Akron, Ohio, October 6, 1901; d. New York, 1988). Historian. Pitkin served as the supervisory historian at the Statue of Liberty National Monument from 1952 until 1964. During this period, he was actively involved in planning the **American Museum of Immigration**, which was installed on Liberty Island. He was author of "Prospectus for the American Museum of Immigration" (1956). He also wrote one of the most important studies on the history of Ellis Island in 1966, which he adapted into a book, the now classic *Keepers of the Gate* (1975). Pitkin served in the army during World War I (1917–1918) and later in the marines (1920–1922). He took degrees from the University of Akron (B.A., 1926), Ohio State University (M.A., 1928), and Western Reserve University (Ph.D., 1935). He worked as a National Park Service historian between 1935 and 1942; 1952 and 1964; and in the same capacity at the War Department (1942–1952). He was the coauthor of *Yorktown: Climax of the Revolution* (1941) and sole author of *Grant the Soldier* (1965) and *The Captain Departs* (1973). Later, he collaborated with Francesco Cordasco on two final books, *The Black Hand* (1977) and *The White Slave Trade and the Immigrants* (1981).

Ports of Departure. The leading foreign ports from which emigrants were shipped to New York harbor were Liverpool and Southampton; Edinburgh; Belfast; Bremerhaven and Hamburg; Rotterdam; Le Havre, Cherbourg, and Marseilles; Antwerp; Oslo; Stockholm; Copenhagen; Danzig (now Gdansk); Libau; Lisbon and the Azores Islands; La Coruña and Barcelona; Naples, Genoa, and Palermo; Trieste; Athens; Constantinople; Alexandria; Beirut; Cape Town; Halifax; Havana; Caracas; Veracruz; Rio de Janeiro; Buenos Aires; Santo Domingo; San Juan; Kingston; and Port of Spain. The busiest ports for emigrants bound for Ellis Island were Liverpool, Southampton, Bremerhaven, Hamburg, Rotterdam, Antwerp, Le Havre, Naples, Genoa, and Trieste, and Athens—not necessarily in that order.

See also **Steamship Companies; Steamships; Steerage**

Ports of Entry. *See* **Immigrant Inspection Stations**

Post, Louis F. [Louis Freeland Post] (b. November 15, 1849, near Danville, New Jersey; d. January 10, 1928, Washington, DC). Writer, lawyer, reformer; assistant secretary of Labor (1913–1921). Louis Post served as assistant secretary during the **red scare**, which followed the end of World War I. He signed the December 1919 deportation orders of the 249 radicals, including **Emma Goldman** and **Alexander Berkman**. During the crisis, he strove to temper the hysteria by blocking every deportation that he could prove excessive. A noted Swedenborgian Christian, Post was also a noted advocate of the single tax economic proposal of his friend Henry George, a well-known economic writer and political activist.

REFERENCE: Post, Louis F. 1923. *The Deportations Delirium of Nineteen Twenty*. Chicago: Kerr.

Postal Cards. In 1910, Commissioner **William Williams** introduced an official postal card that immigrants could use to notify relations and friends of their arrival in the United States. The card was free of charge and saved immigrants the money they would have spent on telegrams. The text read:

> _____ has arrived at Ellis by steamship _____. This immigrant refers to you. If you desire to call on his or her behalf, you may do so. Ferryboat leaves Barge Office (Battery Park) every hour on the hour. You are not required to pay anything to anyone in connection with this matter. If you come to Ellis Island, bring this card with you.

Powderly, Terence V. [Terence Vincent Powderly] (b. Carbondale, Pennsylvania, January 22, 1849; d. Washington, DC, June 24, 1924). Commissioner-general of Immigration (1897–1902). Although Terence Powderly was responsible for a few minor reforms at Ellis Island, the incompetence of Commissioner

Thomas Fitchie and the dishonesty of Assistant Commissioner **Edward McSweeney** and others continued until **Theodore Roosevelt** ascended to the presidency. Powderly took many photographs at Ellis Island during his administration, the bulk of which are currently held by the Catholic University of America. A pioneering trade union leader and labor politician, Powderly served as mayor of Scranton, Pennsylvania (1878–1882), and was Grand Master Workman of the Knights of Labor (1879–1893). In 1906, he studied the causes of emigration in Europe for the U.S. Department of Commerce and Labor.

REFERENCES: Falzone, Vincent J. 1978. *Terence V. Powderly: Middle Class Reformer*; Powderly, Terence V. 1940. *The Path I Trod: the Autobiography of Terence Powderly*. New York: Columbia University Press; *New York Times*. 1924. Terence Powderly, labor leader, dies. June 25.

Power House. Constructed in 1901, the power house on **Island 1** has load-bearing brick walls, a granite base, and a steel-framed floor. It is laid in Flemish bond and also has a granite base and bluestone water table; its quoins and window trim are made of limestone. The second floor reached by means of an iron-framed stairway with slate stairs. In the center of the building rises a chimney stack that is 7 feet in diameter and rises 125 feet high. It was designed in the beaux arts style by architects **William A. Boring** and **Edward L. Tilton**. The plant was originally powered by coal but was converted to fuel oil in 1932. In the 1980s, the plant equipment in the interior was modernized and the Power House was restored to full service.

The power house (1907) on **Island 3** is a two-story building, measuring 49 feet by 66 feet. It is constructed of a masonry and steel frame, and red bricks, stucco, and limestone. Architect **James Knox Taylor** designed it in the neo-Renaissance style. The first floor contains a boiler room, laundry, disinfecting facilities, and a **mortuary and autopsy room**. The

Power House. Photo by M. Johnson. Courtesy of the National Park Service Statue of Liberty National Monument, Ellis Island Immigration Museum.

latter room is located in the southwest corner and is furnished with eight metal-lined cadaver bins and a seating space for observers; its walls are of concrete. Upstairs is a dormitory with a linen room and bathrooms. The building's chimney is on the eastern side of the boiler room and rises 100 feet high.

There is also a boiler room in the **hospital outbuilding** (1901) on **Island 2**.

Pregnancies. Women suspected of being pregnant were taken aside during **line inspection** and later led to the physical examination rooms for a more thorough medical inspection. Women found to be pregnant were certified by the **Public Health Service**. The certifying physician(s) also estimated how many months the woman had been pregnant. Some women had to be hospitalized in the maternity ward on arrival, where they gave birth. The groups most commonly certified for pregnancy in the years 1916–1930 included the Hungarians, Poles, Slovaks; Croats and Slovenians; Ruthenians; Syrians; and Romanians. An estimated 350 babies were born at the station.

See also **Births; Line Inspection; Women**

Primary Inspection. Primary inspection was the heart of the Ellis Island experience and constituted the purpose for which immigrants were brought there. It consisted of an interrogation or "cross-questioning" of aliens in the **Registry Room** and was conducted by a clerk or an interpreter and supervised by an **immigrant inspector**. The inspector had the power to admit, detain, or exclude aliens. The questions he asked each alien were based on the data already recorded on the ship manifest, which he had before him. His task was to determine whether the alien was clearly and beyond

Interpreter questions immigrant in a foreign language while an inspector makes notes. Courtesy of the Ellis Island Immigration Museum.

a doubt entitled to land, which meant that he had to make certain that the person was not in violation of any U.S. immigration laws barring various categories of aliens, such as polygamists, criminals, beggars, and diseased or **feebleminded** persons.

Allan J. McLaughlin, one of the Ellis Island physicians, accurately described the course of primary inspection in an article he wrote late in 1904:

> After passing the doctors, the immigrants are grouped, according to the number of their manifest sheet, into lines of thirty or less. At the head of each line is a registry clerk or interpreter, and an immigration inspector. The clerk or interpreter interrogates each alien and finds his name and verifies the answers on the manifest sheet before him and, if in the opinion of the immigrant inspector the immigrant is not clearly beyond doubt entitled to land, he is held for the consideration of the board of special inquiry. A board of special inquiry, according to the law of 1903, "consists of three members selected from such of the immigrant officials in the service of the commissioner general of immigration, with the approval of the secretary of commerce and labor, shall designate as qualified to serve on such boards."
>
> The decision of any two members of a board shall prevail and be final, but either the alien or any dissenting member of said board may appeal through the commissioner of immigration at the port of arrival, and the commissioner general of immigration to the secretary of commerce and labor, whose decision shall be final, and the taking of such appeals shall operate to stay any action in regard to the final disposal of the alien, whose case is so appealed, until receipt by the commissioner of immigration at the port of arrival of such decision. To this "board of special inquiry" are sent the aliens certified by the medical officers as suffering from loathsome or dangerous contagious disease, idiocy, epilepsy and insanity.
>
> In cases so certified the law is mandatory and the medical certificate is equivalent to exclusion, the board simply applying the legal process necessary for deportation. Aliens certified . . . as suffering from (a) disability likely to make them public charges are also held for examination before the board of special inquiry. The board in these cases takes into consideration the medical certificate and such evidence as may be adduced by the alien or his friends that, in the opinion of the board, would offset the physical disability. In these cases the board has full discretionary powers, and in a great majority of instances the alien is admitted. . . .
>
> Immigrants not detained . . . have their money changed into United States currency and buy their railroad tickets. . . . If they are destined to points beyond New York City, government supervision is maintained until they are taken to one of the great railroad terminals and placed upon the waiting train. These precautions are taken to protect the immigrants from the board house "runners" and other sharpers who lie in wait for them at the Battery. Aliens detained as not clearly entitled to land are brought before the board and, if the evidence is complete, either deported or discharged. When the evidence is incomplete, the immigrant is detained pending the verification of his story, or the arrival of his relatives or friends. All cases are disposed of as rapidly as possible, and immigrants are detained the minimum amount of time required for procuring and carefully considering the evidence in the case. Those ordered deported are returned to the ship as soon as possible after the decision is rendered, providing no appeal is made.

The **Registry Division** handled primary inspections from 1892 to 1918 and 1920 to 1926. The **Boarding Division** handled all primary inspections for cabin class passengers, taking place aboard steamships. From about 1918 until sometime in the 1920s, the Registry Division and Boarding Division were united as the **Primary Inspection Division**. In 1929, the Boarding Division took over primary inspection permanently.

See also **Great Hall; Landing Immigrants; Liable to Become a Public Charge**

REFERENCE: MaLaughlin, Allan. 1905. How immigrants are inspected. *Popular Science Monthly* (February): 359–361.

Prisoners of War (POW). Civilian prisoners of war were held at Ellis Island as enemy aliens during **World War I** (1917–1918) and **World War II** (1941–1945). The aliens held during World War I were largely steamship officers and seamen from the German and Austro-Hungarian steamship lines, although there were also a few spies. During World War II conditions were more complicated, for detainees consisted of thousands of **enemy**

aliens and arriving German and Italian POWs, as well as hundreds of merchant seamen and suspected spies.

Privilege Holders. The privilege holders were contracted for three years by the government to perform such functions as the government could not or preferred not to do. These activities—selling train tickets, cooking and serving food, changing money, and the like—constituted their functions at the station.

The transportation companies sold railway and steamboat tickets to the immigrants who had farther to travel. The companies at Ellis Island included the New York Central & Hudson River Railroad Company; West Shore Railroad Company; New York, Ontario & Western; Erie Railroad Company; Delaware, Lackawanna & Western; Lehigh Valley Railroad; Central Railroad of New Jersey; Philadelphia & Reading Railroad; Baltimore & Ohio Railroad; Central Pacific Railroad; Grand Trunk Railroad; Old Dominion Steamship Company; Southern Pacific Railroad (operated the steamships to New Orleans); the Mallory Line; and the New Haven Railroad.

The baggage service was let to several contractors, including Bernard Biglin (1892–1893; 1897–1907), who had also held the same concession at Castle Garden; American Transportation Company (1896); and Westcott Express (1902).

The restaurant privilege holders were Anderson and Toffey (1892); Felix Livingston (1896); Hudgins and Dumas (1902–1905); Harry Balfe (1905–1908); Fritz Brodt (1908–1911); Hudgins and Dumas (1911–1914).

The **money exchange** concessionaires included Francis J. Scully (1890s); Post & Flagg (1902–1905); and the American Express Company (1905–1954).

The telegraph contracts were let to the Western Union Telegraph Company (1890s–1950s) and its great rival, American Telephone and Telegraph.

Psychopathic Ward. For forty years, the psychopathic ward was used for the mentally ill who came through the Island. The need to house insane or mentally ill patients before their deportation was the driving force that resulted in the construction of the psychiatric ward. In 1906, this hospital building was designed in a simplified beaux arts style by **James Knox Taylor** and built in 1907 by the New York firm of William F. Holding. The two-story building is constructed of Flemish red brick on steel framing with terra cotta and limestone trim; there was an enclosed porch at its south end. The facility could accommodate twenty-five patients. In later years, the building was often called the psychiatric ward.

In a memorandum that was issued in 1922, the medical staff of the psychopathic ward was reminded to keep all doors locked; it forbade patients from leaving the wards without permission of the **medical officer** in charge of the ward or the **chief medical officer**. Chairs, except those for used by the nurse, were not permitted in the wards; an exception to the rule was in allowing rocking chairs in the female wards. The wire frames that covered the windows were kept closed and securely locked at all times. When admitted to the wards, all patients were searched and any items that they might use to harm themselves—such as knives—were placed in the custody of the registrar. Knives and other sharp instruments were not permitted in the wards. Patients were allowed to walk the wards and could go out onto screened porches at the end of the wards. Whenever a patient became excited or unmanageable, a doctor was summoned. Occasionally, it was necessary to forcibly restrain certain patients. This "humane restraint" was done by means of restraining sheets and camisoles. The hospital also had secure isolation rooms for disturbed patients, who had to be observed on a twenty-four-hour basis. Isolation rooms (and, indeed, all other rooms in the building) had steel doors and each door had a small square window through which nurses and doctors could see the patient.

In 1949, the **Public Health Service** ceased

using the psychopathic ward for mental patients and, in 1951, it abandoned the building. The **Coast Guard** was given the building for use as a sick bay and in 1952 began using unoccupied isolation rooms as a brig. When the **Immigration and Naturalization Service** closed Ellis Island late in 1954, the Coast Guard vacated the building.

REFERENCES: Stakely, J. T. 2002. *Cultural Landscape Report for Ellis Island: Site History.* Lowell, Massachusetts: National Park Service; Unrau, Harlan D. 1984. *The Historic Resource Study: Ellis Island/Statue of Liberty.* Vol. 2. Washington, DC: U.S. Department of Interior, National Park Service.

Public Charge. A public charge was an immigrant who had to be cared for by a public charity, such as the municipal or county poor relief, or housed in a public institution, such as a public hospital, orphanage, jail, prison, or almshouse. Immigrants who were cared for in such institutions were subject to deportation, as it violated the grounds of their admission to the country under federal immigration law. **Immigrant inspectors** were required to exclude from the United States any immigrant they believed would become a public charge. This included immigrants certified by medical examiners suffering from Class A diseases or illnesses (e.g., tubercular, trachomatous, mentally defective, insane), who were automatically excluded by immigrant inspectors. Those suffering from Class B illnesses or conditions (e.g., heart disease, poor physique, pregnancy) were usually, but not always, excluded by an immigrant inspector as likely to become public charge. Immigrants were likewise subject to scrutiny by immigrant inspectors on nonmedical matters that might result in exclusion under the heading "likely to become a public charge." Such persons included women, children, and elderly with no adult male able to take care of them and no other likely means of support; mothers with children born out of wedlock, professional beggars; and those with insufficient funds on arrival.

See also **Diseases and Hospitalization; Exclusion; Immigration Act of 1882; Immigration Act of 1891; Line Inspection; Primary Inspection**

Public Health and Marine Hospital Service. This was the official name of the Public Health Service from 1902 through 1912. The name reflected the agency's new work in protecting the public from infectious diseases at immigration and quarantine stations. The name also reflected the origins of the service in its work in caring for sick and injured merchant seamen.

Public Health Service (United States Public Health Service). The Public Health Service carried out all medical examinations of aliens that entered the United States and its largest hospital complex for this activity was at Ellis Island. The agency came into being in 1798 following the passage of an act of Congress that made the federal government provide for the care and relief of sick and injured merchant seamen. Marine hospitals were subsequently opened or designated in Boston and other seaport areas and inland waterways. In 1870, the federal government tightened the control of the **Marine Hospital Service**, as the agency was called, and reorganized it along hierarchical lines, with a head office in Washington, DC. In the following year, John Maynard Woodworth was appointed as head of the agency with title "supervising surgeon." Desiring to create a unique identity for his physicians in order that they might be clearly distinct from civilian physicians, Woodworth organized the service along military lines. Thus he introduced a requirement for them to wear uniforms and instituted disciplinary practices and special examinations for them. In 1889, the uniformed surgeons were according the status of a commissioned corps under an act of Congress. In 1878, the Marine Hospital Service received quarantine authority to prevent infectious diseases from entering the country. Although a number of states gladly handed over this function to the Marine Hospital Service, others, including New York, retained their own quarantine service.

The real expansion for the Marine Hospital Service came with the passage of the **Immigration Act of 1891**, which assigned the agency the responsibility of examining immigrants entering the United States. With the opening of Ellis Island in the next year, the service found itself at last in the limelight of public scrutiny. Surgeons were confronted daily by vast crowds of aliens, so they developed **line inspection** to handle the onslaught. Poor physique, debilitating illnesses, infectious diseases, and mental defects were encountered regularly at Ellis Island. In 1897, the immigrant hospital building was destroyed in a great fire and a new fireproof hospital building was opened at the station in 1901, followed by several more until World War I broke out.

This drastic change in the function of the Marine Hospital Service called into question its identity. Now immigration and, to a lesser degree, quarantine enforcement were more important functions than caring for merchant seamen. To reflect this change in priorities, the agency was renamed the **Public Health and Marine Hospital Service** in 1902. A decade later, in 1912, it the "marine hospital" part of its name was dropped completely, to demonstrate that the service was primarily committed to protecting the general public health of the nation. Nonetheless, seamen and sailors continued to receive the care from the service.

In the mid-1920s, line inspection at Ellis island was discontinued and in 1951 the Public Health Service closed the Ellis Island Hospital and moved its reduced medical services into the Main Building. The last Public Health Service medical team left Ellis Island when the Immigration and Naturalization Service closed the immigrant station completely on November 12, 1951.

See also **Diseases and Hospitalization; Line Inspection**

REFERENCE: Mullan, Fitzhugh. 1989. *Plagues and Politics: The Story of the United States Public Health Service*. New York: BasicBooks.

Purcell, Anna (b. 1890; d. 1981). Head nurse (1939–1948). Nurse Anna Purcell was assigned to the immigrant hospital on **Island 2**. Before her employment with the **Public Health Service**, Purcell had a long career as an army nurse, from 1918 until her discharge from duty in 1939.

See also **Nurses**

Q

Quarantine. Quarantining ships at the Port of New York was controlled by the state of New York. When vessels entered the port, quarantine officials climbed aboard the ship in advance of federal immigration officials from Ellis Island. Immigrants suffering from diseases requiring quarantine—the most common being cholera, yellow fever, smallpox, typhus, typhoid fever, leprosy, and plague—were removed from their vessel and sent to Hoffman and Swinburne Islands in the lower bay. State officials also quarantined the ships and their passengers until the contagion abated. During ship inspection and quarantine all vessels waved the yellow flag. In addition, there was an important quarantine hospital on Staten Island.

Quota Act of 1921 (42 Statute 5). This was the first federal immigration law to reduce mass migration to the United States. A temporary or stop-gap measure, it was passed by the Sixty-seventh Congress of the United States and signed into law by President Warren G. Harding on May 19, 1921; it became effective on June 3, 1921, for one year. The law limited the number of foreign nationals allowed to enter the United States to only 3 percent of the nationality reported to have been living in the United States in the 1910 federal census. Further, the number of aliens arriving monthly could not be more than 20 percent of their homeland's annual quota. The Quota Act took effect in the last few weeks of the fiscal year, June 3 through June 30, 1921. During this brief period, 27,298 immigrants were admitted. In fiscal year 1922 (July 1, 1921 through June 30, 1922), 355,825 were to be admitted. Of that number, the bulk of admissible aliens were 197,000 northern and western Europeans and 155,000 southern and eastern Europeans. Because the majority of immigrants had been coming from southern and eastern Europe in every peacetime year since 1900, this law was highly effective in ending that pattern.

Before it expired on June 30, 1922, the Quota Act was extended to June 30, 1924, by a Joint Resolution of Congress, which President Harding signed into law on May 11, 1922 (42 Stat. 540). Further, to force the steamship companies to observe the new law, a fine of $200 was imposed on them for each immigrant who was brought into the country in excess of the quota. The law also required them to refund the steamship fare of immigrants who exceeded the quota.

See also **Immigration Act of 1924; Quotas**

Quotas. In the 1920s, three important laws allotting quota restrictions were applied to immigrants entering the United States each year. The **Quota Act of 1921** restricted the admission of each immigrant nationality based on 3 percent of their nationality living in the United States in 1910. The **Immigration Act of 1924** restricted admissions to 2 percent of each immigrant nationality living in the country in 1890. The National Origins Act of 1929 made the quota system permanent. The 1921 act allowed 357,803 aliens enter the United States each year, the 1924 act 164,667, and the 1929 act 153,714. Under each law, the largest quotas were allotted to northern and western Europe, especially to Great Britain, Germany, and Ireland. The smallest quotas went to Asia,

Africa, and Oceania. No quotas were assigned to the nations of the Western Hemisphere. In general, most Asian immigrants were barred from entering the United States. These quotas were known as "national origins quotas" or "preferential quotas" because they favored certain regions and countries of the world over others; they continued for many years. The Immigration and Naturalization Act of 1952 (**McCarran-Walter Act**), was the last immigration law to continue this policy. The **Immigration Act of 1965** abolished the preferential quota system based on the national origins of immigrants (effective June 1968). However, it retained an annual quota for immigration, a system that is still used. The 1965 act also introduced a new kind of preference quota that favored refugees, relatives of U.S. citizens, and permanent alien residents.

REFERENCE: LeMay, Michael C. 1987. *From Open Door to Dutch Door: An Analysis of U.S. Immigration Policy since 1820*. New York: Praeger.

R

Races and Peoples. In 1899, the **Bureau of Immigration** began counting immigrants by races or peoples as well as by the nation of which they claimed to be a subject or citizen. These "racial" statistics were gathered from 1899 through 1931. Since the vast majority of these immigrants were coming through Ellis Island, officials such as **Victor Safford** were influential in determining the categories and descriptions used. Most of the races were based on national origin and language. But there were some exceptions. In spite of the fact that Jews came from a variety of countries and often spoke different languages from other Jews, they were all defined as Hebrew and said to be of the same race. Hence Jews were never included in racial statistics of non-Jewish groups, such as Russians, Poles, Ruthenians, Hungarians, French, and Germans.

Another approach to racial classification was applied to Italians. Although all generally came from the Kingdom of Italy and were Roman Catholic, they were divided into two distinct races—South Italians and North Italians. The Bureau of Immigration held that the groups "differed from each other in language, physique, and character as well as geographical distribution." The northern Italians were observed to be natives of regions such as Piedmont, Lombardy, Venetia, and Emilia, as well as from the French, Austrian, and Swiss border regions. The southern Italians were said to be natives of much of the central and southern peninsula as well as the islands of Sicily and Sardinia. Genoans were also counted as southerners. Other peoples counted in a special way in these statistics were the Cubans (African Cubans were not included in the tabulation), Mexicans (Mexicans predominantly of African or Indian descent were not included in the tabulation), Spanish Americans (the people of Central and South America of Spanish descent), Swedes (considered to be a Nordic race distinct from the Danes and Norwegians, due to the linguistic differences), Syrians (only Christians were included in this table), and West Indians (Spanish Cubans and people of African descent were not counted as West Indian).

The races entering the United States between 1899 and 1931 are African (black), 142,559; Armenian, 81,729; Bohemian and Moravian (Czech), 169,646; Bulgarian, Serbian, and Montenegrin, 169,030; Chinese, 66,946; Croatian and Slovenian, 491,407; Cuban, 88,373; Dalmatian, Bosnian, and Herzegovinian, 52,721; Dutch and Flemish, 227,923; East Indian, 8,590; English, 1,313,716; Finnish (and Estonian), 230,833; French, 533,633; German, 1,644,107; Greek, 517,802; Hebrew, 1,911,253; Irish, 1,053,500; North Italian, 621,279; South Italian, 3,310,015; Japanese, 265,092; Korean, 9,458; Lithuanian (and Latvian), 266,029; Magyar, 500,036; Mexican, 700,134; Pacific Islander (including Hawaiian), 1,180; Polish, 1,508,653; Portuguese (including Brazilians), 191,703; Romanian, 151,088; Russian, 267,599; Ruthenian (including Ukrainian, etc.), 268,669; Scandinavian (Norwegians, Swedes, and Danes), 1,065,624; Scotch, 602,355; Slovak, 548,410; Spanish (including Catalan), 196,693; Spanish American, 61,286; Syrian, 106,107; Turkish, 22,942; Welsh, 52,848; West Indian (except Cuban), 32,138; Other Peoples, 42,726.

Other peoples included the following: Arabians (Muslims), Albanians (unless accidentally counted as Greeks or Turks), Georgians, Gypsies (Roma), Maltese, Persians, Semitic-Hamitic (Arabs, Egyptian, Libyan, Berbers, Abyssinians, etc.; Hebrews counted separately). Canadians were not recorded until 1906 and then they were tabulated by their racial origins (e.g., French, English, Scotch, Irish, German).

REFERENCES: *Dictionary of Races or Peoples: Reports of the Immigration Commission.* Vol. 5. 1911. Repr., New York: Arno/New York Times, 1970; Fairchild, Amy L. 2003. *Science at the Borders.* Baltimore: Johns Hopkins University Press.

Radicals. Immigrants associated with political philosophies, parties, and movements labeled as radical were barred from entering the United States under several laws. The **Immigration Act of 1903** barred anarchists or persons who believed in or advocated the overthrow of government and law. Subsequent laws were the **Immigration Act of 1917**, the **Immigration Act of 1918**, the **Internal Security Act of 1950,** and the Immigration Act of 1952. Noted radicals held at Ellis Island included deportees John Turner (English anarchist, 1903), **Alexander Berkman** and **Emma Goldman** (anarchists, 1919). In 1922, world famous dancer American **Isadora Duncan** and her Soviet husband Sergei Esenin (both leftists) were briefly detained at Ellis Island as Bolshevik suspects. In 1933, French communist writer **Henri Barbusse** was held there, and in 1940 Irene Raissa Browder, the Russian wife of Earl Browder, the presidential candidate and leader of the American Communist Party, was deported. During the Cold War, **Ignac Mezei** ("the man without a country"), and West Indian deportees **C. L. R. James** (Marxist, 1953) and Jamaicans Ferdinand Smith and William Strachan (communists, 1952) spent time on Ellis Island. In addition, a German war bride, Ellen Knauff, was mistakenly accused of being a communist and held at Ellis Island for several years before she was finally released.

See also **Red Scare**

Railroad Ticket Office. The railroad ticket office is an extension to the **Main Building** and was more commonly known as the railroad room. Virtually all of the railway companies with terminals in New York City, Jersey City, and Hoboken had agents posted here. These firms included the Southern Pacific, Old Dominion, Canadian Pacific, New York Central, Central Railroad of New Jersey, Pennsylvania railroad lines. In addition, the Trunk Lines Association handled ticketing and contracting to deliver immigrant passengers to a variety of points east of the Mississippi River, while its counterpart, the Western Passenger Association, offered the same services to a large number of travelers going beyond the Mississippi. Great trunk line railroads included the Lackawanna and Lehigh Valley, Erie, Baltimore and Ohio, and the Rock Island Line. Completed and opened in 1904, the single-story railroad ticket office (62 feet by 120 feet) is built on a rusticated granite foundation and has Flemish bond red brick walls trimmed in limestone and iron bay windows. The north side of the roof is distinguished by three gables. The glass skylights were installed in 1931. This section of the Main Building currently houses the **Peopling of America** exhibition.

Razofsky, Cecilia [Cecilia Razofsky Davidson] (b. St. Louis, Missouri, 1891; d. 1968). Social reformer. The **National Council of Jewish Women** (NCJW) posted Cecilia Razofsky to Ellis Island as a social worker (1910–1915). After working as an inspector for the Children's Bureau in Washington, she returned to the NCJW in the 1920s and directed their aid work on Ellis Island for many years. She was particularly adept at helping refugees. She also edited the council's newsletter, the *Immigrant*, and wrote a manual on immigration problems in the 1930s.

REFERENCE: *Encyclopaedia Judaica.* 1972. Cecilia Razofsky. Editorial Staff. Jerusalem: Keter House Publishing, Ltd.

Reagan, Ronald (b. Tampico, Illinois, February 6, 1911; d. June 5, 2004). President of the

United States (1981–1989). President Ronald Reagan launched the **restoration** of Ellis Island in 1982 by taking several steps, including appointing Chrysler chairman Lee A. Iacocca to lead a national fund-raising campaign. These efforts resulted in the establishment of the **Statue of Liberty–Ellis Island Foundation** and creation of the **Ellis Island Immigration Museum**. In April 1987, President Reagan became the first president since **William Howard Taft** to visit Ellis Island.

Before entering politics, Reagan was a popular motion picture actor. His best films include *Dark Victory*, *Knute Rockne-All American*, *International Squadron*, *Santa Fe Trail*, *Kings Row*, *This Is the Army* (with Irving Berlin), *Prisoner of War*, and *The Killers*.

Records. Archives and records pertaining to Ellis Island are largely in the possession of the National Archives and Records Administration (NARA), with headquarters in Washington, DC, and a major branch office in New York City. The records are divided into the following eight groups.

Record Group 36 holds the passenger lists of vessels that arrived at the port of New York from 1820 through 1897. The lists contain each passenger's name, age, sex, occupation, nationality, and destination.

Record Group 51 holds two reports on the Bureau of Immigration and Ellis Island.

Record Group 56 holds the correspondence of the Ellis Island commissioners (1895–1933).

Record Group 65 holds Department of Justice investigative case files on aliens from 1908 through 1922, including suspected enemy aliens.

Record Group 85 is vast and its records cover the years 1789 through 1954. The preponderance of records, however, belong to the Bureaus of Immigration and Naturalization and their successor agency, the Immigration and Naturalization Service. The types of records included are immigration correspondence (1882–1932); World War I records, including enemy alien cases; Americanization and education files (1914–1936); Bureau of Naturalization administrative files (1906–1940); INS alien registration forms; World War II records, including those pertaining to the internment of enemy aliens; deportation cases; crew and passengers of steamship and airplane arrivals.

Record Group 90 holds the medical records of the Public Health Service hospital and medical operations at Ellis Island.

Record Group 121 contains the maintenance and construction records of the buildings and structures on Ellis Island, including correspondence, plans, specifications, contracts, blueprints, and other architectural papers.

Record Group 174 holds the papers of labor secretaries, assistant secretaries, and other officials, including high-level civil servants. The many documents concerning Ellis Island in this group include the Ethelbert Stewart Papers, which contain an investigative report (1918–1919) on Ellis Island immigrant inspectors.

The Bureau of Citizenship and Immigration Services holds lists of passengers who were aboard vessels, and the **National Park Service** at Ellis Island includes oral history interviews, the **John B. Weber** Photograph Album, the **Augustus F. Sherman** Photograph Collection, the **Maud Mosher** Papers, and the **Ludmila K. Foxlee** Papers.

Other repositories of Ellis Island records are held in the following institutions. The Roman Catholic archdiocese of New York holds records of the Mission of the Immaculate Virgin for the Safekeeping of Irish Girls; the Catholic University of America holds the **Terence V. Powderly** Papers; the New York Public Library holds the **William Williams** Papers; Syracuse University Library holds the **Edward Corsi** Papers; the Chicago Historical Society holds the **W. W. Husband** Papers; the American Jewish Historical Society and YIVO Institute in New York hold the **Hebrew Immigrant**

Aid Society records, the industrial removal office, and other Jewish immigration entities; the Center for Migration Studies on Staten Island holds the records of the **Italian Welfare League**; the New York Historical Society holds the **Fiorello LaGuardia** Papers; Louisiana State University, the Wisconsin Historical Society, and the University of California at Riverside hold some original photographs and the American Express Company holds its Ellis Island currency exchange contracts. In addition, some important materials are held abroad, including the **Robert Watchorn** immigrant photographs in Alfreton, England.

REFERENCE: Bolino, August C. 1990. *The Ellis Island Source.* Washington, DC: Kensington Historical Press.

Recreation Hall. The recreation hall was used for entertaining immigrants and others and was primarily used as an auditorium. It was designed in the neocolonial/modern styles by federal architect Louis A. Simon and Chester Aldrich, a consultant. The building has a masonry foundation and the upper levels are limestone and Flemish bond red brick; it measures 43 feet in height by 111 feet in length, and was built during 1936 and 1937. A stage and wings fill the south end of the building and an oak-paneled screened counter runs along the auditorium's north wall. On the second floor are the stage manager's box and two other rooms. During **World War II** many popular stars appeared there to entertain the **Coast Guard**, including Jimmy Durante, **Bob Hope**, and the Lionel Hampton Orchestra.

For several years, the **National Park Service** has used the building as a warehouse for historic Ellis Island furniture.

Recreation Shelter. The recreation shelter or pavilion is located between Islands 2 and 3. It was designed by Louis A. Simon, the super-

Interior of Recreation Hall. Stage shows, radio broadcasts, and concerts were offered to coastguards and detained aliens in the Recreation Hall. Entertainers such as Jimmy Durante, Bob Hope, Lionel Hampton, and Frances Langford performed there during World War II.
Courtesy of the Ellis Island Immigration Museum.

Recreation Hall and Recreation Shelter. Courtesy of the Ellis Island Immigration Museum.

visory architect of the Department of the Treasury. It is one story high and built of red brick and masonry with a terra cotta trim, and measures 81 feet by 17 feet. Its ornamentation includes Flemish brick bond with dark headers, pilasters with terra cotta caps and bases, a terra cotta entablature, and bull's-eye windows. It was completed early in 1937 along with the **recreation hall**. Hospital patients used the shelter as a place to relax.

Red Scare. The post–**World War I** red scare was caused by the Bolshevik Revolution in Russia, which resulted in the violent overthrow of the ancient tsarist monarchy—and the murder of Tsar Nicholas II and the imperial family—and the establishment of a brutal communist dictatorship. The possibility of a similar revolution in the western nations aroused fear in the United States. The federal government responded by taking extreme measures. In 1919 and 1920, Attorney General A. Mitchell Palmer orchestrated the roundup and arrest of hundreds of foreign-born **radicals** and delivered them to the Ellis Island immigrant station, where, under armed guard, they were summarily deported by the **Bureau of Immigration**, with the assistance of the army and Justice Department. Complaints lodged by Commissioner **Frederic C. Howe** were largely ignored. After Howe angrily resigned from office in September 1919, Assistant Commissioner **Byron Uhl** took over as acting commissioner and vigorously handled the deportation cases and issued all the necessary deportation warrants; he was firmly backed in this course by Secretary of Labor William B. Wilson and Assistant Secretary of Labor **Louis F. Post**. The most highly publicized group of deportees were 249 persons, which included the notorious anarchists **Emma Goldman** and **Alexander Berkman**; all of them were deported to Russia aboard the army transport ship ***Buford***, which the newspapers called the Soviet Ark. The ship set sail from New York harbor early on the morning of December 21, 1919. Since the British Royal Navy was blockading Russia's Baltic Sea ports, the ***Buford*** could only sail as far as Finland.

In January 1920, 600 more radicals arrested by the Justice Department were brought for detention at Ellis Island. Nationwide, more than 4,000 suspects were arrested—in some instances, without warrants.

At Ellis Island, **boards of special inquiry** were busy with the deportation cases. Although the most acute stage of the red scare had subsided by the summer of 1920, it lingered until 1923. The following is the memorandum of March 15, 1920, written by Ellis Island's Acting Commissioner **Byron H. Uhl** and sent to Commissioner-General **Anthony Caminetti**. In it, Uhl describes the work of various employees from the Night, Deportation, Registry, Executive, and other divisions, who dealt with the deportees during the most acute stage of the red scare:

It is rather difficult to give you a definite report as called for in your telegram of the 12th instant, no. 54735/411. Inspectors Jacob D. Detwiler, Augustus P. Schell and Charles I. Jones, and Interpreter Reuben Volovick were employed almost exclusively since November 8, 1919 until the present time in reference to cases of anarchistic character. Clerk Alice J. Buckley has devoted the greater part of her time to these cases since the date named. Inspector Frank Hayes devoted his entire attention to the matter between November 8 and December 21, 1919, and since January 3, 1920 has assisted from time to time in the handling of these cases. Interpreter Lucien Daileader gave his entire time to these cases from November 8, 1919 to February 11, 1920, going aboard on the SS "Buford." Interpreter Richard C.N. Wenrich has devoted all of his time to these cases since January 3, 1920 to March 12, 1920. Interpreters Vincent Daukszys and Anthony Dworzecki have devoted their entire time to these cases since January 3, 1920, and are still so employed. Inspector Vivian G. Mackintosh has given his entire time to this matter since January 9, 1920, and is still so engaged. Inspectors Paul F. Morrison and Jeremiah B. Fitzgerald have devoted their entire time to the anarchistic cases since February 25, 1920, but it is anticipated that their assignment to this work will be concluded within a week. In addition, to the above, clerks Louis G. Schwarts and Hyman A. Mintzer have reported several hearings, but this was merely incidental to the general office work and I would not be justified in saying that any considerable portion of their time was devoted to the anarchistic cases. For a portion of time, the entire clerical force of the Executive Division helped on this matter, but it was only for a few hours at a time or, at the most, a few days, and I cannot give you any definite dates.

When it comes to the watchmen, all of them have had something to do with the proper detention of these aliens, but the guards supplied by the Department of Justice were the only ones who gave their entire time to this group of aliens and I do not understand that you want to include them in this estimate. From November 8 to November 29, 1919, the Deporting Division force performed all the labor incident to guard these aliens but, of course, in addition thereto, they had to attend to the regular immigration work. The employees concerned included Inspector-in-Charge John J. McKee, clerks Arch L. Barr, Wright L. Auchmoody and Charles P. Desiderio, and watchmen William T. Benvie, Lake T. Carter, William Dickie, Edgar M. Dugan, Edward E. Hults, Jacob Levit, Henry M. Luick, William McDevitt, Patrick A. McGlynn, John D. Nixon, Peter D. Herrick, Patrick B. Butler, Frank Russell, George N. Watson, Donatus Weber, Alexander L. Curley, Henry C. Christiansen, Frank Devine, Henry C. Ritz, James A. Finn, August W. Muller.

On November 29, 1919, six guards were sent here by the Department of Justice and, later, three additional ones were sent. These remained until December 21, 1919, after which date the number was reduced to four. In the meantime, however, the Watchmen assigned to the Deporting Division had to assist to a large extent. I do not know just how you can separate their time in this report.

Since the delivery here on January 2, 1920, of the Communist and Communist Labor members, the men above named, with the exception of Peter D. Herrick and Patrick B. Butler, have assisted in the work to the date, excepting James A. Finn, who was promoted to the position of Inspector on February 16, 1920, and August Muller, who resigned on March 3, 1920. Watchman William J. McQuillan has been assigned to the Deporting Division since December 4, 1919; Herman J. Grant since February 17; Martin E. Murphy since March 10; Joseph McCormack since March 13; also Joseph G. Hartnett, Frank E. Steward, Arthur Pollack and Edward D.

Cronin since March 13. As heretofore explained, these men must attend to the general duties of an immigration watchman in addition to assisting in the detention and transfer from place to place of the so-called Reds. Once watchman now employed in the Department of Justice and assigned to Ellis Island, Edward Hart, was, I believe, in the employ of the Department of Labor from December 21, 1919 to February 11, 1920, he having gone abroad on the SS "Buford" as one of the guards.

In addition to the above, some consideration must be taken of the Night Force. Here also, from November 8 to November 29, 1919, the Night Force had to take care of these aliens of the anarchistic class. Inspector in Charge Harvey E. Snider and the watchmen below named were on duty during that period, or the portions below indicated. Of course, they assisted in guarding them until the departure of the SS "Buford", December 21, 1919.

Harvey E. Snider, Inspector in Charge
from Nov. 8 to Nov. 29th, inclusive.
Richard W. Conradson,
from Nov. 9, 1919, to Nov. 29, inclusive
Philip Eichorn,
" 10 "
James Fennelly
" 8 "
Charles Masur
" 8 to November 10
William J. McQuillan
" 12 to November 29, inclusive
Charles B. Musgrave
" 8 to 10, and from 26th to 29th
Edward M. Powers
" 8 to November 26th
Alva H. Shipper
" 8 to November 29th
Thomas Wall
" 17th to 29th
Samuel J. Thornton
" 10th to 29th
Ludwig Weppler
" 8th to 29th
Patrick J. Wheeler
" 8th to 29th
Lawrence J. Yeagler
" 8th to 29th

While a comparatively small number were detained here between December 21 and January 3, of course our force did such watching as was necessary. From January 3, 1920 to date, Mr. Snider and the watchmen below have been on duty for a portion of the time stated:

Harvey E. Snider, Inspector in Charge, from
January 3 to March 13
James Ambrose, February 17 to March 13
Philip Eichorn, January 3 to March 3
James Fennelly, January 3 and 4
Clem L. Hensler, February 17 to March 13
Everett E. Lucas, " "
Edward P. Martin, January 3 to March 7
Charles Masur, Jan. 3 to March 8
Charles B. Musgrave, Jan. 3 to March 13
Edward M. Powers " "
Alva H. Shipper, Jan. 3 and 4
Samuel L. Thornton, Jan. 3 to March 13
Thomas Wall, " "
Ludwig Weppler, " "
Adolph Wiessenberger, Feb. 2 to March 13
Lawrence W. Yeagler, January 3–29

Inasmuch as the Department of Justice has had a number of guards here during that period, the proportion of the expense to be charged to the Immigration Service employees must in fairness be reduced correspondingly, and I would say that a very fair estimate would be at least one-third of the time of this force was devoted exclusively in guarding those of the anarchistic type.

The above statement is not satisfactory to me but I trust it will be sufficient to act as a basis for computation. You will realize how utterly impossible it is for me to give you exact figures.

In addition to the above, Superintendent Baker probably gave one-half of his time to signing documents concerning or attending to witnesses who called on behalf of anarchistic aliens detained here. Some of my time was also devoted to this subject. Until you advise me just which of the employees named you conclude to place on a special pay-roll I shall not be able to have this done. In order that there may be no delay in the receipt of salaries due, I trust you will give me this information as quickly as you can, even though the actual appointments may be received somewhat later.

REFERENCE: Ellis Island employees file. Memorandum of Acting Commissioner Byron Uhl, April 1920. Ellis Island, NY: Statue of Liberty and Ellis Island Library.

Reed, David A. [David Aiken Reed] (b. Pittsburgh, Pennsylvania, December 21, 1880; d. Sarasota, Florida, February 10, 1953). Lawyer and politician; U.S. Senator (1922–1935; R-PA). Appointed to the Senate through the influence of financier Andrew Mellon, David Reed quickly emerged as a strong Republican isolationist, opposing both the League of Nations and U.S. diplomatic recognition of the Soviet Union. Most notably, he was a firm restrictionist in the congressional debate over immigration and led a bill through the Senate Immigration Committee and then the full Senate that was to form a part of the **Immigration Act of 1924** (Johnson-Reed Act). The Senate accepted Congressman **Albert Johnson**'s House version of the bill, which restricted immigration quotas to 2 percent of the 1890 census for each foreign nationality living in the country. Although this quota percentage was valid only through 1927, it was not overhauled until the National Origins Act was passed in 1929.

See also **Immigration Restriction League; Immigration Restriction Movement**

REFERENCE: Biographical Directory of the United States Congress. David Aiken Reed. Washington, DC: U.S. Government Printing Office. www.senate.gov/artandhistory/history/common/generic/Historical_Intro_Biographical_Directory.htm (accessed May 12, 2004).

Reentry Permits. Reentry permits were issued to aliens, allowing them to return to the United States after a period of absence abroad. In a story published on October 8, 1933, the *New York Times* described the permit and how it was administered at Ellis Island:

> More than 100 employees on the Island are clerical workers. Every alien here legally here who wishes to travel abroad must have a re-entry permit if he wishes to return; for those who arrived after 1924, application must be made to Washington direct. Each year more than 50,000 re-entry permits are issued. The clerks likewise make 20,000 verifications of landings and arrivals each month for naturalizations and other purposes. And they grant about 200 extensions monthly to visitors here on temporary permits. In the Great Halls where once aliens waited for the ferries to the mainland now stands case after case of immigrants' records. There are records of more than 20,000,000 individuals.

REFERENCE: *New York Times*. 1933. October 8.

Refugees. During Ellis Island's heyday (1892–1924) there was no pressing need to give special status to immigrants who were fleeing to the United States as refugees, since there were few restrictions on entering the country. However, the imposition of the **Immigration Act of 1924** blocked most refugees from legally entering the country just as totalitarianism and war spread in the 1930s and 1940s. Under President Harry S. Truman, Congress enacted the Displaced Persons Act to aid refugees in the aftermath of World War II. In the 1920s the League of Nations issued Nansen passports in an effort to aid stateless persons. These passports were accepted as valid by the U.S. government.

Registry Division. The Registry Division was responsible for admitting immigrants to the United States, a procedure known as **primary inspection**. It carried out this function from 1892 through 1924. The chief inspector of the division or his designated assistant distributed the manifest sheets containing the passengers' names among the inspectors. In the **Registry Room** some twenty **immigrant inspectors** stationed at registry desks interrogated long lines of aliens throughout the day. They were usually assisted by **interpreters** and occasionally **clerks**, who generally interrogated the aliens. Based on the answers, the inspector decided whether the alien was entitled to land. If he was satisfied, the alien was immediately admitted; if he was not, the alien was detained for special inquiry.

Around 1929, the Registry Division was renamed the Inspection Division. It was thought that the term "registry division" was more appropriate for the employees responsible for handling **certificates of registry.** The new Registry Division's clerks investigated certificate applications and interviewed applicants and their witnesses. The clerks of this division also interviewed aliens wishing to be repatriated to their homelands.

From the 1890s through the 1920s, the chief inspectors of the Registry Division included **John Lederhilger**, Vincent F. Jankovski, Michael F. Brophy, William C. Pearsall, and Edward D. Zucker.

See also **Appendix 1: Ellis Island: Its Organization and Some of Its Work**

Registry Room (Great Room), 1903. Courtesy of the Ellis Island Immigration Museum.

Registry Room. Also known as the **Great Hall**, the Registry Room was where the main examination of immigrants took place, which was called **primary inspection**. **Immigrant inspectors** of the **Registry Division** cross-questioned immigrants as to their admissibility, trying to discover if there were any doubts about their eligibility to land. Inspectors admitted most people during this phase of inspection; others they detained or excluded. All immigrants arriving at Ellis Island faced this scrutiny. For this reason the Registry Room was the most significant space on Ellis Island. It was also the largest room in the **Main Building**, measuring 200 feet in length, 100 feet in width, and 56 feet from floor to ceiling.

The room is a two-story barrel-vaulted space. The ceiling is covered with Guastavino tiles (1918), and three brass chandeliers with sectional white globes (1917–1918) are suspended from it. Magnificent semicircular windows provide openings in the north and south walls. This contributes to the overall effect of natural lighting. The floor is laid with Ludowici tiles (1918) in a herringbone pattern in imitation of the ceiling. At the perimeter of its upper level is a balcony that is part of the Main Building's third floor. The balcony's floor is paved with white ceramic tiles; the doors to the dormitory rooms were originally varnished wood but were replaced by sheet-metal doors (1908). The balcony's iron railing has plain balusters and a wooden handrail. The sheet-metal fascia below the railing is studded with electric lights (1911).

A staircase in the middle of the room (from the first floor) was constructed in 1900; it was removed in 1911 and replaced by a new staircase that was built at the east end of the room. In addition, the original iron railing for controlling immigrant crowds, which dated from 1900, was removed in 1911 and replaced by benches. In 1914, the room was decorated with American flags, plants, and pictures.

With the end of mass immigration in 1924, the Registry Room was changed completely. The Registry Division moved out and part of the room was taken over by the **Special Inquiry Division** and part was used for temporarily detained aliens. In addition, the west and south sides of the room were partitioned, the eastern staircase removed, and new toilets added in the general area it occupied.

In 1937, a new staircase in the eastern end of the room was built and some partitions removed. The former Registry Room now became the passenger hall and was used by detainees. During World War II, it was a dayroom for German enemy alien families. It continued as a dayroom for other detainees after the war.

REFERENCES: Chermayeff, Ivan, et al. 1991. *Ellis Island: An Illustrated History of the Immigrant Experience.* New York: Macmillan; Ehrenkrantz Group/Building Conservation Technology. 1978. *Historic Structures Report: Ellis Island.* New York; Unrau, Harlan D. 1984, *The Historic Resource Study: Ellis Island/Statue of Liberty.* Washington, DC: U.S. Department of Interior, National Park Service.

Registry Room Exhibit (C201). The **Registry Room**, which was the main inspection hall for immigrants, is a major part of the **Ellis Island Immigration Museum** and has been restored to the appearance it had between 1918 and 1924. The exhibit features a display of several original benches, the three original chandeliers (1918), and inspectors' desks copied from original designs. The floor and ceiling tiles are original. The ceiling and tiles, made by the Guastavino Company, are especially famous. The Registry Room was also called the **Great Hall** and the passenger hall.

See also **Guastavino, Rafael (I); Guastavino, Rafael (II)**

Registry Room Views (C302). This exhibition of the **Ellis Island Immigration Museum** is located on the balcony overlooking the **Registry Room**. The exhibit features waysides with historic photographs showing the many uses that the Registry Room was put to through the course of decades, including immigrant inspection, festivals, housing naval personnel in **World War I,** and serving as a dayroom for **enemy aliens** in **World War II**. Images also show it in its abandoned state in prior to its restoration.

Reimer, Rudolph (b. East New York district, Brooklyn, New York, September 30, 1875; d. Northport, New York, July 28, 1948). Commissioner of immigration, Ellis Island (1934–1940). A prominent New York Democrat, Rudolph Reimer was President Franklin Roosevelt's commissioner at Ellis Island. During his years at the station, Reimer was credited with modernizing the station and improving conditions among the immigrants there. He concluded his administration with a grand golden jubilee (fiftieth anniversary) celebration of Ellis Island's selection as the country's first federal immigrant control station on April 11, 1940. The event, which included speeches and saw the **ferryboat *Ellis Island*** decorated with bunting, was widely reported in the press. Reimer was the son of German immigrants and graduated from Brooklyn Polytechnic Institute as an engineer and began working in his father's successful coal business. He eventually became president of Brooklyn's Homestead Bank. Beginning in 1923, he began a career in public service that led to important positions in the Delaware River Water Resources Commission, the National Recovery Administration (1933), the New York Port Authority (1933–1943), and the New York Stock Exchange (1946–1947). He was a lifelong resident of Brooklyn.

REFERENCE: *New York Times.* 1948. R. Reimer, 72, dies; aided immigrants; former district commissioner at Ellis Island improved facilities—a civic leader. July 29.

Renkiewicz, Frank (b. New Jersey, 1935; d. New York, 1993). Historian. A respected scholar in Polish American studies, Frank Renkiewicz left academia for the National Park Service and became a historical interpreter at the newly opened **Ellis Island Immigration Museum** in 1990. He remained there until his untimely death. His books include *The Poles in America, 1608–1972* (1973) and *The Polish Presence in Canada and America* (1982). Following his death, his family donated his personal papers and archives to the Piast Institute in New York City.

Restoration. Greater public interest in Ellis Island as a memorial to immigrants emerged with public opposition to the federal government's attempts to sell the island on the open market between 1955 and 1960. Embarrassed by the criticism, officials in the **General Services Administration** unsuccessfully sought other ways of reusing the facility. Several people suggested possible uses for the island, including an immigrant museum.

After Ellis Island became a national monument in May 1965, the **National Park Service** (NPS) was stuck with decaying buildings and virtually no congressional funding. Secretary of the Interior Stewart L. Udall appointed architect **Philip Johnson** to oversee the redevelopment of the island. Johnson suggested razing most of the island's old buildings and creating an expensive park in their place, and erecting the Wall of 16 Million, a memorial to the immigrants who passed through. After lukewarm reviews from the public, the NPS soon dispensed with his services. **Thomas M. Pitkin**, the historian at the monument, wrote an important historic report on Ellis Island in 1966, and in 1968 the NPS issued a master plan for Ellis Island.

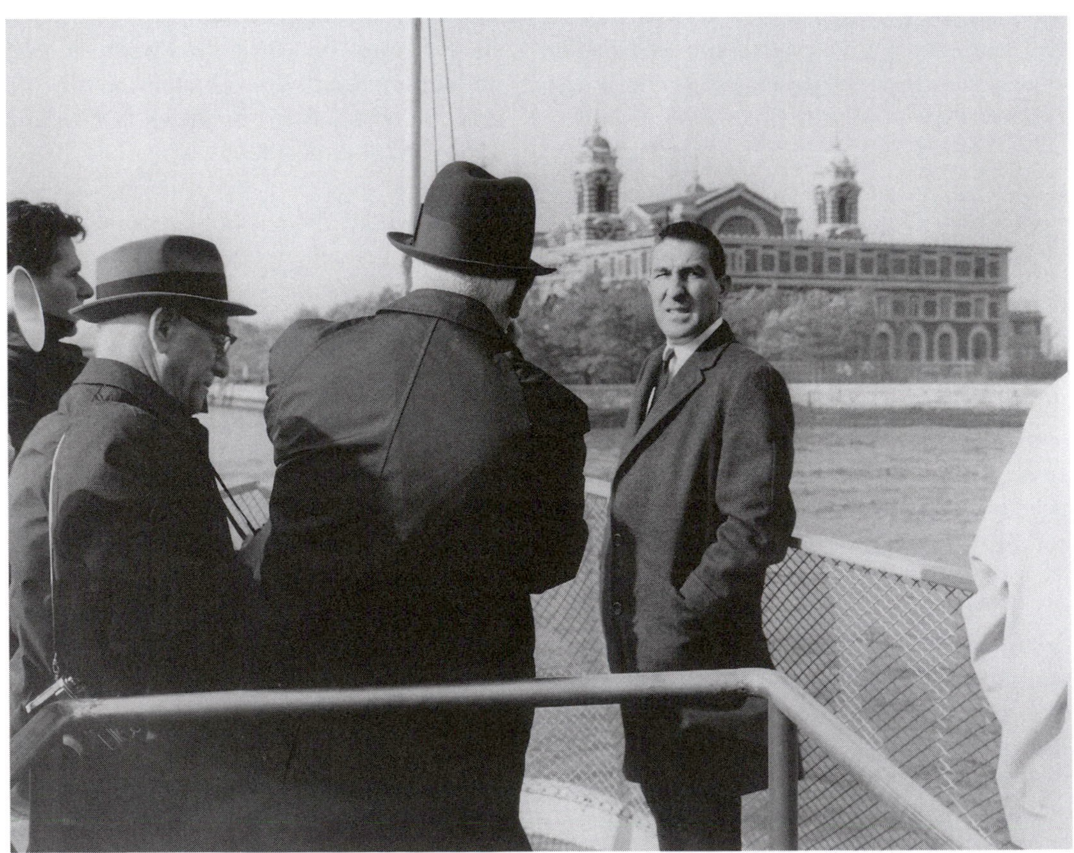

Secretary of the Interior Stewart Udall visits Ellis Island to assess conditions, ca 1967. The restoration of the site did not begin until the Reagan administration in the 1980s.
Courtesy of the Ellis Island Immigration Museum.

Scaffolding in the Registry Room, ca. 1985. Courtesy of the Ellis Island Immigration Museum.

Park Service professionals, including architects, landscape architects, historians, and museum technicians, prepared the master plan. Many of Johnson's ideas were present in the plan, for it included demolishing nearly all of the historic buildings (the **Main Building** was to be spared) and creating a parklike atmosphere with a piazza and plants. The idea was to encourage visitors to stroll and lunch and view the harbor. It was believed that this would be more "inspirational" to them than the island's only real claim to distinction—its buildings.

No action was taken on this proposal either and, meanwhile, as a fantastic symbol of the government's neglect of the monument, the famed **ferryboat *Ellis Island*** sank in its berth on the weekend of August 10–11, 1968. Nonetheless, the master plan was approved and adopted by the NPS in November 1968, but no money came and nothing further was done.

In 1973, **Peter Sammartino**, a retired university chancellor, became interested in the neglected island. In October 1974, he was instrumental in creating the Restore Ellis Island Committee in New Jersey. The committee's goal was to stabilize the old immigration buildings. Through his efforts, volunteers helped the NPS remove more than 40,000 bags of debris from Ellis Island. In 1976, Congress appropriated funds to pay for some maintenance work, and consequently the NPS opened **Island 1** to visitors in May 1976.

In 1977, in spite of carrying out minor improvements such as dredging, the Park Service stood by its position of destroying the majority of the island's buildings.

In December 1980, Secretary of the Interior Cecil Andrus signed an agreement with New Jersey businessman Philip Lax, president of the Ellis Island Restoration Commission, to raise funds through private donations for the restoration of the island. This effort did not meet with success.

The true restoration of Ellis Island began in 1982, when President **Ronald Reagan** appointed Lee A. Iacocca to raise funds in a campaign that included the Statue of Liberty. Subsequently, the **Statue of Liberty–Ellis Island Foundation**, headed by Iacocca, raised millions through a national advertising campaign that brought Ellis Island to the attention of the general public.

In 1982, the NPS issued an interpretive prospectus outlining possible interpretive themes for Ellis Island. These included the immigrant experience at Ellis Island; the story of immigration to the United States; a study of American immigration policy; and the physical development of Ellis Island in the nineteenth and twentieth centuries. This strengthened the resolve to build an immigrant museum in the Main Building and became a key goal of the restoration.

With financial support from the foundation, the Park Service was able to hire a firm to rehabilitate the interior and exterior of the Main Building in 1984. Thus the Ehrenkrantz Group launched the costliest restoration of a historic site in history. Several more contractors were engaged in the restoration project, including the architectural firms of Beyer, Blinder Belle and Notter, Finegold. Island 1 was landscaped, facilities were improved, and a new **canopy** was erected at the entrance to the Main Building. In addition, the **power house** was rehabilitated and put back into use. The NPS was given permission to raze the incinerator and greenhouse, both derelict structures. The two old water towers and the incinerator building were also demolished, and a new water tower was constructed. Meanwhile, park administrative offices (including Museum Services Division) were moved from the **kitchen and laundry building** to the **hospital administration building**. In 1989, permission was granted to the Statue of Liberty–Ellis Island Foundation to build an American Immigrant Wall of Honor along the seawall, just east of the Main Building.

In 1990, **MetaForm,** an exhibit design firm, began installing the exhibits in the Main Building. The **Ellis Island Immigration Museum** was finally dedicated in September 1990. The kitchen and laundry building and the **bakery and carpentry shop** were rehabilitated for use in 1994. The only structure on Island 1 that has yet to be rehabilitated is the **baggage and dormitory building**.

During 1999 and 2002, the buildings on Islands 2 and 3 underwent **stabilization** and plans are under way to restore them completely. The **ferry house** was also stabilized and rehabilitated and was opened to public visitation in 2004.

See also **Save Ellis Island!**

REFERENCES: Stakely, J. Tracy. 2002. *Cultural Landscape Report for Ellis Island: Site History.* National Park Service; Unrau, Harlan D. 1984. *The Historic Resource Study: Ellis Island/Statue of Liberty.* 3 vols. Washington, DC: U.S. Department of Interior, National Park Service.

Roosevelt, Eleanor (b. New York, October 11, 1884; d. New York, November 7, 1962). First Lady to New York State (1929–1933) and the United States (1933–1945). Eleanor Roosevelt, wife of Governor and then President Franklin D. Roosevelt, visited Ellis Island on the morning of December 13, 1932, with a group of girls from the Todhunter School and the Junior League, where she occasionally lectured. They were received by Commissioner **Edward Corsi**, and then Inspector Charles W. Bryant gave them a tour of the facility, most notably the **Main Building** and the physical therapy department run by the **Daughters of the American Revolution**. Then came a lively discussion with Commissioner Corsi in his office about the treatment of communists, the effect of quota laws on immigration at Ellis

Island, the pursuit and capture of illegal aliens, and the legal technicalities that led to their detention.

REFERENCE: *New York Times.* 1932. Mrs. Roosevelt takes students to Ellis Island: Aliens display handiwork for future "First Lady" and her civics class. December 14.

Roosevelt, Theodore (b. New York, October 27, 1858; d. Oyster Bay, New York, January 6, 1919). President of the United States (1901–1909). President Theodore Roosevelt took a great interest in events on Ellis Island and launched investigations that helped remove corrupt officials from the scandal-ridden station. Appointing **William Williams** as the reform commissioner for the station was a stroke of genius. Williams not only proved fully up to the task but also succeeded in introducing strict procedures for each employee and each division, ending the carelessness and capriciousness that had previously been the norm. The president visited the station and was deeply conscious of the masses of immigrants entering at Ellis Island and was uneasy of what he thought it might bode for America.

In 1905, President Roosevelt lost Williams in a dispute over the appointment of Assistant Commissioner **Joseph E. Murray**, one of the president's oldest friends. Williams considered Murray incompetent and worse than useless as his deputy. When Roosevelt insisted that Murray would stay on, Williams resigned. The up-and-coming **Robert Watchorn** replaced him as commissioner. Although Watchorn was not as strong an administrator as Williams, he was able to handle the task and win a measure of popularity as well.

On February 14, 1903, the president placed the **Bureau of Immigration** under the newly created Department of Commerce and Labor. Years later, Theodore Roosevelt's cousin, President Franklin D. Roosevelt (1933–1945), established the **Immigration and Naturalization Service** and, in 1940, transferred that agency to the Department of Justice.

S

Safford, Victor [Moses Victor Safford] (b. 1867; d. 1947). Physician and surgeon, Ellis Island (1895–1905). Victor Safford was a prominent medical officer at Ellis Island in its early years. He was involved in the development of **line inspection** and coauthored the *Dictionary of Races*, used at Ellis Island and at other inspection stations of the **Bureau of Immigration**. His views on identifying heart disease, infections, and loathsome diseases, as well as identifying immigrants' race for statistical purposes, remained influential for years. After leaving Ellis Island, he spent many years at the **Boston Immigrant Inspection Station**.

REFERENCE: Safford, Victor. 1925. Immigration Problems: Personal Experiences of an Official. New York: Dodd, Mead.

St. Joseph's Home for Polish Immigrants. Polish priests in New York founded the St. Joseph's Home in 1893. Priests and agents from the home went regularly to Ellis Island to aid the thousands of Poles arriving. St. Joseph's Home, located at 17 Broad Street, provided free lodging to the immigrants and was maintained by the Felician Sisters. It was financed by donors and received an annual stipend of $1,000 from the Austro-Hungarian government on account of the Galician Poles who often received accommodations there. During the height of immigration, Father Joseph L'Etauche served as the chaplain.

See also **Immigrant Aid Societies; Missionaries**

St. Raphael Society for the Protection of German Immigrants. Also known as the Sankt Raphaelsverein, the society was founded in 1882 and its immigrant home, the Leo House, was opened in 1889. The Sisters of St. Agnes had charge of the Leo House, which was the residence of the chaplain and priests who aided German Catholics arriving at Ellis Island. With the decline of German immigration by 1900, the priests began to help Catholic immigrants from France, Poland, Slovakia, Bohemia, as well as other Slavic Catholics of the Austro-Hungarian monarchy. The society maintained agents in Bremen, Hamburg, Rotterdam, Antwerp, Le Havre, Liverpool, and London.

See also **Immigrant Aid Societies; Missionaries**

St. Raphael Society for the Protection of Italian Immigrants. This was one of the most important immigrant aid societies at Ellis Island and it was present during the height of Italian immigration, from the 1890s through the beginning of **World War I**. It was sponsored by the Roman Catholic Church and was so influential that the Duke of Abruzzi, brother to King Victor Emmanuel III of Italy, visited Ellis Island in 1904 to see how Italians were being treated there. Adolfo Rossi, the prominent Italian emigration commissioner, also inspected conditions and the work of the society at Ellis Island. The society also helped Italians in New York's Little Italy and other Italian communities in the United States. Many priests of the society went to Ellis Island regularly, including Father Pietro Bandini, Father Antonio Demo, and Father **Gaspare Moretti**. The New York branch of this society was active from 1891 through 1923. Its home was managed by the Sisters of Charity (Pallottine) and was located at 8–10 Charlton Street. Only women and children were permitted to lodge there; though given meals and advice, immigrant men were lodged elsewhere.

See also **Immigrant Aid Societies; Italian Welfare League; Missionaries**

Salmon, Thomas W. [Thomas William Salmon] (b. Lansingburgh, New York, January 6, 1876; d. Long Island Sound, New York, August 13, 1927). Psychiatrist; surgeon at Ellis Island (1903–1908). Thomas Salmon was involved in assessing mental defects among immigrants at Ellis Island and produced an influential work on feeblemindedness. In 1906, he was briefly suspended from duty for refusing to do **line inspection**, as it interfered with his mental examinations. Salmon also served as the director of psychiatry in the U.S. Army during World War I and studied cases of shell shock among British and American soldiers. He was called the "father of mental hygiene."

H. D. Geddings, assistant surgeon of the United States, made this report on Salmon in November 1906:

> Dr. Salmon . . . was never instructed to pursue the alienist examinations to the slighting of the line inspection work. He feels aggrieved, maintains that full justice has not been done to him and talks of appealing the matter to higher authority, even to the President. To this end he has enlisted the aid of friends in prominent places, these friends not always the allies or well-wishers of the service, and to these individuals he has magnified the importance of the alienist examinations. . . . It is more than a matter of suspicion that he has formed these alliances with a view to personal, future aggrandizement, and it is my honest conviction that he has outlived any usefulness which he may ever have had at the immigration station at Ellis Island.

In May 1907, Geddings made a return inspection of the hospital service at Ellis Island and included these remarks about Salmon:

> I regret to have to report that since my last visit, Assistant Surgeon Salmon seems to have received the support of another commissioned officer, Assistant Surgeon H.D. Long. . . . The attitude of this latter officer is far from satisfactory. With abilities of more than the average order, with educational advantages . . . favored recently with a detail for special study at the Government Hospital for the Insane in Washington, this young officer appears to have entered into an alliance with Doctor Salmon. . . . In my own opinion, disciplinary measures of the severest character are needed in the case of this officer.

After leaving Ellis Island, Dr. Salmon quickly established himself as a leading psychiatrist, and his contributions to the field are still felt today. He drowned in a boating accident in 1927.

References: Geddings, H. D. *Report to the Surgeon General: Investigations of Medical Policies, Procedures, and Personnel Practices at Ellis Island, 1906 and 1907*; Salmon, Thomas W. 1913. *The Prevention of Mental Diseases*. New York: Appleton; Salmon, T. W. 1905. *The Diagnosis of Insanity in Immigrants*. Public Health Service Report; Salmon, T. W. 1913. Immigration and the Mixture of Races in Relation to the Public Health of the Nation. In *Modern Treatment of Nervous and Mental Diseases*, White and Jeliffe, Philadelphia: Lea & Febiger.

Salvation Army. The Salvation Army, an international Christian charitable organization that was founded in England in 1878, sent missionaries to New York as early as 1880 to aid alcoholics, "fallen women" (i.e., prostitutes), and the poor. Its attention was immediately drawn to the masses of impoverished immigrants living in ghettoes and slums in New York, Chicago, and cities across the country. **Missionaries** were sent to Ellis Island before 1910 to help newcomers. Missionaries included Colonel Helen R. Bastedo, Fritz Nelson, Amelia Fuhr, Katherine Woloschat, a Russian interpreter, and Brigadier General Thomas Johnson.

Sammartino, Peter (b. August 15, 1904; d. Rutherford, New Jersey, March 29, 1992). Educator and author; founder and first chancellor of Fairleigh Dickinson University (1944–1968). In 1973, Peter Sammartino launched a campaign to clean up Ellis Island and open it to visitors. Thanks to the efforts of volunteers and a favorable response from the **National Park Service**, his effort met with success. In November 1975, Sammartino presided over a concert celebrating the reopening of the abandoned station. Entertainment for the occasion included opera singer Licia Albanese. The island opened to tourists in May 1976 and remained open until 1984. Sammartino was the founder and first president of the Restore Ellis Island Committee (1974–1978); Philip Lax, a New Jersey businessman, was elected to succeed him, and Lax renamed the organization the Ellis Island Restoration Commission. After Sammartino died, a plaque was mounted in his memory at the **Ellis Island Immigration Museum** in recognition of his unique role in helping bring about the eventual restoration of Ellis Island.

See also **Restoration**

REFERENCE: Bolino, August C. 1990. *The Ellis Island Source Book.* Washington, DC: Kensington Historical Press.

Sargent, Frank P. (b. East Orange, Vermont, 1854; d. Washington, DC, September 4, 1908). Commissioner-general of immigration (1902–1908). Appointed by President **Theodore Roosevelt** to replace **Terence Powderly**, Frank P. Sargent played an important role in the reform and administration at Ellis Island, working closely with his commissioners there, **William Williams** and **Robert Watchorn**. Along with William Williams, Sargent was a leading figure in President Roosevelt's team of reformers who targeted graft and corruption at the New York station. Sargent firmly backed Commissioner Williams as he rooted out bad employees at Ellis Island and cooperated closely with him in introducing reforms. In Washington, Sargent investigated the rising tide of immigrants and, with assistance from Williams, helped draft the **Immigration Act of 1903**, which expanded the types of immigrants who might be excluded; thus he proved to be a strict interpreter of the immigration laws of his time. In March 1904, his daughter christened the **ferryboat *Ellis Island***. Before heading the **Bureau of Immigration**, Sargent had served as the Grand Master of the Brotherhood of Locomotive Firemen; his caution in negotiations earned him the nickname Safety Valve.

REFERENCE: *New York Times.* 1908. Frank P. Sargent dead: Immigration commissioner, formerly head of the locomotive firemen. September 5.

Save Ellis Island! Save Ellis Island! is a New Jersey–based, national nonprofit organization working in partnership with the **National Park Service** (NPS) to raise funds for rehabilitating and restoring twenty-nine buildings on the south side and the **baggage and dormitory building** on the north side of Ellis Island. In February 2001, the organization entered into an agreement with the NPS for the purpose of coordinating fund-raising activities to benefit the Statue of Liberty National Monument and Ellis Island, a unit of the National Park system. As a part of this agreement, the NPS agrees to recognize Save Ellis Island! as the primary organization raising funds for the preservation, rehabilitation, and enhancement of the south side of Ellis Island. For its part, Save Ellis Island! promises to conduct major fund-raising campaigns to benefit the rehabilitation and eventual reuse of Ellis Island.

See also **Stabilization**

Schooling. The Congregational Church and immigrant aid societies, usually in cooperation, operated nonsectarian schools for detained immigrant children at Ellis Island over the years, especially from 1915 through 1954. The schools were purely voluntary. Every weekday morning and afternoon, the head teacher or her assistant would walk through the detention dayrooms and organize lines of children who wished to attend the school. **Bertha M. Boody** studied the operation in 1922 and wrote:

> The "Head" of the school is from then on responsible until the children are returned at the end of the session. It must be remembered that care must be taken in keeping record of the whereabouts of each immigrant. From the locked gate leading out of the detention rooms, the children are taken up a flight of stairs to the school with its invigorating roof playground. In this was done the psychological testing. . . . It is most interesting to watch at work a group composed of an Arab, a Greek, a Welsh boy, an Armenian and a Russian. The members of such a group do not talk to each other; but they laugh

Children exercise in the schoolroom, 1921. Courtesy of the Ellis Island Immigration Museum.

together and spur each other on. . . . The selection of nationalities and races depended on who happens to be in the detention rooms and on who wanted to come to school. Older girls came sometimes; at others, they preferred to stay in the detention rooms to sew. Older boys, too, came once in a while; but in general they do not come. Children from ten to fourteen predominated. . . . Sometimes [certain] nationalities almost never appear in the school. Practically no Scandinavians . . . yet many pass through Ellis Island.

As to the children who did come to the school, there were many reasons why they were being held. They might be waiting for some member of the family to be discharged from the hospital. They might be waiting for money or for a father to come from Chicago or for legal reasons. . . . Then, of course . . . the children from the Special Inquiry rooms whose cases were pending, were allowed to come to the school, and often the "deports," who were waiting for a ship to carry them back over the ocean again. (pp. 103–104)

Boody encountered the following nationalities in the school: Italians, Poles, Germans, Russians, French, Armenians, Spaniards, Hungarians, Jugoslavs, Welsh, Swedes, Danes, Greeks, Swiss, Albanians, Chinese, Belgians, Lithuanians, Czechs, Slovaks, English, Scots, Irish, Arabs, and Dutch and West Indians of African ancestry (Jamaicans, etc.) whom she identified as "colored from the English Islands." Further, she noted that the various Jews in the schoolroom might come from different countries: Russia, Poland, Germany, England, Scotland, Egypt, and Turkey.

Aside from occasional psychological testing, the children played games, did arts and crafts projects, exercised, read books, sang, drew pictures, learned English and also learned about Ellis Island, what it was and why the immigrant station was there. They also learned about the United States, its symbols, states, cities, geography, and government. The schools continued to the 1950s. On May 22, 1951, a new schoolroom for detained children was officially opened. Prior

Time was spent reading, writing, drawing, and exercising in the old Ellis Island schoolroom. Maltese immigrants are among this group, 1920s. Courtesy of the Ellis Island Immigration Museum.

to 1914, there were no formally organized schools at Ellis Island due to heavy immigration and overcrowding.

REFERENCE: Boody, Bertha M. 1926. *A Psychological Study of Immigrant Children at Ellis Island*. Baltimore: Williams & Walker.

Second Immigrant Station. The second immigrant station comprises the majority of buildings on Ellis Island today. They include the **Main Building**, the **baggage and dormitory building**, the **kitchen and laundry building**, the **bakery and carpentry shop**, the **ferry house**, the new immigration building, the **hospital buildings**, and the **contagious disease wards**.

The supervising architect of the Department of the Treasury designed all of the buildings of the **first immigrant station**. But in 1897 a decision was made to permit a private firm of architects to design the second immigrant station. This innovation was allowed under the newly passed **Tarsney Act of 1893**. Under its provisions Treasury accepted competitive designs from six architectural firms: Alfred E. Barlow, Boring and Tilton, Carrère and Hastings, McKim, Mead and White, and Bruce Price, all of New York City; and John L. Smithmeyer of Washington, DC.

William A. Boring and **Edward L. Tilton** won the competition and designed the chief structures on Island 1: the Main Building, kitchen and laundry building, power house, a corridor, a covered way, and an incinerator; on Island 2 they designed the **general hospital**.

Semsey, Charles [Kalman Semsey] (b. Bartfa, Hungary, 1829; d. New York, June 18, 1911). Immigrant inspector (1892–1911). Immigrated to the United States in 1852. Served in the U.S. Army from 1861 to 1862 (major, 45th New York Infantry) and fought in Virginia. Charles Semsey was employed in the U.S. Customs Service and then with the New York State Emigration Commission as registry clerk (Landing Bureau) at **Castle Garden** until the depot closed in April 1890. Subsequently Semsey was hired as an assistant inspector and registry clerk at Ellis Island. He was transferred to the **Special Inquiry Division**, where one of his cases involved the famous American Theosophical leader Katherine A. Tingley (1847–1929). In November 1902, Gertrude van Pelt brought eleven Cuban boys and girls (aged 8 to 12) to the United States to attend Tingley's Raja-Yoga School of the Universal Brotherhood at Point Loma, near San Diego, California. Prompted by the Society for the Prevention of Cruelty to Children, **immigrant inspectors** detained them at Ellis Island on suspicion that the school was not a fit place for the children. On November 3, Semsey's board of special inquiry, which was handling the case, voted to exclude the children and return them to Cuba. However, Commissioner **William Williams** referred the matter to Washington, and on December 6, the Department of the Treasury ordered the children released.

Semsey was a member of a distinguished family that included the Hungarian nobleman Andor von Semsey, for whom the mineral semseyite was named.

REFERENCE: Beszedits, Stephen. 2004. The life and times of Charles Semsey. Toronto, Canada. Ellis Island, NY: Statue of Liberty and Ellis Island Library.

Senner, Joseph H. [Josef Heinrich Senner] (b. Austria, September 30, 1846; d. New York, September 28, 1908). Commissioner of immigration, Ellis Island (1893–1897).

Senner was educated at the University of Vienna (1867). He practiced law in Brunn until 1880, when he accepted the appointment of foreign correspondent in New York City for various Austrian and German newspapers. He was on the staff of the *New Yorker Staats-Zeitung* (1881–1882) and then served as editor of the *Milwaukee Herald* and became a noted supporter of the Democratic Party, which eventually earned his appointment at Ellis Island.

During his term of office, Commissioner Senner witnessed growing eastern and southern European immigration to the United States and discovered the structural inadequacies of the new station. He had trouble with Italian immigrants who disliked his tactic of locking them in outdoor pens and his policy of deporting anyone who seemed to be penniless. In spite of these confrontations, Senner was interested in the Italians and why so many were coming to America. He wrote an article on this subject for the *North American Review*. He also wrote about the parliamentary elections in Germany for the same publication. His assistant commissioner was **Edward F. McSweeney**.

Senner was not pleased with the quality of the employees under him and petitioned Washington to put the **Bureau of Immigration** under Civil Service certification regulations. This would require that employees take a Civil Service Commission examination before being appointed to their positions. President Grover Cleveland granted the request in 1896, although incumbents were exempted from taking the examinations.

In June 1897, just before the end of his term of office, the Ellis Island station burned to the ground. From 1897 until his death, he owned and published the *National Provisioner*, a journal dedicated to the meat and grocers trade. Senner also gained influence through his service at various times as president of the German Social Scientific Society, the National Organization of German-American Journalists, and the Austrian Society. He died of apoplexy in his office at 116 Nassau Street, in Lower Manhattan.

REFERENCE: *New York Times*. 1908. Joseph Henry Senner. Obituary. September 29.

Sherman, Augustus F. [Augustus Frederick Sherman] (b. Lynn, Susquehanna County, Pennsylvania July 9, 1865; d. New York, February 16, 1925). Clerk (1890s); senior clerk (1898–1909); chief clerk, (1909–1921); confidential secretary to the commissioner (1921–1925); photographer (1900–1925). Augustus F.

Sherman moved to New York City in 1884 and settled permanently in Greenwich Village by 1888. Clerking was the work he followed throughout his long career. At Ellis Island, Sherman was engaged as a clerk but was soon promoted to senior clerk and then chief clerk of the station. He always worked in the Executive Division and the office of the commissioner. His duties as chief clerk included supervising all clerks, stenographers, typists, bookkeepers, the Law Division, and appeals against Special Inquiry exclusion orders that were sent to the commissioner. In April 1910, Sherman's immediate staff consisted of fourteen employees, including assistant chief clerk Paul F. Morrisson, bookkeeper Frederick L. Budde, and typist Emma B. Oosterhoudt.

Sherman is famous for his photographs. The National Park Service has 204 of his pictures in its collection. The images are a combination of portraits of individual immigrants taken as bust shots and full-figure shots; others are group shots. In addition, there are shots of oddities, including "circus freaks," tattooed stowaways, and strongmen. The people photographed are of many nationalities: African, Albanian, Arab, Belgian, Canadian, Chinese, Danish, Dutch, English, Finnish, French, Indian, Italian, German, Guadeloupan, Greek, Gypsy, Hungarian, Jewish, Montenegrin, Polish, Romanian, Russian, Ruthenian, Scottish, Swedish, Turkish, and Wallachian. Some of the sitters are of unknown nationality.

Sherman resided on Bank Street in Greenwich Village, Manhattan. He died unexpectedly in 1925, and his funeral at Grace Episcopal Church (Broadway and 12th Street) was attended by hundreds of immigration employees, including Commissioner **Henry H. Curran**.

Silent Voices (Rooms E313 and E314). This exhibition of the **Ellis Island Immigration Museum** is located on the third floor of the east wing of the **Main Building** and features artifacts found on Ellis Island long after its closing as immigrant station. The items, which are in exhibition cases, include an upright piano, a notice board with instructions in several languages, a stretcher for patients, a medicine cabinet, and furniture.

Society for the Protection of Italian Immigrants. The Society for the Protection of Italian Immigrants was founded in 1901 by a number of wealthy American philanthropists led by Sarah Wool Moore. They were concerned about the plight of the increasing number of Italian peasants who arrived at Ellis Island, often in the tow of unscrupulous bosses called padrones. The society posted representatives to aid them at Ellis Island and remained active there until about 1920. In the early years of its existence, Eliot Norton served as president and Gino Speranza held the post of secretary. The organization was nonsectarian.

See also **Immigrant Aid Societies; Italian Welfare League; Saint Raphael Society for the Protection of Italian Immigrants**

Sovereignty. The landmark decision of the Supreme Court of the United States that assigned the sovereignty of the south side and other parts of Ellis Island to the state of New Jersey was proclaimed on May 26, 1998. Hitherto all 27.5 acres had officially belonged to the State of New York. New Jersey's legal right to all land-filled parts of Ellis Island is based on the Interstate Compact of 1834, in which both states agreed that Ellis Island, then 3.5 acres, and Bedloe's Island, then 10 acres, belonged to the state of New York; the submerged land surrounding the two belonged to the State of New Jersey. Thus all subsequent **landfill** operations enlarging the island became a part of New Jersey. This affects the **Islands 2** and **3** in toto, and a portion of **Island 1**.

The **jurisdiction** of Ellis Island is still held by the federal government.

Special Inquiry Division. This division was created after Congress passed the **Immigration Act of 1893 (II)**. Inspectors of the Special Inquiry Division were engaged in perhaps the most difficult work at Ellis Island and the **Bureau of Immigration** as a whole: they decided problem cases often resulting in exclusion or deportation of aliens seeking to enter the United States or those accused of violating the nation's immigration laws. The division's **immigrant inspectors** were assigned to **boards of special inquiry** and entrusted with great authority. Foreigners sent to the boards included those that were deemed **liable to become public charges**, as well as **anarchists**, criminals, unescorted women, **children**, the **feebleminded**, senile persons, **stowaways**, workaways (passengers who paid their fare by working on board vessels), and **undocumented aliens**.

The Special Inquiry Division was supervised by a chief inspector and included a number of **clerks** as well as **interpreters**. As many as six hearing rooms, as well as offices and detention rooms, were allotted to the division.

In about 1929, the Special Inquiry Division was amalgamated with the **Registry Division** to become the **Inspection Division**.

Special Inspector. The Sundry Civil Act (June 6, 1900; 31 Statute 588, 611) created a special inspector who was detailed in the office of the commissioner general in the **Bureau of Immigration** in Washington, DC. His duties included enforcing the Chinese Exclusion Act and other exclusions of the U.S. government. He was given great authority to investigate a variety of cases. Roger O'Donnell was the first special inspector of the Bureau of Immigration and investigated and resolved many unusual cases at Ellis Island.

See also **Crime and Abuse; Investigations**

Sprague, E. K. [Ezra Kimball Sprague] (b. Milo, Maine, 1866; d. Brooklyn, New York, February 2, 1943). Chief medical officer, Ellis Island (1925–28). E. K. Sprague entered the **Marine Hospital Service** as a surgeon in 1890 after graduating from Bates College. During a long career in public medicine, he worked in many parts of the world, including Calcutta, India, where he studied bubonic plague. After leaving service at Ellis Island, he was promoted to the post of director of the North Atlantic District of the **Public Health Service**. He served in this position until he retired in 1932 with the rank of colonel.

Squatters. After it was abandoned in 1955, Ellis Island attracted not only vandals but also squatters. In March 1970, eight Indians of various tribes unsuccessfully attempted to occupy the island. They left the Jersey City dock on a launch, but engine trouble prevented them from achieving their goal. In a press conference immediately afterward, they explained that they hoped to use Ellis Island as a cultural site for tribal activities and advancement, where young Indians could learn their own cultural life and values and reverse the white man's pollution of air, water, and land. Further, they envisioned a museum on an island that would show the damaging factors Europeans brought to the Native Americans: disease, alcohol, and cultural desecration.

After this incident, the Coast Guard was ordered to protect the island and proclaimed a "zone of security" around it under the Espionage Act of 1917. Two patrol boats were stationed nearby. Trespassers could be imprisoned for as long as ten years. However, this did not prevent another group, **NEGRO**, from occupying the island in the summer of 1970. Eventually, NEGRO was a granted a permit to carry out various activities in the abandoned hospital buildings.

REFERENCE: Novotny, Ann. 1971. *Strangers at the Door.* Riverside, CT: Chatham; Unrau, Harlan D. 1984. *The Historic Resource Study: Ellis Island/ Statue of Liberty.* Vol. 3. Washington, DC: U.S. Department of Interior, National Park Service.

Stabilization. In 1998, the **National Park Service**, with the support of the Governor Christine Todd Whitman of New Jersey, received $8.6 million to complete a stabilization plan for the hospital buildings on the south side of Ellis Island. Stabilization is a way of slowing down decay in a neglected structure until a complete restoration can be undertaken; the lack of funds compelled the National Park Service to take this step.

The first building to be stabilized was the laboratory building on **Island 3**. This was achieved as a pilot project by the New York Landmarks Conservancy and the National Park Service.

The full stabilization plan for Ellis Island is divided into three phases. In phase 1, the **ferry house** and the three general hospital buildings on **Island 2** were stabilized from November 1999 through the summer of 2001. In phase 2, the **psychopathic ward** and the **hospital outbuilding** and laundry on Island 2 were stabilized in 2001. In phase 3, the **contagious disease wards** and the **recreation hall** on Island 3 were stabilized in 2002. The **baggage and dormitory building** on **Island 1** still awaits stabilization. In 2003–2004, the ferry house was completely restored, and its exhibits were opened to the public in 2004. The fund-raising drive to preserve these historic buildings is currently being spearheaded by **Save Ellis Island!**, a nonprofit entity.

Stairs of Separation. The stairs of separation, located in the **Registry Room** of the **Main Building**, is a wide staircase with three lanes down divided by railings. Each stairway led to a different place for the immigrant. The stairs to the right led to the railroad room (**railroad ticket office**), where immigrants could obtain their train tickets and go the railroad dock behind the building to take a boat to the New Jersey Central Railroad terminal in Jersey City. The middle stairway led to the **New York room** for immigrants detained temporarily pending the arrival of family members or friends. The stairway to the left turn was for immigrants who were to take the **ferryboat *Ellis Island*** to Manhattan. The stairs of separation also split up those who had taken passage together aboard the same steamship from a foreign port: friendships struck up at sea often ended abruptly as some walked out to the Ellis Island ferry, another to the railroad room, another to be held in the New York detention room, and another to be sent to the **Special Inquiry** detention rooms just west of the Registry Room.

Statistical Division. The Statistical Division existed from as early as the opening of Ellis Island and its **chief inspector** and many **clerks** were engaged in keeping the tabulations of the hundreds of thousands of foreigners who were inspected at Ellis Island each year. The incoming and outgoing were counted each year. Foreigners leaving the country were required to be counted under the **Immigration Act of 1907**. The Statistical Division carried out this task.

In the late 1920s, the division was renamed the Record Division and, after 1950, it was renamed the Records Unit. The division was also responsible for verifying immigrants' earlier entry into the United States. Verifications were in great demand when aliens filed for naturalization after living in the country for the required number of years. Since most immigrants entered the country through Ellis Island, large numbers of applications were sent to the Statistical/Record Division from all over the nation. Clerks often had difficulty in finding the manifest sheets of immigrants due to inexact dates of entry, misspelled steamship names, and other confusing or inexact information submitted to their office. Sometimes it took months to find the correct record.

Statistics. *See* **Immigration Statistics; Races and Peoples**

Statue of Liberty. The Statue of Liberty, officially called *Liberty Enlightening the World*, is a 151-foot-tall copper statue of the ancient Roman goddess Libertas. She symbolizes freedom from servitude and oppression, friendship between France and the United States (dating from the American War of Independence), independence from England, and American democracy. The goddess holds aloft a torch to enlighten the world with freedom and wears a nimbus, symbolizing her power.

The Statue of Liberty was given to the United States by the people of France on July 4, 1884, in a Parisian ceremony. It was then shipped to New York and reassembled atop a pedestal within the walls of Fort Wood on Bedloe's Island (now Liberty Island) and unveiled to the American people on October 28, 1886. Although not intended to symbolize immigration, the magnificent statue impressed the millions pouring in from Europe and other parts of the world for decades and symbolized their hopes and dreams for a new life in the New World.

In 1883, American poet Emma Lazarus composed a sonnet called "The New Colossus," which proclaimed Liberty Enlightening the World the "Mother of Exiles." A French intellectual, Edouard de Labouleye, and a French sculptor, Frédéric-Auguste Bartholdi, created the Statue of Liberty. President Calvin Coolidge declared it a **national monument** in 1924.

REFERENCE: Moreno, Barry. 2000. *The Statue of Liberty Encyclopedia.* New York: Simon & Schuster.

Statue of Liberty–Ellis Island Foundation. Founded by Richard Rovsek in 1981, the Statue of Liberty–Ellis Island Foundation has been the principal fund-raiser for the restoration for both monuments since 1982. On May 18, 1982, President Ronald Reagan appointed Lee A. Iacocca chairman of the Statue of Liberty Centennial Commission. Iacocca then launched one of the most successful private fund-raising campaigns in American history, enabling the Statue of Liberty to be completely restored and reopened in time for her centennial in 1986, and Ellis Island's **Main Building** to be completely rehabilitated and opened to the public as the **Ellis Island Immigration Museum** in 1990. By 2001, the foundation had raised over $500 million. Since then, it has taken further steps in the direction of memorializing Ellis Island's history. In 1990, it established the American Immigrant Wall of Honor, and in 2001 it opened the **American Family Immigration History Center**, which has a database of the 22 million passengers who entered the Port of New York between 1892 and 1924.

The foundation is working on a project with the **National Park Service** to expand the Ellis Island museum with new exhibits in the **kitchen and laundry building**.

Key executives of the foundation include Lee Iacocca (chairman emeritus), William May (chairman), Steven Briganti (president), Gary Kelley (treasurer), and Peg Zitko (public relations director).

Steamship Companies. Several steamship companies were leaders in bringing emigrant passengers to the United States. The huge traffic in this emigration was exceedingly profitable for them and they took steps to protect and promote it. These included lowering the price of tickets and expanding steamship service by adding more ships at all the major ports of Europe. Growing Italian emigration encouraged the North German Lloyd Line and some other companies to assign older ships to ply the Italian ports of Naples, Genoa, and Palermo, while increasing Slavic and Jewish emigration made the Hamburg Amerika Line and the North German Lloyd Line cooperate with railway companies in order to transport these emigrants to German ports.

The companies attracted Europeans and others to the idea of emigrating through the agents they sent everywhere. These officials worked on commission and drummed up interest in emigrating through their continual visits to villages and towns. Steamship publications also spread the glories of the New World and were read avidly.

To comply with the strict enforcement of U.S. immigration laws that began in the 1890s, the steamship companies instituted medical inspections and deloused emigrant passengers

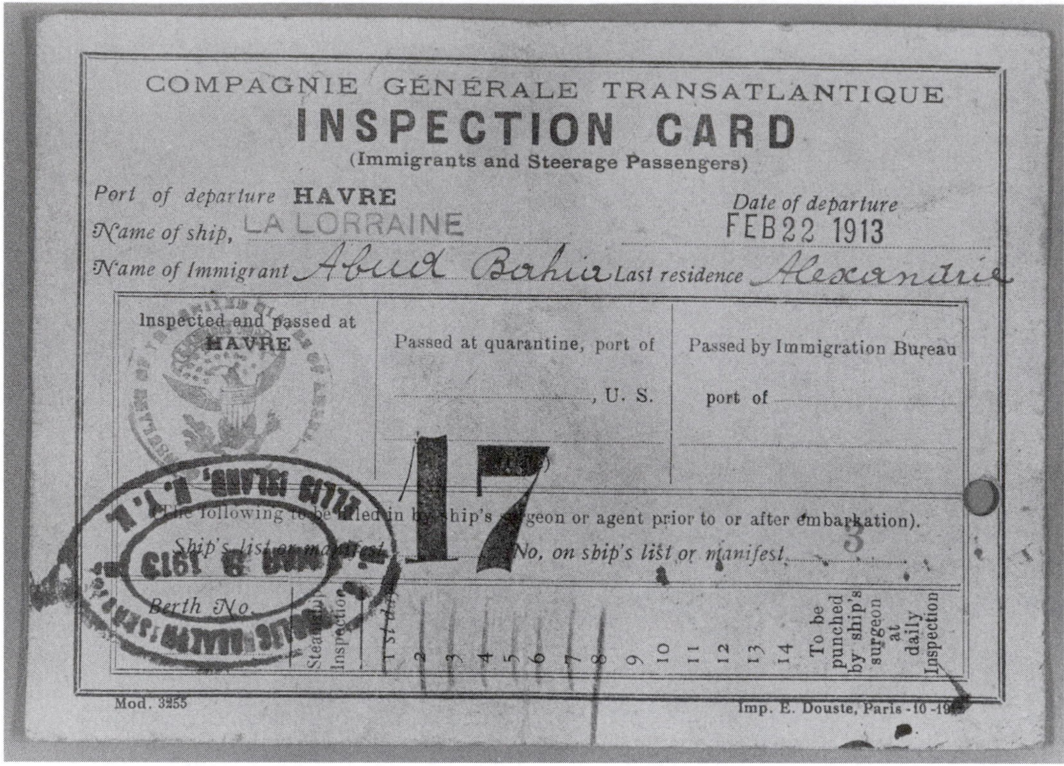
COMPAGNIE GÉNÉRALE TRANSATLANTIQUE

INSPECTION CARD

(Immigrants and Steerage Passengers)

Port of departure HAVRE *Date of departure* FEB 22 1913

Name of ship, LA LORRAINE

Name of Immigrant Abud Bahia *Last residence* Alexandria

Inspected and passed at HAVRE	Passed at quarantine, port of ......, U. S.	Passed by Immigration Bureau port of ......

17

(The following to be filled in by ship's surgeon or agent prior to or after embarkation).

Ship's list or manifest ...... *No. on ship's list or manifest* 3

Berth No.

Steamship | Inspection | 1 | 2 | 3 | 4 | 5 | 6 | 7 | 8 | 9 | 10 | 11 | 12 | 13 | 14 | To be punched by ship's surgeon at daily Inspection

Mod. 3255

Imp. E. Douste, Paris-10-19..

Inspection card for immigrant embarking at Le Havre, France. The ship's surgeon was required to inspect each immigrant daily and punch the card. Courtesy of the Ellis Island Immigration Museum.

before they were permitted to embark. The Germans were especially impressed with the American insistence on hygiene and sanitation and they were often enthusiastic in introducing strict medical examinations. Nonetheless, financial considerations prevented the companies from improving hygienic conditions in the **steerage** accommodations they offered.

The major steamship companies of the day included the Cunard Line, the White Star Line, and the Anchor Line from Great Britain; the North German Lloyd Line (Bremerhaven) and the Hamburg Amerika Line from Germany; the Holland-America Line from The Netherlands; the Red Star Line from Belgium; the Compagnie Transatlantique Générale and Fabre Line from France; the Navigazione Generale Italiana and the La Veloce Line, the Italia Line and the Sicula-American Line (Sicily) from Italy; the Russian East Asiatic Line (Libau) and the Russian Volunteer Fleet (Libau) from Russia; the Austro-American Line (Triest) from Austria-Hungary; the Greek Line (Piraeus) and the Prince Line from Greece; and the Scandinavian-American Line (Copenhagen) from Denmark.

Several other steamship lines were also active during the heyday of immigration. These included the American Line (Southampton, England), the Guion Line, the Spanish Line, the Ward Line, the Scandia Line (Gothenburg, Sweden), Lloyd Italiano, and the Allan Line (Glasgow). After the end of mass migration, the steamship lines switched to world cruising for tourists and cargo shipping.

Steamship Emigration Agents. Steamship agents were primarily salesmen selling steamship tickets on commission to emigrants. Throughout Europe the traveling agents or subagents, as they were more often known, attracted willing audiences to listen to their persuasive pitch about emigrating aboard their company's steamers. Moreover, they were often armed with colorful brochures or interesting leaflets that they distributed to interested persons. They typically received a deposit from clients who paid the balance of the fare when they signed and received an emigration contract (which commonly served as steamship tickets) from a head agent at the steamship a commission of 5 percent or slightly more on each sale. The **steamship companies** also kept representatives on Ellis Island. Known as landing agents, their task was to sort out problem immigrant cases and conflicts with the U.S. immigration authorities, especially the commissioner. They were assigned offices on the first floor of the **Main Building**.

Steamships. The leading ships from 1900 to 1914 included the following:

Cunard Line: (Liverpool and Queenstown) *Carmania*, *Caronia*, *Carpathia*, *Etruria*, *Lucania*, and the *Lusitania* (Liverpool), and the *Slavonia* (Fiume, Triest, and Naples).

White Star Line: (all sailing from Liverpool and Queenstown) *Adriatic*, *Baltic*, *Cedric*, *Majestic*; *Celtic* (Southampton and Cherbourg); *Oceanic* (Southampton); *Cretic* and the *Republic* (Naples).

Anchor Line: (Glasgow) *California*, *Furnessia*; (Liverpool and Queenstown) *Campania*; (Naples and Palermo) *Perugia*.

North German Lloyd Line: (Bremerhaven) *Berlin*, *Bremen*, *Cassel*, *George Washington*, *Friedrich der Grosse*, *Gneisenau*, *Grosse Kurfuerst*, *Hanover*, *Kaiser Wilhelm*, *Kaiser Wilhelm der Grosse*, *Kaiser Wilhelm II*, *Kleist*, *Kronprinzessin Cecilie*, *Kronprinz Wilhelm*, *Neckar*, *Weimar*; (Genoa and Naples) *Koenig Albert*, *Koenigin Luise*.

Hamburg-Amerika Line: *Andalusia*, *Armenia*, *Barbarossa*, *Deutschland*, *Graf Waldersee*, *Imperator*, *Patricia*, *Pretoria*, and the *Victoria Luise*.

Holland-America Line: (Rotterdam; Boulogne) *Nieuw Amsterdam*, *Potsdam*, *Rotterdam*, and the *Ryndam*.

Red Star Line: (Antwerp; Dover) *Gothland*, *Lapland*, *Samland*, *Vaderland*, and the *Zeeland*.

Compagnie Transatlantique Générale: (Le Havre) *Californie*, *France*, *Hudson*, *La Bretagne*, *La Gascogne*, *La Lorraine*, *La Savoie*, *La Touraine*, *Niagara*, *Rochambeau*, and the *St. Laurent*.

Fabre Line: (Marseille) *Sant'Anna*; (Naples) *Madonna*, and the *Roma*.

Navigazione Generale Italiana: (Genoa) *Duca degli Abruzzi*; (Genova and Napoli) *Duca d'Aosta*; (Naples) *Il Piemonte*; (Naples and Palermo) *Lazio*.

La Veloce Line: (Napoli) *Brasile*, *Citta di Torino*, *Europa*, *Nord America*; (Naples and Palermo) *Italia*.

Italia Line: (Genoa, Naples, Palermo) *Ancona*, *Napoli*, and the *Taormina*.

Sicula-American Line: (Messina, Napoli and Palermo) *San Giorgio*; (Napoli) *San Giovanni*.

Russian East Asiatic Line: (Libau) Birma; (Libau and Rotterdam) *Korea*.

Russian Volunteer Fleet: (Libau) *Petersburg*; (Libau and Rotterdam) *Smolensk*.

Austro-American Line: (Triest) *Belvedere*, *Kaiser Franz Josef*; (Triest and Patras) *Alice*, *Francesca*, *Guila*, *Ida*, *Martha Washington*, *Sofia Hohenburg*; (Triest and Palermo) *Argentina*, and the *Eugenia*.

Greek Line: (Piraeus) *Athinai*, *King Alexander*; (Piraeus and Patras) *Themistocles*; (Piraeus and Constantinople) *Acropolis*, and the *Aliza*.

National Greek Line: (Piraeus) *Macedonia*.

Prince Line: (Piraeus, Patras, and Palermo) *Neapolitan Prince*.

Scandinavian American Line: (Copenhagen and Christiania) *Hellig Olaf*, *Oscar II*, and the *United States*.

Übersicht

der Innenräume des Doppelschrauben-Schnellpostdampfers

«Deutschland».

Cross-section of the Hamburg-American line steamship, *Deutschland*. Courtesy of the Ellis Island Immigration Museum.

REFERENCE: Anuta, Michael J. 1983. Ships of our ancestors. *Ancestry*. Baltimore: Genealogical Publishing Co.

Steerage. Steerage was the cheapest accommodation for passengers; the other accommodations were first and second class (and sometimes there was a third class), which together were called cabin class. Steerage accommodations usually ran from $10 to $40, depending on the price wars that were occasionally waged (especially before 1900). Before departing for the United States, physicians vaccinated and examined the eyes of steerage passengers; at German, Dutch, Belgian, French, and Italian

Bustling scene on the steerage deck of a transatlantic steamer.
Courtesy of the Ellis Island Immigration Museum.

ports they were also deloused and sometimes examined for other defects. Passengers' inspection cards were then punched and they were ready to embark.

On board the vessels, steerage passengers usually had contact only with stewards and occasionally stewardesses (who only assisted women and children). Families, single women, and single men usually traveled in separate compartments (often located in the stern). A typical steerage compartment might sleep as many as 194 passengers, although others accommodated as few as 36. The berths were commonly made of iron and had two tiers. Each contained a mattress often filled with straw or seaweed and covered with a slip of canvas. Neither pillows nor storage for personal belongings was provided. Ethnic groups almost always segregated themselves. Thus in a single compartment the Germans were in one area, the Poles in another, and the Jews in yet another. The floors were made of wood and might be swept every morning and the aisles sprinkled with sand. Neither receptacles for refuse nor sick cans for seasickness were provided. Washrooms might contain several large basins and faucets of cold seawater. The basins were used to wash dishes and clothing and served sick passengers. Toilets were near each compartment. Because of the unclean surroundings and lack of bathing facilities, steerage passengers were filthy when they arrived in America.

Steerage passengers were equipped with eating utensils. These often consisted of a fork, a spoon, a tin dinner pail, two small tin dishes, and a tin cup. A steward came to each compartment (or on deck) and rang a bell for each meal. On some vessels, immigrants fetched their meals. On others, the meals were served at table. In any case, the food was stored in large galvanized cans and served by stewards. The meat and vegetables were put on the tables in large plates. Immigrants always queued up for soup, tea, or coffee. Kosher food was served on steamships plying the Jewish emigration traffic. Breakfasts often consisted of a watery boiled cereal, coffee, bread, either butter or jam. This was followed by a dinner (lunch) of macaroni soup, boiled beef, potatoes, and bread. Supper might be boiled fish, potatoes, gravy, tea, black bread and butter. Other foods served at these meals were potato hash, salt pork, stewed liver, rice, sausage, roast beef or mutton, corned beef, pea or lentil soup, pickled herring, sauerkraut, dill pickles, cabbage, and prunes. Milk was given to women and children. Immigrants could buy alcoholic drinks, fruit, and sweets at a bar on many vessels; the men usually bought the drinks and the women the fruit.

A daily medical inspection was required of steerage passengers bound for America. When this was done (often only twice or three times during the voyage) the immigrants passed single file before the ship's doctor. Inspection cards were then punched to show that all inspections for each day of the voyage had been carried out.

Onboard hospitals were also available. Men and women patients were taken to separate hospitals. These had clean berths (with clean white linen) for the patients. Toilets and baths were also available.

In general, it was remarked that steerage passengers acted "like cattle" at meals; the stewards complained that they crowded like swine. But this was brought about by the poor treatment they received while on these vessels.

The smells and general unpleasantness made it impossible to remain below after sleeping or eating hours. Passengers typically spent long hours on the steerage deck, sometimes amid cinders from a smokestack. As there were no deck seats, passengers sat on the machinery (ventilators and other apparatus); some reclined on the floor. The crew often used the same deck during their leisure time. Sailors, stewards, and firemen were often insulting and rude to women. There was no lighting on the steerage deck when night fell, so passengers were reclining in the dark.

See also **Steamship Companies**

REFERENCE: U.S. Immigration Commission Reports. 1911. *Steerage Conditions.* Washington, DC.

Steiner, Edward [Edward Alfred Steiner] (b. near Bratislava, Slovakia, Austria-Hungary, November 1, 1866; d. Claremont, California, June 30, 1956). Congregationalist minister and sociologist. Edward Steiner is famous for his published works and lectures on immigration. Steiner was born a Jew in Slovakia and immigrated to the United States, where he converted to Christianity. His many books on immigration drew attention to Ellis Island and the phenomenon of mass migration to the United States. His publications included *Tolstoy the Man* (1903), *On the Trail of the Immigrant* (1906), *The Immigrant Tide: Its Ebb and Flow* (1909), *From Alien to Citizen; The Story of My Life in America* (1914), and *The Making of a Great Race* (1919).

Sterilization. To prevent the spread of contagion, several instruments were used in the Ellis Island hospital, including mattress steamers and autoclaves, to sterilize medical equipment.

Stowaways. When stowaways were captured by a ship's crew members, they were handed over to the custody of immigration officers and brought to Ellis Island for questioning by a board of special inquiry. Generally, they were legally entitled to enter the country if they could prove that they would not become public charges.

There were many stowaway cases at Ellis Island. Sixteen Chinese stowaways were found aboard the *Ecuador* in January 1925. Immigrant inspectors arrested the stowaways with the help of pier detectives. Illicit liquor and drugs were found in their possession. According to the *New York Times*, they were believed to have been smuggled aboard the vessel at San Francisco. The ship, which belonged to the Pacific Mail Line, sailed through the Panama Canal Zone to Havana and then to New York. The stowaways were deported on the same vessel.

Josef Svoboda was a stowaway aboard the *Queen Mary*. He escaped from the Ellis Island hospital on June 23, 1948, and swam to New Jersey.

Stump, Herman [Herman Stump Jr.] (b. Harford County, Maryland, August 8, 1837; d. Bel Air, Maryland, January 9, 1917). Superintendent of immigration (1893–1895) and commissioner-general of immigration (1895–1897); attorney.

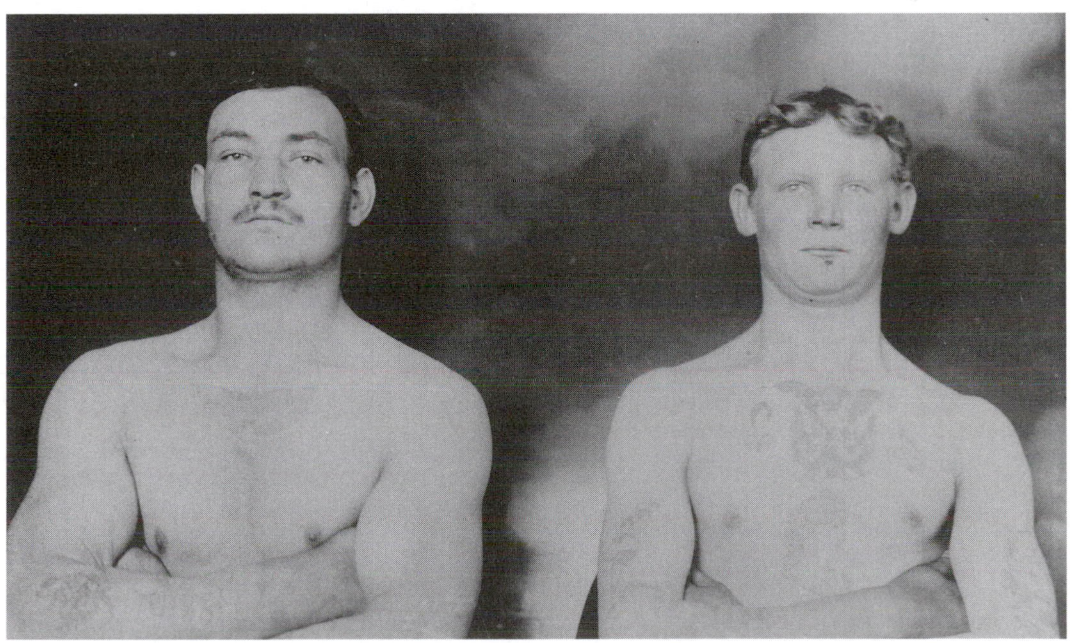

These tattooed German stowaways were deported in May 1911.
Sherman Collection, courtesy of the Ellis Island Immigration Museum.

President Grover Cleveland appointed Herman Stump as head of the Office of Immigration; he was also responsible for having the office elevated to bureau status in the **Immigration Act of 1895**. Stump was a strict enforcer of immigration laws and was especially hostile toward the Chinese. He had participated in extending the **Chinese Exclusion Act** when he served on the House Committee on Immigration. As a member of that committee, he also helped draft the **Immigration Act of 1891**.

A prominent Democrat, Stump served in the Maryland state senate (1878–1880) and was its president in 1880. He also served two terms in the U.S. House of Representatives (1889–1893). After leaving the Bureau of Immigration in 1897, he returned to his law practice in Maryland.

Suicides. Tragedy struck Ellis Island in February 1947, when a Polish woman committed suicide by hanging herself in the detention room. She had just been refused admittance to the United States by a **board of special inquiry**. Her ex-husband, living in Chicago, was asked whether he would accept her and their daughter; he only agreed to take the daughter and so the board admitted the daughter but ordered the mother excluded. There are doubtless more cases of suicide and attempted suicide that have yet to come to light.

REFERENCE: *New York Times.* 1947. Ellis Island suicide. February 12.

Superintendent. This high official was assigned to the **Executive Division** and ran the day-to-day affairs at Ellis Island during its heyday (1890s–1920s). His duties included supervising and coordinating the work of the various **divisions**, particularly **Registry**, **Information**, **Special Inquiry**, and **Janitors' Divisions**. He summoned all division heads for conferences and, upon the approval of the assistant commissioner, assigned and transferred immigration officers to the various divisions when necessary. Additionally, he was responsible for the cleanliness, efficiency, and general safety of the plant and its equipment, and ensured that privilege or concession holders were properly fulfilling their contracts. His immediate superiors were the commissioner and the assistant commissioner. In later years (1930s–1940s), his authority seems to have been restricted to the maintenance of the buildings and so on. The longest serving superintendents included **Alfred Brooks Fry** and **Percy A. Baker**.

See also **Appendix 3: Rules of the U.S. Immigrant Station at Ellis Island**

Superintendent of Immigration. This title was held by the head of the **Office of Immigration**, which was established in 1891. Only two men held the post, **William Dale Owen**, a Republican, and **Herman Stump**, a Democrat. The title was changed to commissioner-general when the office was elevated to bureau status in 1895.

Superintendents (NPS). Superintendents are the highest officials assigned to administer the individual sites of the **National Park Service**. Ellis Island was declared a part of the Statue of Liberty National Monument on May 11, 1965. Since that date, all superintendents assigned to the Statue of Liberty have also been responsible for the care and maintenance of Ellis Island. Since 1965, the following persons have held the office of superintendent or similar post: Lester McClanahan (1965–1969), Arthur Sullivan (1969–1970), James Batman (1970–1973), Howard Crane (1973–1974), Luis García y Curbelo (1974–1976), David L. Moffitt (1976–1987), Kevin C. Buckley (1987–1990), M. Ann Belkov (1990–1996), Diane H. Dayson (1996–), and acting superintendent Cynthia Garrett (2002–). Assistant and deputy superintendents over the years have included Frank Mills, Kevin C. Buckley, Thomas A. Bradley, Lawrence Steeler, and Cynthia Garrett.

Surgeons (Physicians). Surgeons were commissioned officers of the **Public Health Service**. They ran the Ellis Island immigrant hospital. The following is a list of some surgeons who were posted to Ellis Island.

Well-known physicians at Ellis Island included John A. Tonner (chief surgeon, 1892), William A. Wheeler (chief surgeon, 1892–1896), J. H. White (chief surgeon, 1896–1899), L. L. Williams (chief surgeon, 1899–1901 and 1913–1918), George Stoner (chief surgeon, ca. 1901–1913), W. C. Billings (chief surgeon, 1918–1925), J. W. Kerr (chief surgeon, 1920s), C. Knight Aldrich (1940–1941; psychiatrist), F. A. Ashford, L. P. H. Bahrenburg, James L. Baker (1949–1951; psychiatrist), Rose A. Bebb (started 1914; first woman surgeon), R. H. Creel (1901–1903; 1911; 1920s), J. M. Delgado (1903–1915), James P. Dunn (1900–1909), M. H. Foster, H. M. Friedman, E. F. Geddings (1892–1899), M. C. Guthrie, A. B. Hanborn (1892–1899), **Victor Heiser**, R. A. Herring, R. H. Heterick (1920s), Carlisle P. Knight, J. P. Leake, H. D. Long, Allan McLaughlin (1900–1905), John McMullen, Herbert M. Manning, Eugene H. Mullan, A. G. Nute, H. B. Parker, Carl Ramus (1900–1920), Alfred C. Reed, D. E. Robinson, Charles Rubenstein (1920s), **Victor Safford** (1890s–1903), **Thomas W. Salmon** (1903–1908), Roy P. Sandidge (1920s; lived on the island with his wife, Jane), J. J. Shriver (1920s), F. D. Sherwood (1920s), M. Gertrude Slaughter (1920s), William H. Slaughter (1920s; lived on the island with his wife, Mary), E. K. Sprague (1910–1914), R. D. Spratt, H. H. Stearns (1899–early 1900s), Robert Taylor (1951), Walter L. Treadway, **Frederick A. Theiss** (1903–1930s), John C. Thill (mid-1920s), John B. Train (1941–1946), Evans Tremble (1916), Seymour Vestermark (1932–1945; his son, Seymour Jr., was born at Ellis Island in 1933), W. O. Wetmore, J. G. Wilson. Consulting physicians included W. H. Bainbridge (surgery, 1920s), Dr. Nestor Ponce de Leon (1920s, d. 1928), R. F. Sheehan (neuro-psychiatry, 1920s), H. E. Stewart (1920s; physiotherapy), R. L. Waugh (1920s).

Surgeons' House. Located on **Island 2**, the surgeons' house was constructed in 1900–1901. It was two stories high and was used by **Public Health Service** surgeons and assistant surgeons. The first floor included a vestibule, parlor, library, kitchen, pantry, and porches in the front and back. The second floor contained a central hall from which opened five bedrooms and a bathroom. After several years, the house was turned over to the nurses, and so became the "Nurses' Cottage." In 1934, the Ellis Island Investigative Committee recommended that the surgeons' house be razed. This was done in 1936.

Swing, Joseph [Joseph May Swing] (b. Jersey City, New Jersey, February 28, 1894; d. San Francisco, California, December 9, 1984). Commissioner of the Immigration and Naturalization Service (1954–1962). Appointed by President Dwight Eisenhower to head the Immigration and Naturalization Service, one of Swing's first tasks was to inspect the facilities on Ellis Island and determine whether they should remain in operation. Swing quickly advised Attorney **Herbert Brownell** to close them as soon as possible. This was done in November 1954. A strict enforcer of immigration laws, Commissioner Swing also gained attention for the dispatch with which the Border Patrol arrested and deported illegal Mexican immigrants.

A 1915 graduate of West Point, Swing served in the Punitive Expedition in Mexico (1916) and then as an aide-de-camp in France in World War I (1917–1918). Following years of service as a captain and then a major in the peacetime army, he was quickly promoted to colonel and finally general during World War II (1941–1945). His fame rests on his command of the 11th Airborne Division in 1944, in which he successfully launched the Luzon campaign with airborne, amphibious, and ground attacks that were vital in liberating the Philippines from Japanese forces. From 1945 to 1948, Swing served as a commanding general in the occupation of northern Japan, and back in the United States was commander of the U.S. Sixth Army from 1951 until he retired from the Army in 1954.

T

Taft, William Howard (b. Ohio, September 12, 1857; d. Washington, DC, 1930). President of the United States (1909–1913). After assuming office, President William Howard Taft persuaded **William Williams** to return to Ellis Island as its commissioner. The President visited Ellis Island on October 8, 1910, accompanied by his secretary of commerce and labor, Charles Nagel. During the visit, Commissioner Williams invited the president to preside over a case of an alien appealing the order of exclusion he had received from the **Special Inquiry Division** shortly before; such cases were usually handled by the commissioner himself. The following is a report of that appeal case published in the *New York World.* The alien was George Thornton, a Welsh miner traveling with his seven children.

> The President questioned Thornton.
>
> "What have you with which to start life here?"
>
> "One hundred and sixty-five dollars and these two hands, sir." Answered the miner, who did not recognize Mr. Taft. Thornton added he had a sister in Pittsburgh who would care for his children until he and the older of them found work.
>
> "Do you know who is President of the United States?" Commissioner Williams asked.
>
> "William H. Taft," answered Thornton promptly.
>
> "Would it surprise you to know that I am the President?" asked Mr. Taft with that smile of his.
>
> "So you are, sir," said Thornton after studying him for a moment. "I have seen your picture often, sir."
>
> After being admitted to the country, Commissioner Williams learnt that the Welshman was somewhat of a ne'er-do-well having left considerable debts back in his homeland. Shortly after this came out, Thornton was deported at his own request. (p. 204)

REFERENCE: Shapiro, Mary J. 1986. *Gateway to Liberty.* New York: Vintage.

Tarsney Act of 1893. The Tarsney Act of 1893 permitted private architectural firms to design government buildings. The firms were first required to compete with other firms in order to win a government contract. The **second immigrant station** at Ellis Island was one of the first federal buildings to be erected under the provisions of this law.

The law was named for Congressman **John C. Tarsney** of Missouri.

Tarsney, John C. [John Charles Tarsney] (b. Medina, Michigan, November 7, 1845; d. Kansas City, Missouri, September 4, 1920). Politician and lawyer. Congressman John C. Tarsney, chairman of the House Labor Committee, was responsible for the passage of the **Tarsney Act of 1893** allowing private architects to erect public buildings.

Tarsney, a Democrat, served as a U.S. Representative from Missouri between 1889 and 1895.

Taylor, James Knox (b. 1857, Knoxville, Illinois; d. August 27, 1929, Tampa, Florida). Supervising architect, U.S. Public Buildings Service (1898–1912). James Knox Taylor designed several buildings at Ellis Island, including the **baggage and dormitory building** (1909), the **contagious disease wards** (1909), and the **hospital extension** building (1909). Educated at the Massachusetts Institute of Technology, Taylor began his career as an architect in New York City. In 1885, he formed a partnership with Cass Gilbert in St. Paul, Minnesota, which lasted until 1891. After working in Philadelphia for a couple of years, Taylor was hired as a draughtsman in the U.S. Public Buildings

Service; four years later he was promoted to the senior post of supervisory architect. After leaving federal service, he was director of the Department of Architecture at MIT for two years, and then maintained a private practice in Yonkers, New York, until his retirement in 1928. Taylor was noted for his preference for classical designs and left his mark on hundreds of federal buildings across the nation.

Theiss, Frederick A. (b. 1879; d ?). Surgeon; hospital superintendent and personnel officer (1920s and 1930s). Frederick Theiss began working at Ellis Island as an attendant in 1903. He was present during the **Black Tom** Wharf explosions of July 30, 1916. Years later, he told Commissioner **Edward Corsi** about the catastrophe.

About midnight a watchman, after his tour of duty, reported to the Hospital Superintendent that there was a big fire on Black Tom.

I got out and looked out of the window at the mounting mass of flames above the four-story brick piers. The whole sky was transformed into an inferno pierced by deafening explosions and the detonation of shells.

The tide was coming in and a west wind carried the fire toward the barges moored at the Black Tom Wharves. Suddenly I saw that the barges, which had been moored by the usual hemp, had caught fire and were exploding as they drifted toward Ellis Island. Already the Ellis Island windows had been broken, the doors had been jammed inward, and parts of the roof had collapsed.

Acting in conjunction with my associates, I hastened to assist in the removal of our insane patients to the tennis courts. We wrapped them in blankets and carried them out into the open air.

When we had them out of doors, they presented one of the most extraordinary spectacles I have ever seen. As the five-inch shells flared over the island like skyrockets, the poor demented creatures clapped their hands and cheered, laughed, sang and cried, thinking it was a show which had been arranged for their particular amusement.

The immigrants became panicky and were finally loaded upon the ferry and taken to the Barge Office amid scenes of wildest disorder.

We thought for a time that the final explosion had occurred. Then we learned that the barges, which had floated against the Island and set fire to the sea wall, were loaded with munitions. It was then that we who had to care for the patients first realized to what extent our own lives were in danger. Fortunately, the heroism of those who manned the tugs of the Lehigh Valley Railroad saved us. They towed the two flaming barges out to sea, where they sank amid concussions which sounded like the end of the world.

While the explosions were taking place over this period of several hours, the Island was becoming a depository for flaming debris. The New York Fire Department was on the Island stretching hose and putting out fires at every hand. It was not safe to permit anyone inside the buildings. Then came the second and most terrific explosion of all. It lasted about fifteen minutes and ended the series.

We bivouacked on the tennis court for the rest of the night, vainly trying to pacify the insane who were disappointed that the show was over. At 7.00 a.m. we cleaned up and returned the patients to the hospital.

The miracle was that no living thing was injured, except a cat—Chief Clerk Sherman's office pet—who was cut by flying glass. The roof had been lifted from the administration building and smashed to smithereens. Only the work of the Lehigh valley tug boats had saved us. (pp. 118–120)

REFERENCE: Corsi, Edward. 1935. *In the Shadow of Liberty.* New York: Macmillan.

Through America's Gate (Rooms W204–211; 223–224; 227; 230–232). Permanent exhibition of the **Ellis Island Immigration Museum**. It is located on the second floor in the west wing of the **Main Building**, an area that once contained the offices of the **Special Inquiry Division**. The exhibit tells the story of Ellis Island as an immigrant station: the activities of the **Bureau of Immigration**, the **Public Health Service**, and the **missionaries** and **immigrant aid societies** that operated on the station. Through America's Gate comprises fourteen galleries, containing photographs, graphic designs, historic film footage played on television monitors, and historic artifacts. Each gallery tells a part of the history of Ellis Island and contains photographs and oral history recordings. The following is a brief description of each of these galleries.

Arrival (W204) highlights the arrival of immigrants at Ellis Island; includes film footage.

Medical Inspection (W205) highlights the **line inspection**, the **chalk mark code** to indicate suspicion of illness and diseases that might cause exclusion, especially trachoma.

Legal Inspection (W206) This gallery highlights the **primary inspection** of aliens that was handled by **immigrant inspectors** in the **Registry Room**. On display are manifest sheet tags and an inspector's desk and hat.

Board of Special Inquiry (W207). This gallery is located in one of the former board of special inquiry hearing rooms; it deals with the activities of special inquiry cases of aliens whose responses failed to satisfy the immigrant inspector in the Registry Room. The room is restored to its appearance in about 1918.

Watchorn Portraits (W208). These are enlarged photographs of aliens who were at Ellis Island during the tenure of Commissioner **Robert Watchorn**; they come from his private collection in Alfreton, England. A brief comment about the immigrant's case is included with each picture.

Free to Land (W209) concentrates on the departure of aliens admitted to the country. The gallery shows immigrants' telegrams and photographs of those leaving the island via ferryboats.

Money Exchange (W210) features old-fashioned bank notes and coins from Ellis Island days. Includes French, German, Italian, Russian, Austro-Hungarian, British, Dutch, Belgian, Swedish, Spanish, Portuguese, Turkish, Greek, and Polish currency. The exhibit discusses the money exchange service at Ellis Island.

Tickets to All Points (W211) features the railway and steamboat companies that serviced immigrants that were discharged from Ellis Island. Objects on display include original railway timetables.

Mental Testing (W223) shows the various mental tests devised for immigrants by the **Public Health Service**, including wooden puzzles invented by **Howard A. Knox**.

Medical Care (W224) shows the work of the Ellis Island hospitals and features a period wheelchair and other objects.

Immigrant Aid Societies (W227) highlights the services of the social welfare workers, including **Ludmila K. Foxlee**. The exhibit features the phenomenon of picture brides, the old Clothing Room sign and other objects.

Employees. This small room gives a glimpse into the large workforce that ran the Ellis Island station. It features photographs of **Bureau of Immigration** personnel, including interpreter **Fiorello LaGuardia** and photographs of **Public Health Service** surgeons, nurses, attendants, and orderlies.

Detention (W230). This gallery highlights the daily life of detainees, including the notorious detention pens and exclusion.

Food Service (W231) shows menus and original artifacts such as cutlery and crockery from the days when Harry Balfe operated the Ellis Island restaurant.

Island of Hope, Island of Tears (W232). This exhibit highlights the landing of immigrants and the deportation and exclusion of immigrants. In addition, walls inscribed with **graffiti** by detainees are displayed in this room. Much of the text is written in Greek and Italian. The exhibit also highlights the 1980s graffiti preservation work of Christy Cunningham.

Tilson, Richard (b. 1850?; d. Staten Island, November 21, 1917). Chief of the watch and of the Deporting and Night Divisions (1897–1817); watchman (1892–1900). Richard Tilson was hired as a watchman on April 2, 1891. He worked at the Barge Office until he was sent to Ellis Island, which was opened on New Year's Day 1892. Tilson was eventually promoted to superintendent of the watchmen and guards. These employees worked in several divisions, including the **Night Division** and the **Deporting Division**. Fights were all too common in the job.

In April 1910, Commissioner **William Williams** wrote this about Tilson:

> I have already had correspondence with the Bureau in reference to Mr. Tilson. He is a faithful man and has been here for a number of years but his ability is limited. He is usually in charge of the officers

detailed to take aliens aboard ship and for this reason is deserving of a higher compensation than an ordinary watchman. But $1600 per annum is out of proportion to the services rendered and it is not right for him to receive more than the one (Mr. Barr) who acts as chief of the Division in the absence of Mr. McKee, and his ranking officer even when Mr. McKee is present. I feel that $1320 per annum is adequate pay for this position.

Tilson's coworkers referred to are Arch L. Barr, clerk, and John J. McKee, chief of the Deporting, Boarding, and Nights Divisions.

Richard Tilson and his wife and family lived on Staten Island and many of his descendants still live there. The street where he once lived is now called Tilson Place.

REFERENCE: Ellis Island employees file. Ellis Island, NY: Statue of Liberty and Ellis Island Library.

Tilton, Edward L. (b. New York, October 19, 1861; d. Scarsdale, New York, January 5, 1933). Architect. With **William Boring**, Edward Tilton was a designer of the **Main Building** at Ellis Island (1898–1900). Tilton was educated at the Ecole des Beaux-Arts in Paris in the 1880s, where he met fellow architectural student Boring. The two made a tour of southern France, Spain, and Italy before returning to take up duties as architects in the firm of McKim, Mead & White in New York in 1890. In 1891, they went into partnership as Boring & Tilton. Their greatest achievement was the design of the immigrant receiving depot at Ellis Island in 1898. For this, they received the Gold Medal at the Pan-American Exposition of 1900 at Buffalo in 1901, and the Silver Medal at the Louisiana Purchase Exposition in St. Louis in 1904. After his partnership with Boring was dissolved in 1903, Tilton worked independently and became a leading designer of public libraries and theaters. In 1921, he formed a partnership with Alfred Githens in the firm of Tilton & Githens, continuing to design libraries as well as other public buildings. Tilton's early works reveal his debt to the style of the Italian Renaissance, while later designs were chiefly inspired by Greco-Roman classicism. Tilton was the author of *The Architecture of the Small Library* (1911).

See also **Boring, William A.**

Tod, Robert E. [Robert Elliot Todd] (b. Glasgow, Scotland, July 31, 1867; d. Syosset, New York, November 9, 1944). Commissioner of immigration, Ellis Island (1921–1923). Appointed by President Warren G. Harding, Robert Tod was the fourth man of foreign birth to serve as commissioner of immigration at Ellis Island. Before Tod took up his duties, Secretary of Labor James J. Davis appointed him a special commissioner to learn about emigration conditions in Europe. Tod visited American consulates to study the practicality of setting up immigration inspection in those facilities but found diplomatic officials unwilling to take on the responsibility. On his return, he advised that immigration inspectors be named vice consuls. Further, he elaborated on the problem consuls were having with many Europeans who applied for visas to come to the United States. Even when warned that the monthly immigration quota was filled, they still insisted on getting a visa and sailing for the United States. Unimpressed by the newly adopted quota restrictions, they were convinced that they could successfully appeal to government authorities and, where necessary, have influential private organizations intercede for them, winning them admission.

Trachoma. Trachoma, a highly contagious disease of the eyes, was perhaps the most feared disease for an immigrant to be diagnosed with during the first quarter of the twentieth century. It was designated a dangerous contagious disease by the surgeon general in 1897, and in 1898 the surgeons at Ellis Island began examining immigrants with red, watery, or inflamed eyes for signs of the disease. Beginning in 1905, all immigrants entering Ellis Island were examined for trachoma during **line inspection**. The following is a description of the disease from the 1903 edition of the surgeon general's

Physician examines an immigrant's eyes in search of signs of trachoma and other eye diseases. Courtesy of the Ellis Island Immigration Museum.

Book of Instructions for the Inspection of Immigrants.

The term "trachoma" is used to designate a diseased condition of the conjunctiva, characterized by a muco-purulent discharge, firm persistent hyperplastic granulations, and exhibiting a tendency to be associated with atrophy of the conjunctiva with scar formation, roughened corneæ, adhesive bands of cicatricial tissue, entropion, pannus or even marked evidence of inflammatory processes, not due to external traumatism. Examiners are therefore instructed to regard as trachoma any case wherein the conjunctiva presents firm, well-marked granulations which do not have a tendency to disappear when the case is placed in hygienic surroundings a few days, or does not yield rapidly to ordinary treatment, even though there be no evidence of active inflammation at the time of the examination, nor appreciable discharge, nor yet signs of degenerative or destructive processes. Examiners are also instructed to regard as a possible case of trachoma any person who presents an active inflammatory condition of the conjunctiva accompanied by a discharge or a thickened infiltrated condition of the lids, and to hold such case until by treatment or otherwise the examination may be satisfactorily concluded. Cases of acute inflammation of the conjunctiva presenting a granular appearance of the lids should be regarded as suspicious and final judgement be withheld until the case has been under observation for a period of at least two weeks.

In view of the present state of medical science as to the etiology of trachoma, an immigrant should not be regarded as suffering with that disease whose conjunctiva presents only a granular appearance and a discharge both of which rapidly and entirely disappear.

Suggestions—The eyelids should be everted in all cases which show any of the following conditions: roughened cornea, corneal opacities, corneal ulcers, cloudiness of the media, lids which seem thickened at the location of the tarsal cartilage, entropion, lids which have a tendency to droop or do not raise simultaneously with the eyeball as the person looks up, pannus, and any eye which shows signs of acute conjunctival congestion. It should also be remembered that large numbers of cases of trachoma are found among Syrians, Greeks, Armenians, Russians, and Finns, and that, especially among the latter mentioned race, many cases of trachoma are found which give no outward evidence of the disease.

The cul-de-sac should be brought into view, because it frequently happens that an eye which is otherwise normal will have the cul-de-sac filled with granulations. Marginal blepharitis rarely accompanies trachoma. If both are present, the granulations of trachoma will be found farther back on the lid in the cul-de-sac.

Prognosis—The following class of cases may be regarded as practically incurable. Any case showing extensive areas of granulation, associated with any one or all of the following conditions: infiltration, well-marked evidence of degenerative changes, pannus, roughened cornea, entropion, and cases which present numerous so-called "sago-like" bodies. Cases which do not show marked improvement after several weeks' treatment, cases which show a strumous diathesis, cases which present a grayish semitransparent or so-called ground-glass appearance. This is especially true of trachoma found in the Finnish race.

Caution should also be exercised in making definite prognosis even in the most favorable cases, because treatment is generally very disappointing.

In the April 1912 edition of *Popular Science Monthly*, Alfred C. Reed, a medical officer at Ellis Island, described some diseases treated at the station.

> First among these might be placed trachoma, a disease of the eyelids characterized by extreme resistance to treatment, very chronic course and most serious results. Most of the immigrant cases occur in Russians, Austrians and Italians, although it is of common occurrence in oriental and Mediterranean countries. It causes a large percentage of the blindness in Syria and Egypt. Its contagious nature, together with the resulting scarring of the lids and blindness, make its recognition imperative.

Statistically, the immigrant nationalities most often certified for trachoma were the Chinese, Armenians, Syrians, East Indians, Turks, Croatians, Slovenians, and Dalmatians, Bosnians, and Herzegovinians.

The treatment given at the Ellis Island hospital for those afflicted with trachoma was the following. The first stage of treating the disease was to apply cold compresses to the eyes in a dark room at two-hour intervals. In addition to this, the eyes were irrigated with a 20 percent argyrol solution (a weak solution of organic silver compound). Next came an eyewash of water and 4 percent salt or boric acid.

If the first stage of treating trachoma was unsuccessful, surgery followed. Surgery consisted of two procedures. The first surgical procedure was one in which the granules on the eyelids were squeezed of the trachomatous disease by means of rolled forceps; this caused a small hemorrhage or bruise to appear on the eyelids. The second procedure was called scarification. This consisted of making tiny superficial incisions on the eyelids. Following surgery, a new treatment was applied: rubbing the diseased eye tissue with a bluestone, a form of copper sulfate that was found effective in preventing the return of granulations. This surgery and treatment were only provided to patients whose trachomatous condition was not severe. It is credited with having cured some patients. Trachoma patients typically remained in the hospital for six months.

See also **Diseases and Hospitalization**

REFERENCES: Markel, H. 2000. The eyes have it: Trachoma, the perception of disease, the United States Public Health Service and the Jewish American immigration experience, 1897–1924. *Bulletin of the History of Medicine* 74 (3): 525–560; Reed, Alfred C. 1912. The medical side of immigration. *Popular Science Monthly* 5 (April): 383–392; United States Public Health and Marine Hospital Service. 1903. *Book of Instructions for the Medical Inspection of Immigrants.* Washington, DC.

Tracy, Arthur (b. Kamenets-Podolsk, Russia [Abba Tracavutsky], June 25, 1899; d. New York, October 5, 1997). Singer. Arthur Tracy is the most famous immigrant interviewed in the Ellis Island **Oral History Project**. Known as the "Street Singer," Tracy was one of the biggest singing sensations of the 1930s and won acclaim throughout the United States and the British Empire. The National Park Service arranged for Arthur Tracy's return to Ellis Island on February 15, 1995, for an oral history audio interview. In it, he discussed the warmth and vibrancy of life in his native shtetl (Jewish village), his elder brother's drowning in 1905, and the family's exodus from Russia in the spring of 1906. Like many entertainers of his generation (such as Al Jolson), he had long hidden his foreign birth; he always told reporters that he had been born in Philadelphia. It was not until the end of his life that he openly discussed his experiences as an immigrant. Tracy began his career in the Yiddish theater in 1917 but soon switched to vaudeville. Although he continued as a vaudevillian throughout the 1920s, he also toured in the musical comedy *Blossom Time* (1922) and in a production of Beniamino Gigli, the great Italian opera star. In 1931, he moved to radio and won overnight stardom as the Street Singer. As in vaudeville, his specialty was the romantic ballad and his image that of the wandering troubadour and gypsy, with his ever-present accordion. He had a series of nightly shows on the CBS, NBC, and Radio Luxembourg networks. He was just as popular in vaudeville and music hall tours and his records were in demand worldwide. His films included *The Street Singer* (1936), *Command Performance* (1937), and *Follow Your Star* (1938). Although he retired from show business in 1949, he made occasional comebacks on stage, radio, and television; his last film was *Crossing Delancey* (1988).

Arthur Tracy, "the Street Singer," at the height of his fame in the 1930s. The future star immigrated through Ellis Island in 1906. Courtesy of the Ellis Island Immigration Museum.

REFERENCE: Moreno, Barry. 2003. Arthur Tracy. In *Ellis Island*, 100; 110. Charleston, SC: Arcadia.

Treasurer's Office. Located in the **Executive Division**, the personnel of this office maintained the station's accounts, prepared vouchers for payment of services or bills rendered, prepared staff payrolls, and took care of all accounting matters, including receiving and distributing paychecks. They were also responsible for the safekeeping of detainees' valuables, for receiving funds sent by their relatives or friends, for receiving and distributing immigrants' mail, for maintaining the station's lost property office, and for keeping a record of all government property on the island. In 1921, Frederick L. Budde was head of the Treasurer's Office. He had been a clerk there since

Treasures from Home exhibit shows the diversity of immigrant nationalities that passed through Ellis Island. Courtesy of the Ellis Island Immigration Museum.

1900. In a 1910 personnel report, Budde's job as a clerk was described thus: "Mr. Budde is attached to the Treasurer's Office and attends to the . . . preparation of vouchers, accounts, records, etc. . . . The work of that is so heavy as to require long hours of service, which Mr. Budde has always cheerfully rendered." When a large sum of money was reported missing in 1921, Budde lost his post and was demoted to a clerkship in the **Boarding Division**.

See also **Crime and Abuse**

REFERENCE: Ellis Island employees file. Ellis Island, NY: Statue of Liberty and Ellis Island Library.

Treasures from Home (Room E311). Treasures from Home is an exhibition of the **Ellis Island Immigration Museum** and is located on the third floor in the east wing of the Main Building. The exhibit features Family Album Walls of different immigrant nationalities and ethnic groups. Exhibit cases contain a variety of artifacts that were brought through Ellis Island, including clothing and ornaments, personal papers, household goods, and personal items such as a zither, rosary beads, phylacteries, a missal, and Bibles. Many, including the Fiorentino, Jensen, Lipovac, Semerjian, Schneider, and Zauneker families, donated the artifacts.

Trenet, Charles (b. Narbonne, France, May 18, 1913; d. Creteil, France, February 19, 2001). French singer and actor. One of the great French stars since the late 1930s, Charles Trenet was also an international celebrity during much of the twentieth century. In 1948, on Trenet's first visit to the United States, immigration inspectors detained him for twenty-six days at Ellis Island on suspicion of homosexuality and fascist collaboration during the war. He was eventually allowed to enter the country. Trenet, often labeled by American media as the "French Sinatra," appeared in many films, including *Je Chante* (1938), *La Romance de*

Paris (1941), *Adieu Leonard* (1943), *Bouquet de Joie* (1952) and *Printemps à Paris* (1957).

Tuberculosis. Tuberculosis was included on the list of dangerous contagious diseases that, if certified, would lead to exclusion. Certifications resulting in deportation or exclusion, however, were far less common than those for trachoma or parasitic diseases. The immigrant nationalities most often certified with tuberculosis between 1908 and 1930 were the French; Scots; Czechs; Armenians; English; black Africans; Hebrews; Ruthenians; Dalmatians, Bosnians, and Herzegovinians; Welsh; Scandinavians; Croatians and Slovenians; Chinese; Spanish Americans; and Syrians.

See also **Contagious Disease Wards; Diseases and Hospitalization; Line Inspection**

U

Uhl, Byron H. [Byron Hamlin Uhl] (b. Monticello, Indiana, October 1873; d. Hackensack, New Jersey, November 21, 1944). District director, Ellis Island (1933–1942); assistant commissioner (1909–1933); acting commissioner (June 1913–September 1914, September 1919–1931, May 1920). Byron Uhl attained distinction by his long years of service, which took him slowly but steadily to the top. Uhl came to New York at the age of eighteen and took a job as a stenographer at Ellis Island on August 20, 1892; his career at the station was to last fifty years. In 1903, Uhl was promoted to inspector in the **Boarding Division**. After a few months on the job he was promoted to the powerful post of chief clerk, and in 1909 became assistant commissioner. At this level he was often in complete charge of the station in the absence of the commissioner or at times when the post was vacant. When the United States declared war on Germany in April 1917, it was Uhl who personally commanded the immigration squad that rounded up 1,200 officers and seamen from German ships docked in the harbor. Further, in 1919 and 1920, he played a key role in the detention and deportation of hundreds of communists, Bolsheviks, and anarchists, including **Emma Goldman** and **Alexander Berkman**. During this period he worked closely with his superiors, **Frederic Howe** and **Louis F. Post**. Uhl also worked on the failed attempts to exclude **Marie Lloyd**, former Venezuelan president **Cipriano Castro**, **Isadora Duncan**, and Vera, Countess of Cathcart.

Uhl maintained a lifelong friendship with **Fiorello LaGuardia**, dating from LaGuardia's employment as one of the interpreters on the island. In 1933, he was given the title of district director, and in July 1940, when the senior post of commissioner was abolished on **Rudolph Reimer's** retirement, he assumed charge of the station. In his last years, he told reporters that he wished he had become a lawyer instead. On August 20, 1942, his golden jubilee year at Ellis Island, he was feted at a luncheon in the staff dining room. Immigration and Naturalization Service Commissioner Earl G. Harrison came up from Washington just for the occasion; he declared that Ellis Island ought to be renamed "Uhl's Island." Others attending the luncheon included New York City Mayor Fiorello LaGuardia and former Ellis Island commissioners **Benjamin M. Day**, **Edward Corsi**, and Rudolph Reimer, as well as Uhl's top aide, Assistant District Director William J. Zucker. On November 30, 1942, he retired to his Rutherford, New Jersey, home, ending one of the longest and most successful careers in the history of the Immigration Service. In a special commentary published that October, the *New York Times* hailed him as "Keeper of the Gate."

References: *New York Herald Tribune*. 1942. Uhl will mark half-century on Ellis Island. August 18; *New York Herald Tribune*. 1944. Byron Uhl, 71, dies: Ex-head at Ellis Island. November 21.

Ullo, Lorenzo (b. Malta, 1841; d. ?). Admiralty lawyer; legal counsel for Ellis Island Immigrant Station and for the Navigazione Generale Italiana. Lorenzo Ullo played a role in the **Bureau of Immigration** investigations of corruption in 1901 and 1902. The investigations resulted in the fall of Thomas Fitchie, the commissioner, and his assistant, **Edward F. McSweeney**, who had previously dominated the station.

Lorenzo Ullo had immigrated to the United States from Malta in 1873. His law office was in Manhattan.

Undocumented Alien. An undocumented alien was an immigrant without papers, usually indicating illegal presence in a country. After passports became required for entry into the United States after World War I, this category of violator was added to the list of unacceptable immigrants who could be excluded or deported. Such persons were also referred to as being "without papers."

Uniforms. Officers of both the **Bureau of Immigration** and the **Public Health Service** wore uniforms, although the members of the latter agency had a more military appearance, as they were commissioned officers with military ranks (e.g., colonel, major, captain). According to **Department of the Treasury** Circular 31 for the Bureau of Immigration (1903), **immigrant inspectors** were required to wear ordinary sack suits with double-breasted coats. **Interpreters**, assistant inspectors, and **clerks** were required to wear single-breasted coats. All of these Bureau of Immigration employees were authorized to have their measurements taken at the shops of Browning, King & Company, located in Manhattan at 1 Cooper Square as well as in other cities across the country, including Chicago.

In the 1920s and 1930s, immigrant inspectors wore badges and "captain's" caps surmounted by the insignia of the Bureau of Immigration. All male inspectors, interpreters, surgeons, and clerks wore ties. In 1903, when women inspectors were engaged in the **Boarding Division**, special costumes were fashioned to suit Edwardian scruples.

Each Public Health Service surgeon was required to wear a regulation military uniform with all its accoutrements, according to his assignment and the season. Other medical personnel were assigned white coats, aprons, caps, and the like. When appropriate, hats were worn.

Other employees—watchmen, janitors, charwomen, boat personnel, engineers, and so on—wore uniforms appropriate to their assigned duties and status. Most immigrant aid workers and **missionaries** wore no uniforms (except for **Salvation Army** officers), although most conformed to the formal dress of the period.

United Hebrew Charities. The United Hebrew Charities operated an immigration bureau that aided Jewish immigrants arriving at Ellis Island. Additionally, the organization helped the newcomers settle into immigrant neighborhoods, often securing free lodging for them as well as food and medical aid. To encourage Jews to consider settling in other parts of the United States, it sponsored the Jewish Immigrant Information Bureau and the Industrial Removal Office.

Unrau, Harlan D. (b. Los Angeles, California, 1946). Historian. Harlan D. Unrau has been a historian for the National Park Service since 1972 and has authored a large number of historic structure reports, historic resource studies, and administrative histories. Most notably, he is the author of the authoritative *The Historic Resource Study: Ellis Island/Statue of Liberty*, which was issued in three volumes by the National Park Service in 1984.

REFERENCE: Schulz, Karin, ed. 1994. *Hoffnung Amerika: Europaische Auswanderung in die Neue Welt.* Bremerhaven, Germany: NWD.

V

Vandalism. During its years under the care of the General Services Administration, Ellis Island was subject to pilfering and vandalism. With only one guard and watchdog assigned to the once indispensable station, crime and vandalism reached their height in the late 1950s and the 1960s. "Harbor pirates managed to sneak ashore and carry off chairs, desks, metal piling and anything else that was portable." By the time National Park Service rangers were regularly posted to the island in 1966, the place was a ruin.

See also **Graffiti; Squatters**

REFERENCE: Pitkin, Thomas M. 1975. *Keepers of the Gate.* New York: New York University Press.

Waldo, Charles (b. Finland, 1872; d. New York, September 9, 1913). Immigrant inspector. Charles Waldo was tragically killed with four other Ellis Island employees when the railing of the **ferryboat *Ellis Island*** collapsed, causing the men to fall overboard. An investigation proved that repairs made to the railing had been improperly done.

REFERENCES: Bearrs, Edwin. 1969. *The Ferryboat* Ellis Island. Washington, DC: National Park Service; Moreno, Barry. 1992. *Who Was Who at Ellis Island: Officials, Employees & Aliens.* Ellis Island Library, Statue of Liberty N.M.

Wallis, Frederick A. [Frederick Alfred Wallis] (b. Kentucky, 1869; d. Paris, Kentucky, December 22, 1951). Commissioner of immigration, Ellis Island (1920–1921). During his brief reign as commissioner of immigration at Ellis Island, Frederick A. Wallis was overrun with a heavy post–**World War I** immigration, which the station, having fallen into a shabby state, was ill-prepared to handle. In addition, he had to enforce the new **Immigration Act of 1921**, which slightly cut immigration by established preferential annual **quotas** based on the nationality of immigrants. During his watch the distinguished British ambassador Sir Auckland Geddes chose to inspect Ellis Island and found it wanting. Embarrassingly for the U.S. government, Geddes exposed Ellis Island to members of the British Parliament as a place were British immigrants were "inhumanly kept in cages with people of dirtier and inferior nationalities." Throughout much of his career, Wallis worked as a public administrator. He was also a prominent member of the Democratic Party.

See also **Geddes, Lord**

REFERENCES: *New York Times*. 1951. F.A. Wallis dies: Ex-head of prisons . . . once immigration commissioner. December 23; Novotny, Ann. 1971. *Strangers at the Door.* Riverside, CT: Chatham.

Walter, Francis E. [Francis Eugene Walter] (b. May 26, 1894, Easton, Pennsylvania; d. May 31, 1963, Washington, DC). Politician; U.S. Representative (D-PA; 1933–1963). The cosponsor of the Immigration and Naturalization Act of 1952 (McCarran-Walter Act), Congressman Francis Walter chaired both the House Committee on Un-American Activities and the House Judiciary Subcommittee on Immigration Affairs. Throughout his career, Congressman Walter was noted for his investigations of communist subversives and his determination to reform immigration.

See also **Immigration Restriction; McCarran, Patrick A.**

REFERENCE: Biographical Directory of the United States Congress. Francis E. Walter. www.senate.gov/artandhistory/history/common/generic/Historical_Intro_Biographical_Directory.htm (accessed May 12, 2004).

Ward, Robert De Courcy (b. Boston, Massachusetts, November 29, 1867; d. Cambridge, Massachusetts, November 12, 1931). Meteorologist and author. Robert De Courcy Ward was a leading anti-immigrant nativist and a founder of the powerful **Immigration Restriction League**. He strongly opposed the immigration of southern and eastern Europeans, who dominated the "new immigration" of the early twentieth century. In 1895, he and fellow nativist **Prescott Hall** were taken to see the large numbers of Italians detained at the station by Commissioner **Joseph Senner**. When Ward learned that most of the Italians were illiterate in their own language, he realized that a federal law was needed that required immigrants to be literate in their own languages. If such a law were adopted, mass immigration into the United States of "undesirables" or "inferior races" would end. The league's literacy scheme underwent further modification after it was learned that Jewish immigrants (especially males) were literate in Hebrew and Yiddish but not Russian. Thus warned, they made certain that the literacy requirement would require immigrants to be literate in the language of their country of residence. After many years of trial and error, this approach resulted in the adoption of the **Immigration Act of 1917**. Ward was a professor of climatology at Harvard University and authored several books, including *Climate Considered: Especially in Relation to Man* (1908).

References: LeMay, Michael. *From Open Door to Dutch Door: An Analysis of U.S. Immigration Policy since 1820*; Pitkin, Thomas M. 1975. *Keepers of the Gate: A History of Ellis Island*. New York: New York University Press.

Watchmen. Watchmen kept order among the immigrants at Ellis Island, especially those held in detention. They primarily worked in the **Watchmen's and Gatemen's Division**, the **Deporting Division**, and the **Night Division**. For many years—from the 1890s until his death in 1917—**Richard Tilson** was superintendent of the watch. The watchmen often dealt with angry, tense situations caused by misunderstandings, ignorance, distress, or confusion. Regrettably, altercations and physical violence often occurred. Immigrants often complained of being shoved, pushed, insulted, threatened, and exploited, while watchmen were often impatient with the nameless crowds of immigrants demanding help when none was possible. Along with **gatemen**, **messengers**, laborers, and charwomen, watchmen were among the lowest paid employees at Ellis Island.

Watchmen's and Gatemen's Division. This division of the workforce was responsible for crowd control and security at Ellis Island. It was assigned to the **Registry Room**, outside of the **Main Building** at the docks where the barges and the ferry arrived, the **Barge Office** in Manhattan, the **Night Division**, and the **Deporting Division**. This division went by different names at different times. Employees included **watchmen**, **gatemen**, **groupers**, and guards. The work sometimes was rough and violent.

See also **Tilson, Richard**

Watchorn, Robert (b. 1858, Alfreton, Derbyshire, England; d. 1944, Redlands, California). Commissioner of immigration, Ellis Island (1905–1909); oilman. Robert Watchorn began his working life in the coal mines of his native Derbyshire at the age of eleven. He immigrated to the United States in 1880 and went to work as a coal miner in Pennsylvania. He served as the secretary of his trade union and eventually worked as chief clerk to Governor Robert Pattison of Pennsylvania. In 1895, he was hired as an immigrant inspector at Ellis Island. In 1898, he was appointed commissioner of immigration at the Montreal Immigrant Station, and in 1905 President Theodore Roosevelt named him successor to Commissioner **William Williams**, who had resigned suddenly. His swift rise to power made Commissioner-General **Frank P. Sargent** uneasy about his own position as head of the **Immigration Bureau** in Washington.

In a 1905 interview with a reporter from *Success* magazine, Watchorn recalled his immigration twenty-five years before, as they watched a transatlantic liner glide through the harbor.

> It was a ship like that—the good ship "Bothnia"—that brought me to the New World. . . . As we came up the bay that May morning in 1880, I crowded to the rail of the steerage deck to view the shores of the land of promise. I don't know why I thought that it promised much for me, but I did. I was twenty, then, and full of confidence. . . . When I had landed with the rest at Castle Garden, and stood surveying the trees and well-kept lawns of Battery Park, I was full of enthusiasm. (pp. 386–388)

Watchorn's work at the New York station included building the **contagious disease**

wards, coping with the greatest crowds of immigrants in American history, and doing his utmost to alleviate the conditions under which they were received and treated. In addition, he warned certain Protestant **missionaries** to curb their zeal in trying to convert immigrants to their special brand of faith and in 1908 quarreled with aggressive New York City police commissioner Theodore A. Bingham, who accused him of not deporting foreign criminals. To get him out of New York, Oscar Strauss, the commissioner-general of immigration, sent Watchorn to Italy on a "fact-finding mission" to investigate Italian crime. There, Watchorn was granted an audience with H.M. King Victor Emmanuel III. The king dismissed criminal leagues as largely mythical.

At the end of Roosevelt's presidency, in spite of Watchorn's hope of a second term, William Willams got the post at Ellis Island. Watchorn resigned from government service and went into the oil business in Oklahoma. He made his fortune and bought himself an estate in southern California. A devout Methodist and loyal Englishman, he founded Robert Watchorn Charities and donated generously to his native town, Alfreton, England. The Watchorn Methodist Church stands as a tribute to him. He also built Watchorn Hall at the University of Redlands, a Methodist school in California.

REFERENCES: Pitkin, Thomas M. 1975. *Keepers of the Gate.* New York: New York University Press; Watchorn, Robert. 1958. *Autobiography of Robert Watchorn.* Ed. Herbert Faulkner West. Oklahoma City: Robert Watchorn Charities; Welch, J. Herbert. 1905. Robert Watchorn: The man who climbed out: the life-story of a boy immigrant who has become commissioner of immigration. *Success*, June.

Watkins, W. Frank (b. 1887; d. ?). District director, Ellis Island (1942–1949). In 1943, District Director W. Frank Watkins moved the chief administrative offices off Ellis Island to Columbus Circle, Manhattan. Watkins, like his predecessors, handled numerous dramatic cases that attracted the attention of reporters, including **enemy aliens**, communists, **stowaways**, and famous foreigners in trouble, such as French singer **Charles Trenet**.

Watkins entered the **Bureau of Immigration** in 1905 as a stenographer at the Portland, Oregon, immigrant inspection station. In 1913, he was promoted to inspector and some years later came to head the **Chinese Division** at Ellis Island. He also served for a time as the chief clerk in the 1920s. In 1931, Watkins carried out work in the Los Angeles office and was involved in a series of cases, often involving Mexicans.

In December 1933, he returned to Ellis Island at the head of a team of fraud investigators. Secretary of Labor **Frances Perkins** described their work in her annual report for 1935:

> An investigation . . . uncovered evidence of systematic fraud in immigration and naturalization cases in the New York district perpetrated over a period of years by racketeers acting in collusion with employees of this Service. . . . To meet this situation two groups of examiners and inspectors were assigned . . . to conduct the investigation. . . . At the peak, 56 men were assigned to this task. . . . They worked for fifteen months preparing . . . evidence . . . for criminal trials. Five thousand volumes of passenger manifests filed at Ellis Island, covering . . . four million individual aliens were checked for alterations and insertions. . . . The check revealed that manifests had been altered, official documents were missing and files had been stolen. . . . It had been ascertained that up to $100 had been paid in naturalization cases involving false witnesses or the passing of applicants unqualified, and that from $300 to $1,200 had been collected for the alteration of manifests to show legal entry. . . . It is believed that they may have aggregated $1,000,000. The lion's share was retained by racketeers and crooked attorneys and agents who solicited business and were in direct contact with the aliens concerned, while the remainder was paid to employees whose connivance was essential. By the close of the fiscal year, 1,600 alleged illegal entry cases had been investigated, with 424 arrests and 83 deportations, 34 indictments had been obtained in fraudulent naturalizations, 200 cases had been prepared in cancellation of citizenship, and 29 cases against employees. . . . Trial of the most important criminal cases followed later in the year.

In the 1940 annual report, Secretary Perkins reported on the status and results of investigations that had been completed: "During the course of this investigation 37 racketeers were indicted and convicted, 12 government employees were convicted, 13 were dismissed from the Service and 5 resigned rather than face charges. In addition, 151 aliens were prosecuted and convicted (of fraud). . . . Many persons operating steamship agencies were convicted." She also reported that convictions were meted out to many operators of immigrant consulting offices, and crooked lawyers were disbarred.

In 1942, Watkins served briefly as district director at Detroit, but in November of that year, he was brought back to New York as successor to **Byron H. Uhl**, continuing in this position until the end of the decade.

References: U.S. Department of Labor. 1935. *Annual Report of the Secretary of Labor.* Washington, DC: Government Printing Office; U.S. Department of Labor. 1940. *Annual Report of the Secretary of Labor.* Washington, DC: Government Printing Office.

Weber, John B. [John Baptiste Weber] (b. Buffalo, New York, September 21, 1842; d. Lackawanna, New York, December 18, 1926). Commissioner of immigration, Ellis Island; politician and soldier. Colonel John B. Weber was the first head of Ellis Island (1890–1893), first as superintendent and then as commissioner of immigration. Weber, more than any other federal official, was responsible for setting in motion the Ellis Island immigrant station and creating the first practical regulations for the **Bureau of Immigration**. He hired the first executive officers at Ellis Island and the first **immigrant inspectors**, **interpreters**, **clerks**, and **matrons**. He notified the **steamship companies** about what federal law did not tolerate. He dealt with the cholera epidemic of 1892, which immigrants were accused of causing. He instituted new standards for ship passenger **manifests** by increasing the number of questions asked to passengers; he performed the first federal investigation of foreign migration by traveling to eastern Europe

Colonel John B. Weber was the first commissioner of Ellis Island. Courtesy of the National Park Service, Ellis Island Immigration Museum.

to learn why so many Jews were leaving Russia; and he sympathized with and gave fair treatment to the impoverished Jewish refugees who often arrived at Ellis Island in a pitiful condition.

In an article he wrote for the *North American Review*, he observed:

> It is charged that immigrants furnish a larger percentage of paupers and criminals than the native element. This is probably true. But it is hardly because they are foreigners, but because they are the poorer half of society, and consequently less able to cope with misfortune or to withstand temptation. It is not so creditable to a rich man to refrain from stealing a loaf of bread as a hungry one. (p. 424)

Weber entered the Union army at the outbreak of the Civil War and commanded African American soldiers as the colonel of the 89th Colored Infantry. After the war, he became a wholesale grocer in Buffalo and an active member of the Republican Party. Returning to public life, he served as assistant postmaster of Buffalo (1871–1873), as sheriff of Erie

County (1874–1876), and as a U.S. Representative (R-NY; 1885–1889).

Some years after leaving his service at Ellis Island, he was commissioner-general of the Pan American Exposition, held in Buffalo in 1901. In 1912, he called at Ellis Island before making his way to a steamship for a trip to Europe.

Weber's own family emigrated from Alsace-Lorraine and this made him sympathetic to the troubles of immigrants. He published his *Autobiography* in 1924.

See also **Commissioners; First Immigrant Station; Moore, Annie; O'Beirne, James R.**

REFERENCES: Biographical Directory of the United States Congress. John Baptiste Weber. www.senate.gov/artandhistory/history/common/generic/Historical_Intro_Biographical_Directory.htm (accessed May 12, 2004); Markel, Howard. 1892. *Quarantine!* Repr., Baltimore: Johns Hopkins University Press; Weber, John B. 1892. Our national dumping ground: A study of immigration. *North American Review* (April): 424.

Wells, H. G. [Henry George Wells]. British novelist and social commentator. Wells visited Ellis Island during his trip to the United States early in 1906. He described his impressions in his book *The Future in America: A Search after Realities*, which appeared shortly afterward:

> I visited Ellis Island yesterday. . . . For the first time in its history, this filter of immigrant humanity has . . . proved inadequate to the demand upon it. It was choked, and half a score of . . . liners were lying uncomfortably up the harbour, replete with twenty thousand or so . . . from Ireland and Poland, and Italy and Syria, and Finland and Albania; men, women, children, dirt and bags together. . . . I made my way along white passages and through traps and a maze of metal lattices that did for a while succeed in catching and imprisoning me, to Commissioner [Robert] Watchorn, in his quiet, green-toned office. There for a time I sat . . . and heard him deal methodically, swiftly, sympathetically, with case after case, a string of appeals against the sentences of deportation pronounced in the busy little courts below. First would come one dingy and strangely garbed group of wild-eyed aliens, and then another: Roumanian gypsies, South Italians, Ruthenians, Swedes, each under the intelligent guidance of a uniformed interpreter, and a case would be stated, a report made to Washington, and they would drop out again, hopeful or sullen, or fearful. . . . Downstairs we find the courts . . . traverse long refectories, long aisles of tables and close-packed dormitories with banks of steel mattresses, tier above tier, and galleries and passages innumerable. . . . Here is a huge gray waiting-room, like a big railway depot-room, full of a sinister crowd of miserable people, loafing about or sitting dejectedly, whom America refuses, and here a second and third such chamber, each with its tragic or evil-looking crowd that hates us, and that even ventures to groan and hiss at us a little . . . and here, squalid enough, but still . . . hopeful, are the appeal cases . . . At a bank of ranges, works an army of men cooks, in another spins the big machinery of the Ellis Island laundry, washing blankets, drying blankets . . . a big, clean, steamy place of hurry and rotation . . . I recall a neat apartment lined to the ceiling with little drawers, a card index of the names and nationalities . . . and circumstances of upwards of a million and a half people who have gone on . . . (but) yet liable to recall. The central Hall is the key. . . . All day long, through an intricate series of metal pens, the long procession files . . . bearing bundles and trunks and boxes, past this examiner and that, past the quick alert medical officers, the talleymen, and the clerks; at every point immigrants are being picked out and set aside for further medical examination, for further questions, for the little courts; but the main procession satisfies conditions, and passes on. On they go, from this pen to that . . . towards a desk at a little metal wicket—the gate of America . . . The immigration stream . . . goes on past the . . . the money-changing place, past the . . . separating ways that go to this railway or that . . . into a new world. The great majority are young men and young women, between seventeen and thirty, good, youthful, hopeful peasant stock. They stand . . . waiting to go through the wicket, with bundles . . . tin boxes . . . cheap portmanteaus, with odd packages, in pairs, in families, alone, women with children, with strings of dependents, young couples. . . . Yes, Ellis Island is quietly immense. . . . "Look there! said the Commissioner taking me by the arm and pointing, and I saw a monster steamship far way and already a big bulk looming up the Narrows. "It's the Kaiser Wilhelm der Grosse. She's got—I forget the exact figures, but let us say—853 more for us. She'll have to keep them until Friday at the earliest. And there's more behind her and more strung out all across the Atlantic." (pp. 61–65)

REFERENCE: Wells, H. G. 1906. *The Future in America: A Search after Realities.* London: Chapman & Hall.

White Slave Traffic Act (36 Statue 825). Also known as the Mann Act, this law of 1910 barred the "importation and harboring of women for immoral purposes." It authorized the commissioner-general of immigration to investigate and keep files and documents on foreign women who had been brought to the country for prostitution. It further authorized the **Immigration Bureau** to arrest and deport such women. Although this law was not enacted until 1910, the bureau had been dealing with the problem since 1891 and had detailed a number of inspectors to investigate numerous cases.

The adoption of this law was influenced by President Theodore Roosevelt's signing a cooperative agreement with thirteen nations of Europe to break up the traffic in white slavery. The other signatories were France, Great Britain, Germany, Spain, Russia, Italy, Sweden, The Netherlands, Belgium, Denmark, Switzerland, Norway, and Portugal.

See also **American, Sadie; Moral Turpitude**

Williams, William (b. New London, Connecticut, 1862; d. New York, February 8, 1947). Commissioner of immigration, Ellis Island (April 28, 1902–February 1905); attorney. William Williams was the most important commissioner ever appointed to administer Ellis Island. His reforms and policies set the standard by which his successors were judged and influenced the entire **Bureau of Immigration** for years. Williams was a strict and stern manager whose rigid yet just rule caused dishonest or weak employees and privilege holders to exercise caution in any underhanded behavior contemplated. Williams fought and ousted suspect **missionaries** and immigrant aid workers. He organized the **Ellis Island immigrant station** to achieve clarity and intelligence in its work and assigned each employee to tasks that were described in writing and required to be conducted with exactitude.

In 1905, he reached an impasse with President Theodore Roosevelt on the appointment of the new assistant commissioner, Joseph Murray, whom Williams found to be lazy and quite useless. When Roosevelt refused to dismiss his old crony, Williams resigned and returned to his law practice.

In 1910, at the beginning of his second term of office, Williams imposed a $25 financial requirement for immigrants to enter the United States, but Secretary of Commerce and Labor Charles Nagel overruled him. Despite this setback, Williams issued an order declaring "that an alien should have enough to provide for his reasonable wants, and of those of accompanying persons dependent upon him until such time as he is likely to find employment." Nonetheless, Williams dominated **immigrant inspectors** and steamship agents so effectively that the change was not noted; for years immigrants still believed that they needed $25 to enter the United States.

This anti-immigrant policy along with other efforts by Williams to discourage immigrants from coming to America were duly attacked by the German and Jewish immigrant press. Nonetheless, he doubled the rate of exclusions, and in this was sustained by President William H. Taft. Another tactic Williams used was to force second cabin passengers to face inspection at Ellis Island, but in this he was also overruled.

In his first term, Williams's confidential clerk was Allan Robinson, who helped Williams implement his reforms. Commissioner Williams was the author of several vital works on the daily operations of the station, including *Organization of the U.S. Immigrant Station at Ellis Island, New York, Together with a Brief Description of the Work Done in Each of Its Divisions* (1903), *Rules for the Immigrant Station at Ellis Island* (1910–1913) (see Appendix 3), and *Ellis Island: Its Organization and Some of Its Work* (1912) (see Appendix 1).

After leaving Ellis Island, Williams served as the commissioner of water supply, gas, and electricity for New York City (1914–1917). His military record included service in the Spanish

American War in 1898 and with the U.S. army of occupation in Puerto Rico, where he was promoted to major. During World War I, Williams served as a colonel of ordnance in the procurement division in Washington, DC. He then returned to his law practice and worked in his law office at 70 Pine Street until the end of his life. He never married and died in his private quarters at Manhattan's University Club, where he had lived since 1899. Williams was a direct descendant of William Williams, a signer of the Declaration of Independence.

REFERENCES: Pitkin, Thomas M. 1975. *Keepers of the Gate.* New York: New York University Press; *New York Times.* 1947. William Williams, lawyer here, dies—former U.S. commissioner of immigration at Ellis Island—began practice in 1888. February 9; Sullivan, Kerry. 1983. A look at William Williams's first administration as commissioner of Ellis Island. Manuscript Collection, Ellis Island Library, Statue of Liberty N.M.

Within the Quota. This one-act "ballet sketch" was an early musical effort by the composer Cole Porter. Porter and librettist Gerald Murphy used the newly passed **Quota Act of 1921** as an effective background for the production. The ballet opens with an immigrant passing through Ellis Island just within the quota. Next follow a variety of experiences in Manhattan in which he encounters typical Americans from different walks of life. They are an heiress, a "colored" vaudevillian, a flapper, a cowboy. Throughout these delightful encounters, an American puritan continually pops in wearing different guises—a reformer, a revenue agent, an uplifter, and a sheriff. The climax of the ballet arrives when the greenhorn meets none other than silent film star Mary Pickford, "America's Sweetheart," who welcomes and embraces him. She then takes him to Hollywood and transforms him into a movie star, the realization of the American Dream. ***Within the Quota***, which was performed by Les Ballets Suedois, was first presented at the Theatre des Champs Elysees in Paris on October 25, 1923. Its American premiere was at the Century Theater in New York City on November 28, 1923. This was followed by a tour of the country. The show closed in March 1924 after sixty-nine performances. The overture and ballet music were more recently performed by the London Symphony Orchestra (1990) and are available on compact disc (EMI CDC 7 54300 2).

Woman's Home Missionary Society. In 1888, the Woman's Home Missionary Society, an instrument of the Methodist Episcopal Church, opened a shelter for "worthy female immigrants" near **Castle Garden**. In the 1920s and 1930s, its port missionaries at Ellis Island included **Alma Matthews** and Marie Pletzer. Their many tasks included distributing clothing, helping conduct Sunday religious services, and taking admitted immigrant girls and women to the railway stations in Manhattan. In 1927, the Home Missionary Society's shelter for female immigrants was moved to 273 W. 11th Street in Manhattan. It was named Alma Matthews House, in honor of Deaconess Alma Matthews, the society's chief missionary at Ellis Island.

REFERENCES: Jackson, Kenneth T., ed. Methodists. In *Encyclopedia of New York City.* New Haven, Connecticut: Yale University Press.; Pletzer, Marie. 1932. *Ellis Island at the Eastern Gate: Our Work at the Port of New York.* Cincinnati, OH: Woman's Home Missionary Society, Methodist Episcopal Church. Ellis Island, NY: Statue of Liberty and Ellis Island Library.

Women. Unescorted female immigrants were not admitted to the United States on their own account. They were required to be accompanied by an adult male relative (aged 16 or older), who could be responsible for their protection and maintenance. If unaccompanied, a male relative living in the United States was required to meet the immigrant at Ellis Island. On satisfying the inspectors as to his identity, the male relation could be given charge of the immigrant, provided all was suitable and there were no disagreements between the parties.

Because the government was anxious to prevent the immigration of prostitutes, **matrons**

Three peasant women from Slovakia. Courtesy of the Ellis Island Immigration Museum.

Immigrant mother with four children in the 1920s. Courtesy of the Ellis Island Immigration Museum.

were assigned the duty of interrogating suspicious women. Although matrons had no authority in determining an alien's eligibility to enter the country, their judgment in cases of suspicion was often decisive. In addition, the fear of prostitution led to the increased presence of women **missionaries** at Ellis Island after the turn of the century. The continued presence of the **Mission of Our Lady of the Rosary** and the **Woman's Home Missionary Society** and the arrival of groups such as the **Women's Christian Temperance Union** and the **National Council of Jewish Women** were evidence of the heightened concern. A suspected prostitute or a woman traveling under suspicious circumstances with a "strange" man often led to her exclusion for **moral turpitude**.

During the same period, female immigration increased considerably, as men who had immigrated earlier sent for wives, family members, and, in the case of bachelors, picture brides and fiancées. Upon arrival, women were normally met by the men to whom they were betrothed. The **Bureau of Immigration** required these unmarried couples to be legally married before the inspectors could release the women to the custody of the men. As a result, quite a number of marriage contracts were drawn up at Ellis Island and many **marriages** were solemnized in the presence of immigration officers at New York's city hall.

In 1932, a group of American women whose immigrant husbands had left them formed an organization called the League of Abandoned Wives. They pressed charges against the men with the Bureau of Immigration. These cases were nationwide and the men were arrested in cities around the country and brought by train to New York. During deportation hearings at Ellis Island, several of the couples were reconciled. Nonetheless, all the men were ordered deported for violating the terms of their entrance into the country.

World War II found many wives and children of **enemy aliens** interned at Ellis Island for the duration. In December 1945, Congress passed the War Brides Act (59 Statute 659), which allowed mentally or physically defective aliens who were the spouses or children of honorably discharged U.S. citizens who were veterans of World War II to enter the United States as nonquota immigrants. This was followed by the passage of three temporary Alien Fiancées and Fiancés acts (1946–1948), allowing aliens betrothed to U.S. veterans to enter the United States as nonimmigrants for three months in order to be married.

See also **Births; Duncan, Isadora; Food Service and Menus; Foxlee, Ludmila K.; Greenstone, Cecilia; Lloyd, Marie; Mosher, Maud; Nurses; Pregnancies; Public Charge; Razofsky, Cecilia; Steerage; Suicides; White Slave Traffic Act; Women's Home Missionary Society; YWCA**

Women's Christian Temperance Union. This organization provided aid to detained immigrants and was one of the **immigrant aid societies** authorized to send representatives to Ellis Island. One of its early leaders, Margaret Dye Ellis, promoted the appointment of women boarding inspectors at Ellis Island. The officials of the **Bureau of Immigration** met this suggestion with suspicion. Despite their negative response, she persisted and at last persuaded President Theodore Roosevelt to issue an order to that effect in November 1902. Consequently, four women were hired and a matron was assigned by Commissioner **William Williams** to join them. Ellis designed their uniforms, which featured bloomers. This "experiment" of appointing female boarding inspectors was discontinued after three months when Commissioner Williams reported it a failure. Nevertheless, Ellis persisted and finally forced the government to appoint boarding matrons on a permanent basis. One of the first boarding matrons was **Maud Mosher**.

For many years, the Women's Christian Temperance Union was represented at Ellis Island by Athena Marmaroff, a missionary fluent in seven languages who helped deportees at Ellis Island. She began working at the station in 1914 and was still aiding deportees there in the 1940s.

REFERENCE: Unrau, Harlan D. 1984. *The Historic Resource Study: Ellis Island/Statue of Liberty*. Vol. 3. Washington, DC: U.S. Department of Interior, National Park Service.

World Monuments Fund. This preservation organization added the buildings and structures on the south side of Ellis Island to its 1996 list of the world's most threatened culturally significant sites. This act drew public and media attention to the decaying structures on the island. Following in its footsteps, the National Trust for Historic Preservation added the south side to its list of America's Eleven Most Endangered Historic Places in 1997. These acts, followed by the decision of the U.S. Supreme Court to assign the **sovereignty** of the south side and other parts of the island to the State of New Jersey on May 26, 1998, resulted in financial aid coming from New Jersey through Governor Christine Todd Whitman. Whitman also appointed an advisory committee to explore ways of preserving the New Jersey side of the island. The committee's recommendations led to a fund-raising organization called **Save Ellis Island!**, which began working with the **National Park Service** to find ways of restoring the buildings and reusing them.

World War I. The outbreak of the "Great War" in Europe in August 1914 drastically changed conditions at Ellis Island. The nations at war—Austria-Hungary and Germany against Serbia, Russia, France, and Great Britain—had sent scores of immigrants to America. Now things were virtually at a standstill. For the **Bureau of Immigration**, this was especially awkward because the war zone set up by the British and other warring states made it dangerous for ships to cross the Atlantic. Consequently detainees and deportees could not be returned to their home countries as required under immigration law. The entry of Italy and Turkey into the conflict made matters

The 15-year-old Italian soldier boy Enrico Cardi was briefly adopted by vaudeville star Elsie Janis. But when the claim that he was an orphan was proven false, he was promptly deported to Italy. Sherman Collection, courtesy of the Ellis Island Immigration Museum.

much worse. Espionage and sabotage were accessories to the war, and Ellis Island and the Statue of Liberty suffered damage from the **Black Tom** Wharf explosion in 1916. When the United States finally entered the war in April 1917, the large detention and medical facilities at Ellis Island were quickly pressed into war service. In cooperation with the Justice Department, some 300 German and Austro-Hungarian enemy aliens were held prisoner there. In 1918, the War and Navy Departments took over much of the island for the care of wounded and sick soldiers and sailors. From February 1918 until early 1919, the army's Medical Department took over the Ellis Island hospital and the **Registry Room** and other portions of the **Main Building**, while the **navy** used the **baggage and dormitory building** and other rooms in the Main Building for quartering thousands of naval personnel. America's involvement in the war enabled the Bureau of Immigration to curtail its operations, while it played the part of caretaker vis-à-vis the navy, the **army**, and the Justice Department. Nonetheless, the Immigration Bureau retained space necessary for its usual operations on the first floor east wing of the Main Building, occupying all but three medical examination rooms, which were assigned to the navy. The army occupancy of all the hospital buildings caused great trouble for the U.S. **Public Health Service** (PHS). It caused the transfer of medical personnel to other PHS hospitals and the transfer of sick aliens to twenty-eight hospitals scattered throughout the metropolitan area, including the Marine Hospital (NYC), Bayonne Hospital (NJ), Bellevue Hospital (NYC), French Hospital (NYC), Jersey City Hospital, Norwegian Hospital (NYC), St. Luke's Hospital (NYC), St. Vincent's Hospital (NYC), and Ward's Island (NYC) and the West Side Dispensary (NYC). Mental cases were sent to Combes Sanitarium, eye disease cases (including trachoma) were sent to the Manhattan Eye, Ear, and Throat Hospital, and contagious disease cases were sent to Long Island College Hospital. Thousands of military personnel received medical treatment or were assigned to Ellis Island. The **Registry Room**, known as Ward 34, was acclaimed "the biggest ward in the country" in *The Right-About*, an army newspaper. The room contained 260 beds and a corps of surgeons and ward men. In February 1918, 150 contagious disease cases were brought to the **contagious disease ward**. Early in 1919, as war conditions began to wind down, the Young Men's Christian Association opened a victory hut in Battery Park. The hut served as a recreation center for soldiers and sailors in Lower Manhattan, including those at Ellis Island. It was staffed by seven YMCA officials and 200 women volunteers. At the end of June 1919, Commissioner **Frederic Howe** described the end of the military occupation of Ellis Island:

On April 1, 1919, the Navy Department vacated quarters which it had occupied at this station from February 1, 1918, and thereafter removed certain equipment which it had installed, including galley, storerooms, etc. The premises were restored to us in excellent condition. . . . On June 30, 1919, the Army withdrew from the Ellis Island hospitals which had been placed at their disposal on March 1, 1918. On April 1, 1919, they had relinquished that portion of the main building previously assigned to them. Here also the equipment which had been installed for their use was removed and the building restored to the satisfaction of the service.

In the aftermath of the war, an almost hysterical movement to expel radicals from the country took hold. Known as the **red scare**, it symbolized the nation's displeasure with European politics and struggles and reaffirmed America's preference for isolation.

REFERENCES: Howe, Frederic. 1919. *Annual Report of the Commissioner General of Immigration*; Ellis Island during World War I. 1918. File Folder of Naval and Bureau of Immigration Correspondence. Ellis Island, NY: Statue of Liberty and Ellis Island Library; Unrau, Harlan D. 1984. *The Historic Resource Study: Ellis Island/Statue of Liberty*. Vol. 3. Washington, DC: U.S. Department of Interior, National Park Service.

World War II. Although Ellis Island continued to be used as an immigrant detention and deportation station for routine cases throughout the war, it was also used for two other major purposes. The U.S. **Coast Guard** set up an important training station there (1939–1946) and the **Immigration and Naturalization Service** (INS) used the **Main Building** and portions of the **baggage and dormitory building** for processing and housing **enemy aliens**. The resident aliens held were those accused of being **Nazis**, Italian fascists, and espionage agents or potential saboteurs. Germans, Italians, and Japanese were the chief nationalities detained for these reasons.

In 1943, the INS moved its headquarters from the island to 70 Columbus Avenue in Manhattan.

The thousands of routine cases of detainees and deportees handled at Ellis Island were often stateless Europeans (Belgians, Danes, Dutch, Poles, French, Norwegians, and so on), fleeing Germans and Italians, seamen overstaying shore leave (especially those from the British West Indies), illegal Chinese aliens, **stowaways** from Portugal, Spain, and the Latin American nations (especially Cuba), and scores of persons without passports or visas. Many Mexicans and Canadians also found themselves facing deportation at Ellis Island. Other detainees at the island were convicted criminals, persons guilty of **moral turpitude** (including prostitutes and procurers), and the illiterate or insane. All of these types of people were regularly deported—often to any country that would take them.

REFERENCES: Carter, Hugh, LeRoy DePuy, Ernest Rubin, and Marguerite Milan. 1946. *Administrative History of the Immigration and Naturalization Service during World War II*. Washington, DC: U.S. Department of Justice, INS; Moreno, Barry. 1997. *Ellis Island during the Second World War*. National Park Service, Ellis Island Immigration Museum.

Wright, Frank Lloyd (b. Richland Center, Wisconsin, June 8, 1867; d. Phoenix, Arizona, April 9, 1959). Architect. In the late 1950s, Frank Lloyd Wright was approached by broadcaster Jerry Damon and director Elwood M. Doudt, who asked the distinguished architect to draw a design for Ellis Island. Fascinated, Wright dreamed up his last great project: the concept of a perfectly "self-contained supermodern city." In 1962, Wright's son-in-law, William Wesley Peters, presented a design for this "city of tomorrow" to the Senate subcommittee dealing with the fate of the island. The fantastic drawing was reminiscent of Thea von Harbou's classic 1920s science fiction novel, *Metropolis*. The proposed city was to be named "The Key" in memory of the island's famous role as the portal to America. It was Wright's intention that it would inspire casual living without the clamor and haste of big-city life.

Wright wanted all the old buildings demolished and replaced with ultramodern structures. "The Key" was to be furnished with an agora or marketplace, containing shops, banks,

Architect Frank Lloyd Wright's fantastic vision of Ellis Island as the "city of the future." Courtesy of the Ellis Island Immigration Museum.

restaurants, nightclubs, and moving streets in place of the automobile. Huge air-conditioned domes would house auditoriums, churches, and exhibition halls. Above this, there was to be an expansive upper terrace held up by gold-hued steel cables. The island was to house 7,500 permanent residents and a luxury hotel accommodating 500 guests. A yacht marina was to have moorings for 450 pleasure boats. Throughout the city, Wright visualized a radial cable system similar to methods used in suspension bridges. The architect planned the new Ellis Island as a haven for the elderly and the site of a school for Americans who were planning to go into public and private service in foreign countries.

REFERENCES: Benton, Barbara. 1985. *Ellis Island: A Pictorial History.* New York: Facts on File; Novotny, Ann. 1971. *Strangers at the Door.* Riverside, CT: Chelsea; Pitkin, Thomas M. 1975.

Y

YMCA (Young Men's Christian Association). This organization provided an occasional presence at Ellis Island, primarily assisting aliens held in detention. It was especially active from 1915 to 1925. For instance, during the administration of Commissioner **Frederic C. Howe**, the YMCA sent athletic instructors to the island to provide daily classes in calisthenics and sporting activities for men. In addition, the YMCA sponsored classes teaching **Americanization**.

See also **Missionaries**

YWCA (Young Women's Christian Association). **Edith Terry Bremer** brought the YWCA to Ellis Island on a permanent basis sometime around 1919. Bremer had founded the YMCA's National Institute for Immigrant Welfare some years before, and it was her goal to aid immigrant women not only in American cities but also at the place of their entrance. Thus she appointed women fluent in the languages necessary and opened a series of foreign language bureaus at Ellis Island. Among the best-known women posted to the island was **Ludmila K. Foxlee**, who aided Slavs of the former Austro-Hungarian monarchy.

See also **Immigrant Aid Societies; Missionaries**

YWCA social worker Ludmila Foxlee aided these Russian immigrants, 1923. Courtesy of the Ellis Island Immigration Museum.

Z

Zucker, Edward D. (b. 1875; d. New York, July 5, 1943). Administrative assistant to the district director, Ellis Island. Edward Zucker joined the **Bureau of Immigration** as an **immigrant inspector** at Newport, Vermont, in 1910. After serving there and on the Canadian border, he came to Ellis Island in 1920. He served as chief of the **Registry Division** (1929–1942) before assuming his last post as a private secretary to District Director **W. Frank Watkins**. Zucker was also a founder and longtime president of the Association of Immigration and Naturalization Service Officers.

REFERENCE: *New York Times.* 1943. Edward D. Zucker, immigration aide. Obituary. July 6.

Appendix 1

ELLIS ISLAND: ITS ORGANIZATION AND SOME OF ITS WORK

[*Commissioner William Williams wrote this report in December 1912. It provides an excellent description of the general operation of his second administration and the bureaucratic structure that he perfected. Archived among the William Williams papers at the New York Public Library, the following is the full text of his report.*]

The immigration laws (by which expression it is not intended to refer to the Chinese Exclusion Act) prohibit certain classes of aliens from entering the United States and provide a summary means of expelling, usually within three years from the time of entry, all aliens who entered in violation of law, such as have become a public charge "from causes existing prior to landing," and a few other classes more fully referred to later. Prior to 1903, these laws were administered through the Treasury Department, but since that year this has been done through the Department of Commerce and Labor. One of its principal bureaus is the "Bureau of Immigration and Naturalization," presided over by a commissioner-general. Immigrant stations, of which Ellis Island is the largest, are established at several points with commissioners in charge at all of the principal ports. The number of aliens who have arrived at the Port of New York during each of the last ten years has been as follows:

Fiscal year 1902–1903 . . .	689,000
Fiscal year 1903–1904 . . .	633,500
Fiscal year 1904–1905 . . .	821,000
Fiscal year 1905–1906 . . .	935,500
Fiscal year 1906–1907 . . .	1,123,501
Fiscal year 1907–1908 . . .	689,500
Fiscal year 1908–1909 . . .	733,300
Fiscal year 1909–1910 . . .	912,000
Fiscal year 1910–1911 . . .	749,600
Fiscal year 1911–1912 . . .	726,000

The principal excluded classes are these:

Idiots, imbeciles, feeble-minded persons, and epileptics.
Insane persons and those who have been insane within five years.
Persons who at any time have had two or more attacks of insanity.
Persons afflicted with tuberculosis or with a loathsome or dangerous contagious disease (including trachoma).
Persons suffering from any mental or physical defect which may affect their ability to earn a living.
Paupers, persons likely to become a public charge, and professional beggars.

Persons who have been convicted of or admit having committed crimes or misdemeanors involving moral turpitude.
Polygamists and anarchists.
Prostitutes, procurers and "persons who are supported by or receive in whole or in part the proceeds of prostitution."
Persons coming to perform manual labor under contract.
Persons whose ticket of passage has been paid for by any association, municipality, or foreign government.
Children under 16 unaccompanied by either parent, except in the discretion of the Secretary of Commerce and Labor.

Even a cursory glance at this list shows what an important [role] the medical officers must play in any effective administration of the law, and it is their duty to "certify for the information of the immigration officers" all mental and physical defects observed by them. This list further shows that grave administrative difficulties must often be encountered in determining who are paupers, persons "likely to become a public charge" and persons suffering from physical defects which may affect their ability to earn a living. There is no hard and fast rule by which these classes can be detected and yet it is not only the law, but of high importance to the country, that they not be allowed to enter. This subject will be dealt with more fully later, it being desired at this time merely to direct attention to the constant necessity immigration officials are under of exercising sound judgment. Their responsibility is the greater because their decisions are not reviewable by the courts save where it can be shown that they have abused their authority. (The Japanese Immigrant Case, 189 U.S., 86, 102; Chin Yow Case, 208 U.S., 8, 11–13).

Following is a brief outline of the principal processes of inspection. Immigrants pass first before surgeons, then before an immigrant inspector and all who may not appear to the latter to be "clearly and beyond a doubt" entitled to land must be held for "special inquiry" and sent before Boards of Special Inquiry appointed by the Commissioner. At Ellis Island, there are usually from five to eight such boards in session. They have power to admit or exclude, and an appeal lies (in most cases) from their excluding decision through the Commissioner and the Commissioner-General to the Secretary of Commerce and Labor, whose decision is final. All such cases as the examining inspector does not hold for special inquiry he either detains "temporarily" (see *infra*) or permits to land at once. The work incident to the application of a complex law to great numbers of immigrants speaking a variety of foreign tongues must obviously be very difficult, and it requires the services of a large corps of officials. At the present time these number about six hundred and fifty, including one hundred and thirty medical officers and hospital attendants. Most cases must be disposed of through quick and accurate work, while others require careful investigation combined with great patience. As a result of experience the following divisions have been created by the Commissioner for the transaction of official business at Ellis Island.

Executive Division
Medical Division
Boarding Division
Registry Division
Information Division
Special Inquiry Division
Deporting Division
Statistical Division
Mechanical Division
Laborers' Division
Night Division

Each division, other than the Medical Division, is in charge of a "chief of division" or other head responsible to the Superintendent and through him to the Assistant Commissioner and the Commissioner, for the efficient performance of the work of his division. Rules have been prepared for each of the divisions other than the Medical Divisions describing in detail the work thereof, to which rules reference is made for further information concerning the work of Ellis Island beyond that given in this paper.

Executive Division

The Commissioner presides over the station through this division. A number of other important officials serve in it, including the Assistant Commissioner, Superintendent, Chief Clerk, Attorney, Law Clerk, Civil Engineer, Treasurer and Storekeeper. In addition, there are attached to it stenographers, clerks and messengers. Through the Assistant Commissioner and the Superintendent the Commissioner keeps in touch with, and directs to such an extent as he may desire, the internal work and machinery of Ellis Island.

The Assistant Commissioner is required to keep himself well informed as to the work of the station as a whole and of the several divisions and as to the character of services rendered by all employees. He is expected to rectify and correct any error in administration, or if unable to do this, to report the case to the Commissioner. He must hold himself in ready to assume full charge of the conduct of affairs whenever the Commissioner is absent.

The duties of the Superintendent are those usually pertaining to this office and include supervising through the chiefs of division the work of all immigration officials other than those reporting direct to the Commissioner or Assistant Commissioner, co-ordinating the work of the several divisions, calling together the heads of the several divisions from time to time in conference, and satisfying himself that the privilege holders are properly performing their several contracts.

Chiefs of division are appointed by the Commissioner and required amongst other things carefully and impartially to observe the work of the officials under them, to instruct them in their duties, and to establish amongst them a spirit of cooperation. They must see to it that their subordinates shall bear themselves with dignity and treat with courtesy all with whom they have business to transact.

The work of the Executive Division further includes the conduct of the principal external affairs of the station (including all relations with the Washington authorities and the more important relations with other government offices and the transportation companies); receiving and replying to all correspondence, amounting to 300 letters a day, more or less; distributing or disposing of telegrams (twenty or thirty thousand per annum) received on behalf of immigrants; appointing boards of special inquiry; receiving notices of appeal and hearing appeals from board decisions; passing upon requests for hearings before boards; conducting the law work except actual litigation conducted by United States Attorneys; executing warrants to arrest aliens who are improperly in the country and conducting hearings thereon; keeping the government accounts; purchasing and supervising the expenditure of supplies; drawing plans and specifications for and supervising the execution of all construction work; caring for Government property; supervising the operation of the ferryboat and other boats; and supervision (by the Commissioner, Assistant and Superintendent) of all other divisions.

Some of the most difficult and important work which devolves upon the Commissioner is that of hearing appeals from board decisions, dealt with more fully under *Special Inquiry Division*.

An immense amount of law work and work of a quasi-legal character must be done at Ellis Island. In litigated matters the office is represented by the United States Attorneys (usually those of the Southern and Eastern Districts of New York). There may be as many as forty or fifty active matters in the courts at one time relating to a variety [of] subjects. While, as already stated, the Courts have no jurisdiction to review the decisions of the immigration authorities except where abuse of authority can be shown, yet many writs of *habeas corpus* are sued out, almost always, however, improperly so, the Courts being willing to grant the mere sworn conclusion of some one that an alien is being improperly held, without requiring the facts to be stated on which such conclusion is based. The record shows that with rare exceptions these writs are dismissed on the ground that the alien has had the executive hearing which Congress contemplated he should have and been duly excluded by a board of special inquiry. Some of the further classes of litigated matters at the present time are as follows: (a) Sundry breaches of the immigration law by steamship companies for the improper landing of immigrants (failure to detain them on board), for taking on board immigrants with dangerous contagious diseases, for attempting to smuggle immigrants into the country, and for improper manifestation; (b) questions arising out of the fact of former domicile in the United States; (c) status of wives and sons of naturalized United States citizens; (d) suits to recover penalty for importing contract laborers and from bondsmen in public charge cases; (e) prosecutions arising out of the importation of women for immoral purposes and for failing to report inmates of houses of prostitution; (f) prosecutions for perjury committed before boards of special inquiry. While the litigation is conducted by the Department of Justice, yet this office, through its attorney and law clerk, is necessarily and properly called upon to do a great deal of work in preparing the cases.

Some of the non-litigated law work includes drawing numerous contracts (many of them related to improvements), and proceedings incident to the arrest and deportation of certain classes of aliens improperly in the United States. These classes are (a) aliens who have entered the country in violation of law and without inspection and such as have become public charges therein "from causes existing prior to landing", and (b) alien prostitutes and procurers. The former may be deported within three years of the time of entry, the latter at any time. Any alien has entered the United States in violation of law if in fact he belonged to one of the excluded classes, although such fact may at the time of entry have escaped attention. Usual instances in which an alien becomes a public charge are where he enters a public almshouse or a hospital or is sent to jail. What may be a "cause existing prior to landing" depends somewhat on the circumstances of each case. Where the alien is found in a public almshouse or hospital the proof usually required to show that his presence there is due to a "cause existing prior to landing" is a medical certificate establishing the existence of some mental or physical disability prior to the time when he entered the country. Congress has conferred upon the Secretary very great powers in respect of the arrest of all such aliens and his decision is not subject to review by the Courts, which require only (though this is not mentioned in the statute) that prior to deportation there shall have been a hearing, however summary, in order that the alien shall have enjoyed "due process of law". The Secretary is, for practical reasons, compelled to delegate to the immigration authorities the work of conducting such hearings and preparing the records on which deportation occurs. This, though burdensome, is, like so much other work at Ellis Island, very interesting. Wide latitude is given to the officers presiding at such hearings (which the Commissioner himself often conducts). He is not hampered by technical rules of evidence and, with intelligence action, he may render these proceedings a very effective means of ascertaining the truth—in some sense a more effective means than are court proceedings. For further information concerning this matter reference is made to a paper entitled "Explanatory of Warrant Proceedings".

It is of immense importance that immigrants be received in a manner calculated to make upon them a favorable impression. To secure proper treatment on the part of all officials everywhere and at all times an order has been widely posted requiring that they "shall be treated with kindness and civility by everyone at Ellis Island", and the Commissioner requests that any instance of disobedience of this order be brought immediately to his attention. Furthermore, the premises outdoors are made to appear as attractive as possible, through lawns, flowers and hedges; while inside the buildings are kept clean, notwithstanding the conditions render them some of the hardest buildings in the world to keep clean.

So long as immigration occurs there will be on hand unscrupulous persons ready to exploit the ignorant immigrant after he leaves Ellis Island. Usually they are found to be the immigrant's own countrymen. Though the statues authorize the authorities to "protect the United States and aliens migrating thereto from fraud and loss", yet the amount of protection they can give after the immigrant has passed beyond their control is limited. But while unable themselves to give much protection, they can through their influence effectively assist outside agencies engaged in giving it. Much in this direction can be done by the missionaries and immigrant aid societies, referred to later. A new influence for good has recently come into this field through the North American Civic League for Immigrants, composed of high minded citizens who are endeavoring, amongst many other things, to protect immigrants from imposition between the time when they leave federal control and arrive at destination. They provide guides to conduct immigrants, at reasonable charges, to their destination in and about New York City and, from time to time, they are causing notorious swindlers to be sent to jail, thereby deterring a large number of others from plying their trade.

Medical Division

The statute provides (Section 17) that the physical and mental examination of all arriving aliens shall be made by medical officers of the U.S. Public Health Service. They are under the Treasury Department and detailed for service to Ellis Island and other immigrant stations. The statute further provides that these "officers shall certify for the information of the immigration officers and the boards of special inquiry any and all physical and mental defects and diseases" observed by them. The importance of their work has already been alluded to and can hardly be exaggerated. Nearly two thirds of the buildings at Ellis Island are hospitals. These medical officers are relied upon to detect all mental defects and also all physical defects not dealt with by the State Quarantine authorities. The latter remove from the vessel and send to Hoffman and Swinburne islands in the lower bay all immigrants suffering from any quarantineable disease, this principal diseases of the character being cholera, yellow fever, smallpox, typhus fever, leprosy and plague. All other physical disabilities are dealt with by the medical officers at Ellis Island, who are also expected to hold all idiots, imbeciles, feeble-minded persons, epileptics, insane persons, those who have been insane within five years, and those who at any time have had two or more attacks of insanity. One of the contagious diseases of most frequent occurrence is trachoma, a disease of the eye prevalent in many parts of Europe, the result in part of low vitality and filthy surroundings. But for the immigration law this disease would soon spread to many parts of the United States. Further reference to some of the work of the Public Health officers is made under the title *Registry Division.* Immigrants pass before the medical officers before they are inspected by the immigration authorities. Medical officers always accompany the inspectors of the Boarding Division down the Bay to assist in the inspection of cabin aliens, which usually occurs between Quarantine and the docks. Immigrants suffering from disabilities of a serious character are sent to the Ellis Island hospital, and appropriate medical certificates are thereafter issued for the information of the immigration authorities.

Boarding Division

The law provides that it shall be the duty of the immigration officials "to go or send competent assistants" to the vessels arriving with aliens and there inspect such aliens, or "said immigration officers may order a temporary removal of such aliens for examination at a designated time and place"; such temporary removal not to be considered a landing. The Government is thus empowered at its option to inspect all aliens on the vessel or to order all of them, irrespective of class, to Ellis Island. The practice is to order to Ellis Island all who come in the steerage (commonly known as immigrants), but to inspect on the vessels those coming in the cabin, sending to Ellis Island only such of them as it is found necessary to detain for further inquiry.

The first immigration officials to come in contact with arriving aliens are those of this division. Their headquarters are at the Barge Office, Manhattan Island, where the times of probable arrival of vessels at Quarantine on the cutter belonging to the Immigration Service, accompanied by medical officers of the Public Health Service. Upon boarding a vessel the medical and immigration officials proceed to inspect the cabin aliens and are often able to do so by the time the vessel is docked. The process of inspection is the same as at Ellis Island and is described fully under the heading *Registry Division.* Cabin passengers as a rule are less apt to be ineligible as steerage passengers: their inspection can proceed more rapidly and far fewer are held for special inquiry. As to this, however, much depends on the character of the passengers. On some lines, particularly those running on southern routes, the difference in price between the steerage and second-cabin tickets may be as low as $10, resulting in many persons of the immigrant type traveling in the second cabin. Again, some steamship officials (fortunately few) attempt evasion of the immigration law by sending obviously ineligible immigrants in the cabin, and sometimes families are separated in the expectation that the ineligible one traveling in the cabin pass through unnoticed. During three recent months the number of second cabin aliens brought to Ellis Island reached over 2,000.

All aliens brought to the United States must be properly manifested. As to the preparation of the manifests and the proper method to be pursued in procuring the information necessary to complete the same, see section 12 to 16 of the law and office letter of August 23, 1902, addressed to the owners of vessels bringing aliens to New York. To enable inspectors to use the manifests instead of the ship's passenger list (as formerly occurred) in the inspection of second cabin aliens a circular letter was issued under date of October 20, 1902, in the relation of grouping of such aliens. It requested also that first cabin manifests be printed on pink paper, those of the second cabin on light yellow paper and those pertaining to steerage aliens on white paper. The identification cards of second cabin aliens found qualified to land are stamped by the boarding inspector and must be surrendered upon leaving the vessel. See circular letter dated April 8, 1903.

Upon completion of the inspection of cabin aliens it becomes the duty of the immigrant inspectors on board to grant to steerage passengers claiming to be citizens the opportunity to satisfy them that they are such, and if this be the case, to allow them to land at the dock. Those claiming to be native born must make affidavit to this fact. Those claiming to be naturalized citizens must present a passport such as is issued to citizens or a final naturalization certificate, and such as are unable to do this are sent to Ellis Island for inspection. There are many fraudulent naturalization papers and irregular passports in existence, and valid ones are often bought and sold. The task of the inspector who passes upon these cases is often both a difficult and delicate one, since citizens usually resent being brought to Ellis Island with immigrants. It has, however, been decided by the Supreme Court that the immigration authorities have the right to hold arriving passengers for the purpose of determining whether or not they are citizens.

Cattlemen receive special consideration in view of the peculiar character of their work, and certificates are issued to those sailing in charge of live-stock entitling them to re-enter the country without inspection . . . similarly horsemen and birdmen are always inspected at the dock and are not required to go to Ellis Island except for some good cause, such as disease.

It is not practicable or necessary to recite here all of the further matters to which inspectors of this division must give their attention. They are enumerated in the rules.

Suffice it further that their work is of a very responsible nature, and coming as they do in contact with cabin passengers, they are required to use special judgement and tact in its discharge. Criminals and other bad characters, usually bearing no earmarks, seek to enter the country by taking passage in the cabin, and yet the intelligent work of the boarding inspectors often results in their apprehension. These inspectors are put in possession of many confidential notices received in relation to persons about to arrive. While most of them are sent *bona fide* and are of great value in the detention of criminals, yet some of them are lodged here through spite. The duty of determining to which class such a notice relates usually devolves upon these inspectors, and its is greatly to their credit that they apprehend only bad characters and only rarely is their conduct made even the subject of a complaint. In this connexion let it be noted that the power of the immigration officials is so summary that foreign authorities desiring to have an alien apprehended often seek to accomplish through the Immigration Service what should be accomplished through extradition proceedings. This office always declines to allow itself to be used in this fashion.

The further duty devolves upon the boarding inspectors of seeing to it that the steerage aliens (immigrants) are sent to Ellis Island. The rules require that all steerage aliens be sent there, and it is only in very exceptional cases and upon very peculiar facts that the Commissioner consents that one be inspected and released on the pier: for a contrary practice might open the door to great abuses. They proceed to Ellis Island on barges and small steamboats, the steamship companies being responsible for their safe delivery at the immigrant station. It is customary for one of the officials who has boarded the steamer to accompany them and he brings with him the manifests. Where more than one barge or boat is required, he usually comes with the last one and sends the manifests to Ellis Island by the master of the first.

Registry Division

Upon reaching Ellis Island the immigrants first pass before the surgeons and then come before the officials of the Registry Division for inspection. This division should be properly called *Division of Primary Inspection* because the work of registering is only an incident of the important work done here, and registry work is also done in the Boarding Division. But it is not easy to change designations sanctioned by long uses, hence the expression "Registry Division" is allowed to stand. The statute requires that the owners of vessels furnish manifests (sections 12 and 13) containing the names and certain information in relation to all immigrants, and to each immigrant or head of a family there must be given a *ticket* designating the particular manifest sheet in which his name appears. The chief of the division places inspectors at the end of each of the long lines on the registry floor, distributes the manifest sheets amongst them, and thereafter the *groupers* see to it that the immigrants enter the line at the end of which are the manifest sheets containing their names. The examining inspectors question each immigrant as to the information contained in the manifests and correct any errors or omissions, of which there are usually many. Upon the corrected facts and the impression gained by conversation and observation they determine whether or not the immigrant is *clearly and beyond a doubt entitled to land.* If they believe this to be the case he is forthwith landed. But if they entertain the slightest doubt it is their duty not to attempt to solve the doubt but to hold the immigrant for special inquiry. These inspectors are constantly called upon to solve difficult questions and to exercise good judgement upon a brief investigation. The proportion of immigrants held for special inquiry varies greatly sometimes only five percent of those on a given vessel will be so held and again the number may rise to thirty percent. While the inevitable differences of opinion amongst inspectors as to who is and who is not *clearly and beyond a doubt entitled to land* is a factor to be considered in this connexion, yet the chief reasons for these variations lie in the differing personal characteristics of the immigrants. Experience shows that those from southern, south-eastern and eastern Europe are more likely to be ineligible than are those from northern Europe; and this is for many reasons which go to the essence of the immigration problem, including more of them are in more physical, mental and financial condition, more of them illiterate and more of them possess a low standard of living.

Rules have been laid down to guide and assist inspectors in determining who should be held for special inquiry. Immigrants obviously belonging to any of the excluded classes must of course be so held. Included in this category are those certified by the surgeons to be idiots, imbeciles, feeble-minded persons, epileptics, insane persons, and those afflicted with tuberculosis or with a loathsome dangerous or contagious disease. Exclusion (by a board of special inquiry) follows as a matter of course upon all such certificates and cases of this class are from the administrative point of view the simplest ones that come before the office. Immigrants certified by the surgeons for any other mental defect, those who have ever been objects of public charity, those who appear to be devoid of ordinary intelligence, unmarried pregnant women and children under sixteen unaccompanied by either parent, should also be held for special inquiry as a matter of course, but in these cases exclusion may or may not follow. Reference has already been made to the grave administrative difficulties which attach to the application of the law to three of the excluded classes, namely, persons suffering from physical defects which may affect their ability to earn a living, paupers and persons likely to become a public charge. Some of the physical defects that require consideration in this connexion are ankylosis of various joints, arterio-sclerosis, atrophy of extremities, chronic progressive diseases of central nervous system, chronic inflammation of lymph glands of neck, dislocation of hip joints and lameness, double hernia, goiter, poor physical development, locomotor ataxia, psoriasis and lupus (chronic skin diseases), valvular disease of heart, and well-marked varicose veins. It is usually necessary and proper to hold for special inquiry all immigrants certified by the surgeons to be suffering from these are like defects. They are not, however, *per se* grounds for exclusion (as are idiocy, insanity and loathsome or dangerous contagious diseases), though when present in aggravated form they usually affect the immigrant's ability to earn a living (often they render him incapable to do so) and they thus operate to bring him within one of the excluded classes irrespective of whether in addition he is likely to become a public charge. This is a fact not generally understood.

In determining whether or not an immigrant is a pauper or a person likely to become a public charge, inspectors must consider amongst other matters his occupation, his proficiency in the same (including, where relevant, his physical ability to pursue it and his mental aptitude therefor), the demand for labor or the services of the kind he is able to render at the place to which he intends to go, the number of persons who may be dependent upon him for support here or abroad, and the value of his property. The vital questions in these cases usually is whether or not he will be able to secure profitable employment and will be self-supporting before his funds are exhausted. In the absence of a statutory provision no hard and fast rule can be laid down as to the amount of money an immigrant must have, but he should be detained where his funds are not deemed adequate for his maintenance until such time as he is likely to find profitable employment. Cases of wives and minor children going to persons as to whom the examining inspector is satisfied that they are able, willing and legally bound to support them may constitute exceptions to this rule.

The application of the law to criminals, anarchists, contract laborers and some of the classes is somewhat difficult, but for other reasons: such persons rarely bear any earmarks, and many of them are entering the United States because the authorities are ignorant of, and have no means of learning, the facts upon which they should be excluded. This is likely to continue to be the case until Congress perfects the machinery of the law. As to this see the Commissioner's Annual Report for 1912.

Where immigrants are presumably qualified to land but there exists so minor objection to permitting them to do so immediately, which objection is likely to become overcome within a short time, the examining inspector may postpone completion of the process of primary inspection by detaining them *temporarily*, sending them to the Information Division where their cases are disposed of under the rules of that division. Typical instances where such action may be proper are where addresses must be verified or relatives or friends notified to call. Whether or not an immigrant shall be landed, temporarily detained or held for special inquiry often calls, as do so many other things at Ellis Island, for the exercise of sound judgement based upon a knowledge of all relevant facts which may be ascertained.

An immigrant held for special inquiry receives a yellow card with appropriate data inscribed thereon, while one temporarily detained receives a white card similarly inscribed. These cards serve to identify those holding them so long as they remain at Ellis Island. The final disposition of their cases is noted on the back prior to filing.

The inspection of immigrants sent to the hospital may occur either later in the Registry Division or at the hospital, according to the nature of the affliction. Special regard is had for the safety and convenience of small children, young women and aged persons. If they are going to inland points they will be urged to telegraph their relatives or friends before leaving Ellis Island and to insure this being done inspectors pin to them slips of paper bearing the words *Telegraph.* If they are going to New York they are detained until someone calls for them.

Not one of the least difficult features of Ellis Island work is that much of it must be done through a great number of foreign languages. The services of interpreters are required who read, write and speak the following languages and dialects: *Albanian, Armenian, Bohemian, Bulgarian, Croatian, Dalmatian, Danish, Dutch, Finnish, Flemish, French, German, Greek, Italian, Lithuanian, Magyar, Montenegrin, Norwegian, Persian, Polish, Portuguese, Roumanian, Russian, Ruthenian, Servian, Slovak, Slovenian, Spanish, Swedish, Syrian (Arabic), Turkish, Yiddish.*

Interpreters are attached in the first instance to the Registry or Boarding divisions, and upon the application of the chairman of the boards and heads of other divisions requiring their services they are assigned for duty in accordance with such requests.

The question of liability of alien seamen to inspection under the immigration law has always proved a difficult one. Owing to the peculiar nature of their calling they enjoy privileges accorded to no other aliens. Only such as land with intent to abandon their calling are subject to the immigration laws. Thus the door is open to great abuses. When an alien seaman has deserted it is the duty of the owner of the vessel to notify the immigration authorities at once, but he often fails to do so and there is no way of compelling him to. The attention of Congress has been directed to this matter.

Immigrants found by the officials of this division qualified to land forthwith are directed to the ferryboat or to the railroad room, according as their destination is New York or some point beyond.

Information Division

Several hundred thousand persons call annually at Ellis Island for various purposes, some on official business, others as visitors, but the great majority to meet or make inquiries concerning relatives and friends. All such persons are referred to this division; hence its name. To collate and distribute the information called for and direct the persons calling to the particular part of the building to which they must go consumes the time of over twenty officials.

To this division is sent timely information concerning detained immigrants from various other divisions and from the hospital, so that answers may be given to inquiries. There is kept here a record of those held for special inquiry in which is listed opposite each name the action taken by the board and where the immigrant goes upon leaving Ellis Island. This record is referred to when persons call for interviews with excluded immigrants and those whose cases are deferred and when such persons are directed to the Commissioner's office to obtain a rehearing in a case once before a board. There is also kept a record of all the immigrants detained in the hospital or in reference to whom medical certificates have been issued and of the ultimate disposition of their cases. Still another record is that of immigrants turned over to missionaries or immigrant aide societies, the latter being required from time to time to submit a report showing what they have done with such immigrants.

After disposing of inquiries concerning detained immigrants, the addresses of others who have already left Ellis Island without being detained are looked up on the manifests and given to those properly applying therefor.

The records of this division are used also by the clerks of the Executive Division charged with the disposition of telegrams and money orders intended for immigrants. Over 20,000 such telegrams are received annually, and much care must be exercised in distributing them.

Under the heading *Registry Division* reference was made to "temporarily detained" immigrants who are presumably qualified to land but whose inspection it was desirable to postpone a short time to enable them to overcome some minor objection standing in the way of immediate landing. They are sent to this division because usually they are detained to be called for and, as already shown, the persons calling come to this division, their name with certain data entered upon sheets, full inquiry is made as to the cause of temporary detention and official postal-cards or telegrams in proper cases sent to relatives and friends.

A person calling at Ellis Island in response to such telegram or otherwise, must at the outset satisfy the inspectors that he is a proper person to receive the immigrant for whom he calls and that the latter desires to go with him. Touching scenes may often be witnessed when immigrants meet close relatives who have preceded them to this country and whom they have not seen for some time. Immigrants held in this division whose relatives or friends fail to call are sometimes discharged to responsible missionaries and immigrant aid societies, and this action may be proper when it will aid qualified immigrants without relatives or friends here to secure employment.

In allowing temporarily detained immigrants to land, this division completes the work of inspection begun by the Registry Division. A full record of each case is made on the back of the detention card in accordance with a printed form appearing thereon. All who after a reasonable number of days (usually five) are unable to hear from their relatives or friends, or for any other reason fail to satisfy the inspectors of this division that they are entitled to land, are held for special inquiry and sent o the special inquiry room.

Special Inquiry Division

The immigration law (section 24) provides that

> Every alien who may not appear to the examining immigrant inspector at the port of arrival to be clearly and beyond a doubt entitled to land, shall be detained for examination in relation thereto by a board of special inquiry.

No harder work exists at Ellis Island than that required of boards of special inquiry. The task of the primary inspector is a difficult one, but after he is called upon only to detect and hold doubtful cases. Boards must *decide* them. The statute affords them but little aid in doing so, nor have any rules been laid down for their guidance other than those directing the attention to the principal elements to be considered in determining who is a pauper or a person likely to become a public charge. Good board members are not easily found. They must, amongst other things, be intelligent, able [to] exercise sound judgement and to elicit relevant facts from immigrants and witnesses who are often stupid or deceitful. Each of the cases with which they have to deal is likely to present their own peculiar features, and they have fewer precedents to guide them than have courts of law.

Boards are appointed daily by the Commissioner in such numbers as the special inquiry work of the day may require. There may be from five to eight board[s] in session. Each consists of three inspectors and has *authority to determine whether an alien who has been duly held shall be allowed to land or shall be deported* (section 25). The Chief of this division distributes the ones amongst the several boards and sees to it that the immigrants, their witnesses and all documentary evidence are produced as speedily as possible. Boards may dispose of cases upon the facts as they appear at the first hearing but often the interests of justice demand that a case shall be deferred for the production of further evidence. Even after exclusion has occurred a further hearing is granted whenever new and relevant evidence can be produced. Where a board feels itself bound to exclude through believing the case to have great merit, the chairman, in addition to notifying the immigrant of his right of appeal, may submit to the Commissioner a memorandum to this effect. Each board has at its disposal an interpreter, a messenger and a stenographer, and the daily board minutes vary, from 100 to 250 closely typewritten pages.

Each board record should, on its face, justify the action taken. Where the appearance of an alien is a relevant fact, this must be noted; also, the impressions made by witnesses, and before rending its decision the board is directed in most cases in a brief "opinion" to summarize in logical sequence the principal circumstances upon which it bases its decision. It is especially important that it do this where its reasons are conclusions from the evidence, as is usually the case when an immigrant is excluded as a person likely to become a public charge, or where the record is a very long one. These "opinions" are of great assistance to the Commissioner and later to the

Washington authorities, and what is still more important, they are calculated to induce the boards to reason correctly and refrain from rendering decisions unsupported by the facts. . . . Following are samples of some well considered "opinions" on which immigrants were excluded as likely to become public charges taken at random from recent board records.

1. The elder alien is a Syrian widow, by occupation a tailoress. She arrives penniless, encumbered with three helpless children. The testimony shows that she has been unable to support them since her husband's death. All are practically paupers, and if landed would of necessity immediately be recipients of private charity and would probably become public charges.
2. The son because of his age (six years) is dependent upon the father for his support. The father owing to his advance years and poor physical appearance we do not believe capable of self-support—his certified condition alone renders him incapable of supporting himself. They have no one else in the United States legally obliged to provide for them, neither is the money in their possession sufficient to do so. Upon all the facts including, incidentally the medical certificate, we find that the elder alien is suffering from a physical defect of a nature which may and will affect his ability to earn a living.

Where an immigrant has been certified for a physical or mental defect which the board finds will affect his ability to earn a living, it is directed to exclude him on this specific ground in addition to any other ground which may be warranted by the evidence. See, for instance, final paragraph of the "opinion" last above quoted.

The daily number of appeals are heard on the board record with the appellant present and this work constitutes an invaluable means through which the Commissioner and Assistant Commissioner may keep in touch with what the various boards are doing and thus know whether proper standards of inspection are applied in the admission and rejection of immigrants. They can also see whether the questions put to immigrants and witnesses are relevant, fair and so phrased as to elicit the vital facts, also whether the conclusion reached is warranted by the record and many other things bearing on the general character of board work. While boards should be free agents and the Commissioner should studiously refrain from even suggestion how they should decide particular cases, yet as chief executive officer of the station it is his duty to call their attention to errors in their work and also to see to it that their general standards and methods are substantially uniform, so as to ensure the likelihood of cases receiving the same consideration, whether they be sent before one board or the other.

Deporting Division

Immigrants who have once been heard by a board without securing admission are place[d] in the custody of this division irrespective of whether they have been excluded or their case has been deferred. Its work sub-divides itself into two main parts.

1. Guarding such immigrants during the day-time as well as others placed in its custody (as, for instance, persons held under warrant of arrest).
2. Placing excluded immigrants on board ship for deportation.

The Chief of this division usually divides his force into three parts, two of which constitute alternate watches for the guarding of immigrants, the other being known as the *deporting squad.*

Immigrants detained in this division are segregated with reference to sex and, so far as the inadequate facilities permit, persons who occupied cabin quarters during the voyage are placed in separate rooms here. Criminals, procurers, and other persons of bad character are kept separate and apart from all others and, when practical, from each other. Detained immigrants should be still further sub-divided, perhaps with reference to habits, race or nationality, but lack of space prevents this being done. They are frequently removed from the several detention rooms for various purposes, such as going before the boards for a hearing, to the dining room for meals, in warm weather to the roof garden, or to the interview corridor to meet relatives and friends who call upon them, and unless great care is exercised, there is a possibility of their escaping or being returned to the wrong room with resulting confusion. Missionaries and society agents have access to them at all times, also steamship agents and telegraph employees in the presence of an official. So that no unnecessary detention may occur through oversight, the cases of all who have been detained more than five days without final action being taken are discussed by the chief of this division with the superintendent of the chief of the Special Inquiry Division.

As soon as an immigrant has been excluded a blue deportation card is made out for him to which are transcribed the data appearing on the face of the special inquiry card, and before deportation occurs there are added height, color of hair and eyes, time, when, and name of steamer by which deported, and name of deporting officer. Upon notice from the Executive Division that an appeal has been filed, deportation is stayed and the detention card stamped *Appeal filed.* Prompt notice of decisions on appeal is given to this division.

At the end of the day, the Night Division receipts to the Deporting Division for all immigrants in its custody and in the morning the latter division similarly receipts to the former.

The deporting squad consists of six or more men and reports usually on a late boat. Before removing from Ellis Island immigrants subject to deportation all property belonging to them, including baggage and money on deposit with the treasurer, must be collected, the baggage properly tagged, and their passports, if any, stamped *Deported.* They are usually taken to the various steamers or boats of the Moore Towing Company, but sometimes by means of wagons from the Barge Office. Whether the one method or the other be adopted depends on various circumstances, including the number to be deported and the location of piers to be visited. It is customary to place excluded immigrants on board two or three hours prior to sailing, except that when the hour of sailing occurs early in the morning, they are usually placed on board the evening before. The work of this division is usually carried on until late in the night and is one of responsibility and difficulty. An official visits each vessel having on board persons ordered deported immediately prior to the sailing thereof, calls them by name and satisfies himself that all are still there.

In this division, as in all others, it is of the utmost importance that honest and intelligent officials be employed. The friends of excluded immigrants often stand ready to offer a consideration for their release on the way to the vessel, while dishonest petty ship's employees have opportunities to *exchange* an alien put on board for deportation for some one really desiring to go to Europe.

Statistical Division

The preparation of the statistical data required by law and Bureau practice in relation to hundreds of thousands of immigrants of various races and nationalities entails much work. It is performed through a large number of clerks, stenographers and typewriters, in all about fifty five employees. The principal facts given on the ships' manifests are recorded on cards (through electrical punching machines) and forwarded to Washington for tabulation. The data in relation to outgoing aliens (furnished by steamship companies on coupons) are inspected before they are forwarded to Washington.

Since August, 1902, an alphabetical card index of all arriving aliens is kept, each card containing a reference to the sheet of the manifest on which the name appears, so that data not transferred to the card can be readily obtained from the original source. This index is already assuming large proportions.

Another feature of its work consists in what is known as *verifying landings*; that is to say, ascertaining when and by what vessel aliens have arrived to the United States. Thousands of requests for such information are received, particularly from the various naturalization officers throughout the country since the enactment of the law requiring aliens applying for naturalization to show when they arrived in the United States. This division prepares and presents to the steamship companies bills for head-tax in reference to all aliens arriving at New York. It also investigates and acts upon requests from steamship companies that head-tax deposited on account of aliens alleged to be *in transit* be refunded.

This division has the custody of the chief permanent records of the office, excepting correspondence, which is filed in the Chief Clerk's office. Amongst its more important records are the ships' manifests which are from time to time carefully bound and stored in the vault with detention records attached.

Mechanical Division

The work of this division included: (a) caring for the elaborate light, heat and power plant, the refrigerating plant, all electric wires, bells and batteries and all fire lines and apparatus; (b) the heating and lighting of all buildings.

Fifteen thousand tons of coal, more or less, are consumed annually. The mechanical force, numbering approximately fifty men, is under the immediate direction of the Engineer-in-Charge, and composed of engineers, assistant engineers, firemen, wiremen, dynamo tenders, machinists and laborers, divided into three watches, each of which remains on duty eight hours. While this arrangement causes the unpleasant necessity of midnight trips between the Barge Office and Ellis Island, yet it seems preferable to any other. At each change of watch it is necessary to examine the water in the boilers, the feed pumps, engines, dynamos and all other machinery, including during the cold season the heating apparatus; also the condition of the coal bunkers, of the salt and fresh water tanks at the power house and of the emergency tank in the main building. It is the duty of the Engineer-in-Charge to keep himself informed as to the condition of the cable to Manhattan Island and the water main from Communipaw. The latter is (unavoidably) so placed that it is exposed to frequent possibility of damage. . . . Chief Engineer and Superintendent of Repairs to Public Buildings (Mr. A. B. Fry) exercises general supervision over the work and plant of this division.

Janitors' Division (laborers and charwomen)

To keep the buildings on Ellis Island clean is a serious problem owing to the large number of strange people who are constantly coming and going, many of them ignorant of the principles of cleanliness and sanitation; and yet it is both necessary and from every point of view desirable that these buildings be kept clean. In charge of this work is a janitor who has under him some fifty four laborers and seventeen charwomen, a portion of them assigned to duty in the Night Division. Some of the quarters (for instance, the detention rooms, dormitories and dining-room) become dirty much sooner than others. The instructions are that every part of the building shall be cleaned as often as may be necessary. In addition, the employees of this division must empty the refuse cans and wastepaper baskets, fill the ice-coolers, inspect the gutters of down-pipes, and take the soiled blankets to the laundry for disinfection.

Night Division

So heavy and complex is the day work at Ellis Island that the fact of a great deal of work being done during the night is often overlooked. At the head of the night force is an inspector known as the "Night Inspector" and he is assisted by watchmen, matrons, laborers, charwomen and others, in all about thirty two employees. The work consists of guarding and caring for detained immigrants and Government property from the time of departure of the late day force until the arrival on the following morning of the early day force and of cleaning parts of the building during this time.

The number of immigrants detained over night varies greatly, but often reaches 1800 and may reach 2100. Most of these must be conducted in the evening from numerous day detention rooms to various dormitories, while in the morning the process is reversed. In addition, they must be taken to the dining-room for breakfast, and otherwise cared for in a variety of ways. Throughout the night each dormitory is properly guarded and the island patrolled out-of-doors.

The Privilege Holders

The foregoing is an outline of the principal work done at Ellis Island by Government agencies and the machinery and processes by which it is carried on. There remains to be mentioned the work done at Ellis Island by outside agencies, though under Government supervision. The immigrants, especially the detained ones, must be fed; those found qualified to land must be given the opportunity to exchange their foreign money and those going to New York City or vicinity to have their baggage delivered. All such business is done through what are known as "privilege holders" selected by statutory authority usually *after public competition subject to such conditions and limitations* (section 30) as the Washington authorities may prescribe.

Food is supplied by a contractor to two different classes of immigrants and to each class by a different method. To all detained immigrants, meals are furnished at the usual hours at the expense of the steamship companies bringing them, while immigrants who have been passed by the authorities and who are about to leave Ellis Island for points beyond New York may buy packages or separate articles of food at prescribed prices. The gross business done under the feeding contract is a very large one and the records show how badly at times it has been performed. In his annual report for the fiscal year ended June 30, 1902, the then new Commissioner had occasion to score the contractor who held this privilege prior to that date. A new contractor was installed under whom the business was conducted honestly and decently. In 1909, the same Commissioner upon resuming office found it necessary to proceed against another contractor for very serious violations of his contract and as a result it was canceled. It is most unfortunate that the contract for feeding immigrants has so often been the centre of abuses. Its execution may be attended with difficulties; but given an honest contractor (a dishonest one can readily be discovered and dismissed), and a Commissioner who shall insist that the contract be performed efficiently and correctly, and it is quite feasible to have this business carried on in a manner satisfactory to all reasonable persons concerned.

During years of heavy immigration, over twenty million dollars are exhibited by immigrants at Ellis Island, more or less of it being foreign money which it is advantageous for them to exchange before they land. This they are enabled to do at Ellis Island. Here, too, it is possible for a dishonest contractor to make large illegitimate profits, and it is very important that the Government supervise closely the conduct of this business. One contractor it was found necessary to turn out.

The services of a baggage expressman at Ellis Island are required only by immigrants going to points in Greater New York, Jersey City, Hoboken and Staten Island. This business, too, has at times been very badly conducted. In a sense this business is more difficult to supervise than either of the others mentioned, because it is carried on away from Ellis Island. But experience has shown that it is quite possible for the Commissioner, if he will only go about this matter in the right way, to compel a substantially correct execution of the baggage contract and to reduce to a minimum instances of overcharges and improper deliveries.

Still other privilege holders are the two great telegraph companies, each of which has a station at Ellis Island. Both transact a heavy business, though one less heavy than before the official postal-card was placed at the disposal of immigrants desiring to summon relatives and friends from New York City.

It is often necessary to allow petty agents of privilege holders to circulate amongst the immigrants for the purpose of transacting their legitimate business. One means of guarding against abuses on the part of such agents is to let it be known that frequent tests are secretly made as to the manner in which they do their work, and the results recorded. Furthermore, all persons (including particularly the missionaries) who may have knowledge of any wrongdoing are urged and required to inform the Commissioner thereof. Privilege holders should be required to confine their activities strictly to the work for which they are allowed representation. Officials are forbidden to borrow money or receive any consideration from any of them.

The Transportation Companies

These, too, are privilege holders, but of so peculiar and important a character as to render it proper to refer to them under a separate heading. Virtually all of the steamship and railroad companies with termini in Greater New York, Jersey City and Hoboken (including coastwise steamship companies to Norfolk, Savannah, New Orleans and other points) have representation and transact important business at Ellis Island. Together they constitute a notable aggregation of powerful corporations. The railroad passenger business originating at Ellis Island amounts to many millions of dollars annually. As to several matters, the interests of the steamship companies and of the Government are in a sense adverse, and the former must not be permitted to make attempts to interfere with the execution of the law. Under conditions such as exist at Ellis Island there is always danger that subordinate transportation agents will seek (though without criminal intent) through small favors to influence weak Government officials, and it is one of the important duties of the Commissioner to see to it that nothing of this sort occurs.

Prior to 1902, it was the practice for many of the transportation companies to issue passes to Ellis Island officials. Commenting on this practice, the new Commissioner wrote in his annual report for 1902 as follows

> The duty of this office is, and presumably always will be, to execute statues enacted to restrict immigration, while the interests of the powerful transportation companies represented at Ellis Island demand liberal immigration laws and a liberal execution of the

same. Since this office is constantly called upon to assume an attitude more or less at variance with the pecuniary interests of these transportation companies. I believe it should always decline to accept from them any favors not accorded to private persons.

Immigrants going beyond New York City often arrive with "orders" for further transportation. These are as a rule more contracts between them and the steamship companies that the latter will see that they are carried to destination by rail or partly by water and partly by rail. The obligation of the railroad companies arises after these "orders" have been exchanged for "tickets." This occurs at Ellis Island. For many years the *Trunk Line Association*, on which most of these orders were drawn, has distributed the great volume of this business amongst the various trunk lines east of the Mississippi according to percentages determined by them, while west of the Mississippi such business has been distributed by the *Western Passenger Association*. The immigrant is too ignorant to know by what route to proceed, and the Government has thus far contented itself with exercising a general supervision, endeavoring to prevent the selection of improper routes and satisfying itself that immigrants were properly treated while in (the) charge of the railroad companies. For this purpose, inspectors have frequently been detailed to travel incognito on immigrant trains and submit reports, which are on file. In 1911, two of the great trunk lines (the Lackawanna and the Lehigh Valley) broke away from the Association but joined it again in 1912. In July 1911, the practice of renting quarters at Ellis Island to the Trunk Line Association was discontinued, subsequent leases being made with the individual railroad companies.

This office found it necessary to prohibit the railroad companies from making additional charges to immigrants arriving with unconditional "orders" for further transportation at an agreed figure. It has frequently become necessary to regulate the immigrant traffic to the west via (the) Old Dominion Line.

Missionaries and Immigrant Aid Societies

Immigrants who are qualified to land some times require assistance beyond that which the Government is able to give in their efforts to get into quick touch with relatives or friends or to find employment; and in this connexion the missionary may do work of real value. Another field for his work is found amongst the unfortunate immigrants who are excluded and will reach Europe with scant clothing and funds. For many years, a number of earnest missionaries and representatives of immigrant aid societies have been coming to Ellis Island. For the great good they have done and are doing they are entitled to high praise and to every encouragement. It is unfortunate that from time to time so many persons calling themselves missionaries, though in fact more boarding-house keepers (and dishonest ones at that) have found a footing at Ellis Island. The effrontery of some of these persons passed belief. They appeared to think that they could use a Government as a basis for abusing, swindling and otherwise exploiting immigrants and taking them to filthy places where they detained them to swell the revenues of their boarding-houses and exposed even women and girls to coarse and vulgar treatment. At one of the so-called "Homes" a rubber hose filled with shot was kept for the purpose of compelling immigrants to obey. The presence at Ellis Island of persons willing to tolerate such abuses tended not only to lower the tone of the place but was unfair to the real missionary. The files show that at various times the Government has taken very drastic action with a view to ridding Ellis Island of all such parasites. There is reason to believe that the false missionary has now been driven from Ellis Island, but past experience shows that continued vigilance will be necessary to prevent his return.

Conclusion

The foregoing summary, however, incomplete, indicates in some measure the variety, complexity and perhaps the difficulty of Ellis Island work. A few of the duties of the Commissioner have from time to time been referred to. As the executive head of the office, he must exercise general supervision over all of the work and the plant and above all see to it that numerous officials under him perform their several duties in an effective manner. This they can do only if permitted to work through a proper organization, for the creations and maintenance of which the Commissioner is responsible. The machinery of each division must be in good working order and all divisions must work together in harmony. Much depends on the men selected as heads of divisions, but the Commissioner should know enough of the work of each division to satisfy himself that it is properly carried on, and this he must accomplish without so immersing himself in detail as to lack time for the larger questions which are ever before him. How this shall be done is a problem which each Commissioner must solve for himself. The hearing of appeals brings him into direct contact with some of the most important detail work of the office, namely, that of the boards in cases where there has been exclusion with subsequent appeal, but it is not so easy for him to keep himself informed as to other board cases (for instance, those in which admission occurs) or to the no less important work of the Registry Division, which admits the great majority of immigrants after a brief examination. In closing this summary, it may be pointed out that the number and variety of people from all quarters of Europe, with some from Asia and Africa, many of them most interesting and with customs varying widely from our own, who annually come to Ellis Island for inspection under the immigration law, result in making this a great human nature office, with a long list of comedies and tragedies, and an office very interesting to administer.

William Williams
Commissioner
Ellis Island, December 1912

Appendix 2

PERSONNEL REPORT OF 1909

[*Roger O'Donnell, a special immigrant inspector in the Bureau of Immigration and directly reporting to the secretary of commerce and labor, "proceeded on March 30, 1909 to Ellis Island and carefully went over the question of the personnel . . . and the sufficiency thereof" and wrote the following report for the secretary of Commerce and Labor, dated April 15, 1909. The following is an excerpt.*]

Increases in the Force and the Reasons Thereof.

Recommendations for the Commissioner of Immigration at New York are . . . for additional help:

Ten clerks at $900 per annum.
Two stenographers for board of special inquiry, at $1,000 per annum.
Eleven watchmen at $840 each per annum.
Four Inspectors at $1,400 each per annum.
One Interpreter at $1,200 per annum.

Without doubt there is a necessity for all this additional help, with the exception of the one Interpreter, although the reasons for certain of the proposed appointments are susceptible of more complete explanation than the Commissioner's letter give and in some instances they are predicated upon quite different grounds that those represented to the Department.

a. Ten Clerks at $900 each per annum for the following reasons and for the particular duties indicated, viz: The card indexing of the alien manifests has almost ceased, eight clerks having been withdrawn from this work, consequent upon the Department requirements that statistics, similar in all respects to those prepared covering inward bound aliens, be compiled as to outward bound aliens, in relation to whom manifests are furnished under the provision of Section 12 of the Act of February 20, 1907, thus constituting an entirely new feature of the work also the great increase in the number of requests for verification of landing growing out of the enforcement of the naturalization Act of June 29, 1906, which requires the applicants for citizenship shall have their admission verified from the official records. The importance of this latter work being done with absolute accuracy is obvious, since an incomplete search (in many cases with the most meagre date for guide) may perpetrate an injustice upon an applicant for naturalization. These requests average from 50 to 100 per diem and as instances occur where several hours time of one man is required to locate the record in the manifests the condition speaks for itself. Furthermore, the preparations of the returns in presentable typewritten form for certification by the Commissioner or the Department adds greatly to the work. Eight of the proposed new clerks are needed in this division, so that the eight card writers withdrawn from that duty may return thereto and bring the index up to date; it is now over 300,000 in arrears and an adequate index will certainly be necessary unless a change can be made in the law, with a suitable penalty to back it up, whereby steamship companies will be required to furnish complete and accurate alphabetical books as indices to the manifests of aliens.

b. One additional clerk is required in connection with handling the money of detained aliens. The Commissioner took the wise precaution, several months ago, to perfect an arrangement whereby detained persons shall temporarily surrender their valuables for safe-keeping until discharged or deported, thereby preventing fraud and loss and providing an absolute check to prevent complaints, which had been numerous . . . Until the recent increase in immigration the operation of this system did not impose an amount of work beyond that which the regular force could handle, but during the rush period such as the present there is great need for one more man, whose services will do much to guard against . . . mistakes. . . .

c. One additional clerk is needed for the Information and Discharging Division for the same reason; the number of "temporarily detained" persons far exceeds . . . those detained upon statutory grounds, and the discharge of these persons makes it necessary that their valuables be obtained prior thereto. Even with the one addition recommended, the force of clerks in the division will be one less than it was in the rush season of 1907, when the process was not quite as complicated as at present.

d. Two additional stenographers for the boards of special inquiry are needed to prevent breaking down the health of employees assigned regularly to this hard, grinding work, which is very wearing at best. The present force consists of thirteen men and with fifteen the quota will be as large as should be required, allowances for leave of absence considered.

e. The eleven new watchmen requested by the Commissioner really represent an increase of but eight (8) men, three of the existing staff being nominated for advancement to clerkships, for which they have qualified in the civil service examination. These three men, last referred to, are in the Executive, Deportation and Night Divisions respectively, and three of the new watchmen will replace them. These eight new appointees should be divided as follows:

Registry Division. 4;	*Total: 11;*	*In 1907: 12*
Special Inquiry Division. 1;	*Total: 8;*	*In 1907: 9*
Inf'n and Disch'g Div 2;	*Total: 10;*	*In 1907: 11*
Night Division. 1;	*Total: 13;*	*In 1907: 15*

f. The Commissioner's request for the assignment of four new inspectors at Ellis Island is based upon the proposed designation of four officers to do special investigating in connection with the "white slave traffic"; this premise is a trifle misleading, as the four proposed assignments (Inspectors Tedesco, Bawor, Piaggo and Inspectress Bullis) do not withdraw a single employee from the division where more help is really needed, viz: the Registry Division, where primary examinations take place and where there are now but sixteen (16) inspectors, aside from the inspector in charge, to handle about the same volume of immigration as that of 1907, when there were twenty (20) inspectors in this division aside from the inspector in charge. Furthermore, Inspectors Tedesco and Bawor have been on "special duty" for the greater part of the time for months past; Miss Bullis has never been on anything else, and Inspector Piaggio is in the Information and Discharging Division where his services are believed to be more valuable than they are likely to be in connection with the "white slave" investigations.

g. Four inspectors added to the Registry Division will greatly expedite the inspection work; three of these men might be assigned from elsewhere in the service, or newly appointed, but the fourth can be otherwise obtained in a manner indicated in the second general caption of this report, entitled "Possible decreases and explanation thereof."
h. No more interpreters at Ellis Island are needed at present; the request therefor, like that relating to the four inspectors grows out of a suggestion from the Department of that Interpreter D.J. Andreaccio might be a good man in the "white slave" investigation. On the other hand, Italian Interpreter F.C. di Giovanni has since July 8, 1908, been doing the work of a draftsman and latterly supervising the laying of cement floors in the new hospital extension. He may have been withdrawn from this work since April 12th, because I understand the Commissioner learned (probably as a result of my inquiry) that di Giovanni had been assigned to work other than that contemplated by his appointment. It should be added that his detail in July, 1908, was ordered personally by the Commissioner, at the request of Civil Engineer (Frank S.) Howell who simply wanted the man, asked for his services, got them and retained them.

"Possible Decreases and the Explanation Thereof"

In canvassing the entire official force at Ellis Island, so far as concerns retaining the services of certain employees whose salaries represent an annual outlay almost sufficient to pay for the additional help needed, I ran across the following cases, and my reason for calling your attention to them is briefly set forth in each instance not in a spirit of criticism but because the facts exist and were unmistakable to one who looked below the surface.

a. Two wiremen at $1000 each, viz: Robert W. Fearing and J.S. Van Horne. There are now FIVE wiremen at Ellis Island and there (were) duties for all of them until the original electric wiring in the older buildings had been replaced by new material, properly installed. Civil Engineer Howell reported in writing to the Commissioner in October, 1908, that two wiremen could be spared, but the Commissioner nominated but one (Van Horne) in his letter of October 5, 1908, for transfer or furlough. Why the other was not included I failed to ascertain.
b. 1 Pilot, J.J. Halpin. $1200 per annum; I engineer, Chas. Fink, $1000 p. a. These two men constitute the crew of the launch "Samoset", which I will refer to again in my supplementary "confidential" report. If this vessel is placed out of commission, the crew will no longer be needed.
c. 1 Inspector (R.W. Conradson) at $1,825 per annum; change to Watchman. Commissioner Watchorn recommended on January 21, 1909, that the title of this man be changed to that of Watchman, and his salary reduced to $840 per annum; that was the first official intimation received that Conradson was not doing the work for which he was appointed, although the Commissioner nominated him on October 5, 1908 for

transfer to an *inspector*. His duties are those of simple watchman on the Night Force and his over-payment of salary is an established fact.

d. 1 Foreman of Carpenters (J.J. Daly) $4.50 p. d. ($1642.50 p.a.). Inquiry failed to disclose any reasons for continuing this office, which is, plainly speaking, a sinecure for the man who occupies it. There are four carpenters at Ellis Island, supposed to be supervised by the civil engineer (Chief of the Structural, Mechanical and Marine Division). The latter frankly informed me, in reply to my inquiry, that the foreman was not needed and in his absence the work proceeds more smoothly than when he is present.

e. 1 Senior Engineer (Wm. F. Foist) $120 p.m. ($1440 per annum). This is a position which is in existence by reason of the maintenance of the marine and power house forces as separate units, instead of treating them as one unit, for the purpose of providing "relief men" during absences of the regular force. The duties of the Senior Engineer (Marine) consists of sitting in an office on the ferry-boat "Ellis Island" every day and doing nothing, unless an engineer regularly on day duty is, perchance, absent or sick. On the other hand, there are engineers in the power house holding marine licenses, any one of whom could be temporarily assigned to the ferry-boat, if required.

f. 1 Law Clerk (Charles H. Paul) $2,500 per annum. The duties of this office have degenerated in late years. It was formerly thought that a law officer at Ellis Island should be furnished to prepare cases for the United States Attorney. A Mr. Paddock filled this position. He resigned and Hugh Govern, jr., held the place and filled it fairly well. He was transferred to the Naturalization Service and Charles H. Paul was raised from the grade of Immigrant Inspector (member of the board of special inquiry) to Law Clerk at a salary of $2,500 per annum, the same as the amount received by the various "chiefs of division" at Ellis Island. The duties contemplate supervising the handling of warrant cases, in probably 98% of which only questions of fact are involved, requiring good judgment rather than legal education; also preparing forms of contract, every one of which is reviewed by the Solicitor of the Department prior to becoming effective; the blank forms are also edited by the Solicitor and filling in the same is mostly a mechanical operation. The certifying of papers to the United States Attorney for use in habeas corpus cases is a mere administrative detail and the Chief Clerk at Ellis Island is really the man who closely supervises the entire work of the Law Division. Furthermore, the habits and temperamental qualifications of the man occupying this office have led to its decadence and, if the position were abolished altogether, the work would be carried on by the Executive Division proper, to which the four clerks and three inspectors nominally under direction of the Law Clerk would be assigned. Mr. Paul is eligible to reinstatement as an Immigrant Inspector, which office he is reported to have filled ordinarily well. . . .

g. 1 Cook (P.R.J. Bertrand), $60 per month; ($720 per annum). The duties of this man are intended to be the preparation of meals for the crew of, and officers using, the boarding cutter "Immigrant". The cook is permitted to charge the men for what they order and his employment was sanctioned upon the theory that a man would not undertake the work without a fixed salary, owing to the small number of customers. It is aided by the officers concerned that the cooking is unsatisfactory and that they are little benefited by the arrangement. If the Department elected to abolish this position, perhaps the restaurant privilege holder at Ellis Island would meet the needs of the situation, the galley apparatus, utensils, etc., being the property of the Government and available for use by whoever may be assigned the work.

h. The number of stationary firemen at $925 each may be reduced by two if an arrangement is made whereby the men may work in three shifts, instead of as at present, the alternate shifts of 116 and 8 hours at a time. Lack of means of reaching Ellis Island is the basis of the present arrangement, but as the entire crew of the ferryboat remains thereon at night, and the same is true of the boarding cutter except as to the pilot, it could readily be arranged to have the smaller boat (the cutter) leave the Barge Office every night at 11.30 p.m. with the power house relief gang, leaving Ellis Island shortly after 12 midnight with the gang relieved. The advantages of this suggestion are five-fold, viz:
    1. Security that exhausted employees will not be in charge of the boilers and machinery in the power house (16 hour shifts are dangerous and in case the "relief men" do not report, 24 hours continuous duty is required).
    2. A regular night service to and from Ellis Island, instead of 3 nights per week as at present.
    3. A probable reduction in the amount of sick leaves taken by the firemen who are overstrained by 16 and 24 hour shifts.
    4. Opportunity to make machine repairs to the ferryboat at night and thus cut down expenses of maintenance of broken machinery.
    5. Saving $1850 per annum in the salaries of firemen.

Feasibility of Regrading and advantages thereof

Officers now serving on boards of special inquiry receive from $1825 to $2500 per annum, no fixed basis existing in this regard and the selections for board duty being made by the Commissioner. There is grave doubt as to whether the pure question as to excellence of judgment enters into the selection board members, whose duties are generally regarded as second to none in importance. Proper allowance for the high character of this duty would be equitable, but it is suggested that the system should be changed so that capabilities for board duty may be ascertained competitively among the officers, the selection of permanent chairmen to be made by the Commissioner from the highest qualified of the men and the next in rank, up to the prescribed number, from the next highest upon the list, *seriatim* . . . and fixing compensation at a salary of $2100 pr annum for board chairmen and $1980 for board members. . . .

Matrons

At the present time there is one female interpreter at $720 per annum, acting as a matron; 14 regular matrons at $840 per annum and 7 at $720 per annum. The work of these employees at Ellis Island being supervised by one Matron-Inspectress at $1400 per annum and, on the Boarding Division, by one Matron at $1,200 per annum.

Laborers (61 laborers)

The arrangement of salaries of unskilled laborers at Ellis Island is very unequal, different rates being paid without essential difference in the work performed. . . .

The position of laborer on the Night Division is a particularly unpleasant assignment . . .
Charwomen (1 Head Charwoman; 18 charwomen)
The same comments as to laborers apply to the charwomen . . .

Marine and Mechanical Employees

In taking up this subject, I found that the salaries paid are about the same as those allowed in similar lines in New York City . . .

Employees: 1 consulting engineer (Mr. Fry); 7 marine firemen ($900 per annum.); 18 stationary firemen ($925 p.a.); 1 head wireman ($1200 p.a.); 4 wiremen ($1,000 p.a.); 4 general mechanics (1 at $900; 2 at $1,000; 1 new at 960); plumber and gasfitter ($1200); refrigerating machinists (1,000); 2 dynamo tenders ($1,000); 1 elevator conductor ($840); 1 cook ($60 p.m.); 6 marine engineers (4 at $1440; 1 at $1200; 1 at $1,000); 1 head stationary engineer ($1400); 5 assistant engineers ($1200); 5 pilots (4 at $1620; 1 at $1200); 3 quartermasters (1 at $840; 2 at $900); 3 marine oilers ($900); 1 foreman of carpenters ($3.75 per diem); 15 deckhands [laborers] ($780); 2 draftsmen, temporary, ($6 p.d.).

Special Inspector O'Donnell summed up his regrading of employees by stating that the current salaries paid per year be reduced from $441,105.25 to $422,170.00.

Appendix 3

RULES FOR THE U.S. IMMIGRANT STATION AT ELLIS ISLAND

[*This set of rules was laid down by Commissioner William Williams from 1910 through 1913 and describes the bureaucratic structure at Ellis Island at the height of mass immigration early in the twentieth century, 1900 through the 1920s. The full text follows.*]

General Rules

The work of the Immigrant Station shall be performed through the following divisions:

1. Executive Division
2. Medical Division
3. Boarding Division
4. Registry Division
5. Information Division
6. Special Inquiry Division
7. Deporting Division
8. Statistical Division
9. Mechanical Division
10. Janitors' Division
11. Night Division

Chiefs of division are responsible to the Commissioner, through the Assistant Commissioner and Superintendent, for the efficient performance of the work of their several divisions. They shall carefully and impartially observe the work of the officials under them, shall instruct them in their duties, establish amongst them a spirit of co-operation and endeavor at the same time to secure respect and good-will.

They shall have the care of all Government property in their several divisions and report to the Superintendent any damage thereto and any unsanitary conditions prevailing in any part thereof.

They are charged with the execution of the rules pertaining to their several divisions and required to exact from their subordinates knowledge thereof, as well as of those portions of the Immigration Laws and Bureau Rules which relate to their work.

Each chief of division shall see to it that at least one of his subordinates is qualified to act temporarily in his place, but any designation so to act shall be made by the Commissioner.

In the absence of the Commissioner, the Assistant Commissioner and any other person authorized by the Department to act as Commissioner, the following named officials shall in the order named have charge of detained immigrants and Government property, shall maintain order at Ellis Island and conduct any business of so urgent a character that it must be transacted at once (in which case, however, effort should first be made to communicate with the Commissioner or Assistant Commissioner by telephone):

Chief of Registry Division
Chief of Special Inquiry Division

Chief of Information Division
Chief of Deporting Division
The "early day" or "late day" inspector appointed pursuant to the rules of the Registry Division
The Night Inspector

The Superintendent shall so arrange that at least one of the officials in this section named is always on Ellis Island.

This rule has no application to hospital patients or property.

Work shall be carried on at such times, including Sundays and holidays, may be necessary. In the absence of directions from the chiefs of their divisions officials in the classified service shall report daily by the boat leaving the Barge Office at 9 a.m. and remain at Ellis Island until 4.40 p.m. Laborers and charwomen shall work during such times as the Janitor, with the approval of the Superintendent, shall direct.

While on duty, whether at Ellis Island, on vessels or elsewhere, officials shall bear themselves with dignity and treat with courtesy all with whom they may have business to transact. Slouching is forbidden, as well as slovenly speech. Officials shall endeavor to use correct English and to acquire the habit of expressing themselves with directness and precision. While on duty during day hours, they shall not smoke.

Criticism of the work of one official by another, except in the line of official duty and through official channels, is forbidden.

Information concerning official matters shall not be made public except with the knowledge of the Commissioner or his authorized representative.

Immigrants shall be treated with kindness and civility by everyone at Ellis Island. Neither harsh language nor rough handling will be tolerated. It is the duty of every official on Ellis Island actively to assist the Commissioner in carrying out this order and to bring any violation thereof to his attention.

The Superintendent and the chiefs of divisions shall familiarize themselves thoroughly with the fire apparatus and regulations and see to it that those under them possess a general knowledge thereof and understand what is expected of them in the event of fire. The Superintendent from time to times will conduct a fire drill.

Borrowing money or receiving any gift from anyone having business relations with the Immigration Service at Ellis Island or elsewhere, including privilege holders, societies or their agents, is forbidden; also all financial or business transactions with aliens detained at Ellis Island except with the knowledge and approval of the Commissioner.

Particular attention is called to Civil Service Rule XII, which reads as follows.

> No recommendation for the promotion of a classified employee shall be considered by any officer concerned in making promotions, unless it be made by the person under whose supervision such employee has served; and such recommendation by any other person, if made with the knowledge and consent of the employee, shall be sufficient cause for debarring him from the promotion proposed, and a repetition of the offence shall be sufficient cause for removing him from the Service.

The name of an alien shall always be written as it appears on the corrected manifest, the surname being placed first. Any serious error detected in any division shall be corrected and reported by the chief of that division to the Superintendent who will cause all records thereby affected to be corrected.

Stationery and other office supplies will be furnished only to the chiefs of the several divisions to be used only for official work in such divisions. Formal requisition therefor must be made in the afternoon on Mondays and Thursdays, unless the Storekeeper, with the approval of the Superintendent, shall designate other times.

Employees shall report a change in address to the Assistant Commissioner through the Chief of their division. They shall seek to prevent personal mail from being addressed to them at Ellis Island. Their use of the telephone for personal business is governed by special written directions on this subject.

Rules for the Executive Division

The work of this division includes:

a. The conduct of the principal external affairs of this Station. These include all relations with the Washington authorities and the more important relations with other Government offices and the transportation companies.
b. Receiving a replying to all correspondence.
c. Appointing boards of special inquiry.
d. Receiving notices of appeal and hearing appeals from board decisions and applications of aliens for admission on bond.
e. Passing upon requests for rehearings before boards.
f. Conducting the law work, except actual litigation conducted by U.S. Attorneys.
g. Executing warrants to arrest aliens who are improperly in the country and conducting hearings thereon.
h. Keeping the Government accounts.
i. Purchase and supervision of the expenditure of supplies.
j. Caring for Government property.
k. Supervision (by the Commissioner, Assistant Commissioner and Superintendent) of all other divisions.

The Commissioner presides over the Station through this division. The following officials serve in this division.

Assistant Commissioner
Superintendent
Chief Clerk (clerks, including clerk in charge of requests for rehearings) and stenographers immediately attached to his office
Attorney
Law Clerk (and inspectors and stenographers under him)
Treasurer
Civil Engineer
Storekeeper
Matrons
Messengers
Time Clerk

Telegram Clerks (stationed near Information Division)
Telephone Operator
Plumbers
Carpenters
Painters
Tile Setter
Elevator Operator
Gardeners
Pilots
All other employees not specifically assigned to other divisions

The Superintendent, Chief Clerk, the Attorney and the Law Clerk shall report to the Commissioner and the Assistant Commissioner. The Treasurer and all clerks, stenographers, and messengers shall report to the Chief Clerk and through him to the Superintendent. The other officials in this division shall report to the Superintendent.

The *Assistant Commissioner* shall keep himself well informed as to the work of the station as a whole and of the several divisions and as to the general character of the services rendered by all employees. He shall rectify and correct any errors in administration or, if unable to do this, report the same to the Commissioner. He shall perform such special duties as from time to time are assigned to him by the Commissioner and be prepared in the absence of the Commissioner to assume full charge of the conduct of affairs.

The duties of the *Superintendent* shall be those usually pertaining to this office and shall include supervising through the chiefs of division the work of all immigration officials other than reporting direct to the Commissioner or Assistant Commissioner; co-ordinating the work of the several divisions (particularly that of the Registry, Information and Special Inquiry divisions); calling together the heads of divisions from time to time in conference; determining in what divisions officers shall serve and transferring them (with the approval of the Assistant Commissioner) whenever necessary from one to the other; seeing to it that the plant and equipment are kept clean and in good condition; adopting precautionary measures against fire; and satisfying himself that the privilege holders are properly performing their several contracts.

The duties of the *Law Clerk* include:

a. Investigation of requests that warrants issue for the arrest and deportation of aliens already in the United States.
b. Conduct of hearings upon such warrants.
c. Investigating probable infraction of the immigration law and preparing cases thereunder for submission to U.S. Attorneys.
d. Preparation of contracts relating to improvements and other matters.
e. Reading and filing copies of all Court decisions pertaining to immigration matters.

The *Chief Clerk* shall perform the duties of Chief of Division with reference to all employees who report to him. His further duties shall be those usually pertaining to this office and shall include the custody of the correspondence records and files and the supervision of the receipt, distribution, filing and answering of official mail.

He shall caused to be made a carbon and a letter press copy of all outgoing letters, the former to be filed with the letter to which it is a reply, the latter to be numbered and from time to time bound in a book form in chronological order.

He shall from time to time destroy all stenographic notebooks used in connection with correspondence, and superfluous copies of board minutes.

He shall authorize board stenographers to make . . . copies of board minutes in cases covered by the written instructions on file.

The duties of the Chief Clerk further include supervision of all clerical matters pertaining to appeals. Upon receipt of notice of appeal he shall cause the time of receipt to be stamped thereon, shall cause deportation of appellant and any accompanying persons to be stayed and copies of the board minutes to be prepared and the case presented to the Commissioner as soon as practicable. On receipt of the decision on appeal he shall direct the Deporting Division to comply with the terms thereof.

The Chief Clerk shall see to the correctness of immigrants' bonds prior to their transmittal to the Department and, whenever practicable, shall compel their preparation by those offering to furnish them.

The duties of the Chief Clerk further include supervision of all matters pertaining to requests for rehearings before boards. The work of his assistant in immediate charge of such matters includes the following:

a. Answering inquiries (made in person) in relation to immigrants held for special inquiry.
b. Passing upon oral applications for rehearings in excluded cases. Such applications shall usually be granted when responsible persons offer to present new, material evidence.
c. Permitting persons thereto entitled, upon written request, to inspect board minutes (other than minutes relating to aliens arrested on warrant). Such persons include steamship agents and attorneys for aliens who have filed appeals. But prior to appeal, no one shall inspect the minutes in a contract labor case unless alleged contractor has appeared and final decision rendered by the board.
d. Reading the board minutes of the previous day, causing to be corrected (through the Chief of the Special Inquiry Division) typographical errors, and calling the Commissioner's attention to important and difficult cases.
e. Filing two bound copies of board minutes for a period of one year, and transferring earlier minutes to the record vault.

The duties of the *Treasurer* include the following:

a. Keeping accounts of all receipts, which include payments from privilege holders under their contract; from steamship companies in settlement of hospital bills; from steamship companies to reimburse Government employees for expenses incurred in placing immigrants aboard ship for deportation. The first two items are deposited with the Assistant Treasurer, the third turned over to the employees concerned.
b. Keeping accounts of all expenditures, including expenditures under special congressional appropriations and allotments by the Bureau.
c. Preparation of payrolls, of vouchers as to all expenditures and of bills against steamship companies and privilege holders.
d. Receiving, entering and paying over remittances made to immigrants through the Commissioner, and caring for money and valuables of detained immigrants at owner's risk.

The duties of the *Civil Engineer* include:

a. Drawing plans and specifications for and supervising the execution of all new construction work, also all contracts pertaining to repair and maintenance work.
b. Supervising the execution of such other repair and maintenance work as he may be directed to supervise.
c. Examining from time to time the physical condition of the plant (including boats) with reference to defects and necessary repairs and reporting the same to the Superintendent.
d. Giving advice on any other matters of a technical nature which may be referred to him.

The Storekeeper shall solicit bids for supplies as required, shall receive such supplies and distribute them to the several divisions in which they shall be used, taking receipts therefore from the chiefs of division. He shall maintain an inventory of the personal property belonging to the Government at Ellis Island.

The matrons shall report for duty to such chiefs of division as from time to time the Chief Matron, with the approval of the Superintendent, shall direct.

Rules for the Boarding Division

The work of this division includes:

a. The inspection of first and second cabin aliens on board vessels.
b. Discharging American citizens in the steerage at the piers.
c. Inspecting and discharging caretakers of live stock and birds at the piers.
d. Supervising the transfer of aliens from the docks to Ellis Island.
e. Issuing cattlemen's certificates and inspecting and discharging cattlemen at the docks upon their return to the United States with proper certificates.
f. Ascertaining the status, under the immigration law, of members of crews.

All incoming vessels from a foreign port, from Porto Rico and from the Canal Zone, shall be boarded by medical officers and immigrant inspectors. Where such vessel has touched at a U.S. port en route, those of its passengers who have come on board at such port shall not be inspected.

When several inspectors are sent to one vessel, the chief of this division shall designate one of them as *Officer-in-Charge.* Where the vessel is boarded by only one inspector, the duties of the Officer-in-Charge hereinafter referred to shall devolve upon such inspector in addition to his other duties.

The duties of the Officer-in-Charge shall include the following:

a. Obtaining from the purser the manifest (cabin and steerage), the alphabetical index book, any consular reports, copy of custom's list of passengers, report of births or deaths on the voyage, of stowaways, passage workers, cattlemen, birdmen, Chinamen and Japanese, of steerage passengers transferred to the cabin during the voyage, of passengers removed at Quarantine (including the manifest numbers of the latter), and all affidavits relating to aliens claming to be in transit or to have resided in Canada, Cuba, Mexico or Newfoundland during the statutory period.
b. Causing the manifest to be verified by the proper ship's officers.
c. Requiring the ship's officers to furnish suitable space and sufficient light for the

proper inspection of cabin aliens and to group them (by the use of letters or otherwise) according to the manifest sheets on which their names appear.

d. Distributing the second-cabin manifest sheets amongst the inspectors, and directing the production of second-cabin aliens first before the medical examiners and thereafter before the inspectors.
e. Causing the first-cabin aliens to be inspected who do not appear to be clearly and beyond a doubt entitled to land. Where the purser fails upon request to supply statutory information which may be lacking, the Officer-in-Charge shall obtain from the alien passengers.
f. Examining the first cabin manifest to ascertain whether alien concerning whom notices have been issued are on the vessel, and similarly examining the second cabin manifest in reference to such aliens or, where this is impracticable, satisfying himself that this is done by the several inspectors, the latter always to be under the duty of endeavoring to locate such aliens irrespective of whether or not the Officer-in-Charge does so.
g. Receiving from the inspectors and medical officers all papers in their custody pertaining to cabin passengers and disposing of such papers, as well as any others obtained from the purser, as follows: the affidavits relating to aliens claiming to be in transit and to those claiming the statutory residence in Canada, Cuba, Mexico and Newfoundland shall be returned to the purser; the first and second cabin manifests, the ship's report (yellow card) and the medical certificates of cabin aliens who have been discharged at the pier shall, together with the reasons for such discharge, be delivered to the Chief of the Boarding Division; all other papers shall be delivered to the Registry Division at Ellis Island not later than the arrival of the aliens to whom they pertain.
h. Serving the proper ship's officer with any notices relating to the detention of aliens on board, or their delivery at Ellis Island or to a designated ambulance, and calling attention to the penalties accruing for failure to comply with such notices.
i. Furnishing to the medical officer the appropriate form on which the ship's surgeon shall report diseases, injuries, births and deaths occurring on the next voyage.
j. Causing the baggage of all aliens going to Ellis Island to be examined before they leave the pier, and in the case of cabin aliens specifically requesting the dock superintendent to see that this be done.
k. Supervising the transfer to Ellis Island of all steerage aliens and of all cabin aliens ordered sent there, and seeing to it that in the meantime they receive proper treatment. During this period only Government officials or proper steamship employees may communicate with steerage aliens.
l. Notifying as soon as possible the Chinese Inspector-in-Charge of the presence of any Chinaman on board and ordering his detention pending official action.

The examining inspectors shall question each second cabin alien as to the matters mentioned in the manifest and correct any error or omission. Where New York City is given as the *final destination* the inspector shall before accepting it as correct, satisfy himself that this is not done as a means of concealing the real destination. Upon the ascertained relevant facts, including the alien's appearance and general demeanor, the examining inspector shall determine whether or not he is *clearly and beyond doubt entitled to land*, and if not he shall hold him for special inquiry.

Aliens obviously belonging to any of the excluded classes shall, as a matter of course, be held for special inquiry. Included in this category are those certified by the surgeons to be idiots, imbeciles, feeble-minded persons, epileptics, insane persons, and those afflicted with tuberculosis or a loathsome or dangerous contagious disease. Aliens certified by the surgeons for any *mental* defect, those who have been objects of public charity, those who appear to be devoid of ordinary intelligence, unmarried pregnant women and children under sixteen unaccompanied by either parent and neither being in this country, shall also be held for special inquiry as a matter of course.

It shall usually be necessary and proper to hold for special inquiry an alien in respect of whom the surgeons have issued a certificate for any physical defect affecting in their opinion his ability to earn a living. But if with a knowledge of the alien's occupation the examining inspector is of the opinion that the alien is clearly and beyond a doubt entitled to land, he may permit him to land, submitting his reasons for such action to the chief of this division.

In determining whether or not an alien is a pauper or a person likely to become a public charge, inspectors must consider amongst other matters his occupation, his proficiency in the same (including, where relevant, his physical ability to pursue it and his mental aptitude therefor), the demand for labor or services of the kind he is able to render at the place to which he intends to go, the number of persons who may be dependent upon him for support either here or abroad, and the value of his property. The vital question in these cases usually is whether or not he will be able to secure profitable employment and be self-supporting before his funds are exhausted.

In the absence of a statutory provision no hard and fast rule can be laid down as to amount of money an alien must have, but he should be held for special inquiry where his funds are not deemed adequate for his maintenance until such time as he is likely to find profitable employment. Cases of wives and minor children going to persons as to whom the examining inspector is satisfied that they are *able, willing and legally bound* to support them may constitute exceptions to this rule.

Where aliens are presumably qualified to land but there exists some minor objection to permitting them to do so immediately, which objection is likely to be overcome within a short time, the examining inspector may postpone completion of the process of primary inspection by detaining them temporarily, thus sending them to the Information Division where their cases will be disposed of under the rules of that division. Typical instances where such action is proper are where addresses must be verified or relatives or friends notified to call.

Whether or not an alien shall be landed, temporarily detained, or held for special inquiry often calls for the exercise of good judgement and a sound discretion based upon a knowledge of all relevant facts which is possible to ascertain. The chief of this division shall report to the Superintendent the names of inspectors who after a fair trial have proven themselves unable to exercise such judgement and discretion.

Each alien shall be asked specifically whether or not he is traveling alone. If not, and he is detained, the name of the accompanying person shall be written on the detention card. Where the surgeon or the examining inspector considers the detained alien helpless from sickness, mental or physical disability or infancy, at least one of the accompanying persons shall also be detained.

Inspectors shall note upon the manifest whether aliens not permitted to land immediately, are temporarily detained or held for special inquiry. In the former case, a cross shall be made opposite the name and a white card issued. In the latter case, the letters *S.I.* shall be placed opposite their name, and a yellow card issued. The cause or causes of detention shall be noted on the card, also any important admissions or information given by an alien. There shall also be noted on the manifest all medical certificates or surgeon's memoranda. Upon completion of this examination, to sign his name to the manifest sheets before him, inserting also the time when inspection began and when ended. He shall report in writing to the chief of this division (who in turn shall report to the Law Clerk) any alien named in the manifest sheets before him who has not appeared for inspection and who has not been sent to hospital; also any whom he has detained as accompanying one placed in hospital.

Whenever a first cabin passenger has been detained for special inquiry notice hereof must be given to the Superintendent or Chief of the Registry Division as soon as possible. Aliens who are sent to Ellis Island *for further examination* shall be given a white detention card with an appropriate notation to this effect.

The identification cards of second cabin aliens found eligible to land shall be stamped *Inspected by Immigration Authorities at New York*, and only those whose cards are so stamped may land at the pier.

Cabin aliens claiming to be in transit and those entering the United States after an uninterrupted residence of at least one year immediately preceding such entrance, in the Dominion of Canada, Newfoundland, Mexico or Cuba, may take affidavit to this effect, the same to be left with the purser. In the case of first cabin aliens, the boarding inspector may, in lieu of the affidavit, accept their signature witnessed by the purser.

Diplomatic and consular officers and other accredited officials of foreign governments, their suites, families and guests, coming to the United States to reside or in transit, being exempt from the provisions of the Immigration Act, no detailed statistical information is required concerning them; but their names and titles should be grouped together on the manifest.

When at the request of the medical officer or ship's surgeon a sick passenger remains on board, the Officer-in-Charge will endeavor personally to ascertain whether such passenger is a citizen or an alien and, if the latter, notice either to deliver him at Ellis Island or detain him on shipboard will be served on the appropriate ship's officer.

Permission to send an alien so ordered held on board to a private hospital for treatment will be granted only in cases deemed by the medical officer to be urgent and upon receipt from an agent of the vessel of proper written assurances as to payment of hospital expenses and delivery for inspection when health is restored.

As soon as inspection of cabin aliens has been completed, the Boarding Inspector shall grant to the steerage passengers claiming to be citizens the opportunity to satisfy him that they are such. Those claiming to be native born citizens must make affidavit to this effect. Those claiming to be naturalized citizens must present a passport such as is issued to citizens or a final naturalization certificate, and such as are unable to do this will be sent to Ellis Island for inspection. If, notwithstanding such documents, the Inspector has reason to believe that the passenger is not a citizen, or that naturalization paper is fraudulent, or that he is not the lawful owner thereof, he will send the passenger to Ellis Island for further inspection, making appropriate notation on his card.

Steerage passengers who prove that they are citizens will be discharged at the pier. A full record, including addresses in the United States, of all naturalized citizens so discharged will be made and entered on the manifest or in a book.

The Officer-in-Charge is further responsible for the following matters:

a. He shall deliver to the Registry Division all cabin aliens, entering their names in the cabin book of that division and marking on their cards the hour of arrival, and shall report to that division in writing (which shall in turn transmit this information to the Law Clerk) all missing cabin aliens with their manifest list and number, noting such report in the cabin book of the Registry Division. He shall also deliver to the Registry Division the identification (doctor's) cards of steerage passengers discharged at the pier, and a list of all aliens (cabin or steerage) who are either detained on the vessel or sent directly to a hospital other than that of Ellis Island.

b. He shall deliver to the Chief Clerk a report upon cases concerning which special notices were issued.
c. He shall furnish to the Information Division in writing the names of all cabin aliens temporarily detained or held for special inquiry.
d. He shall submit (a) written report of his work to the chief of this division forthwith upon reaching the Barge Office.

Immigrant inspectors who have occasion to administer oaths under the law shall do so in a manner showing appreciation of the character of the act.

Immigration officials while on shipboard shall not drink any intoxicating liquor, nor shall they take any meals at the expense of the ship's owners, unless than cannot otherwise obtain a meal at the usual time.

This chief of this division shall point out to new inspectors the advantage which they will possess if they are able to converse personally with aliens presenting themselves for inspection, and he shall endeavor to induce each one to learn at least one foreign language.

In addition to his other duties, the chief of this division shall be further responsible as follows:

a. Upon the arrival of vessels at Quarantine, with immigrants who can presumably be landed the same day, he shall notify the Registry Division of the probable time when such immigrants will reach Ellis Island.
b. He shall transmit daily to the Statistical Division his report showing in detail the vessels boarded and by whom, the number of passengers by classes from each port of departure and the disposition made of them, together with the other information called for by the appropriate form.
c. He shall detail inspectors to attend the sailing of cattle ships for the purpose of issuing certificates to expert cattlemen. He shall keep a record of all such certificates issued and caused to be taken up and canceled those pertaining to returning cattlemen.
d. He shall instruct the gatemen at the Barge Office as to the rules governing the admission of persons to Ellis Island, including the times at which various classes thereof may come to Ellis Island.
e. He shall supervise the exercise by any privilege holder of his privilege on the premises used by the Immigration Service on Manhattan Island.
f. He shall supervise the receipt at the Barge Office of goods for the Ellis Island Immigrant Station and see that they are properly forwarded.

Rules for the Registry Division

The principal work of this division is known as *primary inspection.* It consists in inspecting all aliens brought to Ellis Island except those (principally cabin aliens) who may have been temporarily detained or held for special inquiry by an inspector of the Boarding Division. All aliens coming under the jurisdiction of this division shall either be landed, temporarily detained or held for special inquiry.

Whenever aliens reach Ellis Island, gatemen or watchmen shall receive and conduct them to the medical officers. Upon completion of the medical examination, they will again come under the control of this division.

Upon receipt of manifests, the chief of this division shall detail an official to examine the same and call attention of the examining inspector to groups of persons going to the same place but listed on different sheets and to any other matters which might escape the notice of the several inspectors. He shall also ascertain through the manifest, alphabetical book and otherwise, whether persons concerning whom notices have been issued have come to Ellis Island, in which case the examining inspector shall be directed to consult such notices. He shall see to it that matrons are stationed near the medical officers who shall pin to the cards of female aliens any special information concerning their physical condition, stamping on the cards the words *See Matron's Remarks.* He shall distribute the manifest sheets amongst the examining inspectors whom he has selected for service on the various lines. He shall place *groupers* at proper points to direct aliens who have passed the medical examiners to the lines at the end of which are the manifest sheets containing their names. Groupers may be instructed to place aliens holding medical certificates and women with small children at the head of the inspection lines.

The examining inspectors shall question each alien as to the matters mentioned in the manifest and correct any error or omission. Where New York City is given as the *final destination* the inspector shall, before accepting it as correct, satisfy himself that this is not done as a means of concealing the real destination. No inspector shall attempt to inspect an alien with whom he cannot converse either personally or through an interpreter. Upon the ascertained relevant facts, including the alien's appearance and general demeanor, the examining inspector shall determine whether or not he is *clearly and beyond a doubt entitled to land*, and if not, he shall hold him for special inquiry.

Aliens obviously belonging to any of the excluded classes shall, as a matter of course, be held for special inquiry. Included in this category are those certified by the surgeons to be idiots, imbeciles, feeble-minded persons, epileptics, insane persons, and those afflicted with tuberculosis or with a loathsome or dangerous contagious disease. Aliens certified by the surgeons for any *mental* defect, those who have been objects of public charity, those who appear to be those who have been objects of public charity, those who appear to be devoid of ordinary intelligence, unmarried pregnant women and children under sixteen unaccompanied by either parent and neither being in this country, shall also be held for special inquiry as a matter of course.

It will usually be necessary and proper to hold for special inquiry an alien in respect of whom the surgeons have issued a certificate for any physical defect affecting in their opinion his ability to earn a living. But if with a knowledge of the alien's occupation the examining inspector is of the opinion that he should nevertheless be landed at primary inspection, he shall consult with the chief of this division, and if they agree, then the alien need not be held for special inquiry.

Where the medical certificate does not state that a physical defect in the surgeon's opinion affect the alien's ability to earn a living, the examining inspector may, if he deem the alien clearly and beyond a doubt entitled to land, permit him to do so, but must be prepared to justify such action.

In determining whether or not an alien is a pauper or a person likely to become a public charge, inspectors must consider amongst other matters his occupation, his proficiency in the same (including, where relevant, his physical ability to pursue it and his mental aptitude therefor), the demand for labor or services of the kind he is able to render at the place to which he intends to go, the number of persons who may be dependent upon him for support either here or abroad, and the value of his property. The vital question in these cases usually is whether or not he will be able to secure profitable employment and be self-supporting before his funds are exhausted.

In the absence of a statutory provision no hard and fast rule can be laid down as to amount of money an alien must have, but he should be held for special inquiry where his funds are not deemed adequate for his maintenance until such time as he is likely to find profitable employment. Cases of wives and minor children going to persons as to whom the examining inspector is satisfied that they are *able, willing and legally bound* to support them may constitute exceptions to this rule.

Where aliens are presumably qualified to land but there exists some minor objection to permitting them to do so immediately, which objection is likely to be overcome within a short time, the examining inspector may postpone completion of the process of primary inspection by detaining them temporarily, thus sending them to the Information Division where their cases will be disposed of under the rules of that division. Typical instances where such action is proper are where addresses must be verified or relatives or friends notified to call.

Whether or not an alien shall be landed, temporarily detained, or held for special inquiry often calls for the exercise of good judgement and a sound discretion based upon a knowledge of all relevant facts which is possible to ascertain. The chief of this division shall report to the Superintendent the names of inspectors who after a fair trial have proven themselves unable to exercise such judgement and discretion.

Where an examining inspector immediately after holding an alien for special inquiry discovers that he has done so through an inadvertence, he shall report the case forthwith through the chief of this division to the Superintendent, who shall bring it to the attention of the Commissioner for such action as the latter may deem proper; but the examining inspector shall never release an alien once held for special inquiry.

Inspectors shall note upon the manifest whether aliens not permitted to land at once are temporarily detained or held for special inquiry. In the former case, a cross shall be made opposite the name and a white card issued; in the latter case, the letters *S.I.* shall be placed opposite them name and a yellow card issued. The cause or causes of detention shall be concisely noted on the card, also any important admissions or information given by an alien. They shall also note on the manifest all medical certificates, memoranda or remarks, including matron's remarks, together with (the) name or (the) initial of (the) matron making them.

Aliens who have been to hospital prior to inspection shall upon their return be inspected upon the floor of the Registry Division or, if it be necessary to inspect them while still in hospital, through shall occur through affidavits or taken an inspector of this division. In the latter case where an alien is held for special inquiry the affidavit or statement shall be delivered to the Chief of the Special Inquiry Division together with the detention card.

Each alien shall be asked specifically whether or not he is traveling alone. If not, and he is detained, the name of the accompanying person or persons shall be written on the detention card. Where the surgeon or the examining inspector considers the detained alien helpless from sickness, mental or physical disability or infancy, at least one of the accompanying persons shall also be detained.

Unattended females, young children and aged persons who have been admitted, particularly where they are bound for a large inland city, shall be urged to telegraph their relatives or friends before leaving Ellis Island. There shall be pinned to them a piece of paper with the word *Telegraph* marked thereon. Young children shall also be tagged.

Effort should be made to reduce to a minimum the instances in which aliens who have been brought to Ellis Island and are bound for points beyond New York City shall go to such city for any purpose. Whenever an alien insists on doing this his case should be referred to the chief of this division for such action as the latter deems proper.

The examining inspectors shall inform themselves of the hours at which aliens must leave Ellis Island to take steamers or trains leaving on the day of their arrival and shall detain and give a temporary detention card marked *Too late for . . . (specify route)* to all qualified persons unable to proceed on such day.

Should an alien bound for an inland point but holding no ticket or order for transportation beyond Ellis Island request of the examining inspector information as to how to proceed, he shall be referred to the chief of this division who will inform him as to the various routes where more than one exists, cost of transportation and approximate duration of journey, leaving him to decide by which route he will proceed, the route selected to be noted on the manifest. The routes taken by all aliens going beyond New York City shall be shown by appropriate entry on the manifest.

Aliens arriving at Ellis Island with prepaid tickets, orders or contracts entitling them unconditionally to transportation to any point, shall not be compelled by any one at Ellis Island to pay any additional sum for such transportation. Report shall be made to the Commissioner of any violation of this rule or of the refusal of the representative of any steamship company to approve any such orders or contracts.

After inspection, aliens shall be directed to the special inquiry room, the temporary detention room, the railroad room, or to the ferryboat to New York, according to the disposition made of them by the examining inspectors on the line.

Any challenge under the statute shall be reported to the chief of this division, who will note on the card to be given the fact that such challenge has been made.

Steerage claiming to be naturalized citizens, being required to come to Ellis Island, the examining inspector shall sift the proof of citizenship offered by them, and when in doubt require them to state under oath or even verify an affidavit stating when and where naturalization papers were secured, the Court which issued them and their addresses in the United States. Notation as to such data and oath or affidavit shall be made on the manifest.

When a naturalization paper is presented the inspector shall enter on the manifest a brief record, to include date of paper, name of Court issuing the same, and future address: If the name on the manifest does not correspond with that in the paper, the latter shall also be written on the manifest. Where naturalization papers appear to be fraudulent or defective the matter shall be referred to the chief of this division.

Minors born in the United States of alien parents shall be entered in the *Nationality* and *Race* columns as *U.S. Born.*

All corrections and notations on the manifests shall be neatly made in red ink. Upon completion of the examination, the inspector shall sign his name to the manifest sheets before him and report in writing to the chief of this division (who in turn shall report to the Law Clerk) any alien named therein who has not appeared for inspection and who is not in hospital.

Inspectors shall note on detention cards any important information obtained from the alien, including particularly his admissions, with [the] name of [the] interpreter; or in lieu hereof, he may request to be called by the board.

The chief of this division shall point out to new inspectors the advantage which they will possess if they are able to converse personally with aliens presenting themselves for inspection, and he shall endeavor to induce each one to learn at least one foreign language.

Interpreters shall report to the chief of this division. Upon request, he shall detail those not required in connection with primary inspection to serve temporarily in other divisions.

A recess for luncheon may be taken from noon till 12.30 p.m., but the chief of this division shall designate some other appropriate time whenever at or about noon large numbers of immigrants are awaiting registration and by so doing he can expedite primary inspection.

Watchmen, gatemen and messengers serving in this division shall assist women, children and aged persons in carrying their hand baggage from one part of the building to another to the extent of their ability to do so without interfering with other work.

The chief of this division shall before the expiration of each month prepare lists of so-called *early-day* and *late-day* men. The former shall consist of at least one inspector who will report before the night inspector leaves the island and remain on duty until dismissed for the day. The latter shall consist of at least one inspector and one interpreter who shall report by a late morning boat and remain on duty until relieved by the officials of the Night Division.

Rules for the Information Division

The work of this division includes (1) giving appropriate information and directions to persons calling at Ellis Island, including such as come (a) on official business, (b) on behalf of immigrants, (c) to testify before boards of inquiry, (d) as visitors; (2) disposing of the cases of aliens detained temporarily by the Registry Division and taking charge of such aliens during the day hours.

Officials stationed at the ferry-slip shall receive all persons coming from New York and direct those calling on behalf of immigrants to the waiting room in the covered way or to main Information Office, as instructed from time to time by the chief of this division. Information pertaining to immigrants, particularly those who have been detained, shall be secured as promptly as possible and given without unnecessary delay to those calling on their behalf.

Officials stationed at the entrance to the temporary detention room shall secure the prescribed data concerning all who have been temporarily detained, take up their detention cards, inquire fully into the causes for which they have been detained and supervise the sending of official post-cards or telegrams to their relatives or friends. The name of the telegraph company and the signature of the agent shall appear on the detention card, also the time when sent and the charge therefor. A carbon copy of the message, showing also the amount collected, shall be delivered to the alien.

Temporarily detained aliens shall either be landed or held for special inquiry. They shall be held for special inquiry as soon as it becomes evident that they cannot be landed by this division. The rules of the Registry Division pertaining to eligibility and detention for special inquiry are generally applicable in this division and must be known to its inspectors. A daily report of all cases held for special inquiry in this division shall be submitted to the Statistical Division.

In the discretion of the Commissioner, missionaries, agents of immigrant aid societies, telegraph company employees and transportation agents shall, to facilitate [the] performance of their respective duties . . . be admitted to the temporary detention rooms. Addresses may be furnished only through the chief of this division. At no time during detention shall anyone other than officials have possession of the detention card.

Each day the chief of this division shall discuss with the Superintendent the cases of any immigrants who have been detained in this division for over five days (exclusive of those held as accompanying patients in the hospital) with a view to determining whether or not they should be further held in this division.

No immigrant shall be discharged to anyone as to whom the inspector is not satisfied that he is a fit person to receive the immigrant and that the latter wishes to go to him. Such person may be first required to verify an affidavit. A record of each discharge shall be made on the back of the detention card.

In discharging immigrants to missionaries and immigrant aid societies, inspectors shall be held to the exercise of sound discretion. Such action may be proper when it will aid qualified immigrants to secure stated remunerative employment. They shall be informed of any additional expense to which they will be thereby subjected. A daily report of such discharges shall be made in writing to the Chief Clerk.

All information concerning action taken in any case shall be entered of record as soon as possible. Detention cards shall be preserved and dealt with in accordance with written instructions thereto pertaining. The number of meals had by each immigrant in this division shall be entered on his card.

Immigrants may, with the consent of the chef of this division, visit relatives or friends detained in hospital, or upon inquiry, they shall be informed as to their condition.

All changes of destination, names, ages, nationalities of immigrants admitted by this division shall be reported daily in writing to the Statistical Division.

The chief of this division shall keep the Boarding Division advised of the hours during which persons desiring to call on behalf of immigrants arriving on stated ships should come to Ellis Island.

Rules for the Special Inquiry Division

The chief of this division shall have the custody of all aliens in the special inquiry detention room. He shall station officials at the entrance who shall secure the prescribed data concerning them, take up their detention cards and supervise the sending of official postal cards or telegrams to relatives or friends. But no one held for suspected violation of the contract labor law may communicate with anyone prior to a first hearing.

The chief of this division shall distribute the cases amongst the several boards in session, shall see to it that aliens, witnesses and documentary evidence are produced before boards as speedily as possible, shall assign stenographers and shall supervise the preparation of boards records. He shall study the work of the several boards and shall time to time report to the Superintendent any lack of uniformity in their standards.

The official designated by the Commissioner as chairman is responsible for the proper, expeditious and efficient conduct of the proceedings over which he presides. He shall see to it that the prescribed questions are put and the inquiry is confined to relevant matters. He shall cause to be kept a daily record showing the number of cases admitted, deferred and excluded. Subject to the foregoing, each member shall do his full share of the work of the board and is held to the exercise of correct judgement as to all matters pertaining to each case.

Boards have the right to dispose of cases upon the facts as they appear when the aliens first come before them, and it is proper for them to do so unless it is likely that additional evidence will alter the decision. Cases may be deferred once by a majority vote. They shall not be deferred more than once except by a unanimous vote.

The case of an alien who has been excluded shall be reconsidered only upon a recommendation from the Commissioner. Where immediately after admission, and while the alien is still in the custody of the immigration authorities, new evidence is discovered which, if known, would probably have brought about a different decision, this fact shall be reported at once to the Commissioner.

In determining whether or not an alien is a pauper or a person likely to become a public charge, boards should consider, amongst other matters, his occupation, his proficiency in the same (including, where relevant, his physical ability to pursue it and his mental aptitude therefore), his chances of securing employment, his general appearance, the number of persons who may be dependent upon him for support and the value of his property. Nothing herein contained applies to wives, minor children, or others going to persons *able, willing and legally bound* to support them.

Boards may give such consideration as they desire to pecuniary assistance furnished an alien after arrival by one not legally bound to give it, bearing in mind that such assistance usually renders him to a certain extent an object of charity.

> *NOTE: The testimony of relatives and friends is often relevant upon the question whether or not an alien is likely to become a public charge. But, if after hearing such testimony, the board still believes that he is likely to become a public charge, then it should not admit him merely because oral and written assurances are given that he will not become such: for to do so would give such assurances the effect of a bond, whereas the Secretary alone, under Section 26, has the power to admit on bond aliens "likely" to be excluded because likely to become a public charge.*

Where an alien is under a moral or legal obligation to support absent persons, inquiry should be made as to their condition and whether they or not they are objects of public or private charity. The fact that a portion of a man's earnings will be consumed in the support of others may be taken into consideration in passing upon his right to land.

Whenever it is relevant to ascertain what the alien stated at primary inspection, the examining inspector may be summoned, through the chief of his division, to testify.

Whenever a board desires that further evidence be procured or an investigation be made before it decides a case, written request shall be made therefor through the chief of this division to the Superintendent or Chief Clerk, specifying what is desired.

The record of each case shall, on its face value, justify the decision. Where relevant (as it often is) the appearance or impression made by the aliens or witnesses shall be noted.

Before rendering its decision, the board shall, in a brief *opinion*, summarize in logical sequence the principal circumstances upon which it will base the same. Usually, it will be necessary and proper to state of record whether or not the alien will be able to secure employment and perform the work incident thereto. Where the decision is to one of exclusion, the opinion shall cite as many of the statutory disabilities as exist in the case, summarizing as to each the principal circumstances which show the existence thereof.

The decision shall be in the words *Alien Admitted* or *Alien Excluded and Ordered Deported*, as the case may be.

Where the board feels itself bound to exclude though believing that the case has great merit, the chairman, in addition to notifying the alien of his right of appeal, may submit to the Commissioner through the chief of this division, a written memorandum in regard to the case.

A brief record of the action of the board shall be made on the back of the detention card over the signature of the chairman, which record shall include disposition made of the case, date and hour when made, name of stenographer and page in his book where shorthand record may be found. In the case of exclusion, the ground or grounds thereof shall be stated. These cards shall thereafter be dealt with in accordance with written directions on file and shall eventually be lodged with the chief of the Statistical Division. The data above mentioned, except the grounds of exclusion, shall be stamped also on all documentary evidence considered by the board.

The board messengers shall personally supervise the delivery to the Deporting Division of those who are excluded or whose cases are deferred.

Board secretaries shall prepare six typewritten sets of minutes in full. Sets 1, 2, 3 and 4 shall be signed by them and filed in the Executive Division. The remaining sets shall be delivered to the chief of this division, who shall retain one and deliver the other to the board which heard the case, the last named set to be used by the board in connection with any rehearing and at the close of business each day to be returned to the chief of this division, who shall retain possession thereof until again required by the board. The sets so delivered to the boards shall at the end of sixty days be delivered to the Chief Clerk for destruction.

Any detained alien expression desire to deposit valuables for safe-keeping shall be conducted to the Treasurer's office for this purpose; and whenever it is deemed desirable that valuables be so deposited, the alien shall be urged to do so. Steerage aliens going to points beyond New York City, whom the board is disposed to admit, will be discouraged from stopping over in this city.

Where otherwise qualified immigrants are unable to locate relatives or friends or to find employment, boards may consult with the accredited missionaries and immigrant aid societies. Details should be required as to the employment tendered and where immigrants are turned over to such missionaries of societies they should be informed of the appropriate expense to which they will be subjected.

Rules for the Deporting Division

The work of this division shall include (1) guarding during day time aliens who have been excluded, those whose cases have been deferred by a board, those held under Department warrant and such others as may be placed in its custody; (2) placing those ordered deported on board ship.

The chef of this division shall divide his force into three parts, two of which shall constitute alternate watches (to be known respectively as the *first watch* and the *second watch*) for the guarding of detained aliens. The third shall be known as the *deporting squad.* The first watch shall report in time to relieve the Night Division and the second watch shall remain on duty till relieved by the Night Division.

Aliens detained in this division shall be segregated with reference to sex except that young male children may be placed in the female detention room. So far as existing facilities permit aliens who occupied cabin quarters during the voyage shall be segregated from those who came in steerage, and the latter shall be separated with reference whether they were excluded or deferred. Ex-convicts, procurers, prostitutes and other bad characters held under Department warrant shall always be kept separate and apart from any others. All in the custody of this division shall be counted frequently and checked by calling their names. If anyone be found missing the fact shall forthwith be reported to the Superintendent.

Immigrants in the custody of this division shall be taken to the dining-room for meals. When the weather permits, they shall be taken to the roof garden. Upon request, they shall be permitted to bathe. Those desiring to send articles of clothing to the laundry may do so from time to time.

With the consent of the chief of this division, they may visit relatives of friends detained in hospital or, upon inquiry, they shall be informed of their condition.

Missionaries and society agents shall have access to them under the supervision of the chief of this division, who also may grant steamship agents and telegraph employees the same privilege, but only in the presence of an official. Addresses may be furnished them only through the chief of this division and only officials may be in possession of their detention cards.

Upon request from the Special Inquiry Division, immigrants shall be temporarily turned over to it for the purpose of further board hearings.

The chief of this division shall daily call attention of the Superintendent of the Chief of the Special Inquiry Division to the cases of all who have been detained more than five days without final action having been taken.

As soon as an immigrant is excluded a blue *deportation card* shall be made out for him. There shall be transcribed to it the data appearing on the face of the *special inquiry card* and before deportation there shall be added the following: height, color of hair, color of eyes, date when and name of steamer by which deported and name of deporting officer. After deportation, these cards shall be dealt with in accordance with the written instructions pertaining to detention cards.

On receipt of notice that an appeal has been filed, deportation shall be forthwith stayed and the detention cards stamped *Appeal filed.* Upon receipt of notice of decision in any case the terms thereof shall be carried out as soon as possible.

Aliens having the right of appeal shall though they fail to exercise such right, not be deported within forty eight hours after arrival nor within twenty four hours after exclusion by a board except with the consent of the Assistant Commissioner or the Superintendent. No excluded member of a family who is without [the] right of appeal shall be deported until [the] decision has been rendered as to other members of the same family who may have filed an appeal; nor shall excluded as and accompanying alien be deported until final action is taken as to his or her ward. An excluded who has no right of appeal and is unaccompanied by any relative shall be deported as soon as possible.

Where an alien about to be deported is in hospital, this division shall make timely request to the Medical Division for his surrender, together with his baggage. If afflicted with a loathsome or contagious disease he shall be isolated.

Before removing an alien from Ellis Island for deportation, all property belonging to him, including baggage and money on deposit with the Treasurer, shall be collected. The baggage shall be properly tagged and, upon arrival at the pier, receipt shall be secured therefor from the baggage agent.

Any passports shall be stamped *Deported* with the date of deportation. Detention card shall be similarly stamped. At the time of delivery on board the vessel a receipt for the immigrant shall be secured from the proper officer.

An employee of this division shall visit each vessel having on board persons ordered deported on the date of the sailing thereof. He shall call them by name and satisfy himself that all are actually on board at the time of sailing and make report to the chief of this division.

Rules for the Statistical Division

The work of this division includes:

a. Transferring certain prescribed statistical data of all arriving and departing aliens from the ship's manifest to cards and forwarding such cards at proper intervals to the Bureau.

b. Preparing from the manifests an alphabetical card-index of each alien passenger arriving at New York, and of each third class passenger manifested as a citizen.
c. Preparing and submitting to the steamship companies bills of head tax assessed on account of aliens arriving at New York.
d. Investigating and acting upon requests from the steamship companies for the refund of head tax in the cases mentioned in the statute and the rules.
e. Filing in this division the permanent official records, other than correspondence.
f. Verifying the amounts charged the steamship companies for subsistence of detained aliens (by considering such amounts in connection with the time of detention).
g. Ascertaining the amounts from the records in response to inquiries whether states aliens have landed at New York and, if so, when and by what steamer (commonly called *verifying landings*).
h. Entering on the manifests the disposition made of all aliens temporarily detained, held for special inquiry or placed in the hospital, an comparing the final destination noted on the corrected manifest with the final destination given by the alien before a board of special inquiry or in the Information Division, and in the event of a discrepancy, correcting the manifest.
i. Preparing and keeping on file a record of aliens who entered without inspection, who have been in the United States for a period longer than three years and who are petitioners for naturalization. The certificate of arrival shall, as required by the Bureau, be forwarded to the Chief of the Division of Naturalization in Washington, D.C. on a form prepared for this purpose.

Index cards of the card-index shall show the name and age of each passenger, the number of the bound volume containing the manifest upon which the name is listed, also the name of such manifest and the list or sheet number of each such passenger. Whenever there is doubt as to which is the surname, the name shall be indexed both ways.

Bills for head tax shall be submitted to the steamship company within twenty-four hours after the arrival. One copy of each bill shall be sent to the Collector of Customs and a press copy retained for the file.

Carbon copies of verifications of landing are to be attached to the correspondence to which they relate. All requests for verifications of landing shall be card-indexed, numbered and filed in such a manner as to be easily available for reference.

Before compiling statistical data from the manifests, the entries thereon shall be compared with reports pertaining thereto received from the Information Division. The manifests shall from time to time be bound in convenient form and with them shall be bound the appropriate special inquiry and temporary detention sheets. The bound volumes shall be numbered consecutively and filed.

Rules for the Mechanical Division

The work of this division includes: (a) caring for the light, heat and power plant and its appurtenances, the refrigerating plant and all fire lines and apparatus; (b) the heating and lighting of all buildings.

Its force shall be divided into three *watches* as follows:

1. A day watch which shall leave the Barge Office at 7.20 a.m. and remain at Ellis Island until 3.30 p.m.

2. An afternoon watch which shall leave the Barge Office at 3 p.m. and remain at Ellis Island until 11.30 p.m.
3. A morning watch which shall leave the Barge Office at 11 p.m. and remain at Ellis Island until 7.40 a.m.

Each watch shall remain on duty in its entirety until relieved by the succeeding watch. A watch going off duty shall turn over all parts of [the] plant in good running order or, if derangements beyond the ability of the watch to repair have occurred, they shall be reported in detail by the Assistant Engineer relieved to the Assistant Engineer relieving.

The Engineer-in-Charge shall designate at least one assistant engineer, one dynamo tender, one wireman, two firemen, one refrigerating machinist and one laborer to perform duty on each watch. Such assistant engineer shall direct the work of all other employees assigned to his watch and is responsible for the proper performance of such work.

The duties of assistant engineers further include the following:

a. Upon taking charge they shall personally examine the water in the boilers, the feed-pumps, engines, dynamos and all other machinery including during the cold season the heating apparatus in the buildings.
b. They shall frequently inspect the ground detector to determine whether or not there is any loss of current on any circuit.
c. They shall also inspect the condition of the coal bunkers. Should the temperature be unduly high, indicating (the) possibility of spontaneous combustion, they shall proceed to overhaul coal and extinguish any fire and report the matter at once by telephone to the Chief Engineer and Superintendent of Repairs to Public Buildings at his office or residence and writing to the Engineer-in-Charge.
d. They shall note on the log-block and report to the Engineer-in-Charge in writing any inferior coal which may come to their notice.
e. They shall see to it that the six water tanks at the power house and the emergency tank in the main building are kept full.
f. They shall inspect the water gauge on the water main from Comunipaw and, if the pressure is below normal, they shall enter this fact in the log-book and, if the situation warrants such action, communicate by telephone with Chief Engineer and Superintendent of Repairs.
g. They shall cause any minor repairs becoming necessary during their respective watches to be made at once, noting the same in the log-book and, they shall report by telephone to the Chief Engineer and Superintendent of Repairs and in writing to the Engineer-in-Charge any serious accident, fire or derangement of the plant, making also appropriate entry thereof in the log-book. The assistant engineers shall call upon the Superintendent for the services of plumbers and such other employees not under their immediate direction as they may require.

The Engineer-in-Charge shall designate an assistant engineer to take charge of the Engineer's work at the hospital and its adjoining buildings during the usual hours of business. Such assistant engineer shall be guided by these rules as far as applicable, and shall each morning inspect the flush tanks in all toilet rooms of the hospital buildings.

The dynamo tenders shall oil and clean all dynamos and engines during its watch, see that proper voltage is maintained on the voltameter at the switchboard, and note hourly in the log-book the voltage, amperage and steam pressure on boilers.

The wiremen shall inspect and maintain in proper condition wires, electric bells, batteries, motor fans and other electrical appliances throughout the station, including the hospital buildings. They shall report to the Engineer-in-Charge or assistant engineer such repairs as they are unable to make on the spot.

The firemen shall attend to the fires, endeavor to maintain a steady steam pressure, maintain the water in the boilers at such height as the Engineer-in-Charge or assistant engineer shall from time to time direct, and clean the brass work and boiler fronts at least once during each watch.

The duties of refrigerating machinists shall include making ice, taking care and keeping clean the refrigerating machinery, keeping the ice boxes at a proper temperature and maintaining a sufficient quantity of ice in the storage box.

The laborers shall supply the firemen with coal, remove ashes, clean the pumps and brass work in the pump-pit and the floors of the fire room clean and orderly. They shall keep a tally of the amount of coal and ashes wheeled to and from the boilers, delivering the same at the end of each watch to the assistant engineer for entry in the log-book.

The employees of this division shall also perform further work, in addition to any herein specifically described, as may be directed by the Engineer-in-Charge.

The Engineer-in-Charge is responsible for the maintenance of the fire alarm system in proper condition and shall daily cause the same to be tested.

The Engineer-in-Charge is responsible for the maintenance of the fire apparatus in proper condition and shall from time to time cause the same to be tested, recording the fact in the log-book. His duties hereunder include testing the relief valve and setting the same at the proper pressure, maintaining valves, nozzles and panels at each rack in proper state, keeping hose racks filled with hose in good condition and keeping fire extinguishers, properly charged, in their proper places, recharging to occur at intervals of not to exceed six months, also immediately after use. Neither axes and picks shall be removed from the panels nor hose from the racks for any purpose other than fire.

The assistant engineer in charge of each watch shall see to it that the stop valve in the power house vestibule in the covered way is kept shut during freezing weather; that the wrench providing for the quick opening of this valve is kept available and attached to such valve so that it may be opened at any time; that all valves above hose reels and controlling hose lines throughout the covered-way are kept closed at all times save when the hose lines are in use; that in the absence of specific orders to the contrary the shut-off valve in the middle of the ferry-slip over the gate is kept open at all times; and that the small drips draining fire line in the power house vestibule are always open except when the main valve is opened, in which case these drips must be immediately thereafter shut off.

In the event of a fire alarm necessitating of any of the lines in the covered-way system, both of the large salt water pumps and, if necessary, the small auxiliary salt water pumps, shall all be worked in order to maintain a fire line pressure. The stop-valve on the fire line shall be opened and the stop-valve on the flushing line closed. All fresh water pumps shall be run if necessary at full speed in order to build up the pressure in the fresh water tanks and thereby secure good stream from the fresh water lines of hose and stand pipes.

As to all other matters which may arise should fire occur, the employees of this division shall, in addition to observing the specific instructions above given, act in accordance with the requirements of the Fire Drill in so far as they are able.

Rules for the Night Division

The work of this division includes: (a) guarding and caring for detained immigrants and government property from the time of the departure of the *long day* force until the arrival on the following morning of the early day force, and (b) cleaning the building during this time.

There shall be two watches composed of such officials and reporting at such hours as shall be from time to time determined. Either the Inspector-in-Charge or his assistant (selected by him) shall be on duty throughout the night.

Upon reaching Ellis Island, the Night Inspector shall cause to be made a count of all detained aliens, classifying them as (a) temporarily detained; (b) excluded and deferred; (c) held for special inquiry; (d) cabin and warrant cases.

In a book kept for the purpose, he shall receipt to the Deporting Division for classes "b", "c" and "d."

The detained aliens shall be counted on the following morning, when the Night Inspector shall turn the classes "b", "c" and "d" to the first watch of the Deporting Division, upon a written receipt to be entered in the same book.

Aliens temporarily detained (class "a") to be turned over to the first watch of the Information Division.

Bibliography

Books

Adamic, Louis. *From Many Lands.* New York: Harper and Brothers, 1940.

Antin, Mary. *The Promised Land.* Boston: Houghton Mifflin, 1912.

———. *They Who Knock at Our Gates: A Complete Gospel of Immigration*. Boston: Houghton Mifflin, 1914.

Benton, Barbara. *Ellis Island: A Pictorial History.* New York: Facts on File, 1985.

Bolino, August C. *The Ellis Island Source Book.* 2nd ed. Washington, DC: Kensington Historical Press, 1990.

Brandenburg, Broughton. *Imported Americans.* New York: Stokes, 1904.

Brownstone, David M., Irene M. Franck, and Douglass L. Brownstone. *Island of Hope, Island of Tears.* New York: Rawson, Wade, 1979.

Burdick, John. *Ellis Island: Gateway of Hope.* New York: Smithmark, 1997.

Chermayeff, Ivan, Fred Wasserman, and Mary J. Shapiro. *Ellis Island: An Illustrated History of the Immigrant Experience.* New York: Macmillan, 1991.

Coan, Peter Morton. *Ellis Island Interviews: In Their Own Words.* New York: Facts on File, 1997.

Corsi, Edward. *In the Shadow of Liberty: The Chronicle of Ellis Island*. New York: Macmillan, 1935.

Cowen, Philip. *Memories of an American Jew.* New York: International, 1932.

Curran, Henry H. *Pillar to Post.* New York: Charles Scribner's Sons, 1941.

Daniels, Roger. *American Immigration.* New York: Oxford University Press, 2001.

———. *Coming to America.* New York: Harper Collins, 1990.

———. *Guarding the Golden Door.* New York: Hill & Wang, 2004.

Fairchild, Amy L. *Science at the Borders: Immigrant Inspection and the Shaping of the Modern Industrial Labor Force*. Baltimore: Johns Hopkins University Press, 2003.

Foner, Nancy. *From Ellis Island to JFK.* New Haven: Yale University Press, 2001.

Graham, Stephen. *With Poor Immigrants to America.* New York: Macmillan, 1914.

Hamblin, B. Colin. *Ellis Island: The Official Souvenir Guide.* Santa Barbara, CA: Companion, 1991.

Handlin, Oscar. *The Uprooted: The Epic Story of the Great Migrations that Made the American People*. Boston: Little, Brown, 1951.

Heaps, Willard. *The Story of Ellis Island.* New York: Seabury, 1976.

Heiser, Victor. *Odyssey of an American Doctor.* New York: W.W. Norton, 1936.

Holland, F. Ross. *Idealists, Scoundrels, and the Lady: The Memoirs of an Insider in the Statue of Liberty–Ellis Island Project*. Urbana: University of Illinois Press, 1993.

Hoobler, Dorothy, and Thomas Hoobler. *We Are Americans: Voices of the Immigrant Experience.* New York: Scholastic, 2003.

Howe, Frederick C. *The Confessions of a Reformer.* New York: Charles Scribner's Sons, 1925.

Kotker, Norman, Susan Jonas, and Robert Twolmby. *Ellis Island: Echoes of a Nation's Past.* New York: Aperture Foundation, 1989.

Kraut, Alan M. *Silent Travelers: Germs, Genes, and the "Immigrant Menace."* New York: Basic Books, 1994.

LaGuardia, Fiorello H. *The Making of an Insurgent: An Autobiography, 1882–1919.* Philadelphia: Lippincott, 1948.

Moreno, Barry. *Ellis Island.* Charleston, SC: Arcadia, 2003.

———. *Italian Americans.* New York: Barron's Educational Series, 2003.

———. *The Statue of Liberty Encyclopedia.* New York: Simon & Schuster, 2000.

Morrison, Joan, and Charlotte Fox Zabusky. *American Mosaic: The Immigrant Experience in the Words of Those Who Lived It.* New York: Dutton, 1980.

Mullan, Fitzhugh. *Plagues and Politics: The Story of the United States Public Health Service.* New York: Basic Books, 1989.

Novotny, Ann. *Strangers at the Door: Ellis Island, Castle Garden and the Great Migration to America.* Riverside, CT: Chatham, 1971.

Palmer, Carleton H., ed. *Report of the Ellis Island Committee.* Washington, DC: U.S. Department of Labor, 1934. Reprint, New York: Ozer, 1971.

Pauli, Hertha E. *The Golden Door.* New York: Knopf, 1949.

Perec, Georges. *Ellis Island.* New York: New Press, 1995.

Pitkin, Thomas M. *Keepers of the Gate: A History of Ellis Island.* New York: New York University Press, 1975.

Post, Louis F. *Deportations Delirium of Nineteen Twenty.* Chicago: Charles H. Kerr, 1923.

Powderly, Terence V. *The Path I Trod: The Autobiography of Terence Powderly.* New York: Columbia University Press, 1940.

Preston, William, Jr. *Aliens and Dissenters: Federal Suppression of Radicals, 1903–1933.* Cambridge: Harvard University Press, 1963.

Safford, Victor. *Immigration Problems: Personal Experiences of an Official.* New York: Dodd, Mead, 1925.

Schulz, Karin, ed. *Hoffnung Amerika: Europaische Auswanderung in die Neue Welt.* Bremerhaven, Germany: Nordwestdeutsche Verlagsgesellschaft, 1994.

Shapiro, Mary J. *Gateway to Liberty: The Story of the Statue of Liberty and Ellis Island.* New York: Vintage Books, 1986.

Smith, Darrell H., and H. Guy Herring. *The Bureau of Immigration: Its History, Activities and Organization.* Baltimore: Johns Hopkins University Press, 1924.

Steiner, Edward A. *The Immigrant Tide: Its Ebb and Flow.* New York: Fleming H. Revell, 1909.

———. *On the Trail of the Immigrant.* New York: Fleming H. Revell, 1906.

Tifft, Wilton. *Ellis Island.* Chicago: Contemporary Books, 1990.

Tifft, Wilton, and Thomas Dunne. *Ellis Island: A Picture Text History.* New York: W.W. Norton, 1971.

Vecoli, Rudolph. "The Lady and the Huddled Masses: The Statue of Liberty as a Symbol of Immigration." In *The Statue of Liberty Revisited: Making a Universal Symbol*, edited by Wilton S. Dillon and Neil G. Kotler, 39–69. Washington, DC: Smithsonian Institution Press, 1994.

Watchorn, Robert. *The Autobiography of Robert Watchorn.* Edited by Herbert Faulkner West. Oklahoma City: Robert Watchorn Charities, 1958.

Weber, John B. *Autobiography.* New York: privately printed, 1925.

Weiss, Feri Felix. *The Sieve, or, Revelations of the Man Mill, Being the Truth about American Immigration*. Boston: Page, 1921.

Wepman, Dennis. *Immigration: From the Founding of Virginia to the Closing of Ellis Island.* New York, Facts on File, 2002.

Yans-McLaughlin, Virginia, and Marjorie Lightman. *Ellis Island and the Peopling of America.* New York: New Press, 1997.

Yew, Elizabeth. "Medical Inspection of Immigrants at Ellis Island, 1892–1924." *Bulletin of the New York Academy of Medicine* 56 (June 1980).

Government Reports

Bearss, Edwin C. *The Ferryboat "Ellis Island": Transport to Hope.* Washington, DC: National Park Service, 1969.

Berengarten, Sidney. *Ellis Island.* Washington, DC: Civil Works Administration of the National Parks, 1934.

Beyer, Blinder, Belle/Anderson, Notter, Finegold. *Ellis Island, Historic Structure Report, The Main Building.* 14 vols. Washington, DC: National Park Service, 1984.

Immigration and Naturalization Service. *History of Ellis Island.* 2 reports. Washington, DC: Immigration and Naturalization Service, October 1947 and December 1952.

National Park Service. *Master Plan for Ellis Island.* Washington, DC: National Park Service, 1968.

———. *A Study Report on Ellis Island.* Washington, DC: National Park Service, June 1964.

Pike, Henry H. *Ellis Island: Its Legal Status.* Washington, DC: Office of the Counsel General, General Services Administration.

Pitkin, Thomas M. *Report on Ellis Island as an Immigrant Depot, 1890–1954.* Washington, DC: National Park Service, 1966.

Pousson, John F. *An Overview and Assessment of Archeological Resources on Ellis Island.* Washington, DC: National Park Service, 1986.

Reimer, Rudolph. *History of Ellis Island.* New York: Immigration and Naturalization Service, 1934. Available in the New York Public Library.

Stakely, J. Tracy. *Cultural Landscape Report for Ellis Island.* Olmsted Center for Landscape Preservation. Brookline, MA: National Park Service, 2002.

United States Public Health Service. *Ellis Island: America's Immigration Cornerstone.* Washington, DC: U.S. Department of Health and Human Services, 1993.

Unrau, Harlan, D. *Historic Structure Report: Ellis Island, Historical Data.* Denver Service Center. Denver: National Park Service, 1978.

Films and Documentaries

Ellis Island. Story by Arthur T. Horman, Directed by Phil Rosen. Hollywood, CA: Invincible Pictures, 1936. Feature film.

Ellis Island: Everyman's Monument. Narrated by Telly Savalas. Beverly Hills, CA: Panorama International Productions, 1991. Includes interviews with Ellis Island curators, librarians, and rangers. Documentary.

Gateway. Story by Walter Reisch. Screenplay by Lamar Trotti. Hollywood, CA: Twentieth Century Film Corporation, 1938. Feature film.

An Island Called Ellis. Narrated by Jose Ferrer. New York: NBC Project Twenty, 1967. Documentary.

Island of Hope, Island of Tears. Washington, DC: Guggenheim Productions, 1991. Documentary.

Index

Boldface numerals refer to main entries; italics refer to illustrations.

abandonment, 37–38, 95–96
abbreviations, **1**
Abruzzi, Duke of the, 214
abuses, 47–48
Adamic, Louis, **1–2**, 61, 80
Administration. *See* commissioners; Executive Division
administration building, 41
aerial views of Ellis Island, *26–27*
African Americans, **2**, 14–15, 46–47, 55, 129, 180, 181, 221
Africans, 14–15, 120, 220
Albanians, 109, 120, 217, 220
Albera, Charles (accordionist), 36
Albright, Horace M., 3
alcoholics, 115, 163
Aldrich, Chester H., 73, 85, 117, 203
alien enemies. *See* enemy aliens
Alien Registration Act, 75
alien seamen, 35, 37–38, 132, 190, 254
Alsatians, 248
Ameche, Don, 93
American, Sadie, **2**, 46, 100, 170
American Dream, 250
American Express, 172, 203
American Family Immigration History Center (AFIHC), **2**, 73, 223
American Immigrant Wall of Honor, 12, 73, 212, 223
American Library Association, 4, 141
American Museum of Immigration (AMI), **2–4**, 45, 177, 191
American Red Cross, **4**, 8, 108, 109, 141, 184, 185
American Tract Society, **4**, 141, 170
Americanization Movement, **4–5**, 25, 51, 63
anarchists, **5**, 14, 17, 26, 61, 78, 97, 114, 115, 116, 120, 201, 241
Anderson (pirate), xii, xxi
Anderson's Island, xii, xxi
Andros, Sir Edmund, xii, xxi
Andrus, Cecil, 212
Angel Island Immigrant Station, **6**, 35
Anglicans. *See* Protestant Episcopal Church
Animal House, **6**, 27, 41, 127
Antin, Mary, 80
Anything Can Happen (Papashvily), 85
appeals, **6–7**, 18, 33, 48, 56, 79, 118, 220, 232, 248; right of appeal denied, 115
Arabs, 47, 80, 83, 96, 112, 120, 132, 159, 169, 200, 216, 220
Arbeely, Najeeb, 112, 126
archaeology, 53, 90
architects, xxv, 13, 19, 29, 85, 86, 95, 96, 106, 117, 203, 212, 232–233, 235, 254–255
architectural competition, 218
architecture, xxv, 6, 13, 208
Argentineans, 61, 85, 169
aristocrats, 61
Armenians, 15, 64, 81, 120, 169, 200, 216, 237
Army, xii–xiii, xxii, xxiii, **7–8**, 26, 75, 76, 89–90
Army Corps of Engineers, xii, 29
arrival, **8–10**, 16, 20–25, 29, 70, 92–93
Arthur, Johnny, 72
Asians, 6, 12, 55, 115, 121, 169
Asiatic Barred Zone, 115
Asimov, Isaac, 81
assimilation. *See* Americanization Movement
assistant commissioners, **10**, 138, 159–160, 186
Association of Immigration and Naturalization Officers, 257
Astor, Mrs. Vincent, 73
Atlas, Charles, 80
Austria-Hungary, 1, 4, 10, 194, 214, 252
Austrian Society, xvii, **10**, 48, 169, 219
Austrians, 61, 69, 219, 237
Austro-Hungarian Society, 110
autopsy room, 140
awards for main building design, 19

Bachmeyer, J., 86
bacteriological research. *See* office building and laboratory

Baer, Beulah, **11**
baggage, 9, 158–159
Baggage and Dormitory Building, **11–12**, 27, 38, 97, 127, 212, 216, 254
baggage room, 47, 61, 86
Baggage Room (exhibit), **12**
bail bonds. *See* bonds
Baker, Percy A., 10, **12**, 112, 206
Baker, S. Josephine, 73
Bakery and Carpentry Shop, **13**, 27, 127, 212
balcony. *See* Main Building; registry room
Bandini, Pietro, 214
Baptists. *See* missionaries
barber shop, 133
Barbieri, Fedora, 61
Barbusse, Henri, **13**, 201
Barge Office, xxii, **13**, 25, 38, 47, 81, 85, 100, 140, 182
barges, 8, 53, *82*
Barnes, Binnie, 94
Bartholdi, Frédéric-Auguste, 223
Bass, Sydney H., 57–60
Bastedo, Helen R., 170, 215
bathhouse, 133
The Battery (Battery Park), **13–14**, 25, 29, 38, 100–101, 253
Bawor, Karl, 112
Beame, Abraham, 80
Bedloe's Island, xii, xxii, 13, 220, 223
beds. *See* dormitories
Behlert, Charles L., 112
Behnkin, Frank, 48
Belarsky, Isabel, 187
Belarsky, Sidor, 61, 81
Belgian Bureau, xvi, **14**, 109
Belgians, 14, 63, 200, 220, 254
Belkov, M. Ann, 172, 230
Berkman, Alexander, 5, 12, **14**, 26, 61, 97, 204
Berlin, Irving, 80
Bernardin, Tom (ranger), 85
Berry, John A., xxii
Besant, Annie, 135
Beyer, Blinder, Belle, 212
"beyond a doubt qualified to land," 112
Biddle, Francis, **14**, 75
Births, **14**, 193
Bishara, Habib A., 112, 125
Black Americans. *See* African Americans
Black Hand (*la mano nera*), 126
Black Immigrants, **14–15**, 55, 61, 81, 120, 200, 217
Black Tom Explosion, xxiii, **15–16**, 81, 233, 253
Blegen, Theodore, 3
Board of Review, **16**, 18
Boarding Division, 8, 13, **16**, 70, 81, 124, 140, 173–175
boards of special inquiry, 6, **17–18**, 46, 55, 58–59, 63, 78, 117, 124, 205
boats. *See* ferries and boats
Boiardi, Ettore, 80
Bolsheviks, xxiv, 17, 29, 61, 114, 120, 201, 204
Bond Office, **18**
bonds, **18–19**, 79, 140
Boody, Bertha M., **19**, 164, 216–217
border crossings, 32
Boring, William A., xxiii, **19**, 95, 192, 218, 235
Boston Immigrant Station, **19–20**, 35, 214
Boundary dispute, xxii, xxv
Brandenburg, Broughton, **20–25**
Brazilians, 200
Bremer, Edith Terry, **25**, 109, 110, 256
Briganti, Steven A., 223
British subjects, 5, 49–50, 57–60, 61, 94, 98–99, 128–129, 216, 220, 232
Browder, Irene, 61, 201
Brown, William W., 112
Brownell, Herbert, 25, 37
Buck, Pearl S., **25–26**, 38
Bucking Island, xii, xxi
Budde, Frederick L., 48, 238
Buford, 26, 97, 205, 206
buildings, *26–27*, **27**
Bulgarian Society, 109
Bulgarians, 75, 141, 200
Bureau of Citizenship and Immigration Services, 117
Bureau of Customs and Border Protection, 117
Bureau of Immigration, xiii–xv, xxiii, 6, 13, 16, 19, **27–28**, 31, 34, 39, 40, 53, 75, 78, 102, 104, 114, 117, 131, 139, 200, 204, 213
Bureau of Immigration and Customs Enforcement, 117
Bureau of Immigration and Naturalization, **28**, 117, 131
Bureau of Naturalization, 117
bureaucracy. *See* divisions
burials. *See* cemeteries; deaths and burials
Burkhardt, Louis, 48
Burmese, 169
buttonhook, 79

cabin passengers, 16, 54–56, 57–61, 249
Cable Act, 71
cafeteria, 123
California, 6, 57, 219
Caminetti, Anthony, **29**, 40, 205
Canada and Canadians, 5, 32, 35, 55, 57, 89, 103, 117, 200, 220, 254

canopy, **29**, 212
Capra, Frank, 80
Cardi, Enrico, *253*
Carey, Harry, 93
Caribbean Immigrants. *See* West Indians
Carnera, Primo, 61
Carol, Charles A., **29**, 35, 109, 170
carpentry, 13
Carradine, John, 94
Caruso, Enrico, xvii, 107
Cassells, David H., 39, 187
Castle Clinton, **29–30**
Castle Garden, 3, 13, 14, **30–31**, 42, 89, 97, 109, 124, 138, 156, 165, 166, 169, 183, 218, 250
Castro, Cipriano, **31**, 61, 80, 241
Catalan, 101, 200, 208
Cathcart, Vera, countess of, 173, 241
Catholics, 4, 8, 10, 47, 62, 90, 100–101, 120–121, 169–170, 214–215
ceiling (registry room), 101
Celebrations and ceremonies, **31**, 35–36, 53, 77
cemeteries, 52
Central Jersey Rail Road Terminal, 70
certificates, **32**, 64–68 *passim*
certificates of registry, **32**, 207
Chalk Mark Code, **32–33**, *33*
chapel, 63, 133
Chaplin, Sir Charles (Charlie), xvii
charwomen, 2, 47, 129
Chermayeff, Ivan, 164
Chicago, xvii–xviii
chief clerk, **33**, 37, 79, 140, 219
children, 17, **33–34**, 51, 54–56, 62, 88, 115, 216–217, *218*, 219
Chinatown, 35, 126
Chinese, 6, 12, 20, 112, 115, 126, 182, 188, 200, 217, 220, 254
Chinese Division, **34–35**, 70, 126
Chinese Exclusion Act, 6, 34, **35**, 112, 230
Christian Science, 62
Christians, 4, 29, 35–36, 62, 100–101, 169–171
Christmas, xvii, 31, **35–36**, 63, 137, 173
chronology, xxi–xxv
Church of Jesus Christ of Latter-Day Saints, 2
Circle Line, 30, 40, 85
citizens, 4–5, 14, 25, 28, **36**, 70–71
Civil War, 89, 186, 247
Clara de Hirsch Home for Immigrant Girls, 109
Clark, Jane Perry, 109
cleaning, 129, 133, 139
clergymen, 35
clerks, 1, 2, 11, **36–37**, 46–47, 56, 57, 79, 187, 207, 219
Cleveland, Grover, xxiii, 20, 45, 105
Clive, E. E., 80, 94
closing of Ellis Island, 25–26, **37–38**
Coast Guard, xxiv, **38–39**, 117, 203, 221, 254
Coastguardsmen, *38*, 187
codes, 1, 32–33
Cohen, Maury M., 72
Cohrsen, Johanna, 25, 110
Colbert, Claudette, 80
Cold War, **39**
Commerce and Labor, Department of, 28, 45, 108, 131, 213, 249
commissioners, xxiii–xxiv, **39–40**, 43–45, 47–48, 49–50, 51, 79, 107–109, 209, 219, 235, 244, 245–246, 247–248
commissioners-general, 2, 28, 29, **40**, 50, 108, 132, 191–192, 216
communicable diseases. *See* contagious diseases
communists, 13, 39, 61, 71, 114, 123, 201, 204
complaints. *See* criticism
computer databases, 2, 73, 189
concerts, xvii, 107
concessions, **40**. *See also* privilege holders
Congregational Church, 170–171, 216
Congressional Resolution of 1890, **40**, 104
conjunctivitis, 79
consuls, 116, 188
contagious disease wards, 7, 27, **40–41**, 184
contagious diseases, 41, **42**, 64–66, 68–69, 235–237, 240
Contract Labor Division, 42, 86, 108
contract labor laws, **42**
contracted laborers, 78, 114, 115
Cook, Donald, 72
Coolidge, Calvin, xxiv, 108, 223
Corcoran, Emma, **42–43**, 187
corridors and covered passages, 27, **43**
corruption, 47–48, 126–127, 131, 140, 246–247
Corsi, Edward, xxiv, 3, 12, 13, 40, **43–45**, 73, 126, 132, 156, 187, 202, 212, 233, 241
Cortelyou, George, **45**, 83
Cortez, Ricardo, 81
Costello, Frank, 80
Coudert, Frederic R., 73
Cowen, Philip, **45–46**, 112, 126
Craigwell, Ernest, 2, **46–47**
crematory, **47**, 53
Crespi, Muriel, 53
crime and abuse, **47–48**
criminals, 53, 61, 78, 115
criticism, 18, 25, 38, 47, 54–56, 57–61, 94, 248
Croats, 5, 200, 237
crowd control, 101
Cubans, 80, 97, 169, 200, 219, 254
Cugat, Xavier, 80

Cunard Line, 136
Curran, Henry H., xxiv, 40, 49–50, 220
Customs Service, 13, 85, 86, 117
Cynalewski, S., 35
Czechs (Bohemians, Moravians, etc.), 61, 90–91, 141, 200

Dalmatians, Bosnians and Herzegovinians, 200, 237
Danes, 200
databases. *See* computer databases
Daughters of the American Revolution (DAR), 4, **51**, 109, 141, 212
Davis, James, J., 94
Day, Benjamin M., xxiv, 40, **51**, 135, 187, 241
Dean, Millvina (*Titanic* survivor), 187
deaths and burials, **51–52**, 53, 244
deferred cases, 56
Delaware Indians, xi, **52–53**
Demo, Antonio, 214
demolished structures, **53**
demolishing buildings, proposals for, xxv
deportation, xxiv, 26, 39, **53–54**, 63, 70, 78, 114
deportation cases, 14, **54–56**, 140, 205–206
deportees, 35, 54–56, 57–60, 61, 77, 97, 116, 229
Deporting Division, 33, 37, **56–57**, 70, 88–89, 126, 205–206, 234
deporting squad, 56, 72
destinations, 15, **57**
detainees, 34, 53–56, 57–61, 70–71, 126, 190
detention cases, 5, 13, 31, 53–56, **57–61**, 75–77
detention conditions, 1930s, **61–62**
detention conditions, 1949, **62–63**
detention conditions, 1950s, **63**
Dewey, Thomas, 44
dialects. *See* languages and dialects
diet and dieticians, 133, 162, 185
Dillingham, William P., 57, 108
Dillingham Commission, 115
dining room, 12
diphtheria, 34, 40
discharging aliens at piers, 16, 47
Discharging Division, 37, **64**, 70
discrimination, 35, 47, 99, 116, 120
diseases and hospitalization, **64–70**
dispensary, 95, 186
Displaced Persons Act, 207
district directors, 40, **70**, 241, 246–247. *See also* New York District
divisions, 39, **70**
Doak, William N., 51, **70**
docks, 13, 53, **70**, 92
doctors. *See* surgeons
documents, 18, 25–26, 27–28, 32, 56–57, 205–206, *224*, 259–304
Dominicans, 169
dormitories, 47, 55, 58, 60, 61, 62, 63, 117, 182
Dormitory (exhibit), **70**
Dubinsky, David, 80, 183
Duncan, Isadora, **70–71**, 201, 241
DuPont, Pierre S. III, 2
Dutch, 63, 200, 217, 220, 254
Dutch colonialism, xi, xxi
Dutch Reformed Church, xvi, 170
Dutch West India Company, 52–53, 187
Dyre, William, xii, xxi
Dyre's Island, xxi

Eastern Orthodox churches, 35, 90
Edison, Thomas A., 85
Egyptians, 120, 168–169, 200
Eichler, Charles G., 31, 112
Einsiedler case, 50
Eisenhower, Dwight D., 44
Elevators, 13, **72**, 106
Ellis, Samuel, xii, xxi, **72**, 73, 131
Ellis Island (film), **72–73**, 85
Ellis Island: Everyman's Monument (documentary), 85
Ellis Island: historical overview, xi–xix; chronology, xxi–xxv
Ellis Island Chronicles (exhibit), **73**
Ellis Island Committee, xxiv, **73**, 188, 231
Ellis Island Foundation. *See* Statue of Liberty–Ellis Island Foundation
Ellis Island Immigration Museum, xix, 4, 12, 40, **73–74**, 133, 178, 188–189, 201, 212, 223
Ellis Island: Its Organization and Some of Its Work (Williams), 18, 259–276
Ellis Island Oral History Project. *See* Oral History Project
Ellis Island Resolution of 1890. *See* Congressional Resolution of 1890
Ellis Island Restoration Commission, 212, 216
emigration statistics, 115
employees' quarters, **74–75**, 106, 184
employees and workers: assistant commissioners, 10; boat captains, 83; charwomen, 129; chief inspectors of registry, 207; commissioners, 39–40; deckhands, 132; district directors, 70; immigrant aid workers, 109–110; immigrant inspectors, 112–113, 126; interpreters, 125, 136; laborers, 129; nurses, 184–185; surgeons, 230–231; watchmen, 234
enemy aliens, xxiii, xxiv, 6, 14, **75–77**, 97, 127, 179–181, 190, 194–95, 209, 251–252, 253, 254
engineers, 91
English colonialism, xii, xxi

English immigrants, 12, 56, 59–60, 61, 80, 105, 163, 200
entertainment, 8, 31–32, 36, 63, 107–108, 203, 217
epileptics, 121
Episcopalians. *See* Protestant Episcopal Church
Eppler, Samuel J., 31, 33, 112
escapees, 63, 89
Escobar, José Dias d', **77**, 125
espionage, 126, 195, 254
Estes, Elizabeth, 51, 110
Evans-Gordon, Sir William, **77–78**
exclusion, 5, 6–7, 42, 56, 70, **78–79**, 109, 241
executions, xii, xxi–xxii
Executive Division, 33, 37, 39, 70, **79**, 140, 205
exhibits, 73–74; Baggage Room, 12, 73; Dormitory, 70, 73; Ellis Island Chronicles, 74; graffiti columns, 74; Oral History Listening Room, 74; Peak Immigration Years, 74, 188–189; Peopling of America, 189–190; Registry Room, 73; Registry Room Views, 74; Through America's Gate, 74, 233–234; Treasures from Home, 74, 238; Silent Voices, 74, 220
expulsion. *See* deportation; exclusion
eye examinations/eyesight, 68, 79, 235–237, *236*

Factor, Max, 80
Fairbanks, Douglas, xvii
famous immigrants, 4, 31, 61, **80–81**, 105, 135, 190, 238
Faris, James Edge, **81**
fascists, 123, 254
favus, 41, 65
FBI (Federal Bureau of Investigation), xviii, 39, 75
feeblemindedness, **81**, 115, 215
Feeney, Brian, 187
Ferrer, José, 85
ferries and boats, 8, *16*, 53, 70, **81**
Ferro, Edward, **81**, 112, 125
Ferry House, 27, 38, 70, 73, **83–85**, *84*, 93, 117, 127, 137, 212
ferry service, 30, 40, **85**
ferryboat *Ellis Island*, xxiii, xxv, 13, 37–38, 73, **81-83**, *82*, 85, 136, 209, 211, 244
fiction, 92. *See also* literature and reminiscences
films and documentaries, 63, 72–73, **85**, 93
Finns, 65, 200, 220, 237
fire of 1897, **85**
Firpo, Luis, 61, 85
first immigrant station, 85, **86–88**, *87*
Fitchie, Thomas, xxiii, 39, 47, 110, 126, 159, 192, 241
Flanagan, Edward, 80
fog bell, 70
food service and menus, 12, 55, 61, 62, **88**, *88*, 133, 145, 234
foreign languages. *See* languages and dialects
foreign workers, 42
forgeries, 48
Forman, Philip, **88–89**, 112
Fort Gibson, xii–xiii, xxii, **89–90**, 96
Fort Wadsworth, xxii, 89
Fort Wood, xxv
fortifications, xii–xiii, xxii
Foxlee, Ludmila K., 25, 36, **90–91**, 110, 203, 234, 256
France, 60, 222–223, 224, 252
Francis Joseph, 10
Frankfurter, Felix, 80
Franklin, John Hope, 3
Fraser, Douglas, 80
French, 13, 61, 80, 132, 217, 220, 254
Fry, Alfred Brooks, 13, **91**
fuel dock, 27
funding, 104

Gallico, Paul, **92**
Galveston, Texas, 112
Galvin, Thomas P., **92**, 112
games, xvii, 8, 34
garbage and refuse, 47
Gardiner, Elizabeth G., 110
Garrett, Cynthia, 230
Garvey, Marcus, 15, 183
gatemen, 47, **47–48**
Gateway (film), 85, **93–94**
Geddes, Lord, 49–50, **94**, 244
Geddings, H. D., 215
genealogy, 2
general hospital building, 27, **94–95**
General Services Administration, xviii, xxiv, 38, **95-96**, 131, 210
Geneva Convention (1929), 76, 180
Georgians, 81, 169, 200
German-American Bund, 77
German Lutheran Church, xvi, 35, 136–137, 169
German Society, 109
Germans, xviii, 57, 75, *76*, 77, 81, 200, 209, 214, 219, 220, 226, 228, *229*, 249, 254
Germany, 4, 14, 15, 75, 252
Gibbet Island, xii, xxi
Gibbs, George (pirate), xii
Gibran, Kahlil, 80, **96**
Gibson, James, xii, xxii, 89, **96**
Gilum, Louise, 185
Glanvill case, 54–56
Gloucester City Immigrant Station, **96–97**
Goddard, H. H., 134

Goldman, Emma, 5, 12, 14, 26, 61, **97**, 204, 241
Gorky, Arshile, 81
Governor's Island, xii, xxii, 13
graffiti, 6, **97–98**, 234
Graham, Stephen, **98–99**
Grant, Madison, **99**, 120
Great Britain, 77, 89, 94, 252
Great Hall, 31, **100**, 208
Greek Society, 109–110, 169
Greeks, 12, 55, 64, 120, 141, 159, 188, 216, 220
Greene, Graham, 39
greenhorns, 46, 90
greenhouses, 53
Greenstone, Cecilia, 2, **100**, 170, 177
Grogan, Anthony J., xvi, 4, 8, 35, **100–101** 109, 169, *170*
groupers, **101**
guard houses, 127
guards and watchmen, 48, 55, 56, 57, 61, **101**
Guastavino, Rafael (I), **101–102**
Guastavino, Rafael (II), **102**
Gull Island. *See Kioshk*
Gypsies, 120, 169, 200, 220, 248

Hackman, Gene, 85
Haig, Chester R., 7
halal meals, 62
Halifax Immigrant Station, **103**
Hall, Prescott, **103**, 120, 244
Hamburg-Amerika Line, *226*
Handlin, Oscar, 3
hangings. *See* executions
Hanlon, Edward V., 48
Harbor defence, 29–30, 89–90
Harding, Warren G., xxiv, 49, 108, 198, 235
Hardwick, Mary Angela, 164
Harkavy, Alexander, **103**, 104, 170
Harland & Hollingsworth, 83
Harriman, W. Averill, 45
Harrison, Benjamin, xxii, 40, 89, **103–104**, 105
Hart, William S., xvii
head tax, 32, **104**, 113, 115, 117
health inspections (Europe), 226–227
heart disease, 51, 67–68
Hebrew Immigrant Aid Society, xvi–xvii, 46, 48, 100, 103, **104–105**, 109, 145, 169, 202
Heiser, Victor, **105**
Hendley, Charles M., **105**
Herrlich, Philip E., 31, 47, 112
Higham, John, 3
Hill, James G., 13
Hindus, 85, 135, 169, 220
Hine, Lewis, **105**
Hispanics. *See* Spanish Americans; *individual nationalities*
Hitler, Adolf, 77, 98
Hitler Youth, 123
Hodur, Francis, 80
Home Missions Council, 107
Homeland Security, Department of, 28, 117
Hoover, Herbert C., xxiv, 44, 70, 108
Hoover, J. Edgar, 75
Hope, Bob, 80, **105**, 203
Hospital Administration Building, 27, 74–75, **106**, 142, 212
hospital buildings, 40–41, **106**, 127
Hospital Extension, 27, **106–107**
Hospital Outbuilding, 140
hospitals (NY and NJ), 253
Howe, Frederic C., xxiii–xxiv, 40, **107–108**, 109, 141, 204, 241, 253, 256
Hsu, Dick, 53
Hudson River, 52
Hull, Harry, **108**
Hungarian Home, 110
Hungarian Relief Society, 110
Hungarians, xviii, 5, 75, 80, 120, 133, 166–167, 200, 217, 218–219, 220
Hurok, Sol, 71, 80
Husband, W.W., 40, 50, **108**, 202

Iacocca, Lee A., xix, xxv, 177, 212, 223
idiots, 67, **109**, 114, 115
illegal aliens, 32, 35, 78, 80, 254
illiteracy, 78, 145, 244–245, 254
imbeciles, **109**, 115
immigrant aid societies, 29, 50, **109**, 126, 136–137, 141, 256
immigrant inspection. *See* primary inspection
immigrant inspection stations, 6, 96–97, **110–112**
immigrant inspectors, 1, 2, 6, 17, 19–20, 37, 48, 81, 92, **112–113**, 126, 131, 207, 208, 219
immigrant writings. *See* literature and reminiscences
Immigration Act of 1882, 104, **113**
Immigration Act of 1891, 27, 40, 53, 104, **113–114**, 197
Immigration Act of 1893 (I), **114**
Immigration Act of 1893 (II), 17, **114**
Immigration Act of 1895, **114**, 230
Immigration Act of 1903, 5, 17, **114–115**, 201, 216
Immigration Act of 1907, 104, **115**
Immigration Act of 1917, 104, **115–116**, 201
Immigration Act of 1918, **116**, 201
Immigration Act of 1924, **116**, 121, 207
immigration building, **117**, 142, 182
Immigration and Nationality Act of 1965, **116–117**, 199

Immigration and Naturalization Act (1952), 121, 157–158, 199, 201
Immigration and Naturalization Service (INS), 6, 28, 37–38, 39, 75–77, 95, 117, 131, 182
immigration records, 2
Immigration Regulations, **117–120**
Immigration Restriction League, 78, 99, 103, **120**, 244
Immigration Restriction Movement, 77–78, 99, 116 **120–121**, 130, 157, 198, 206–207, 244
Immigration Service Beneficial Association, 132
immigration statistics, **122**
immorality. *See* moral turpitude
Impellitteri, Vincent R., 44, 80
imposters, 48, 61, 94
incinerator, 47, 53, 127
Indians. *See* Hindus, Sikhs; or Native Americans
Information Bureau, 37, 45, 70, 86, **122–123**
insane persons, 66–67, 114, 115, **123**, 195, 254
inspection. *See* diseases and hospitalization; line inspection; primary inspection
Inspection Division, **123**
inspectors. *See* immigrant inspectors
Interior, Department of the, 28, 130, 131, 210, 212
Internal Security Act, xxiv, 121, **123–124**, 201
internment. *See* enemy aliens; Nazis; World War I; World War II
interpreters, 17–18, 47, 57, 77, 89, **124–126**, 136, 139, 156, **167–168**, *193*, 207
Interview Corridor, **126**,
investigations, 47–48, 73, **126–127**, 140, 246–247
IQ tests, 134
Irish, 57, 80, 85, 100–101, 129, 163, 169, 172, 182, 200, 217
Island 1 (One), 13, 43, 53, 70, **127**, 137
Island 2 (Two), 39, 43, 74, **127**, 137
Island 3 (Three), 6, 40–41, 43, 74, **127**, 137
Island Called Ellis, An (documentary), 85
Island of Hope, Island of Tears (documentary), 85
Island of Tears, xiii
isolation wards. *See* contagious disease wards
Italian Welfare League, xvii, 109, 110, 127, 170, 203
Italians, xiv, xvi, xviii, 5, 12, 20–25, 35–36, 43–45, 47, 48, 57, 60, 69, 75–77, 80–81, 120, 126, 133, 163, 190, 200, 214–215, 217, 219, 220, *253*, 254
Italy, xviii, 105, 126, 188, 214, 246

jails, 25–26, 37–38
James, C. L. R., 15, 39, 61, **128**, 201
James, Henry, **128–129**
Janis, Elsie, 253
Janitors' Division, **129**
Japanese, xviii, 75, 76, 115, 120, 169, 188, 200, 254
Japanese Exclusion League 121
Jersey City, NJ, xv, 47, 70
Jewish aid workers, 2, 48, 63, 100, *100*, 103, 104–105, 109, 242
Jewish emigration investigation, 247
Jewish organizations. *See* Hebrew Immigrant Aid Society; National Council of Jewish Women; United Hebrew Charities
Jews, 5, 14, 31, 45–46, 62, 77, 80–81, 88, 97, 98, 99, 104–105, 133, 146, 168, 177, 200, 228, *238*, 242, 249
Johnson, Albert, **130**, 207
Johnson, Hiram, 121
Johnson, Lyndon B., xviii, xxv, 96, 117, **130**
Johnson, Philip, xxv, **130**, 210–211
Johnson, Solomon, 2, 46, 113
Johnson-Reed Act. *See* Immigration Act of 1924
Joliet-Curie, Irene, 61
Jolson, Al, 80, 238
Junker, William E., 112, **131**
Jurisdiction, 38, 40, 89–90, 95–96, **131**, 220
Justice, Department of, 14, 28, 37, 75–76, 123, 131, 204

Keefe, Daniel J., 40, **132**
Kerensky, Alexandr, 60
Kerr, Frances W., 62–63
Khodja, Murad Mohammed, 83, **132**
Kioshk (Gull Island), xi, xxi, 52
kissing post, **132–133**
Kitchen Building, 41, 127, **133**
Kitchen and Laundry Building, 7, 27, 74, 127, **133**, 212
kitchens, 62
Kluge, John, 81
Knauff, Ellen, 39, 201
Knox, Howard A., **133–134**, 164, 234
Koreans, 200
kosher meals, xvii, 12, 31, 62, 88, 104, 105, 145, 228
Kosutic, August, 61
Koussa, Joseph el, 47
Koussa, Kahlil el, 47
Kramer, Samuel Noah, 80
Krishnamurti, Jiddu, 81, **135**, 173
Kropotkin, Prince Peter, 5
Krout, John A.
Kuhn, Fritz, 77, 180

LaBonde, Agatha, 18
Labor, Department of, 7, 16, 29, 38, 51, 70, 73, 94, 108, 131, 188, 190, 191, 204
laboratory. *See* office building and laboratory
laborers (male), 2, 47, 55, 129
Laboulaye, Edouard de, 223

LaGuardia, Fiorello, 44, 50, 125, **136**, 156, 203, 234, 241
Lalande, F. M., 57
Land, Paul H., **136–137**
landfill, *26–27*, 73, 85, 117, 127, **137**, 220
landing agents, 54, **138**
landing cards, 32
landing immigrants, 17–18, 118, **138**
Landis, Harry R., 10, **138**
landscape and vegetation, **138–139**
languages and dialects, 5, 15, 61, 62, 89, 90, 97–98, 100, 103, 124–126, 136, **139**, 141, 145, 189, 193
Laning, Edward, 73
Lansky, Meyer, 80
Larned, Frank H., **139**
Larned, Ruth, 109
LaRue, Jack, 72
Lasker, Florina, 46
Latin America and Latinos, 77, 85, 169, 200, 254. *See also individual nationalities*
Latvians (Letts), 200
laundries, 62, 133, **139**
Laundry and Linen Exchange, 27, **140**
Law Division, 70, 92, **140**, 220
Lax, Philip, 212, 216
Lazarus, Emma, 45, 223
League of Abandoned Wives, 251
League of Nations, 207
Lebanese, 15, 47, 80, 96
Lederhilger, John, 47, **140**, 159, 207
Lenni Lenape, xi, xxi, 52–53
L'Etauche, Joseph, 48, 214
Levitt, Alfred, 80
liable to become a public charge, 1, 17, 67, 78, 116, **140–141**
Liberty Island, 2, 52, 53, 142, 223
libraries, 4, 29, 35, 63, 133, **141–142**, 162
Lilier-Steinheil, Baroness Mara de, 61
Lind, Jenny, 30
line inspection, xiv, 32, 64, 79, **142–144**, 197, 214, 235; ceased, 116
linen exchanges, 140, **145**
Lipsitch, I. Irving, 104, **145**, 170
literacy bill veto (1909), 132
literacy tests, 115, 121, **145**, 244–245
literature and reminiscences, 1–2, 11, 12–13, 20–25, 44–45, 49, 54–56, 57–61, 90–91, 97, 98–99, 128–129, 136, **145–146**
Lithuanians, 61, 167–168, 200
Little Italy, 20, 214–215
Little Oyster Island, xii, xxi, 53
Lloyd, Marie, **146**, 173, 241
Lloyd, Thomas, xii, xxi
loathsome and/or contagious diseases, 65, 115, **146**
Lodge, Henry Cabot, 120, 121
Lodsin, Michael, 170, **146**
Los Angeles, 35, 80, 246
LPC. *See* liable to become a public charge; public charge
Luciano, Charles "Lucky," 61, 80
luggage. *See* baggage
Lugosi, Bela, 80, **147**
Lutherans, 62, 63, 169–170

MacCormack, Daniel W.
Main Building, 7, 8, 9, 10, 27, 29, 97, 100, 127, 132, 142, 208, 211
maintenance, 73, 83, 182. *See also* Janitors' Division; Matrons' Division; Mechanical Division
Maltese, 126, 200, 241–242
manifests, 2, 118, 247
Manning, H. H., 69
marine hospital, 52
Marine Hospital Service, 105
Marmaroff, Athena, 252
marriages, **155–156**, 251
Martoccia, Francesco, xiv, 125, 132–133, 136, **156**
matrons, 47, 61, 79, 133, **156**, 173–175, 252
Matrons' Division, 70, **156–157**
Matthew, Thomas W., 181
Matthews, Alma, 109, **156**, 170, 250
Mazurki, Mike, 80
McCarran, Patrick A., 123–124, **157**
McCarran-Walter Act, **157–158**, 199, 201
McCarthy period, 39
McComb, John, 29
McCool, Patrick, 100
McDonald, Peter, 31, **158–159**, *159*
McKay, Claude, 15, 81
McKinley, William, xxiii, 5, 45
McLaughlin, Allan J., 194
McSweeney, Edward F., 10, 47, 140, **159–160**, 192, 219, 242
meals. *See* food service and menus; halal meals; kosher meals
measles, 34, 40, 41, **160**
Mechanical Division, 32, 37, 39, 70, **160**
medical certificates, 32, 64–68 *passim*, **160**
Medical Division, 70, **160–162**
medical officers, **162–163**
Meir, Golda, 189
mental deficiency, 78, 81, 109, 115, **163**
mental room, **163**
mental testing, 133–134, **163–164**, 215, 217, 234
messengers, 56, 79, 101, **164**
MetaForm Incorporated, 73, **164**, 212
MetaForm Research Collection, **164–166**
Methodist Church, xvi, 57, 156

Mexico and Mexicans, 32, 117, 169, 200, 254
Mezei, Ignac, 39, **166–167**
Mikolainis, Peter, 125, **167–168**
military use, xii–xiii, xxi–xxii, 89–90
Miller, Watson B., **168**
minorities, 14–15, **168–169**
Mission of Our Lady of the Rosary, 100, **169**, 251
missionaries, 29, 34, 35–36, 48, 90–91, 100–101, 109, 136–137, 139, 141, 156, **169–171**, 214–215, 216, 249
models of Ellis Island, 73
Money Exchange, 24, 86, **171–172**
money requirement, 249
Montenegrins, 200, 220
Montgomery, Phyllis, 164
Moore, Annie, xxiii, 80, 105, **172**, 182
moral turpitude, 1, 17, 78, 114, 115, 126, **172–173**, 239–240, 251, 254
Moreno, Antonio, 80
Moretti, Gaspare, xvi, 35–36, 170, **173**, 214
Mormons, 2, 12, 85
mortuaries, 6, 51
mortuary and autopsy room, 41, 127, **173**
Mosher, Maud, 133, 156, **173–175**, 203, 252
motion pictures. *See* films and documentaries
Mowbray, Alan, 80
Mulholland, Thomas F., 109, 170
Mullan, Eugene H., 32, 81, 143–144, 162, 163, 164
mural, 73
murder, 47
Murray, Joseph E., 10, 159, 175, 213
Museum Services Division, 74, 212
museums. *See* American Museum of Immigration; Ellis Island Immigration Museum
music, 36, 238, 250
Muskie, Edmund S., xviii, 96
Muslims, 2, 12, 62, 200
Mussolini, Benito, 98
My Boy (film), 85, **175**

Nagel, Charles, 31, 249
name change legend (aliens), **176**
names (Ellis Island), **176**
names of employees (selected). *See* employees and workers
Nansen Passports, 207
Narragansett, 81, **177**
National Archives, 2, 34, 202
National Catholic Welfare Conference, 169
National Council of Jewish Women, xvi, 2, 46, 100, 109, 169, **177**, 201, 251
National Institutes of Immigrant Welfare, 25, 90, 110, 256
National Liberal Immigration League, 120
national monument, xviii, xxv
National Origins Act (1929), 121, 198, 207
National Park Service, xviii, xxv, 2, 30, 40, 45, 53, 73, 74, 96, 131, 133, 139, 142, **177–178**, 191, 202, 209–210, 210–212, 216
National Register for Historic Places, 177
Native Americans, xi, xxi, 52–53, 221
nativists, 4–5, 99, 103, 120–121
naturalization, 28, 35, 48
Navy, xiii, xxii, xxiii, 7, 40, 83, 86, 89, 131, **178–179**
Nazis, 77, 123, **179–181**, 254
NEGRO, **181**, 221
Nevada, **182**
Nevins, Allan, 3
New Immigration Building. *See* immigration building
New Jersey, xxii, xxiii, xxv, 52, 57, 63, 70, 89, 216, 220
New Netherlands, xi, xxi, 53
New Orleans, 35, 53, 80
New Year's Day, 31
New York, xi, xv, xxi–xxii, xxv, 13–14, 15, 25–26, 35, 57, 89, 99, 108, 140, 141, 182–183, 220
New York Bible Society, 35, 170
New York Chinese Office, 112, **182**
New York City Mission Society, **182**
New York Detention Dormitory, **182**
New York District, **182**
New York Room (temporarily detained), 86, **183**
New York State Construction Co., 11
New York University, 51
Newman, Pauline, 80
Nicknames, **183**
Night Division, 37, 70, 75, 85, **183**, 206, 234
Nixon, Richard M., 2
Non-quota immigrants, 116
Norkus, Constantine, 61
North American Civic League for Immigrants, **183**
Norwegians, 37–38, 80, 190, 200, 254
notice against swindling, 47–48
Novotny, Ann, **183–184**
nurses, 51, 75, 82, 106, 133, **184–185**, 197, 231

O'Beirne, James R., 10, **186**
Oberoutcheff, Constantin and Olga, 57, 60
obstetrics, 106
occupational therapy, 51
O'Donnell, Roger, 37, 47, 113, 126, 277–282
O'Dwyer, William, 80
office building and laboratory, 27, 41, 127, **186**, 222
Office of Immigration, xxii, xxiii, 27, 114, 131, 186
Oland, Warner, 80
Oosterhoudt, Emma B., 11, **187**, 220
opera singers, 61

Oral History Project, 74, **187**, 238
orphans, 33, *253*
Orthodox churches, 35
Owen, William Dale, **187**
Ownership, xi–xii, xxi–xxii, 72, 131
Oyster Island, xii, xxi–xxii, 53

Paauw, Michael, xi, xxi, 53, **188**
Palmer, A. Mitchell, 204
Palmer, Carleton H., 73, **188**
Pan American Exposition, 19
Panama, 6, 14
Pankhurst, Emmeline, 61
Papashvily, George, 81
passenger lists, xiii, 2
Passover, xvii
Passport Division, **188**
passports, 1, 48, 85, 126, **188**, 207, 254
paupers, 114, 115, 126, 196
Peak Immigration Years (exhibit), **188–189**
Pennsylvania, 57, 97
Peopling of America (exhibit), **189–190**, 201
Perec, Georges, 85
Perkins, Frances, 38, 73, 188, **190**
Persians, 120, 169, 200
Personnel Report (1909), 277–282
Peterssen, Arne, 37–38, **190**
physical defect, 17, 78, 115
physicians. *See* medical officers; surgeons
Pickford, Mary, xvii, 250
picture brides, 251
Pinza, Ezio, 77, 127, **190**
pirates, xii, xxi–xxii
Pitkin, Thomas M., xvi, 3, 177, 183, **191**, 210
Poles, 159, 200, 209–210, 220, 228, 254
Polish Home, 48, 214
Polish National Alliance, 110
Polish Society, xvi
political detainees, 31, 61, 75–77, 114, 190
polygamy, 114, 115, 126
Porter, Cole, 250
Portland, Oregon, 35
ports of departure, **191**
ports of entry. *See* immigrant inspection stations
Portuguese, 77, 120, 200, 254
Post, Louis F., **191**, 204, 241
postal cards, **191**
Powderly, Terence V., 40, 126, **191–192**, 216
Power House, 27, **192**
preferential quotas, 116
pregnancies, 68, **193**
Presbyterian Church, 170
presidents, 53. *See also* Cleveland; Coolidge; Eisenhower; Harding; Harrison; Hoover; McKinley; Nixon; Reagan; Roosevelt, F. D.; Roosevelt, T.; Taft; Truman
priests, 10, 35, 54, 100–101, 214
primary inspection, xv, 36, 78, **193–194**, 32, 207, 208
prisoners of war, xii, **194–195**
privilege holders, 40, 88, **195**
professional beggars, 114, 115, 121, 194, 196
proselytization, 35, 246
prostitution, 2, 53, 114, 116, 121, 172, 249, 251, 254
Protestant Episcopal Church, xvi, 29, 35, 63, 141, 169, 169–171, 182
Protestants, xvi, 29, 35, 62–63, 90, 136–137, 141, 169–171, 182, 246
psychology, 19
Psychopathic Ward, 27, **195–196**
psychopaths, 106, 115, 163, 195
public charge, 17, 67, 78, 114, **196**
Public Health and Marine Hospital Service, 69, **196**
Public Health Service, xiv, 6, 14, 32, 39, 42, 51–52, 64, 184–185, 193, **196–197**
Puerto Rico and Puerto Ricans, 31, 39, 166
Purcell, Anna, 185, **197**

quarantine, xiii, xxi, **198**
Quayle, J. Danforth, 178
questioning immigrants, 118, 124, 193–194, 208
Quota Act, 121, **198**
quotas, xxiv, 51, 63, 116, **198–199**, 207, 235

races and peoples, 134, **200–201**
racism, 99, 115, 120
radicals, 5, 13, 14, 26, 97, 166–167, **201**, 204–206
railroad dock, 70
Railroad Ticket Office, 61, 73, **201**
railways and terminals, xvii, 12, 47, 70, 201
Rand, Ayn, 81
Ratoff, Gregory, 94
Razofsky, Cecilia, 2, 46, 109, 170, 177, **201**
Reagan, Ronald, xix, xxv, 177, **201–202**, 212, 223
records, 2, **202–203**, 222
Recreation Hall, 27, **203**
Recreation Shelter, 27, **203**
Red Cross House, 4, 53, 73, 127, 141
red scare, xxiv, 14, 26, 29, 39, 71, 97, 107, 191, 201, **204–206**, 241, 254
Reed, Alfred C., 68–69, 142–143, 164, 237
Reed, David A., **206–207**
reentry permits, 140, **207**
refugees, 199, **207**
Registry Division, 7, 17, 32, 70, 124, 136, 145, **207**
registry room, 62, 63, 86, 100, 107, **208–209**
Registry Room (exhibit), **209**

Registry Room Views (exhibit), **209**
Reimer, Rudolph, xxiv, 11, 40, 70, 187, **209**, 241
Reisch, Walter, 94
religious observances, xvii, 4, 61, 62, 63, 239
Renkiewicz, Frank, **209–210**
Report of Excess Real Property, 37
resident alien certification, 32
restaurant. *See* food service and menus
Reston, James, 80
restoration, xviii–xix, xxv, 177, 201, **210–212**, 215–216
Restore Ellis Island Committee, xviii, 211, 216
Rickover, Hyman G., 80
robberies, 47–48
Robinson, Allen, 23, 249
Robinson, Edward G., 2, 80
Rockne, Knute, 80
Rölvaag, Ole, 80
Roman Catholic Church, xvi, 35, 100–101, 214–215
Romanians, xviii, 75, 120, 141, 188, 200, 220, 248
Romanoff, "Prince" Michael, 61, 89, 94
Roosevelt, Eleanor, **212–213**
Roosevelt, Franklin D., 28, 75, 112, 209, 212, 213
Roosevelt, Theodore, xxiii, 31, 45, 47, 69, 175, 192, **213**, 216, 249
Rossi, Adolfo, 214
Roth, Henry, 80
Rothko, Mark, 81
rules and regulations, 6–7, 17, 18–19, 33, 39, 56–57, 78, 138, 283–304
Russell, Lillian, 127
Russia, 45, 97, 100, 204, 247, 252
Russians, 57, 60, 61, 64, 69, *256*
Ruthenians, 31, 200, 220

Sabata, Victor de, 61
sabotage and saboteurs, xxii, 15, 116, 254
Sacco and Vanzetti, 5
Sadeleer, Louis de, 14
safekeeping, 63
Safford, Victor, 160, 200, **214**
St. Joseph's Home for Polish Immigrants, 48, 110, 169, **214**
St. Raphael Society for the Protection of German Immigrants, 169, **214**
St. Raphael Society for the Protection of Italian Immigrants, 169, 173, **214–215**
St. Raphael Society for the Protection of Ruthenian Immigrants, 169
salaries, 2, 136
Salmon, Thomas W., 164, **215**
Salvation Army, xvi, 35, 63, 169, **215**, 242
Sammartino, Peter, xviii, xxv, 177, 211, **215–216**
San Francisco, 6
San Marino, xviii
Sanitary Division, 37
sanitation, 51–52, 55, 58, 59–60, 61, 62, 63, 129, 133
Sargent, Frank P., 2, 5, 40, 45, 83, 139, **216**, 245
Savalas, Telly, 85
Save Ellis Island!, **216**, 222
scandals, 47–48, 110, 126, 127, 135
Scandinavians, xvi, 12, 57, 200, 217, 254
scarlet fever, 6, 34, 40, 51
schooling, 19, 25, 34, 63, 133, **216–218**, *218*
Schumann-Heink, Ernestine, xvii
scientific experiments, 6
Scots, 200, 201, 235
seamen, 35, 37, 132
second immigrant station, **218**
Secret Service, 5
sell Ellis Island, attempts to, xxiv, 95–96
Semsey, Charles, 31, 113, **218–219**
Senner, Joseph H., xvi, xxiii, 39, 85, 103, 120, 126, 140, **219**, 244
Serbs, *5*, 141, 200
sewing and darning, 51
sexual offences. *See* moral turpitude; White Slave Traffic Act
Shahn, Ben, 183
Shapiro, Mary, 164
Shaughnessy, Edward J., xxiv, 25–26, 40, 70
Sheehan, Dennis P., 48
Sherman, Augustus F., 7, 16, 33, 43, 59, 202, **219–220**, 233
Sherman gallery, 74
Sigrist, Paul, 187
Sikhs, *168*, 169
Sikorsky, Igor, 80
Silent Voices (exhibit), **220**
Simon, Louis A., 85, 117, 203
Simpson, John J., 31, 138
Skouras, Spyros P., 2, 183
Slavonic Immigrant Society, 110
Slavs, 120, 133, 168, 200, 256
Slovaks, 90–91, 200, 217, *251*
Slovenians, 1–2, 141, 200
Smith, Mrs. H. Stebbins, 51, 110
social service workers, 48, 63, 90–91, 100, 139, 201
socialism, 120
Society for the Protection of Italian Immigrants, 110, **220**
South Africans, 54–56
South Slavs, 200
Southern Pacific, 53
sovereignty, xxv, **220**
Soviet Union, 39, 61, 207
Spaniards, 61, 63, 80, 101–102, 120, 200, 217, 254
Spanish Americans, 120, 200

Special Inquiry Division, 7, 12, 17–18, 32, 33, 36, 37, 39, 45, 70, 72, 92, 182, 219, **220–221**, 232
special inspector, **221**
Speranza, Gino, 142, 220
sponsors, 33
Sprague, E. K., **221**
squatters, 181, **221**
stabilization, 212, **221–222**
staff house, 27, 41, 127
stairs of separation, 24, **222**
stateless persons, 254
Staten Island, 13, 38, 40, 89, 235
Statistical Division, 2, 7, 37, 46, 70, 138, **222**
Statistics. *See* immigration statistics; races and peoples
Statue of Liberty, xi, xxv, 3, 13, 30, 44, 85, 100, **222–223**
Statue of Liberty–Ellis Island Foundation, xix, xxv, 2, 12, 73, 201, 212, **223**
steamship companies, 1, 115, 118, 136, 138, 194, **223–224**, 241, 247
steamship emigration agents, **224–225**
steamships, 1, 13, 20–21, 31, 43, 54, 60, 85, 132, 135, 182, **225–226**
steerage, 16, 20–21, 90–91, **226–228**
Steiner, Edward, **228–229**
stenographers, 36–37, 79
stereotypes, 163
sterilization, **229**
Stevens, Ebenezer, xxi
Stoner, George W., 41, 161
stories. *See* literature and reminiscences
stowaways, 17, 33, 35, 41, 63, 78, **229**, *229*, 254
Strauss, Oscar S., 45
Stucklen, Regina, 31
Stump, Herman, 40, 85, **229–230**
subversives, 78
suicides, 56, **230**
superintendent, 12, 79, **230**
superintendent of immigration, 39, 40, 187, 229, **230**
superintendents (NPS), 133, 172, **230**
Supreme Court (United States), xxv, 220
Surgeon's House (a.k.a. nurses' cottage), 53, 74, *82*, 107, 127, **231**
surgeons, 32, 64, 81, 105, **133–134**, 142–144, 162, 214, 215, 221, **230–231**, 233
Svejda, George, 183
Swanson, Gloria, xvii
Swedes, 80, 200, 217, 248
Swedish Immigrant Home, 48, 110
swindling, 47–48
Swing, Joseph M., 37, **231**
syndicalism, 120
Syrians, 64, 200

Taft, William Howard, xxiii, 132, 145, 201, **232**, 249
tags, 53, 119
Tarsney, John C., **232**
Tarsney Act of 1893, 218, **232**
Taylor, James Knox, 6, 11, 13, 41, 106, 186, 192, 195, **232–233**
telegraph office, 12, 47, 56, 58, 86, 122
telephone, 79, 86, 123
Termini, Isadore, 47
Theiss, Frederick A., **233**
Theosophists, 135, 219
Through America's Gate (exhibit), **233–234**
tickets. *See* tags
tiles, 101, 208, 209
Tilson, Richard, 101, **234–235**, 245
Tilton, Edward L., xxiii, 19, 95, 192, 218, **235**
Tingley, Katherine A., 219
Titanic, 132
Tod, Robert E., xxiv, 40, 50, **235**
Tompkins, Daniel D., xxii
tourists, 39, 73–74, 85, 216
trachoma, 34, 41, 64–65, 68–69, 79, 120, **235–237**
Tracy, Arthur, 80, 187, **238**
transport, 8–10, 13, 16, 81–83, 136
Trapp family singers, 61, 81
Travelers' Aid Society (port department) 110
Treasurer's Office, 48, 70, 86, **238–239**
Treasures from Home (exhibit), **239**
Treasury, Department of the, xxii, 13, 28, 40, 42, 90, 105, 131, 203–204
Treasury Division, 61, 70
Trenet, Charles, 61, 173, **239–240**
Trigère, Pauline, 81
Trinidadians, 14–15, 61
Trotti, Lamar, 94
Truman, Harry S., xxiv, 30, 77, 207
tuberculosis, 41, 51, 65, 115, 120, 240
Turks, 2, 120, 141, 169, 200, 220, 237
Turner, John, 5, 201
typhus, 120
typists, 36

Udall, Stewart L., 130, 210, *210*
Uhl, Byron H., xxiv, 10, 11, 33, 40, 48, 70, 136, 138, 187, 204–206, **241**
Ukrainians and Ruthenians, 31, 200, 220
Ullo, Lorenzo, 126, **241–242**
Un-American activities, 39
undertakers, 52
undesirable aliens, 62
undocumented aliens, 35, 78, **242**

uniforms, **242**, 252
United Hebrew Charities, **242**
U.S. attorneys, 75, 79
U.S. Debarkation Hospital, 7–8
Unrau, Harlan D., **242**

vaccinations, 106
vagabonds and vagrants, 108, 115
Valentino, Rudolph, 4
Valtin, Jan, 77
vandalism, 97–98, **243**
vaudeville, 8, 105, 238, 250, 253
Vecoli, Rudolph, 3
venereal diseases, 41, 65
Venezuelans, 14, 31
visas, 1, 51, 63, 75, 116, 254
visitation, xviii
visitors, 61, 94, 122–123, 128–129, 212–213, 248
Vittorio Emmanuel III, 246
Voskovec, George, 61, 81
voyages, 90–91

Wadsworth, James, 49
waiting rooms, 64, 86, 127
Waldo, Charles, 83, 125, **244**
Wall, Thomas, 47, 101
Wall of Honor. *See* American Immigrant Wall of Honor
Wallis, Frederick A., 40, 48, **244**
Walter, Francis E., 157, **244**
Wank, Albert, 47, 113, 126
Wansley, Thomas (pirate), xii
War of 1812, xii, xxii, 3, 30, 89, 96
war brides, 201, 252
War Department, xxii, 7, 131
Ward, Robert DeCourcy, 120, **244–245**
warrants, 41, 79, 205
Wasserman, Fred, 164
watchmen, **245**. *See also* guards and watchmen
Watchmen's and Gatemen's Division, 70, 93, 101, **245**
Watchorn, Robert, xxiii, 7, 39, 41, 45, 126, 175, 203, 213, 216, 234, **245–246**, 248
water tanks, 53
Watkins, W. Frank, xxiv, 40, **246–247**, 257
Weber, John B., xxiii, 39, 104, 126, 202, *247*, **247–248**,
Weiss, Feri Felix, 19–20
Wells, H. G., **248**
Welsh, 72, 200, 232
West Indians, 14–15, 128, 169, 200, 217, 220, 254
White Slave Traffic Act (Mann Act), **249**
white slavery, 2, 113
Wilhelms, Cornelius (pirate), xii, xxii
Williams, Jonathan, xii, 29, 89
Williams, L. L., 126, 185
Williams, William, xxiii, 18, 23, 35, 39–40, 47–48, 49, 59, 72, 83, 103, 110, 115, 124–125, 126, 128, 136, 175, 187, 191, 213, 216, 219, 232, **249–250**, 259–276, 283–304
Wilson, Woodrow, xxiii, xxiv, 29, 115
Windom, William, 105
Within the Quota, 250
Wittke, Carl, 3
Woman's Home Missionary Society, 156, 170, **250**
women, 11, 17, 51, 53, 54–56, 61, 62, 90–91, 97, 100, 101, 129, 156–157, 172, 187, 193, **250–251**
Women's Christian Temperance Union, 170, 251, **252**
workers. *See* employees and workers
Works Progress Administration (WPA), 117, 137
World Monuments Fund, **252**
World War I, xxiii, 7–8, 10, 14, 15, 26, 38–39, 100, 101, 108, 109, 141, 178–179, 194, 204, **252–253**,
World War II, xxiv, 6, 14, 75–77, 127, 137, 179–181, 190, 194–195, 203, 251, **254**
Wouters, Garrett, xii
Wright, Frank Lloyd, 96, **254–255**

Yezierska, Anzia, 80
YMCA, 4, 8, 54, 56, 108, 170, 253, **256**
Yugoslavs, 61. *See also* Croats; Dalmatians; Slovenians; South Slavs
YWCA, xvi, 25, 36, 90, 141, 170, **256**

Zanuck, Darryl F., 94
Zielenska, Constancia, 47
Zucker, Edward D., 35, 113, 207, **257**
Zucker, William J., 241

About the Author

BARRY MORENO is Librarian and Historian, Museum Services Division, at the Ellis Island Immigration Museum in New York. He is the author of *The Statue of Liberty Encyclopedia* (2000).